Supreme Court DRAMA

Cases That Changed America

Supreme Court DRAMA

Cases That Changed America

Daniel E. Brannen, &
Dr. Richard Clay Hanes
Elizabeth Shaw, Editor

VOLUME 2

CAPITAL PUNISHMENT
CRIMINAL LAW AND PROCEDURE
FAMILY LAW
JURIES
JUVENILE LAW AND JUSTICE
SEARCH AND SEIZURE

U•X•L®

AN IMPRINT OF THE GALE GROUP

DETROIT · NEW YORK · SAN FRANCISCO
LONDON · BOSTON · WOODBRIDGE, CT

Supreme Court Drama: Cases That Changed America

DANIEL E. BRANNEN
RICHARD CLAY HANES

Staff

Elizabeth M. Shaw, U•X•L Editor
Carol DeKane Nagel, U•X•L Managing Editor
Thomas L. Romig, U•X•L Publisher

Shalice Shah-Caldwell, Permissions Associate (Pictures)
Maria Franklin, Permissions Manager
Robyn Young, Imaging and Multimedia Content Editor

Rita Wimberley, Senior Buyer
Evi Seoud, Assistant Manager, Composition Purchasing and Electronic Prepress
Dorothy Maki, Manufacturing Manager
Mary Beth Trimper, Production Director
Michelle DiMercurio, Senior Art Director

Pamela A. Reed, Imaging Coordinator
Randy Basset, Image Database Supervisor
Barbara Yarrow, Imaging and Multimedia Content Manager

Linda Mahoney, LM Design, Typesetting

Cover photographs: Reproduced by permission of the Library of Congress and the Supreme Court of the United States.

Library of Congress Cataloging-in-Publication Data

Brannen, Daniel E., 1968-
Supreme Court drama: cases that changed the nation / Daniel E. Brannen, Jr. and Richard Clay Hanes ; Elizabeth M. Shaw, editor.
p. cm.
Includes bibliographical references and index.
ISBN 0-7876-4877-9 (set) – ISBN 0-7876-4878-7 (v.1) – ISBN 0-7876-4879-5 (v.2) –ISBN 0-7876-4880-9 (v.3) – ISBN 0-7876-4881-7 (v.4)
1.Constitutional law–United States–Cases–Juvenile literature. 2. United States. Supreme Court–Juvenile Literature. [1. Constitutional law–United States–Cases. 2. United States. Supreme Court.] I. Hanes, Richard Clay, 1946- II. Shaw, Elizabeth M., 1973- III. Title.

KF4550.Z9 B73 2001
347.73'26'0264–dc21

00-056380

Printed in Canada

10 9 8 7 6 5 4 3 2

Contents

Contents

Contents

Contents

VOLUME 2: CRIMINAL JUSTICE AND FAMILY LAW

CAPITAL PUNISHMENT

CRIMINAL LAW AND PROCEDURE

Contents

Contents

Contents

Contents

Trials Alphabetically

A

B

C

D

E

F

G

H

I

J

K

L

M

N

O

P

R

S

T

U

V

W

Y

Trials Chronologically

Trials Chronologically

1911

1915

1918

1919

1925

1927

1931

1932

1934

1936

1937

1938

1940

1941

1942

1943

Trials Chronologically

1960

1961

1962

1963

1964

1965

1966

1967

1968

1969

1970

1971

1972

1973

1974

1975

1976

1977

1978

1979

1980

1981

1982

1984

1985

1986

1987

1988

1989

1990

Trials Chronologically

1991

1992

1993

1994

1995

1996

1997

1998

1999

2000

Reader's Guide

U.S. citizens take comfort and pride in living under the rule of law. Our elected representatives write and enforce the laws that cover everything from family relationships to the dealings of multi-billion-dollar corporations, from the quality of the air to the content of the programs broadcast through it. But it is the judicial system that interprets the meaning of the law and makes it real for the average citizen through the drama of trials and the force of court orders and judicial opinions.

The four volumes of *Supreme Court Drama: Cases that Changed America* profile approximately 150 cases that influenced the development of key aspects of law in the United States. The case profiles are grouped according to the legal principle on which they are based, with each volume covering one or two broad areas of the law as follows:

- **Volume : Individual Liberties** includes cases that have influenced such First Amendment issues as freedom of the press, religion, speech, and assembly. It also covers the right to privacy.
- **Volume 2: Criminal Justice and Family Law** covers many different areas of criminal law, such as capital punishment, crimnal procedure, family law, and juvenile law.
- **Volume 3: Equal Protection and Civil Rights** includes cases in the areas of affirmative action, reproductive rights segregation, and voting rights, as well as areas of special concern such as immigrants, the disabled, and gay and lesbian citizens. Sexual harassment and the right to die are also represented in this volume.

- **Volume 4: Business and Government Law** also encompasses two major spheres of the law. Monopolies, antitrust, and labor-related cases supplement the business fundamentals of corporate law. The government cases document the legal evolution of the branches of the federal government as well as the federal government's relation to state power. Separate topics address military issues, taxation, and legal history behind some Native American issues.
- **Appendixes** to all volumes also present the full text of the U.S. Constitution and its amendments and a chronological table of Supreme Court justices.

Coverage

Issue overviews, averaging 2,000 words in length provide the context for the case profiles that follow. Case discussions range from 750 to 2,000 words according, to their complexity and importance. Each provides the background of the case and issues involved, the main arguments presented by each side, and an explanation of the Supreme Court's decision, as well as the legal, political, and social impact of the decision. Excerpts from the Court's opinions are often included. Within each issue section, the cases are arranged from earliest to most recent.

When a single case could be covered under several different areas—the landmark reproductive rights decision in *Roe v. Wade,* for example, is also based upon an assertion of privacy rights—the case is placed with the issue with which it is most often associated. Users should consult the cumulative index that appears in each volume to find cases throughout the set that apply to a particular topic.

Additional Features

- The issues and proceedings featured in *Supreme Court Drama* are presented in language accessible to middle school users. Legal terms must sometimes be used for precision, however, so a Words to Know section of more than 300 words and phrases appears in each volume.
- A general essay providing a broad overview of the Supreme Court of the United States and the structure of the American legal system.
- **Bolded** cross-references within overview and case entries that point to cases that appear elsewhere in the set.

- Tables of contents to locate a particular case by name or in chronological order.
- A cumulative index at the end of each volume that includes the cases, people, events and subjects that appear throughout *Supreme Court Drama.*

Suggestions Are Welcome

We welcome your comments on *Supreme Court Drama: Cases That Changed America.* Please write, Editors, *Supreme Court Drama,* U•X•L, 27500 Drake Road, Farmington Hills, MI 48331-3535; call toll-free: 1-800-877-4253; fax to 248-414-5043; or send e-mail via http://www.galegroup.com.

Advisors

The editor is grateful for all the assistance and insight offered by the advisors to this product.

- Mary Alice Anderson, Media Specialist, Winona Middle School, Winona, Minnesota
- Sara Brooke, Librarian, Ellis School, Pittsburgh, Pennsylvania
- Marolynn Griffin, Librarian, Desert Ridge Middle School, Albuquerque, New Mexico
- Dr. E. Shane McKee, Instructor, The Putney School at Elm Lea Farm, Putney, Vermont

The editor and writers would also like to acknowledge the tireless review and copy editing work done by:

- Aaron Ford, The Ohio State University, Columbus, Ohio
- Kathleen Knisely, Franklin County Courts, Columbus, Ohio
- Courtney Mroch, Freelance Writer, Jacksonville, Florida
- Melynda Neal, Franklin County Courts, Columbus, Ohio
- Berna Rhodes-Ford, Franklin County Courts, Columbus, Ohio
- Gertrude Ring, Freelance Writer, Los Angeles, California
- Lauren Zupnic, Franklin County Courts, Columbus, Ohio

Guide to the Supreme Court of the United States

The United States Supreme Court is the highest court in the judicial branch of the federal government. That means the Supreme Court is equal in importance to the president, who heads the executive branch, and Congress, which heads the legislative branch. Congress makes laws, the president enforces them, and the Supreme Court interprets them to make sure they are properly enforced.

The Supreme Court's main job is to review federal (national) and state cases that involve rights or duties under the U.S. Constitution, the document outlining the laws and guidelines for lawmaking and enforcement in the United States. The Court does this to make sure that all federal and state governments are obeying the Constitution.

For example, if Congress passes a law that violates the First Amendment freedom of speech, the Supreme Court can strike the law down as unconstitutional. If the president violates the Fourth Amendment by having the Federal Bureau of Investigation search a person's home without a warrant, the Supreme Court can fix the violation. If a state court violates the Constitution by convicting someone of a crime in an unfair trial, the Supreme Court can reverse the conviction.

As the highest court in the United States government, the Supreme Court also has the job of interpreting federal law. Congress creates law to regulate crimes, drugs, taxes, and other important issues across the nation. When someone is accused of violating a federal law, a federal

court must interpret the law to decide whether the accused has broken the law. In this role, the Supreme Court makes the final decision about what a federal law means.

The Federal Court System

The Supreme Court was born in 1789, when the United States adopted the Constitution. Article III of the Constitution says, "The judicial Power of the United States, shall be vested in one supreme Court, and in such inferior Courts as the Congress may from time to time ordain and establish." With this sentence, the Constitution made the Supreme Court the highest Court in the judicial branch of the federal government. It also gave Congress the power to create lower courts.

Congress used that power to create a large judicial (court) system. The system has three levels. Trial courts, called federal district courts, are at the lowest level. There are ninety-four federal district courts covering different areas of the country. Each federal district court handles trials for cases in its area.

Federal district courts hold trials in both criminal and civil cases. Criminal trials involve cases by the government against a person who is accused of a crime, like murder. Civil trials involve cases between private parties, such as when one person accuses another of breaking a contract or agreement.

When a party loses a case in federal district court, she usually may appeal the decision to a U.S. court of appeals. Federal courts of appeals are the second level in the federal judicial system. There are twelve courts of appeals covering twelve areas, or circuits, of the country. For example, the district courts in Connecticut, New York, and Vermont are part of the Second Circuit. Appeals from district courts in those states go to the U.S. Court of Appeals for the Second Circuit.

During an appeal, the losing party asks the court of appeals to reverse or modify the trial court's decision. In essence, she argues that the trial court made an error when it ruled against her.

The party who loses before the court of appeals must decide whether to take her case to the U.S. Supreme Court. The Supreme Court is the third and highest level of the federal judicial system. The process of taking a case to the U.S. Supreme Court is described below.

State Court Systems

Most states have a judicial system that resembles the federal system. Trial courts hold trials in both criminal and civil cases. Most states also have special courts that hear only certain kinds of cases. Family, juvenile, and traffic courts are typical examples. There also are state courts, such as justices of the peace and small claims courts, that handle minor matters.

Appeals from all lower courts usually go to a court of appeals. The losing party there may take her case to the state's highest court, often called the state supreme court. When a case involves the U.S. Constitution or federal law, the losing party sometimes may take the case from the state supreme court to the U.S. Supreme Court.

Bringing a Case to the U.S. Supreme Court

There are three main ways that cases get to the U.S. Supreme Court. The most widely used method is to ask the Supreme Court to hear the case. This is called filing a petition for a writ of *certiorari.* The person who files the petition, usually the person who lost the case in the court of appeals, is called the petitioner. The person on the other side of the case is called the respondent. The Court only grants a small percentage of the writ petitions it receives each year. It usually tries to accept the cases that involve the most important legal issues.

The second main way to bring a case to the Supreme Court is by appeal. An appeal is possible only when the law that the case involves says the parties may appeal to the Supreme Court. The losing party who files the appeal is called the appellant, while the person on the other side of the case is a called the appellee.

The third main way to bring a case to the Supreme Court is by filing a petition for a writ of habeas corpus. This petition is mainly for people who have been imprisoned in violation of the U.S. Constitution. For example, if an accused criminal is convicted and jailed after the police beat him to get a confession (a police act that is illegal), the prisoner may ask the Supreme Court to release him by filing a petition for a writ of habeas corpus. The person who files the petition is called the petitioner, while the person holding the petitioner in jail is called the respondent.

The process of arguing and deciding a case in the Supreme Court is similar no matter how the case gets there. The parties file briefs that

explain why they think the lower court's decision in their case is either right or wrong. The Supreme Court reviews the briefs along with a record of the evidence presented during trial in the federal district court or state trial court. The Supreme Court also may allow the parties to engage in oral argument, which is a chance for the lawyers to explain their clients' cases. During oral argument, the Supreme Court justices can ask questions to help them make the right decision.

After the justices read the briefs, review the record, and hear oral argument, they meet privately in chambers to discuss the case. Eventually, the nine justices vote for the party they think should win the case. A party must receive votes from five of the nine justices to win the case. The justices who cast the votes for the winning party are called the majority, while the justices who vote for the losing party are called the minority.

After the justices vote, one justice in the majority writes an opinion to explain the Court's decision. Other justices in the majority may write concurring opinions that explain why they agree with the Court's decision. Justices in the minority may write dissenting opinions to explain why they think the Court's decision is wrong.

The Supreme Court's decision is the final word in a case. Parties who are unhappy with the result have no place to go to get a different ruling. The only way to change the effect of a Supreme Court decision is to have Congress change the law, have the entire nation change, or amend, the Constitution, or have the president appoint a different justice to the Court when one retires or dies. This is part of the federal government's system of checks and balances, which prevents one branch from becoming too strong.

Supreme Court Justices

Supreme Court justices are among the greatest legal minds in the country. Appointment to the job is usually the high point of a career that involved some combination of trial work as a lawyer, teaching as a professor, or service as a judge on a lower court.

Under the Constitution, the president appoints Supreme Court justices with the advice and consent of the Senate when one of the nine justices retires, dies, or is removed from office. Supreme Court justices cannot be removed from office except by impeachment and conviction by Congress for serious crimes. That means the process of appointing a new justice usually begins when one of the justices retires or dies.

The president begins the process by nominating someone to fill the empty seat on the Court. The president usually names someone who he thinks will interpret the Constitution favorably to his political party's wishes. In other words, democratic presidents typically nominate liberal justices, while republican presidents nominate conservative justices.

The next step in the process is for the Senate Judiciary Committee to review the president's recommendation. If the Senate is controlled by the president's political party, the review process usually results in Senate approval of the president's selection.

If the president's political opposition controls the Senate, the review process can be fierce and lengthy. The Judiciary Committee calls the nominee before it to answer questions. The Committee's goal is to determine whether the nominee is qualified to be a Supreme Court justice. The Committee also uses the investigation to try to figure out how the nominee will decide controversial cases, such as cases involving abortion. After its investigation, the Committee recommends whether the Senate should confirm or reject the president's nomination. Two-thirds of the senators must vote for the nominee to confirm him as a new Supreme Court justice.

The Supreme Court has changed greatly over the years. One of the Court's greatest liberal periods was when Chief Justice Earl Warren headed the Court from 1953 to 1969. In 1954, the Warren Court decided one of its most famous cases, *Brown v. Board of Education,* in which it forced public schools to end the practice of separating black and white students in different schools.

The Warren Court was followed by one of the Court's greatest conservative periods, under Chief Justice Warren E. Burger from 1969 to 1986, followed by Chief Justice William H. Rehnquist from 1986 onward. In one of the Rehnquist Court's most important decisions, *Clinton v. Jones* (1997), the Court said the president may be sued while in office for conduct unrelated to his official duties. The decision allowed Paula Jones to sue President William J. Clinton for sexual harassment.

Unfortunately, the justices on the highest court in a nation of diversity have not been very diverse themselves. Until 1916, all Supreme Court justices were white, Christian men. That year, Louis D. Brandeis became the first Jewish member of the Supreme Court. In 1967, Thurgood Marshall became the first African American justice. Clarence Thomas became just the second in 1991. In 1981, President Ronald Reagan nominated Sandra Day O'Connor to be the first woman on the Supreme Court. Ruth Bader Ginsburg joined her there in 1993.

Research and Activity Ideas

Activity 1: New School Rule

Assignment: Imagine that your school principal has just announced a new school rule for detention. Students who get detention are not allowed to explain themselves, even if they did nothing wrong. Instead, they must sit in the principal's office during lunch. They are not allowed to eat lunch, not allowed to talk at all, and must listen to Frank Sinatra music during the entire period. Your teacher has asked you to prepare a written report on whether this new rule violates the U.S. Constitution.

Preparation: Begin your research by reading the Bill of Rights, which contains the first ten amendments to the U.S. Constitution, along with the Fourteenth Amendment. These amendments contain many rights that might apply to the principal's new rule. Do you see any that might help? Continue your research by looking in *Supreme Court Drama: Cases That Changed America* for essays and cases on the freedom of speech, cruel and unusual punishment, and students' rights in school. Consult the library and Internet web sites for additional research material. Does it seem to matter whether you are in a public or private school?

Presentation: After you have gathered your information, prepare a report that explains what you found. Does the principal's new rule violate the Constitution? Why or why not? Explain your conclusions by referring to specific amendments from the Constitution and specific cases from *Supreme Court Drama.*

Activity 2: Taking a Case to Court

Assignment: Pretend you were in a bookstore that was being robbed. When the police arrived to arrest the criminal, they accidentally arrested you. During the arrest they treated you roughly and broke your arm. Your lawyer has informed you that you may sue the police to recover damages in either state or federal court. Before deciding which court system to use, you must do some research about both systems.

Preparation: Begin by reading the Introduction to *Supreme Court Drama: Cases That Changed America* so you can learn about the federal and state court systems in general. Continue with library and Internet research for more information about these systems. Then figure out which courts you need to use for your case. For the state system, use the library and Internet to find your local trial court for civil cases. Then find your state court of appeals and supreme courts in case you lose in the trial court. For the federal system, find the federal district court and U.S. court of appeals for your area. Write to the state supreme court and the U.S. court of appeals to find out what percentage of cases make it from those courts to the U.S. Supreme Court each year.

Presentation: Write a letter to your attorney explaining what you found. Tell her where you need to file your case if you choose the state system, and where you need to take appeals in that system. Do the same for the federal system. Tell her what your chances are of getting to the U.S. Supreme Court with your case.

Activity 3: Oral Argument

Activity: Imagine that a new religious group called Planterism has moved into your community. Planters are a group of men who worship trees, flowers, and other plant life. Once every week they hold an all-night ceremony during which they burn a tree as a sacrifice for all living plants. The ceremony disturbs neighbors who are trying to sleep and threatens to eliminate rare trees in your town.

Your mayor or other local leader decides he does not like Planters, so he enacts the following law:

> **Everyone in this town must follow Christianity, Judaism, or some other popular religion. Anyone who follows a false religion, including Planterism, is guilty of a felony. Anyone who burns a tree as a**

> **sacrifice during a religious ceremony is guilty of a felony. Anyone who disturbs the peace with a religious ceremony at night is guilty of a felony.**
>
> **Violation of this law by men is punishable by life in prison without a trial. If the local police suspect a man is violating this law, they shall enter his house immediately without a warrant, arrest him, and take him to jail for imprisonment. Violation of this law by women is punishable by thirty days in jail only after a jury finds the woman guilty in a fair trial.**

Your teacher has instructed the class to convene a Supreme Court to determine whether this law violates the U.S. Constitution.

Preparation: Select nine members of your class to be justices on the Court. The rest of your class should divide into three teams. One team will represent the mayor, who will argue in favor of the law. The second team will represent a group of Planters who want to challenge the law. The third team will represent a group of Christians, who want to burn palms on Palm Sunday, a religious holiday that happens once a year.

The justices and all three teams should begin by reading the Bill of Rights and the Fourteenth Amendment of the U.S. Constitution. Continue by reading *Supreme Court Drama: Cases That Changed America* for essays and cases on the freedom of religion, the establishment clause, search and seizure, cruel and unusual punishment, governmental power, due process of law, and gender discrimination. Supplement this with research from library materials and Internet web sites. You may want to assign small groups from each team to handle specific issues.

Presentation: When everyone has completed the research, all three teams should prepare to argue before the Supreme Court. The team representing the mayor should explain why the law should be upheld. The teams representing the Planters and the Christians should explain why the law should be struck down as unconstitutional. During the argument, the justices are allowed to ask questions of each team. After every team has made its argument, the justices should meet to discuss the case and to make a ruling. Is the law unconstitutional? Which parts are valid and which are not?

Words to Know

A

Accessory Aiding or contributing in a secondary way to a crime or assisting in or contributing to a crime.

Accomplice One who knowingly and voluntarily helps commit a crime.

Acquittal When a person who has been charged with committing a crime is found not guilty by the courts.

Admissible A term used to describe information that is allowed to be used as evidence or information in a court case.

Adultery Voluntary sexual relations between an individual who is married and someone who is not the individual's spouse.

Affidavit A written statement of facts voluntarily made by someone in front of an official or witness.

Affirmative action Employment programs required by the federal government designed to eliminate existing and continuing discrimination, to remedy lingering effects of past discrimination, and to create systems and procedures to prevent future discrimination; commonly based on population percentages of minority groups in a particular area. Factors considered are race, color, sex, creed (religious beliefs), and age.

Age of consent The age at which a person may marry without parental approval.

Words to Know

Age of majority The age at which a person, formerly a minor or an infant, is recognized by law to be an adult, capable of managing his or her own affairs and responsible for any legal obligations created by his or her actions.

Aggravated assault A person is guilty of aggravated assault if he or she tries to cause serious bodily injury to another or causes such injury purposely, knowingly, or recklessly without any concern for that person or without remorse.

Alien Foreign-born person who has not been naturalized to become a U.S. citizen under federal law and the Constitution.

Alimony Payment a family court may order one person in a couple to make to the other when the couple separates or divorces.

Amendment An addition, deletion, or change to an original item, such as the additions to the Constitution.

Amicus curiae Latin for "friend of the court"; a person with strong interest in, views on, or knowledge of the subject matter of a case, but is not a party to the case. A friend of the court may petition the court for permission to file a statement about the situation.

Amnesty The action of a government by which all persons or certain groups of persons who have committed a criminal offense—usually of a political nature that threatens the government (such as treason)—are granted immunity from prosecution.

Appeal Timely plea by an unsuccessful party in a lawsuit to an appropriate superior court that has the power to review a final decision on the grounds that the decision was made in error.

Appellate court A court having jurisdiction to review decisions of a lower court.

Apportionment The process by which legislative seats are distributed among those who are entitled to representation; determination of the number of representatives that each state, county, or other subdivision may send to a legislative body.

Arbitration Taking a dispute to an unbiased third person and agreeing in advance to comply with the decision made by that third person, after both parties have had a chance to argue their side of the issue.

Arraignment The formal proceeding where the defendant is brought before the trial court to hear the charges against him or her and to enter a plea of guilty, not guilty, or no contest.

Arrest The taking into custody of an individual for the purpose of answering the charges against him or her.

Arrest warrant A written order issued by an authority of the state and commanding that the person named be taken into custody.

Arson The malicious burning or exploding of a house, building, or property.

Assault Intentionally harming another person.

Attempt Unsuccessfully preparing and trying to carry out a deed.

B

Bail An amount of money the defendant needs to pay the court to be released while waiting for a trial.

Bankruptcy A federally authorized procedure by which an individual, corporation, or municipality is relieved of total liability for its debts by making arrangements for the partial repayment of those debts.

Battery An intentional, unpermitted act causing harmful or offensive contact with another person.

Beneficiary One who inherits something through the last will and testament (will) of another; also, a person who is entitled to profits, benefits, or advantage from a contract.

Bigamy The offense of willfully and knowingly entering into a second marriage while married to another person.

Bill A written declaration that one hopes to have made into a law.

Bill of rights The first ten amendments to the U.S. Constitution, ratified (adopted by the states) in 1791, which set forth and guaranteed certain fundamental rights and privileges of individuals, including freedom of religion, speech, press, and assembly; guarantee of a speedy jury trial in criminal cases; and protection against excessive bail and cruel and unusual punishment.

Black codes Laws, statutes, or rules that governed slavery and segregation of public places in the South prior to 1865.

Bona fide occupational qualification An essential requirement for performing a given job. The requirement may even be a physical condition beyond an individual's control, such as perfect vision, if it is absolutely necessary for performing a job.

Brief A summary of the important points of a longer document.

Burden of proof The duty of a party to convince a judge or jury of their position, and to prove wrong any evidence that damages the position of the party. In criminal cases the party must prove their case beyond a reasonable doubt.

Burglary The criminal offense of breaking and entering a building illegally for the purpose of committing a crime.

Bylaws The rules and regulations of an association or a corporation to provide a framework for its operation and management.

C

Capacity The ability, capability, or fitness to do something; a legal right, power, or competency to perform some act. An ability to comprehend both the nature and consequences of one's acts.

Capital punishment The lawful infliction of death as a punishment; the death penalty.

Cause A reason for an action or condition. A ground of a legal action.

Censorship The suppression of speech or writing that is deemed obscene, indecent, or controversial.

Certiorari Latin for "to be informed of"; an order commanding officers of inferior courts to allow a case pending before them to move up to a higher court to determine whether any irregularities or errors occurred that justify review of the case. A device by which the Supreme Court of the United States exercises its discretion in selecting the cases it will review.

Change of venue The removal of a lawsuit from one county or district to another for trial, often permitted in criminal cases in which the court finds that the defendant would not receive a fair trial in the first location because of negative publicity.

Charter A grant from the government of ownership rights of land to a person, a group of people, or an organization, such as a corporation.

Circumstantial evidence Information and testimony presented by a party in a civil or criminal case that allows conclusions to be drawn about certain facts without the party presenting concrete evidence to support their facts.

Citation A paper commonly used in various courts that is served upon an individual to notify him or her that he or she is required to appear at a specific time and place.

Citizens Those who, under the Constitution and laws of the United States, owe allegiance to the United States and are entitled to the enjoyment of all civil rights awarded to those living in the United States.

Civil law A body of rules that spell out the private rights of citizens and the remedies for governing disputes between individuals in such areas as contracts, property, and family law.

Civil liberties Freedom of speech, freedom of press, freedom from discrimination, and other rights guaranteed and protected by the Constitution, which were intended to place limits on government.

Civil rights Personal liberties that belong to an individual.

Class action A lawsuit that allows a large number of people with a common interest in a matter to sue or be sued as a group.

Clause A section, phrase, paragraph, or segment of a legal document, such as a contract, deed, will, or constitution, that relates to a particular point.

Closing argument The final factual and legal argument made by each attorney on all sides of a case in a trial prior to the verdict or judgment.

Code A collection of laws, rules, or regulations that are consolidated and classified according to subject matter.

Collective bargaining agreement The contractual agreement between an employer and a labor union that controls pay, hours, and working conditions for employees which can be enforced against both the employer and the union for failure to comply with its terms.

Commerce Clause The provision of the U.S. Constitution that gives Congress exclusive power over trade activities between the states and with foreign countries and Native American tribes.

Commercial speech The words used in advertisments by commercial companies and service providers. Commercial speech is protected under the First Amendment as long as it is not false or misleading.

Common law The principles and rules of action, embodied in case law rather than legislative enactments, applicable to the government and protection of persons and property, Common laws derive their authority from the community customs and traditions that evolved over the centuries as interpreted by judicial tribunals (types of courts).

Common-law marriage A union of two people not formalized in the customary manner but created by an agreement by the two people to consider themselves married followed by their living together.

Community property The materials and resources owned in common by a husband and wife.

Complaint The possible evidence that initiates a civil action; in criminal law, the document that sets in motion a person's being charged with an offense.

Concurring opinion An opinion by one or more judges that provides separate reasoning for reaching the same decision as the majority of the court.

Conditional Subject to change; dependent upon the occurrence of a future, uncertain event.

Confession A statement made by an individual that acknowledges his or her guilt of a crime.

Conflict of interest A term used to describe the situation in which a public official exploits his or her position for personal benefit.

Consent Voluntary agreement to the proposal of another; the act or result of reaching an agreement.

Conspiracy An agreement between two or more persons to engage in an unlawful or criminal act, or an act that is innocent in itself but becomes unlawful when done by those participating.

Constituent A person who gives another person permission to act on his or her behalf, such as an agent, an attorney in a court of law, or an elected official in government.

Constitution of the United States A document written by the founding fathers of the United States that has been added to by Congress over

the centuries that is held as the absolute rule of action and decision for all branches and offices of the government, and which all subsequent laws and ordinances must be in accordance. It is enforced by representatives of the people of the United States, and can be changed only by a constitutional amendment by the authority that created it.

Contempt An act of deliberate disobedience or disregard for the laws or regulations of a public authority, such as a court or legislative body.

Continuance The postponement of an action pending (waiting to be tried) in a court to a later date, granted by a court in response to a request made by one of the parties to a lawsuit.

Corporations Business entities that are treated much like human individuals under the law, having legally enforceable rights, the ability to acquire debt and pay out profits, the ability to hold and transfer property, the ability to enter into contracts, the requirement to pay taxes, and the ability to sue and be sued.

Counsel An attorney or lawyer.

Court of appeal An intermediate court of review that is found in thirteen judicial districts, called circuits, in the United States. A state court of appeal reviews a decision handed down by a lower court to determine whether that court made errors that warrant the reversal of its final decision.

Covenant An agreement, contract, or written promise between two individuals that frequently includes a pledge to do or refrain from doing something.

Criminal law A body of rules and statutes that defines behavior prohibited by the government because it threatens and/or harms public safety, and establishes the punishments to be given to those who commit such acts.

Cross-examination The questioning of a witness or party during a trial, hearing, or deposition by the opposing lawyer.

Cruel and unusual punishment Such punishment as would amount to torture or barbarity, any cruel and degrading punishment, or any fine, penalty, confinement, or treatment so disproportionate to the offense as to shock the moral sense of the community.

Custodial parent The parent to whom the court grants guardianship of the children after a divorce.

Words to Know

D

Death penalty See Capital punishment.

De facto Latin for "in fact"; in deed; actually.

Defamation Any intentional false communication, either written or spoken, that harms a person's reputation; decreases the respect, regard, or confidence in which a person is held; or causes hostile or disagreeable opinions or feelings against a person.

Defendant The person defending or denying; the party against whom recovery is sought in an action or suit, or the accused in a criminal case.

Defense The forcible reaction against an unlawful and violent attack, such as the defense of one's person, property, or country in time of war.

De jure Latin for "in law"; legitimate; lawful, as a matter of law. Having complied with all the requirements imposed by law.

Deliberate Willful; purposeful; determined after thoughtful evaluation of all relevant factors. To act with a particular intent, which is derived from a careful consideration of factors that influence the choice to be made.

Delinquent An individual who fails to fulfill an obligation or otherwise is guilty of a crime or offense.

Domestic partnership laws Legislation and regulations related to the legal recognition of nonmarital relationships between persons who are romantically involved with each other, have set up a joint residence, and have registered with cities recognizing said relationships.

Denaturalization To take away an individual's rights as a citizen.

Deportation Banishment to a foreign country, attended with confiscation of property and deprivation of civil rights.

Deposition The testimony of a party or witness in a civil or criminal proceeding taken before trial, usually in an attorney's office.

Desegregation Judicial mandate making illegal the practice of segregation.

Disclaimer The denial, refusal, or rejection of a right, power, or responsibility.

Discrimination The grant of particular privileges to a group randomly chosen from a large number of people in which no reasonable dif-

ference exists between the favored and disfavored groups. Federal laws prohibit discrimination in such areas as employment, housing, voting rights, education, access to public facilities, and on the bases of race, age, sex, nationality, disability, or religion.

Dismissal A discharge of an individual or corporation from employment.

Dissent A disagreement by one or more judges with the decision of the majority on a case before them.

Divorce A court decree that terminates a marriage; also known as marital dissolution.

Double jeopardy A second prosecution for the same offense after acquittal or conviction or multiple punishments for the same offense. The evil sought to be avoided by prohibiting double jeopardy is double trial and double conviction, not necessarily double punishment.

Draft A mandatory call of persons to serve in the military.

Due process of law A fundamental, constitutional guarantee that all legal proceedings will be fair and that one will be given notice of the proceedings and an opportunity to be heard before the government acts to take away one's life, liberty, or property. Also, a constitutional guarantee that a law shall not be unreasonable, random, or without consideration for general well-being.

Duress Unlawful pressure exerted upon a person to force that person to perform an act that he or she ordinarily would not perform.

E

Emancipation The act or process by which a person is liberated from the authority and control of another person.

Entrapment The act of government agents or officials that causes a person to commit a crime he or she would not have committed otherwise.

Equal Pay Act Federal law that commands the same pay for all persons who do the same work without regard to sex, age, race, or ability.

Equal protection The constitutional guarantee that no person or class of persons shall be denied the same protection of the laws that is enjoyed by other persons or other classes in like circumstances in their lives, liberty, property, and pursuit of happiness.

Establishment Clause The provision in the First Amendment that provides that there will be no laws created respecting the establishment of a religion, inhibiting the practice of a religion, or giving preference to any or all religions. It has been interpreted to also denounce the discouragement of any or all religions.

Euthanasia The merciful act or practice of terminating the life of an individual or individuals inflicted with incurable and distressing diseases in a relatively painless manner.

Exclusionary rule The principle based on federal constitutional law that evidence illegally seized by law enforcement officers in violation of a suspect's right to be free from unreasonable searches and seizures cannot be used against the suspect in a criminal prosecution.

Executive agreement An agreement made between the head of a foreign country and the president of the United States. This agreement does not have to be submitted to the Senate for consent, and it supersedes any contradicting state law.

Executive orders When the president uses some part of a law or the Constitution to enforce some action.

Executor The individual legally named by a deceased person to administer the provisions of his or her will.

Ex parte Latin for "on one side only"; done by, for, or on the application of one party alone.

Expert witness A witness, such as a psychological statistician or ballisticsexpert, who possesses special or superior knowledge concerning the subject of his or her testimony.

Ex post facto laws Latin for "after-the-fact laws"; laws that provide for the infliction of punishment upon a person for some prior act that, at the time it was committed, was not illegal.

Extradition The transfer of a person accused of a crime from one state or country to another state or country that seeks to place the accused on trial.

F

Family court A court that presides over cases involving: (1) child abuse and neglect; (2) support; (3) paternity; (4) termination of custody due to constant neglect; (5) juvenile delinquency; and (6) family offenses.

Federal Relating to a national government, as opposed to state or local governments.

Federal circuit courts The twelve circuit courts making up the U.S. Federal Circuit Court System. Decisions made by the federal district courts can be reviewed by the court of appeals in each circuit.

Federal district courts The first of three levels of the federal court system, which includes the U.S. Court of Appeals and the U.S. Supreme Court. If a participating party disagrees with the ruling of a federal district court in its case, it may petition for the case to be moved to the next level in the federal court system.

Felon An individual who commits a felony, a crime of a serious nature, such as burglary or murder.

Felony A serious crime, characterized under federal law and many state statutes as any offense punishable by death or imprisonment in excess of one year.

First degree murder Murder committed with deliberately premeditated thought and malice, or with extreme atrocity or cruelty. The difference between first and second degree murder is the presence of the specific intention to kill.

Fraud A false representation of a matter of fact—whether by words or by conduct, by false or misleading allegations, or by concealment of what should have been disclosed—that deceives and is intended to deceive another so that the individual will act upon it to her or his legal injury.

Freedom of assembly See Freedom of association.

Freedom of association The right to associate with others for the purpose of engaging in constitutionally protected activities, such as to peacefully assemble.

Freedom of religion The First Amendment right to individually believe and to practice or exercise one's religious belief.

Freedom of speech The right, guaranteed by the First Amendment to the U.S. Constitution, to express beliefs and ideas without unwarranted government restriction.

Freedom of the press The right, guaranteed by the First Amendment to the U.S. Constitution, to gather, publish, and distribute information and ideas without government restriction; this right encompasses

freedom from prior restraints on publication and freedom from censorship.

Fundamental rights Rights that derive, or are implied, from the terms of the U.S. Constitution, such as the Bill of Rights, the first ten amendments to the Constitution.

G

Gag rule A rule, regulation, or law that prohibits debate or discussion of a particular issue.

Grandfather clause A portion of a statute that provides that the law is not applicable in certain circumstances due to preexisting facts.

Grand jury A panel of citizens that is convened by a court to decide whether it is appropriate for the government to indict (proceed with a prosecution against) someone suspected of a crime.

Grand larceny A category of larceny—the offense of illegally taking the property of another—in which the value of the property taken is greater than that set for petit larceny.

Grounds The basis or foundation; reasons sufficient in law to justify relief.

Guardian A person lawfully invested with the power, and charged with the obligation, of taking care of and managing the property and rights of a person who, because of age, understanding, or lack of self-control, is considered incapable of administering his or her own affairs.

Guardian ad litem A guardian appointed by the court to represent the interests of infants, the unborn, or incompetent persons in legal actions.

H

Habeas corpus Latin for "you have the body"; a writ (court order) that commands an individual or a government official who has restrained another to produce the prisoner at a designated time and place so that the court can determine the legality of custody and decide whether to order the prisoner's release.

Hate crime A crime motivated by race, religion, gender, sexual orientation, or other prejudice.

Hearing A legal proceeding in which issues of law or fact are tried and evidence is presented to help determine the issue.

Hearsay A statement made out of court that is offered in court as evidence to prove the truth of the matter asserted.

Heir An individual who receives an interest in, or ownership of, land or tenements from an ancestor who died through the laws of descent and distribution. At common law, an heir was the individual appointed by law to succeed to the estate of an ancestor who died without a will. It is commonly used today in reference to any individual who succeeds to property, either by will or law.

Homicide The killing of one human being by another human being.

Hung jury A trial jury selected to make a decision in a criminal case regarding a defendant's guilt or innocence that is unable to reach a verdict due to a complete division in opinion.

I

Immunity Exemption from performing duties that the law generally requires other citizens to perform, or from a penalty or burden that the law generally places on other citizens.

Impeachment A process used to charge, try, and remove public officials for misconduct while in office.

Inalienable Not subject to sale or transfer; inseparable.

Incapacity The absence of legal ability, competence, or qualifications.

Income tax A charge imposed by government on the annual gains of a person, corporation, or other taxable unit derived through work, business pursuits, investments, property dealings, and other sources determined in accordance with the Internal Revenue Code or state law.

Indictment A written accusation charging that an individual named therein has committed an act or admitted to doing something that is punishable by law.

Indirect tax A tax upon some right, privilege, or corporation.

Words to Know

Individual rights Rights and privileges constitutionally guaranteed to the people as set forth by the Bill of Rights; the ability of a person to pursue life, liberty, and property.

Infant Persons who are under the age of the legal majority—at common law, twenty-one years, now generally eighteen years. According to the sense in which this term is used, it may denote the age of the person, the contractual disabilities that nonage entails, or his or her status with regard to other powers or relations.

Inherent rights Rights held within a person because he or she exists.

Inheritance Property received from a person who has died, either by will or through state laws if the deceased has failed to execute a valid will.

Injunction A court order by which an individual is required to perform or is restrained from performing a particular act. A writ framed according to the circumstances of the individual case.

In loco parentis Latin for "in the placeof a parent"; the legal doctrine under which an individual assumes parental rights, duties, and obligations without going through the formalities of legal adoption.

Insanity defense A defense asserted by an accused in a criminal prosecution to avoid responsibility for a crime because, at the time of the crime, the person did not comprehend the nature or wrongfulness of the act.

Insider Relating to the federal regulation of the purchase and sale of stocks and bonds, anyone who has knowledge of facts not available to the general public.

Insider trading The trading of stocks and bonds based on information gained from special private, privileged information affecting the value of the stocks and bonds.

Intent A determination to perform a particular act or to act in a particular manner for a specific reason; an aim or design; a resolution to use a certain means to reach an end.

Intermediate courts Courts with general ability or authority to hear a case (trial, appellate, or both) but are not the court of last resort within the jurisdiction.

Intestate The description of a person who dies without making a valid will.

Involuntary manslaughter The act of unlawfully killing another human being unintentionally.

Irrevocable Unable to cancel or recall; that which is unalterable or irreversible.

J

Judicial Relating to courts and the legal system.

Judicial discretion Sound judgment exercised by a judge in determining what is right and fair under the law.

Judicial review A court's authority to examine an executive or legislative act and to invalidate (cancel) that act if it opposes constitutional principles.

Jurisdiction The geographic area over which authority (such as a cout) extends; legal authority.

Jury In trials, a group of people selected and sworn to inquire into matters of fact and to reach a verdict on the basis of evidence presented to it.

Jury nullification The ability of a jury to acquit the defendant despite the amount of evidence against him or her in a criminal case.

Just cause A reasonable and lawful ground for action.

Justifiable homicide The killing of another in self-defense or in the lawful defense of one's property; killing of another when the law demands it, such as in execution for a capital crime.

Juvenile A young individual who has not reached the age whereby he or she would be treated as an adult in the area of criminal law. The age at which the young person attains the status of being a legal majority varies from state to state—as low as fourteen years old, as high as eighteen years old; however, the Juvenile Delinquency Act determines that a youthful person under the age of eighteen is a juvenile in cases involving federal jurisdiction.

Juvenile court The court presiding over cases in which young persons under a certain age, depending on the area of jurisdiction, are accused of criminal acts.

Juvenile delinquency The participation of a youthful individual, one who falls under the age at which he or she could be tried as an adult, in illegal behavior.

L

Larceny The unauthorized taking and removal of the personal property of another by a person who intends to permanently deprive the owner of it; a crime against the right of possession.

Legal defense A complete and acceptable response as to why the claims of the plaintiff should not be granted in a point of law.

Legal tender All U.S. coins and currencies—regardless of when coined or issued—including (in terms of the Federal Reserve System) Federal Reserve notes and circulating notes of Federal Reserve banks and national banking associations that are used for all public and private debts, public charges, taxes, duties, and dues.

Legislation Lawmaking; the preparation and enactment of laws by a legislative body.

Liability A comprehensive legal term that describes the condition of being actually or potentially subject to (responsible for) a legal obligation.

Libel and slander The communication of false information about a person, a group, or an entity, such as a corporation. Libel is any defamation that can be seen, such as in print or on a film or in a representation such as a statued. Slander is any defamation that is spoken and heard.

Litigation An action brought in court to enforce a particular right; the act or process of bringing a lawsuit in and of itself; a judicial contest; any dispute.

Living will A written document that allows a patient to give explicit instructions about medical treatment to be administered when the patient is terminally ill or permanently unconscious; also called an advance directive.

Lobbying The process of influencing public and government policy at all levels: federal, state, and local.

M

Magistrate Any individual who has the power of a public civil officer or inferior judicial officer, such as a justice of the peace.

Majority Full age; legal age; age at which a person is no longer a minor. The age at which, by law, a person is capable of being legally respon-

sible for all of his or her acts (i.e., contractual obligations) and is entitled to manage his or her own affairs and to the enjoy civic rights (i.e., right to vote). Also the status of a person who is a major in age.

Malice The intentional commission of a wrongful act, without justification, with the intent to cause harm to others; conscious violation of the law that injures another individual; a mental state indicating a disregard of social responsibility.

Malpractice When a professional, such as a doctor or lawyer, fails to carry out their job correctly and there are bad results.

Mandate A judicial command or order from a court.

Manslaughter The unjustifiable, inexcusable, and intentional killing of a human being without deliberation, premeditation, or malice.

Material Important; significant; substantial. A description of the quality of evidence that possesses such value as to establish the truth or falsity of a point in issue in a lawsuit.

Mediation Settling a dispute or controversy by setting up an independent person between the two parties to help them settle their disagreement.

Minor An infant or person who is under the age of legal competence. In most states, a person is no longer a minor after reaching the age of eighteen (though state laws might still prohibit certain acts until reaching a greater age; i.e., purchase of liquor).

Misdemeanor Offenses lower than felonies and generally those punishable by fine, penalty, or imprisonment other than in a penitentiary.

Mistrial A courtroom trial that has been ended prior to its normal conclusion. A mistrial has no legal effect and is considered an invalid trial. It differs from a new trial, which recognizes that a trial was completed but was set aside so that the issues could be tried again.

Mitigating circumstances Circumstances that may be considered by a court in determining responsibility of a defendant or the extent of damages to be awarded to a plaintiff. Mitigating circumstances do not justify or excuse an offense but may reduce the charge.

Monopoly An economic advantage held by one or more persons or companies because they hold the exclusive power to carry out a particular business or trade or to manufacture and sell a particular task or produce a particular product.

Moratorium A suspension (ending) of activity or an authorized period of delay or waiting. A moratorium is sometimes agreed upon by the interested parties, or it may be authorized or imposed by operation of law.

Motion A written or oral application made to a court or judge to obtain a ruling or order directing that some act be done in favor of the applicant.

Motive An idea, belief, or emotion that causes a person to act in a certain way, either good or bad.

Murder The unlawful killing of another human being without justification or excuse.

N

National origin The country in which a person was born or from which his or her ancestors came. One's national origin is typically calculated by employers to provide equal employment opportunity statistics in accordance with the provisions of the Civil Rights Act.

Naturalization A process by which a person gains nationality and becomes entitled to the privileges of citizenship. While groups of individuals have been naturalized in history by treaties or laws of Congress, such as in the case of Hawaii, typically naturalization occurs on the individual level upon the completion of a list of requirements.

Necessary and Proper Clause The statement contained in Article I, Section 8, Clause 18 of the U.S. Constitution that gives Congress the power to pass any laws that are necessary and proper to carrying out its specifically granted powers.

Negligence Conduct that falls below the standards of behavior established by law for the protection of others against unreasonable risk of harm.

Nonprofit A corporation or an association that conducts business for the benefit of the general public rather than to gain profits for itself.

Notary public A public official whose main powers include administering oaths and witnessing signatures, both important and effective ways to minimize fraud in legal documents.

O

Obscenity An act, spoken word, or item tending to offend public morals by its indecency or lewdness.

Ordinance A law, statute, or regulation enacted by a municipality.

P

Palimony The settlement awarded at the end of a non-marital relationship, where the couple lived together for a long period of time and where there was an agreement that one partner would support the other in return for the second making a home and performing domestic duties.

Pardon When a person in power, such as a president or governor, offers a formal statement of forgivenss for a crime and takes away the given punishment.

Parental liability A statute (law), enacted in some states, that makes parents responsible for damages caused by their children if it is found that the damages resulted from the parents' lack of control over the acts of the child.

Parole The release of a person convicted of a crime prior to the end of that person's term of imprisonment on the condition that they will follow certain strict rules for their conduct, and if they break any of those rules they will return to prison.

Patents Rights granted to inventors by the federal government that permit them to keep others from making, using, or selling their invention for a definite, or restricted, period of time.

Peremptory challenge The right to challenge the use of a juror in a trial without being required to give a reason for the challenge.

Perjury A crime that occurs when an individual willfully makes a false statement during a judicial proceeding, after he or she has taken an oath to speak the truth.

Petition A formal application made to a court in writing that requests action on a certain matter.

Petit larceny A form of larceny—the stealing of another's personal property—in which the value of the property that is taken is generally less than $50.

Words to Know

Plaintiff The party who sues in a civil action.

Plain view doctrine In the context of searches and seizures, the principle that provides that objects that an officer can easily see can be seized without a search warrant and are fair to use as evidence.

Plea The phase in a court case where the defendant has to declare whether they are guilty or not guilty.

Police power The authority that states to employ a police force and give them the power to enforce the laws and protect the community.

Poll tax A specified sum of money to be paid by each person who votes.

Polygamy The offense of having more than one wife or husband at the same time.

Precedent A court decision that is cited as an example to resolve similar questions of law in later cases.

Preponderance of evidence A rule that states that it is up to the plaintiff to convince the judge or the jury of their side of the case in or to win the case.

Prima facie [*Latin,* On the first appearance.]A fact presumed to be true unless it is disproved.

Prior restraint Government violating freedom of speech by not allowing something to be published.

Privacy In constitutional law, the right of people to make personal decisions regarding intimate matters; under the common law, the right of people to lead their lives in a manner that is reasonably secluded from public scrutiny, whether such scrutiny comes from a neighbor's prying eyes, an investigator's eavesdropping ears, or a news photographer's intrusive camera; and in statutory law, the right of people to be free from unwarranted drug testing and electronic surveillance.

Privilege An advantage or benefit possessed by an individual, company, or class beyond those held by others.

Privileges and immunities Concepts contained in the U.S. Constitution that place the citizens of each state on an equal basis with citizens of other states with respect to advantages resulting from citizenship in those states and citizenship in the United States.

Probable cause Apparent facts discovered through logical inquiry that would lead a reasonably intelligent person to believe that an accused person has committed a crime.

Probate court Called Surrogate or Orphan's Court in some states, the probate court presides over wills, the administration of estates, and, in some states, the appointment of guardians or approval of the adoption of minors.

Probation A sentence whereby a convict is released from confinement but is still under court supervision; a testing or a trial period. It can be given in lieu of a prison term or can suspend a prison sentence if the convict has consistently demonstrated good behavior.

Procedural due process The constitutional guarantee that one's liberty and property rights may not be affected unless reasonable notice and an opportunity to be heard in order to present a claim or defense are provided.

Property A thing or things owned either by government—public property—or owned by private individuals, groups, or companies—private property.

Prosecute To follow through; to commence and continue an action or judicial proceeding to its conclusion. To proceed against a defendant by charging that person with a crime and bringing him or her to trial.

Prosecution The proceedings carried out before a court to determine the guilt or innocence of a defendant. The term also refers to the government attorney charging and trying a criminal case.

Punitive damages Money awarded to an injured party that goes beyond that which is necessary to pay for the individual for losses and that is intended to punish the wrongdoer.

Q

Quorum A majority of an entire body; i.e., a quorum of a legislative assembly.

Quota The number of persons or things that must be used, or admitted, or hired in order to be following a rule or law.

R

Rape A criminal offense defined in most states as forcible sexual relations with a person against that person's will.

Ratification The confirmation or adoption of an act that has already been performed.

Words to Know

Reapportionment The realignment of voting districts done to fulfill the constitutional requirement of one person, one vote.

Referendum The right reserved to the people to approve or reject an act of the legislature, or the right of the people to approve or reject legislation that has been referred to them by the legislature.

Refugees Individuals who leave their native country for social, political, or religious reasons, or who are forced to leave as a result of any type of disaster, including war, political upheaval, and famine.

Rehabilitation Work to restore former rights, authority, or abilities.

Remand To send back.

Replevin A legal action to recover the possession of items of personal property.

Reprieve The temporary hold put on a death penalty for further review of the case.

Rescind To declare a contract void—of no legal force or binding effect—from its beginning and thereby restore the parties to the positions they would have been in had no contract ever been made.

Reservation A tract of land under the control of the Bureau of Indian Affairs to which a Native American tribe retains its original title of ownership, or that has been set aside from the public domain for use by a tribe.

Reserve Funds set aside to cover future expenses, losses, or claims. To retain; to keep in store for future or special use; to postpone to a future time.

Resolution The official expression of the opinion or will of a legislative body.

Retainer A contract between attorney and client specifying the nature of the services and the cost of the services.

Retribution Punishment or reward for an act. In criminal law, punishment is based upon the theory that every crime demands payment.

Reverse discrimination Discrimination against a group of people that is generally considered to be the majority, usually stemming from the enforcement of some affirmative action guidlelines.

Revocation The recall of some power or authority that has been granted.

Robbery The taking of money or goods in the possession of another, from his or her person or immediate presence, by force or intimidation.

S

Sabotage The willful destruction or impairment of war material or national defense material, or harm to war premises or war utilities. During a labor dispute, the willful and malicious destruction of an employer's property or interference with his or her normal operations.

Search warrant A court order authorizing the examination of a place for the purpose of discovering evidence of guilt to be used in the prosecution of a criminal action.

Second degree murder The unlawful taking of human life with malice, but without premeditated thought.

Sedition A revolt or an incitement to revolt against established authority, usually in the form of treason or defamation against government.

Seditious libel A written communication intended to incite the overthrow of the government by force or violence.

Segregation The act or process of separating a race, class, or ethnic group from a society's general population.

Self-defense The protection of one's person or property against some injury attempted by another.

Self-incrimination Giving testimony in a trial or other legal proceeding that could subject one to criminal prosecution.

Sentencing The post-conviction stage of a criminal justice process, in which the defendant is brought before the court for penalty.

Separate but equal The doctrine first accepted by the U.S. Supreme Court in *Plessy v. Ferguson* establishing that different facilities for blacks and whites was valid under the Equal Protection Clause of the Fourteenth Amendment as long as they were equal.

Separation of church and state The separation of religious and government interest to ensure that religion does not become corrupt by government and that government does not become corrupt by religious conflict. The principle prevents the government from supporting the practices of one religion over another. It also enables the government to do what is necessary to prevent one religious group from violating the rights of others.

Separation of powers The division of state and federal government into three independent branches.

Words to Know

Settlement The act of adjusting or determining the dealings or disputes between persons without pursuing the matter through a trial.

Sexual harassment Unwelcome sexual advances, requests for sexual favors, and other verbal or physical conduct of a sexual nature that tends to create a hostile or offensive work environment.

Share A portion or part of something that may be divided into components, such as a sum of money. A unit of stock that represents ownership in a corporation.

Shield laws Statutes that allow journalists not to disclose in legal proceedings confidential information or sources of information obtained in their professional capacities.

Statutes that restrict or prohibit the use of certain evidence in sexual offense cases, such as evidence regarding the lack of chastity of the victim.

Shoplifting Theft of merchandise from a store or business establishment.

Small claims court A special court that provides fast, informal, and inexpensive solutions for small claims.

Solicitation The criminal offense of urging someone to commit an unlawful act.

Statute An act of a legislature that declares, or commands something; a specific law, expressed in writing.

Statute of limitations A type of federal or state law that restricts the time within which legal proceedings may be brought.

Statutory law A law which is created by an act of the legislature.

Statutory rape Sexual intercourse by an adult with a person below a designated age.

Subpoena Latin for "under penalty"; a formal document that orders a named individual to appear before an officer of the court at a fixed time to give testimony.

Suffrage The right to vote at public elections.

Summons The paper that tells a defendant that he or she is being sued and asserts the power of the court to hear and determine the case. A form of legal process that commands the defendant to appear before the court on a specific day and to answer the complaint made by the plaintiff.

Supreme court The highest court in the U.S. judicial system.

Surrogate mother A woman who agrees under contract to bear a child for an infertile couple. The woman is paid to have a donated fertilized egg or the fertilized egg of the female partner in the couple (usually fertilized by the male partner of the couple) artificially placed into her uterus.

Suspended sentence A sentence that states that a criminal, in waiting for their trial, has already served enough time in prison.

Symbolic speech Nonverbal gestures and actions that are meant to communicate a message.

T

Testify To provide evidence as a witness in order to establish a particular fact or set of facts.

Testimony Oral evidence offered by a competent witness under oath, which is used to establish some fact or set of facts.

Trade secret Any valuable commercial information that provides a business with an advantage over competitors who do not have that information.

Trade union An organization of workers in the same skilled occupation or related skilled occupations who act together to secure for all members favorable wages, hours, and other working conditions.

Treason The betrayal of one's own country by waging war against it or by consciously or purposely acting to aid its enemies.

Treaty A compact made between two or more independent nations with a view to the public welfare.

Trespass An unlawful intrusion that interferes with one's person or property.

Trial A judicial examination and determination of facts and legal issues arising between parties to a civil or criminal action.

Trial court The court where civil actions or criminal proceedings are first heard.

Truancy The willful and unjustified failure to attend school by one required to do so.

U

Unenumerated rights Rights that are not expressly mentioned in the written text of a constitution but instead are inferred from the language, history, and structure of the constitution, or cases interpreting it.

Unconstitutional That which is not in agreement with the ideas and regulations of the Constitution.

Uniform commercial code A general and inclusive group of laws adopted, at least partially, by all of the states to further fair dealing in business.

V

Valid Binding; possessing legal force or strength; legally sufficient.

Vandalism The intentional and malicious destruction of or damage to the property of another.

Venue A place, such as a city or county, from which residents are selected to serve as jurors.

Verdict The formal decision or finding made by a jury concerning the questions submitted to it during a trial. The jury reports the verdict to the court, which generally accepts it.

Veto The refusal of an executive officer to approve a bill that has been created and approved by the legislature, thereby keeping the bill from becoming a law.

Voir dire Old French for "to speak the truth"; the preliminary examination of possible jurors to determine their qualifications and suitability to serve on a jury, in order to ensure the selection of a fair and impartial jury.

Voluntary manslaughter The unlawful killing of a person where there is no malice, premeditation or deliberate intent but too near to these standards to be classified as justifiable homicide.

W

Waive To intentionally or voluntarily give up a known right or engage in conduct that caused your rights to be taken away.

Ward A person, especially an infant or someone judged to be incompetent, placed by the court in the care of a guardian.

Warrant A written order issued by a judicial officer commanding a law enforcement officer to perform a duty. This usually includes searches, seizures and arrests.

White collar crime Term for nonviolent crimes that were committed in the course of the offender's occupation.

Will A document in which a person explains the management and distribution of his or her estate after his or her death.

Workers' compensation A system whereby an employer must pay, or provide insurance to pay, the lost wages and medical expenses of an employee who is injured on the job.

Writ An order issued by a court requiring that something be done.

Z

Zoning Assigning different areas within a city or county different uses, whereby one area cannot be used for any other purpose other than what it is designated. For example, if an area is assigned as residential, an office building could not be built there.

Capital punishment, also called the death penalty, means killing a person as punishment for a crime. By the end of 1999, thirty-eight states and the federal government allowed the death penalty for criminal homicide, or murder. The District of Columbia and the following states did not allow the death penalty: Alaska, Hawaii, Iowa, Maine, Massachusetts, Michigan, Minnesota, North Dakota, Rhode Island, Vermont, West Virginia, and Wisconsin.

In 1999 ninety-eight executions occurred in the United States, up from sixty-eight in 1998. Ninety-four were by lethal injection, which kills the criminal with a deadly chemical solution. Three were by electrocution in an electric chair. Just one was with lethal gas, by which the state locks the criminal in a room with deadly gas. The only other methods allowed in the United States, hanging and firing squad, were not used in 1999.

History

Colonists brought the death penalty to America from England. The first recorded execution in America happened in the Jamestown Colony of

Virginia in 1608. Death penalty laws varied widely in the colonies. In 1636, the Massachusetts Bay Colony allowed capital punishment for a long list of crimes that included witchcraft and blasphemy. Pennsylvania, by contrast, initially allowed the death penalty only for treason and murder.

In the wake of the American Revolution in 1776, eleven colonies became states with new constitutions. Nine of the states prohibited cruel and unusual punishment, but all allowed the death penalty. In 1790, the first U.S. Congress passed a law allowing the death penalty for crimes of robbery, rape, murder, and forgery of public securities (notes and bonds for the payment of money). Under most of these laws, the death penalty was an automatic punishment for murder and other serious crimes.

Ever since the United States was established, many Americans have opposed the death penalty. In 1845, the American Society for the Abolition of Capital Punishment was formed. In 1847, Michigan became the first state to abolish capital punishment for all crimes except treason. By 1850, nine states had societies working to abolish capital punishment. Reflecting this trend, many states and other countries began to reduce the crimes punishable by death to murder and treason. Nevertheless, nearly 1400 recorded executions took place in the United States in the 1800s.

The movement to abolish capital punishment had both high and low points in the 1900s. On the up side, by the beginning of the century most states had changed their laws. Instead of making the death penalty automatic, new laws allowed juries to choose between death or imprisonment.

A low point, however, was in the 1930s and 1940s when between one hundred and two hundred prisoners were executed each year. Executions then declined in the 1950s and 1960s, partly because more prisoners began fighting their sentences in court. This trend led to a series of U.S. Supreme Court cases in the 1970s about whether the death penalty violates the U.S. Constitution.

Cruel and unusual punishment

The Eighth Amendment of the U.S. Constitution says that the government may not use "cruel and unusual punishments." Death penalty opponents say that this makes capital punishment unlawful. However, supporters argue that the Eighth Amendment only prevents torture and other barbaric punishments. They point out that the Fifth and Fourteenth Amendments say that the government may not take a person's life without "due process of law." Due process of law means using fair procedures to give a defendant a fair trial. For death penalty supporters, this means capital punishment is lawful if the government follows fair procedures.

Beginning in 1967, the nation stopped executions so the courts could examine whether the death penalty violated the U.S. Constitution. At that time, no guidelines were in effect to help juries decide between life or death. Studies showed that juries randomly chose the death penalty. For example, in cases that were similar some defendants got the death penalty, while others just went to prison.

Other studies suggested that the death penalty treated whites better than blacks. Blacks were sentenced to death more often than whites. Criminals who killed white people received the death penalty more often than those who killed black people.

In ***Furman v. Georgia*** (1972), the defendant argued to the Supreme Court that these random and racial results made the death penalty unconstitutional. With a 5–4 decision, the Supreme Court agreed. Justice William O. Douglas said that death penalty laws are cruel and unusual when they are unfair to African Americans and to poor, uneducated, and mentally ill people. Justice Douglas said America's laws were unfair because they did not give juries any guidance for choosing between life or death.

States reacted to *Furman* in two different ways. Some states passed new laws that made the death penalty automatic. In other words, if a defendant was found guilty of murder, he automatically got the death penalty. This was a return to the system that existed in 1776.

Most states passed new laws that created a two–phase approach to the death penalty. In the first phase, the jury decided whether the defendant was guilty, just like in a regular trial. In the second phase, the jury heard new evidence to determine if the defendant deserved the death penalty. This new evidence would tell the jury about the defendant's character, childhood, criminal record, and other background information, plus information about the severity of the murder. The jury then had to follow certain guidelines to decide whether to choose the death penalty.

In 1976, the Supreme Court heard a series of cases involving the new laws. In ***Woodson v. California*** (1976), the Court said that automatic death penalty laws are unconstitutional because they do not respect human dignity, as they do not consider each defendant's case on its own merits. In *Gregg v. Georgia* (1976), however, the Court said the new two–phase system in most states was constitutional. The two–phase system was a good way to make sure defendants facing the death penalty got a fair trial. Justice Potter Stewart specifically said that the death penalty is not a "cruel and unusual" punishment. Rather, it is a severe punishment fit for a severe crime.

One year later, in *Coker v. Georgia* (1977), the Supreme Court said that the death penalty is an unfair punishment for rape. (Rape is when a person forces someone else to have sexual intercourse.) After *Coker,* the death penalty in the United States is mostly limited to murder cases.

Death penalty debate

Between 1976 and the end of 1999, there were 598 executions in the United States. As of September 1, 1999, there were 3,625 inmates on death row waiting to be executed.

Studies suggest that seventy-five percent of Americans support the death penalty. Whether America should keep the death penalty, however, is a hotly debated question. Supporters say the death penalty makes the punishment fit the crime. Opponents say that killing murderers does not teach people that killing is wrong. Here are some of the issues that divide Americans in this debate.

Accuracy

Death penalty opponents argue that the system is not entirely accurate. They fear that innocent people are put to death when judges and juries make mistakes, and when the government frames the wrong person. Sometimes after a defendant is convicted, for instance, another person admits to being the real murderer. For instance, in 1999 alone, eight people were released from death row after new evidence suggested they were not guilty. In one of these cases in Illinois, Anthony Porter came within hours of being executed before he was released. Death penalty opponents wonder how many innocent people are not saved in time.

Death penalty supporters say the chance for an innocent person to be executed is small. On the other hand, they say murderers who are allowed to live are likely to kill again. For them, the death penalty is a choice between victims and criminals.

Fairness

As noted above, studies in the mid-1900s suggested that the death penalty treated whites better than blacks. Some say that the situation has not improved under the new laws after *Furman.* While African Americans make up less than fifteen percent of the general population, they made up 42 percent of the death row population in 1997. Although blacks and whites are murder victims in roughly equal numbers, for the ninety-eight people executed in 1999, one hundred and four of their victims were white, while only fifteen were black. Death penalty opponents say that these statistics show that the system treats whites better than blacks, and punishes people who murder whites more severely.

Data also suggests a gender bias in the death penalty system. Although women commit thirteen percent of all murders, they account for only two percent of all death sentences and less than one percent of actual executions. Death penalty opponents also say that poor people are executed more often than wealthy people, and uneducated people more than educated people. As Supreme Court Justice William O. Douglas said in *Furman* when referring to wealthy people, "The Leopolds and Loebs are given prison terms, not sentenced to death."

Death penalty supporters reject this data. They say studies show that people who get the death penalty are the ones who commit the worst murders, such as murder during rape, murder of children, and murder of more than one person.

In *McCleskey v. Kemp* (1987), the U.S. Supreme Court rejected a racial bias challenge to the death penalty. The Court said that as long as the system is designed to be fair, and as long as a jury does not convict a defendant just because of his race, the death penalty is constitutional. Numerical studies that suggest the system is unfair do not mean that it is.

Juveniles

In the United States, most young people are minors, or juveniles, until they reach the age of eighteen. The Supreme Court, however, has said that people who are sixteen when they commit murder may receive the death penalty. In the 1990s, the United States was one of only six countries to allow juvenile offenders to be executed. The other countries were Iran, Nigeria, Pakistan, Saudi Arabia, and Yemen.

Death penalty opponents say that it is barbaric to execute juvenile offenders. They say juveniles are too young to understand what they are doing when they kill another person. Some juvenile murderers are themselves victims of crime, including physical and sexual child abuse. Death penalty opponents say these juveniles need love, caring, and reform to nurture them into responsible adults.

Death penalty supporters argue that a person who is old enough to kill is old enough to die for it. They also say gangs use juveniles for crimes if juveniles cannot get the death penalty. In 1999, just one juvenile offender was executed in the United States.

Cost

Death penalty cases spend many years in the court system because defendants appeal their convictions and sentences many times. The average inmate spends eleven years on death row during this process. Because the state often pays expenses for both the prosecution and defense, one estimate says that death penalty cases cost states between two and four million dollars per inmate. By comparison, it costs about one million dollars to keep a criminal in prison for life. Opponents say that death penalty cases are wasting taxpayer dollars.

Death penalty supporters disagree with these numbers. They say inmates on death row are costly and take up valuable space in already overcrowded jails.

In 1996, Congress passed the Anti -Terrorism and Effective Death Penalty Act. The law is designed to speed up death penalty cases so they do not take as long or cost as much. Some fear, however, that quicker executions will cause more mistakes.

Prevention

Death penalty supporters say that capital punishment prevents murderers from killing again and discourages other people from ever killing. They point to the example of Kenneth McDuff, who was sentenced to death for two murders in 1966. When the Supreme Court temporarily got rid of the death penalty in *Furman* in 1972, McDuff's sentence was reduced to life in prison. After being released on parole in 1989, McDuff raped, tortured, and murdered at least nine women before being caught again in 1992.

Death penalty opponents argue that capital punishment does not stop criminals from committing murder. They point to studies that show that the murder rate in states without the death penalty is half the murder rate of states with capital punishment. For death penalty opponents, this is evidence that capital punishment increases violence in society by setting a bad example.

Suggestions for further reading

Almonte, Paul. *Capital Punishment.* New York: Crestwood House, 1991.

"Death Penalty." *Issues and Controversies on File.* May 1, 1998.

Gottfried, Ted. *Capital Punishment: The Death Penalty Debate.* Enslow Publishers, Inc., 1997.

Nardo, Don. *Death Penalty.* Lucent Books, 1992.

O'Sullivan, Carol. *The Death Penalty: Identifying Propaganda Techniques.* San Diego: Greenhaven Press, 1989.

Steins, Richard. *The Death Penalty: Is It Justice?* Twenty First Century Books, 1995.

Wawrose, Susan C. *The Death Penalty: Seeking Justice in a Civilized Society.* Millbrook Press, 2000.

Winters, Paul A., ed. *The Death Penalty: Opposing Viewpoints.* San Diego: Greenhaven Press, 1997.

Wolf, Robert V. *Capital Punishment.* Philadelphia: Chelsea House Publishers, 1997.

Furman v. Georgia 1972

Appellant: William Henry Furman

Appellee: State of Georgia

Appellant's Claim: That the Georgia death penalty was cruel and unusual punishment under the Eight and Fourteenth Amendments.

Chief Lawyer for Appellant: Anthony G. Amsterdam

Chief Lawyer for Appellee: Dorothy T. Beasley, Assistant Attorney General of Georgia

Justices for the Court: William J. Brennan, Jr., William O. Douglas, Thurgood Marshall, Potter Stewart, Byron R. White

Justices Dissenting: Harry A. Blackmun, Warren E. Burger, Lewis F. Powell, Jr., William H. Rehnquist

Date of Decision: June 29, 1972

Decision: Georgia's death penalty statute was unconstitutional.

Significance: *Furman* said death penalty laws that allow random, racial results are unconstitutional.

On the night of August 11, 1967, 29-year-old William Joseph Micke, Jr., came home from work to his wife and five children in Savannah, Georgia. He went to bed around midnight. Two hours later, the Mickes were awakened by strange noises in the kitchen. Thinking that one of his children was sleepwalking, William Micke went to the kitchen to investigate.

Micke found 26-year-old William Henry Furman in the kitchen. Furman was a poor, uneducated, mentally ill African American who had broken into the house and was carrying a gun. When he saw Micke, Furman fled the house, shooting Micke as he left. The bullet hit Micke in the chest, killing him instantly.

Micke's family immediately called the police. Within minutes, the police searched the neighborhood and found Furman still carrying his gun. Furman was charged with murder. Before Furman's trial, the court committed Furman to the Georgia Central State Hospital for psychological examination. After studying Furman, the hospital decided he was mentally ill and psychotic.

On Trial

Furman's trial was on September 20, 1968. Because he was poor, Furman got a poor man's trial. His court-appointed lawyer, B. Clarence Mayfield, received the regular court-approved fee of just $150. Furman testified in his own defense. He said that when Micke caught him in the kitchen, he started to leave the house backwards and tripped over a wire. When Furman tripped, the gun fired. Furman said he did not mean to kill anyone.

Although murder cases can be complicated, Furman's trial lasted just one day. The court rejected Furman's insanity plea and the jury found Furman guilty of murder. Although the evidence suggested Furman killed Micke accidentally, the jury sentenced Furman to death.

Furman Appeals

Furman appealed his conviction and sentence. The Georgia Supreme Court affirmed both on April 24, 1969. On May 3, however, the court stayed (delayed) Furman's execution so Furman could appeal to the U.S. Supreme Court. Because Furman's case attracted a lot of publicity, several lawyers, including Anthony G. Amsterdam, joined Mayfield to help with the appeal.

Before the Supreme Court on January 17, 1972, Amsterdam argued that the death penalty in Georgia violated the Eighth Amendment of the U.S. Constitution. The Eighth Amendment says the federal government may not use "cruel and unusual punishments." States, including Georgia, must obey the Eighth Amendment under the Due Process Clause of the Fourteenth Amendment.

Amsterdam said the death penalty was "cruel and unusual" for several reasons. At the time, juries received no guidance about choosing the death penalty. They simply listened to the evidence on guilt or innocence and decided whether the defendant deserved to die. Studies showed that juries acted randomly when choosing the death penalty. In cases that were similar, some defendants got the death penalty while others just went to prison.

Other studies showed that defendants who were black, uneducated, poor, or mentally ill received the death penalty more often than those who were white, educated, wealthy, and mentally healthy. Amsterdam said these random, racial, unfair results made the death penalty cruel and unusual.

Supreme Court Rules

With a 5–4 decision, the Supreme Court reversed Furman's conviction. Five of the justices agreed that Furman's death sentence was cruel and unusual punishment. The justices, however, could not agree on a reason for their decision. All five justices in the majority, then, wrote separate opinions explaining the result.

Justice William O. Douglas wrote an opinion that best explained the Court's decision. Justice Douglas reviewed the history of the death penalty in England and America. He noted that under English law, the death penalty was unfair if it was applied unevenly to minorities, outcasts, and unpopular groups. Douglas decided the death penalty in the United States is "unusual" under the Eighth Amendment if it discriminates against a defendant because of his "race, religion, wealth, social position, or class."

Douglas then reviewed many studies about how the death penalty was applied in America. He decided that African Americans and the poor, sick, and uneducated members of society received the death penalty most often. Douglas believed this happened because juries had no guidance when applying the death penalty. This allowed juries to act on their prejudices by targeting unpopular groups with the death penalty. Douglas suggested death penalty laws would have to be rewritten to prevent such results.

Justices William J. Brennan, Jr., and Thurgood Marshall also wrote opinions. They believed the death penalty was cruel and unusual punishment in all cases and should be outlawed forever. Four justices wrote dissenting opinions, meaning they disagreed with the Court's decision. Chief Justice Warren E. Burger said if the public did not like the death

FLORIDA'S ELECTRIC CHAIR

Debate over the death penalty heated up again in Florida in 1999. The issue was whether the electric chair is cruel and unusual punishment. In July 1999, blood poured from Allen Lee Davis's nose as he was executed in Florida's electric chair. The incident followed two others in Florida in 1990 and 1997, when inmates caught fire as they were killed in the chair.

Death penalty opponents said the electric chair is cruel and unusual punishment. They called for Florida to stop all such executions. Meanwhile, the U.S. Supreme Court agreed to review a case to determine whether Florida may continue to use the electric chair.

Death penalty supporters said the electric chair is a fair way to execute convicted murderers. Davis had been convicted of murdering a pregnant woman and her two young daughters. Florida Governor Jeb Bush said Davis's nosebleed was nothing compared to the savage murders he committed.

In January 2000, the Florida state legislature considered a law to switch the death penalty from the electric chair to lethal injection. Florida State Senator Locke Burt (R) once said he did not want to make the switch because "a painless death is not punishment." On January 7, 2000, however, the legislature passed the law, and Governor Bush was expected to sign it

penalty or thought it was being used unfairly, they could rewrite the law or get rid of it altogether.

Impact

Furman did not outlaw the death penalty. It just required states to prevent random, racial, unfair results by giving juries guidance to apply the death penalty fairly. After *Furman,* most states rewrote their death penalty laws to do this. The new laws created a two-phase system for death penalty cases. In the first phase, the jury decides if the defendant is guilty of murder. In the second phase, the jury hears new evidence to decide if the defendant deserves the death penalty. The new laws gave juries guidance for making this decision. In *Gregg v. Georgia* (1976), the Supreme Court said the new laws were valid under the Eighth Amendment. America was allowed to keep the death penalty.

Some people believe the death penalty is still unfair under the new laws. For the ninety-eight people executed in the United States in 1999, 104 of their victims were white while only fifteen of their victims were black. Death penalty opponents say this means the system treats whites better by punishing their attackers more severely. Death penalty supporters disagree. They say studies prove that criminals who get the death penalty are the ones who commit the worst murders, such as murder during rape, murdering children, and murdering more than one person.

Suggestions for further reading

Almonte, Paul. *Capital Punishment.* New York: Crestwood House, 1991.

Bragg, Rick. "Florida's Messy Executions Put the Electric Chair on Trial." *New York Times,* November 18, 1999.

"Death Penalty." *Issues and Controversies on File.* May 1, 1998.

Gottfried, Ted. *Capital Punishment: The Death Penalty Debate.* Enslow Publishers, Inc., 1997.

Henson, Burt M., and Ross R. Olney. *Furman v. Georgia: The Death Penalty and the Constitution.* New York: Franklin Watts, Ind., 1996.

Herda, D.J. *Furman v. Georgia: The Death Penalty Case.* Enslow Publishers, Inc., 1994.

Nardo, Don. *Death Penalty.* Lucent Books, 1992.

O'Sullivan, Carol. *The Death Penalty: Identifying Propaganda Techniques.* San Diego: Greenhaven Press, 1989.

Steins, Richard. *The Death Penalty: Is It Justice?* Twenty First Century Books, 1995.

Wawrose, Susan C. *The Death Penalty: Seeking Justice in a Civilized Society.* Millbrook Press, 2000.

Winters, Paul A., ed. *The Death Penalty: Opposing Viewpoints.* San Diego: Greenhaven Press, 1997.

Wolf, Robert V. *Capital Punishment.* Philadelphia: Chelsea House Publishers, 1997.

Woodson v. North Carolina 1976

Petitioners: James Tyrone Woodson and Luby Waxton

Respondent: State of North Carolina

Petitioners' Claim: That North Carolina's automatic death penalty for first degree murder violated the Eighth Amendment.

Chief Lawyer for Petitioners: Anthony G. Amsterdam

Chief Lawyer for Respondent: Sidney S. Eagles, Jr., Special Deputy Attorney General of North Carolina

Justices for the Court: William J. Brennan, Jr., Thurgood Marshall, Lewis F. Powell, Jr., John Paul Stevens, Potter Stewart

Justices Dissenting: Harry A. Blackmun, Warren E. Burger, William H. Rehnquist, Byron R. White

Date of Decision: July 2, 1976

Decision: North Carolina's automatic death penalty was cruel and unusual punishment under the Eighth Amendment.

Significance: *Woodson* said death penalty laws must let juries choose between death and imprisonment. To make that decision, juries must consider the defendant's character, his prior criminal record, and the circumstances of the murder he committed.

CAPITAL PUNISHMENT

Using the death penalty, governments kill people as punishment for crime. In the United States, most states allow the death penalty for first degree murder. Before 1972, most states allowed juries to decide death penalty cases with no guidance. Juries had total control to choose life or death for defendants who committed murder.

Associate Justice Potter Stewart.
Courtesy of the Supreme Court of the United States.

The Eighth Amendment prevents the government from using cruel and unusual punishments. In ***Furman v. Georgia*** (1972), the U.S. Supreme Court said death penalty laws that give juries total control are cruel and unusual under the Eighth Amendment. Many states, including North Carolina, changed their laws to take control away from juries. Under the new laws, defendants who were convicted of first degree murder automatically got the death penalty. In *Woodson v. North Carolina,* the question was whether these new laws were cruel and unusual.

Killing for Cash

James Tyrone Woodson and three other men in North Carolina had discussed robbing a convenience food store. On June 3, 1974, Woodson had been drinking alcohol in his trailer. At 9:30 p.m., Luby Waxton and Leonard Tucker arrived at Woodson's trailer. Waxton hit Woodson in the face and threatened to kill him if he did not join the robbery.

Woodson got into the car and the three men drove to Waxton's trailer, where they met Johnnie Lee Carroll. Waxton got a handgun, Tucker gave Woodson a rifle, and the four men drove to a convenience food store in one car. Tucker and Waxton entered the store while Carroll and Woodson stayed in the car as lookouts.

Inside the store, Tucker bought a pack of cigarettes. Waxton also asked the clerk for cigarettes. When she handed them over, Waxton shot her at point blank range. Waxton then removed money from the cash register and gave it to Tucker, who rushed back to the parking lot. From outside, Tucker heard another shot and then saw Waxton appear holding a wad of money. The four men drove away together.

As it turned out, the clerk died and a customer was seriously wounded. This made it a case of first degree murder. Tucker and Carroll pled guilty to crimes lesser than murder in exchange for testifying for the prosecution at Woodson and Waxton's trial. At trial, Waxton claimed that Tucker, not he, had shot the clerk and customer. Woodson, who was forced to go along that night and sat in the car during the robbery, refused to admit to any wrongdoing.

The jury found both Woodson and Waxton guilty of first degree murder. Under North Carolina's new law, they automatically got the death penalty. The judge and jury had no choice. Woodson and Waxton appealed their death sentences. They argued that the death penalty is cruel and unusual punishment under the Eighth Amendment. The U.S. Supreme Court agreed to review their case.

Automatic Death Penalty Unconstitutional

With a 5–4 decision, the Supreme Court reversed Woodson and Waxton's death sentences. Writing for the Court, Justice Potter Stewart first decided that the death penalty is not cruel and unusual punishment in all cases. When a criminal commits first degree murder, the death penalty makes the punishment fit the crime.

The Court decided, however, that automatic death penalties are cruel and unusual punishment. Stewart said punishment is cruel and unusual when it offends America's standards of decency. To determine these standards, Justice Stewart analyzed the history of the death penalty.

CRUEL AND UNUSUAL PUNISHMENT

The Eighth Amendment of the U.S. Constitution prevents the government from using cruel and unusual punishment. Most people agree that torture and other barbaric punishments are cruel and unusual. Does this mean the death penalty is cruel and unusual?

To answer this question, the Supreme Court uses the test from a non-death penalty case. In *Trop v. Dulles* (1958), Albert L. Trop lost his U.S. citizenship after deserting the U.S. army during World War II. The U.S. Supreme Court decided that taking away Trop's citizenship was cruel and unusual punishment under the Eighth Amendment. To decide what is cruel and unusual, the Court said it must consider American standards of decency as the country grows and matures.

In *Woodson,* the question was whether the death penalty is indecent in American society. The Court decided that when a criminal commits murder, the death penalty is not indecent. The death penalty cannot, however, be automatic. The law must allow juries to decide whether each criminal should live or die.

When the United States was born in 1776, many states had automatic death penalties for crimes such as murder, rape, and robbery. Juries, however, thought automatic death was too serious for certain crimes. This led most states to change their death penalty laws to give juries the choice between death and imprisonment. Stewart said this meant automatic death penalties offended American society.

In *Furman v. Georgia,* the U.S. Supreme Court struck down laws giving juries too much control over the death penalty. But Stewart said automatic death penalties did not solve the problem. Instead, juries needed to decide the death penalty in each case based on the defendant's character and criminal record and the circumstances of his crime. Only such individual consideration would respect the humanity of each defendant. Justice Stewart said the Eighth Amendment required such respect in a civilized society.

Impact

After *Furman* outlawed the death penalty in 1972, *Woodson* and other cases decided on July 2, 1976 made it legal again. From 1976 through 1999, 598 people were executed in the United States. Protesters still say the death penalty is cruel and unusual punishment in any case. Supporters say people who commit murder deserve to die. Under *Woodson,* juries deciding death penalty cases must be guided by the defendant's character and background and the circumstances of his murder.

Suggestions for further reading

Almonte, Paul. *Capital Punishment.* New York: Crestwood House, 1991.

Gottfried, Ted. *Capital Punishment: The Death Penalty Debate. Enslow Publishers, Inc., 1997.*

Henson, Burt M., and Ross R. Olney. *Furman v. Georgia: The Death Penalty and the Constitution.* New York: Franklin Watts, Inc., 1996.

Herda, D.J. *Furman v. Georgia: The Death Penalty Case.* Enslow Publishers, Inc., 1994.

Mikula, Mark, and L. Mpho Mabunda, eds. *Great American Court Cases.* Vol. II. Detroit: The Gale Group, 1999.

Nardo, Don. *Death Penalty.* Lucent Books, 1992.

O'Sullivan, Carol. *The Death Penalty: Identifying Propaganda Techniques.* San Diego: Greenhaven Press, 1989.

Steins, Richard. *The Death Penalty: Is It Justice?* Twenty First Century Books, 1995.

Tushnet, Mark. *The Death Penalty.* New York: Facts on File, 1994.

Wawrose, Susan C. *The Death Penalty: Seeking Justice in a Civilized Society.* Millbrook Press, 2000.

Winters, Paul A., ed. *The Death Penalty: Opposing Viewpoints.* San Diego: Greenhaven Press, 1997.

Wolf, Robert V. *Capital Punishment.* Philadelphia: Chelsea House Publishers, 1997.

Booth v. Maryland
1987

Petitioner: John Booth

Respondent: State of Maryland

Petitioner's Claim: That Maryland violated the Eighth Amendment by letting the jury hear evidence about how his crime affected his victim's family.

Chief Lawyer for Petitioner: George E. Burns, Jr.

Chief Lawyer for Respondent: Charles O. Monk II, Deputy Attorney General of Maryland

Justices for the Court: Harry A. Blackmun, William J. Brennan, Jr., Thurgood Marshall, Lewis F. Powell, Jr., John Paul Stevens

Justices Dissenting: Sandra Day O'Connor, William H. Rehnquist, Antonin Scalia, Byron R. White

Date of Decision: June 15, 1987

Decision: The Supreme Court reversed Booth's death sentence.

Significance: With *Booth,* the Supreme Court said it is cruel and unusual to let juries hear evidence about how a murder affected the victim's family.

Using the death penalty, governments kill people as punishment for crime. In the United States, most states allow the death penalty for first degree murder. Before 1972, most states allowed juries to decide death penalty cases with no guidance. Juries had total control to choose life or death for defendants who committed murder.

The Eighth Amendment prevents the government from using cruel and unusual punishments. In ***Furman v. Georgia*** (1972), the U.S. Supreme Court said death penalty laws that give juries total control are cruel and unusual. The Court said juries must be guided to decide between life or death based on the defendant's character, his background, and the circumstances of the murder he committed.

As violent crime increased in the 1980s, a victims rights movement began in the United States. The movement's goal was to make sure the criminal justice system takes care of victims instead of just protecting the rights of defendants and criminals. During this movement, many states passed laws allowing juries to hear victim impact evidence during the sentencing phase of death penalty cases. Victim impact evidence is information that tells the jury how a murder has affected the victim's family and community. In *Booth v. Maryland,* the U.S. Supreme Court had to decide whether victim impact evidence violates the Eighth Amendment.

Killing for Drugs

Irvin Bronstein, 78, and his wife Rose, 75, lived a happy life of retirement in West Baltimore, Maryland. John Booth lived three houses away in the same neighborhood. In 1983, Booth and Willie Reid entered the Bronsteins' home to steal money to buy heroin. During the crime, Booth and Reid bound and gagged the Bronsteins and then stabbed them to death with a kitchen knife. The Bronsteins' son found his dead parents two days later.

Booth and Reid faced separate trials in Maryland. The jury convicted Booth of two counts of first-degree murder, two counts of robbery, and conspiracy to commit robbery. Maryland's prosecutor requested the death penalty, and Booth chose to have the jury make the decision. A Maryland law required the prosecutor to prepare a victim impact statement (VIS) before the death penalty hearing. The purpose of the VIS was to describe the effect the crime had on the Bronsteins' family.

The prosecutor prepared a VIS based on interviews with the Bronsteins' son, daughter, daughter-in-law, and granddaughter. The Bronsteins' son, who discovered his murdered parents, said they were "butchered like animals." He said he suffered from lack of sleep and depression ever since finding them. The Bronsteins' daughter also suffered from lack of sleep and constant crying. She felt like a part of her died with her parents and that the joy in life was gone. The Bronsteins' granddaughter told how a family wedding four days after the murders was ruined. The Bronsteins expressed their desire that Booth be put to death.

The prosecutor read the VIS at Booth's death penalty hearing. Booth objected, arguing that it would prevent the jury from fairly deciding whether he deserved to die. The trial court rejected this objection and the jury sentenced Booth to death. Booth appealed to the Maryland Court of Appeals, again arguing that the VIS was cruel and unusual under the Eighth Amendment. The court disagreed and said the VIS helped the jury determine the punishment Booth deserved based on the harm he had done. Booth took his case to the U.S. Supreme Court.

Focus on the Criminal

With a 5–4 decision, the Supreme Court reversed Booth's death sentence. Writing for the Court, Justice Lewis F. Powell, Jr., said the jury's job in a death penalty case is to decide whether the criminal deserves to die based on his character and background and the circumstances of the murder. The jury is supposed to focus on the criminal's personal responsibility and moral guilt. Victim impact statements make the jury focus on the victim instead of the criminal.

Powell said murderers usually have no idea how their crimes will affect their victims' families. That means those effects have nothing to do with a criminal's blameworthiness. Victim impact evidence makes juries evaluate how much a victim is worth. That implies that people deserve to die more when they kill a valuable person who has a big family than when they kill a bad person who is alone. That did not feel right to the Supreme Court.

The Supreme Court said the death penalty is cruel and unusual when given by a jury that has been inflamed by victim impact evidence. Because the jury received such evidence in Booth's case, his death sentence violated the Eighth Amendment and had to be reversed.

Make the Punishment Fit the Crime

Four justices dissented, which means they disagreed with the Court's decision. Justice Byron R. White said that "just as the murderer should be considered as an individual, so too the victim is an individual whose death represents a unique loss to society and in particular to his family." Justice Antonin Scalia agreed. He said the jury's job is to determine

DRUGS AND CRIME

The murderers in *Booth v. Maryland* were stealing money to buy heroin, an illegal narcotic drug. Studies show a link between crime and frequent drug use. In a 1988 study, eighty-two percent of daily narcotic drug users said they committed some form of property crime, such as theft, shoplifting, and burglary. Violent crime, such as assault, robbery, rape, and murder, was less frequent among narcotic drug users.

Crime among non-narcotic drug users is a little different. Studies say cocaine users frequently commit both property and violent crime. In a 1991 study of 1,725 teenagers, cocaine users accounted for sixty percent of minor thefts, fifty-seven percent of felony thefts, forty-one percent of robberies, and twenty-eight percent of felony assaults. By contrast, people who use marijuana do not appear to commit more crime than non-users. In fact, there is evidence that marijuana use reduces violent crime.

whether a murderer deserves to die. How can the jury do that without knowing the harm the murderer did to his victim's family.

Impact

Booth was a setback for the victims rights movement in the United States. Four years later, however, the Supreme Court decided ***Payne v. Tennessee*** (1991). In *Payne,* the jury was allowed to hear evidence about how a mother's murder affected her son, who was with her and injured himself while his mother was killed. The Supreme Court said that because the boy was one of the victims, it did not violate the Eighth Amendment to tell the jury how the crime affected his life.

Suggestions for further reading

Almonte, Paul. *Capital Punishment.* New York: Crestwood House, 1991.

Gottfried, Ted. *Capital Punishment: The Death Penalty Debate.* Enslow Publishers, Inc., 1997.

Henson, Burt M., and Ross R. Olney. *Furman v. Georgia: The Death Penalty and the Constitution.* New York: Franklin Watts, Inc., 1996.

Herda, D.J. *Furman v. Georgia: The Death Penalty Case.* Enslow Publishers, Inc., 1994.

Jaffe, Jerome H., ed. *Encyclopedia of Drugs and Alcohol.* New York: Macmillan Library Reference USA, 1995.

Nardo, Don. *Death Penalty.* Lucent Books, 1992.

O'Sullivan, Carol. *The Death Penalty: Identifying Propaganda Techniques.* San Diego: Greenhaven Press, 1989.

Steins, Richard. *The Death Penalty: Is It Justice?* Twenty First Century Books, 1995.

Tushnet, Mark. *The Death Penalty.* New York: Facts on File, 1994.

Wawrose, Susan C. *The Death Penalty: Seeking Justice in a Civilized Society.* Millbrook Press, 2000.

Winters, Paul A., ed. *The Death Penalty: Opposing Viewpoints.* San Diego: Greenhaven Press, 1997.

Wolf, Robert V. *Capital Punishment.* Philadelphia: Chelsea House Publishers, 1997.

Thompson v. Oklahoma 1988

Appellant: William Wayne Thompson

Appellee: State of Oklahoma

Appellant's Claim: That executing him for committing murder when he was fifteen years old would be cruel and unusual punishment.

Chief Lawyer for Appellant: Harry F. Tepker, Jr.

Chief Lawyer for Appellee: David W. Lee

Justices for the Court: Harry A. Blackmun, William J. Brennan, Jr., Thurgood Marshall, Sandra Day O'Connor, John Paul Stevens

Justices Dissenting: William H. Rehnquist, Antonin Scalia, Byron R. White (Anthony M. Kennedy did not participate)

Date of Decision: June 29, 1988

Decision: The Supreme Court reversed Thompson's death sentence.

Significance: *Thompson* said the Eighth Amendment forbids executing people for crimes they commit when they are less than sixteen years old.

In 1983, when he was fifteen years old, William Wayne Thompson had a brother-in-law named Charles Keene. Keene was married to Thompson's sister, Vicki, whom Keene beat and abused. Thompson decided to end his sister's suffering.

On the night of January 22, 1983, Thompson left his mother's house with his half-brother and two friends to kill Charles Keene. In the early morning hours of January 23, a neighbor named Malcom "Possum" Brown was awakened by the sound of a gunshot on his porch. Someone pounded on Brown's door shouting, "Possum, open the door, let me in. They're going to kill me." Brown called the police and then opened the door to see Keene being beaten by four men. Before the police arrived, the four men took Keene away in a car.

Thompson and his friends shot Keene twice, cut his throat, chest, and stomach, broke one of his legs, chained him to a concrete block, and threw him into the Washita River. One of Thompson's friends said Thompson cut Keene "so the fish could eat his body." Authorities did not find Keene's body until almost four weeks after the murder.

Lawyer David W. Lee argued the state's case against William Thompson. Reproduced by permission of AP/Wide World Photos.

Child or Adult Murderer?

As most states do, Oklahoma had a juvenile justice system. The system's goal was to reform childhood criminals in juvenile justice centers rather than punish them in prisons. Oklahoma, however, allowed childhood murderers to be tried and punished as adults if they understood what they were doing and had no hope for reform.

Prior to the murder, Thompson had been arrested four times for assault and battery and once for attempted burglary. Mary Robinson, who worked for the juvenile justice system, said the counseling Thompson received in the juvenile justice system did not improve his behavior. The court decided Thompson understood the severity of murder and could not be reformed by the juvenile justice system. Thompson was tried as an adult, convicted of murder, and sentenced to death.

Thompson appealed his conviction and sentence. The Eighth Amendment of the U.S. Constitution prevents the federal government from using "cruel and unusual punishment." States, including Oklahoma, must obey the Eighth Amendment under the Due Process Clause of the Fourteenth Amendment. During his appeals, Thompson argued that executing him for a crime he committed when he was fifteen years old would be cruel and unusual.

The court of criminal appeals ruled in favor of Oklahoma. It said if Thompson was old enough to commit murder and old enough to be tried as an adult, he was old enough to be punished as an adult. Thompson appealed to the U.S. Supreme Court. The Child Welfare League of America and others filed briefs (official documents giving evidence on Thompson's behalf) urging the Court to outlaw the death penalty for juvenile offenders.

Court Spares Thompson's Life

With a 5–3 decision, the Supreme Court reversed Thompson's death sentence. Writing for the Court, Justice John Paul Stevens said executing people for childhood crimes is cruel and unusual punishment. In short, the Eighth Amendment forbids executing people for crimes they commit when under sixteen years old.

Justice Stevens said the Constitution does not explain what it means by "cruel and unusual punishment." Instead, the Supreme Court must decide based on what American society thinks is cruel and unusual. To do this, the Court reviewed laws affecting juveniles.

In the United States at the time, eighteen states set sixteen as the minimum age for the death penalty. In most of the fifty states, people under sixteen could not vote, sit on a jury, marry, buy alcohol or cigarettes, drive, or gamble. Stevens said those laws meant people under sixteen lack the intelligence, experience, and education to make adult decisions. If children cannot make adult decisions, it is cruel and unusual to punish them as adults, especially when the punishment is death.

Cruel and Unusual Children

Three justices dissented, which means they disagreed with the Court's decision. Justice Antonin Scalia wrote a dissenting opinion. Scalia said the Eighth Amendment does not require a strict rule that nobody can be executed for crimes committed under sixteen. Scalia pointed out that when the United States adopted the Eighth Amendment, children could be executed for crimes committed at age fourteen.

Scalia said courts should be able to decide each case separately. The question is whether a childhood murderer has the ability to understand and control his conduct like an adult. If so, he should be punished like an adult. Scalia said the Court's decision would allow hardened criminals who are just one day short of sixteen to escape severe punishment for the most severe crimes. In a society that says people should pay for murder with their lives, that result may be cruel and unusual.

Suggestions for further reading

Almonte, Paul. *Capital Punishment.* New York: Crestwood House, 1991.

Gottfried, Ted. *Capital Punishment: The Death Penalty Debate.* Enslow Publishers, Inc., 1997.

Henson, Burt M., and Ross R. Olney. *Furman v. Georgia: The Death Penalty and the Constitution.* New York: Franklin Watts, Inc., 1996.

Herda, D.J. *Furman v. Georgia: The Death Penalty Case.* Enslow Publishers, Inc., 1994.

Nardo, Don. *Death Penalty.* Lucent Books, 1992.

O'Sullivan, Carol. *The Death Penalty: Identifying Propaganda Techniques.* San Diego: Greenhaven Press, 1989.

SEAN SELLERS

At age sixteen in 1985, Sean Sellers murdered his mother, stepfather, and a convenience store clerk in Oklahoma. Around that time, Sellers worshiped Satan and played the game "Dungeons and Dragons." He told a friend that he killed the clerk just to know what it felt like to kill. There was evidence that Sellers killed his parents to escape their supervision.

Sellers, however, said his mother abused him verbally and physically. In 1992, a psychiatric test said Sellers suffered from multiple personality disorder. Some say this prevented Sellers from controlling his behavior when he committed murder.

In prison for his crimes, Sellers rejected Satan and became a Christian. He wrote poems and a Christian comic book. A Christian ministry helped Sellers make a video urging young people not to follow his bad deeds. His stepfather's family and prison guards, however, said Sellers' Christianity was an act to help him escape the death penalty.

If it was an act, it did not work. On February 4 1999, when Sellers was twenty-nine years old, Oklahoma executed him by lethal injection. It was the first time since 1959 that a state executed someone for committing murder at age sixteen. The execution revived the debate over whether the death penalty is appropriate for juvenile offenders.

Romano, Lois. "Reaching Out as Time is Running Out; Teenage Killer of 3 Becomes Christian Book Writer and Contributor to Web Site." *Washington Post,* January 22, 1999.

Steins, Richard. *The Death Penalty: Is It Justice?* Twenty First Century Books, 1995.

Tushnet, Mark. *The Death Penalty.* New York: Facts on File, 1994.

Wawrose, Susan C. *The Death Penalty: Seeking Justice in a Civilized Society.* Millbrook Press, 2000.

Winters, Paul A., ed. *The Death Penalty: Opposing Viewpoints.* San Diego: Greenhaven Press, 1997.

Wolf, Robert V. *Capital Punishment.* Philadelphia: Chelsea House Publishers, 1997.

Penry v. Lynaugh
1989

Petitioner: Johnny Paul Penry

Respondent: James A. Lynaugh, Director, Texas Department of Corrections

Petitioner's Claim: That executing mentally retarded criminals is cruel and unusual punishment under the Eighth Amendment.

Chief Lawyer for Petitioner: Curtis C. Mason.

Chief Lawyer for Respondent: Charles A. Palmer, Assistant Attorney General of Texas

Justices for the Court: Harry A. Blackmun, William J. Brennan, Jr., Thurgood Marshall, Sandra Day O'Connor, John Paul Stevens

Justices Dissenting: Anthony M. Kennedy, William H. Rehnquist, Antonin Scalia, Byron R. White

Date of Decision: June 26, 1989

Decision: The Supreme Court reversed Penry's conviction and death sentence.

Significance: In *Penry,* the Supreme Court said it is not cruel and unusual to give the death penalty to mentally retarded criminals. Juries, however, must be allowed to decide whether defendants should get a prison sentence instead of the death penalty because of their mental retardation

CAPITAL PUNISHMENT

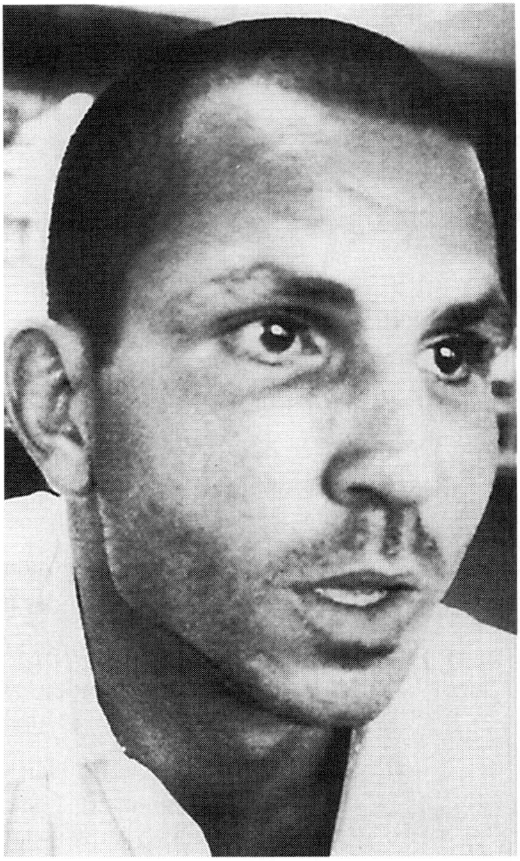

The Court decided that it would be cruel and unusual to sentence Johnny Paul Penry to death. Reproduced by permission of AP/Wide World Photos

Johnny Paul Penry was mildly mentally retarded. At age twenty-two, he had the mental age of a six year old child. Brain damage during his birth probably caused Penry's mental retardation. Penry's mother, however, beat and abused Penry when he was a child. The abuse also may have caused Penry's retardation.

On the morning of October 25, 1979, Pamela Carpenter was raped, beaten, and stabbed with a pair of scissors in her home in Livingston, Texas. She died a few hours later during emergency treatment. Before her death, Carpenter described her attacker to two sheriff's deputies. The deputies suspected Penry, who was on parole after raping another woman. Under questioning, Penry admitted to killing Carpenter.

Texas charged Penry with capital murder. At his trial, Penry's lawyer argued that Penry was innocent because he was insane and unable to control his behavior. As an expert witness, Dr. Jose Garcia testified that Penry had a limited mental capacity. Garcia said Penry did not know right from wrong and could not control his behavior to obey the law. The state of Texas presented its own testimony from two psychiatrists. The psychiatrists said that while Penry was mentally retarded, he was not insane and could control his behavior.

The jury rejected Penry's insanity defense and found him guilty of murder. The jury's next step was to decide whether Penry should get life in prison or the death penalty. Penry's lawyer argued that because of

Penry's mental retardation and childhood abuse, Penry did not deserve the death penalty. Under Texas law, however, the jury had to give the death penalty if it decided that Penry killed Carpenter on purpose, was not provoked, and probably would commit more crimes.

The jury answered all these questions in Texas's favor and sentenced Penry to death. Relying on the Eighth Amendment, which forbids cruel and unusual punishment, Penry's lawyer appealed the sentence. His lawyer said the jury should have been allowed to give Penry life in prison instead of the death penalty because of his mental retardation and childhood abuse. He also argued that executing mentally retarded people should be banned as cruel and unusual punishment. The Texas Court of Criminal Appeals and two federal courts rejected these arguments, so he took his case to the U.S. Supreme Court.

Executing mentally retarded murderers constitutional

With a 5–4 decision, the Supreme Court reversed Penry's death sentence. Writing for the Court, Justice Sandra Day O'Connor said the jury should have been allowed to consider mitigating evidence when it determined Penry's sentence. Mitigating evidence is information about a defendant's character and background that suggests he should not get the death penalty.

In Penry's case, the jury might have decided that because of his mental retardation and childhood abuse, Penry deserved less punishment than someone with a happy background and full mental ability. Under Texas's death penalty law, the jury was not allowed to make that decision. That made Penry's death sentence cruel and unusual punishment that had to be reversed.

The Supreme Court, however, decided that executing mentally retarded criminals is not always cruel and unusual under the Eighth Amendment. O'Connor said whether a punishment is cruel and unusual depends on the standards of decency in American society. To determine what those standards are, the Supreme Court looks at American laws. At the time, only two states made it illegal to execute mentally retarded criminals. That meant most Americans did not think such executions were cruel and unusual.

O'Connor said some mentally retarded people who cannot control their behavior should not get the death penalty. Courts can make those

CAPITAL PUNISHMENT

FORD V. WAINWRIGHT

In 1974, a jury in Florida found Alvin Bernard Ford guilty of murder and sentenced him to death. Ford was not insane at the time. In early 1982, however, Ford's behavior changed while he awaited execution. Ford claimed he was the target of a conspiracy. He thought prison guards were killing people and sealing the bodies into concrete prison beds. Ford began calling himself Pope John Paul III.

Two doctors examined Ford and decided he had become insane. Ford's lawyer asked Florida to declare Ford legally insane and cancel Ford's execution. Florida's governor refused and, in April 1984, signed Ford's death warrant. Meanwhile, Ford's lawyer took the case to the Supreme Court. There he argued that executing insane people is cruel and unusual punishment under the Eighth Amendment.

The Supreme Court reversed Ford's death sentence. The Court said insane people are unable to defend themselves because they cannot tell their side of the story. Executing insane people will not prevent others from committing crimes. It also offends religion, because an insane person cannot make peace with God before being executed. For all these reasons, the Supreme Court ruled that executing insane people is cruel and unusual punishment that is outlawed by the Eighth Amendment.

decisions in individual cases. When a jury decides that a mentally retarded criminal was able to control his behavior, however, the jury is allowed to give the death sentence. Until more Americans decide it is cruel and unusual, executing mentally retarded criminals does not violate the Eighth Amendment.

Impact

When the Supreme Court decided *Penry* in 1989, only two states with the death penalty made it illegal to execute mentally retarded criminals. After *Penry,* organizations such as the American Association on Mental

Retardation (AAMR), the Association for Retarded Citizens (ARC), and the American Psychological Association (APA) formally spoke out against death sentences for the mentally retarded. Ten years later, twelve of the thirty-eight death penalty states outlawed death sentences for the mentally retarded.

If this trend continues, the Supreme Court might someday decide that such executions violate the Eighth Amendment. Meanwhile, thirty-four mentally retarded persons have been executed in the United States since the Supreme Court found the death penalty constitutional in 1976.

Suggestions for further reading

Almonte, Paul. *Capital Punishment.* New York: Crestwood House, 1991.

Gottfried, Ted. *Capital Punishment: The Death Penalty Debate.* Enslow Publishers, Inc., 1997.

Henson, Burt M., and Ross R. Olney. *Furman v. Georgia: The Death Penalty and the Constitution.* New York: Franklin Watts, Inc., 1996.

Herda, D.J. *Furman v. Georgia: The Death Penalty Case.* Enslow Publishers, Inc., 1994.

Mikula, Mark, and L. Mpho Mabunda, eds. *Great American Court Cases.* Vol. II. Detroit: Gale Group, 1999.

Nardo, Don. *Death Penalty.* Lucent Books, 1992.

O'Sullivan, Carol. *The Death Penalty: Identifying Propaganda Techniques.* San Diego: Greenhaven Press, 1989.

Steins, Richard. *The Death Penalty: Is It Justice?* Twenty First Century Books, 1995.

Tushnet, Mark. *The Death Penalty.* New York: Facts on File, 1994.

Wawrose, Susan C. *The Death Penalty: Seeking Justice in a Civilized Society.* Millbrook Press, 2000.

Winters, Paul A., ed. *The Death Penalty: Opposing Viewpoints.* San Diego: Greenhaven Press, 1997.

Wolf, Robert V. *Capital Punishment.* Philadelphia: Chelsea House Publishers, 1997.

Stanford v. Kentucky 1989

Petitioner: Kevin N. Stanford

Respondent: State of Kentucky

Petitioner's Claim: That executing him for committing murder when he was seventeen years old would be cruel and unusual punishment.

Chief Lawyer for Petitioner: Frank W. Heft, Jr.

Chief Lawyer for Respondent: Frederic J. Cowan, Attorney General of Kentucky

Justices for the Court: Anthony M. Kennedy, Sandra Day O'Connor, William H. Rehnquist, Antonin Scalia, Byron R. White

Justices Dissenting: Harry A. Blackmun, William J. Brennan, Jr., Thurgood Marshall, John Paul Stevens

Date of Decision: June 26, 1989

Decision: The Supreme Court affirmed Stanford's death sentence.

Significance: Under *Stanford,* the government may execute people who are sixteen years old or older when they commit murder.

On January 7, 1981, Kevin Stanford was seventeen years and four months old. That night, he and an accomplice robbed a gas station in Jefferson County, Kentucky, where Barbel Poore worked as an attendant. During the robbery Stanford and his accomplice repeatedly raped Poore. After taking 300 cartons of cigarettes, two gallons of fuel, and a small

Associate Justice Antonin Scalia.
Courtesy of the Supreme Court of the United States.

amount of cash, they drove Poore to a hidden area near the gas station. There Stanford killed Poore by shooting her once in the face and once in the back of the head.

After he was arrested, Stanford admitted to the murder to a corrections officer. Stanford said he killed Poore because she lived next door and would recognize him. The corrections officer said Stanford laughed when he told the story.

Kentucky state law allowed juveniles to be tried as adults for committing murder. A juvenile court conducted a hearing to determine if Stanford should be tried as an adult. The court learned that Stanford had a history of juvenile offenses and did not respond well to reform efforts. Because Stanford was charged with a disgusting murder, had many prior crimes, and did not seem capable of being reformed, the court ordered Stanford to be tried as an adult.

Stanford was convicted of murder and sentenced to death. The Eighth Amendment of the U.S. Constitution, however, prevents the government from using cruel and unusual punishment. Stanford used the Eighth Amendment to appeal his death sentence. He said it would be cruel and unusual to execute him for a crime he committed as a juvenile.

The Kentucky Supreme Court rejected Stanford's appeal. Relying on Stanford's criminal history and his failure to respond to reform, the court affirmed his death sentence. Stanford took his case to the U.S. Supreme Court.

Death penalty for juveniles approved

Just one year before the Supreme Court ruled in Stanford's case, it decided that executing people for crimes they commit under sixteen years old violates the Eighth Amendment. With a 5–4 decision, however, the Supreme Court affirmed Stanford's death sentence. Writing for the Court, Justice Antonin Scalia said executing people for crimes they commit when sixteen or older is not cruel and unusual punishment.

Scalia said whether a punishment is cruel and unusual depends on the standards of decency in American society. To determine what those standards were, Scalia studied American laws and cases.

In 1988, thirty-seven states had laws that allowed the death penalty. Twenty-two of those states allowed the death penalty to be given to people who committed crimes when they were sixteen or seventeen years old. In other words, most of the states with the death penalty allowed it to be given to juvenile offenders. Moreover, between 1982 and 1988, forty-five juvenile offenders received death sentences in the United States.

For Scalia, this data meant American society approved of executing juvenile offenders. If such executions do not offend the standards of decency in the United States, they do not violate the Eighth Amendment.

Children too young to know better

Four justices dissented, meaning they disagreed with the Court's decision. Justice William J. Brennan, Jr., wrote a dissenting opinion. Brennan believed it was cruel and unusual to take someone's life for committing a crime as a child. When he counted the states that outlawed the death penalty completely, Brennan found that a total of twenty-seven states said nobody under eighteen could get the death penalty. He also learned that between 1982 and 1988, less than three percent of death sentences in the United States were for juvenile crimes.

Brennan did not stop with analyzing the data. He pointed out that many important organizations opposed the death penalty for juvenile offenders. Most countries in the world had outlawed the death penalty completely or at least for juvenile offenders. The United States even had signed international treaties that prohibited juvenile death penalties.

Finally, Brennan said the reason for the death penalty is to punish offenders and discourage other criminals. Executing juvenile offenders

INTERNATIONAL LAW ON JUVENILE OFFENDERS

Treaties and conventions are agreements between different countries. These agreements form an international law. If a country ratifies a convention, it must obey the agreement or be in violation of international law.

Many international conventions prevent countries from using the death penalty for juvenile offenders—people who commit crimes and are under eighteen years old. The countries that ratify these agreements believe children under eighteen are too young to understand the meaning of their crimes. They also believe that children can change and grow into lawful adults if the government helps rather than executes them.

Although the United States has signed and ratified some of these agreements, it has reserved the right to execute juvenile offenders. Since the U.S. Supreme Court approved the death penalty in 1976, the United States has executed sixteen juvenile murderers, including three in January 2000. At the start of 2000, the only other countries that allowed the death penalty for juvenile offenders were Iran, Nigeria, Pakistan, and Saudi Arabia.

does not serve these purposes. Because juveniles are not old enough to understand their crimes and control their conduct, reform is more appropriate than punishment. Because juveniles often believe they will never die, the death penalty does not discourage them from committing murder. In Brennan's opinion, the best thing to do with juvenile murderers is to try to reform them into lawful adults.

Suggestions for further reading

Almonte, Paul. *Capital Punishment.* New York: Crestwood House, 1991.

Gottfried, Ted. *Capital Punishment: The Death Penalty Debate.* Enslow Publishers, Inc., 1997.

Henson, Burt M., and Ross R. Olney. *Furman v. Georgia: The Death Penalty and the Constitution.* New York: Franklin Watts, Inc., 1996.

Herda, D.J. *Furman v. Georgia: The Death Penalty Case.* Enslow Publishers, Inc., 1994.

Nardo, Don. *Death Penalty.* Lucent Books, 1992.

O'Sullivan, Carol. *The Death Penalty: Identifying Propaganda Techniques.* San Diego: Greenhaven Press, 1989.

Steins, Richard. *The Death Penalty: Is It Justice?* Twenty First Century Books, 1995.

Tushnet, Mark. *The Death Penalty.* New York: Facts on File, 1994.

Wawrose, Susan C. *The Death Penalty: Seeking Justice in a Civilized Society.* Millbrook Press, 2000.

Winters, Paul A., ed. *The Death Penalty: Opposing Viewpoints.* San Diego: Greenhaven Press, 1997.

Wolf, Robert V. *Capital Punishment.* Philadelphia: Chelsea House Publishers, 1997.

Payne v. Tennessee
1991

Petitioner: Pervis Tyrone Payne

Respondent: State of Tennessee

Petitioner's Claim: That allowing the jury to consider evidence of how his crimes affected his victims violated the Eighth Amendment.

Chief Lawyer for Petitioner: J. Brooke Lathram

Chief Lawyer for Respondent: Charles W. Burson, Attorney General of Tennessee

Justices for the Court: Anthony M. Kennedy, Sandra Day O'Connor, William H. Rehnquist, Antonin Scalia, David H. Souter, Byron R. White

Justices Dissenting: Harry A. Blackmun, Thurgood Marshall, John Paul Stevens

Date of Decision: June 27, 1991

Decision: The Supreme Court affirmed Payne's death sentence.

Significance: In *Payne,* the Supreme Court said prosecutors in death penalty cases may use victim impact evidence—evidence about how the crime affected the victim and her family. This decision overruled earlier decisions that the Supreme Court had made concerning victim impact evidence.

CAPITAL PUNISHMENT

On Saturday, June 27, 1987, Pervis Tyrone Payne visited the apartment of his girlfriend, Bobbie Thomas, in Millington, Tennessee. Thomas was on her way home from her mother's house in Arkansas. While Payne waited for Thomas to arrive, he spent the morning and early afternoon injecting cocaine into his body and drinking beer. Then he and a friend drove around town while reading a pornographic magazine. Payne returned to Thomas's apartment complex around 3 p.m.

Across the hall from Thomas, twenty-eight year old Charisse Christopher lived with her three year old son Nicholas and two year old daughter Lacie. Payne entered Christopher's apartment and made sexual advances toward her. When Christopher resisted and screamed "get out," Payne grabbed a butcher's knife and stabbed her forty-one times, causing eighty-four separate wounds. Christopher died from massive bleeding. Payne also stabbed Christopher's children, Nicholas and Lacie. Nicholas survived by a miracle, but Lacie died with her mother.

When she heard the blood-curdling scream from Christopher's apartment, a neighbor called the police. The police officer who arrived saw Payne leaving the building soaked in blood and carrying an overnight bag. When the officer asked Payne what was happening, Payne hit him over the head with the bag and escaped. Later that day, the police found Payne hiding in the attic at a former girlfriend's home.

The Trial

The state of Tennessee charged Payne with two counts of murder and one count of assault with intent to commit murder. At trial, Payne said he had not hurt anyone. The evidence against him, however, was strong. At the murder scene, his baseball cap was strapped around Lacie's arm. There were cans of beer with Payne's fingerprints on them. The jury convicted Payne on all counts.

At the sentencing phase of the trial, the jury had to decide whether to give Payne the death penalty or life in prison. Payne presented evidence from his parents, his girlfriend, and a doctor. Payne's parents said he was a good person who did not use drugs or alcohol and who never had been arrested. Thomas called Payne a loving person who would not commit murder. The doctor testified that Payne was mentally handicapped.

The state presented victim impact evidence (evidence about how the crime affected one of the victims). Nicholas's grandmother testified that Nicholas cried for his mother and did not understand why she never came home. Nicholas also asked his grandmother if she missed his sister, Lacie, and said he was worried about Lacie.

During closing arguments to the jury, lawyers are allowed to explain the verdict if they want. The prosecutor for Tennessee said the jury should remember all the people who would miss Charisse Christopher and Lacie, especially Nicholas. He also said the jury should give Payne the death penalty so that when Nicholas grew up, he would know that his mother and sister's murderer received justice. The jury gave Payne the death penalty for both murders and a thirty year prison sentence for assaulting Nicholas.

Cruel and Unusual Evidence

The Eighth Amendment of the U.S. Constitution prevents the government from using cruel and unusual punishment. In ***Booth v. Maryland*** (1987) and *South Carolina v. Gathers* (1989), the Supreme Court said it is cruel and unusual to allow juries to hear victim impact evidence during a death penalty hearing and closing arguments. The Supreme Court said such evidence makes the jury focus on the victim instead of the defendant. Under the Eighth Amendment, the jury is supposed to decide whether a defendant deserves the death penalty by focusing on the defendant's crime, character, and background.

Payne appealed his death sentences. He said that under *Booth* and *Gathers,* it was illegal for the state of Tennessee to use evidence about how the crime affected Nicholas. The Supreme Court of Tennessee rejected Payne's argument. It said that when a man picks up a butcher's knife and stabs a mother and her two children, the effect on the child that survives helps the jury determine the criminal's punishment. Payne took his case to the U.S. Supreme Court.

Victims' Rights

With a 6–3 decision, the Supreme Court affirmed the death penalty for Payne. Writing for the Court, Chief Justice William H. Rehnquist said the Court decided to overrule its decisions in *Booth* and *Gathers.* When the Supreme Court overrules earlier decisions, it announces a new rule of law.

Rehnquist said that one of the goals of criminal justice in the United States is to make the punishment fit the crime. A jury cannot

VICTIMS' RIGHTS

The criminal justice system in the United States usually focuses on the criminal by asking who broke the law and what should be her punishment. Victims often are ignored in this process. That began to change, however, during the victims' rights movement.

Today, prosecutors' offices have entire units that keep victims informed about the progress of criminal cases. The federal government and most states allow juries to determine the punishment for a crime by using victim impact evidence—information about how the crime affected the victim and her family. Victims often present this evidence as a statement to the jury during the sentencing phase of a trial.

Some criminal justice systems use a practice called a victim-offender conference (VOC). At a VOC, the criminal and victim meet in a safe place to explore how the crime affected their lives. The criminal has a chance to apologize to the victim. The victim can ask questions and even forgive the criminal. Like other parts of the victims' rights movement, the VOC is supposed to help victims get on with their lives after suffering through crime.

do this if it does not know how the crime affected the victim and her family. In a murder case, victim impact evidence helps the jury determine how a family and community suffer and what they lose from the death of a loved one. As long as the evidence is not so unrelated to the crime as to become unfair, the Eighth Amendment allows victim impact evidence.

In the long run

As of 1999, forty-nine states and the federal government had laws allowing juries to hear victim impact evidence. After signing a victims' rights law in 1997, President William J. Clinton said, "when someone is a victim, he or she should be at the center of the criminal justice process, not on the outside looking in."

Suggestions for further reading

Almonte, Paul. *Capital Punishment.* New York: Crestwood House, 1991.

Gottfried, Ted. *Capital Punishment: The Death Penalty Debate.* Enslow Publishers, Inc., 1997.

Henson, Burt M., and Ross R. Olney. *Furman v. Georgia: The Death Penalty and the Constitution.* New York: Franklin Watts, Inc., 1996.

Herda, D.J. *Furman v. Georgia: The Death Penalty Case.* Enslow Publishers, Inc., 1994.

Lerman, David. "Restoring Dignity, Effecting Justice." *Human Rights,* Fall 1999.

Nardo, Don. *Death Penalty.* Lucent Books, 1992.

O'Sullivan, Carol. *The Death Penalty: Identifying Propaganda Techniques.* San Diego: Greenhaven Press, 1989.

Steins, Richard. *The Death Penalty: Is It Justice?* Twenty First Century Books, 1995.

Tushnet, Mark. *The Death Penalty.* New York: Facts on File, 1994.

Wawrose, Susan C. *The Death Penalty: Seeking Justice in a Civilized Society.* Millbrook Press, 2000.

Winters, Paul A., ed. *The Death Penalty: Opposing Viewpoints.* San Diego: Greenhaven Press, 1997.

Wolf, Robert V. *Capital Punishment.* Philadelphia: Chelsea House Publishers, 1997.

The American criminal justice system has two legal parts: law and procedure. Criminal law defines crime and punishment. It protects society by discouraging harmful conduct and punishing wrongdoers. Criminal procedure controls the process of investigating crime, arresting a suspected criminal, and convicting him in a court of law. Criminal procedure protects the rights of the accused, whether guilty or innocent.

Criminal Law

Criminal law in the United States has its roots in Great Britain. When the United States was born in 1776, criminal law in England existed in the common law. Under common law, judges developed definitions for crimes on a case-by-case basis. Criminal law in the United States originally came from the common law. Today the federal government and most states have statutes that define crime and punishment. Many of these definitions, however, come from the common law.

Under federal law and that of most states, crimes are categorized as felonies, misdemeanors, and petty offenses. A felony is a crime, such as murder, that is punishable by death or imprisonment for more than one year. Misdemeanors are less serious crimes, punishable by imprisonment for up to one year, a monetary fine, or both. Petty offenses are punishable by imprisonment for less than six months, a small fine, or both. Infractions, such as minor traffic and parking violations, are punishable only by a fine and are not considered crimes.

Most crimes are against either people or property. Crimes against people include murder, assault, battery, rape, and kidnapping. Crimes against property include arson, trespass, and burglary. The definitions for most crimes include both a bad act and a guilty mind. The bad act requirement makes sure people are not punished just for bad thoughts. The guilty mind requirement makes sure people are not punished when they do something bad accidentally. A person must intend to do something wrong to be guilty of a crime.

People charged with crimes can use many defenses to avoid being convicted and punished. Capacity defenses are for people who did not have the ability to control their behavior. Capacity defenses include insanity, infancy, and intoxication. Defenses such as duress, coercion, and necessity are for people who were forced to commit a crime. Entrapment is a defense for people whom the government tricks into committing a crime. Self defense is for people who respond to an attack with the force necessary to stop it and end up hurting or killing their attacker.

The U.S. Constitution says "No . . . *ex post facto* Law shall be passed." An *ex post facto* (after the fact) law makes a crime out of something a person did when it was not a crime. For example, imagine that it was legal in 1999 to protest outside an abortion clinic. If a state passed a law in 2000 that made it a crime to have protested outside abortion clinics in 1999, the law would be *ex post facto* and invalid under the Constitution.

Criminal Procedure Before Trial

Criminal procedure controls the process of investigating crime and convicting criminals. Supreme Court cases deal with criminal procedure more than criminal law. That is because the U.S. Constitution contains many provisions that make up the law of criminal procedure. The most general provision says "No Bill of Attainder . . . shall be passed." A bill of attainder is a law that convicts and punishes a person without a trial. The framers of the Constitution wanted to assure that people could only be convicted of crimes after fair, individual trials.

Criminal procedure, however, protects Americans well before a trial begins. When the police investigate a crime, the Fourth Amendment limits their investigation. Police may not search a private place without a warrant and probable cause. Probable cause means good reason to believe the place has evidence to be seized or criminals to be arrested. The Fourth Amendment also requires the police to have a warrant to arrest a criminal suspect.

There are exceptions to these rules. The police may arrest a person without a warrant when they have probable cause to believe she has committed a felony. Because felons can be dangerous to society, arresting them quickly is more important than making the police get a warrant. The police also may arrest a person without a warrant when he commits a crime in the officer's presence.

When the police arrest a suspect, the Fifth and Sixth Amendments protect the suspect's rights. One of those is the right not to be a witness against oneself. This is called the right against self-incrimination. It prevents the government from forcing a suspect to talk about a crime, make a confession, or share any evidence that could be used against him.

The Sixth Amendment gives all suspects the right to have an attorney. If the suspect cannot afford an attorney, the government must pay one to defend him. The suspect is allowed to have the attorney present during all police questioning. The attorney also must be allowed to watch if the police conduct a line-up. A line-up is when the suspect stands among a group of people to see if the victim can identify him. The suspect's attorney is allowed to be there to make sure the line-up is fair.

In ***Miranda v. Arizona*** (1966), the U.S. Supreme Court used the right against self-incrimination and the right to an attorney to create the famous warning that police officers must give when they arrest a suspect. It is called reading the suspect her rights. Police must tell the suspect she has the right to remain silent, and that anything she says will be used against her in court. The police also must tell the suspect she has the right to have an attorney, and that the government will appoint one if she cannot afford one. If the suspect says she wants to remain silent and get an attorney, the police cannot ask her any questions about the crime.

After the police arrest a suspect, the court conducts a preliminary hearing. There the government presents its evidence to a magistrate to show that it has probable cause to believe the defendant has committed a crime. It the magistrate agrees, she requires the suspect to enter a plea of guilty or not guilty. If the plea is guilty, the case goes right to the sentencing phase. If the plea is not guilty, the magistrate sets bail. Bail is an amount of money the defendant needs to pay the court to be released while waiting for a trial. The Eighth Amendment says bail may not be too high. If the defendant pays his bail and shows up for trial, he gets his money back. If he fails to show up for trial, he forfeits the money and the court issues a warrant for his arrest.

Before there is a trial in federal court for serious crimes, the Fifth Amendment requires a grand jury to indict the defendant. A grand jury is a large group of citizens, usually as many as twenty-three, that reviews the government's case to make sure it has enough evidence to charge the defendant with a crime. If the grand jury hands down an indictment, the defendant faces a trial on criminal charges.

Criminal Procedure During Trial

The Sixth Amendment gives the defendant many rights during a criminal trial. The defendant has a right to know the charges against him. The right to have an attorney continues through the trial. The trial must involve an impartial jury that determines whether or not the defendant is guilty. The Sixth Amendment says the trial must be speedy and open to the public.

The Sixth Amendment gives the defendant the right to see witnesses against him. In other words, witnesses must face the defendant when they testify against him. They cannot give their testimony in private. Courts sometimes make an exception when the witness is a young child whom the defendant is charged with sexually abusing. In any case, the defendant has a right to cross-examine all witnesses to challenge their testimony.

The defendant has the right to force witnesses in her favor to testify in court. The court accomplishes this with a subpoena (pronounced SUH-PEE-NUH), a document that orders the witness to appear in court to give testimony. The government also must give the defendant any evidence it has that suggests she is innocent. The defendant, however, need not share evidence that suggests he is guilty. In fact, the Fifth Amendment right against self-incrimination prevents the government from forcing the defendant to testify at all. The defendant cannot lie, but she can choose not to answer the government's questions.

The burden of proof is an important part of American criminal procedure. The burden of proof says a defendant is presumed innocent until proven guilty. The government has the burden of proving the defendant's guilt beyond a reasonable doubt. That does not mean there must be no doubt about the defendant's guilt. It means the government must present enough evidence of guilt so that no reasonable person would have any doubt that the defendant is guilty.

Criminal Procedure After Trial

If the jury finds the defendant guilty, the defendant receives a punishment, called a sentence. The judge usually determines the sentence. Sometimes the jury does so when it determines guilt. Sentences can include imprisonment, a fine, community service, and probation. Probation happens when the court allows the defendant to go free with orders to follow certain rules and obey all laws. If the defendant violates the terms of his probation by breaking a rule or law, the court can send the defendant back to jail.

Sometimes the court holds a separate hearing to determine a sentence. That is particularly true when the defendant faces the death penalty for first degree murder. In such cases, the defendant has a right to present evidence at the sentencing hearing about his character, background, and the circumstances of the crime to convince the jury he does not deserve the death penalty.

The Eighth Amendment limits the sentence a defendant can receive. It says the government may not impose "excessive fines" or "cruel and unusual punishments." The Eighth Amendment is supposed to make sure the punishment fits the crime. Applying the Eighth Amendment, the Supreme Court eliminated the death penalty for the crime of rape. As of 2000, most states restrict the death penalty to murder cases.

Sometimes a jury convicts a defendant and sends him to jail after a trial that was unfair. In such cases, the Constitution says the defendant may use a device called a writ of *habeas corpus.* The writ is a lawsuit the defendant files against his jailer. To win, the defendant must prove the government convicted him by violating one or more of his constitutional rights. If the defendant succeeds, the court orders the government to set him free.

Besides *habeas corpus,* most defendants can challenge their convictions by filing an appeal. In the federal system and most state systems, the first appeal to a court of appeals is a statutory right. The right to have an attorney still applies at this stage. If the defendant loses on appeal, her last hope is to appeal to the state supreme court or U.S. Supreme Court.

In most cases, the defendant does not have a right to file such an appeal. Instead, the supreme court must agree to hear the defendant's case. If the defendant loses all appeals, she must serve her sentence.

The Fifth Amendment contains an important protection called the Double Jeopardy Clause. It prevents the government from trying or punishing a person twice for the same crime. That means the government cannot hold another trial for burglary against the same defendant if it loses the first one. The Double Jeopardy Clause, however, does not prevent a different government from trying the defendant for the same crime. For example, if a federal court finds a defendant not guilty of murdering a federal law enforcement officer, the state in which the murder happened can hold a second murder trial.

Suggestions for further reading

Fireside, Harvey. *The Fifth Amendment: The Right to Remain Silent.* Enslow Publishers, Inc., 1998.

Force, Eden. *The Sixth Amendment.* Silver Burdett Press.

Franklin, Paula A. *The Fourth Amendment.* Englewood Cliffs: Silver Burdett Press, 1991.

Galloway, John. *The Supreme Court & the Rights of the Accused.* New York: Facts on File, 1973.

Holmes, Burnham. *The Fifth Amendment.* Silver Burdett Press, 1991.

Johnson, Joan. *Justice.* New York: Franklin Watts, 1985.

Karson, Jill, ed. *Criminal Justice: Opposing Viewpoints.* San Diego: Greenhaven Press, 1998.

Owens, Lois Smith, and Vivian Vedell Gordon. *Think about Prisons and the Criminal Justice System.* Walker & Co., 1992.

Wetterer, Charles M.*The Fourth Amendment: Search and Seizure.* Enslow Publishers, Inc., 1998.

Powell v. Alabama 1932

Petitioners: Ozzie Powell, Willie Roberson, Andy Wright, Olen Montgomery, Haywood Patterson, Charley Weems and Clarence Norris

Respondent: State of Alabama

Petitioner's Claim: The Sixth Amendment right to legal counsel for criminal defendants includes the effective help of counsel at the critical stages of investigation and preparation before the trial.

Chief Lawyer for Petitioner: Walter H. Pollack

Chief Lawyer for Respondents: Thomas E. Knight, Jr.

Justices for the Court: Louis D. Brandeis, Benjamin N. Cardozo, Charles Evans Hughes, Owen Josephus Roberts, Harlan Fiske Stone, George Sutherland Willis Van Devanter

Justices Dissenting: Pierce Butler, James Clark McReynolds

Date of Decision: November 7, 1932

Decision: That the right to the effective assistance of an attorney applies even before the trial.

Significance: The Scottsboro trials gave the American public insight into the prejudices and procedures of Southern courts in their treatment of blacks and other minorities. This case was the first time that the United States Supreme Court interpreted the Sixth Amendment of the Constitution and its guaranty to a criminal defendant of "the Assistance of Counsel for his defense". The Court decided this meant "effective" assistance of counsel.

On March 25, 1931, seven young white men entered a railroad stationmaster's office in northern Alabama. They claimed that while they were riding the rails, a "bunch of Negroes" picked a fight with them and threw them off the train. The stationmaster phoned ahead to the next station, near Scottsboro, Alabama. A Scottsboro deputy sheriff made deputies of every man in town with a gun. When the train stopped, the posse (group of people legally authorized keep the peace) rounded up nine young black men and two young white women. The women, Ruby Bates and Victoria Price, were dressed in men's caps and overalls.

The deputy sheriff tied the black youths together and started questioning them. All of them were from other states. Five of them were from Georgia. Twenty-year-old Charlie Weems was the oldest. Clarence Norris was nineteen. Ozie Powell was sixteen. Olin Montgomery, seventeen, was blind in one eye and had only 10 percent of his vision in the other eye. Willie Roberson, seventeen, suffered from the sexually-transmitted diseases syphilis and gonorrhea, which made him walk with a cane. The other four boys were from Chattanooga, Tennessee. Haywood Patterson and Andy Wright were nineteen. Eugene Williams was thirteen. Wright's brother, Roy, was twelve. None of them could read.

Accused of Rape

As the deputy sheriff loaded his prisoners onto an open truck, one of the women, Ruby Bates, spoke up. She told the deputy sheriff that she and her friend had been raped by the nine black youths.

In Scottsboro, the sheriff sent the women off to be examined by two doctors. Meanwhile, news of the rape had spread throughout the county. By nightfall, a mob of several hundred people stood before the Scottsboro jail, promising to lynch (hang) the prisoners. The sheriff, barricaded inside with twenty- one deputies, called the governor. The governor sent out twenty-five National Guardsmen, but by the time they arrived at the jail, the crowd had given up and drifted away.

The First Trial Begins

Only a few days after their arrest, their trial began on April 6, 1931, with the National Guard keeping a crowd of several thousand people at bay only 100 feet away from the courthouse. On the trial date, Judge Alfred E. Hawkins offered the job of defending the nine black youths to any attorney in the room who would take it. He selected Tennessee attorney Stephen R. Roddy, who volunteered but had not had an opportunity to prepare a defense and admitted he did not know much about Alabama law. A local attorney, Milo Moody offered to assist him with the trials. The defendants were tried in three separate trials.

Prosecutor H. G. Bailey tried Norris and Weems first. Victoria Price described how she and Ruby Bates had gone to Chattanooga to look for jobs. When they found none, they hopped freight trains to go home. After the black boys had thrown the whites off the train, Price said that the blacks turned on the women. She described how she was "beaten up" and "bruised up" as she was repeatedly raped until she lost consciousness.

Dr. R. R. Bridges examined the girls after the incident. He testified that he saw no evidence of violence when he examined the girls. A second doctor agreed and noted that both girls showed signs of having had sexual intercourse, it had occurred at least twelve hours before his physical examination.

Nonetheless, all of the defendants except twelve-year-old Roy Wright were found guilty and sentenced to die in the electric chair. Due to Roy Wright's age, the prosecution had asked for a life sentence for him rather than the death penalty. In spite of this request, seven of the jurors wanted to give Roy the death penalty. The judge was forced to declare a mistrial.

A Legal Lynching

A nationwide dispute arose as the news of the trials spread around the country. The Central Committee of the Communist Party of the United States called the sentences "legal lynching" and called the defendants the "victims of 'capitalist justice.'" Its International Labor Defense (ILD) section pushed the National Association for the Advancement of Colored People (NAACP) to push the case through the legal system to the U.S. Supreme Court. In Harlem (a part of New York City), 300,000 people marched in the streets with the slogan "The Scottsboro Boys Shall Not Die."

The ILD hired a famous Chattanooga lawyer George W. Chamlee. He and his co-counsel, Joseph Brodsky, asked for a new trial for the Scottsboro boys. To support this request, they showed the court sworn statements from Chattanooga blacks. These statements alleged that Victoria Price had been seen "embracing Negro men in dances in Negro houses," and that Ruby Bates had bragged that she could "take five Negroes in one night and that Victoria had rented a room for prostitution." The local press declared these statements false, but a Huntsville detective confirmed that both women were prostitutes.

"You Can't Mix Politics with Law"

The court refused to give the boys a new trial. Nationally celebrated attorney Clarence Darrow turned down the NAACP's request that he argue the appeal all the way up to the Supreme Court. "You can't mix politics with law," he said, adding that eventually the cases would have to be won in an Alabama trial. After that, the NAACP withdrew its support.

In March, the Alabama Supreme Court upheld the convictions of all but Eugene Williams. As a juvenile, he was granted a new trial. In November, the U.S. Supreme Court ruled that seven of the defendants had been denied due process of law under the Fourteenth Amendment due to the belated and casual treatment of the appointment of their attorneys by Judge Hawkins. The Court noted that until the very morning of trial no lawyer had been named to represent the defendants. The Court concluded that during the most critical time of the trial, from their arraignment to the start of the trial, the defendants were without the aid of any attorney. They were entitled to legal advice, a thorough investigation and most important preparation. The Supreme Court found that it was the duty of the trial court to give the defendants a reasonable time and chance to hire attorneys or to appoint counsel under such circumstances which prevents counsel from giving effective aid in the preparation and trial of the case. This failure of the trial court was a clear denial of their right to due process of law.

For the retrial, the ILD turned to noted New York criminal lawyer Samuel Leibowitz. Claiming that the defendants could not get a fair trial in Scottsboro, Leibowitz succeeded in having the trial transferred to Decatur, Alabama, before Judge James Edward Horton, Jr. Haywood Patterson was tried first. Leibowitz produced several surprises. Bates took back her earlier testimony, saying she had lied to avoid being arrested. The arresting posse had found the defendants in several different cars of the forty-two-car train. Willie Roberson's medical condition made it impossible for him to engage in sexual activity, and Olin Montgomery's blindness also made him an unlikely rapist. Victoria Price, who was married, had been convicted and served time for other sex related crimes.

Dr. Bridges repeated his testimony that neither girl had been raped. The second doctor, Marvin Lynch, privately told Judge Horton that he had confronted the girls with the fact that they knew they had not been raped "and they just laughed at me." But, he added, if he testified for the boys, "I'd never be able to go back into Jackson County." The judge believed the defense would prove Patterson innocent, so he said nothing.

Defense attorney Leibowitz now lived with National Guardsmen to protect him against threats of lynching. Prosecutor Wade Wright added to the tense atmosphere when he told the jury, "Show them that Alabama justice cannot be bought and sold with Jew money from New York."

The jury found Patterson guilty and he was sentenced to death. Judge Horton granted a new trial based on his review of the evidence. Then, under pressure from Attorney General Thomas Knight, he withdrew from the case.

Another New Trial

Opening the new trial, Judge William Washington Callahan, dismissed the National Guard and banned cameras from inside and outside the courtroom. He rejected Leibowitz's motion to dismiss Patterson's indictment because no blacks were on the jury list. He ran twelve-hour days in the courtroom. He refused to allow in testimony about Victoria Price's sexual activities in two nights before the train ride. When he gave the jury its instructions on the law, he told them that any intercourse between a black man and a white woman was rape. Until Leibowitz reminded him, Judge Callahan neglected to give the jury instructions on how to acquit the defendant if he was found not guilty.

Again Patterson was found guilty and sentenced to death. Next Clarence Norris was found guilty. Leibowitz discovered that two ILD attorneys were caught trying to bribe Price to change her testimony. The ILD attorneys told Leibowitz that a changed story would be "good for their cause." Furious, Leibowitz threatened to withdraw from the case "unless all Communists are removed from the defense." Attorney Brodsky withdrew.

Supreme Court Overturns Convictions Again

The U.S. Supreme Court overturned all the convictions under the equal protection clause of the Constitution because the state of Alabama excluded African Americans from all juries at the time. In November 1935, a grand jury of thirteen whites and one black brought new indictments. At his fourth trial, in January 1936, a jury again found Patterson guilty. Sentenced this time to seventy-five years in jail, he said, "I'd rather die."

The next trial was delayed until July 1937. Clarence Norris was found guilty and sentenced him to death. Then Andy Wright was found guilty and received ninety-nine years in jail. Charlie Weems was declared guilty and given seventy-five years' imprisonment. The charges against Ozie Powell were dropped in exchange for his guilty plea to stabbing a deputy sheriff. He was sentenced to twenty years. After these convictions, prosecutor Thomas Lawson, suddenly dropped the charges against Olin Montgomery, Roy Wright, Willie Roberson, and Eugene Williams.

All Guilty or All Free

The U.S. Supreme Court refused to review Patterson's conviction. Alabama Governor Bibb Graves, asked to pardon the four convicted Scottsboro boys, agreed that "all were guilty or all should be freed." However, after setting a date for the pardon, he changed his mind.

Weems was freed in November 1943. Wright and Norris were released from jail in January 1944 on parole. They were sent back to prison after they broke the terms of their parole by moving north. Wright was paroled again in 1950. Patterson escaped from prison in 1948. He was arrested in Detroit, but Michigan Governor G. Mennen Williams refused a request to send him back to Alabama. Patterson was later convicted of manslaughter. He died of cancer in prison in 1952. Alabama Governor George Wallace pardoned Norris at the age of 64 in 1976.

Suggestions for Further Reading

Carter, Dan T. *Scottsboro: A Tragedy of the American South.* Baton Rouge: Louisiana State University Press, 1969.

Goodman, James. E. *Stories of Scottsboro.* New York: Vintage Books, 1995.

Haskins, James. *The Scottsboro Boys.* New York: Henry Holt, 1994.

Nash, Jay Robert. *Encyclopedia of World Crime.* Wilmette, IL: CrimeBooks, Inc., 1990.

Patterson, Haywood. *Scottsboro Boy.* Garden City, NY: Doubleday & Co., 1950.

Reynolds, Quentin. *Courtroom.* New York: Farrar, Straus and Cudahy, 1950.

Palko v. Connecticut 1937

Appellant: Frank Palko

Appellee: State of Connecticut

Appellant's Claim: That when Connecticut tried him a second time for murder, it violated the Double Jeopardy Clause of the Fifth Amendment.

Chief Lawyers for Appellant: David Goldstein and George A. Saden

Chief Lawyer for Appellee: William H. Comley

Justices for the Court: Hugo Lafayette Black, Louis D. Brandeis, Benjamin N. Cardozo, Charles Evans Hughes, James Clark McReynolds, Owen Josephus Roberts, Harlan Fiske Stone, George Sutherland

Justices Dissenting: Pierce Butler

Date of Decision: December 6, 1937

Decision: The Supreme Court affirmed Palko's second conviction for murder.

Significance: With *Palko,* the Supreme Court said the Bill of Rights does not automatically apply to the states. It took many cases over the next few decades for the Court to reverse this decision and apply most of the Bill of Rights to the states.

Associate Justice Benjamin N. Cardozo.
Courtesy of the Supreme Court of the United States.

Palko v. Connecticut

The Fifth Amendment of the U.S. Constitution says no person "shall . . . be twice put in jeopardy of life and limb" for the same crime. This is called the Double Jeopardy Clause. It prevents the federal government from trying or punishing a person twice for the same crime.

The Fifth Amendment is part of the Bill of Rights, which contains the first ten amendment to the Constitution. The United States adopted the Bill of Rights in 1791 to give American citizens rights against the federal government. State and local governments did not have to obey the Bill of Rights.

In 1868, after the American Civil War, the United States adopted the Fourteenth Amendment. The Fourteenth Amendment contains a phrase called the Due Process Clause. It says states may not "deprive any person of life, liberty, or property, without due process of law." Ever since 1868, the Supreme Court has struggled to define what is meant by "due process of law." In *Palko v. Connecticut* (1937), the Supreme Court had to decide whether "due process of law" means states must obey the Double Jeopardy Clause of the Fifth Amendment.

Murder

Frank Palko was charged with first degree murder in Fairfield County, Connecticut, where he could get the death penalty. The jury found Palko guilty of second degree murder, a lesser crime that was punishable only with imprisonment. The court sentenced Palko to life in prison. A state law, however, allowed Connecticut to appeal the decision in a criminal case if there were errors during the trial. Connecticut appealed Palko's conviction.

The Supreme Court of Errors decided the trial judge made three errors during Palko's trial. The judge had refused to allow the jury to hear testimony about Palko's confession. He also refused to allow Connecticut to cross-examine Palko to impeach Palko's credibility, which means to challenge his truthfulness and believability. Finally, the trial judge erred when he instructed the jury about the difference between first and second degree murder. Based on these errors, the Supreme Court of Errors reversed Palko's conviction and ordered a new trial.

At the second trial, the jury found Palko guilty of first degree murder and the court sentenced him to death. Palko appealed his conviction. He said trying him twice for the same murder violated the Double Jeopardy Clause of the Fifth Amendment. Palko argued that the Due Process Clause of the Fourteenth Amendment required Connecticut to obey the entire Bill of Rights, including the Double Jeopardy Clause. The Connecticut Supreme Court of Errors rejected this argument and affirmed Palko's conviction, so he took his case to the U.S. Supreme Court.

Fundamental Justice

With an 8–1 decision, the Supreme Court affirmed Palko's conviction and death sentence. Writing for the Court, Justice Benjamin N. Cardozo rejected the argument that the Due Process Clause requires the states to obey the entire Bill of Rights. Cardozo said states only must obey those parts of the Bill of Rights that are fundamental. A right is fundamental when a system of justice would not be fair without it.

Cardozo said the First Amendment freedom of speech and the Sixth Amendment right to a jury trial in criminal cases are examples of fundamental rights. Without them, a fair system of justice would be impossible. In contrast, the Seventh Amendment right to jury a trial in civil cases—cases between private citizens—is not fundamental. A person cannot lose his life or freedom in a civil case.

The Supreme Court decided that in Palko's case, the rights under the Double Jeopardy Clause were not fundamental. Connecticut retried Palko because his first trial had serious errors. Defendants are allowed to get retrials when their first trials have errors. Cardozo said it made the system more fair to give both defendants and states the right to have error free trials.

BENTON v. MARYLAND

The Supreme Court overturned *Palko* in *Benton v. Maryland* (1969). In 1965, a jury in Maryland found John Benton guilty of burglary but not guilty of larceny. Afterwards, the Maryland Court of Appeals struck down a law that required jurors to swear to their belief in God. Maryland then gave Benton the chance to have a second trial. At that trial, the jury found Benton guilty of both larceny and burglary.

Benton took the case to the U.S. Supreme Court, arguing that two trials violated the Double Jeopardy Clause. The Supreme Court agreed and reversed Benton's larceny conviction. The Court overruled *Palko,* saying it no longer accepted the idea that the Fourteenth Amendment applied only a "watered down" version of the Bill of Rights to the states. After *Benton,* states must obey the Double Jeopardy Clause.

Impact

Thirty-two years later, the Supreme Court overturned *Palko* in ***Benton v. Maryland*** (1969). By then, the Supreme Court had decided that the Due Process Clause requires states to obey most of the Bill of Rights.

Suggestions for further reading

Galloway, John. *The Supreme Court & the Rights of the Accused.* New York: Facts on File, 1973.

Holmes, Burnham. *The Fifth Amendment.* Silver Burdett Press, 1991.

Johnson, Joan. *Justice.* New York: Franklin Watts, 1985.

Krull, Kathleen. *A Kids' Guide to America's Bill of Rights: Curfews, Censorship, and the 100-Pound Giant.* Avon Books, 1999.

Mikula, Mark, and L. Mpho Mabunda. *Great American Court Cases.* Detroit: The Gale Group, 1999.

Stein, Richard Conrad. *The Bill of Rights.* Children's Press, 1994.

Gideon v. Wainwright
1963

Petitioner: Clarence Earl Gideon

Respondent: Louie L. Wainwright

Petitioner's Claim: The Sixth Amendment right to legal counsel for defendants unable to afford an attorney should apply equally to the states.

Chief Lawyer for Petitioner: Abe Fortas

Chief Lawyer for Respondents: Bruce R. Jacob

Justices for the Court: Hugo Lafayette Black, William J. Brennan, Jr., Tom C. Clark, William O. Douglas, Arthur Goldberg, John Marshall Harlan II, Earl Warren, Byron R. White.

Justices Dissenting: None

Date of Decision: March 18, 1963

Decision: The Sixth Amendment applies to the states and they are required to provide defendants charged with serious crimes and unable to afford an attorney with legal counsel.

Significance: In taking his case to the United States Supreme Court, Clarence Gideon brought about an historic change in the way American criminal trials are conducted. Before this case, state courts only appointed attorneys for capital cases (cases with the possibility of the death penalty). Now all defendants charged with felony crimes (cases with the possibility of one year or more in prison) that cannot afford to pay for an attorney are entitled to court-appointed legal representation.

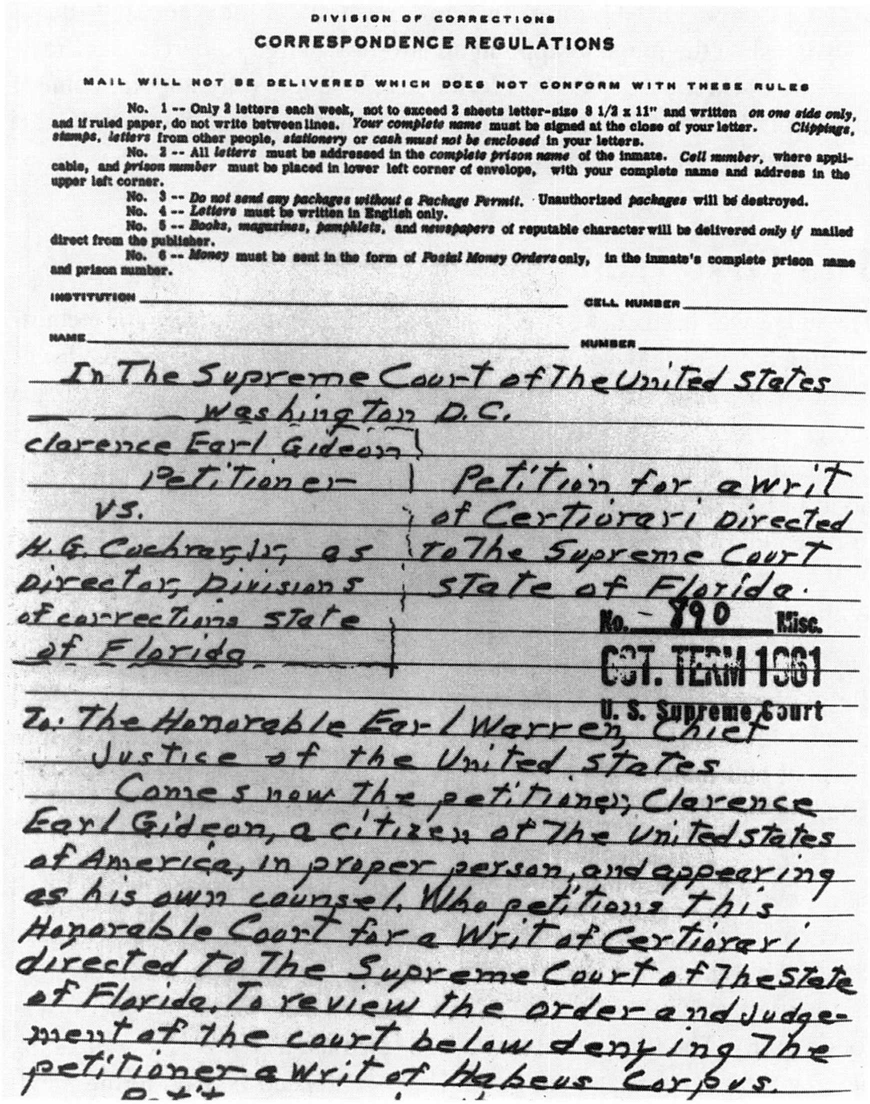
DIVISION OF CORRECTIONS

CORRESPONDENCE REGULATIONS

MAIL WILL NOT BE DELIVERED WHICH DOES NOT CONFORM WITH THESE RULES

No. 1 -- Only 2 letters each week, not to exceed 2 sheets letter-size 8 1/2 x 11" and written *on one side only*, and if ruled paper, do not write between lines. *Your complete name* must be signed at the close of your letter. *Clippings, stamps, letters* from other people, *stationery* or *cash must not be enclosed* in your letters.

No. 2 -- All *letters* must be addressed in the *complete prison name* of the inmate. *Cell number*, where applicable, and *prison number* must be placed in lower left corner of envelope, with your complete name and address in the upper left corner.

No. 3 -- *Do not send any packages without a Package Permit.* Unauthorized *packages* will be destroyed.

No. 4 -- *Letters* must be written in English only.

No. 5 -- *Books, magazines, pamphlets,* and *newspapers* of reputable character will be delivered *only if* mailed direct from the publisher.

No. 6 -- *Money* must be sent in the form of *Postal Money Orders* only, in the inmate's complete prison name and prison number.

INSTITUTION ____ CELL NUMBER ____

NAME ____ NUMBER ____

In The Supreme Court of The United states
Washington D.C.
clarence Earl Gideon
Petitioner — | Petition for a writ
VS. | of Certiorari Directed
H.G. Cochran, Jr, as | To The Supreme Court
Director, Divisions | state of Florida.
of corrections state |
of Florida |

No. 890 Misc.
OCT. TERM 1961
U. S. Supreme Court

To: The Honorable Earl Warren, Chief Justice of the United states

Comes now the petitioner, Clarence Earl Gideon, a citizen of The United states of America, in proper person, and appearing as his own counsel. Who petitions this Honorable Court for a Writ of Certiorari directed to The Supreme Court of The State of Florida. To review the order and Judgement of the court below denying The petitioner a writ of Habeus Corpus.

Clarence Earl Gideon petitioned the Supreme Court himself to urge them to consider his case. Courtesy of the Supreme Court of the United States.

At eight o'clock on the morning of June 3, 1961, a police officer in Panama City, Florida, noticed that the door of the Bay Harbor Poolroom was open. Stepping inside, he saw that someone had burglarized the pool hall, breaking into a cigarette machine and jukebox. The evidence gathered by police led to the arrest of Clarence Gideon, a fifty-one-year-old drifter who sometimes worked at the poolroom. Gideon declared that he was innocent. Nonetheless, two months later he faced trial in the Panama City courthouse. No one present had any idea that they were about to witness history in the making.

Clarence Earl Gideon, in court without money and without a lawyer, asked the judge to appoint an attorney. Judge Robert L. McCrary, Jr. denied his request as under Florida law, he could only appoint counsel in a capital case. Gideon argued that the United States Supreme Court said he had a right to counsel.

The First Trial

The judge was correct. At that time, Florida law did not allow for a court-appointed defense lawyer. A 1942 Supreme Court decision, *Betts v. Brady,* had extended this right only to those state court defendants facing a charge punishable with the death sentence. Many other states voluntarily provided all defendants accused of a felony with a lawyer. Florida did not. So at the start of the trial on August 4, 1961, Clarence Gideon was alone in defending himself. Gideon, a man of limited education, performed as well as he could, but he was not the equal of the Assistant State Attorney William E. Harris.

Prosecution witness Henry Cook claimed to have seen Gideon inside the poolroom at 5:30 on the morning of the robbery. He had watched Gideon for a few minutes through a window. When Gideon came out of the pool hall he had a pint of wine in his hand, he made a telephone call from a nearby booth. Soon afterward a cab arrived and Gideon left.

During cross-examination Gideon questioned Cook's reasons for being outside the bar at 5:30 in the morning. Cook replied that he had "just come from a dance, had been out all night." An attorney might have checked out this story further, but Gideon let it pass. Eight other witnesses testified on Gideons behalf. None proved helpful, and Gideon was found guilty. The whole trial had lasted less than a day. At the sentencing hearing three weeks later Judge McCrary sentenced Gideon to the maximum sentence of five years in prison.

Gideon Fights Back

Gideon was outraged at the verdict. He applied to the Florida Supreme Court for an order freeing him because he had been illegally imprisoned (a writ of *habeas corpus*). When this application was denied, Gideon handwrote a five page appeal of this denial to the United States Supreme Court.

Each year the United States Supreme Court receives thousands of petitions. Most are rejected without any hearing. Against the odds, the

HABEAS CORPUS: A CONSTITUTIONAL RIGHT

Clarence Gideon claimed that he had not had a fair trial because he could not afford an attorney and the court refused to give him one. Based on that he argued he was being held illegally and he sought a writ of *habeas corpus*. The privilege of the writ of *habeas corpus* is guaranteed by Article I, Section 9 of the U.S. Constitution. *Habeas corpus* is a Latin term that means "you have the body." It refers to a prisoner's right not to be held except under circumstances outlined by law. In other words, the police cannot simply pick up someone and hold him or her in prison. To legally hold a person in jail, the person must either be legally arrested and awaiting trial or convicted of a crime and serving a sentence. Moreover, the Fifth Amendment guarantees that citizens cannot be "deprived of life, liberty, or property, without due process of law." So Gideon claimed that since he had not had an attorney for his trial, he had not received due process of law.

Supreme Court decided to hear Gideon's petition. The case was heard as *Gideon v. Wainwright* (the director of Florida's Division of Corrections). Bruce R. Jacob, Assistant Attorney General of Florida argued the case for the State of Florida. Abe Fortas, Gideon's appointed counsel for the appeal (and later a Supreme Court justice himself) argued Gideon's suit. The court heard the oral argument on January 14, 1963.

On March 18, 1963, the Supreme Court unanimously overruled the prior case law *Betts v. Brady,* saying that all felony defendants are entitled to legal representation and sent Gideon's case back to the Florida trial court for a second trial. Justice Hugo L. Black wrote the opinion that set aside Gideon's conviction:

> **Reason and reflection requires us to recognize that in our adversary system of criminal justice, any person haled [hauled] into court, who is too poor to hire a lawyer, cannot be assured a fair trial**

unless counsel is provided for him. This seems to us to be an obvious truth.

The Second Trial

On August 5, 1963, Clarence Gideon again appeared before Judge Robert L. McCrary in the Panama City courthouse, but at his new trial he had an experienced trial lawyer, W. Fred Turner, to defend him. Due to all of the publicity surrounding his Supreme Court victory there was an even stronger prosecution team against him at the second trial. State Attorney J. Frank Adams and J. Paul Griffith joined William Harris in an effort to convict Gideon a second time. Cook was again the main prosecution witness, Henry Cook, fell apart under Turner's expert questioning. Particularly damaging was Cook's admission that he had withheld details of his criminal record at the first trial. The jury found Gideon not guilty of all charges.

Clarence Earl Gideon died a free man in 1973 at age sixty-one.

Suggestions for further reading

Lewis, Anthony. *Gideons Trumpet.* New York: Random House, 1964.

Schwartz, Bernard. *History of the Law in America.* New York: American Heritage, 1974.

West Publishing Company Staff. *The Guide to American Law.* St. Paul, MN: West Publishing Co., 1985.

Robinson v. California 1962

Appellant: Lawrence Robinson

Appellee: State of California

Appellant's Claim: That convicting him for having a drug addiction was cruel and unusual punishment.

Chief Lawyer for Appellant: Samuel Carter McMorris

Chief Lawyer for Appellee: William E. Doran

Justices for the Court: Hugo Lafayette Black, William J. Brennan, Jr., William O. Douglas, John Marshall Harlan II, Potter Stewart, Earl Warren

Justices Dissenting: Tom C. Clark, Byron R. White (Felix Frankfurter did not participate)

Date of Decision: June 25, 1962

Decision: The Supreme Court reversed Robinson's conviction.

Significance: With *Robinson,* the Supreme Court said it is cruel and unusual to convict someone for having an illness, such as drug addiction. *Robinson* helped eliminate status crimes such as vagrancy and homelessness.

Lawrence Robinson was on the streets of Los Angeles one evening when Officer Brown confronted him. Although Robinson was not doing anything wrong, Officer Brown questioned and searched Robinson for evidence of a crime. Brown found needle marks, scar tissue, and discoloration on Robinson's arms. Under questioning, Robinson admitted that he occasionally used illegal drugs. Officer Brown arrested Robinson and took him to the Central Jail in Los Angeles.

The next morning, Officer Lindquist examined Robinson's arms, both in person and in photographs taken the night before. Based on ten years of experience in the Narcotics Division of the Los Angeles Police Department, Officer Lindquist concluded that Robinson was injecting illegal drugs into his arms. According to Lindquist, Robinson admitted this under questioning.

Despite the marks on Robinson's arms, there was no evidence that he was under the influence of illegal drugs or having withdrawal symptoms when he was arrested. California, however, had a law that made it a crime to be addicted to drugs. People convicted under the law got a minimum of ninety days in jail. California charged Robinson with being a drug addict.

At his trial, Robinson said the marks on his arms were an allergy condition he got from shots in the military. Two witnesses for Robinson said the same thing. Robinson denied that he ever used or admitted to using illegal drugs. Officers Brown and Lindquist, however, testified to what they saw on Robinson's arms. The judge instructed the jury that even if there was no evidence that Robinson had used drugs in California, it could convict Robinson for being addicted to drugs while in California. The court said the law made the "condition or status" of drug addiction a crime.

The jury convicted Robinson, so he appealed to the Appellate Department of the Los Angeles County Superior Court. When that court ruled against him too, Robinson appealed to the U.S. Supreme Court.

Cruel and Unusual Punishment

With a 6–2 decision, the Supreme Court reversed Robinson's conviction. Writing for the Court, Justice Potter Stewart said drug addiction is an illness, not a crime. Punishing someone for an illness violates the Eighth Amendment of the U.S. Constitution, which bans cruel and unusual punishments.

Justice Stewart said states can fight against America's serious drug problem by making it illegal to manufacture, sell, buy, use, or possess illegal drugs. States also may protect their citizens from criminal activity by drug addicts by requiring addicts to get medical treatment.

MANDATORY MINIMUM DRUG SENTENCES

When a jury convicts a criminal, the judge usually has the power to select a punishment, or sentence, to fit the crime. In the 1970s, however, America's war on drugs led to the enactment of mandatory minimum drug sentence laws. These laws forced judges to give drug offenders long prison sentences.

New York was the first state to enact a mandatory drug sentence law. Called the Rockefeller law after then Governor Nelson Rockefeller, it required a fifteen year sentence for anyone convicted of having at least four ounces or selling at least two ounces of an illegal drug. Thomas Eddy, one of the first to be convicted under New York's law, received 15 years to life in prison for selling two ounces of cocaine when he was a sophomore at State University of New York, Binghamton.

After over twenty-five years with such laws in the United States, many people call them a failure. The big drug dealers the laws were supposed to stop often escape punishment by turning in smaller dealers and users. America's jails are filled with first-time drug offenders serving stiff mandatory sentences. Meanwhile, overcrowded jails are forced to release rapists, robbers, and murderers to make room for drug users.

Supporters say mandatory minimum sentences are working. They say crime in the United States dropped in the 1990s because so many drug offenders were in jail. They also say tough mandatory sentences are the only way to fight drugs in the nation with the world's biggest drug problem.

California's law was different. It was meant to punish drug addicts, not cure them. Justice Stewart said punishing someone for having a drug addiction is like punishing someone for having a mental illness, leprosy, venereal disease, or the common cold. "Even one day in prison would be a cruel and unusual punishment for the 'crime' of having a common cold."

Losing the War on Drugs

Justices Tom C. Clark and Byron R. White dissented, which means they disagreed with the Court's decision. In a dissenting opinion, Justice Clark said California's law was not designed to punish people for drug addiction. It was designed to put them in jail for at least 90 days to help them break the addiction.

In addition, Justice Clark said there is no difference between a person who uses drugs and a person who is addicted to drugs. Both are dangerous to society because drug use leads to health problems and criminal behavior. Convicting someone for a drug addiction is the same as convicting an alcoholic for public drunkenness. They are not status crimes, they are crimes that endanger societal health and welfare. Justice Clark said California should be allowed to protect people from such dangers.

Impact

Robinson could have been used to eliminate all crimes resulting from a person's voluntary use of drugs and alcohol. In *Powell v. Texas* (1968), however, the Supreme Court said addiction to alcohol cannot be used as a defense the crime of public drunkenness. Instead, *Robinson* has been used to strike down other types of status crimes, such as vagrancy and homelessness.

Suggestions for further reading

Bernards, Neal. *The War on Drugs: Examining Cause and Effect Relationships.* San Diego: Greenhaven Press, 1991.

Brennan, Michael. "A Case for Discretion." *Newsweek,* November 13, 1995.

Gottfried, Ted. *Should Drugs Be Legalized?* Twenty First Century Books, 2000.

Hansen, Mark. "Mandatories Going, Going . . . Gone." *ABA J ournal,* April 1999.

Johnson, Joan. *America's War on Drugs.* New York: Franklin Watts, 1990.

Kronenwetter, Michael. *Drugs in America: The Users, the Suppliers, the War on Drugs.* Englewood Cliffs: Messner, 1990.

Marks, Alexandra. "Rolling Back Stiff Drug Sentences." *Christian Science Monitor,* December 8, 1998.

Powell, Jillian. *Drug Trafficking.* Copper Beach Books, 1997.

Santamaria, Peggy. *Drugs and Politics.* Rosen Publishing Group, 1994.

Stefoff, Rebecca. *The Drug Enforcement Administration.* New York: Chelsea House, 1989.

Terkel, Susan Neiburg. *Should Drugs Be Legalized?* New York: Franklin Watts, 1990.

Thompson, Stephen P., ed. *The War on Drugs: Opposing Viewpoints.* San Diego: Greenhaven Press, 1998.

Wier, William. *In the Shadow of the Dope Fiend: America's War on Drugs.* Archon, 1997.

Miranda v Arizona
1966

Petitioner: Ernesto Miranda

Respondent: State of Arizona

Petitioner's Claim: That the Fifth Amendment privilege against self-incrimination protects a suspect's right to be informed of his constitutional rights during police questioning and applies to the states through the Due Process Clause of the Fourteenth Amendment.

Chief Lawyer for Petitioner: John Flynn

Chief Lawyer for Respondents: Gary K. Nelson

Justices for the Court: Hugo Lafayette Black, William J. Brennan, Jr., William O. Douglas, Abe Fortas, Earl Warren

Justices Dissenting: Tom C. Clark, John Marshall Harlan II, Potter Stewart, Byron R. White

Date of Decision: June 13, 1966

Decision: The Fifth Amendment protection from self-incrimination requires that suspects be informed of their constitutional rights before questioning by the police when they are in police custody.

Significance: Few events have altered the course of American criminal law more than the events surrounding the 1963 rape conviction of Ernesto Miranda. The only strong evidence against him was a confession he made while in police custody. The events surrounding that confession captured the nations attention and prompted a landmark United States Supreme Court decision.

Miranda v. Arizona

In Phoenix, Arizona, during the early hours of March 3, 1963, an eighteen-year-old movie theater attendant was kidnapped by a stranger while on her way home from work. The stranger dragged her into his car, drove out into the desert, and raped her. Afterwards, he dropped her off near her home.

The young woman's story of the events was vague and confusing. She described her attacker as a Mexican in his late twenties wearing glasses. He drove an early 1950s car, either a Ford or Chevrolet.

By chance, one week later, the woman and her brother-in-law saw what she believed was the car of her attacker, a 1953 Packard, license plate number DFL-312. License records showed that this plate was actually registered to a late model Oldsmobile. But plate number DFL-317 was a Packard, registered to a woman, Twila N. Hoffman. Further investigation showed that her boyfriend, Ernesto Miranda, age twenty-three, fit the attacker's description almost exactly.

Ernesto Miranda had a long history of criminal behavior. He had served a one-year jail term for attempted rape. Police put him into a line-up with three other Mexicans of similar height and build, though none wore glasses. The victim did not positively identify Miranda, but told detectives that he looked most like her attacker.

Detectives Carroll Cooley and Wilfred Young took Miranda into another room for questioning. They told him, incorrectly, that the victim had identified him as her attacker from the line-up. They asked him to make a statement. Two hours later, Ernesto Miranda signed a written confession. He was not forced to sign the statement. The detectives did not physically or verbally abuse him. The confession even included a section stating that he understood his rights.

Miranda was given a lawyer, appointed by the court, to represent him because he did not have enough money to hire his own attorney. His lawyer, Alvin Moore, studied the evidence against Miranda. The case against him was very strong, with the most damaging evidence being his confession to the crime. Moore found the events surrounding the statement troubling. Convinced it had been obtained improperly, he intended to ask the court suppress this evidence and not permit his admission of guilt to come into evidence and be heard by the jury.

Only four witnesses appeared to testify for the prosecution: the victim, her sister, and Detectives Cooley and Young. In his closing argument to the jury, the prosecutor, Deputy County Attorney Laurence Turoff, told the jury that Ernesto Miranda, by the use of force and violence, raped the victim.

In Miranda's defense, Attorney Moore was able to point out several inconsistencies in the victim's story, including the fact that she had no physical injuries after her supposed attack. In his cross-examination of Detective Cooley, Attorney Moore made his most important point:

> **Question: Officer Cooley, in the taking of this statement, what did you say to the defendant to get him to make this statement?**
>
> **Answer: I asked the defendant if he would . . . write the same story that he just told me, and he said that he would.**
>
> **Question: Did you warn him of his rights?**
>
> **Answer: Yes, sir, at the heading of the statement is a paragraph typed out, and I read this paragraph to him out loud.**
>
> **Question: I don't see in the statement that it says where he is entitled to the advice of an attorney before he made it.**
>
> **Answer: No, sir.**
>
> **Question: Is it not your practice to advise people you arrest that they are entitled to the services of an attorney before they make a statement?**
>
> **Answer: No, sir.**

Based on this testimony, Moore asked the judge to keep the jury from hearing Miranda's confession. Judge Yale McFate overruled him. The judge gave the jury a well-balanced and fair account of the law as it stood at the time and permitted them to hear the confession. In 1963, the law did not include a constitutional right to remain silent at any time before the beginning of a trial.

Consequently, on June 27, 1963, Ernesto Miranda was convicted of both crimes and sentenced to two concurrent sentences of twenty-to-thirty years imprisonment. Concurrent sentences run at the same time.

However, Alvin Moore's arguments about the confession touched off a legal debate. Miranda's conviction was appealed all the way to the U.S. Supreme Court. On June 13, 1966, Chief Justice Earl Warren, writing the decision for a 5–4 majority, established guidelines about what is and what is not acceptable police behavior in an interrogation:

INFLUENTIAL CHIEF JUSTICE

Earl Warren was Chief Justice of the U.S. Supreme Court from 1953 to 1969. During this time, the "Warren Court" made some of the most influential decisions in modern U.S. history, establishing many civil rights and individual liberties issues. No one expected such landmark decisions from Warren whose previous history was as a rather unremarkable Republican politician. Warren was California's attorney general from 1939 to 1943 and its governor from 1943 to 1953, involving himself in a shameful chapter in the state's history. As attorney general during World War II, he pressed for the internment of Japanese Americans in detention camps, based on the fear that they might be enemy agents and spies. As governor, he presided over the internment process. In 1948, he was an unsuccessful vice-presidential candidate, running with Republican Thomas Dewey against President Harry S Truman. Yet as Chief Justice, Warren led the court to establish new precedents that outlawed school segregation, established the right to court-appointed attorneys, and asserted the right of arrested men and women to know their rights. While serving as Chief Justice, Warren also headed the "Warren Commission," established by President Lyndon Johnson on November 29, 1963, to investigate the assassination of President John F. Kennedy.

> **Prior to any questioning, the person must be warned that he has a right to remain silent, that any statement he does make may be used as evidence against him, and that he has a right to the presence of an attorney, either retained or appointed . . .**

With Miranda's conviction overturned, the State of Arizona was forced to free its now famous prisoner. Without his confession, the state stood little chance of getting a second conviction.

It was Ernesto Miranda himself who brought about his own downfall. He expected to be released after the Supreme Court decision so he had begun a battle for custody of his daughter with Twila Hoffman, his common-law wife. A common-law marriage is an informal marriage where the couple has no license or ceremony but live together, with the intent to be married and tell others that they are married. Hoffman, angry and fearful, told authorities about a conversation with Miranda after his arrest, in which he had admitted the rape. This new evidence was all Arizona needed.

Miranda's second trial began February 15, 1967. Most of the arguments took place in the judge's private chambers. This time the main issue was whether Hoffman, his common-law wife could testify against Miranda, her common-law husband. Judge Lawrence K. Wren ruled that Hoffman's testimony could be allowed as evidence and Hoffman was allowed to tell her story to the jury. Miranda was convicted for a second time and sentenced him to twenty-to-thirty-years in jail.

On January 31, 1976, four years after his released from prison on parole, Ernesto Miranda was stabbed to death in a bar fight. The killer fled but his accomplice (helper) was caught. Before taking him to police headquarters for questioning, the arresting officers read the suspect his "Miranda rights."

The importance of this case cannot be overstated. Although presidents from Richard Nixon to Ronald Reagan have publicly disagreed with it, the *Miranda* decision remains law. Originally intended to protect the poor and the ignorant, the practice of "reading the defendant his rights" has become standard procedure in every police department in the country. The practice is seen so frequently in police movies and shows that the Miranda warnings are as familiar to most Americans as the Pledge of Allegiance.

Suggestions for further reading

Baker, Liva. *Miranda: Crime, Law and Politics.* New York: Atheneum, 1983.

Graham, Fred P. *The SelfInflicted Wound.* New York: Macmillan Co., 1970.

Skene, Neil. "The Miranda Ruling." *Congressional Quarterly* (June 6, 1991): 164.

Tucker, William. "The Long Road Back." *National Review* (October 18, 1985): 28–35.

Arizona v. Evans
1995

Petitioner: State of Arizona

Respondent: Issac Evans

Petitioner's Claim: That marijuana found during an illegal arrest caused by a computer error could be used to convict Evans.

Chief Lawyer for Petitioner: Gerald Grant

Chief Lawyer for Respondent: Carol Carrigan

Justices for the Court: Stephen Breyer, Anthony M. Kennedy, Sandra Day O'Connor, William H. Rehnquist, Antonin Scalia, David H. Souter, Clarence Thomas

Justices Dissenting: Ruth Bader Ginsburg, John Paul Stevens

Date of Decision: March 1, 1995

Decision: The Supreme Court said Arizona could use the evidence if the computer error was not the police department's fault.

Significance: *Evans* makes it easier for states to use evidence they get in violation of the Fourth Amendment.

The Fourth Amendment of the U.S. Constitution protects privacy. It requires federal law enforcement officers to get a warrant to arrest and search a suspected criminal. To get a warrant, law enforcement must have probable cause, which means good reason to believe the person to be arrested has committed a crime. State law enforcement officers must obey the Fourth Amendment under the Due Process Clause of the Fourteenth Amendment.

To enforce the Fourth Amendment, the U.S. Supreme Court created the exclusionary rule. This rule prevents the government from convicting a defendant with evidence found during an arrest or search that violates the Fourth Amendment. Without the exclusionary rule, the police would be encouraged to disobey the Fourth Amendment because they still could use any evidence they found.

Computer Glitch

Bryan Sargent was a police officer in Phoenix, Arizona. In January 1991, Sargent saw Issac Evans driving the wrong way on a one-way street in front of a police station. Sargent stopped Evans and asked to see his driver's license. Evans told Sargent he did not have a license because it had been suspended.

Sargent went back to his police car to enter Evans's name into a computer data terminal. The computer told Sargent that Evans's license had been suspended. It also said there was a warrant for Evans's arrest for failure to appear in court for traffic violations. On the strength of the warrant, Sargent returned to Evans's car and arrested him. While he was being handcuffed, Evans dropped a hand-rolled cigarette that smelled like marijuana, an illegal drug. The police searched Evans's car and found a whole bag of marijuana under the passenger seat.

The state of Arizona charged Evans with illegal possession of marijuana. It soon learned, however, that the warrant to arrest Evans did not exist when Sargent made the arrest. Evans had appeared in court seventeen days before the arrest to resolve his traffic violations. Unfortunately, the court clerk forgot to call the sheriff's office to tell it to erase the warrant from its computer system. When the computer told Sargent there was a warrant for Evans's arrest, the computer was wrong. That made the arrest illegal under the Fourth Amendment.

Without the arrest, the police never would have found Evans's marijuana. At Evans's trial, his lawyer made a motion to enforce the exclusionary rule by getting rid of the marijuana evidence. Without that evidence, the court would have to dismiss Arizona's case against Evans. The trial court granted the motion, so Arizona took the case all the way up to the U.S. Supreme Court.

Good Faith Exception

With a 7–2 decision, the Supreme Court ruled in favor of Arizona. Writing for the Court, Chief Justice William H. Rehnquist said the exclusionary rule does not apply to every violation of the Fourth Amendment. The Supreme Court designed the exclusionary rule to discourage police misconduct. If the police believe in good faith that they are obeying the Fourth Amendment, there is no reason to apply the exclusionary rule.

Officer Sargent thought he had a valid warrant to arrest Issac Evans. The fact that there was a computer error was the court clerk's fault. The clerk was the one who failed to tell the sheriff's office to erase the warrant for Evans's arrest. Since Officer Sargent thought he was obeying the Fourth Amendment when he arrested Evans, there was no reason to apply the exclusionary rule. Arizona was allowed to proceed with its case against Evans for illegal possession of marijuana.

Big Brother

Two justices dissented, which means they disagreed with the Court's decision. Justice John Paul Stevens did not think the Fourth Amendment and the exclusionary rule were designed to discourage police misconduct alone. He said they were designed to prevent all state actors, including courts, from violating the Fourth Amendment.

In her own dissent, Justice Ruth Bader Ginsburg cautioned against allowing the police to rely on new computer systems that might contain lots of errors. Quoting the Arizona Supreme Court, Ginsburg said, "It is repugnant to the principles of a free society that a person should ever be taken into custody because of a computer error [caused] by government carelessness."

Impact

When the Supreme Court created the exclusionary rule for the federal government in *Weeks v. United States* (1914), it strengthened the Fourth Amendment for American citizens. The Court strengthened the amendment even further when it applied the exclusionary rule to state governments in ***Mapp v. Ohio*** (1961). Since then, the Court has weakened the Fourth Amendment by creating exceptions such as the "good faith" exception in *Arizona v. Evans.* Some think the exceptions are necessary to help law enforcement protect society from dangerous criminals. Others think the exceptions allow law enforcement officers to harass American citizens with warrantless searches and illegal arrests.

RUTH BADER GINSBURG

Justice Ruth Bader Ginsburg, who dissented in *Arizona v. Evans,* set an example of excellence for women and men in the legal profession. Born on March 15, 1933 in Brooklyn, New York, Ginsburg grew up in a middle class family. Along with the opportunity that brought, Ginsburg fought through gender discrimination to work her way to the nation's highest court.

When Ginsburg attended Harvard Law School in 1956, she was told that she and her eight female classmates were taking places away from qualified men. After transferring to Columbia Law School and graduating top in her class, Ginsburg failed to receive a job offer from any law firm. Even Supreme Court Justice Felix Frankfurter refused to hire Ginsburg as a law clerk because he was not ready to hire a woman.

Ginsburg did not let the discrimination stop her. After working for a district court judge in New York, Ginsburg taught law at Rutgers University, Harvard, and then Columbia. From 1973 to 1980, she worked as an attorney on the Women's Rights Project for the American Civil Liberties Union. In that role, Ginsburg surprised people by taking on cases supporting equal rights for both men and women. Ginsburg did not think equal rights meant greater rights for women than for men.

Ginsburg served as a judge on the U.S. Court of Appeals for the District of Columbia from 1980 to 1993. As a judge, Ginsburg again surprised many people by being more conservative than she was as a lawyer. Still, President William J. Clinton appointed Ginsburg to the U.S. Supreme Court in 1993. In 1996, Justice Ginsburg wrote an opinion that ended gender discrimination by all-male state military colleges in the United States.

Suggestions for further reading

Franklin, Paula A. *The Fourth Amendment.* Englewood Cliffs: Silver Burdett Press, 1991.

Mooney, Louise, ed. *Newsmakers: The People Behind Today's Headlines.* Detroit: Gale Research Inc., 1993.

Persico, Deborah A. *Mapp v. Ohio: Evidence and Search Warrants.* Enslow Publishers, Inc., 1997.

—-*New Jersey v. T.L.O: Drug Searches in Schools.* Enslow Publishers, Inc., 1998.

Shattuck, John H.F. *Rights of Privacy.* Skokie: National Textbook Co., 1977.

Wetterer, Charles M.*The Fourth Amendment: Search and Seizure.* Enslow Publishers, Inc., 1998.

United States v. Ursery
1996

Petitioner: United States

Respondent: Guy Ursery

Petitioner's Claim: That convicting Ursery for growing marijuana and then taking the house in which he grew the marijuana did not violate the Double Jeopardy Clause of the Fifth Amendment.

Chief Lawyer for Petitioner: Drew S. Days III, U.S. Solicitor General

Chief Lawyers for Respondent: Lawrence Robbins, David Michael, Jeffry K. Finer

Justices for the Court: Stephen Breyer, Ruth Bader Ginsburg, Anthony M. Kennedy, Sandra Day O'Connor, William H. Rehnquist, Antonin Scalia, David H. Souter, Clarence Thomas

Justices Dissenting: John Paul Stevens

Date of Decision: June 24, 1996

Decision: The Supreme Court affirmed Ursery's conviction and approved the forfeiture proceeding against his house.

Significance: On one level, *Ursery* said a civil forfeiture that is not punitive does not raise Double Jeopardy concerns. On another level, the case indicated the Supreme Court would give Congress as much power as possible to fight the war on drugs.

Guy Ursery grew marijuana in his home in Flint, Michigan. Marijuana is an illegal drug that people smoke to get "high." Ursery grew the marijuana for himself and his family and friends. He worked as an autoworker, however, not a drug dealer.

Double Trouble

Based on a tip from Ursery's former girlfriend, Michigan police raided Ursery's home and found marijuana seeds, stems, stalks, and a light for growing the plants. Under federal law, the government is allowed to take away personal property that is used to make illegal drugs. This is called forfeiture because it makes a person forfeit his property. The federal government began a forfeiture proceeding against Ursery's home. Ursery eventually settled the case by paying the government $13,250.

Federal law also makes it a crime to make illegal drugs. Before the forfeiture proceeding was over, the United States charged Ursery with

People are often caught and prosecuted for growing marijuana, an illegal drug, on thier property. Reproduced by permission of AP/Wide World Photos.

violating the law by growing marijuana. A jury found Ursery guilty and the judge sentenced him to five years and three months in prison.

The Double Jeopardy Clause of the Fifth Amendment says no person "shall . . . be twice put in jeopardy of life and limb" for the same crime. This means the government cannot prosecute or punish a person twice for the same crime. Ursery appealed his conviction to the U.S. Court of Appeals for the Sixth Circuit. He argued that the forfeiture proceeding and criminal conviction were double punishment that violated the Double Jeopardy Clause. The Sixth Circuit agreed and reversed Ursery's conviction, so the United States took the case to the U.S. Supreme Court.

Forfeiture Not Punishment

With an 8–1 decision, the Supreme Court ruled in favor of the United States and affirmed Ursery's conviction. Writing for the Court, Chief Justice William H. Rehnquist said the Double Jeopardy Clause forbids successive punishments for the same crime. Imprisonment after a criminal conviction is certainly punishment. The question, then, was whether the forfeiture proceeding was punishment.

Rehnquist said there are two types of civil forfeitures. "In personam" forfeitures are cases in which the government fines a person for unlawful behavior. Rehnquist said these fines can be a form of punishment, meaning they count as punishment under the Double Jeopardy Clause.

"In rem" forfeitures are cases in which the government directly sues the property to be forfeited. The government punishes the property that was being used for criminal activity by taking it away from the criminal. In such cases, the government does not punish the criminal. "In rem" forfeiture cases, then, do not usually count as punishment under the Double Jeopardy Clause.

Rehnquist analyzed the history of Supreme Court forfeiture cases. The most important example was *Various Items of Personal Property v. United States* (1931). In that case, a corporation was using property to make alcohol during Prohibition in the 1920s, when making alcohol was illegal. After convicting the corporation on criminal charges, the government sued the property in a forfeiture action. The Supreme Court said that did not violate the Double Jeopardy Clause. It said, "the forfeiture is not part of the punishment for the criminal offense."

DRUG ENFORCEMENT ADMINISTRATION

The Drug Enforcement Administration (DEA) is an office in the U.S. Department of Justice. Formed in 1973, the DEA enforces federal drug laws in the United States. Its primary goal is to prevent criminals from making, smuggling, and transporting illegal drugs in the country. The DEA works with individual states and foreign countries to stop drugs at their source in the United States and around the world. It also works to enforce regulations on prescription drugs.

Asset forfeiture is an important tool for the DEA. Federal laws allow the DEA to seize valuable property that is used to violate drug laws. The DEA sells most of the property at auctions and puts the money into an Asset Forfeiture Fund. That fund helps victims and crime fighting programs across the nation.

The DEA also uses seized property to help communities with drug problems. In Philadelphia, Pennsylvania, for example, the DEA gave two drug stash houses to an organization called United Neighbors Against Drugs. The organization uses the homes to run drug abuse prevention, job training, and education programs for neighborhood adults and children.

For the same reasons, the Court decided that Ursery's conviction and the forfeiture proceeding against his home did not violate the Double Jeopardy Clause. The forfeiture proceeding was not designed to punish Ursery for growing marijuana. It was designed to take away property that was being used to commit a crime. In effect, the government punished Ursery once with imprisonment and his property once with forfeiture. The government punished nobody twice, so it did not violate the Double Jeopardy Clause.

Taking Property is Punishment

Justice John Paul Stevens wrote a dissenting opinion, which means he disagreed with the Court's decision. Stevens said there was no way to characterize forfeiture of Ursery's home as anything other than punishment. The house was neither illegal by itself nor bought with illegal money. It was not harming society. The only reason to take it was to punish Ursery and discourage others from breaking the law. Stevens said such forfeitures should count as punishment under the Double Jeopardy Clause.

Impact

Forfeiture laws are a weapon in the war on drugs in the United States. *Ursery* was a sign the Supreme Court would give Congress all the power it could to fight that war. In another case the same year, *Bennis v. Michigan* (1996), the Supreme Court said the government could seize a car that was used for illegal sex with a prostitute even when the car's co-owner did not know about the illegal activity. With forfeiture laws, then, the government hopes to take a bite out of crime.

Suggestions for further reading

Bernards, Neal. *The War on Drugs: Examining Cause and Effect Relationships.* San Diego: Greenhaven Press, 1991.

Drug Enforcement Administration website, [Online] http://www.usdoj.gov/dea/programs/af.htm (Accessed August 8, 2000).

Gottfried, Ted. *Should Drugs Be Legalized?* Twenty First Century Books, 2000.

Holmes, Burnham. *The Fifth Amendment.* Silver Burdett Press, 1991.

Jaffe, Jerome H., ed. *Encyclopedia of Drugs and Alcohol.* 1995 ed., s.v. "U.S. Government."

Johnson, Joan. *America's War on Drugs.* New York: Franklin Watts, 1990.

Kronenwetter, Michael. *Drugs in America: The Users, the Suppliers, the War on Drugs.* Englewood Cliffs: Messner, 1990.

Powell, Jillian. *Drug Trafficking.* Copper Beach Books, 1997.

Santamaria, Peggy. *Drugs and Politics.* Rosen Publishing Group, 1994.

Stefoff, Rebecca. *The Drug Enforcement Administration.* New York: Chelsea House, 1989.

Terkel, Susan Neiburg. *Should Drugs Be Legalized?* New York: Franklin Watts, 1990.

Thompson, Stephen P., ed. *The War on Drugs: Opposing Viewpoints.* San Diego: Greenhaven Press, 1998.

Wier, William. *In the Shadow of the Dope Fiend: America's War on Drugs.* Archon, 1997.

"Not so many years ago, the law considered a man's wife and children as little more than his property, and he was free to treat them accordingly. Few areas of the law have undergone as much change in the past half century as the area known as family law, and few areas of the law affect so many people." (From *The 21st Century Family Legal Guide,* p. 19)

The importance of families to maintaining order in society has long been recognized. However, throughout much of history, most domestic (within the household) family matters were considered separate from general public law and not subject to government regulation. Family issues, including finances and disputes between family members, were almost always left for the family to resolve. Exceptions would include criminal cases of murder or assault, or other severe occurrences.

By the late twentieth century, fears were growing that a decline in "family values" was occurring. A greater desire to regulate family grew. In addition, medical advances in the 1980s and 1990s opened new avenues for both creating life and extending life. These advances led to new legal issues no one imagined only a few decades earlier. To further complicate matters, the character of American families was radically changing as well. Family law developed as a mix of diverse legal issues.

History of Family Law

Dating back to early historic times of the European feudal period and later English common law, the husband was legally considered the dominant person in a family. He owned all property and held certain rights not enjoyed by the wife. The husband controlled all of the wife's property after the marriage, but was obligated to provide support for the wife and children. Marriage and divorce were considered private matters. In fact, the biggest issue prior to 1900 was the recognition by one state of marriages performed in another.

By the middle of the nineteenth century, the Industrial Revolution led to many fathers working away from the household during a large part of the day. Wives assumed larger roles in raising children and taking care of the home. As a result, various states began passing laws giving wives greater legal standing. The earliest laws, like the Married Women's Property Acts, allowed wives to own and sell the property they held before marriage, to enter into contracts, and to sue others and be sued. A wife had become more of a person before the law. Then, by outlawing polygamy (having two or more marriage partners at the same time) in ***Reynolds v. United States*** (1879), the Court began to create national standards for marital (marriage) rights.

The American Family

Traditionally, many Americans normally thought of families as consisting of a husband, wife, and one or two children. However, by 1970 only half of American households met that idea. A later University of Chicago study showed that by 1998 only one-fourth of households had a husband, wife, and child. The study also showed that only fifty-six percent of adults were married in 1998, a dramatic drop from seventy-five percent in 1972. Similarly, the percentage of children living in a household with two parents had dropped from seventy-three percent in 1972 to just over half by 1998. The number of children living with single parents in the same time span rose from less than five percent to over eighteen percent. And finally, the number of households composed of two unmarried adults with no children had more than doubled from 1972 to 1998 to thirty-three percent of American homes, actually outnumbering households meeting the earlier ideal family model.

One contributing factor to these statistics is the aging U.S. population. Grown children of married couples of the post-World War II (1939–1945) "baby-boom" generation had left home. However, this study and others clearly showed that the character of the American family had indeed changed significantly.

Marriage

Various aspects of marriage are addressed by family law. Known also as a "consortium," a marital relationship is a contract through which both partners have a right to support, cooperation, and companionship. Marriages require both governmental and public recognition. A governmental license to marry must be obtained and advanced public notice given to the community, commonly through local newspaper notices. These are followed by a public wedding overseen by an governmentally authorized person and one additional witness. Specific legal rights and duties are then established.

Increasingly looking at marriage as a public contract between two individuals, states sought to regulate most conditions of marriage. The Supreme Court affirmed this right of the states. State laws commonly set minimum ages for marriage, identifies duties and obligations of the husband and wife, how property is controlled including inheritance, limits who one may marry regarding incest and mental illness, and how a marriage may be ended. For example, bigamy (marrying a second time while still married) is considered a crime. A decreasing number of states legally recognize common law marriages in which a couple has lived together for a certain length of time and have consistently represented themselves as married to others.

Historically, husbands held the right to have physical control over wives, including physical punishment. Courts traditionally avoided involvement in such matters until the concern over domestic violence came to the forefront as a national issue in the 1980s. States made domestic violence a criminal offense. In 1994 Congress passed the Violence Against Women Act increasing penalties for domestic violence and making such gender-related crimes violations of constitutional civil rights laws.

The sexual relationship between spouses (marriage partners) has also come under family law. Historically, if one partner was unable to engage in sexual relations, it was grounds for divorce. In a birth control case, the Supreme Court ruled in ***Griswold v. Connecticut*** (1965) that state laws could not unreasonably intrude in sexual relationships of marriage. Marriage, they ruled, is protected by Constitutional rights of privacy. Similarly, in ***Loving v. Virginia*** (1967) the Court ruled that state laws prohibiting interracial marriages was unconstitutional, violating equal protection of the laws.

As late as 1953 the Supreme Court in *McGuire v. McGuire* was unwilling to define minimum living standards. It is a matter of the family. Adequacy of support by one spouse for the other and their children, however, began to be addressed in courts through the "doctrine of necessities." Under this doctrine, the state can hold one or the other spouse, or both, responsible for providing essential support, such as clothing, shelter, food, education, and medical care. In many states it became a criminal offense to not provide minimum support.

When the death or severe injury of a spouse occurs such as a car accident or doctor's error, the other spouse can sue those responsible for the death or injury. These suits are called wrongful injury or death lawsuits. The spouse can win money awards to cover expenses for the care of the injured spouse as well as for loss of love, affection, companionship, and future income.

Neither the husband or wife may be forced to testify in court against the other. This privileged communication is recognized as part of the constitutionally protected privacy. The Court did rule in *Trammel v. United States* (1980) that one can testify against the other in a federal criminal trial if they so choose.

Property

Property issues related to marriage are also controlled by state laws. Therefore, disputes over property is handled differently around the nation. Types of property often involved in disputes include real estate, bank savings, stocks and bonds, retirement benefits, personal items, and savings plans. Usually, courts are reluctant to get involved in family property disputes except in divorce cases.

Two legal standards are used. Some states use a "title" standard which connects ownership of each piece of property to the spouse who controls it. Often it is the spouse who earned the money to purchase it unless given as a gift to the other. At death, the deceased (dead) spouse may have willed their property to someone other than the surviving (still living) spouse. However, to promote fairness under the title standard, state laws have established that the surviving spouse is entitled to some portion of the deceased spouse's property, often one-third, depending on the state.

Other states apply a "community property" standard which considers marriage to be a partnership of equal partners. This second standard assumes each spouse contributed equally to the accumulation of the property and, therefore, it is equally owned. The husband and wife can also have separate property including gifts from others and inheritance prior to marriage. In an important development, a new approach to fairly distribute property at divorce under community property law considers the non-economic as well as economic contributions of the spouses to the marriage. Non-economic contributions would include maintaining a home and tending to the children while the other spouse works.

Divorce

Divorce (the ending of marriage) creates a new legal relationship between previous spouses, leading to different rights and responsibilities particularly when children are involved. Divorce was rare in eighteenth century colonial times. In the new nation, divorce actually required action by a state legislature, a difficult process. The only exception was Massachusetts which had passed a law in 1780 allowing court justices to grant divorces rather than state legislature. The U.S. Constitution, adopted in 1789, did not address divorce, leaving it to the states to regulate. By 1900 all states except South Carolina had passed laws like Massachusetts, greatly changing the way in which divorces could be granted. Special divorce courts were established to deal with the cases.

However, divorce was still strongly discouraged by religious groups. To seek divorce, the husband or wife commonly had to charge the other with some wrong doing, such as adultery (having sexual relations with someone other than spouse), desertion (walking out), or cruelty. The California Family Law Act of 1969 introduced yet another important change to divorce law with creation of "no-fault" divorces. Marriages could be ended through mutual agreement rather than one having to accuse the other of a wrong doing. Consideration of wrong doing was reserved for child custody and support and alimony (allowance to the former spouse) decisions. By the late 1980s all states had adopted no-fault divorce. Many critics charged that divorce had become too easy, not forcing couples to work hard enough to solve their problems and hurting many more children.

In 1970 Congress passed the Uniform Marriage and Divorce Act establishing national standards for marriage, divorce, property, and child custody and support. Still, the individual states vary considerably in regard to divorce law. As with marriages, states are required by the Constitution to recognize divorces granted in other states.

The Family's Children

Issues surrounding child custody and support are central to divorce law. Until the nineteenth century, fathers commonly retained custody of their children following divorce. In the early agricultural societies, fathers, owning the family property, needed the children to help with the farm he retained. However, during the nineteenth century the courts established two principles leading to mothers having the primary right to retain custody: the "best-interests-of-the-child" and the "tender years" doctrines. Such custody decisions at the time of divorce have important influence on a child's future. The parent retaining custody holds almost complete control over key decisions affecting the child's life. In contrast, the parent having visitation rights holds almost no control. @p:Responding to calls for custody reform, in 1980 Congress amended the Judiciary Act to establish greater governmental oversight of custody disputes. With each state having different divorce laws, parents would sometimes move to another state where they might get a more favorable custody decision. Sometimes the actual kidnaping of the child to another state might occur. To address this growing problem Congress passed the Parental Kidnapping Prevention Act of 1980 to stop the trend. Also, all states passed various forms of the Uniform Child Custody Jurisdiction Act to help resolve interstate (between different states) custody disputes.

Regarding child support, the divorced parent not having custody usually must provide financial support to help with expenses in the raising the children. With concerns over the rising incidents of non-payment and the effects on state government budgets because of growing welfare roles, the states and federal government have taken several measures to help locate parents (often referred to as deadbeat dads) that have not provided the court-ordered support. To enhance cooperation in tracking deadbeat dads, all states have adopted various versions of the Uniform Reciprocal Enforcement of Support Act. In 1975 Congress also established the Office of Child Support Enforcement to oversee collection of overdue child support. By the 1990s family law allowed for various collection methods, including employers withholding money from paychecks, taking away drivers licenses, placing liens (ownership claims) on property and bank accounts, withhold welfare and retirement benefits, and make deductions from tax refunds. The Welfare Reform Act of 1996 also provided for more aggressive child support collection.

In the late twentieth century women increasingly pursued careers outside the home and many families had both the father and mother working. The father became more involved in child rearing. As a result, a joint custody option arose in which both parents keep decision-making powers. Actual physical custody can go with either parent, or shared as well. By the close of the twentieth century, women, however, still predominately retained custody of children at divorce.

The rights of children also expanded late in the twentieth century. Historically considered as property, by the 1990s the courts recognized the right of children to end their relationship with parents in *Kingsley v. Kingsley* (1992). Children could now sue parents for lack of support, property loss, and personal injury. They could also sue to maintain a relationship with foster parents when challenged by the biological parents as recognized in *Mays v. Twigg* (1993). Some states have taken measures to protect parents against lawsuits, establishing "reasonable parent" standards.

Family Issues Multiply

By the late twentieth century, various means of conceiving babies had developed. These included artificial insemination in which sperm of a father are medically placed in the mother and in vitro fertilization which involves fertilizing an egg outside the womb then medically placing the resulting embryo in the mother. Use of surrogate (substitute) mothers also emerged. All of these medical advances brought with them new legal issues in family law. Who are the legal parents of children conceived with donated sperm or eggs, or given birth by a surrogate (substitute) mother? Family law normally does not recognize donors as legal parents. The famous case of "Baby M" known as *In re Baby M* (1988) involved the custody dispute between the surrogate mother and a married couple who had paid her to be artificially inseminated and give birth to a child for them. The New Jersey Supreme Court ruled that such financial arrangements are improper. But, using the "best interests of the child" doctrine, the court awarded custody to the couple and visitation rights to the surrogate mother.

In addition, efforts to legally recognize same-sex marriages grew. Key issues involved protection of such benefits as inheritance, property rights, and tax and social security benefits. The Minnesota Supreme Court in *Baker v. Nelson* (1971) ruled that marriage could only be legally recognized between people of the opposite sex. In 1996 Congress passed the Defense of Marriage Act defining marriage as only being between people of opposite sex. Same-sex marriage advocates argued the Fourteenth Amendment's "equal protection of the laws" was violated due to discrimination based on sex by denying the same protections and benefits to gays and lesbians. The issue rose to the Hawaii Supreme Court in 1999 which denied the legality of same-sex marriages. However, in December of 1999 the Vermont Supreme Court ruled that the state constitution guarantees the same rights to gay and lesbian couples as to opposite-sex couples.

Saving the Family

Though studies indicate Americans have become increasingly accepting of the many social changes and although these opinions are being reflected in family law applications, efforts are still popular to promote the traditional family idea and look for ways it could work in the twenty-first century. Child care, family leave programs under the Family and Medical Leave Act of 1993, non-traditional workweek arrangements, and "telecommuting" from home in the electronic age have raised new family legal issues.

Suggestions for further reading

Battle, Carl W. *Legal-Wise: Self-Help Legal Guide for Everyone.* New York: Allworth Press, 1996.

Binder, Julee, Harvey Loomis, and Nancy Nicholas, eds. *Know Your Rights and How to Make Them Work for You.* Pleasantville, NY: The Reader's Digest Association, Inc., 1995.

Gregory, John De Witt, Peter N. Swisher, and Sheryl L. Scheible. *Understanding Family Law.* New York: Matthew Bender, 1993.

Mierzwa, Joseph W. *The 21st Century Family Legal Guide.* Highlands Ranch, CO: Prose Associates, Ince., 1994.

Very, Donald L. *The Legal Guide for the Family.* Chicago: J. G. Ferguson Publishing Co., 1989.

Moore v. East Cleveland
1977

Appellant: Inez Moore

Appellee: City of East Cleveland, Ohio

Appellant's Claim: That restrictions in an East Cleveland housing ordinance concerning which family members could occupy the same household violates a basic liberty of choice protected by the Fourteenth Amendment of the U.S. Constitution.

Chief Lawyers for Appellant: Edward R. Stege, Jr.

Chief Lawyers for Appellee: Leonard Young

Justices for the Court: Harry A. Blackmun, William J. Brennan, Jr., Thurgood Marshall, Lewis F. Powell, Jr., Potter Stewart,

Justices Dissenting: Chief Justice Warren E. Burger, William H. Rehnquist, John Paul Stevens, Byron R. White

Date of Decision: May 31, 1977

Decision: Ruled in favor of Moore by finding that government through zoning restrictions cannot prohibit an extended family from living together merely to prevent traffic problems and overcrowding.

Significance: The Court determined that the protection of the "sanctity of the family" guaranteed by the U.S. Constitution extended beyond the nuclear family consisting of a married couple and dependent children. Also protected are extended families that can include various other related family members. The right of relatives to live under the same roof was recognized.

FAMILY LAW

"This Court has long recognized that freedom of personal choice in matters of marriage and family life is one of the liberties protected by the Due Process Clause of the Fourteenth Amendment." Written by the U.S. Supreme Court in *Cleveland Board of Education v. LaFleur* (1974).

Families

The family is one of the oldest and most basic aspects of human societies. The family provides protection and training for children. It also provides emotional and economic support for all its members. Most families are based on kinship ties established through birth, marriage, or adoption. About sixty-six million families lived in the United States in the 1990s.

Various types of families exist. Extended families have been historically common in many societies through time. These families include various combinations of grandparents, aunts, uncles, cousins, or grandchildren sharing the same household with a married couple and their dependent children. However, the industrial revolution of the nineteenth

It has become increasingly hard to place a boundary around what defines a family. Reproduced by permission of Index Stock Imagery.

century dramatically changed patterns of family life. Americans began to think of families being restricted to a husband, wife, and one or two children, known as the nuclear family.

Faced with scientific, economic, and social changes in the 1960s and 1970s, family relationships began to once more change away from the ideal nuclear family pattern, to a much more diverse grouping including many single parent families. By 1970 only half of American households met the earlier twentieth century ideal. By 1998 only one-fourth of households had a husband, wife, and child.

The East Cleveland Housing Ordinance

Concerned about the livability of their community as its population increased, the city of East Cleveland, a suburb of Cleveland, Ohio, passed a zoning ordinance (city law) in 1966 describing who may occupy individual residences. Rather than drawing a line simply to include only persons related by blood, marriage, or adoption, the city chose to draw a tighter, more complicated line. The city established that only certain combinations of relatives could occupy a residence. Besides a husband and wife, the household could also include unmarried dependent children, but only one dependent child having a spouse and dependent children themselves, and only one parent of either the husband or wife. The ordinance gave the city's Board of Building Code Appeals authority (power) to grant variances (deviations) "where practical difficulties and unnecessary hardships shall result from the strict compliance with or the enforcement of the . . . ordinance." Violation of the ordinance was a misdemeanor criminal offense subject to a maximum of six months in prison and a fine not to exceed $1,000. Each day the ordinance was violated could be considered a separate offense. The ordinance essentially selected what types of kin could live together.

Inez Moore

In the early 1970s Inez Moore owned a two and a half story wood frame house in East Cleveland. The house was split into two residences in which Moore lived in one side with an unmarried son, Dale Moore, Sr., and his son Dale, Jr., and John Moore, Jr., another grandson of Inez. John had joined the household following the death of his mother. John and Dale, Jr., were, therefore, cousins. In January of 1973 a city housing inspector issued a violation notice to Inez Moore for occupying the residence with a combination of family members not allowed by the city ordinance. John could not legally live in his grandmother's household as long as his uncle and cousin lived there. The notice directed Moore to correct the situation.

As the city continued to complain of the violation, Moore resisted changing the situation or applying for a variance. Sixteen months after the notice was first issued, Moore was brought before a city court. She filed a motion to dismiss the charge claiming the restrictions on family choice in the city ordinance violated the U.S. Constitution. The city court rejected her claim and found Moore guilty. She was sentenced to five days in jail and fined $25. Moore appealed to the Ohio Court of Appeals which ruled in favor of the city. After the Ohio Supreme Court refused to hear the case, Moore appealed to the U.S. Supreme Court which accepted her case.

Freedom to Make Family Decisions

Before the Court in November of 1976, East Cleveland claimed its housing ordinance was designed to protect the city's quality of life by preventing overcrowding, minimizing traffic and parking congestion, and limiting the financial burden on the city's school system. The city argued that the Court had supported a similar ordinance in *Village of Belle Terre v. Boraas* (1974). Moore argued that the ordinance deprived her of a basic liberty (freedom) without due process of law (fair legal hearing). The Fourteenth Amendment specifically states that no state may "deprive any person of life, liberty, or property, without due process of law." More specifically, the zoning ordinance denied her the right to make important family choices about where and with whom her grandson could live.

First, the Court sought to determine if such a family choice is a constitutionally protected liberty. Justice Lewis F. Powell, Jr., in writing for the Court, reviewed the history and tradition of family life in American society. Powell noted that extended families, ordinarily consisting of close relatives and family friends, would come together to raise children and care for the elderly and disabled. This tradition, strongly founded in America's agricultural society in its early history, was reinforced by the waves of immigrants in the late nineteenth century. Powell noted that such a drawing together has been "virtually a means of survival . . . for large numbers of the poor and deprived minorities of our society (involving the) . . . pooling of scant resources" and has been critical "to maintain or rebuild a secure home life." Powell concluded,

Ours is by no means a tradition limited to respect for the bonds uniting the members of the nuclear family. The tradition of uncles, aunts, cousins, and especially grandparents sharing a household along with parents and children has roots equally venerable [ancient] and equally deserving of constitutional recognition.

Powell concluded the right to live in an extended family household is recognized in the Fourteenth Amendment's freedom of personal choices. Other private family life freedom include the right to marry, to bear and raise children, and the right to education. Extended families were entitled to the same constitutional protections as nuclear families. Inez's choice to raise John, Jr. was a private family matter.

Finding that indeed living in extended families is a constitutional right, Lewis next examined the ordinance to determine if it served an important government purpose. If so, then the ban on certain family households would be valid. Powell quickly concluded the ordinance was ineffective in achieving its goals. If John and Dale had been brothers they both could have lived in the residence, but as cousins they could not. East Cleveland did not show a substantial relationship of the ordinance to protecting public health, safety, or general welfare. Powell added that the ordinance supported in the *Belle Terre* decision affected only unrelated individuals, not kinship ties.

By a 5–4 decision, the Court ruled the housing ordinance unconstitutional. The Court concluded,

the zoning power is not a license for local communities to enact senseless and arbitrary restrictions which cut deeply into private areas of protected family life . . . [T]his ordinance displays a depressing insensitivity toward the economic and emotional needs of a very large part of our society.

A Closer Look

The decision expanded the liberties enjoyed under the Fourteenth Amendment. The government could not unreasonably intrude in decisions concerning family living arrangements. This meant family choices would come under closer review (strict scrutiny) in future cases involving such issues. A family of any type would be protected by the right to due process of law.

MAKING FAMILY CHOICES

Interpretation of the Fourteenth Amendment's Due Process Clause has expanded through the years to include fundamental rights and liberties not specifically identified in the U.S. Constitution and Bill of Rights but considered essential to freedom in a democracy. Deeply rooted in U.S. legal and social traditions, these include the right to privacy in maintaining certain family relations. The 1977 decision in *Moore v. East Cleveland* expanded on these liberties. Earlier, the Court recognized a right to an education in *Meyer v. Nebraska* (1923) and a right to bear children in *Skinner v. Oklahoma* (1942). Later, in ***Griswold v. Connecticut*** (1965) the Court described "zones of privacy" created by these liberties. In ***Loving v. Virginia*** (1967) the Court upheld the right to freely choose a marriage partner. The landmark case of ***Roe v. Wade*** (1973) extended the zone of privacy to include the right to abortions. Shortly after the *Moore* decision, the Court ruled parents had the right to commit children to mental hospitals without a hearing in *Parham v. J.R.* (1979). Later in 1990 the Court ruled in ***Cruzan v. Director, Missouri Department of Health*** that competent individuals could refuse medical treatment, even if their death might result.

In sum, the Court has determined that personal choice in almost all family matters is a fundamental right. The Due Process Clause serves to protect these basic liberties. Consequently, any law or regulation that limits such choices must be shown to have a highly important (compelling) government purpose and be designed to affect as few people as need be (narrowly tailored).

Suggestions for further reading

Coontz, Stephanie. *The Way We Never Were: American Families and the Nostalgia Trap.* New York: Basic Books, 1992.

Eshleman, J. Ross. *The Family: An Introduction.* Boston: Allyn and Bacon, 1997.

Skolnick, Arlene. *Embattled Paradise: The American Family in an Age of Uncertainty.* New York: Basic Books, 1991.

Stacey, Judith. *Brave New Families: Stories of Domestic Upheaval in Late Twentieth Century America.* Berkeley, CA: University of California Press, 1998.

Orr v. Orr
1979

Appellant: William H. Orr

Appellee: Lillian M. Orr

Appellant's Claim: That Alabama's alimony law requiring only husbands, not wives, to pay alimony violated the Equal Protection Clause of the Fourteenth Amendment.

Chief Lawyers for Appellant: John L. Capell III

Chief Lawyers for Appellee: W. F. Horsley

Justices for the Court: Harry A. Blackmun, William J. Brennan, Thurgood Marshall, John Paul Stevens, Potter Stewart, Byron R. White

Justices Dissenting: Chief Justice Warren E. Burger, Lewis F. Powell, Jr., William H. Rehnquist

Date of Decision: March 5, 1979

Decision: Ruled in favor of William Orr by agreeing that Alabama's alimony law fostered unconstitutional sex discrimination by requiring only husbands, not wives, to pay alimony.

Significance: The decision changed the way in which family court judges determine alimony payments during divorce proceedings. Both the husband's and wife's circumstances must be considered, rather than only the wife's situation, as before.

"No longer is the female destined solely for the home and the rearing of the family, and only the male for the marketplace [employment] and the world of ideas [important decision-making roles]." Statement by the U.S. Supreme Court in *Stanton v. Stanton* (1975).

Alimony is regular payments of money that a family court judge determines one spouse (husband or wife) owes the other after divorce. The purpose of the payments is to make divorce more fair for the spouse who is most economically affected. Alimony is different from property settlements or child support. Alimony payments are not considered punishment by the courts.

Alimony and Divorce Through Time

In early English history, divorce between a married couple was not permitted. Unhappy married couples would often live apart with the husband still responsible for providing ongoing financial (money) support for the wife. As divorce became more acceptable through time, the traditional responsibility of the husband providing support continued. This monetary support became known as alimony.

Traditionally in America, husbands and wives took on certain set roles in the family that society expected of them. The wife was responsible for taking care of the home and raising the kids. College educations and professional careers were discouraged. The husband was expected to provide the primary source of income supporting the family. Some states wrote their alimony laws to match this expected family norm.

During proceedings divorce judges would often follow general state guidelines in determining the amount of financial support (alimony) needed by the wife, if any. The divorce judges exercised a great deal of flexibility to determine what was fair. If the ex-husband failed to make the alimony payments, one of the few options the former wife had available to her to correct the situation was to file contempt-of-court charges against the former husband.

An example of state laws reflecting these family norms was the Alabama gender-based (based on sex of the person) alimony law. The law read, "If the wife has no separate estate [possessions] or if it be insufficient for her maintenance, the judge, upon granting a divorce, at his discretion, may order to the wife an allowance out of the estate of the husband, taking into consideration the value thereof and the condition of his family." The law assumes that the wife is always dependent on the husband's income, and never the reverse. The husband's needs were not important. The Alabama Supreme Court had noted in 1966 that for situations where the wife had been the primary source of family income "there is no authority in this state for awarding alimony to the husband."

Gender Discrimination and Equal Protection

Such gender-based state laws began to increasingly reach the attention of the U.S. Supreme Court in the 1970s. In *Reed v. Reed* (1971) the Court for the first time struck down a state law by extending the Equal Protection Clause of the Fourteenth Amendment to gender discrimination. The clause requires equal treatment of all citizens by state laws unless sufficient reasons support otherwise. In *Craig v. Boren* (1976) the Court expressed a more modern vision of the American woman having her own political and economic identity in striking down an Oklahoma law. Importantly, the Court ruled that gender discrimination cases must be more closely examined (scrutiny) by the Court than in the past. The government must now prove that the challenged law serves an important government objective (goal) and the law must substantially (significantly) relate to reaching that objective.

The Orrs

In February of 1974, Lillian and William Orr obtained a divorce in the Lee County Circuit Court of Alabama. As part of the divorce settlement, the court ordered William to pay Lillian $1,240 each month in alimony. After a couple of years William stopped making the required payments. In July of 1976 Lillian went back to the Circuit Court and filed contempt of court charges. She demanded he begin making the payments again, plus provide missing payments. The court responded by ordering William to begin making payments again. The court also told him to pay back payments and Lillian's court expenses, a total of over $5,500.

William appealed the decision to the Alabama's Court of Civil Appeals claiming Alabama's alimony law was not valid. He asserted that because the law only required husbands to pay alimony and not wives, the law violated the Equal Protection Clause of the Fourteenth Amendment. In March of 1977, the appeals court rejected William's argument and agreed with the circuit court's decision. William appealed again, first to the Alabama Supreme Court which declined to accept the case, and then to the U.S. Supreme Court which agreed to hear it.

An Important Government Purpose

As in the lower courts, Lillian Orr simply argued that the Alabama law was indeed constitutionally valid under the Equal Protection Clause. Because the state law treated males and females differently therefore not equally protecting the two groups, it must serve some important government purpose to be considered constitutionally valid. Lillian asserted the alimony law served three important government purposes, she contended: (1) to support the traditional structure of families by making the husband always economically responsible for the family; (2) to lessen the cost of divorce for needy wives; and, (3) to repay women for past economic discrimination within traditional American marriages. In arguing against the law's constitutionality, William Orr did not claim that Lillian should pay him alimony. He did argue, however, that if the circuit court was required to consider his circumstances too, then the amount of alimony payments might have been less. He contended the law was unconstitutional based on lack of equal protection.

Justice William J. Brennan, writing for the Court, noted that previous Supreme Court rulings had established that "classifications by gender must serve important governmental objectives and must be substantially related to achievement of those objectives." In reviewing the Alabama law, Brennan disagreed with the first government purpose of supporting traditional family structure. He asserted that the ideas of what the state thought a family should be did not apply to many families in modern America. Though agreeing the law's other two purposes had some merit, the law's approach requiring only husbands to pay alimony was clearly not valid.

Brennan pointed out that the process of review by a family law judge in determining alimony makes the process very personalized. The Alabama law need not be gender-based. The Alabama law more likely served to uphold outdated role models than correct past social injustices. Brennan concluded, "it would cost the State nothing more, if it were to treat men and women equally by making alimony burdens independent of sex."

In the 6–3 decision, the Court ruled the Alabama law unconstitutional in violation of the Equal Protection Clause of the Fourteenth

ALIMONY FACTORS

A key effect of the Supreme Court decision in *Orr v. Orr* was how judges determine alimony payments in divorce proceedings. The amount and length of payment can be determined through a court-approved agreement between the former husband and wife, or it could be set by the court, especially when agreement was not possible.

The amount a husband or wife owes usually depends on several complex factors. These include the person's financial needs who is requesting alimony whether it be the husband or wife, the ability of the other person to pay alimony, the standard of living they had been use to in marriage, their age and health, how long they were married, and how long it would take the person requesting alimony to become more self-sufficient through education or job-training. Court decisions often consider the non-monetary contributions of both husband and wife to the marriage, including neglecting their own careers to support the spouse's.

Alimony payments end if the former wife dies or remarries. However, alimony payments could continue from the estate of a former husband, even after his death, through trusts or insurance policies. Payments can always been changed, as well, if basic conditions of either person changes.

Amendment. The Court also sent William Orr back to the lower courts to determine his alimony situation.

Who Was Injured?

In dissent, Justice William Rehnquist asserted that there was no case existed because no one was wronged by the Alabama law in this instance. William Orr is "a divorced male who has never sought alimony, who is . . . not entitled to alimony even if he had, and who contractually bound himself to pay alimony to his former wife and did so without objection for over two years." The case would have been more appropriate if brought by a man deserving support, but denied alimony by the state gender-based law. Orr had little to gain from the decision.

Changing Alimony Standards

The decision provided a major change in how American marriages were legally viewed. Factors concerning both the husband and wife would have to be equally considered in divorce settlements. Sometimes the woman might have to pay alimony to the man if she was the primary income provider. Though the procedures actually changed greatly, the results of alimony decisions changed far less. Despite making alimony laws not gender-oriented, still by the mid-1990s few women were ordered to pay alimony to former husbands.

Suggestions for further reading

Horgan, Timothy J. *Winning Your Divorce: A Man's Survival Guide.* New York: Dutton, 1994.

Miller, Kathleen A. *Fair Share Divorce for Women.* Bellevue, WA: Miller, Bird Advisors, Inc., 1995.

Pistotnik, Bradley A. *Divorce War! 50 Strategies Every Woman Needs to Know to Win.* Holbrook, MA: Adams Media, 1996.

Woodhouse, Violet, Victoria F. Collins, and M. C. Blakeman. *Divorce and Money: How to Make the Best Financial Decisions During Divorce.* Berkeley, CA: Nolo.com, 2000.

DeShaney v. Winnebago County Department of Social Services 1989

Petitioner: Melody DeShaney for her son, Joshua DeShaney

Respondent: Winnebago County Department of Social Services

Petitioner's Claim: That Winnebago County in Wisconsin violated the due process clause of the Fourteenth Amendment by failing to protect Joshua DeShaney from the violent abuse of his father.

Chief Lawyer for Petitioner: Donald J. Sullivan

Chief Lawyer for Respondent: Mark J. Mingo

Justices for the Court: Anthony M. Kennedy, Sandra Day O'Connor, Chief Justice William H. Rehnquist, Antonin Scalia, John Paul Stevens, Byron R. White

Justices Dissenting: Harry A. Blackmun, William J. Brennan, Jr., Thurgood Marshall

Date of Decision: February 22, 1989

Decision: Ruled in favor of Winnebago County by finding the county was not responsible for Joshua's severe beating.

Significance: The ruling raised considerable concern among advocates for protecting children from abusive parents. The Court's decision approved the inaction of a government welfare agency, even when aware of ongoing abuse.

Well into the nineteenth century, children were considered property of the father. However, later in the century concern increased over the well-being of the nation's children. The relationship between child and parent received more special legal attention. Cases of neglect or abuse attracted particular public interest.

In the United States, state laws primarily govern the parent-child relationship, protecting the relationship as well as the rights of both. Ordinarily, the parent holds a constitutional right to custody (making key life decisions for another) of their child as well as the duty to care for the child. A child has the right to receive sufficient care, including food, clothing, shelter, medical care, and presumably love and affection. Through time states have assumed greater responsibility for making sure children are receiving this proper care. The growing responsibilities include greater powers to intervene (come in to settle) in family matters, particularly in cases of neglect or abuse. Parents not adequately performing their duties may be criminally charged. In determining custody of children, a rule known as the "best interest of the child" is often used by the court for cases that come before them.

Joshua's Plight

Joshua was born to Randy and Melody DeShaney in 1979 in Wyoming. Soon after, in 1980, the DeShaneys divorced with Randy receiving custody of Joshua. Randy and Joshua moved to Wisconsin and before long Randy remarried. With a break up of the second marriage soon occurring, a pattern of child abuse began to emerge. In 1982 the second wife, shortly before divorce, reported regular physical abuse of Joshua to Wisconsin child welfare agencies. The Winnebago County Department of Social Services (DSS) began to investigate. However, denials of the accusations by Randy DeShaney led to the county taking no action at the time.

In January of 1983, Joshua arrived at a hospital emergency with bruises that an attending physician believed resulted from abuse. The doctor notified DSS and a team of child care workers were assembled to tackle the case. Joshua was temporarily placed in custody of the hospital for three days. However, no charges against Randy were made and Joshua was returned to him. The county did make several recommendations, including that Joshua be enrolled in a pre-school program and Randy attend counseling. Also, a social worker, Ann Kemmeter, was assigned to the case to watch over Joshua through regular visits to his home.

CHILD ABUSE: SIGNS AND SYMPTOMS

Although these signs do not necessarily indicate that a child has been abused, they may help adults recognize that something is wrong. The possibility of abuse should be investigated if a child shows a number of these symptoms, or any of them to a marked degree:

Sexual Abuse

Being overly affectionate or knowledgeable in a sexual way inappropriate to the child's age
Medical problems such as chronic itching, pain in the genitals, venereal diseases
Other extreme reactions, such as depression, self-mutilation, suicide attempts, running away, overdoses, anorexia
Personality changes such as becoming insecure or clinging
Regressing to younger behavior patterns such as thumb sucking or bringing out discarded cuddly toys
Sudden loss of appetite or compulsive eating
Being isolated or withdrawn
Inability to concentrate
Lack of trust or fear someone they know well, such as not wanting to be alone with a babysitter
Starting to wet again, day or night/nightmares
Become worried about clothing being removed
Suddenly drawing sexually explicit pictures
Trying to be "ultra-good" or perfect; overreacting to criticism

Physical Abuse

Unexplained recurrent injuries or burns
Improbable excuses or refusal to explain injuries
Wearing clothes to cover injuries, even in hot weather
Refusal to undress for gym
Bald patches
Chronic running away
Fear of medical help or examination
Self-destructive tendencies
Aggression towards others
Fear of physical contact—shrinking back if touched
Admitting that they are punished, but the punishment is excessive (such as a child being beaten every night to "make him/her study")
Fear of suspected abuser being contacted

Emotional Abuse

Physical, mental, and emotional development lags
Sudden speech disorders
Continual self-depreciation ("I'm stupid, ugly, worthless, etc.")
Overreaction to mistakes
Extreme fear of any new situation
Inappropriate response to pain ("I deserve this")
Neurotic behavior (rocking, hair twisting, self-mutilation)
Extremes of passivity or aggression

Neglect

Constant hunger
Constant tiredness
Emaciation
Poor personal hygiene
Poor state of clothing
Untreated medical problems
No social relationships
Compulsive scavenging
Destructive tendencies

A child may be subjected to a combination of different kinds of abuse. It is also possible that a child may show no outward signs and hide what is happening from everyone.

Source: Kidscape, http://www.solnet.co.uk/kidscape/kids5.htm. Reprinted by permission.

Through the following year Kemmeter visited the DeShaneys approximately twenty times. She made notes of bumps and bruises on occasion including injuries to the head. She also noted that Randy never enrolled Joshua in pre-school or attended counseling sessions. During this time period Joshua visited emergency rooms twice more where doctors observed more suspicious injuries. Despite Kemmeter later admitting she feared for Joshua's life, the state still took no action to intervene in the father and child relationship.

Finally, in March of 1984, one day after yet another visit by Kemmeter, the four year old boy fell into a coma after a severe beating. Joshua came out of his coma, but was suffering from severe brain damage leaving him permanently paralyzed and mentally retarded. Joshua had to be placed in an institution for full-time care for the rest of his life at public expense.

Mother Sues the Child Welfare Agency

Randy DeShaney was charged with child abuse and found guilty. He was sentenced for up to four years in prison, but actually served less than two years before receiving parole. Disappointed with the conviction and sentencing, Joshua's mother, Melody, filed suit against DSS for not rescuing Joshua from his father before the fateful beating. Melody charged that Winnebago County and its social workers had violated Joshua's due process rights under the Fourteenth Amendment to the Constitution by not taking action.

The due process clause of the Fourteenth Amendment declares that states shall not "deprive any person of life, liberty, or property, without due process of law." Melody DeShaney charged the state had denied Joshua his rights to liberty by not taking action when it was fully aware of the situation. The federal district court, however, ruled in favor of Winnebago County. Melody DeShaney appealed the decision to the federal court of appeals which affirmed the district court's decision. DeShaney next appealed to the U.S. Supreme Court which agreed to hear the case. DeShaney again argued that the county had a responsibility to protect the child since it not only knew of the situation and had even held custody of Joshua for three days. She claimed the state had established a "special relationship" with Joshua and that relationship created a responsibility to protect him from known dangers.

OPPOSITE PAGE: *There are many signs that may indicate child abuse.* Reproduced by permission of Kidscape.

State Not Constitutionally Responsible

Chief Justice William Rehnquist delivered the opinion of the Court. Rehnquist found that the due process clause of the Fourteenth Amendment only applies to states, not private citizens. Rehnquist wrote that the purpose of the due process clause "was to protect the people from the State, not to ensure that the State protected them from each other." He found neither "guarantee of certain minimal levels of safety and security" for the nation's citizens through the clause nor did he find a "right to governmental aid." Therefore, "the State cannot be held liable under the Clause for the injuries" that might have been prevented if it had more fully used its protective services.

Rehnquist further explained that the due process clause would only apply in cases where the state had assumed custody of a person against their will and then had not adequately provided for their "safety and general well-being." Then a deprivation (withholding) of liberty by the state would have occurred.

In summary, the Court concluded the state had neither played any part in directly causing the injuries nor had made him more vulnerable. Rehnquist wrote, "Under these circumstances, the State had no constitutional duty to protect Joshua." In fact, if the state had acted to take custody of Joshua away from Randy DeShaney, it may have been charged with "improperly intruding into the parent-child relationship" under the same due process clause. Rehnquist did add, however, that the state may have been guilty of some duty under Wisconsin law, but that was not the subject of DeShaney's charges.

State Has Responsibility By Its Very Existence

Three of the Court justices dissented (disagreed) with the majority's decision. Justice Brennan, writing for the other two, asserted that the very existence of the Wisconsin child-welfare system means that its citizens have a certain level of dependence on the services in provides. Public expectations create a state responsibility to act when conditions come to its attention, such as with Joshua. If the services did not exist, then those concerned with Joshua might have taken other action to help which might have made a major difference in his life.

As Justice Blackmun, also dissenting, added,

BEST INTEREST OF THE CHILD

Well into the nineteenth century, fathers normally received custody of children following divorce. Then, following the American Civil War (1861–1865), the "tender years" standard began to be applied by the courts in justifying awarding custody to the mother who was believed to provide better nurturing to the child during its earliest years. However, before long another standard was adopted, known as "best interests of the child." This second standard which weighs the right of the mother to custody against the needs of the child became the most important standard used by the courts to determine child custody.

Among the factors considered by judges in determining the best interest of the child are: (1) which parent can best provide daily care; (2) what special needs might the child have; (3) what is the health and fitness of each parent; (4) where are their brothers or sisters; (5) is one parent keeping the home or staying in the community the child is used to living in; and, (6) what does the child herself want. Still, most often the mother has been the child's primary caretaker and is awarded custody. But, increasingly fathers have been granted custody in certain situations.

Poor Joshua! Victim of repeated attacks by an irresponsible, bullying, cowardly, and intemperate father, and abandoned by respondents who placed him in a dangerous predicament and who knew or learned what was going on, and yet did essentially nothing except . . . 'dutifully recorded these incidents in [their] files.'

Concern for Children's Safety Raised

The Court's ruling raised considerable concern among child welfare advocates. They claimed the rights of the child to a safe, nurturing home environment were ignored. The decision, they believed, set a dangerous precedent for future rulings in similar cases of abuse. They reasoned, what if the police knew of a murder about to happen, but chose to do nothing to stop it? Similar to the county's inaction to help Joshua, the police would not have caused the death directly, nor made the victim worse off. Yet many would consider the police negligent (failing to do take the required action) in their duties to protect the citizens in their jurisdiction.

Suggestions for further reading

Helfer, Mary Edna, Ruth S. Kempe, and Richard D. Krugman, eds. *The Battered Child.* Chicago: University of Chicago Press, 1997.

Pelzer, David J. *A Child Called "It:" An Abused Child's Journey from Victim to Victor.* Deefield Beach, FL: Health Communications, 1995.

Trickett, Penelope K., and Cynthia D. Schellenbach, eds. *Violence Against Children in the Family and the Community.* Washington, DC: American Psychological Association, 1998.

Besharov, Douglas. *Recognizing Child Abuse: A Guide for the Concerned.* New York: Free Press, 1990.

Haskins, James. *The Child Abuse Help Book.* Reading, MA: Addison-Wesley, 1982. (for adolescent readers)

Troxel v. Granville
2000

Petiotioners: Jenifer and Gary Troxel

Respondent: Tommie Granville

Petitioner's Claim: That the Washington Supreme Court's denial of their petition for visitation of their grandchildren was in error.

Chief Lawyer for Petitioner: Mark D. Olson

Chief Lawyer for Respondent: Catherine W. Smith

Justices for the Court: Stephen Breyer, Ruth Bader Ginsburg, Sandra Day O'Connor, Chief Justice William Rehnquist, David H. Souter, Clarence Thomas.

Justices Dissenting: Anthony M. Kennedy, Antonin Scalia, John Paul Stevens

Date of Decision: June 5, 2000

Decision: Ruled in favor of Granville by stating that Washington statute, as applied to the case at hand, unconstitutionally infringed upon her right to care for her children.

Significance: Reaffirmed the constitutionally protected right to raise one's children free from overly evasive interference from government.

In today's society, it is difficult to describe the "average" American family. "While many children may have two married parents and grandparents who visit regularly, many other children are raised in single-parent households." In the latter case, both maternal (the parents of the mother)

FAMILY LAW

and paternal (the parents of the father) grandparents of the children may desire to have visitation. On June 5, 2000, the United States Supreme Court decided *Troxel v. Granville,* a case involving paternal grandparents seeking visitation of their two grandchildren.

Troxel involved an unmarried couple, Tommie Granville and Brad Troxel, who had two children together, Isabelle and Natalie. In 1991, Tommie and Brad's relationship ended. Two years later, Brad committed suicide. After Brad's death, his parents, Jenifer and Gary, desired to visit their grandchildren. They sought two weekends of overnight visitation per month and two weeks of visitation each summer. Though Tommie allowed some visitation, she did not allow visitation in the amount that Isabelle and Natalie's grandparents wanted. She prefered that the Troxels have only one night of visitation a month with no overnight stays. Because of the differences in opinion, Jenifer and Gary sued Tommie in Washington state court to obtain visitaiton of their grandchildren.

The Troxels sued Tommie under a Washington Revised Code, which permitted "any person," including grandparents, to petition a superior court for visitation rights "at any time." The statute also allowed a court to grant visitation whenever it might "serve the best interest of the child" regardless

Custody is a matter that concerns not only parents, but grandparents as well. Reproduced by permission of Stock Boston, Inc.

of whether there had been a change in circumstances of the children. The Troxels won their initial suit against Tommie in Washington Superior Court, and the judge entered an oral ruling (which was later put into writing). In finding for the Troxels, the superior court judge determined that visitation was in the best interest of Isabelle and Natalie. In particular, the court noted that "[t]he Petitioners [the Troxels] are part of a large, central, loving family, all located in this area, and the Petitioners can provide opportunities for the children in the areas of cousins and music." The court "took into consideration all factors regarding the best interest of the children and considered all the testimony."

Though the court decided that the children would benefit from spending time with their grandparents, it also determined that the children would benefit from spending time with their mother and stepfather's other six children. Thus, the court ordered visitation in the amount of one weekend per month, one week in the summer, and four hours on both of the grandparents birthdays. Tommie appealed from this decision to the Washington Court of Appeals. During this time, Tommie married Kelly Wynn, who eventually adopted both Isabelle and Natalie.

The Washington Court of Appeals reversed the lower court's decision and dismissed the Troxels' petition for visitation. The court determined that the Washington statute only allowed people to sue for visitation when there was a custody action pending. Since this was no such action, the court opined, the Troxels did not have standing (permission) to sue for visitation.

The Washington Supreme Court disagreed with the court of appeals' determination that the statute did not give the Troxels standing to sue. Instead, the Washington Supreme Court said, the statute's plain language authorized "any person" to petition a superior court for visitation rights "at any time." The Washington Supreme Court, however, agreed with the appellate court's ultimate conclusion that the Troxels could not obtain visitation of Isabelle and Natalie, as it violated the Constitution's fundamental right of parents to rear their children.

The Washington Supreme Court found two problems with the statute. First, the Constitution permitted a State to interfere with the right of parents to rear their children only to prevent harm or potential harm to a child. Since the statute provided no requirement that a petitioner show harm, it violated the Constitution. Second, the statute was too broad because it allowed "'any person' to petition for forced visitation of a child at 'any time' with the only requirement being that the visitation serve the best interest of the child." The Washington Supreme Court felt that a parent had the right to limit visitation with their children of third parties. In that court's opinion, parents, not judges, "should be the ones to choose whether to expose their children to certain people or ideas."

The Troxels appealed the Washington Supreme Court's decision to the United States Supreme Court. The Supreme Court granted certiorari (agreed to hear the case), and affirmed the Washington Supreme Court's decision. Announcing the judgment of the Court, Justice O'Connor first pointed out that the government cannot interfere "with certain fundamental rights and liberty interests." Included in these rights and interests is a parent's ability to care for and control her children. According to Justice O'Connor, Supreme Court decisions such as *Meyer v. Nebraska, Pierce v. Society of Sisters,* and *Prince v. Massachusetts,* had long established the right of parents to "establish a home and bring up children" and "to direct the upbringing and education of children under their control." Indeed, Justice O'Connor added, "the custody, care and nurture of the child reside[s] first in the parents."

Given these facts, the Supreme Court decided that the Washington statute was too intrusive on a parent's right to determine what was in the best interest of her child. Specifically, the Supreme Court concluded that the statute "placed the best-interest determination solely in the hands of the [court]." Thus, if a judge merely disagreed with a parent as to whether visitation by a third party was in the best interest of a child, she could simply order that it occur. This, the Supreme Court opined, exceeded the bounds of the Constitution.

Moreover, the Superior Court Judge gave no "special weight at all to Granville's determination of her daughters' best interst." Instead, the judge "applied exactly the opposite presumption." He presummed that the grandparents' request for visitation should be granted "unless the children would be 'impact[ed] adversely.'" Indicative of this fact was the judge's statement: "I think [visitation with the Troxels] would be in the best interst of the children and I haven't been shown it is not in [the] best interest of the children."

Thus, the Supreme Court concluded that the visitation order in this case was an unconstitutional infringment of Tommie's fundamental right to make decisions concerning the care, custody and control of her children, Isabelle and Natalie. The Supreme Court, however, did not decide whether all visitation statutes were unconstitutional. Instead, it decided to allow state courts to determine, on a case-by-case basis, whether or not a visitation staute unconstitutionally infringed upon the parental right.

OTHER TYPES OF THIRD-PARTY VISITATION STATUTES

All fifty states have third-party visitation statutes. The statutes primarily allow petitions from persons who are: (1) stepparent; (2) grandparent - death of their child; (3) grandparent - child divorce; (4) (grand)parent of child born out of wedlock; and (5) any interested party. Only three states allow all of the above to petition the court for visitation. Twelve states allow only grandparents of either type to petition. Twelve additional states allow grandparents of either type and relatives of babies born out of wedlock to petition for visitation. The remaining allow various combinations of third parties to petition a court for visitation. In light of *Troxel,* the status of each of these statutes is uncertain.

Only three other Supreme Court Justices agreed with Justice O'Connor: Justice Rehnquist, Justice Ginsburg and Justice Breyer. Justices Souter and Thomas filed opinions concurring (agreeing) in the judgment. Both of these Justices felt that the ultimate decision of the Court was correct, but that the logic was incorrect. Justices Stevens, Scalia and Kennedy, however, dissented (disagreed), and filed separate opinions. Each of these Justices outlined why they felt the Court had come to the wrong conclusion, and laid out what he felt the correct outcome should be. Regardless of the split in the Court, one this is apparant from this decision, a parent's right to raise his children and to make decision for them can be violated by the government only with caution.

Suggestions for further reading

American Bar Association, *Grandparent visitation disputes: A legal resource manual*, June 1998.

Boland, Mary, *Your right to child custody, visitation and support (Legal survival guide),* Sphinx Publication, February 2000.

Truly, Traci, *Grandparent rights,* Sphinx Publication, March 1999.

A jury is a group of ordinary citizens that hears and decides a legal case. The jury's decision is called a verdict. Juries base their verdicts on testimony from witnesses and other evidence. A jury's verdict represents a community's opinion about who should win a legal case. Jurors, then, play an important role in the American system of justice.

History of the Jury

Historians have traced the jury system back to Athens, Greece, around 400 BC. Aristotle, a Greek philosopher, recorded that juries decided cases based on their understanding of general justice. The ancient Roman Empire, however, did not use juries. A professional court system decided cases without ordinary citizens. The Dark Ages that followed the fall of the Roman Empire had little law and no use for juries.

Great Britain did not use a jury system until the twelfth century AD. Prior to then, the Catholic Church's courts controlled the legal system. The ordeal was a popular way of deciding criminal cases. If the accused could survive physical torture, the court declared him innocent.

Compurgation was a method of resolving civil cases, those between individual citizens. The person who brought the most friends to support his side of the case won.

In the twelfth century AD, King Henry II gave Great Britain its first jury system for deciding disputes over land. Later, his son King John was a ruthless monarch who regularly seized the land and families of landowners who could not pay their debts on time. In 1215, a group of landowners confronted King John at knifepoint and forced him to sign the Magna Carta. That historic document gave British citizens the right to have a jury trial before being "imprisoned or seized or exiled or in any way destroyed."

The Right to Jury Trials in the United States

The English jury system migrated to the American colonies. Great Britain, however, did not allow jury trials in all cases in the colonies. Some cases were bench trials, which means a judge decided them from his bench. Because colonial judges depended on the British monarch for their jobs and the amount of their salaries, they often were unfair to the colonists. When Thomas Jefferson and the Second Continental Congress wrote the Declaration of Independence in 1776, they listed unfair judges and the lack of jury trials among their reasons for breaking ties with Great Britain.

The U.S. Constitution mentions jury trials in three places. Article III says that all criminal trials, except for impeachment, must be jury trials. The Sixth Amendment repeats this right and adds that juries must be impartial, which means fair, neutral, and open-minded. In *Duncan v. Louisiana* (1968), the Supreme Court said the right to a jury trial applies in all criminal cases in which the penalty can be imprisonment for more than six months.

The Seventh Amendment guarantees a jury trial in all civil cases in which the amount in dispute is greater than twenty dollars. This amendment applies only to the federal government and not to the states. Most state constitutions, however, give citizens the right to jury trials in both criminal and civil cases.

Jury Selection

Choosing a jury for a case happens in two stages. The first stage is called assembling the venire. The venire is a large group of citizens selected from voting, tax, driving, or address records. This group acts as a pool from which the court selects juries for individual cases. To be selected for the venire, citizens must satisfy certain requirements. For example, many states require jurors to be over eighteen, able to read, and without any serious criminal convictions.

Federal and state courts used to restrict jury service to white males. The U.S. Supreme Court ended that with two important cases. In ***Strauder v. West Virginia*** (1879), the Court said the Fourteenth Amendment makes it illegal to exclude African Americans from jury service. In ***Taylor v. Louisiana*** (1975), the Court struck down a law that tended to exclude women from jury service in Louisiana. With the Federal Jury Service and Selection Act of 1968, Congress required federal jury venires to contain a fair cross section of the community.

The second stage in jury selection is called voir dire. Judges conduct voir dire by asking the members of the venire questions to make sure they can consider a case impartially and deliver a fair verdict. Under the jury system in England, jurors usually were selected because of their knowledge of the case. The American system of impartiality requires that jurors know as little as possible about a case before serving on a jury. That way they can render a verdict based on the evidence in court rather than what they have learned on the outside.

Attorneys also participate in voir dire. Sometimes they ask questions through the judge, while other times they pose questions directly to potential jurors. After questioning, the parties can strike people from the jury using jury challenges. Attorneys can make an unlimited number of challenges "for cause." A challenge is for cause when the attorney has a good reason to excuse a potential juror from service. For example, if a potential juror is the defendant's brother, the prosecutor can challenge him for cause and dismiss him from service on the case.

Attorneys also get a limited number of peremptory challenges. Attorneys do not have to explain their reason for using a peremptory challenge. It gives them a chance to get rid of jurors they think will be against their clients' case. The U.S. Supreme Court, however, has limited the use of peremptory challenges. In ***Batson v. Kentucky*** (1986), the Court said prosecutors cannot use peremptory challenges to dismiss potential jurors because of their race. In ***J.E.B. v. Alabama*** (1994), the

Court said attorneys may not use peremptory challenges to dismiss potential jurors because of their gender.

Voir dire ends when the court finds the right number of jurors who can render a fair decision and are not challenged by the attorneys. The English jury system typically used twelve jurors. Legend says this number came from the number of Jesus Christ's apostles in the Bible's New Testament. Most juries in America have twelve jurors. Some states use as few as six jurors. In *Ballew v. Georgia* (1978), the U.S. Supreme Court said a five member jury is too small to decide a case fairly.

Jury Verdicts

After the jury hears the evidence in a case, the judge instructs the jury on what law to apply. The jury then retires to the jury room to deliberate, which means to discuss the case and reach a verdict. The jury reaches a verdict by deciding what really happened in the case, called determining the facts, and then applying the law to those facts to determine who wins.

At the federal level and in most states, a jury verdict must be unanimous. That means all twelve jurors must agree on the verdict. Some states allow jury verdicts by super majorities of ten or eleven out of the twelve jurors. If the jury cannot agree on a verdict, it is called a hung jury. A hung jury requires the judge to dismiss the entire case without a decision.

The jury's verdict is not always the final decision in the case. If the judge thinks the verdict is wrong, she can either order a new trial or enter the verdict she thinks is correct. There is one important exception. When a jury finds a defendant not guilty in a criminal case, the judge must accept the verdict.

When the jury reaches a verdict in a civil case, it also decides how much money the winning party receives. In a criminal case, the jury usually only decides guilt or innocence. If the verdict is guilty, the judge determines the criminal's sentence. Many southern states allow the jury to determine the sentence within certain guidelines. In cases in which the defendant faces the death penalty, however, the federal government and most states allow the jury to determine the sentence or at least make a recommendation.

Suggestions for further reading

Guinther, John. *The Jury in America.* New York: Facts on File Publications, 1988.

Summer, Lila E. *The American Heritage History of the Bill of Rights: The Seventh Amendment.* New Jersey: Silver Burdett Press, Inc., 1991.

Wolf, Robert V. *The Jury System.* Philadelphia: Chelsea House Publishers, 1999.

Zerman, Melvyn Bernard. *Beyond a Reasonable Doubt: Inside the American Jury System.* New York: Crowell, 1981.

Strauder v. West Virginia 1879

Appellant: Taylor Strauder

Appellee: State of West Virginia

Appellant's Claim: That West Virginia violated his constitutional rights by excluding African Americans from the jury selection process.

Chief Lawyers for Appellant: Charles Devans and George O. Davenport

Chief Lawyers for Appellee: Robert White, Attorney General of West Virginia, and James W. Green

Justices for the Court: Joseph P. Bradley, John Marshall Harlan, Ward Hunt, Samuel Freeman Miller, William Strong, Noah Haynes Swayne, Morrison Remick Waite

Justices Dissenting: Nathan Clifford, Stephen Johnson Field

Date of Decision: March 1, 1880

Decision: The Supreme Court reversed Strauder's murder conviction.

Significance: With *Strauder,* the Supreme Court said African American men have the same right as white men to serve on juries.

The American Declaration of Independence, written in 1776, says all men are created equal. Shamefully, the United States of America did not treat all men equally when it was born that year. White men owned

African Americans as slaves, forcing them to work on plantations to make the white men wealthy.

The United States finally outlawed slavery with the Thirteenth Amendment in 1865. Prejudice against African Americans remained high, however, in the former slave states. There was concern that these states would discriminate against newly freed slaves by treating them differently under the law. To prevent that, the United States adopted the Fourteenth Amendment in 1868.

The Equal Protection Clause is an important part of the Fourteenth Amendment. It says states may not deny anyone "the equal protection of the laws." This means states must apply their laws equally to all citizens. In *Strauder v. West Virginia,* the U.S. Supreme Court had to decide whether a law that prevented African Americans from serving on juries violated the Equal Protection Clause.

White Men Only

Taylor Strauder was an African American who was charged with murder in Ohio County, West Virginia, on 20 October 1874. A West Virginia law said only white men could serve as jurors. Strauder did not think he could get a fair trial in a state that did not allow African Americans to serve on juries. In fact, he thought West Virginia's law violated the Equal Protection Clause by treating African Americans unequally.

A federal law said a defendant could have his case moved from state court to federal court whenever the state court was violating its citizens' equal rights. Strauder used this law to ask the state court to move his trial to a federal court. The state court refused and forced Strauder to stand trial in West Virginia. After he was convicted, Strauder appealed his case to the Supreme Court of West Virginia. When he lost there too, Strauder appealed to the U.S. Supreme Court.

Jury of His Peers

With a 7-2 decision, the Supreme Court reversed Strauder's conviction. Writing for the Court, Justice William Strong said West Virginia violated the Equal Protection Clause by preventing African Americans from serving as jurors. Strong said under the Equal Protection Clause, "the law in the States shall be the same for the black as for the white; that all persons, whether colored or white, shall stand equal before the laws of the

JURIES AND RACE

Selecting a jury is a two-stage process. In the first stage, a court uses local records to create a pool of people from the community. This pool is called a venire. The venire must contain a cross-section of the community. That means all races of Americans must be eligible to be selected for the venire. In the second stage, the judge and lawyers select twelve people from the venire to be the jury for a specific case. The jury does not have to contain a cross-section of the community. That means juries often are dominated by people from one race. When that happens, the public sometimes wonders whether race affected a jury's decision.

For example, in 1991, four white Los Angeles police officers beat an African American motorist named Rodney G. King. In 1992, the officers faced criminal charges in the mostly white Los Angeles suburb of Simi Valley. The jury, which contained no African Americans, found the officers not guilty of almost all charges against them. Many Americans thought racial prejudice affected the jury's verdict.

Two years later, football star O.J. Simpson's ex-wife, Nicole Brown Simpson, was murdered in Los Angeles along with her boyfriend, Ronald L. Goldman. Simpson, an African American, faced murder charges for the crime in 1995. At his trial, nine of the twelve jurors were African American. When the jury found Simpson not guilty, many Americans again believed racial prejudice affected the verdict. Some even thought the verdict was payback for the King verdict three years earlier.

States, and . . . that no discrimination shall be made against [African Americans] because of their color."

A law that allows only whites to be jurors treats citizens unequally. Justice Strong asked what white men would think about a law that allowed only African Americans to be jurors, or that excluded Irish Americans from being jurors. Such laws would defeat the very purpose of a criminal trial, which is to allow a man to be judged by a jury of his peers-his neighbors, fellows, and associates.

Justice Strong made it clear that Strauder did not have a right to have a certain number of African Americans on his jury. He only had the right to have the jury selected from a group of citizens that included African Americans. Moreover, West Virginia was free to apply non-racial requirements for jurors. For example, West Virginia could require jurors to be men who had reached a certain age and received an education. It simply could not exclude entire races of people from ever serving as jurors.

Impact

With *Strauder,* the Supreme Court gave African Americans the right to serve as jurors in the United States. States, however, often got around this by requiring jurors to have a certain education and reading ability. Newly freed slaves in the late 1800s usually could not afford a good education. African Americans spent many more decades fighting through such prejudice to enjoy their right to serve as jurors. Moreover, it was not until 1975 in ***Taylor v. Louisiana*** that the Supreme Court struck down all laws that made it difficult for women to serve as jurors.

Suggestions for further reading

Claireborne, William. "Acquitted, O.J. Simpson Goes Home." *Washington Post,* October 4, 1995.

Guinther, John. *The Jury in America.* New York: Facts on File Publications, 1988.

Morin, Richard. "Polls Uncover Much Common Ground on L.A. Verdict." *Washington Post,* May 11, 1992

Summer, Lila E. *The American Heritage History of the Bill of Rights: The Seventh Amendment.* New Jersey: Silver Burdett Press, Inc., 1991.

Wolf, Robert V. *The Jury System.* Philadelphia: Chelsea House Publishers, 1999.

Zerman, Melvyn Bernard. *Beyond a Reasonable Doubt: Inside the American Jury System.* New York: Crowell, 1981.

Taylor v. Louisiana 1975

Appellant: Billy Jean Taylor

Appellee: State of Louisiana

Appellant's Claim: That by excluding women, Louisiana's jury selection system violated his Sixth Amendment right to have an impartial jury.

Chief Lawyer for Appellant: William M. King

Chief Lawyer for Appellee: Kendall L. Vick

Justices for the Court: Harry A. Blackmun, William J. Brennan, Jr., Warren E. Burger, William O. Douglas, Thurgood Marshall, Lewis F. Powell, Jr., Potter Stewart, Byron R. White (writing for the Court)

Justices Dissenting: William H. Rehnquist

Date of Decision: January 21, 1975

Decision: The Supreme Court reversed Taylor's conviction.

Significance: With *Taylor,* the Supreme Court said juries must be selected from a fair cross section of the community, including both men and women.

The Sixth Amendment of the U.S. Constitution gives every American the right to be tried by an impartial jury when accused of a crime. An impartial jury is one that is fair, neutral, and open-minded. The use of juries in criminal trials allows defendants to be judged by their peers from the community.

Selecting a jury for a case is a two-stage process. In the first stage, the court creates a large pool of people from the community to serve as jurors. This pool is called a venire. In the second stage, the court selects twelve people from the venire to be the jury for a specific case. In *Taylor v. Louisiana,* the U.S. Supreme Court had to decide whether Louisiana's jury selection system violated the Sixth Amendment.

Mostly Men

On September 28, 1971, police arrested Billy Jean Taylor, a twenty-five year old convict in St. Tammany parish, Louisiana. (In Louisiana, a parish is a county.) The police charged Taylor with aggravated kidnapping, armed robbery, and rape. Taylor's trial was scheduled to begin on April 13, 1972.

Louisiana had a law that said women could not be selected for jury service unless they registered with the court. Men did not have to register to serve as jurors. The law had the effect of making women a rare sight on juries in St. Tammany parish. Only one out of every five women registered for jury service. Although women made up fifty-three percent of the people eligible for jury service in St. Tammany, the venire of one hundred seventy-five people selected before Taylor's trial contained no women.

The day before his trial, Taylor filed a motion to get rid of the venire. He argued that excluding women from jury service violated his Sixth Amendment right to have an impartial jury. Taylor said a venire without women did not represent the community of his peers.

The trial court rejected Taylor's motion and selected an all-male jury to try his case. The jury convicted Taylor and the court sentenced him to death. Taylor appealed, but the Supreme Court of Louisiana affirmed his conviction. As his last resort, Taylor appealed to the U.S. Supreme Court.

Fair Cross Sections

With an 8–1 decision, the Supreme Court reversed Taylor's conviction. Writing for the Court, Justice Byron R. White said Louisiana violated the Sixth Amendment by excluding women from juries. Louisiana and all states must obey the Sixth Amendment under the Due Process Clause of the Fourteenth Amendment.

Before the Supreme Court, Louisiana argued that as a man, Taylor had no right to complain about the lack of women on his jury. Justice

FEDERAL JURY SELECTION AND SERVICE ACT OF 1968

In the Civil Rights Act of 1957, Congress gave most Americans the right to serve on juries in federal court cases. In the Federal Jury Selection and Service Act of 1968, Congress went one step further. It said federal courts must select juries from a fair cross section of the community. The Act specifically prevents federal courts from excluding citizens from jury service based on their race, color, religion, sex, national origin, or economic status.

The Act has some qualifications. Federal jurors must be American citizens, eighteen years of age or older, and able to read, write, and speak English. If a federal court selects a citizen as a possible juror, he must fill out a form to allow the court to decide whether he satisfies these requirements. An American who refuses to fill out a juror qualification form or fails to appear as a juror when called can be fined $one-hundred and imprisoned for three days.

White rejected this argument. He said all Americans, male and female, have a right under the Sixth Amendment to be tried by an impartial jury. An impartial jury is one that is "drawn from a fair cross section of the community." A venire with no women in a parish that is half female does not represent the community.

White explained the importance of impartial juries. They make sure a defendant is judged by his peers. If a prosecutor wants to convict an innocent man, the jury can prevent that. Juries also can prevent a biased judge from doing injustice. A jury cannot properly do its job unless it is the voice of the entire community. Jury service by all members of a community also creates public confidence in the criminal justice system.

Louisiana said it was protecting women from having to leave the important position of taking care of families at home. Justice White pointed out that as of 1974, fifty-two percent of all women between eighteen and sixty-four worked outside the home. It no longer was right to assume that women cannot be interrupted from taking care of a home. The courts would have to handle each person individually to determine if jury service would be too much of a burden.

Justice White closed by emphasizing that individual juries do not have to contain a cross section of the community. That would be impossible to do with every jury of twelve people. Juries, however, must be selected from venires that fairly represent the community. Only then can defendants be fairly judged by their peers.

Suggestions for further reading

Guinther, John. *The Jury in America.* New York: Facts on File Publications, 1988.

Summer, Lila E. *The American Heritage History of the Bill of Rights: The Seventh Amendment.* New Jersey: Silver Burdett Press, Inc., 1991.

Wolf, Robert V. *The Jury System.* Philadelphia: Chelsea House Publishers, 1999.

Zerman, Melvyn Bernard. *Beyond a Reasonable Doubt: Inside the American Jury System.* New York: Crowell, 1981.

Batson v. Kentucky 1986

Petitioner: James Kirkland Batson

Respondent: State of Kentucky

Petitioner's Claim: That by striking African Americans from his jury, the prosecutor violated his constitutional rights.

Chief Lawyer for Petitioner: J. David Niehaus

Chief Lawyer for Respondent: Rickie L. Pearson, Assistant Attorney General of Kentucky

Justices for the Court: Harry A. Blackmun, William J. Brennan, Jr., Thurgood Marshall, Sandra Day O'Connor, Lewis F. Powell, Jr., John Paul Stevens, Byron R. White

Justices Dissenting: Warren E. Burger, William H. Rehnquist

Date of Decision: April 30, 1986

Decision: The Supreme Court sent Batson's case back to the trial court to determine whether the prosecutor had race-neutral reasons for striking African Americans from the jury.

Significance: With *Batson,* the Supreme Court said striking jurors because of their race violates the Equal Protection Clause of the Fourteenth Amendment.

The Sixth Amendment of the U.S. Constitution gives every American the right to be tried by an impartial jury when accused of a crime. An impartial jury is one that is fair, neutral, and open-minded. The use of impartial juries allow defendants to be judged fairly by their peers from the community.

Associate Justice Lewis F. Powell.
Courtesy of the Supreme Court of the United States.

Selecting a jury for a case is a two-stage process. In the first stage, the court creates a large pool of people from the community to serve as jurors. This pool is called a venire. In the second stage, the court and lawyers select twelve people from the venire to be the jury for a specific case. During this stage the lawyers for both parties get to make jury challenges. A jury challenge allows the parties to exclude specific people from the jury.

There are two kinds of jury challenges. A challenge "for cause" happens when a party has a good reason to believe a potential juror might not be able to decide a case fairly. For example, if a potential juror is the defendant's brother, the prosecutor can use a for cause challenge to prevent the brother from serving on the jury. There is no limit to the number of for cause challenges a party can make during jury selection.

The second kind of challenge is called a peremptory challenge. Each party gets a limited number of peremptory challenges. They allow the parties to exclude potential jurors who the lawyers feel will be against their cases. Traditionally, a lawyer could use peremptory challenges without giving a good reason. All he needed was a hunch that a potential juror would rule against his client. Peremptory challenges were one way for defendants to make sure they got an impartial jury.

Jury of His White Peers

In 1981, James Kirkland Batson stood trial in Jefferson county, Kentucky, on charges of second-degree burglary and receipt of stolen goods. Batson was an African American. During jury selection, the prosecutor used his peremptory challenges to strike the only four African Americans from the jury venire. The resulting jury had only white people.

Batson made a motion to dismiss the jury and get a new one. (When a party makes a motion, he asks the court to do something.) Batson argued that the prosecutor violated his right to an impartial jury by eliminating African Americans. Batson also argued that using peremptory challenges to get rid of jurors based on race violates the Equal Protection Clause of the Fourteenth Amendment. The Equal Protection Clause says states may not discriminate against citizens because of race.

The trial court denied Batson's motion and the jury convicted him on both counts. Batson appealed to the Supreme Court of Kentucky, but it affirmed his conviction. As his last resort, Batson took his case to the U.S. Supreme Court. There he got help from the Legal Defense and Education Fund of the National Association for the Advancement of Colored People.

Discrimination Disallowed

With a 7-2 decision, the Supreme Court ruled in favor of Batson. Writing for the Court, Justice Lewis F. Powell, Jr., said dismissing African American jurors because of their race suggests that African Americans are incapable of being jurors or deciding a case fairly. The Supreme Court could not allow prosecutors to reinforce such ignorant, old-fashioned ideas.

The Equal Protection Clause prevents Kentucky and all states from discriminating against races of people. When a prosecutor uses a peremptory challenge to strike an African American from a jury, he hurts the defendant, the potential juror, and society. The defendant loses the right to have a jury free from discrimination. The potential juror loses the right to serve on a jury. Society loses confidence in the fairness of the criminal justice system.

The Supreme Court sent Batson's case back to the trial court in Kentucky. That court had to determine whether the prosecutor had race-neutral reasons for striking the four African Americans from the jury. If not, the court would have to reverse Batson's conviction.

Justice Thurgood Marshall filed a concurring opinion, which means he agreed with the Court's decision. Justice Marshall said, however, that he would go one step further by eliminating peremptory challenges entirely. He thought it would be too difficult to determine whether a pros-

NORRIS V. ALABAMA

In March 1931, Clarence Norris and eight other African American boys were indicted in Scottsboro, Alabama, for raping two white girls. The case of the Scottsboro boys drew national attention. Locals bent on revenge were determined to see the nine boys convicted. Evidence of the boys' innocence, however, led people around the work, including scientist Albert Einstein, to sign a petition requesting Alabama to release the boys.

Alabama rejected the petition and tried the Scottsboro boys in court. The U.S. Supreme Court overturned the first trial because Alabama failed to appoint a good lawyer for the boys. Clarence Norris was convicted and sentenced to death in a second trial. Norris appealed the conviction because the grand jury that indicted him and the jury that convicted him had no African Americans.

The U.S. Supreme Court reversed Norris's second conviction. If found that Morgan and Jackson counties in Alabama, where Norris was indicted and tried, regularly excluded African Americans from jury service. There even was evidence that local authorities were tampering with jury lists to make it look like they were considering African Americans for jury service when in fact they were not. The evidence proved that in a generation, no African Americans had served on a grand or petit jury in Morgan and Jackson counties. For that reason, Norris deserved a new trial.

ecutor used a peremptory challenge for a race-neutral reason. Marshall said the only way to get rid of the evil of discrimination is to get rid of peremptory challenges.

Leaving Long Traditions Behind

Chief Justice Warren E. Burger and Justice William H Rehnquist filed dissenting opinions, which means they disagreed with the Court's decision. Burger and Rehnquist said peremptory challenges were one of the most important parts of America's criminal justice system. They stated very frankly that people tend to favor other people of their own race, religion, age, and ethnicity. Peremptory challenges make sure such favoritism does not affect a jury's decision. Making prosecutors use these challenges for race-neutral reasons would force them to keep biased people on juries.

Impact

Batson only applied to prosecutors in criminal cases. Eventually, however, the courts extended the decision to civil cases, which are between individual citizens. Eight years later in ***J.E.B. v. Alabama*** (1994), the Supreme Court said lawyers may not use peremptory challenges to exclude jurors based on their sex either. As of 1999, however, the Court has declined to prevent religious discrimination in the selection of jurors.

Suggestions for further reading

Guinther, John. *The Jury in America.* New York: Facts on File Publications, 1988.

Mikula, Mark, and L. Mpho Mabunda, eds. *Great American Court Cases.* Detroit: The Gale Group, 1999.

Summer, Lila E. *The American Heritage History of the Bill of Rights: The Seventh Amendment.* New Jersey: Silver Burdett Press, Inc., 1991.

Wolf, Robert V. *The Jury System.* Philadelphia: Chelsea House Publishers, 1999.

Zerman, Melvyn Bernard. *Beyond a Reasonable Doubt: Inside the American Jury System.* New York: Crowell, 1981.

Lockhart v. McCree
1986

Petitioner: A.L. Lockhart

Respondent: Ardia V. McCree

Petitioner's Claim: That Arkansas did not violate the constitution in death penalty cases by removing prospective jurors who could not vote for death under any circumstances.

Chief Lawyer for Petitioner: John Steven Clark, Attorney General of Arkansas

Chief Lawyer for Respondent: Samuel R. Gross

Justices for the Court: Harry A. Blackmun, Warren E. Burger, Sandra Day O'Connor, Lewis F. Powell, Jr., William H. Rehnquist, Byron R. White

Justices Dissenting: William J. Brennan, Jr., Thurgood Marshall, John Paul Stevens

Date of Decision: May 5, 1986

Decision: The Supreme Court said Arkansas did not violate the constitution.

Significance: *Lockhart* allows states to use death-qualified juries during the guilt phase of death penalty cases even though evidence suggests that death-qualified juries are more likely to convict defendants.

JURIES

The Sixth Amendment of the U.S. Constitution gives every American the right to be tried by an impartial jury when accused of a crime. An impartial jury is one that is fair, neutral, and open-minded. A jury cannot be fair unless it is selected from a fair cross-section of the community. Using impartial juries allow defendants to be judged fairly by their peers from the community.

Selecting a jury for a case is a two-stage process. In the first stage, the court creates a large pool of people to serve as jurors. This pool is called a venire. It is supposed to contain a cross-section of the community. In the second stage, the court and lawyers select twelve people from the venire to be the jury for a specific case.

During the second stage, lawyers for both parties get to make jury challenges. A jury challenge allows the parties to exclude specific people from the jury. One kind of jury challenge is called "for cause." Parties use for cause challenges to strike jurors who might not be able to decide a case fairly. For example, if a potential juror is the defendant's brother, the prosecutor can use a for cause challenge to prevent the brother from serving on the jury.

Jurors take an oath promising to apply the law when deciding a case. In states that use the death penalty, that means jurors must be able to impose the death penalty if the defendant deserves it. Often a juror says she opposes the death penalty and could not sentence a person to die under any circumstances. In *Witherspoon v. Illinois* (1968), the U.S. Supreme Court said prosecutors may use for cause challenges to exclude such jurors. This is called selecting a death-qualified jury. In *Lockhart v. McCree,* the Supreme Court had to decide whether death-qualified juries violate the defendant's Sixth Amendment right to have an impartial jury.

Bloody Valentine

Evelyn Boughton owned and operated a service station with a gift shop in Camden, Arkansas. On Valentine's Day in 1978, Boughton was murdered during a robbery. Eyewitnesses said the getaway car was a maroon and white Lincoln Continental.

Later that afternoon, police in Hot Springs, Arkansas, arrested Ardia McCree, who was driving a maroon and white Lincoln Continental. McCree admitted to being at Boughton's shop during the murder. He claimed, however, that he had given a ride to a tall black stranger who was wearing an overcoat. McCree said the stranger took McCree's rifle from the back seat of the car and used it to kill Boughton, then rode with McCree to a nearby dirt road and got out of the car with the rifle.

Two eyewitnesses disputed McCree's story. They saw McCree's car with only one person in it between Boughton's shop and the place where McCree said the black man got out. The police found McCree's rifle and a bank bag from Boughton's shop alongside the dirt road. The Federal Bureau of Investigation determined that the bullet that killed Boughton came from McCree's rifle.

Life in Prison

Arkansas charged McCree with capital felony murder. Felony murder is a murder committed in the course of a felony, such as a robbery. At McCree's trial, the prosecutor used jury challenges to remove eight prospective jurors who said they could not impose the death penalty under any circumstances. The jury convicted McCree but gave him life in prison instead of the death penalty.

McCree filed a habeas corpus lawsuit against his jailer, the Arkansas Department of Corrections. A habeas corpus lawsuit is for people who are in jail because their constitutional rights have been violated. McCree said Arkansas violated his Sixth Amendment right to an impartial jury by excluding jurors who would not impose the death penalty. He said it also violated his Sixth Amendment right to have the jury selected from a fair cross-section of the community.

At a hearing, McCree presented evidence that people who favor the death penalty are more likely to convict than are people who oppose it. By excluding people who oppose the death penalty, Arkansas increased the chance that the jury would find McCree guilty of murder. McCree said that violated the Sixth Amendment. The federal trial court and court of appeals both agreed and ordered Arkansas to release McCree from prison. Arkansas thought the courts were wrong, so it took the case to the U.S. Supreme Court.

Juries Must Apply the Law

With a 6–3 decision, the Supreme Court reversed and ruled in favor of the Arkansas Department of Corrections. Writing for the Court, Justice

William H. Rehnquist rejected the evidence that death-qualified juries are more likely to convict defendants. Rehnquist said the evidence was faulty and did not prove anything. Rehnquist, however, did not base the Court's decision on the evidence alone. Even assuming that death-qualified juries are more likely to convict, Rehnquist said they do not violate the Sixth Amendment.

Rehnquist gave two reasons for the Court's decision. First, he said the Sixth Amendment only guarantees that a jury will be drawn from a fair cross-section of the community. That means the venire from which a jury is selected must be a cross-section of the community. The Sixth Amendment does not require each jury to represent the entire community. Rehnquist said it would be impossible to make sure that every jury of twelve people represented the various viewpoints of all members of the community.

Second, Rehnquist said the Sixth Amendment requires juries to be impartial. There was no evidence that any member of McCree's jury did not decide his case fairly and impartially. Indeed, there was no reason to believe that death-qualified juries cannot be impartial when deciding whether defendants are guilty. Because death-qualified juries can be impartial, they do not violate the Sixth Amendment.

In the end, Rehnquist said states have a good reason for using death-qualified juries. Jurors must apply the law. In death penalty states, jurors must be able to impose the death penalty if the defendant deserves it. Excluding jurors who cannot ensures that all jurors in death penalty cases can obey their oaths. McCree's conviction did not violate the Sixth Amendment, so he had to serve his sentence of life in prison.

Organized to Convict

Three justices dissented, which means they disagreed with the Court's decision. Justice Thurgood Marshall wrote a dissenting opinion. He believed the evidence was overwhelming that death-qualified juries are more likely to convict defendants. Marshall said that means death-qualified juries are "organized to return a verdict of guilty." Marshall did not understand how such juries satisfy the Sixth Amendment guarantee of a fair, impartial jury.

Marshall even proposed a solution to the whole problem. In death penalty cases, states can use two juries. The first jury can decide guilt or innocence. Citizens can serve on that jury even if they oppose the death

WITHERSPOON V. ILLINOIS

In 1960, Illinois had a law that allowed prosecutors to exclude jurors who had conscientious, religious, or other general objections to the death penalty. William C. Witherspoon was convicted and sentenced to death by such a death-qualified jury. When Witherspoon appealed his case, the Supreme Court affirmed his conviction but reversed his death sentence. The Court said prosecutors may exclude jurors who say they could never vote for the death penalty. But a juror who simply is opposed to the death penalty may serve as a juror if he promises to apply the law as instructed by the judge. According to the Court, "A man who opposes the death penalty, no less than one who favors it, can ... obey the oath he takes as a juror."

penalty. If the first jury decides the defendant is guilty, a second jury can determine the sentence. Only citizens who are able to impose the death penalty can serve on the second jury. Marshall criticized the Court for rejecting this solution in favor of allowing death-qualified juries to convict defendants.

Suggestions for further reading

Guinther, John. *The Jury in America.* New York: Facts on File Publications, 1988.

Mikula, Mark, and L. Mpho Mabunda, eds. *Great American Court Cases.* Detroit: The Gale Group, 1999.

Wolf, Robert V. *The Jury System.* Philadelphia: Chelsea House Publishers, 1999.

Zerman, Melvyn Bernard. *Beyond a Reasonable Doubt: Inside the American Jury System.* New York: Crowell, 1981.

J.E.B. v. Alabama ex rel. T.B. 1994

Petitioner: J.E.B.

Respondent: Alabama ex rel. T.B.

Petitioner's Claim: That by striking men from his jury, Alabama violated his constitutional rights.

Chief Lawyer for Petitioner: John F. Porter III

Chief Lawyer for Respondent: Lois B. Brasfield

Justices for the Court: Harry A. Blackmun, Ruth Bader Ginsburg, Anthony M. Kennedy, Sandra Day O'Connor, David H. Souter, John Paul Stevens

Justices Dissenting: William H. Rehnquist, Antonin Scalia, Clarence Thomas

Date of Decision: April 19, 1994

Decision: The Supreme Court sent J.E.B.'s case back to the trial court to determine whether Alabama had gender-neutral reasons for striking men from the jury.

Significance: With *J.E.B.,* the Supreme Court said striking jurors because of their gender violates the Equal Protection Clause of the Fourteenth Amendment.

The American system of justice uses jury trials. A jury is a group of citizens, usually numbering twelve, that hears and decides a legal case. Juries are supposed to be impartial, which means fair, neutral, and open-minded. The use of impartial juries allows parties to be judged fairly by their peers from the community.

Selecting a jury for a case is a two-stage process. In the first stage, the court creates a large pool of people from the community to serve as jurors. This pool is called a venire. In the second stage, the court and lawyers select twelve people from the venire to be the jury for a specific case. During this stage the lawyers for both parties get to make jury challenges. A jury challenge allows the parties to exclude specific people from the jury.

There are two kinds of jury challenges. A challenge "for cause" happens when a party has a good reason to believe a juror might not be able to decide a case fairly. For example, if a juror is one litigant's brother, the other side can use a for cause challenge to strike the juror from the jury. There is no limit to the number of for cause challenges a party can make during jury selection.

The second kind of challenge is called a peremptory challenge. Each party gets a limited number of peremptory challenges. They allow the parties to exclude jurors who the lawyers feel will be against their cases. Traditionally, a lawyer could use peremptory challenges without giving a good reason. All he needed was a hunch that a potential juror would rule against his client. Peremptory challenges were one way for parties to make sure they got an impartial jury.

In ***Batson v. Kentucky*** (1986), the Supreme Court decided that lawyers are not allowed to use peremptory challenges to strike jurors just because of their race. For example, a lawyer who represents an African American cannot strike white jurors because he thinks white people will be against his client. That violates the Equal Protection Clause of the Fourteenth Amendment, which prevents states from allowing discrimination based on race. In *J.E.B. v. Alabama ex rel. T.B.,* the Supreme Court had to decide whether the Equal Protection Clause prevents lawyers from using peremptory challenges to strike jurors because of their gender.

Jury of His Female Peers

T.B. was the mother of a young child in Alabama. She believed that J.E.B. was the child's father. (The courts used the parents' initials to protect their privacy.) J.E.B. denied that he was the father, so Alabama sued J.E.B. for T.B. Alabama wanted to prove that J.E.B. was the father and then force him to pay child support, which is money to take care his child.

On 21 October 1991, the case went to trial and the parties began jury selection. They had to pick a jury of twelve from thirty-six people in the venire. Alabama believed women would be better for its case against J.E.B., so it used its peremptory challenges to strike nine male jurors. The resulting jury had no men on it.

J.E.B. believed Alabama violated the Equal Protection Clause by eliminating men from the jury. He urged the court to extend *Batson,* which prohibited race-based peremptory challenges, to gender-based challenges too. The trial court denied J.E.B.'s request and held the trial with the all-female jury. The jury decided J.E.B. was the father of T.B.'s child, and the court ordered J.E.B. to pay child support. J.E.B. appealed the decision, but the Alabama Court of Civil Appeals affirmed and the Supreme Court of Alabama refused to review the case. J.E.B. finally took the case to the U.S. Supreme Court.

Equal Protection Includes Men and Women

With a 6–3 decision, the Supreme Court ruled in favor of J.E.B. Writing for the Court, Justice Harry A. Blackmun said gender-based peremptory challenges violate the Equal Protection Clause.

Although the case involved peremptory challenges against men, lawyers in other cases used challenges to strike women from juries. Blackmun said striking women reinforces the old-fashioned idea that women are less capable than men. In fact, it sends America back to the 1800s, when laws prevented women from serving on juries. Men made such laws because they thought trials were too ugly for ladies, who belonged at home taking care of their families.

The Supreme Court refused to support such "outdated misconceptions concerning the roles of females in the home rather than in the marketplace and world of ideas." Women, like African Americans, went too long in the United States without equal rights. Women were not allowed to vote until 1920, when the United States adopted the Nineteenth Amendment. Women were not allowed to serve on juries in some states until the 1960s.

In American history, then, women suffered discrimination just like African Americans. The United States adopted the Equal Protection Clause of the Fourteenth Amendment in 1868 to prevent

HESTER VAUGHAN TRIAL

Hester Vaughan was a housekeeper in Philadelphia, Pennsylvania, in the mid-1800s. When she became pregnant from being raped by a member of the household, Vaughan left to rent a small, unheated room where she waited for her child to be born. Because she had little money, Vaughan became malnourished. She gave birth around February 8, 1868.

Two days later, Vaughan asked a neighbor to give her a box in which to put her baby, who was dead. The neighbor reported this to the police, who arrested Vaughan and charged her with murder. At the time, women were not allowed to be jurors in Pennsylvania. Vaughan's all-male jury convicted her of murder and the court sentenced her to death.

Prominent women leaders stepped in to ask Pennsylvania Governor John W. Geary to pardon Vaughan, which means to forgive her and get rid of her death sentence. Dr. Susan A. Smith told Governor Geary that she believed Vaughan's baby died during childbirth. Women's rights leaders Susan B. Anthony and Elizabeth Cady Stanton objected to convicting Vaughan with a jury that contained no women. In the summer of 1869, Governor Geary pardoned Vaughan on the condition that she return to England, which she did.

discrimination against African Americans. Likewise, the Equal Protection Clause must protect women too. Gender-based peremptory challenges could not survive in a society that wanted to end illegal discrimination.

Justice White said ending gender-based peremptory challenges would benefit litigants, jurors, and society. Litigants get impartial juries that contain a fair cross section of the community. Jurors get the right to participate in the justice system regardless of sex. Society gains confidence in a system that does not discriminate against men or women.

Suggestions for further reading

Frost-Knappman, Elizabeth, Edward W. Knappman, and Lisa Paddock, eds. *Courtroom Drama: 120 of the World's Most Notable Trials.* Detroit: Gale Research, 1998.

Guinther, John. *The Jury in America.* New York: Facts on File Publications, 1988.

Summer, Lila E. *The American Heritage History of the Bill of Rights: The Seventh Amendment.* New Jersey: Silver Burdett Press, Inc., 1991.

Wolf, Robert V. *The Jury System.* Philadelphia: Chelsea House Publishers, 1999.

Zerman, Melvyn Bernard. *Beyond a Reasonable Doubt: Inside the American Jury System.* New York: Crowell, 1981.

JUVENILE COURTS AND LAW

Juvenile law is the body of law that applies to young people who are not yet adults. These people are called juveniles or minors. In most states, a person is a juvenile until eighteen years old. Juvenile cases are handled in a special court, usually called a juvenile court. Before the American juvenile justice system was created in the late 1800s, juveniles who broke the law were treated like adult criminals.

Historical Background

When the United States was born in 1776, children under seven years of age were exempt from the criminal laws. Courts, however, treated juveniles seven years and older like miniature adults. Juveniles could be arrested, tried, and convicted of crimes. If convicted, they received prison sentences just like adults. Children convicted of minor crimes found themselves in jails with adult murderers and rapists, where children learned the ways of these criminals.

In the early 1800s, immigrants from Europe filled American cities such as New York. Neglected immigrant children often roamed city streets and got into trouble while their parents looked for work. In 1818, the Society for the Prevention of Pauperism created the term "juvenile delinquents" to describe these children.

Social awareness led people to search for a better way to handle young people who broke the law. In the 1820s, the Society for the Prevention of Juvenile Delinquency suggested separating adult and juvenile criminals. The Society for the Reformation of Juvenile Delinquents worked to reform juvenile delinquents instead of punishing them. It sent them to live in dormitories and to go to school to learn to work in factories. Unfortunately, these programs often did more harm than good. Manufacturers overworked the young children while school directors kept the children's wages.

In the late 1800s, Americans decided it was time to treat juvenile criminals differently than adult criminals. As one man put it, "Children need care, not harsh punishment." Many people believed that if cared for properly, juvenile criminals could become law-abiding citizens. In 1872, Massachusetts became the first state to hold separate court sessions for children. In the 1890s, the Chicago Women's Club urged Illinois to create an entirely separate justice system for juveniles. Illinois did so by creating the world's first juvenile court in 1899.

By 1925, all but two states had juvenile justice systems. As of 1999, all states have such systems. The federal government even has a juvenile justice system for people under eighteen who violate federal law. The goal of all juvenile justice systems is to protect society from young people who break the law while reforming them into lawful adults.

Juvenile Law

Juvenile courts handle cases involving three kinds of problems: crimes, status offenses, and child abuse or neglect. Criminal cases involve the same kinds of crimes that adults commit, such as burglary, robbery, and murder. For serious cases such as murder, some states allow juveniles over a certain age, often fourteen, to be tried as adults. In such cases, if the court decides a juvenile cannot be reformed by the juvenile justice system, it sends him to the regular court system to be tried as an adult.

Status offenses are things that are illegal for juveniles but not for adults. Truancy (missing school), running away from home, smoking cigarettes, and drinking alcohol are status offenses. Abuse and neglect cases are lawsuits by states against parents or guardians who are abusing or not taking care of their children. In these cases, the parent or guardian is on trial, not the child. States can order parents and guardians to stop abusing children and to care for them properly with food, shelter, and clothing. States also can take children away from abusive parents and place them with loving relatives or in child care centers and foster homes.

Juvenile Courts

A juvenile case usually begins with a police investigation in response to a complaint by a citizen, parent, or victim of juvenile crime. In many cases, the police resolve the problem themselves by talking to the juvenile, his parents, and the victim. The police can give the juvenile a warning, arrange for him to pay for any damage he caused, make him promise not to break the law again, and make sure the victim is alright.

If the police think a juvenile case needs to go to court, they arrest the juvenile and take him to the police station. If the juvenile committed a serious crime, such as rape or murder, the police may keep him in jail until the juvenile court decides how to handle the case. After the police arrest a juvenile, an intake officer in the juvenile court decides whether there really is a case against the juvenile. If not, the police give the juvenile back to his parents or guardians.

If there is a case, the intake officer may arrange an informal solution. If the intake officer thinks the state needs to file a case against the juvenile, she makes this recommendation to the state district attorney. The district attorney then files a petition against the juvenile, charging him with specific violations. While a juvenile waits for his hearing to begin, the state prepares a social investigation report about the juvenile's background and the circumstances of his offense.

In court, a juvenile case is called a hearing or adjudication instead of a trial. Most hearings are closed to the public to protect the juvenile's privacy. The judge decides the case instead of a jury. As in a regular trial, the judge listens to testimony from witnesses for both the state and the juvenile. If the state has charged the juvenile with a crime, it must prove its case beyond a reasonable doubt. That means the case must be so strong that no reasonable person would doubt that the juvenile committed the crime.

After the judge hears all the evidence, she decides whether the juvenile has committed the offense charged. If so, the juvenile is called delinquent instead of guilty of a crime. The judge next holds a dispositional hearing instead of a sentencing. At the dispositional hearing, the judge uses the state's social investigation report to decide how to reform the juvenile while protecting society from him. The judge may require probation, community service, a fine, restitution, or confinement in a juvenile detention center. Probation allows the juvenile to go home but requires him to obey certain rules under court supervision. Restitution requires the juvenile to pay for any damage he caused. Juveniles who commit the most serious crimes find themselves in juvenile detention centers. Although they resemble jails, detention centers are supposed to rehabilitate juvenile delinquents, not punish them.

Constitutional Rights

The U.S. Constitution gives adult defendants many rights in criminal cases. For example, defendants have the right to know the charges against them, to be represented by an attorney, and to have a jury trial in cases in which they face imprisonment for more than six months. When states created juvenile justice systems in the early 1900s, they did not give these same rights to juvenile defendants. Juvenile justice systems were supposed to help juveniles rather than punish them, so people did not think juveniles needed constitutional rights.

As the century passed, people began to question whether juveniles need constitutional protection. The Fourteenth Amendment says states may not deprive a person of liberty, meaning freedom, without due process of law. Due process of law means a fair trial. Juveniles who are found delinquent and either placed on probation or confined in juvenile detention centers lose their freedom.

In a series of cases beginning in the 1960s, the U.S. Supreme Court decided that the Fourteenth Amendment requires states to give juveniles many of the constitutional rights that criminal defendants have. In the first case, *Kent v. United States* (1966), the Supreme Court said the due process clause of the Fourteenth Amendment applies to juveniles. One year later in ***In re Gault*** (1967), the Court said juveniles have the right to know the charges against them and to be represented by an attorney. Juveniles also have the right to cross-examine witnesses against them and the right not to testify against themselves. Three years later in *In re Winship* (1970), the Court said states must prove criminal charges against juveniles beyond a reasonable doubt.

In *McKeiver v. Pennsylvania* (1973), the Supreme Court decided that juveniles do not have the right to jury trials. The Court said jury trials would turn the juvenile justice system into the criminal justice system, making it senseless to run two systems. The trend in favor of juveniles continued, however, in *Breed v. Jones* (1975). There the Court said juveniles who are found delinquent cannot be tried again for the same offense as adults. Then in *Thompson v. Oklahoma* (1988), the Supreme Court said states may not execute a defendant who is younger than sixteen at the time of his offense.

The Future

At the end of the twentieth century, the American juvenile justice system received low marks from many critics. Extending constitutional rights to juveniles made hearings seem more like criminal trials. That made it harder to use the system to reform delinquents instead of treating them like adult criminals. The availability of drugs and weapons led to increased juvenile crime. According to *Congressional Quarterly,* "Between 1985 and 1995, the juvenile arrest rate for violent crimes rose 69 percent. For murders it rose 96 percent." Finally, some say the juvenile justice system is racist because minority youths are more likely to find themselves in detention centers.

Many people wonder whether the juvenile justice system is doing, or can do, its job of helping juvenile delinquents. A rash of juvenile shootings in schools across the country forced Americans to look at whether families are taking care of their children. Frustrated and scared, Americans looked to the future of juvenile justice with more questions and concerns than solutions.

Suggestions for further reading

Berry, Joy. *Every Kid's Guide to Laws that Relate to Parents and Children.* Chicago: Children's Press, 1987.

—. *Every Kid's Guide to the Juvenile Justice System.* Chicago: Children's Press, 1987.

Burns, Marilyn. *I Am Not a Short Adult: Getting Good at Being a Kid.* Boston: Little, Brown, & Co. 1977.

Greenberg, Keith Elliot, and Jeanne Vestal. *Adolescent Rights: Are Young People Equal under the Law?* Twenty First Century Books, 1995.

Hyde, Margaret O. *Juvenile Justice and Injustice.* New York: Franklin Watts, 1977.

Kowalski, Kathiann M. *Teen Rights: At Home, at School, Online.* Enslow Publishers Inc., 2000.

Landau, Elaine. *Your Legal Rights: From Custody Battles to School Searches, the Headline-Making Cases That Affect Your Life.* Walker & Co., 1995.

Marx, Trish, and Sandra Joseph Nunez. *And Justice for All: The Legal Rights of Young People.* Millbrook Press, 1997.

Olney, Ross R., and Patricia J. Olney. *Up against the Law: Your Legal Rights as a Minor.* New York: E.P. Dutton, 1985.

Riekes, Linda, Steve Jenkins, and Armentha Russell. *Juvenile Responsibility and Law.* St. Paul: West Publishing Co., 1990.

In Re Gault
1967

Appellants: Paul L. Gault and Marjorie Gault, parents of Gerald Francis Gault, a minor

Appellee: State of Arizona

Appellants' Claim: That states must give juvenile defendants the same constitutional rights as adult criminal defendants.

Chief Lawyer for Appellants: Norman Dorsen

Chief Lawyer for Appellee: Frank A. Parks, Assistant Attorney General of Arizona

Justices for the Court: Hugo Lafayette Black, William J. Brennan, Jr., Tom C. Clark, William O. Douglas, Abe Fortas, John Marshall Harlan II, Earl Warren, Byron R. White.

Justices Dissenting: Potter Stewart

Date of Decision: May 15, 1967

Decision: The Supreme Court held that Arizona violated Gault's constitutional rights.

Significance: With *Gault,* the Supreme Court said juvenile defendants must have notice of the charges against them, notice of their right to have an attorney, the right to confront and cross-examine witnesses against them, and the right not to testify against themselves.

JUVENILE COURTS AND LAW

Gerald Francis Gault was a boy who lived in Gila County, Arizona. Early in 1964, police arrested him for being with a friend who stole a wallet from a woman's purse. For that offense, the juvenile court ordered Gault to be on probation for six months. Probation lets the court supervise someone who has broken the law.

Associate Justice Abe Fortas.
Reproduced by permission of Archive Photos, Inc.

On June 8, 1964, while Gault was still on probation, a neighbor named Mrs. Cook complained to the police that Gault and a friend made an obscene telephone call to her. Police arrested Gault while his parents were at work and took him to the Children's Detention Home. When Gault's mother arrived home, she had to search to find her son in the detention home. There Superintendent Flagg told Mrs. Gault that there would be a hearing the next day in juvenile court.

The juvenile court held two hearings for Gault's case, one on June 9 and one on June 15. The police and the court never told Gault what law he was accused of breaking. They did not explain that he could have an attorney represent him in court. The court did not even require Mrs. Cook to testify against Gault. Instead, it relied on testimony by Superintendent Flagg that Gault admitted to making an obscene telephone call to Mrs. Cook. According to Judge McGhee, Gault even confessed during the second hearing to making obscene comments on the telephone. Gault's parents denied this, saying that Gault only dialed Mrs. Cook's number and then handed the telephone to his friend.

Based on the testimony, Judge McGhee decided that Gault was a juvenile delinquent. He ordered Gault to be confined in the State Industrial School, a juvenile detention center, until he was twenty-one. Gault was only fifteen at the time, so he faced six years in detention. If Gault had been an adult, his crime would have been punishable by only two months in prison.

The Rights of the Accused

The Fourteenth Amendment of the U.S. Constitution says states may not take away a person's liberty, meaning freedom, without due process of law. Due process means a fair trial. Under the Sixth Amendment, a trial is not fair unless the defendant has notice of the charges against him, the right to have an attorney, and the chance to face and cross-examine witnesses against him. Under the Fifth Amendment, the right against self-incrimination says defendants cannot be forced to make confessions or to testify against themselves.

Juvenile courts are not supposed to be run like criminal courts. They are supposed to help juvenile delinquents become lawful adults by reforming them, not punishing them. For this reason, Arizona's juvenile courts did not give juvenile defendants the same constitutional rights as criminal defendants.

Arizona, however, sent Gault to a detention center for six years for making an obscene telephone call. Gault's parents did not think the state should be allowed to do that without giving their son the same rights as criminal defendants. The Gaults filed a lawsuit against Arizona for holding their son in detention without giving him a fair trial. The Arizona Superior Court dismissed the case and the Arizona Supreme Court affirmed, so the Gaults appealed to the U.S. Supreme Court.

Justice for All

With an 8–1 decision, the Supreme Court ruled in favor of the Gaults, releasing their son from detention. Writing for the Court, Justice Abe Fortas said "neither the Fourteenth Amendment nor the Bill of Rights is for adults alone." Even though a juvenile case is not a criminal case, sending a juvenile to a detention center takes away his liberty and freedom. "Instead of mother and father and sisters and brothers and friends and classmates, his world is peopled by guards, custodians, state employ-

JUVENILE MURDER

On February 29, 2000, a six-year-old boy in Michigan shot and killed his classmate with a .32 caliber semi-automatic handgun. The victim, Kayla Rolland, died from a single gunshot wound to her chest. Both children attended Theo J. Buell Elementary School in Mount Morris Township, where they had an argument the day before the shooting. The boy said Kayla slapped him on the arm during the argument and that he brought the gun to school to scare her.

Investigators learned that the boy was living with his uncle and a nineteen-year-old man named Jamelle Andrew James in a house where drug deals were common. The boy, whose mother had been evicted from her home and whose father was in jail, slept in the house without a bed. Police arrested James for allegedly letting the boy get the stolen gun to take to school. James faced a charge of involuntary manslaughter for Kayla's death, a crime punishable by up to fifteen years in prison.

Because the law says children under seven cannot intend to commit a crime, the boy probably will not face criminal charges. Prosecutor Arthur A. Busch said the boy "is a victim in many ways and we need to put our arms around him and love him." Sadly, friends and family can no longer put their arms around Kayla, who a relative described as a "very well-behaved little girl, loved by everybody."

ees, and 'delinquents' confined with him for anything from waywardness to rape and homicide."

The state cannot deprive a person, even a juvenile delinquent, of liberty without a fair trial. Fortas said Gault's trial was not fair because he did not know which crime he was accused of breaking. Without such notice and an attorney to help him, Gault could not defend himself properly. Without the right to confront and cross-examine witnesses, Gault could not test whether Mrs. Cook had told the truth. Without the right against self-incrimination, Gault may have been pressured to admit to a crime he did not commit. Justice Fortas said that when a juvenile faces detention, he must have these rights and protections during his hearing.

The End of an Era

Justice Potter Stewart filed a dissenting opinion, which means he disagreed with the Court's decision. Justice Stewart agreed that juveniles deserve rights during their hearings. He disagreed, however, that they need the same rights as criminal defendants. The whole purpose of the juvenile justice system is to treat juveniles differently than adult criminals. Stewart feared the Court's decision would turn juvenile cases into criminal trials, sending America back to the days when twelve-year-old boys were sentenced to death like adults.

Suggestions for further reading

Berry, Joy. *Every Kid's Guide to the Juvenile Justice System.* Chicago: Children's Press, 1987.

Claiborne, William. "A 'Life in Chaos' Shaped Young Shooter." *Washington Post,* March 2, 2000.

Claiborne, William. "Man Charged in Schoolgirl's Slaying." *Washington Post,* March 3, 2000.

Gora, Joel M. *Due Process of Law.* National Textbook Co., 1982.

Greenberg, Keith Elliot, and Jeanne Vestal. *Adolescent Rights: Are Young People Equal under the Law?* Twenty First Century Books, 1995.

Hyde, Margaret O. *Juvenile Justice and Injustice.* New York: Franklin Watts, 1977.

Johnson, Joan. *Justice.* New York: Franklin Watts, 1985.

Kowalski, Kathiann M. *Teen Rights: At Home, at School, Online.* Enslow Publishers Inc., 2000.

Landau, Elaine. *Your Legal Rights: From Custody Battles to School Searches, the Headline-Making Cases That Affect Your Life.* Walker & Co., 1995.

Marx, Trish, and Sandra Joseph Nunez. *And Justice for All: The Legal Rights of Young People.* Millbrook Press, 1997.

Olney, Ross R., and Patricia J. Olney. *Up against the Law: Your Legal Rights as a Minor.* New York: E.P. Dutton, 1985.

"Pupils Return to Site of Child's Slaying." *Washington Post,* March 7, 2000.

Riekes, Linda, Steve Jenkins, and Armentha Russell. *Juvenile Responsibility and Law.* St. Paul: West Publishing Co., 1990.

Goss v. Lopez
1975

Appellants: Norval Goss, et al.

Appellees: Dwight Lopez, et al.

Appellants' Claim: That Ohio schools did not violate the Due Process Clause of the Fourteenth Amendment by suspending public school students without a hearing.

Chief Lawyer for Appellants: Thomas A. Bustin

Chief Lawyer for Appellees: Peter D. Roos

Justices for the Court: William J. Brennan, Jr., William O. Douglas, Thurgood Marshall, Potter Stewart, Byron R. White

Justices Dissenting: Harry A. Blackmun, Warren E. Burger, Lewis F. Powell, Jr., William H. Rehnquist

Date of Decision: January 22, 1975

Decision: The Supreme Court decided that the Ohio schools did violate the Due Process Clause.

Significance: *Goss* requires public schools to give students a chance to explain their conduct before or soon after suspending them from school.

The American justice system is supposed to be fair. When a person is accused of breaking a law, fairness means giving him notice of the charges against him. Fairness also means holding a hearing or trial to give the accused a chance to defend himself. Punishing a person without notice and a hearing is very un-American.

The Due Process Clause of the Fourteenth Amendment protects Americans from unfair treatment by state governments. It says states may not take away life, liberty, or property without "due process of law." Due process usually means notice and a hearing. In *Goss v. Lopez,* the U.S. Supreme Court had to decide whether public schools may suspend students for up to ten days without notice or a hearing.

School Riot

In the early 1970s, an Ohio law allowed public school principals to suspend students for up to ten days without a hearing. Demonstrations related to the Vietnam War and other public issues of the day resulted in a lot of suspensions. Dwight Lopez was a student at Central High School in Columbus, Ohio. Lopez was suspended along with 75 other students after a lunchroom disturbance that damaged school property. Although Lopez said he did not destroy anything, the school suspended him without a hearing and without explaining what he did wrong.

Betty Crome, who attended McGuffey Junior High School in Columbus, attended a demonstration at another high school. The police arrested Crome and many others during the demonstration, but released Crome without charges at the police station. The next day, Crome learned that she had been suspended from school for ten days. Crome also did not get a hearing or an explanation of what she had done wrong.

Lopez and Crome joined a group of other students to sue the Columbus Board of Education and the Columbus Public School System. They wanted the court to strike down the Ohio law that allowed principals to suspend students without a hearing. Lopez and the students said the law violated the Due Process Clause of the Fourteenth Amendment. When the trial court ruled in favor of the students and ordered the schools to remove the suspensions from the students' records, the school system and school board appealed to the U.S. Supreme Court.

High Court Rules

With a 5–4 decision, the Supreme Court ruled in favor of the students. Writing for the Court, Justice Byron R. White said public schools must obey the Due Process Clause. "The Fourteenth Amendment, as now

CALIFORNIA JUSTICE

In the late 1990s, statistics said crime by juveniles was declining. In spite of this trend, violent juvenile crime captured headlines and horrified the nation. In April 1999, two teenagers shot and killed classmates and a teacher at Columbine High School in Colorado before killing themselves. In early 2000, a thirteen-year-old boy in Michigan was convicted for a murder he committed at age eleven. On February 29, 2000, a six-year-old boy in Michigan shot and killed Kayla Rolland, his six-year-old classmate.

On March 7, 2000, voters in California went to the polls to take a stand against juvenile crime. Voting that day in the presidential primary, Californians approved a new law called Proposition 21. The new law toughened California's laws for juvenile crime.

Most juveniles charged with crimes face delinquency proceedings in juvenile court instead of trials in criminal court. For serious crimes, Proposition 21 allowed prosecutors to try teenagers as young as fourteen like adults in criminal courts. Convicted juveniles could receive long sentences in adult prisons. The law also created mandatory jail sentences for minor crimes committed by gang members.

A spokesman for California governor Gray Davis called the new laws necessary. "Just because you're fourteen doesn't mean you're immune to picking up a gun and shooting someone anymore." State Senator Tom Hayden, however, questioned whether the law was a good idea. "If [juveniles] aren't antisocial when they go into prison, that's what they are going to be when they come out."

applied to the States, protects the citizen against the State itself and all of its creatures—Boards of Education not excepted." Students are citizens just like adults, so the Fourteenth Amendment protects them at school.

The Court said the right to attend public school is a property right because it is something valuable that the state provides all students.

When a school suspends a student, it takes away her property right for a certain number of days. Suspension also harms a student's reputation, which is a part of liberty and freedom. Because suspension takes away both a property right and liberty, schools may not suspend students without "due process of law."

Due process usually requires notice and a hearing. The Court decided, however, that it would be impossible to conduct a full hearing for every suspension. It would take too much time and money, both of which are scarce resources in public schools.

The Court decided that schools cannot suspend students without notifying them of the charges, explaining the evidence against them, and giving them an informal hearing. Without notice, a student may not know why he is being suspended. Without a hearing, he cannot explain his conduct or convince the school that he did nothing wrong. The Court said, "Fairness can rarely be obtained by secret, onesided determination of facts decisive of rights."

In most cases, the hearing can be a discussion with the principal before the student is suspended. Something more formal may be appropriate in serious cases. If the student is endangering other students, the hearing may happen soon after the school dismisses the student. In any event, students must get notice of the charges against them and a chance to explain why they should not be suspended. Otherwise, students may not learn the procedures that are supposed to make American justice fair.

Suggestions for further reading

Berry, Joy. *Every Kid's Guide to the Juvenile Justice System.* Chicago: Children's Press, 1987.

Gora, Joel M. *Due Process of Law.* National Textbook Co., 1982.

Greenberg, Keith Elliot, and Jeanne Vestal. *Adolescent Rights: Are Young People Equal under the Law?* Twenty First Century Books, 1995.

Hyde, Margaret O. *Juvenile Justice and Injustice.* New York: Franklin Watts, 1977.

Johnson, Joan. *Justice.* New York: Franklin Watts, 1985.

Kowalski, Kathiann M. *Teen Rights: At Home, at School, Online.* Enslow Publishers Inc., 2000.

Landau, Elaine. *Your Legal Rights: From Custody Battles to School Searches, the Headline-Making Cases That Affect Your Life.* Walker & Co., 1995.

Marx, Trish, and Sandra Joseph Nunez. *And Justice for All: The Legal Rights of Young People.* Millbrook Press, 1997.

Olney, Ross R., and Patricia J. Olney. *Up against the Law: Your Legal Rights as a Minor.* New York: E.P. Dutton, 1985.

Riekes, Linda, Steve Jenkins, and Armentha Russell. *Juvenile Responsibility and Law.* St. Paul: West Publishing Co., 1990.

Sanchez, Rene, and William Booth. "California Toughens Juvenile Crime Laws." *Washington Post,* March 13, 2000.

Ingraham v. Wright
1977

Petitioners: James Ingraham and Roosevelt Andrews

Respondents: Willie J. Wright, et al.

Petitioners' Claim: That officials at Drew Junior High School violated the Eighth and Fourteenth Amendments by spanking them.

Chief Lawyer for Petitioners: Bruce S. Rogow

Chief Lawyer for Respondents: Frank A. Howard, Jr.

Justices for the Court: Harry A. Blackmun, Warren E. Burger, Lewis F. Powell, Jr., William H. Rehnquist, Potter Stewart

Justices Dissenting: William J. Brennan, Jr., Thurgood Marshall, John Paul Stevens, Byron R. White

Date of Decision: April 19, 1977

Decision: The Supreme Court dismissed the case against Drew Junior High School, saying the school did not violate the students' constitutional rights.

Significance: With *Ingraham,* the Court said corporal punishment, or spanking, is not cruel and unusual punishment. It also said schools can use corporal punishment without giving students a chance to explain their conduct or otherwise defend themselves. If a student is injured by corporal punishment, he may file civil or criminal charges against the school.

The American justice system is supposed to be fair. When a person is accused of breaking a law, fairness means giving him notice of the charges against him. Fairness also means holding a hearing or trial to give the accused a chance to defend himself. Notice and a hearing are part of "due process of law." The Fourteenth Amendment requires states to use due process of law before taking away a person's liberty or freedom.

When a defendant is found guilty after a criminal trial, the Eighth Amendment prevents the government from using cruel and unusual punishments—punishments that are barbaric in a civilized society. Under the Due Process Clause of the Fourteenth Amendment, states must obey the Eighth Amendment and avoid cruel and unusual punishments.

Public schools often punish students who misbehave in school. The punishment can be detention, suspension, expulsion, or corporal punishment. Corporal punishment is punishment inflicted on a student's body, such as spanking. In *Ingraham v. Wright,* the Supreme Court had to decide whether corporal punishment is cruel and unusual under the Eighth Amendment. The Court also had to decide whether schools must give students notice and a hearing before using corporal punishment.

Paddle Licks

In the early 1970s, a Florida law allowed public schools to use corporal punishment to maintain discipline. In Dade County, Florida, a local law said teachers could punish students using a flat wooden paddle measuring less than two feet long, three to four inches wide, and one-half inch thick. Teachers were supposed to get permission from the principal before paddling a student, and then were supposed to limit the paddling to one to five licks on the student's buttocks. Teachers, however, paddled students without getting permission and used more than five licks.

During the 1970-71 school year, James Ingraham and Roosevelt Andrews were students at Drew Junior High School in Dade County. On one occasion in October 1970, Ingraham was slow to respond to his teacher's instructions. As punishment, Ingraham received twenty licks with a paddle while being held over a table in the principal's office. The paddling was so severe that Ingraham missed several days of school with a hematoma, a pool of blood in his buttocks.

That same month, school officials paddled Andrews several times for breaking minor school rules. On two occasions the school paddled

Corporal punishment, such as spanking, was an acceptable form of discipline in the United States for a long time.
AP/Wide World Photos.

Andrews on his arms. One paddling was so bad that Andrews lost full use of his arm for a week. Other students also received severe paddlings. One student got fifty licks for making an obscene telephone call.

Ingraham and Roosevelt filed a lawsuit against the principals of Drew Junior High and the superintendent of the Dade County School System. Ingraham and Roosevelt thought the school violated the Eighth Amendment by using cruel and unusual punishment and the Fourteenth Amendment by paddling them without a hearing. Ingraham and Roosevelt wanted to recover damages and to prevent the school from using corporal punishment in the future. The trial court dismissed the lawsuit, however, and the court of appeals affirmed, so the students took their case to the U.S. Supreme Court.

Corporal Punishment Approved

With a 5–4 decision, the Supreme Court ruled in favor of Drew Junior High. Writing for the Court, Justice Lewis F. Powell, Jr., first addressed whether the Eighth Amendment applies to public schools. The Eighth Amendment says, "Excessive bail shall not be required, nor excessive fines imposed, nor cruel and unusual punishments inflicted." Powell said bail, fines, and punishment are part of the criminal justice system. Public schools are not part of that system, so they do not have to obey the Eighth Amendment.

Bruce S. Rogow, Ingraham and Roosevelt's lawyer, urged the court to apply the Eighth Amendment to corporal punishment in public schools. He said there were few public schools when the United States adopted the amendment in 1791 because most children were educated privately. Americans did not know that someday students would be forced to attend public schools in which corporal punishment would be used. Rogow said it would be absurd to protect criminals but not school children from cruel and unusual punishment.

The Court rejected Rogow's argument. It said public schools are different from prisons. Public schools are open environments where children are free to go home at the end of each day. That means parents are likely to learn if schools are beating their children too severely. That alone is enough to protect the students in most cases.

Attorney Rogow also argued that schools should have to give students a hearing and a chance to defend themselves before using corporal punishment. After all, in ***Goss v. Lopez*** (1975), the Supreme Court said schools must give students notice and a hearing before suspending them from school for up to ten days. Students should get the same due process rights before being paddled.

The Supreme Court also rejected this argument. Florida laws allowed students who were injured by severe beatings to sue school officials to recover their damages. School officials also could face criminal charges in such cases. Justice Powell said civil and criminal charges are enough to protect students who receive beatings that are unfair or too harsh. Forcing schools to hold a hearing in every case would make cor-

CRUEL AND UNUSUAL MUSIC?

When the Supreme Court decided *Ingraham v. Wright,* only two states outlawed corporal punishment in schools. In the 1990s, twenty-one states banned the practice. As opposition to corporal punishment grew, schools were forced to become more creative with their punishments.

Bruce Janu, a teacher at Riverside High School near Chicago, Illinois, made students in detention listen to Frank Sinatra music. Janu said students grimaced and begged for leniency when hearing the legendary singer croon classic American songs. Teachers at Cedarbrook Middle School in Cheltenham Township, Pennsylvania, sent fighting students to a nature center to work out their differences while caring for plants and animals.

Other teachers chose punishments more traditional yet just as effective. At T.C. Williams High School in Alexandria, Virginia, students who used rainbow colors to spray paint a parking lot had to repaint it black. Joyce Perkins, a teacher in Sour Lake, Texas, forced students who cursed on the playground to call their mothers to repeat the bad language.

poral punishment too expensive and time-consuming. The Supreme Court was not willing to end corporal punishment by making it so costly.

Uncle Sam the Barbarian

Four justices dissented, which means they disagreed with the Court's decision. Justice Byron R. White wrote a dissenting opinion. He thought the Eighth Amendment prevented the government from using cruel and unusual punishment anywhere, not just in the criminal justice system. The United States adopted the amendment because "there are some punishments that are so barbaric and inhumane that we will not permit them to be imposed on anyone." White said that under the Court's decision, the Eighth Amendment protects "a prisoner who is beaten mercilessly" but not "a schoolchild who commits the same breach of discipline."

Suggestions for further reading

Berry, Joy. *Every Kid's Guide to the Juvenile Justice System.* Chicago: Children's Press, 1987.

Gora, Joel M. *Due Process of Law.* National Textbook Co., 1982.

Greenberg, Keith Elliot, and Jeanne Vestal. *Adolescent Rights: Are Young People Equal under the Law?* Twenty First Century Books, 1995.

Hyde, Margaret O. *Juvenile Justice and Injustice.* New York: Franklin Watts, 1977.

Jordan, Mary. "Instead of a Hit, Sinatra." *Washington Post,* February 7, 1993.

Kowalski, Kathiann M. *Teen Rights: At Home, at School, Online.* Enslow Publishers Inc., 2000.

Landau, Elaine. *Your Legal Rights: From Custody Battles to School Searches, the Headline-Making Cases That Affect Your Life.* Walker & Co., 1995.

Marx, Trish, and Sandra Joseph Nunez. *And Justice for All: The Legal Rights of Young People.* Millbrook Press, 1997.

Olney, Ross R., and Patricia J. Olney. *Up against the Law: Your Legal Rights as a Minor.* New York: E.P. Dutton, 1985.

Riekes, Linda, Steve Jenkins, and Armentha Russell. *Juvenile Responsibility and Law.* St. Paul: West Publishing Co., 1990.

New Jersey v. T.L.O.
1985

Petitioner: State of New Jersey

Respondent: T.L.O.

Petitioner's Claim: That the assistant vice principal did not violate the Fourth Amendment when he searched T.L.O.'s purse after she had been caught smoking in the restroom.

Chief Lawyer for Petitioner: Allan J. Nodes, Deputy Attorney General of New Jersey

Chief Lawyer for Respondent: Lois De Julio

Justices for the Court: Harry A. Blackmun, Warren E. Burger, Sandra Day O'Connor, Lewis F. Powell, Jr., William H. Rehnquist, Byron R. White

Justices Dissenting: William J. Brennan, Jr., Thurgood Marshall, John Paul Stevens

Date of Decision: January 15, 1985

Decision: The Supreme Court approved the principal's search and affirmed the decision that T.L.O. was a juvenile delinquent.

Significance: With *T.L.O.,* the Supreme Court said public school officials can search students' private belongings without a warrant or probable cause. To conduct a search, public schools need only a reasonable suspicion that a student has violated the law or a school rule.

The Fourth Amendment of the U.S. Constitution protects privacy. It requires the police to get a warrant to search a person, house, or other private place for evidence of a crime. To get a warrant, police must have probable cause, which means good reason to believe the place to be searched has evidence of a crime. In *New Jersey v. T.L.O.,* the Supreme Court had to decide whether public schools needed a warrant and probable cause to search a student's purse.

Smoking in the Girl's Room

On March 7, 1980, a teacher at Piscataway High School in Middlesex County, New Jersey, found two girls smoking in a restroom. One of the girls was T.L.O. (The courts used the girl's initials to protect her privacy.) Smoking in the restroom was against school rules, so the teacher took the girls to the principal's office.

There the girls spoke to Assistant Vice Principal Theodore Choplick. T.L.O.'s friend admitted that she had been smoking in the restroom, but T.L.O. denied it. In fact, T.L.O. said she never smoked. Choplick did not believe this, so he took T.L.O. into his private office. There he demanded to see T.L.O.'s purse. When she gave it to him, Choplick opened it and found a pack a cigarettes inside. Choplick pulled the cigarettes out and accused T.L.O. of lying.

When Choplick looked back into the purse, he saw a package of cigarette rolling papers. In Choplick's experience, students with rolling papers often used marijuana, an illegal drug. Without getting permission, Choplick searched the rest of T.L.O.'s purse. Inside he found a small amount of marijuana, empty plastic bags, a lot of one dollar bills, an index card with a list of students who owed T.L.O. money, and two letters that suggested T.L.O. was selling marijuana.

Choplick notified T.L.O.'s mother of what he found and gave the evidence to the police. T.L.O.'s mother took her to the police station, where T.L.O. confessed that she had been selling marijuana. Using the confession and the evidence from T.L.O.'s purse, the state of New Jersey filed a delinquency lawsuit against T.L.O. in the Juvenile and Domestic Relations Court.

T.L.O.'s lawyer tried to get the evidence against her thrown out of court. The Fourth Amendment requires a warrant and probable cause for most searches. States, including public schools, must obey the Fourth Amendment under the Due Process Clause of the Fourteenth

Amendment. T.L.O.'s lawyer argued that Choplick violated the Fourth Amendment by searching T.L.O.'s purse without a warrant or any reason to believe she had marijuana.

The trial court ruled against T.L.O., found her delinquent, and put her on probation for one year. (Probation allows the court to supervise someone who has broken the law.) T.L.O. appealed to the Supreme Court of New Jersey. That court reversed the judgment against her because it thought Choplick violated her rights by searching her purse. As its last resort, New Jersey took the case to the U.S. Supreme Court.

Students Get Less Privacy Than Adults

With a 6–3 decision, the Supreme Court ruled in favor of New Jersey. Writing for the Court, Justice Byron R. White said the first question was whether public schools must obey the Fourth Amendment. White said they must. The United States adopted the Fourth Amendment to protect Americans from invasion of privacy by the government, not just by the police. Public schools are part of the government.

The next question was whether Choplick violated the Fourth Amendment by searching T.L.O.'s purse without a warrant. The answer depended on balancing T.L.O.'s interest in privacy against the school's interest in maintaining discipline. T.L.O. obviously had an interest in keeping her purse private. Students often carry love letters, money, diaries, and items for grooming and personal hygiene in their purses. Unlike prisoners, who cannot expect much privacy in jail, students do not shed their right to privacy at the schoolhouse gate.

Schools, however, need to maintain discipline for the sake of education. Justice White noted that schools face increasing problems with drugs, guns, and violence. School officials must react quickly to those problems to protect other students and to prevent interference with education. Forcing a school official to get a warrant with probable cause to conduct a search would frustrate quick discipline.

Balancing these interests, the Court decided schools do not need a warrant or probable cause to conduct a search. As Justice Lewis F. Powell, Jr., said in a concurring opinion, "It is simply unrealistic to think that students have the same subjective expectation of privacy as the population generally." Schools cannot, however, search anyone, anywhere, anytime for any reason. To conduct a search, schools must have a reasonable suspicion that a student has broken the law or a school rule.

HORTON V. GOOSE CREEK INDEPENDENT SCHOOL DISTRICT

In 1978, the Goose Creek Independent School District made a plan to fight drugs in school. It decided to bring drug-sniffing dogs to school to sniff students and their lockers and cars. The searches were unannounced and random. The school district used the dogs to sniff anybody, even if there was no reason to believe a student used drugs.

Heather Horton was a student in the Goose Creek school district. One day while she was in the middle of a French test, drug-sniffing dogs entered the room, went up and down the aisles, and sniffed all the students and their desks. Because Heather was afraid of big dogs, the sniff search destroyed her concentration. Although the dogs found nothing on Heather, they reacted after sniffing Robby Horton and Sandra Sanchez. School officials searched Sandra's purse and Robby's pockets, socks, and pant legs. These embarrassing searches revealed no drugs or illegal substances.

Heather, Bobby, and Sandra sued Goose Creek for violating their Fourth Amendment rights. The trial court found in favor of the school, so the students appealed to the U.S. Court of Appeals for the Fifth Circuit. That court said it was all right for the school to use drug-sniffing dogs to search lockers and cars, but not students. Sniffing people with dogs is an invasion of privacy. The court said schools cannot do that without having individual suspicion that a student is carrying drugs or alcohol.

Under this test, Choplick did not violate the Fourth Amendment when he searched T.L.O.'s purse. A teacher saw T.L.O. smoking in the restroom. When T.L.O. denied it, Choplick had good reason to suspect she was lying and that her purse would have evidence of the lie. When Choplick opened T.L.O.'s purse and found rolling papers, he had good reason to believe T.L.O. was either smoking or selling marijuana. Searching her purse to find more evidence was reasonable.

Smokescreen in the Courtroom

Three justices dissented, which means they disagreed with the Court's decision. Justice William J. Brennan, Jr., said school officials, just like the police, should need probable cause to search a student's private belongings. Brennan said, "The Fourth Amendment rests on the principle that a true balance between the individual and society depends on the recognition of 'the right to be let alone-the most comprehensive of rights and the right most valued by civilized men.'"

In his own dissenting opinion, Justice John Paul Stevens said it was wrong to give students less Fourth Amendment protection than adults. "If the Nation's students can be convicted through the use of arbitrary [random] methods destructive of personal liberty, they cannot help but feel that they have been dealt with unfairly."

Suggestions for further reading

Berry, Joy. *Every Kid's Guide to the Juvenile Justice System.* Chicago: Children's Press, 1987.

Franklin, Paula A. *The Fourth Amendment.* Englewood Cliffs: Silver Burdett Press, 1991.

Greenberg, Keith Elliot, and Jeanne Vestal. *Adolescent Rights: Are Young People Equal under the Law?* Twenty First Century Books, 1995.

Hyde, Margaret O. *Juvenile Justice and Injustice.* New York: Franklin Watts, 1977.

Kowalski, Kathiann M. *Teen Rights: At Home, at School, Online.* Enslow Publishers Inc., 2000.

Landau, Elaine. *Your Legal Rights: From Custody Battles to School Searches, the Headline-Making Cases That Affect Your Life.* Walker & Co., 1995.

Marx, Trish, and Sandra Joseph Nunez. *And Justice for All: The Legal Rights of Young People.* Millbrook Press, 1997.

Mikula, Mark, and L. Mpho Mabunda, eds. *Great American Court Cases.* Detroit: The Gale Group, 1999.

Olney, Ross R., and Patricia J. Olney. *Up against the Law: Your Legal Rights as a Minor.* New York: E.P. Dutton, 1985.

Persico, Deborah A. *Mapp v. Ohio: Evidence and Search Warrants.* Enslow Publishers, Inc., 1997.

—. *New Jersey v. T.L.O: Drug Searches in Schools.* Enslow Publishers, Inc., 1998.

Riekes, Linda, Steve Jenkins, and Armentha Russell. *Juvenile Responsibility and Law.* St. Paul: West Publishing Co., 1990.

Wetterer, Charles M. *The Fourth Amendment: Search and Seizure.* Enslow Publishers, Inc., 1998.

Search and seizure are tools used by law enforcement officers to fight crime. When a police officer investigates a murder at the scene of the crime, she searches the place. If she finds the murder weapon, she seizes it as evidence. If the police officer finds the criminal, she arrests him. An arrest is a seizure of a person.

Before the United States was born, Great Britain conducted searches and seizures in the American colonies using general warrants and writs of assistance. These were documents that allowed British officer to enter anyone's home to look for smugglers and others who violated trade laws. British officers used these warrants to search homes and arrest people even when there was no evidence of a crime.

America's founders did not want the federal government to have such power. Privacy was something most Americans cherished. They decided to protect privacy by adopting the Fourth Amendment to the U.S. Constitution. The Fourth Amendment says law enforcement officials may conduct searches and seizures only when they have good reason to believe there has been a crime.

The Fourth Amendment was written to limit the power of federal law enforcement. Until the mid-1900s, state and local law enforcement did not have to obey the Fourth Amendment. The Fourteenth Amendment, however, says states may not take away liberty, or freedom, unfairly. In *Wolf v. Colorado,* the U.S. Supreme Court decided that the Fourteenth Amendment means state and local law enforcement officials must obey the Fourth Amendment.

Warrants and Probable Cause

The Fourth Amendment says, "The right of the people to be secure in their persons, houses, papers, and effects, against unreasonable searches and seizures, shall not be violated, and no Warrants shall issue, but upon probable cause, supported by Oath or affirmation, and particularly describing the place to be searched, and the persons or things to be seized." In short, the Fourth Amendment requires law enforcement to have a warrant and probable cause to conduct a search and seizure or to make an arrest.

A warrant is a document issued by a neutral person, such as a judge or magistrate. If law enforcement officials were allowed to issue their own warrants, the Fourth Amendment would not give Americans much protection. Police officers could just write a warrant anytime they wanted to enter a house or arrest a person, just like Great Britain did with general warrants. If a neutral person issues the warrant, he can make sure the police have a good reason to conduct the search or seizure.

Under the Fourth Amendment, a warrant must describe the place to be searched and the person or things to be seized. This was meant to end the British practice of using general warrants to search anywhere and arrest anyone. In the United States, for example, a warrant might specify that a police officer may search a person's business. If the officer does not find evidence of a crime, he cannot search the business owner's house and car, too.

To get a warrant, law enforcement officials must prove to the neutral judge or magistrate that they have probable cause. This is a legal term that means the officers have good reason to believe that a crime has been committed. It also means there is good reason to believe the place to be searched has either evidence of the crime or criminals to be arrested. If police officers, informants, or other citizens swear under oath to such information, a neutral magistrate can find probable cause to issue a warrant.

The warrant and probable cause requirements are the general rule under the Fourth Amendment. There are two main exceptions for arrests and automobiles.

Arrests

When a police officer sees someone commit a crime, she may arrest him without getting a warrant. For example, if an officer sees one man attacking another, she may arrest him on the spot. Making the officer get a warrant would allow the criminal to escape. The same rule applies when the police see someone who is wanted for committing a felony. (A felony is a serious crime, such as murder.) To make an arrest without a warrant, however, the officer still needs probable cause to believe the person she arrests has committed a crime.

When an officer makes an arrest, she may conduct a limited search without a warrant. The purpose of the search is to protect her safety and make sure the person she is arresting cannot destroy any evidence. This means the officer may search the person she is arresting and the area right around him. Without a search warrant, the officer cannot arrest someone and then search his entire house. That would violate the privacy the Fourth Amendment is supposed to protect.

Sometimes police officers see suspicious activity without seeing a crime. For example, an officer might see three men pacing back and forth outside a store like they are going to rob it. That is what happened in ***Terry v. Ohio*** (1968), in which the Supreme Court created the "stop and frisk" rule. This rule allows police officers to stop suspicious persons, frisk them to make sure they have no weapons, and ask a few questions. As long as the police have a good reason to be suspicious, they do not need a warrant or probable cause. If the stop and frisk reveals no wrongdoing, the police must quickly let the person go without making an arrest or conducting a full search of the person's clothes or surroundings.

Automobiles

The invention and widespread use of automobiles in the early 1900s presented a challenge to the Fourth Amendment. People expect to have privacy in their cars. Cars, however, are easy to move. If police officers had to get warrants to search cars, drivers could leave the state to avoid being caught.

In ***Carroll v. United States*** (1925), the U.S. Supreme Court created an automobile exception to the Fourth Amendment's warrant requirement. Under *Carroll,* if a police officer has probable cause to search a car, he need not get a search warrant. For example, if a police officer sees a car speeding away from a bank that was just robbed, he may stop the car and search it for stolen money without getting a search warrant. The automobile exception even allows the officer to search bags and other closed compartments in the car if he has probable cause to believe he will find evidence of a crime in them.

When police stop a car for a traffic violation, they sometimes see evidence of crimes in plain view in the car. In *Whren v. United States* (1996), police officers saw crack cocaine on the seat of a car they had stopped for making a turn without a signal. Even though the officers did not have probable cause to believe there was a drug violation when they stopped the car, they were allowed to seize the drugs that were in plain view.

There is one automobile exception that allows police to search a car without a warrant or probable cause. Police is some states use checkpoints to search for drunk drivers. At the checkpoint they stop cars and interview drivers, even if they have no reason to believe the driver is drunk. In *Michigan v. Sitz* (1990), the Supreme Court said police may use checkpoints to catch drunk drivers. The Court said checkpoint stops are a small invasion of privacy with the potential to do a lot of good by stopping drunk drivers.

Electronic Searches

The Fourth Amendment mentions people and their "houses, papers, and effects." Until 1967, the Supreme Court said the Fourth Amendment did not apply to electronic searches, such as wiretapping to hear telephone conversations. That changed in *Katz v. United States* (1967). In *Katz,* the federal government learned about illegal gambling by listening to telephone conversations in a public phone booth through a device attached outside the booth. The defendant challenged his conviction, saying the government violated the Fourth Amendment by "searching" his telephone conversations without a warrant and probable cause.

The U.S. Supreme Court agreed. It said the Fourth Amendment was not designed to protect just houses and papers. It was written to protect privacy. When a person has a telephone conversation in a closed booth, he expects it to be private. The federal government cannot invade that privacy without a warrant and probable cause.

Exclusionary Rule

The reason law enforcement officials conduct searches and seizures is to arrest criminals and find evidence to convict them in court. If an officer finds evidence by searching without a warrant, he suffers the penalty of the exclusionary rule. This rule prevents prosecutors from using evidence seized without a valid search warrant. Sometimes that means the prosecutor does not have enough evidence to convict a person who really is guilty. When that happens, the criminal is set free.

Many people have criticized the exclusionary rule. They say criminals should not be allowed to go free just because police officers make an error. The Supreme Court, however, says the exclusionary rule is necessary to make sure the government follows the law. As the Court said in ***Mapp v. Ohio*** (1961), "Nothing can destroy a government more quickly than its failure to observe its own laws."

Most rules, of course, have an exception, and the exclusionary rule is no different. The good faith exception applies when law enforcement uses a warrant that turns out to be invalid. A warrant is invalid, for example, if the judge issues it without probable cause. In *United States v. Leon* (1984), the Supreme Court said if law enforcement believes in good faith that a warrant is valid, prosecutors can use the evidence to convict the defendant, even if the warrant was not valid. This means criminals will not go free just because a judge or magistrate makes an error when issuing a warrant.

Suggestions for further reading

Franklin, Paula A. *The Fourth Amendment.* Englewood Cliffs: Silver Burdett Press, 1991.

Persico, Deborah A. *Mapp v. Ohio: Evidence and Search Warrants.* Enslow Publishers, Inc., 1997.

—-*New Jersey v. T.L.O: Drug Searches in Schools.* Enslow Publishers, Inc., 1998.

Shattuck, John H.F. *Rights of Privacy.* Skokie: National Textbook Co., 1977.

Wetterer, Charles M. *The Fourth Amendment: Search and Seizure.* Enslow Publishers, Inc., 1998.

Carroll v. United States
1925

Appellants: George Carroll and John Kiro

Appellee: United States

Appellants' Claim: That searching their car for illegal liquor without a search warrant violated the Fourth Amendment.

Chief Lawyer for Appellants: Thomas E. Atkinson and Clare J. Hall

Chief Lawyers for Appellee: John G. Sargent, Attorney General, and James M. Beck, Solicitor General

Justices for the Court: Louis D. Brandeis, Pierce Butler, Joseph McKenna, Edward Terry Sanford, William Howard Taft, Willis Van Devanter

Justices Dissenting: James Clark McReynolds, George Sutherland

Date of Decision: March 2, 1925

Decision: The Supreme Court affirmed appellants' convictions.

Significance: In *Carroll,* the Supreme Court decided that law enforcement officers do not need to get a warrant to search an automobile or other movable vehicle. Law enforcement only needs probable cause to believe the automobile has evidence of a crime.

The Fourth Amendment of the U.S. Constitution protects privacy. It requires law enforcement officers to get a warrant to search a house or other private place for evidence of a crime. To get a warrant, officers must have probable cause, which means good reason to believe the place to be searched has evidence of a crime. In *Carroll v. United States,* the Supreme Court had to decide whether officers need a warrant to search an automobile.

Chief Justice William Howard Taft.
Courtesy of the Library of Congress.

Bootlegging

In January 1919 the United States adopted the Eighteenth Amendment to the U.S. Constitution. The Eighteenth Amendment made it illegal to manufacture, sell, and transport alcohol in the United States. Because many Americans still wanted to drink alcohol, gangs of organized criminals entered the liquor trade. They made their own alcohol for sale in the United States and smuggled alcohol in from other countries.

Under the Volstead Act, Congress gave federal law enforcement the power to seize vehicles and arrest persons illegally transporting alcohol. Fred Cronenwett was a federal law enforcement officer. On September 29, 1921, Cronenwett went undercover to an apartment in Grand Rapids, Michigan. There he met John Carroll, who took Cronenwett's order for three cases of whiskey. Although Carroll never delivered the whiskey, Cronenwett remembered what Carroll and his car looked like.

A few months later on December 15, Cronenwett and two other officers were driving down the highway from Grand Rapids to Detroit, Michigan, when they passed Carroll and John Kiro going the other way. Smugglers frequently used that road to bring alcohol into the country from Canada. The officers turned around, caught up to Carroll and Kiro, and told them to pull over. The officers then searched the car without a warrant and found 69 quarts of whiskey. The United States convicted Carroll and Kiro of violating the Volstead Act and the Eighteenth Amendment.

The Automobile Exception

Carroll and Kiro appealed their convictions to the U.S. Supreme Court. They said searching their car without a warrant violated the Fourth Amendment. With a 7-2 decision, the Supreme Court disagreed and affirmed their convictions.

Chief Justice William Howard Taft wrote the opinion for the Court. Taft said the Fourth Amendment protects privacy by requiring searches to be reasonable. It does not, however, require a warrant for all searches. When police believe a private home has evidence of a crime, it is reasonable to require them to get a warrant before searching the place. The house cannot go anywhere.

The case is different with automobiles and other moving vehicles. When a police officer sees an automobile that might contain evidence of a crime, there is no time to get a search warrant. The driver can hide the car or leave the state and escape the police officer's jurisdiction, or area of power. That means it is unreasonable to require the police to get a warrant to search an automobile.

Taft emphasized, however, that officers enforcing the Volstead Act could not stop and search cars at random. To conduct any search, the Fourth Amendment requires probable cause, which means good reason to believe the place to be searched has evidence of a crime. That meant officers enforcing the Volstead Act were limited to searching cars that probably contained illegal alcohol.

The Supreme Court decided that Cronenwett and his fellow officers had probable cause to search Carroll and Kiro's car. Cronenwett knew Carroll was involved in the liquor trade because Cronenwett went undercover to order illegal whiskey from Carroll. Cronenwett also knew that alcohol smugglers often used the road between Detroit and Grand Rapids. Chief Justice Taft said that when Cronenwett saw Carroll driving on that road, Cronenwett had good reason to believe the car contained illegal alcohol, which it did.

PROHIBITION

The United States adopted the Eighteenth Amendment to the U.S. Constitution in January 1919. The Eighteenth Amendment made it illegal to manufacture, sell, and transport alcohol, including liquor, beer, and wine, in the United States. This was the beginning of the period of time known as Prohibition.

Prohibition happened for many reasons. Some religious groups, especially Protestants, believed alcohol was immoral. Medical reports suggested that alcohol caused health problems and early death. Politicians in favor of prohibition said it would reduce crime. Prejudice against foreigners who used alcohol also fueled the movement for Prohibition. This was especially true of prejudice toward Germans, against whom the United States fought in World War I from 1917 to 1918.

Prohibition, however, did not work very well. Crime increased as organized criminals supplied illegal alcohol to those who wanted it. Poor people who could not afford good alcohol often were poisoned by bad alcohol. Closing saloons eliminated a popular meeting place for working class Americans. When the Great Depression hit the United States in the 1930s, Americans decided legalizing alcohol would help the economy. The United States ended prohibition with the Twenty-First Amendment to the Constitution in 1932.

Uncommon Law

Two justices dissented, meaning they disagreed with the Court's decision. Justice James Clark McReynolds wrote a dissenting opinion. McReynolds disagreed that the Fourth Amendment allows law enforcement to search a car without a warrant.

Under English common law at the time the United States adopted the Fourth Amendment, police could arrest and search a man without a warrant only if he was wanted for a felony or had committed a misdemeanor in front of the officer. (Felonies are serious crimes such as murder, while misdemeanors are less serious crimes such as reckless driving.) Because violating the Volstead Act was a misdemeanor, McReynolds thought Cronenwett needed a warrant to arrest Carroll and Kiro and search their car.

McReynolds also did not think Cronenwett had probable cause to search the car. McReynolds asked, "Has it come about that merely because a man once agreed to deliver whiskey, but did not, he may be arrested whenever thereafter he ventures to drive an automobile on the road to Detroit!"

Despite McReynolds's concerns, *Carroll* has remained good law. Federal and state law enforcement officers with probable cause to believe a car has evidence of a crime may stop and search it without a warrant.

Suggestions for further reading

Baughman, Judith S., ed. *American Decades: 1920-1929.* Detroit: Gale Research, 1996.

Franklin, Paula A. *The Fourth Amendment.* Englewood Cliffs: Silver Burdett Press, 1991.

Persico, Deborah A. *Mapp v. Ohio: Evidence and Search Warrants.* Enslow Publishers, Inc., 1997.

—. *New Jersey v. T.L.O: Drug Searches in Schools.* Enslow Publishers, Inc., 1998.

Shattuck, John H.F. *Rights of Privacy.* Skokie: National Textbook Co., 1977.

Vile, John R. *Encyclopedia of Constitutional Amendments, Proposed Amendments, and Amending Issues.* Santa Barbara: ABC-CLIO, Inc., 1996.

Wetterer, Charles M. *The Fourth Amendment: Search and Seizure.* Enslow Publishers, Inc., 1998.

Mapp v. Ohio 1961

Appellant: Dollree Mapp

Appellee: State of Ohio

Appellant's Claim: That convicting her with evidence obtained during an illegal search violated the Fourth Amendment.

Chief Lawyer for Appellant: A.L. Kearns

Chief Lawyer for Appellee: Gertrude Bauer Mahon

Justices for the Court: Hugo Lafayette Black, William J. Brennan, Jr., Tom C. Clark, William O. Douglas, Potter Stewart, Earl Warren

Justices Dissenting: Felix Frankfurter, John Marshall Harlan II, Charles Evans Whittaker

Date of Decision: June 19, 1961

Decision: The Supreme Court reversed Mapp's conviction.

Significance: Until *Mapp,* states did not have to obey the exclusionary rule, which prevents the government from using evidence its gets during an illegal search and seizure. By forcing states to obey the exclusionary rule, the Supreme Court strengthened the Fourth Amendment's protection of privacy for Americans.

A persons privacy is protected by the Fourth Amendment of the U.S. Constitution. The Fourth Amendment requires law enforcement officers to get a warrant to search a house or other private place for evidence of a

Associate Justice Tom C. Clark.
Courtesy of the Supreme Court of the United States.

crime. In *Weeks v. United States* (1914), the U.S. Supreme Court created the exclusionary rule. That rule prevents the federal government from convicting a defendant with evidence the government finds during an illegal search without a warrant.

In *Wolf v. Colorado* (1949), the Supreme Court said state and local governments must obey the Fourth Amendment by getting a warrant to conduct a search. The Court also said, however, that the exclusionary rule does not apply to the states. That allowed state prosecutors to use evidence seized during illegal searches without warrants. *Mapp v. Ohio* gave the Supreme Court the chance to overrule *Wolf* and apply the exclusionary rule to the states.

Breaking and Entering

On May 23, 1957, police officers in Cleveland, Ohio, had information that a bombing suspect was hiding in the house of Dollree Mapp. They also thought the house had illegal gambling equipment. When the police went to Mapp's house to search it, however, Mapp called her attorney and then refused to let the police in without a search warrant.

The police stationed themselves outside Mapp's home to watch the place. Three hours later they sought entrance again. When Mapp did not

SEARCH AND SEIZURE

come to the door immediately, the police forced it open and entered the house. Mapp demanded to see a search warrant and grabbed the piece of paper the police waved at her. The police struggled with Mapp to get the paper back, hurting her in the process, and then put her in handcuffs. The paper was not really a search warrant.

The police searched Mapp's entire house, looking in rooms, leafing through photo albums and personal papers, and opening a trunk. They never found the bombing suspect or any gambling equipment. They did, however, find obscene materials that were illegal to have under Ohio's obscenity law. The police charged Mapp with violating that law and the court convicted her and put her in prison.

Mapp appealed her conviction. Her main argument was that Ohio's obscenity law violated her right to freedom of thought under the First Amendment. The Ohio Supreme Court rejected this argument. Mapp also argued that Ohio should not be allowed to convict her with evidence found during an illegal search without a warrant. Relying on *Wolf,* the Ohio Supreme Court also rejected this argument and affirmed Mapp's conviction. Mapp appealed her case to the U.S. Supreme Court.

The police entered Dollree Mapp's house without a search warrant. Reproduced by permission of AP/Wide World Photos.

EXCLUSIONARY RULE EXCEPTIONS

The exclusionary rule prevents the government from using evidence at trial that it gets during and illegal search and seizure. There are, however, two exceptions to this rule. The good faith exception applies when law enforcement uses a search warrant that turns out to be illegal. If law enforcement truly believed the warrant was valid, the government may use the illegally obtained evidence at a criminal trial.

The second exception is called the inevitable discovery rule. It applies when law enforcement conducts an illegal search and seizure to get evidence that it eventually would have found legally. Again, the government may use such evidence at trial. Under both exceptions, the Supreme Court considers the violation of the defendant's constitutional rights to be harmless compared to the cost of letting the defendant go free.

Law Over Anarchy

With a 6–3 decision, the Supreme Court reversed Mapp's conviction. Writing for the Court, Justice Tom C. Clark ignored the First Amendment issue and focused on the illegal search and seizure. Clark and the rest of the majority decided to overrule *Wolf* and apply the exclusionary rule to the states.

Clark emphasized that the Fourth Amendment was designed to protect privacy for Americans in their homes. Without the exclusionary rule, state police are encouraged to invade privacy with illegal searches and seizures. It also encourages federal law enforcement to violate the Fourth Amendment and then give the illegal evidence to the states.

Clark said the exclusionary rule not only protects privacy, but also fosters respect for the law. "Nothing can destroy a government more quickly than its failure to observe its own laws. . . . If the Government becomes a lawbreaker, it breeds contempt [disrespect] for the law; it invites every man to become a law unto himself; it invites anarchy."

Suggestions for further reading

Franklin, Paula A. *The Fourth Amendment.* Englewood Cliffs: Silver Burdett Press, 1991.

Persico, Deborah A. *Mapp v. Ohio: Evidence and Search Warrants.* Enslow Publishers, Inc., 1997.

—. *New Jersey v. T.L.O: Drug Searches in Schools.* Enslow Publishers, Inc., 1998.

Shattuck, John H.F. *Rights of Privacy.* Skokie: National Textbook Co., 1977.

Wetterer, Charles M. *The Fourth Amendment: Search and Seizure.* Enslow Publishers, Inc., 1998.

Witt, Elder, ed. *Guide to the U.S. Supreme Court,* 2d ed. Washington, D.C.: Congressional Quarterly, 1990.

Terry v. Ohio
1968

Petitioner: John W. Terry

Respondent: State of Ohio

Petitioner's Claim: That Officer Martin McFadden violated the Fourth Amendment when he stopped and frisked petitione r on the streets of Cleveland without probable cause.

Chief Lawyer for Petitioner: Louis Stokes

Chief Lawyer for Respondent: Reuben M. Payne

Justices for the Court: Hugo Lafayette Black, William J. Brennan, Jr., Abe Fortas, John Marshall Harlan II, Thurgood Marshall, Potter Stewart, Earl Warren, Byron R. White

Justices Dissenting: William O. Douglas

Date of Decision: June 10, 1968

Decision: The Supreme Court affirmed Terry's conviction for carrying a concealed weapon.

Significance: In *Terry,* the Supreme Court said police officers do not need probable cause to stop and frisk suspicious people who might be carrying weapons.

The Fourth Amendment of the U.S. Constitution protects privacy. It requires law enforcement officers to have probable cause before they seize or arrest a person and search his belongings. Probable cause means good reason to believe that the person has committed a crime. In *Terry v.*

Ohio, the Supreme Court had to decide whether the police can stop and frisk a suspicious person in public without probable cause.

Casing the Joint

Martin McFadden, a police officer and detective for 39 years, was patrolling the streets of Cleveland, Ohio, on October 31, 1963. That afternoon, McFadden saw two men, John W. Terry and Richard D. Chilton, standing on a street corner. McFadden's experience told him the men looked suspicious, so he began to observe them from a nearby store entrance.

As McFadden watched, Terry and Chilton took turns walking past and looking inside a store window. Between them the men walked back and forth past the store twelve times. At that point a third man joined them for a brief discussion on the street corner. When the third man left, Terry and Chilton continued to take turns walking past the same store window to peer inside. Ten minutes later they headed down the street in the same direction as the third man whom they had met.

McFadden believed the three men were getting ready to rob the store they were watching. Because it was daytime, he also suspected they were armed and dangerous. McFadden followed Terry and Chilton and found them in front of Zucker's store with the third man. McFadden introduced himself as a police officer and asked for their names. When the men only mumbled in response, McFadden grabbed Terry, spun him around to face the other two men, and frisked him. McFadden felt a gun inside Terry's coat. He immediately ordered the three men to go into Zucker's store.

When everyone was inside, McFadden removed Terry's overcoat and found a .38 caliber revolver inside. McFadden ordered the three men to put their hands up on the wall. He then patted down Chilton and the third man to find a revolver in Chilton's overcoat. Ohio convicted Terry and Chilton of carrying concealed weapons.

Terry and Chilton appealed their convictions. They argued that McFadden's stop and frisk was a search and seizure under the Fourth Amendment. McFadden conducted the stop and frisk without probable cause to believe that Terry and Chilton had committed a crime. After all, there was nothing illegal about walking around the streets of Cleveland. Without probable cause, Terry and Chilton said the stop and frisk was illegal under the Fourth Amendment. If that was true, Ohio was not

ILLINOIS V. WARDLOW

In 1995, Sam Wardlow was on the streets of Chicago in an area known for drug deals. When a caravan of four police cars appeared, Wardlow fled on foot. Officers Nolan and Harvey chased and caught Wardlow on a nearby street. When Officer Nolan frisked Wardlow, he found a .38 caliber handgun. Illinois convicted Wardlow of unlawful use of a weapon by a felon.

Wardlow appealed his conviction. Wardlow argued that the police did not have any reason to be suspicious of him. That meant the stop and frisk was an illegal search and seizure under the Fourth Amendment. The Supreme Court disagreed and affirmed Wardlow's conviction. Writing for the Court, Chief Justice William H. Rehnquist said police are allowed to stop a man who flees from them in a high crime area. The circumstances of the flight give the police reason to be suspicious and to investigate.

allowed to use the evidence of the concealed weapons, meaning the cases should have been dismissed for lack of evidence.

The court of appeals rejected this argument and affirmed Terry's and Chilton's convictions. When Terry and Chilton appealed to the Ohio Supreme Court, it dismissed the appeal without considering the case. Terry and Chilton finally asked the U.S. Supreme Court to review the case. Before it did, Chilton died, so the Supreme Court was left to consider Terry's case.

Stop and Frisk Approved

With an 8–1 decision, the Supreme Court affirmed Terry's conviction. Writing for the Court, Chief Justice Earl Warren approved the stop-and-frisk tactic as a legal police procedure.

Warren said the Fourth Amendment is designed to protect privacy. A stop and frisk is a search and seizure that invades a person's privacy.

When the police stop and frisk someone who is innocent of a crime, it is especially offensive. Police, however, need to investigate suspicious activity. When they do, they need to protect themselves from people who might be armed and dangerous.

Warren rejected Terry's argument that police need probable cause to conduct a stop and frisk. He said the Fourth Amendment does not require probable cause for all searches and seizures. It only requires that a search and seizure be reasonable. When police see suspicious activity by people who might be armed and dangerous, it is reasonable to stop them for questions and frisk them for weapons. If the stop and frisk reveals no illegal activity, the police must let them go immediately. Warren said this result created the best balance between the right of privacy and needs of law enforcement.

Justice William O. Douglas wrote a dissenting opinion, meaning he disagreed with the Court's decision. Douglas said the Fourth Amendment requires probable cause for every search and seizure. When the Court creates an exception, Americans lose protection for privacy. Despite Douglas's concern, *Terry* remains the law of the land. Police are allowed to stop suspicious people and frisk them for weapons without reason to believe they have committed a crime.

Suggestions for further reading

Franklin, Paula A. *The Fourth Amendment.* Englewood Cliffs: Silver Burdett Press, 1991.

Greenhouse, Linda. "Supreme Court Roundup; Flight Can Justify Search By Police, High Court Rules." *New York Times,* January 13, 2000.

Persico, Deborah A. *Mapp v. Ohio: Evidence and Search Warrants.* Enslow Publishers, Inc., 1997.

—. *New Jersey v. T.L.O: Drug Searches in Schools.* Enslow Publishers, Inc., 1998.

Shattuck, John H.F. *Rights of Privacy.* Skokie: National Textbook Co., 1977.

Wetterer, Charles M. *The Fourth Amendment: Search and Seizure.* Enslow Publishers, Inc., 1998.

United States v. Santana 1976

Petitioner: United States

Respondents: Mom Santana, et al.

Petitioner's Claim: That the police did not violate the Fourth Amendment when they arrested Mom Santana in her home and searched her for drug money.

Chief Lawyer for Petitioner: Frank H. Easterbrook

Chief Lawyer for Respondent: Dennis H. Eisman

Justices for the Court: Harry A. Blackmun, Warren E. Burger, Lewis F. Powell, Jr., William H. Rehnquist, John Paul Stevens, Potter Stewart, Byron R. White

Justices Dissenting: William J. Brennan, Jr., Thurgood Marshall

Date of Decision: June 24, 1976

Decision: The Supreme Court said the police did not violate the Fourth Amendment.

Significance: With *Santana,* the Supreme Court said police officers in hot pursuit of a criminal suspect do not need a warrant to chase her into her home and arrest her.

The Fourth Amendment of the U.S. Constitution protects privacy. It requires police officers to have a warrant and probable cause before they arrest a person and search her in her home. A warrant is a document that a neutral magistrate issues when there is probable cause to arrest someone. Probable cause means good reason to believe the person has committed a crime. In *United States v. Santana* (1976), the Supreme Court had to decide whether the police need a warrant to arrest a person who retreats into her home after the police begin to chase her.

Drug Bust

Michael Gilletti was an undercover officer with the Philadelphia Narcotics Squad. On August 16, 1974, Gilletti arranged to buy heroin, a narcotic drug, from Patricia McCafferty. McCafferty told Gilletti the heroin would cost $115 and that they would get it from Mom Santana.

Gilletti told his supervisors about the plan and the Narcotics Squad planned a drug bust. Gilletti recorded the serial numbers for $110 in marked bills and went to meet McCafferty, who got into Gilletti's car and directed him to Mom Santana's house. There McCafferty took the money from Gilletti and went inside. When she returned a short time later, McCafferty got into Gilletti's car and they drove away together. When McCafferty pulled envelopes with heroin out of her bra, Gilletti stopped the car, showed McCafferty his badge, and arrested her.

McCafferty told Gilletti that Mom Santana had the marked money. Gilletti told this to Sergeant Pruitt, who went with his officers back to Mom Santana's house while Gilletti took McCafferty to the police station. At the house, Pruitt and his officers saw Mom Santana standing in the doorway holding a brown paper bag. The police stopped their car fifteen feet from Santana and got out of the car shouting "police" and showing their badges. As the officers approached Santana, she retreated into her home.

The police followed Mom Santana inside and caught her in the foyer. During a brief struggle, two bundles of packets with powder fell out of the brown paper bag. The powder turned out to be heroin. When the police ordered Santana to empty her pockets, she produced $70 of Gilletti's marked money.

The United States filed criminal charges against Mom Santana for possessing heroin with the intention of selling it. At her trial, Santana made a motion to exclude the evidence of the heroin and the marked money. Santana said the police violated her Fourth Amendment rights by arresting and searching her in her home without a warrant. The government is not allowed to use evidence it finds when it violates the Fourth Amendment. Without the heroin and the marked money, the government would not have a case against Santana.

MINNESOTA V. OLSON

On July 18, 1987, Joseph Ecker robbed an Amoco gasoline station in Minneapolis, Minnesota, killed the station manager, and escaped in a car driven by Rob Olson. Police found and arrested Ecker that same day. The next day, police received a call from a woman who said Olson was hiding in a house where he was staying with two women.

Police surrounded the house and then telephoned to ask Olson to come out. The woman who answered the phone said Olson was not there, but police heard Olson tell her to say that. Without a warrant, the police entered the home, found Olson hiding in a closet, and arrested him. Olson soon confessed to the crime and was convicted of murder, robbery, and assault.

On appeal, the Minnesota Supreme Court reversed Olson's conviction and the U.S. Supreme Court agreed. The Supreme Court said Olson expected privacy in the house where he was staying. The Fourth Amendment protects that privacy by requiring police officers to get a warrant before entering a home. Unlike in *Santana,* the police were not in hot pursuit of Olson. Instead, they surrounded the home to prevent Olson from escaping. There was plenty of time to get a warrant before entering the home to arrest Olson. Because the police failed to get a warrant, Olson's arrest and confession were illegal under the Fourth Amendment.

The trial court granted Santana's motion. It said the government cannot enter a person's house to arrest her without a warrant. The court of appeals affirmed this decision, so the United States took the case to the U.S. Supreme Court.

Mom Busted

With a 7–2 decision, the Supreme Court ruled in favor of the United States. Writing for the Court, Justice William H. Rehnquist said the Fourth Amendment protects privacy by requiring probable cause before an arrest. From what McCafferty told Gilletti, the police had probable cause to believe Mom Santana was selling drugs.

Justice Rehnquist said the Fourth Amendment does not require police to have a warrant for every arrest. Police only need a warrant to enter a private place, such as a home. Mom Santana was not in her home when Sergeant Pruitt and his team tried to arrest her. She was standing in the doorway in full view of the public. Anything people choose to expose to the public is not private.

Rehnquist said Santana could not frustrate a legal arrest by retreating into her home. Rehnquist called this the "hot pursuit" doctrine. When police are in hot pursuit of a criminal suspect, they may follow her into her home if stopping to get a warrant would frustrate the arrest. In this case, Santana could have gotten rid of the marked money while police went to get a warrant. Under those circumstances, the police were allowed to follow Santana into her house. They did not violate the Fourth Amendment.

Suggestions for further reading

Franklin, Paula A. *The Fourth Amendment.* Englewood Cliffs: Silver Burdett Press, 1991.

Persico, Deborah A. *Mapp v. Ohio: Evidence and Search Warrants.* Enslow Publishers, Inc., 1997.

—. *New Jersey v. T.L.O: Drug Searches in Schools.* Enslow Publishers, Inc., 1998.

Shattuck, John H.F. *Rights of Privacy.* Skokie: National Textbook Co., 1977.

Wetterer, Charles M. *The Fourth Amendment: Search and Seizure.* Enslow Publishers, Inc., 1998.

Arkansas v. Sanders
1979

Petitioner: State of Arkansas

Respondent: Lonnie James Sanders

Petitioner's Claim: That the police did not violate the Fourth Amendment by searching Sanders's suitcase without a search warrant.

Chief Lawyer for Petitioner: Joseph H. Purvis, Deputy Attorney General of Arkansas

Chief Lawyer for Respondent: Jack T. Lassiter

Justices for the Court: Warren E. Burger, Thurgood Marshall, Lewis F. Powell, Jr., John Paul Stevens, Potter Stewart, Byron R. White

Justices Dissenting: Harry A. Blackmun, William H. Rehnquist

Date of Decision: June 20, 1979

Decision: The Supreme Court said the search violated the Fourth Amendment.

Significance: With *Sanders,* the Supreme Court said police may not search luggage without a warrant unless there are exigent, or urgent, circumstances.

A person's privacy is protected by the Fourth Amendment of the U.S. Constitution. The Fourth Amendment requires searches and seizures by the government to be reasonable. In most cases, law enforcement officers must get a warrant to search a house or other private place for evidence of a crime. To get a warrant, officers must have probable cause, which means good reason to believe the place to be searched has evidence of a crime.

There are exceptions to the warrant requirement. The automobile exception allows police to stop and search a car without a warrant when they have probable cause to believe the car is holding evidence of a crime. There are two reasons for the automobile exception. First, because a car can be moved, police might lose the evidence if they were forced to get a warrant. Second, Americans have less privacy in their cars than in their homes. In *Arkansas v. Sanders,* the U.S. Supreme Court had to decide whether police could search a suitcase in the trunk of a car without a warrant.

The Man With the Green Suitcase

David Isom was an officer with the police department in Little Rock, Arkansas. On April 23, 1976, an informant told Isom that at 4:35 in the afternoon, Lonnie James Sanders would arrive at the Little Rock airport carrying a green suitcase with marijuana inside. Isom believed the informant because just three months earlier, the informant gave the police information that led to Sanders's arrest and conviction for possessing marijuana.

Acting on the informant's tip, Isom and two other police officers placed the airport under surveillance. As the informant predicted, Sanders appeared at gate No. 1, deposited some luggage in a taxicab, and then went to the baggage claim area. There Sanders met a man named David Rambo. Rambo waited while Sanders retrieved a green suitcase from the airport baggage service. Sanders gave the suitcase to Rambo and then went to his taxicab, where Rambo joined him a short while later. Rambo put the suitcase into the trunk and rode off in the taxicab with Sanders.

Isom and one of his fellow officers pursued the taxicab. With help from a patrol car, they stopped the taxicab several blocks from the airport. At the request of the police, the taxi driver opened the trunk of the car, where the officers found the green suitcase. Without asking for permission, the police opened the suitcase and found 9.3 pounds of marijuana in ten plastic bags.

On October 14, 1976, Arkansas charged Sanders and Rambo with possession of marijuana with intent to deliver. Before trial, Sanders made a motion to suppress, or get rid of, the marijuana evidence. When the government violates the Fourth Amendment, it is not allowed to use the evidence it finds to convict the defendant. Sanders said the police violated his Fourth Amendment rights by opening the suitcase without a search warrant. Arkansas argued that the search was legal under the automobile exception to the warrant requirement.

The trial court denied Sanders's motion, the jury convicted him, and the court sentenced him to ten years in prison and fined him $15,000. Sanders appealed to the Supreme Court of Arkansas. That court ruled in his favor, saying the trial court should have suppressed the marijuana evidence because the police violated the Fourth Amendment. Faced with having to dismiss the case against Sanders, Arkansas took the case to the U.S. Supreme Court.

Privacy Prevails

With a 7–2 decision, the Supreme Court ruled in favor of Sanders. Writing for the Court, Justice Lewis F. Powell, Jr., said the automobile exception did not apply to the search of Sanders's suitcase. Once the police had the suitcase, there was no danger that it would be taken away like an automobile.

Powell said people usually keep personal belongings in their luggage. That means they expect the luggage to be private. The Fourth Amendment protects privacy by requiring the police to get a warrant by proving they have probable cause to search a private item. After seizing Sanders's suitcase, Isom and his fellow officer should have asked a judge or magistrate for a warrant before searching it. Because they did not, Arkansas could not use the marijuana evidence to convict Sanders of a crime.

Criminal Justice Fails?

Two justices dissented, which means they disagreed with the Court's opinion. Justice Harry A. Blackmun wrote a dissenting opinion. Blackmun thought Isom was allowed to search the suitcase under the automobile exception to the warrant requirement. Why should Isom have stopped the search when he found a piece of luggage that was supposed to contain criminal evidence? Blackmun thought the Court's decision created an unrealistic difference between searching cars and searching things found in cars. He feared this would allow many guilty people to go free.

THE WAR ON DRUGS

The South American country of Colombia is a major battleground in the war on drugs. According to estimates by the U.S. Drug Enforcement Administration, 80 percent of the cocaine and heroin in the United States comes from Colombia.

In January 2000, President William J. Clinton announced a plan to make the Colombian government a partner in the war on drugs. Clinton asked Congress to approve a $1.3 billion aid package to Colombia. Most of the aid would equip and fund the Colombian military. Clinton's request included thirty Black Hawk helicopters and fifteen UH-1N Huey helicopters.

Clinton's plan received criticism from members of Congress. Many Republicans think the United States should fund American drug-fighting police instead of the Colombian military. They say the Colombian military uses aid packages to fight guerrillas (independent bands of soldiers) who are trying to overthrow the Colombian government. Amnesty International and many Democrats added concerns that the Colombian military is responsible for many human rights violations, including restricting military service to uneducated people. The Clinton administration, however, believes fighting Colombian guerrillas is a necessary part of winning the war on drugs.

Suggestions for further reading

Deyoung, Karen. "Clinton Plans to Seek $1.3 Billion to Stem Colombian Drug Flow." *Washington Post,* January 12, 2000.

Deyoung, Karen. "Colombia Anti-Drug Plan Draws Hill Fire." *Washington Post,* February 16, 2000.

Franklin, Paula A. *The Fourth Amendment.* Englewood Cliffs: Silver Burdett Press, 1991.

Persico, Deborah A. *Mapp v. Ohio: Evidence and Search Warrants.* Enslow Publishers, Inc., 1997.

Peters, Ralph. "The U.S. Is Setting a Trap for Itself in Colombia." *Washington Post,* March 5, 2000.

Shattuck, John H.F. *Rights of Privacy.* Skokie: National Textbook Co., 1977.

Wetterer, Charles M. *The Fourth Amendment: Search and Seizure.* Enslow Publishers, Inc., 1998.

New York v. Belton 1981

Petitioner: State of New York

Respondent: Roger Belton

Petitioner's Claim: That a police officer did not violate the Fourth Amendment by searching Belton's jacket in a car without a search warrant.

Chief Lawyer for Petitioner: James R. Harvey

Chief Lawyer for Respondent: Paul J. Cambria, Jr.

Justices for the Court: Harry A. Blackmun, Warren E. Burger, Lewis F. Powell, Jr., William H. Rehnquist, John Paul Stevens, Potter Stewart

Justices Dissenting: William J. Brennan, Jr., Thurgood Marshall, Byron R. White

Date of Decision: July 1, 1981

Decision: The Supreme Court approved the police officer's search.

Significance: With *Belton,* the Supreme Court said whenever the police arrest people in a car, they may search the passenger compartment without a warrant.

The Fourth Amendment of the U.S. Constitution protects privacy. Any searches and seizures undertaken by the government are required to be reasonable. In most cases, law enforcement officers must get a warrant to search a house or other private place for evidence of a crime. To get a warrant, officers must have probable cause, which means good reason to believe the place to be searched has evidence of a crime.

There are exceptions to the warrant requirement. When police officers see a person commit a felony or misdemeanor, they may arrest the person without a warrant. During the arrest, the police need to protect themselves from any weapons the criminal might have. Police also need to make sure the criminal does not destroy any evidence during the arrest. Because of these needs, police are allowed to search a person and his surroundings without a warrant when they arrest him. In *New York v. Belton,* the Supreme Court had to decide whether police could search inside a car after arresting the car's occupants.

Smoking

On April 9, 1978, New York State Trooper Douglas Nicot was driving an unmarked police car on the New York Thruway. An automobile passed Nicot going well over the speed limit. Nicot chased the car and ordered it's driver to pull off the road. There were four men in the car, including Roger Belton.

Nicot asked to see the driver's license and automobile registration. He learned that none of the four men owned the car or was related to its owner. During the stop, Nicot smelled burnt marijuana and saw an envelope marked "Supergold" on the floor of the car. In Nicot's experience, Supergold meant marijuana. Because possessing marijuana was illegal, Nicot ordered the four men to get out of the car and arrested them.

After separating the men outside the car and patting them down, Nicot returned to the car to search it. Inside the envelope he found marijuana, just as he suspected he would. Nicot then searched the entire passenger compartment. On the back seat he found a black leather jacket. Nicot unzipped the pockets and found cocaine and Belton's identification card inside. Nicot finally took everyone to a nearby police station.

New York charged Belton with criminal possession of cocaine, a controlled substance. At Belton's trial, he made a motion to get rid of the cocaine evidence. Belton argued that Nicot violated the Fourth Amendment by searching his jacket without a search warrant. Belton said Nicot did not need to search the jacket to protect himself or the evidence because the four men already were out of the car.

The trial court denied Belton's motion. Belton pleaded guilty to a lesser offense and reserved his right to appeal the issue of whether Nicot

POTTER STEWART

Potter Stewart, who wrote the Supreme Court's opinion in *New York v. Belton,* was born on January 23, 1915, in Jackson, Michigan. After graduating from Yale Law School in 1941, Stewart worked in law firms in New York City and Cincinnati before entering Cincinnati politics in 1949. After Stewart supported Dwight D. Eisenhower's presidential campaign in 1952, Eisenhower appointed Stewart to the Sixth Circuit Court of Appeals in 1954. At thirty-nine, Stewart was the youngest federal judge in the country.

Eisenhower appointed Stewart to the Supreme Court in 1958. Stewart was a moderate justice, often casting the deciding vote in close cases. In 1962, he was the only dissenter in a case banning prayer in public schools. In an obscenity case in 1964, Stewart said that while he could not define obscenity, "I know it when I see it." In 1969, press reports suggested that Stewart was being considered to succeed Earl Warren as chief justice of the Supreme Court. Privately, Stewart asked President Richard M. Nixon not to name him to that post. In 1981 at age sixty-six, Stewart became the youngest justice to resign from the Supreme Court. He died on December 7, 1985, after suffering a stroke.

violated the Fourth Amendment. On appeal, the Appellate Division said Nicot's search was lawful. The New York Court of Appeals, however, reversed. It said Nicot did not need to search Belton's jacket to protect himself or the evidence. Belton, then, should have gotten a warrant before searching the jacket. Faced with having to dismiss Belton's case, New York took the case to the U.S. Supreme Court.

Bright-Line Rules

With a 6–3 decision, the Supreme Court reversed again and ruled in favor of New York. Writing for the Court, Justice Potter Stewart said confusing cases were making it hard for police officers to know what they could search without a warrant. The Supreme Court decided to change that with a clear, bright-line rule. It held that when police officers lawfully arrest the occupants of an automobile, they may search the entire passenger compartment and anything in it without a search warrant. With a clear rule, police would have no doubt what their powers are under the Fourth Amendment.

This new rule made Nicot's search lawful under the Fourth Amendment. Nicot was allowed to arrest Belton and his companions without a warrant because he saw them with marijuana. That arrest allowed Nicot to search the passenger compartment of the car, including Belton's jacket in the back seat. Because Nicot found the cocaine without violating the Fourth Amendment, New York was allowed to use the cocaine to charge Belton with criminal possession of a controlled substance.

Fourth Amendment Falls

Three justices dissented, which means they disagreed with the Court's decision. Justice William J. Brennan wrote a dissenting opinion. Brennan said the Fourth Amendment is an important tool for protecting privacy in the United States. Exceptions to the warrant requirement must be narrow if privacy is to survive. The Court's decision hurt privacy by allowing police officers to search cars without a warrant, probable cause, or any danger to police officers and evidence. Brennan did not think helping police officers with a bright-line rule was a good reason for disregarding the Fourth Amendment.

Suggestions for further reading

Franklin, Paula A. *The Fourth Amendment.* Englewood Cliffs: Silver Burdett Press, 1991.

Gareffa, Peter M., ed. *Contemporary Newsmakers.* Detroit: Gale Research Company, 1986.

Persico, Deborah A. *Mapp v. Ohio: Evidence and Search Warrants.* Enslow Publishers, Inc., 1997.

Shattuck, John H.F. *Rights of Privacy.* Skokie: National Textbook Co., 1977.

Wetterer, Charles M. *The Fourth Amendment: Search and Seizure.* Enslow Publishers, Inc., 1998.

Washington v. Chrisman 1982

Petitioner: State of Washington

Respondent: Neil Martin Chrisman

Petitioner's Claim: That a police officer did not violate the Fourth Amendment by searching Chrisman's dormitory room for illegal drugs without a warrant.

Chief Lawyer for Petitioner: Ronald R. Carpenter

Chief Lawyer for Respondent: Robert F. Patrick

Justices for the Court: Harry A. Blackmun, Warren E. Burger, Sandra Day O'Connor, Lewis F. Powell, Jr., William H. Rehnquist, John Paul Stevens

Justices Dissenting: William J. Brennan, Jr., Thurgood Marshall, Byron R. White

Date of Decision: January 13, 1982

Decision: The Supreme Court approved the police officer's search and seizure.

Significance: With *Chrisman,* the Supreme Court said if police are lawfully in a person's private home, they may seize any criminal evidence they see in plain view.

A person's privacy is protected under the Fourth Amendment of the U.S. Constitution. The Fourth Amendment requires searches and seizures by the government to be reasonable. In most cases, law enforcement officers must get a warrant to search a house or other private place for evidence of a crime. To get a warrant, officers must have probable cause, which means good reason to believe the place to be searched has evidence of a crime. The warrant must specifically describe the evidence the police may look for.

There are exceptions to the warrant requirement. One of the exceptions is called the "plain view" doctrine. Under this doctrine, police who have a warrant to look for specific evidence may seize any other evidence that is in plain view in the place they are searching. In *Washington v. Chrisman,* the U.S. Supreme Court had to decide whether a policeman in a dormitory room without a search warrant could seize evidence in plain view.

Party Time

Officer Daugherty worked for the Washington State University police department. On the evening of January 21, 1978, Daugherty saw Carl Overdahl, a student, leave a dormitory carrying a half-gallon bottle of gin. University regulations outlawed alcoholic beverages on university property. State law also made it illegal for anyone under twenty-one to possess alcoholic beverages.

Because Overdahl appeared to be under twenty-one, Daugherty stopped him and asked for identification. Overdahl said he would have to go back to his room to get it. Daugherty arrested Overdahl and said he would have to accompany Overdahl back to the room. Overdahl's roommate, Neil Martin Chrisman, was in the room when Overdahl and Daugherty arrived. Chrisman, who was putting a small box into a medicine cabinet, became nervous.

Daugherty stood in the doorway while Overdahl went to get his identification. While in the doorway, Daugherty noticed seeds and a seashell pipe sitting on a desk. Without asking for permission or getting a search warrant, Daugherty entered the room to examine the seeds, which were marijuana seeds. Daugherty arrested Chrisman and read both gentlemen their rights, including the right to remain silent. He then asked whether they had any other drugs in the room. Chrisman handed Daugherty the small box he had been putting away. The box had three small plastic bags with marijuana and $112 in cash.

Daugherty radioed for a second officer to help him. Both officers said they would have to search the whole room, but that Chrisman and

Overdahl could force them to get a search warrant first. After discussing the matter in whispers, Chrisman and Overdahl allowed the officers to search the whole room without a warrant. Daugherty and his fellow officer found more marijuana and some LSD, another illegal drug.

Time to Pay the Piper

The State of Washington charged Chrisman with one count of possessing more than 40 grams of marijuana and one count of possessing LSD, both felonies. Before his trial, Chrisman made a motion to exclude the drug evidence that Daugherty had seized. Chrisman said the entire search was illegal under the Fourth Amendment because Daugherty entered the room to look at the seeds without a search warrant. The trial court denied Chrisman's motion and the jury convicted him on both counts.

The Washington Court of Appeals affirmed the convictions, but the Supreme Court of Washington reversed. It said although Overdahl was under arrest, Daugherty had no reason to enter the dormitory room. There was no indication that Overdahl was getting a weapon, destroying evidence, or trying to escape. Absent such problems, Daugherty was

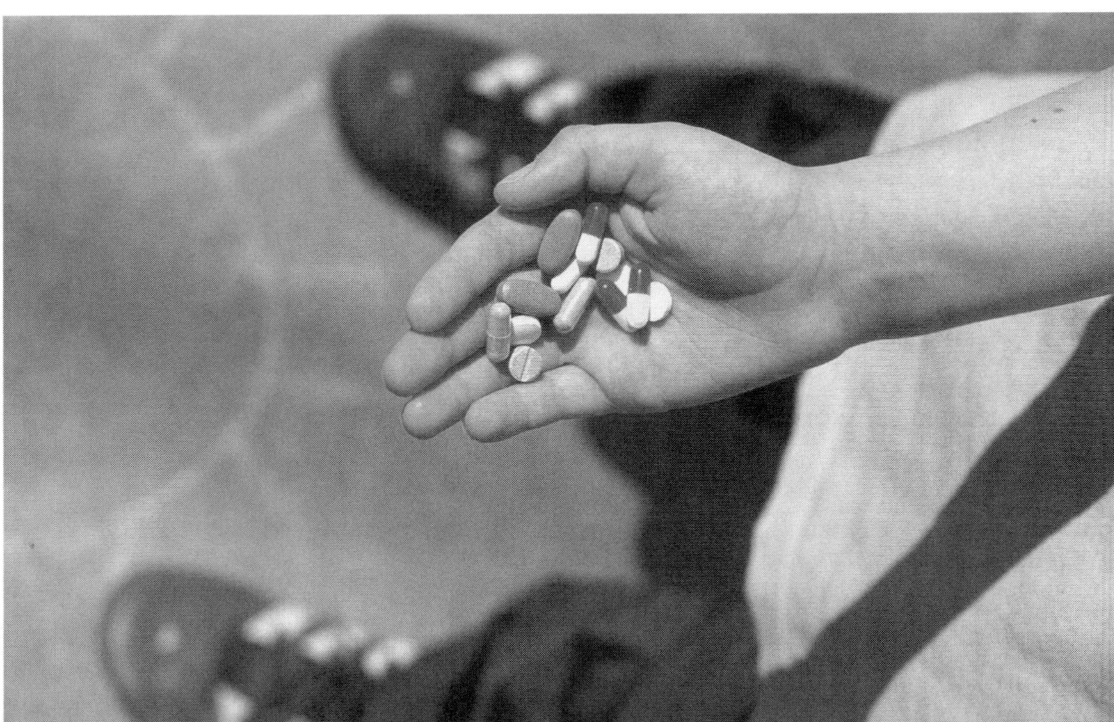

Illegal drugs can come in many shapes and forms, but the police are trained to recognize them all. AP/Wide World Photos.

DRUG SNIFFING DOGS

The U.S. Customs Service guards the United States's borders to prevent illegal drugs from getting into the country. In 1970, Customs faced increasing drug traffic with a shrinking staff. That year, a manager suggested that dogs could sniff for illegal drugs. Working with dog experts from the U.S. Air Force, Customs developed a program to train dogs for drug detection.

Customs selects dogs that are natural-born retrievers for drug detection programs. The dogs it uses most often are golden retrievers, Labrador retrievers, and German short-hair retrievers. Customs trains the dogs to detect a drug by linking drug detection with positive feedback. In effect, the dog learns that it will get praise if it finds a certain drug. Trainers must make sure that all items used during training smell like the drug to be found. Otherwise the dog might look for odors that are not associated with an illegal drug.

obliged to remain outside the room. Without a warrant, he was not allowed to enter to search for illegal drugs. Faced with having to dismiss the charges against Chrisman, Washington took the case to the U.S. Supreme Court.

The Plain View Rule

With a 6–3 decision, the Supreme Court reversed again and ruled in favor of Washington. Writing for the Court, Chief Justice Warren E. Burger applied the plain view doctrine to decide the case. He said Officer Daugherty legally arrested Overdahl for having alcohol. After arresting Overdahl, Daugherty was allowed to stay with him wherever Overdahl went. Police need to stay with arrested people to protect themselves, to protect evidence, and to prevent escape.

Because Daugherty was allowed to stay with Overdahl, he was allowed to go into Overdahl's room when Overdahl went to get his identification. Once in the room, the plain view doctrine allowed Daugherty to seize any evidence of a crime that he saw in plain view. After he seized the marijuana seeds, Chrisman voluntarily handed over three bags of marijuana and then gave Daugherty permission to search the entire room. The whole search was lawful under the Fourth Amendment.

Invasion of Privacy

Three justices dissented, which means they disagreed with the Court's decision. Justice Byron R. White wrote a dissenting opinion. Justice White disagreed that Daugherty was allowed to go into Overdahl's private home just because Daugherty had arrested him. White said Daugherty could go in only if necessary to protect himself or prevent escape. There was no indication that Overdahl was getting a weapon, and Daugherty was preventing escape by standing in the doorway.

White said that without a valid reason to enter the room, Daugherty was not allowed to enter just because he saw seeds that looked like marijuana seeds. Otherwise, police officers can snoop around people's homes looking inside for evidence of a crime. That would destroy the privacy the Fourth Amendment is supposed to protect.

Suggestions for further reading

Franklin, Paula A. *The Fourth Amendment.* Englewood Cliffs: Silver Burdett Press, 1991.

Jaffe, Jerome H., ed. *Encyclopedia of Drugs and Alcohol.* New York: Macmillan Library Reference USA, 1995.

Persico, Deborah A. *Mapp v. Ohio: Evidence and Search Warrants.* Enslow Publishers, Inc., 1997.

Shattuck, John H.F. *Rights of Privacy.* Skokie: National Textbook Co., 1977.

Wetterer, Charles M. *The Fourth Amendment: Search and Seizure.* Enslow Publishers, Inc., 1998.

Hudson v. Palmer
1984

Petitioner: Ted S. Hudson

Respondent: Russel Thomas Palmer. Jr.

Petitioner's Claim: That the Fourth Amendment does not apply to prison inmates.

Chief Lawyer for Petitioner: William G. Broaddus, Deputy Attorney General of Virginia

Chief Lawyer for Respondent: Deborah C. Wyatt

Justices for the Court: Warren E. Burger, Sandra Day O'Connor, Lewis F. Powell, Jr., William H. Rehnquist, Byron R. White

Justices Dissenting: Harry A. Blackmun, William J. Brennan, Jr., Thurgood Marshall, John Paul Stevens

Date of Decision: July 3, 1984

Decision: The Supreme Court said the Fourth Amendment does not apply to prison inmates.

Significance: After *Hudson,* prisoners who are treated unfairly during cell searches must sue under state law to recover their damages.

The Fourth Amendment of the U.S. Constitution protects privacy. It requires searches and seizures by the government to be reasonable. In most cases, law enforcement officers must get a warrant to search a house or other private place for evidence of a crime. To get a warrant,

SEARCH AND SEIZURE

officers must have probable cause, which means good reason to believe the place to be searched has evidence of a crime. Requiring law enforcement officers to get a warrant prevents them from harassing people for no good reason. In *Hudson v. Palmer,* the U.S. Supreme Court had to decide whether the Fourth Amendment protects prisoners in their jail cells.

Shakedown

Russel Thomas Palmer, Jr,. was an inmate at the Bland Correctional Center in Bland, Virginia. Palmer was serving sentences for forgery, grand larceny (theft), and bank robbery convictions. Ted S. Hudson was an officer at the correctional center.

On September 16, 1981, Hudson and a fellow officer searched Palmer's prison locker and cell. They were looking for contraband, which means illegal items such as weapons. During the search they found a ripped prison pillow case in a trash can near Palmer's bed. The prison filed a disciplinary charge against Palmer for destroying state property. Palmer was found guilty. The prison forced him to pay for the pillow case and entered a reprimand on his prison record.

Afterwards, Palmer filed a lawsuit against Hudson. He said Hudson searched his cell just to harass him. Palmer accused Hudson of destroying some of Palmer's personal property during the search. Palmer said the harassing and destructive search violated his constitutional rights. He sought to recover his damages under a federal statute for people whose constitutional rights are violated.

Without holding a trial, the federal court entered judgment in Hudson's favor. The court said Hudson did not violate any of Palmer's constitutional rights. It said if Hudson destroyed personal property, Palmer could file a property damage lawsuit under state law.

The federal court of appeals, however, reversed. It said Palmer had a constitutional right of privacy in his jail cell under the Fourth Amendment. If Hudson violated that privacy with a harassing and destructive search, Palmer could recover damages for violation of his constitutional rights. The trial court would have to hold a trial to determine if that is what happened. Wishing to avoid the trial, Hudson took the case to the U.S. Supreme Court.

ATTICA TORTURE CASE

On September 9, 1971, prison inmates at the Attica Correctional Facility near Buffalo, New York, rioted. They took control of an exercise yard and held forty-nine prison guards hostage. The prisoners rioted because of inhumane conditions at the facility. Prisoners had to work in a metal shop where the temperature was over 100 degrees Fahrenheit. They got only one shower and one roll of toilet tissue each month. Spanish-speaking prisoners could not get their mail, and Muslim prisoners demanded meat other than pork.

After four days of unsuccessful negotiations to end the crisis, New York governor Nelson Rockefeller ordered state troopers to take control of the situation. After bombing the yard with tear gas, troopers stormed in, shooting blindly through the gas. In the end, thirty-two inmates and eleven prison officers were dead.

After regaining control of the facility, prison guards punished and tortured the inmates. They forced inmates to strip and crawl over broken glass. They shoved a screwdriver up one man's rectum. They forced another man to lie naked for hours with a football under his chin. Guards told the inmate he would be killed or castrated if he dropped the ball.

In 1974, lawyers for the inmates filed a lawsuit seeking $100 million for injuries suffered during the torture. On February 16, 2000, a judge finally approved a settlement to end the case. Under the settlement, New York State will pay $8 million, to be divided among the inmates who were injured.

Struck Down

With a 5–4 decision, the Supreme Court ruled in favor of Hudson. Writing for the Court, Chief Justice Warren E. Burger began by saying prisoners do not give up all of their constitutional rights. For example, prisoners have First Amendment rights to freedom of speech and religion. The Eighth Amendment says prisoners cannot receive cruel and unusual punishments. In short, there is no "iron curtain" separating prisoners from all constitutional rights.

Prisoners, however, do give up some constitutional rights. Prisoners are confined because they have broken the law. Prisons need to maintain order and discipline among these criminals. Prison officials especially need to protect themselves, visitors, and other inmates from violence by the prisoners.

The ultimate question, then, was whether the Fourth Amendment protects prisoners from unreasonable searches and seizures. The Supreme Court said it does not. Because prison officials need to search jail cells for weapons, drugs, and other dangers, prisoners have no right of privacy in their cells. That means Hudson did not violate Palmer's Fourth Amendment rights by conducting a harassing and destructive search. As a prisoner, Palmer had no Fourth Amendment rights in his jail cell.

Chief Justice Warren emphasized that Palmer had other remedies available. If Hudson destroyed his property, Palmer could file a property damage suit under state law. He just could not recover for violation of constitutional rights.

Imprisoning Property Rights

Four justices dissented, which means they disagreed with the Court's decision. Justice John Paul Stevens wrote a dissenting opinion. He did not think the Fourth Amendment protects only privacy. He said it also protects property from unreasonable seizures. Surely it is unreasonable for a prison official to seize and destroy personal property such as personal letters, photographs of family members, a hobby kit, a diary, or a Bible. Justice Stevens said that for prisoners, holding onto such personal items marks "the difference between slavery and humanity."

Suggestions for further reading

Boyd, Herb. "Long Time Coming, but Welcome." *New York Amsterdam News,* January 6, 2000.

Chen, David W. "Judge Approves $8 Million Deal for Victims of Attica Torture." *Washington Post,* February 16, 2000.

Franklin, Paula A. *The Fourth Amendment.* Englewood Cliffs: Silver Burdett Press, 1991.

Haberman, Clyde. "Attica: Exorcising Demons, Redeeming the Deaths." *Washington Post,* January 9, 2000.

Persico, Deborah A. *Mapp v. Ohio: Evidence and Search Warrants.* Enslow Publishers, Inc., 1997.

Shattuck, John H.F. *Rights of Privacy.* Skokie: National Textbook Co., 1977.

Wetterer, Charles M. *The Fourth Amendment: Search and Seizure.* Enslow Publishers, Inc., 1998.

California v. Ciraolo 1986

Petitioner: State of California

Respondent: Dante Carlo Ciraolo

Petitioner's Claim: That the police did not violate the Fourth Amendment by searching Ciraolo's backyard from an airplane without a warrant.

Chief Lawyer for Petitioner: Laurence K. Sullivan, Deputy Attorney General of California

Chief Lawyer for Respondent: Marshall Warren Krause

Justices for the Court: Warren E. Burger, Sandra Day O'Connor, William H. Rehnquist, John Paul Stevens, Byron R. White

Justices Dissenting: Harry A. Blackmun, William J. Brennan, Jr., Thurgood Marshall, Lewis F. Powell, Jr.

Date of Decision: May 19, 1986

Decision: The Supreme Court said the search did not violate the Fourth Amendment.

Significance: With *Ciraolo,* the Supreme Court said people in enclosed yards cannot expect privacy from air traffic above.

A person's right to privacy is guaranteed under the Fourth Amendment of the U.S. Constitution. The Fourth Amendment requires any searches and seizures by the government to be reasonable. In most cases, law enforcement officers must get a warrant to search a house or other private place for evidence of a crime. To get a warrant, officers must have probable cause, or believe the place to be searched has evidence of a crime.

In *Oliver v. United States* (1984), the Supreme Court said people can expect privacy not just inside their houses, but in the curtilage too. The curtilage is the yard that a person encloses or considers to be private. Because the curtilage is private, law enforcement officers usually must have a warrant and probable cause to search it. In *California v. Ciraolo,* the U.S. Supreme Court had to decide whether the police violated the Fourth Amendment by searching a backyard from an airplane without a warrant.

Flying Low

Dante Carlo Ciraolo lived in Santa Clara, California. On September 2, 1982, Santa Clara police received an anonymous tip that Ciraolo was growing marijuana in his backyard. The police could not see the backyard from the ground because Ciraolo enclosed it with a six-foot outer fence and a ten-foot inner fence. Later that day, Officer Shutz hired a private plane to fly him and Officer Rodriguez over Ciraolo's backyard at an altitude of 1,000 feet.

Shutz and Rodriguez both were trained in marijuana identification. From the airplane they saw marijuana plants growing eight- to ten-feet high in a fifteen-by-twenty-five-foot plot. The officers photographed Ciraolo's backyard and those of surrounding neighbors. Six days later they used the photographs and their observations to get a warrant to search Ciraolo's entire house and yard. During the search they seized seventy-three marijuana plants.

Florida charged Ciraolo with cultivating, or growing, marijuana. At his trial, Ciraolo asked the court to suppress, or get rid of, the marijuana evidence against him. When the government violates the Fourth Amendment, it may not use the evidence it finds to convict the defendant. Ciraolo said Officers Shutz and Rodriguez violated the Fourth Amendment by searching his backyard from an airplane without a warrant.

The trial court denied Ciraolo's motion, so he pleaded guilty to the charge against him and appealed to the California Court of Appeals. That court reversed his conviction, saying the police violated the Fourth Amendment. Faced with having to dismiss its case against Ciraolo, California took the case to the U.S. Supreme Court.

FLORIDA V. RILEY

Three years after deciding *Ciraolo,* the Supreme Court decided another case involving aerial surveillance. In *Florida v. Riley,* police used a helicopter to hover 400 feet over a greenhouse that had two panels missing from its roof. From the helicopter they were able to see and photograph marijuana plants through the open panels. At his trial for possession of marijuana, Michael A. Riley asked the court to suppress the marijuana evidence because the police violated the Fourth Amendment.

The trial court ruled in Riley's favor, but the Supreme Court reversed. Relying on its decision in *Ciraolo,* the Court said Riley could not expect privacy from helicopters hovering above his greenhouse. In a dissenting opinion, Justice William J. Brennan, Jr., warned that the Court was creating a dictatorial society such as George Orwell described in his novel *1984:*

> **The black-mustachio'd face gazed down from every commanding corner. There was one on the house front immediately opposite. BIG BROTHER IS WATCHING YOU, the caption said. . . . In the far distance a helicopter skimmed down between the roofs, hovered for an instant like a bluebottle, and darted away again with a curving flight. It was the Police Patrol, swooping into people's windows.**

High Court Rules

With a 5–4 decision, the Supreme Court reversed and ruled in favor of California. Writing for the Court, Chief Justice Warren E. Burger said the Fourth Amendment only protects reasonable expectations of privacy. By putting a fence around his yard, Ciraolo had a reasonable expectation that nobody would invade his privacy from the ground.

Ciraolo did not, however, cover his yard from the airspace above. It was unreasonable for Ciraolo to think that nobody would see his yard from airplanes and other flying machines. After all, public airplanes were allowed to fly over Ciraolo's yard at the same height flown by Officers Shutz and Rodriguez. Quoting from a prior Supreme Court case, Burger said, "What a person knowingly exposes to the public, even in his own home or office, is not a subject of Fourth Amendment protection."

Because Ciraolo could not expect privacy from above his backyard, the police did not need a warrant to search from the airplane. "The Fourth Amendment simply does not require the police traveling in the public airways at this altitude to obtain a warrant to observe what is visible to the naked eye."

Low Down Dirty Shame

Four justices dissented, which means they disagreed with the Court's decision. Justice Lewis F. Powell, Jr., wrote a dissenting opinion. He said Ciraolo did all he needed to do to protect privacy in his backyard by erecting fences. The Court's decision called Ciraolo's privacy expectation reasonable on the ground but unreasonable from the air. That meant police could not use a ladder to see into Ciraolo's yard, but they could use an airplane.

Powell said that in reality, public and commercial airplane passengers cannot see backyards very well from the air. That means people do not expect invasions of privacy from airplanes. The police were able to see Ciraolo's backyard only because they hired a plane that positioned them to see the marijuana plot. Letting them do that without a search warrant was unfaithful to privacy, which is what the Fourth Amendment is supposed to protect.

Suggestions for further reading

Franklin, Paula A. *The Fourth Amendment.* Englewood Cliffs: Silver Burdett Press, 1991.

Mikula, Mark, and L. Mpho Mabunda, eds. *Great American Court Cases.* Detroit: The Gale Group, 1999.

Persico, Deborah A. *Mapp v. Ohio: Evidence and Search Warrants.* Enslow Publishers, Inc., 1997.

Shattuck, John H.F. *Rights of Privacy.* Skokie: National Textbook Co., 1977.

Wetterer, Charles M. *The Fourth Amendment: Search and Seizure.* Enslow Publishers, Inc., 1998.

General Bibliography

Aaseng, Nathan. *Great Justices of the Supreme Court.* Minneapolis: Oliver Press, 1992.

Arthur, Joe. *Justice for All: The Story of Thurgood Marshall.* New York: Yearling Books, 1995.

Bains, Rae. *Thurgood Marshall: Fight for Justice.* Mahwah, NJ: Troll Assoc., 1993.

Bernstein, Richard, and Jerome Agel. *Into the Third Century: The Supreme Court.* New York: Walker & Co., 1989.

Cornelius, Kay. *The Supreme Court.* New York: Chelsea House Publishers, 2000.

Coy, Harold. *The Supreme Court.* New York: Franklin Watts, 1981.

Deegan, Paul J. *Anthony Kennedy.* Edina, MN: Abdo & Daughters, 1992.

——. *Antonin Scalia.* Edina, MN: Abdo & Daughters, 1992.

——. *Chief Justice William Rehnquist.* Edina, MN: Abdo & Daughters, 1992.

——. *David Souter.* Edina, MN: Abdo & Daughters, 1992.

——. *Supreme Court Book.* Edina, MN: Abdo & Daughters, 1992.

Deegan, Paul J., and Bob Italia. *John Paul Stevens.* Edina, MN: Abdo & Daughters, 1992.

——. *Sandra Day O'Connor.* Edina, MN: Abdo & Daughters, 1992.

Feinburg, Barbara Silberdick. *Constitutional Amendments.* Twenty First Century Books, 1996.

General Bibliography

Friedman, Leon. *The Supreme Court.* New York: Chelsea House, 1987.

Friedman, Leon, and Fred L. Israel. *The Justices of the United States Supreme Court: Their Lives and Major Opinions.* New York: Chelsea House Publishers, 1995.

Goldish, Meish. *Our Supreme Court.* Brookfield: Millbrook Press, 1994.

Harrison, Michael. *Landmark Decisions of the United States Supreme Court.* San Diego: Excellent Books, 1991.

Health, David. *The Supreme Court of the United States.* New York: Capstone, 1998.

Holland, Gini. *Sandra Day O'Connor.* Austin: Raintree/Steck Vaughn, 1997.

Irons, Peter H. *The Courage of Their Convictions: Sixteen Americans Who Fought Their Way to the Supreme Court.* New York: Penguin, 1990.

Italia, Bob, and Paul Deegan. *Ruth Bader Ginsburg.* Edina, MN: Abdo & Daughters, 1994.

Kallen, Stuart A. *Thurgood Marshall.* Edina, MN: Abdo & Daughters, 1993.

Kent, Deborah. *Thurgood Marshall and the Supreme Court.* Chicago: Children's Press, 1997.

Krull, Kathleen. *A Kids' Guide to America's Bill of Rights: Curfews, Censorship, and the 100-Pound Giant.* New York: Avon Books, 1999.

Macht, Norman L., Christopher E. Henry, and Nathan I. Huggins. *Clarence Thomas: Supreme Court Justice.* New York: Chelsea House Publishers, 1995.

Peterson, Helen Stone. *The Supreme Court in America's Story.* Scarsdale: Garrard Pub. Co., 1976.

Prentzas, G.S. *Thurgood Marshall.* New York: Chelsea House Publishers, 1994.

Prolman, Marilyn. *The Constitution.* Chicago: Children's Press, Inc., 1995.

Reef, Catherine. *The Supreme Court.* New York: Dillon Press, 1994.

Rierden, Anne B. *Reshaping the Supreme Court: New Justices, New Directions.* New York: Franklin Watts, 1988.

Sagarin, Mary. *Equal Justice under Law: Our Court System and How It Works.* New York: Lothrop, Lee & Shephard Co., Inc., 1966.

Stein, R. Conrad. *The Powers of the Supreme Court.* Chicago: Children's Press, Inc., 1995.

——. *The Bill of Rights.* Chicago: Children's Press, Inc., 1992.

White, G. Edward. *Oliver Wendell Holmes: Sage of the Supreme Court.* New York: Oxford University Press Children's Books, 2000.

Justices of the Supreme Court

The Justices are listed by year of appointment and in what way they served the court—as an Associate Justice or Chief Justice.

John Jay (Chief: 1789 - 1795)

John Rutledge (Associate: 1790 - 1791, Chief: 1795 - 1795)

William Cushing (Associate: 1790 - 1810)

James Wilson (Associate: 1789 - 1798)

John Blair (Associate: 1790 - 1795)

James Iredell (Associate: 1790 - 1799)

Thomas Johnson (Associate: 1792 - 1793)

William Paterson (Associate: 1793 - 1806)

Samuel Chase (Associate: 1796 - 1811)

Oliver Ellsworth (Chief: 1796 - 1800)

Bushrod Washington (Associate: 1799 - 1829)

Alfred Moore (Associate: 1800 - 1804)

John Marshall (Chief: 1801 - 1835)

William Johnson (Associate: 1804 - 1834)

Brockholst Livingston (Associate: 1807 - 1823)

Thomas Todd (Associate: 1807 - 1826)

Gabriel Duvall (Associate: 1811 - 1835)
Joseph Story (Associate: 1812 - 1845)
Smith Thompson (Associate: 1823 - 1843)
Robert Trimble (Associate: 1826 - 1828)
John McLean (Associate: 1830 - 1861)
Henry Baldwin (Associate: 1830 - 1844)
James M. Wayne (Associate: 1835 - 1867)
Roger B. Taney (Chief: 1836 - 1864)
Philip P. Barbour (Associate: 1836 - 1841)
John Catron (Associate: 1837 - 1865)
John McKinley (Associate: 1838 - 1852)
Peter V. Daniel (Associate: 1842 - 1860)
Samuel Nelson (Associate: 1845 - 1872)
Levi Woodbury (Associate: 1845 - 1851)
Robert C. Grier (Associate: 1846 - 1870)
Benjamin R. Curtis (Associate: 1851 - 1857)
John A. Campbell (Associate: 1853 - 1861)
Nathan Clifford (Associate: 1858 - 1881)
Noah Swayne (Associate: 1862 - 1881)
Samuel F. Miller (Associate: 1862 - 1890)
David Davis (Associate: 1862 - 1877)
Stephen J. Field (Associate: 1863 - 1897)
Salmon P. Chase (Chief: 1864 - 1873)
William Strong (Associate: 1870 - 1880)
Joseph P. Bradley (Associate: 1870 - 1892)
Ward Hunt (Associate: 1873 - 1882)
Morrison R. Waite (Chief: 1874 - 1888)
John M. Harlan (Associate: 1877 - 1911)
William B. Woods (Associate: 1881 - 1887)
Stanley Matthews (Associate: 1881 - 1889)
Horace Gray (Associate: 1882 - 1902)

Samuel Blatchford (Associate: 1882 - 1893)
Lucius Q.C. Lamar (Associate: 1888 - 1893)
Melville W. Fuller (Chief: 1888 - 1910)
David J. Brewer (Associate: 1890 - 1910)
Henry B. Brown (Associate: 1891 - 1906)
George Shiras, Jr. (Associate: 1892 - 1903)
Howell E. Jackson (Associate: 1893 - 1895)
Edward D. White (Associate: 1894 - 1910, Chief: 1910 - 1921)
Rufus Peckham (Associate: 1896 - 1909)
Joseph McKenna (Associate: 1898 - 1925)
Oliver W. Holmes, Jr. (Associate: 1902 - 1932)
William R. Day (Associate: 1903 - 1922)
William H. Moody (Associate: 1906 - 1910)
Horace H. Lurton (Associate: 1910 - 1914)
Charles E. Hughes (Associate: 1910 - 1916, Chief: 1930 - 1941)
Willis Van Devanter (Associate: 1911 - 1937)
Joseph R. Lamar (Associate: 1911 - 1916)
Mahlon Pitney (Associate: 1912 - 1922)
James C. McReynolds (Associate: 1914 - 1941)
Louis D. Brandeis (Associate: 1916 - 1939)
John H. Clarke (Associate: 1916 - 1922)
William Howard Taft (Chief: 1921 - 1930)
George Sutherland (Associate: 1922 - 1938)
Pierce Butler (Associate: 1923 - 1939)
Edward T. Sanford (Associate: 1923 - 1930)
Harlan Fiske Stone (Associate: 1925 - 1941, Chief: 1941 - 1946)
Owen J. Roberts (Associate: 1930 - 1945)
Benjamin N. Cardozo (Associate: 1932 - 1938)
Hugo L. Black (Associate: 1937 - 1971)
Stanley Reed (Associate: 1938 - 1957)
Felix Frankfurter (Associate: 1939 - 1962)

Justices of the Supreme Court

William O. Douglas (Associate: 1939 - 1975)

Frank Murphy (Associate: 1940 - 1949)

James F. Byrnes (Associate: 1941 - 1942)

Robert H. Jackson (Associate: 1941 - 1954)

Wiley B. Rutledge (Associate: 1943 - 1949)

Harold Burton (Associate: 1945 - 1958)

Fred M. Vinson (Chief: 1946 - 1953)

Tom C. Clark (Associate: 1949 - 1967)

Sherman Minton (Associate: 1949 - 1956)

Earl Warren (Chief: 1953 - 1969)

John M. Harlan (Associate: 1955 - 1971)

William J. Brennan (Associate: 1956 - 1990)

Charles E. Whittaker (Associate: 1957 - 1962)

Potter Stewart (Associate: 1959 - 1981)

Byron R. White (Associate: 1962 - 1993)

Arthur J. Goldberg (Associate: 1962 - 1965)

Abe Fortas (Associate: 1965 - 1969)

Thurgood Marshall (Associate: 1967 - 1991)

Warren E. Burger (Chief: 1969 - 1986)

Harry A. Blackmun (Associate: 1970 - 1994)

Lewis F. Powell, Jr. (Associate: 1972 - 1987)

William H. Rehnquist (Associate: 1972 - 1986, Chief: 1986 -)

John Paul Stevens (Associate: 1975 -)

Sandra Day O'Connor (Associate: 1981 -)

Antonin Scalia (Associate: 1986 -)

Anthony Kennedy (Associate: 1988 -)

David H. Souter (Associate: 1990 -)

Clarence Thomas (Associate: 1991 -)

Ruth Bader Ginsburg (Associate: 1993 -)

Stephen Gerald Breyer (Associate: 1994 -)

The Constitution of the United States

On February 21, 1787, Congress adopted the resolution that a convention of delegates should meet to revise the Articles of Confederation. The Constitution was signed and submitted to Congress on September 17 of that year. Congress then sent it to the states for ratification; the last state to sign, Rhode Island, did so May 29, 1790.

We The People of the United States, in Order to form a more perfect Union, establish Justice, insure domestic Tranquility, provide for the common defence, promote the general Welfare, and secure the Blessings of Liberty to ourselves and our Posterity, do ordain and establish this Constitution for the United States of America.

Art. I

Sec. 1. All legislative Powers herein granted shall be vested in a Congress of the United States, which shall consist of a Senate and House of Representatives.

Sec. 2. The House of Representatives shall be composed of Members chosen every second Year by the People of the several States, and the Electors in each State shall have the Qualifications requisite for Electors of the most numerous Branch of the State Legislature.

No Person shall be a Representative who shall not have attained to the Age of twenty five Years, and been seven Years a Citizen of the

United States, and who shall not, when elected, be an Inhabitant of that State in which he shall be chosen.

Representatives and direct Taxes shall be apportioned among the several States which may be included within this Union, according to their respective Numbers, which shall be determined by adding to the whole Number of free Persons, including those bound to Service for a Term of Years, and excluding Indians not taxed, three fifths of all other Persons. The actual Enumeration shall be made within three Years after the first Meeting of the Congress of the United States, and within every subsequent Term of ten Years, in such Manner as they shall by Law direct. The Number of Representatives shall not exceed one for every thirty Thousand, but each State shall have at Least one Representative; and until such enumeration shall be made, the State of New Hampshire shall be entitled to chuse three, Massachusetts eight, Rhode-Island and Providence Plantations one, Connecticut five, New-York six, New Jersey four, Pennsylvania eight, Delaware one, Maryland six, Virginia ten, North Carolina five, South Carolina five, and Georgia three.

When vacancies happen in the Representation from any State, the Executive Authority thereof shall issue Writs of Election to fill such Vacancies.

The House of Representatives shall chuse their Speaker and other Officers; and shall have the sole Power of Impeachment.

Sec. 3. The Senate of the United States shall be composed of two Senators from each State, chosen by the Legislature thereof, for six Years; and each Senator shall have one Vote.

Immediately after they shall be assembled in Consequence of the first Election, they shall be divided as equally as may be into three Classes. The Seats of the Senators of the first Class shall be vacated at the Expiration of the second Year, of the second Class at the Expiration of the fourth Year, and of the third Class at the Expiration of the sixth Year, so that one third may be chosen every second Year; and if Vacancies happen by Resignation, or otherwise, during the Recess of the Legislature of any State, the Executive thereof may make temporary Appointments until the next Meeting of the Legislature, which shall then fill such Vacancies.

No Person shall be a Senator who shall not have attained to the Age of thirty Years, and been nine Years a Citizens of the United States, and who shall not, when elected, be an Inhabitant of that State for which he shall be chosen.

The Vice President of the United States shall be President of the Senate, but shall have no Vote, unless they be equally divided.

The Senate shall chuse their other Officers, and also a President protempore, in the Absence of the Vice President, or when he shall exercise the Office of President of the United States.

The Senate shall have the sole Power to try all Impeachments. When sitting for that Purpose, they shall be on Oath or Affirmation. When the President of the United States is tried, the Chief Justice shall preside: And no Person shall be convicted without the Concurrence of two thirds of the Members present.

Judgment in Cases of Impeachment shall not extend further than to removal from Office, and disqualification to hold and enjoy any Office of honor, Trustor Profit under the United States: but the Party convicted shall nevertheless be liable and subject to Indictment, Trial, Judgment and Punishment, according to Law.

Sec. 4. The Times, Places and Manner of holding Elections for Senators and Representatives, shall be prescribed in each State by the Legislature thereof; but the Congress may at any time by Law make or alter such Regulations, except as to the Places of chusing Senators.

The Congress shall assemble at least once in every Year, and such Meeting shall be on the first Monday in December, unless they shall by Law appoint a different Day.

Sec. 5. Each House shall be the Judge of the Elections, Returns and Qualifications of its own Members, and a Majority of each shall constitute a Quorum to do Business; but a smaller Number may adjourn from day to day, and may be authorized to compel the Attendance of absent Members, in such Manner, and under such Penalties as each House may provide.

Each House may determine the Rules of its Proceedings, punish its Members for disorderly Behaviour, and, with the Concurrence of two thirds, expel a Member.

Each House shall keep a Journal of its Proceedings, and from time to time publish the same, excepting such Parts as may in their Judgment require Secrecy; and the Yeas and Nays of the Members of either House on any question shall, at the Desire of one fifth of those Present, be entered on the Journal.

Neither House, during the Session of Congress, shall, without the Consent of the other, adjourn for more than three days, nor to any other Place than that in which the two Houses shall be sitting.

Sec. 6. The Senators and Representatives shall receive a Compensation for their Services, to be ascertained by Law, and paid out of the Treasury of the United States. They shall in all Cases, except Treason, Felony and Breach of the Peace, be privileged from Arrest during their Attendance at the Session of their respective Houses, and in going to and returning from the same; and for any Speech or Debate in either House, they shall not be questioned in any other Place.

No Senator or Representative shall, during the Time for which he was elected, be appointed to any civil Office under the Authority of the United States which shall have been created, or the Emoluments whereof shall have been encreased during such time; and no Person holding any Office under the United States, shall be a Member of either House during his Continuance in Office.

Sec. 7. All Bills for raising Revenue shall originate in the House of Representatives; but the Senate may propose or concur with Amendments as another Bills.

Every Bill which shall have passed the House of Representatives and the Senate, shall, before it become a Law, be presented to the President of the United States; If he approve he shall sign it, but if not he shall return it, with his Objections to that House in which it shall have originated, who shall enter the Objections at large on their Journal, and proceed to reconsider it. If after such Reconsideration two thirds of that House shall agree tapes the Bill, it shall be sent, together with the Objections, to the other House, by which it shall likewise be reconsidered, and if approved by two-thirds of that House, it shall become a Law. But in all such Cases the Votes of both Houses shall be determined by yeas and Nays, and the Names of the Persons voting for and against the Bill shall be entered on the Journal of each House respectively. If any Bill shall not be returned by the President within ten Days (Sundays excepted) after it shall have been presented to him, the Same shall be a Law, in like Manner as if he had signed it, unless the Congress by their Adjournment prevent its Return, in which Case it shall note a Law.

Every Order, Resolution, or Vote to which the Concurrence of the Senate and House of Representatives may be necessary (except on a question of Adjournment) shall be presented to the President of the United States; and before the Same shall take Effect, shall be approved by him, or being disapproved by him, shall be repassed by two thirds of the Senate and House of Representatives, according to the Rules and Limitations prescribed in the Case of a Bill.

Sec. 8. The Congress shall have Power To lay and collect Taxes, Duties, Imposts and Excises, to pay the Debts and provide for the common Defence and general Welfare of the United States; but all Duties, Imposts and Excises shall be uniform throughout the United States;

To borrow Money on the credit of the United States;

To regulate Commerce with foreign Nations, and among the several States, and with the Indian Tribes;

To establish an uniform Rule of Naturalization, and uniform Laws on the subject of Bankruptcies throughout the United States;

To coin Money, regulate the Value thereof, and of foreign Coin, and fix the Standard of Weights and Measures;

To provide for the Punishment of counterfeiting the Securities and current Coin of the United States;

To establish Post Offices and post Roads;

To promote the Progress of Science and useful Arts, by securing for limited Times to Authors and Inventors the exclusive Right to their respective Writings and Discoveries;

To constitute Tribunals inferior to the supreme Court;

To define and punish Piracies and Felonies committed on the high Seas, and Offences against the Law of Nations;

To declare War, grant Letters of Marque and Reprisal, and make Rules concerning Captures on Land and Water;

To raise and support Armies, but no Appropriation of Money to that Use shall be for a longer Term than two Years;

To provide and maintain a Navy;

To make Rules for the Government and Regulation of the land and naval forces;

To provide for calling forth the Militia to execute the Laws of the Union, suppress Insurrections and repel Invasions;

To provide for organizing, arming, and disciplining, the Militia, and for governing such Part of them as may be employed in the Service of the United States, reserving to the States respectively, the Appointment of the Officers, and the Authority of training the Militia according to the discipline prescribed by Congress;

To exercise exclusive Legislation in all Cases whatsoever, over such District (not exceeding ten Miles square) as may, by Cession of particular States, and the Acceptance of Congress, become the Seat of the Government of the United States, and to exercise like Authority over all Places purchased by the Consent of the Legislature of the State in which the Same shall be, for the Erection of Forts, Magazines, Arsenals, dock-Yards, and other needful Buildings;—And

To make all Laws which shall be necessary and proper for carrying into Execution the foregoing Powers, and all other Powers vested by this Constitution in the Government of the United States, or in any Department or Officer thereof.

Sec. 9. The Migration or Importation of such Persons as any of the States now existing shall think proper to admit, shall not be prohibited by the Congress prior to the Year one thousand eight hundred and eight, but a Tax or daytime be imposed on such Importation, not exceeding ten dollars for each Person.

The Privilege of the Writ of Habeas Corpus shall not be suspended, unless when in Cases of Rebellion or Invasion the public Safety may require it.

No Bill of Attainder or ex post facto Law shall be passed.

No Capitation, or other direct, Tax shall be laid, unless in Proportionate the Census or Enumeration herein before directed to be taken.

No Tax or Duty shall be laid on Articles exported from any State.

No Preference shall be given by any Regulation of Commerce or Revenue to the Ports of one State over those of another: nor shall Vessels bound to, or from, one State, be obliged to enter, clear, or pay Duties in another.

No Money shall be drawn from the Treasury, but in Consequence of Appropriations made by Law; and a regular Statement and Account of the Receipts and Expenditures of all public Money shall be published from time to time.

No Title of Nobility shall be granted by the United States: And no Person holding any Office of Profit or Trust under them, shall, without the Consent of the Congress, accept of any present, Emolument, Office, or Title, of any kind whatever, from any King, Prince or foreign State.

Sec. 10. No State shall enter into any Treaty, Alliance, or Confederation; grant Letters of Marque and Reprisal; coin Money; emit

Bills of Credit; make any Thing but gold and silver Coin a Tender in Payment of Debts; pass any Bill of Attainder, ex post facto Law, or Law impairing the Obligation of Contracts, or grant any Title of Nobility.

No State shall, without the Consent of the Congress, lay any Impostor Duties on Imports or Exports, except what may be absolutely necessary for executing it's inspection Laws: and the net Produce of all Duties and Imposts, laid by any State on Imports or Exports, shall be for the Use of the Treasury of the United States; and all such Laws shall be subject to the Revision and Controul of the Congress.

No State shall, without the Consent of Congress, lay any Duty of Tonnage, keep Troops, or Ships of War in time of Peace, enter into any Agreement or Compact with another State, or with a foreign Power, or engage in War, unless actually invaded, or in such imminent Danger as will not admit of delay.

Art. II

Sec. 1. The executive Power shall be vested in a President of the United States of America. He shall hold his Office during the Term of four Years, and, together with the Vice President, chosen for the same Term, be elected, as follows.

Each State shall appoint, in such Manner as the Legislature thereof may direct, a Number of Electors, equal to the whole Number of Senators and Representatives to which the State may be entitled in the Congress: but no Senator or Representative, or Person holding an Office of Trust or Profit under the United States, shall be appointed an Elector.

The Electors shall meet in their respective States, and vote by Ballot for two Persons, of whom one at least shall not be an Inhabitant of the same State with themselves. And they shall make a List of all the Persons voted for, and of the Number of Votes for each; which List they shall sign and certify, and transmit sealed to the Seat of the Government of the United States, directed to the President of the Senate. The President of the Senate shall, in the Presence of the Senate and House of Representatives, open all the Certificates, and the Votes shall then be counted. The Person having the greatest Number of Votes shall be the President, if such Number be a Majority of the whole Number of Electors appointed; and if there be more than one who have such Majority, and have an equal Number of Votes, then the House of Representatives shall immediately chuse by Ballot one of them for

President; and if no personae a Majority, then from the five highest on the List the said House shallon like Manner chuse the President. But in chusing the President, the Votes shall be taken by States, the Representation from each State having one Vote; A quorum for this Purpose shall consist of a Member or Members from two thirds of the States, and a Majority of all the States shall be necessary to a Choice. In every Case, after the Choice of the President, the Person having the greatest Number of Votes of the Electors shall be the Vice President. But if there should remain two or more who have equal Votes, the Senate shall chuse frothed by Ballot the Vice President.

The Congress may determine the Time of chusing the Electors, and the day on which they shall give their Votes; which Day shall be the same throughout the United States.

No Person except a natural born Citizen, or a Citizen of the United States, at the time of the Adoption of this Constitution, shall be eligible the Office of President; neither shall any Person be eligible to that Office who shall not have attained to the Age of thirty five Years, and been fourteen Years a Resident within the United States.

In Case of the Removal of the President from Office, or of his Death, Resignation, or Inability to discharge the Powers and Duties of the said Office, the Same shall devolve on the Vice President, and the Congress may by Law provide for the Case of Removal, Death, Resignation or Inability, both of the President and Vice President, declaring what Officer shall then act as President, and such Officer shall act accordingly, until the Disability be removed, or a President shall be elected.

The President shall, at stated Times, receive for his Services, a Compensation, which shall neither be encreased nor diminished during the Period for which he shall have been elected, and he shall not receive within that Period another Emolument from the United States, or any of them.

Before he enter on the Execution of his Office, he shall take the following Oath or Affirmation:—"I do solemnly swear (or affirm) that I will faithfully execute the Office of President of the United States, and will to the bestow my Ability, preserve, protect and defend the Constitution of the United States."

Sec. 2. The President shall be Commander in Chief of the Army and Navy of the United States, and of the Militia of the several States, when called into the actual Service of the United States; he may require the Opinion, in writing, of the principal Officer in each of the executive

Departments, upon any Subject relating to the Duties of their respective Offices, and he shall have Power to grant Reprieves and Pardons for Offences against the United States, except in Cases of Impeachment.

He shall have Power, by and with the Advice and Consent of the Senate, to make Treaties, provided two thirds of the Senators present concur; Andie shall nominate, and by and with the Advice and Consent of the Senate, shall appoint Ambassadors, other public Ministers and Consuls, Judges of the supreme Court, and all other Officers of the United States, whose Appointments are not herein otherwise provided for, and which shall be established by Law: but the Congress may by Law vest the Appointment of such inferior Officers, as they think proper, in the President alone, in the Courts of Law, or in the Heads of Departments.

The President shall have Power to fill up all Vacancies that may happen during the Recess of the Senate, by granting Commissions which shall expire at the End of their next Session.

Sec. 3. He shall from time to time give to the Congress Information of the State of the Union, and recommend to their Consideration such Measures as he shall judge necessary and expedient; he may, on extraordinary Occasions, convene both Houses, or either of them, and in Case of Disagreement between them, with Respect to the Time of Adjournment, he may adjourn them to such Time as he shall think proper; he shall receive Ambassadors and other public Ministers; he shall take Care that the Laws be faithfully executed, and shall Commission all the Officers of the United States.

Sec. 4. The President, Vice President and all civil Officers of the United States, shall be removed from Office on Impeachment for, and Conviction of, Treason, Bribery, or other high Crimes and Misdemeanors.

Art. III

Sec. 1. The judicial Power of the United States, shall be vested none supreme Court, and in such inferior Courts as the Congress may from time to time ordain and establish. The Judges, both of the supreme and inferior Courts, shall hold their Offices during good Behaviour, and shall, at stated Times, receive for their Services, a Compensation, which shall not be diminished during their Continuance in Office.

Sec. 2. The judicial Power shall extend to all Cases, in Law and Equity, arising under this Constitution, the Laws of the United States,

and Treaties made, or which shall be made, under their Authority;—to all Cases affecting Ambassadors, other public Ministers and Consuls;—to all Cases of admiralty and maritime Jurisdiction;—to Controversies to which the United States shall be a Party;—to Controversies between two or more States;—between a State and Citizens of another State;—between Citizens of different States,—between Citizens of the same State claiming Lands under Grandson different States, and between a State, or the Citizens thereof, and foreign States, Citizens or Subjects.

In all Cases affecting Ambassadors, other public Ministers and Consuls, and those in which a State shall be Party, the supreme Court shall have original Jurisdiction. In all the other Cases before mentioned, the supreme Court shall have appellate Jurisdiction, both as to Law and Fact, with such Exceptions, and under such Regulations as the Congress shall make.

The Trial of all Crimes, except in Cases of Impeachment, shall be by Jury; and such Trial shall be held in the State where the said Crimes shall have been committed; but when not committed within any State, the Trial shall be at such Place or Places as the Congress may by Law have directed.

Sec. 3. Treason against the United States, shall consist only in levying War against them, or in adhering to their Enemies, giving them Aid and Comfort. No Person shall be convicted of Treason unless on the Testimony of two Witnesses to the same overt Act, or on Confession in open Court.

The Congress shall have Power to declare the Punishment of Treason, but no Attainder of Treason shall work Corruption of Blood, or Forfeiture except during the Life of the Person attainted.

Art. IV

Sec. 1. Full Faith and Credit shall be given in each State to the Public Acts, Records, and judicial Proceedings of every other State. And the Congressman by general Laws prescribe the Manner in which such Acts, Records and Proceedings shall be proved, and the Effect thereof.

Sec. 2. The Citizens of each State shall be entitled to all Privileges and Immunities of Citizens in the several States.

A Person charged in any State with Treason, Felony, or other Crime, who shall flee from Justice, and be found in another State, shall on

Demand of the executive Authority of the State from which he fled, be delivered up, to be removed to the State having Jurisdiction of the Crime.

No Person held to Service or Labour in one State, under the Laws thereof, escaping into another, shall, in Consequence of any Law or Regulation therein, be discharged from such Service or Labour, but shall be delivered up on Claim of the Party to whom such Service or Labour may be due.

Sec. 3. New States may be admitted by the Congress into this Union; but no new States shall be formed or erected within the Jurisdiction of another State; nor any State be formed by the Junction of two or more States, or Parts of States, without the Consent of the Legislatures of the States concerned as well as of the Congress.

The Congress shall have Power to dispose of and make all needful Rules and Regulations respecting the Territory or other Property belonging to the United States; and nothing in this Constitution shall be so construed as to Prejudice any Claims of the United States, or of any particular State.

Sec. 4. The United States shall guarantee to every State in this Union a Republican Form of Government, and shall protect each of them against Invasion; and on Application of the Legislature, or of the Executive (when the Legislature cannot be convened) against domestic Violence.

Art. V

The Congress, whenever two thirds of both Houses shall deem it necessary, shall propose Amendments to this Constitution, or, on the Application of the Legislatures of two thirds of the several States, shall call a Convention for proposing Amendments, which, in either Case, shall be valid to all Intents and Purposes, as Part of this Constitution, when ratified by the Legislatures of three fourths of the several States, or by Conventions in three fourths thereof, as the one or the other Mode of Ratification may be proposed by the Congress; Provided that no Amendment which may be made prior to the Year One thousand eight hundred and eight shall in any Manner affect the first and fourth Clauses in the Ninth Section of the first Article; and that no State, without its Consent, shall be deprived of it's equal Suffrage in the Senate.

Art. VI

All Debts contracted and Engagements entered into, before the Adoption of this Constitution, shall be as valid against the United States under this Constitution, as under the Confederation.

This Constitution, and the Laws of the United States which shall be made in Pursuance thereof; and all Treaties made, or which shall be made, under the Authority of the United States, shall be the supreme Law of the Land; and the Judges in every State shall be bound thereby, any Thing in the Constitution or Laws of any State to the Contrary notwithstanding.

The Senators and Representatives before mentioned, and the Members of the several State Legislatures, and all executive and judicial Officers, both of the United States and of the several States, shall be bound by Oath or Affirmation, to support this Constitution; but no religious Test shall ever be required as a Qualification to any Office or public Trust under the United States.

Art. VII

The Ratification of the Conventions of nine States, shall be sufficient for the Establishment of this Constitution between the States so ratifying the Same.

The Bill of Rights

Articles in addition to, and Amendment of the Constitution of the United States of America, proposed by Congress, and ratified by the Legislatures of the several States, pursuant to the fifth Article of the original Constitution.

[The first ten amendments went into effect November 3, 1791.]

Art. I

Congress shall make no law respecting an establishment of religion, or prohibiting the free exercise thereof; or abridging the freedom of speech, or of the press; or the right of the people peaceably to assemble, and to petition the government for a redress of grievances.

Art. II

A well regulated Militia, being necessary to the security of a free State, the right of the people to keep and bear Arms, shall not be infringed.

Art. III

No Soldier shall, in time of peace be quartered in any house, without the consent of the Owner, nor in time of war, but in a manner to be prescribed by law.

Art. IV

The right of the people to be secure in their persons, houses, papers, and effects, against unreasonable searches and seizures, shall not be violated, and no Warrants shall issue, but upon probable cause, supported by Oath or affirmation, and particularly describing the place to be searched, and the persons or things to be seized.

Art. V

No person shall be held to answer for a capital, or otherwise infamous crime, unless on a presentment or indictment of a Grand Jury, except in cases arising in the land or naval forces, or in the Militia, when in actual service in time of War or public danger; nor shall any person be subject for the same offence to be twice put in jeopardy of life or limb; nor shall be compelled in any criminal case to be a witness against himself, nor be deprived of life, liberty, or property, without due process of law; nor shall private property be taken for public use, without just compensation.

Art. VI

In all criminal prosecutions, the accused shall enjoy the right to a speedy and public trial, by an impartial jury of the State and district wherein the crime shall have been committed, which district shall have been previously ascertained by law, and to be informed of the nature and cause of the accusation; to be confronted with the witnesses against him; to have compulsory process for obtaining witnesses in his favor, and to have the Assistance of Counsel for his defence.

Art. VII

In Suits at common law, where the value in controversy shall exceed twenty dollars, the right of trial by jury shall be preserved, and no fact tried by a jury, shall be otherwise re-examined in any Court of the United States, than according to the rules of the common law.

Art. VIII

Excessive bail shall not be required, nor excessive fines imposed, nor cruel and unusual punishments inflicted.

Art. IX

The enumeration in the Constitution, of certain rights, shall not be construed to deny or disparage others retained by the people.

Art. X

The powers not delegated to the United States by the Constitution, nor prohibited by it to the States, are reserved to the States respectively, or to the people.

Further Amendments to the Constitution

Art. XI
Jan. 8, 1798

The Judicial power of the United States shall not be construed to extend to any suit in law or equity, commenced or prosecuted against one of the United States by Citizens of another State, or by Citizens or Subjects of any Foreign State.

Art. XII
Sept. 25, 1804

The Electors shall meet in their respective states, and vote by ballot for President and Vice-President, one of whom, at least, shall not be an inhabitant of the same state with themselves; they shall name in their ballots the person voted for as President, and in distinct ballots the person voted for as Vice-President, and they shall make distinct lists of all persons voted for as President, and of all persons voted for as Vice-

President, and of the number of votes for each, which lists they shall sign and certify, and transmit sealed to the seat of the government of the United States, directed to the President of the Senate;—The President of the Senate shall, in the presence of the Senate and House of Representatives, open all the certificates and the votes shall then be counted;—The person having the greatest number of votes for President, shall be the President, if such number be a majority of the whole number of Electors appointed; and if no person have such majority, then from the persons having the highest numbers not exceeding three on the list of those voted for as President, the House of Representatives shall choose immediately, by ballot, the President. But in choosing the President, the votes shall be taken by states, the representation from each state having one vote; a quorum for this purpose shall consist of a member or members from two-thirds of the states, and a majority of all the states shall be necessary to a choice. And if the House of Representatives shall not choose a President whenever the right of choice shall devolve upon them, before the fourth day of March next following, then the Vice-President shall act as President, as in the case of the death or other constitutional disability of the President.—The person having the greatest number of votes as Vice-President, shall be the Vice-President, if such number be a majority of the whole number of Electors appointed, and if no person have a majority, then from the two highest numbers on the list, the Senate shall choose the Vice-President; a quorum for the purpose shall consist of two-thirds of the whole number of Senators, and a majority of the whole number shall be necessary to a choice. But no person constitutionally ineligible to the office of President shall be eligible to that of Vice-President of the United States.

Art. XIII
Dec. 18, 1865

Sec. 1. Neither slavery nor involuntary servitude, except as a punishment for crime whereof the party shall have been duly convicted, shall exist within the United States, or any place subject to their jurisdiction.

Sec. 2. Congress shall have power to enforce this article by appropriate legislation.

Art. XIV
July 28, 1868

Sec. 1. All persons born or naturalized in the United States, and subject to the jurisdiction thereof, are citizens of the United States and of the State wherein they reside. No State shall make or enforce any law which shall abridge the privileges or immunities of citizens of the United States; nor shall any State deprive any person of life, liberty, or property, without due process of law; nor deny to any person within its jurisdiction the equal protection of the laws.

Sec. 2. Representatives shall be apportioned among the several States according to their respective numbers, counting the whole number of persons in each State, excluding Indians not taxed. But when the right to vote at any election for the choice of electors for President and Vice President of the United States, Representatives in Congress, the Executive and Judicial officers of a State, or the members of the Legislature thereof, is denied to any of the male inhabitants of such State, being twenty-one years of age, and citizens of the United States, or in any way abridged, except for participation in rebellion, or other crime, the basis of representation therein shall be reduced in the proportion which the number of such male citizens shall bear to the whole number of male citizens twenty-one years of age in such State.

Sec. 3. No person shall be a Senator or Representative in Congress, or elector of President and Vice President, or hold any office, civil or military, under the United States, or under any State, who, having previously taken an oath, as a member of Congress, or as an officer of the United States, or as a member of any State legislature, or as an executive or judicial officer of any State, to support the Constitution of the United States, shall have engaged in insurrection or rebellion against the same, or given aid or comfort to the enemies thereof. But Congress may by a vote of two-thirds of each House, remove such disability.

Sec. 4. The validity of the public debt of the United States, authorized by law, including debts incurred for payment of pensions and bounties for services in suppressing insurrection or rebellion, shall not be questioned. But neither the United States nor any State shall assume or pay any debt or obligation incurred in aid of insurrection or rebellion against the United States, or any claim for the loss or emancipation of any slave; but all such debts, obligations and claims shall be held illegal and void.

Sec. 5. The Congress shall have power to enforce, by appropriate legislation, the provisions of this article.

Art. XV
March 30, 1870

Sec. 1. The right of citizens of the United States to vote shall not be denied or abridged by the United States or by any State on account of race, color, or previous condition of servitude.

Sec. 2. The Congress shall have power to enforce this article by appropriate legislation.

Art. XVI
February 25, 1913

The Congress shall have power to lay and collect taxes on incomes, from whatever source derived, without apportionment among the several States and without regard to any census or enumeration.

Art. XVII
May 31, 1913

The Senate of the United States shall be composed of two senators from each State, elected by the people thereof, for six years; and each Senator shall have one vote. The electors in each State shall have the qualifications requisite for electors of the most numerous branch of the State legislature.

When vacancies happen in the representation of any State in the Senate, the executive authority of such State shall issue writs of election to fill such vacancies: *Provided*, That the legislature of any State may empower the executive thereof to make temporary appointments until the people fill the vacancies by election as the legislature may direct.

This amendment shall not be so construed as to affect the election or term of any senator chosen before it becomes valid as part of the Constitution.

Art. XVIII
January 29, 1919

After one year from the ratification of this article, the manufacture, sale, or transportation of intoxicating liquors within, the importation thereof into, or the exportation thereof from the United States and all territory subject to the jurisdiction thereof for beverage purposes is hereby prohibited.

The Congress and the several States shall have concurrent power to enforce this article by appropriate legislation.

This article shall be inoperative unless it shall have been ratified as an amendment to the Constitution by the legislatures of the several States, as provided in the Constitution, within seven years from the date of the submission thereof to the States by Congress.

Art. XIX
August 26, 1920

The right of citizens of the United States to vote shall not be denied or abridged by the United States or by any States on account of sex.

The Congress shall have power by appropriate legislation to enforce the provisions of this article.

Art. XX
February 6, 1933

Sec. 1. The terms of the President and Vice-President shall end at noon on the twentieth day of January, and the terms of Senators and Representatives at noon on the third day of January, of the years in which such terms would have ended if this article had not been ratified; and the terms of their successors shall then begin.

Sec. 2. The Congress shall assemble at least once in every year, and such meeting shall begin at noon on the third day of January, unless they shall by law appoint a different day.

Sec. 3. If, at the time fixed for the beginning of the term of the President, the President-elect shall have died, the Vice-President-elect shall become President. If a President shall not have been chosen before

the time fixed for the beginning of his term, or if the President-elect shall have failed to qualify, then the Vice-President-elect shall act as President until a President shall have qualified; and the Congress may by law provide for the case wherein neither a President-elect nor a Vice-President-elect shall have qualified, declaring who shall then act as President, or the manner in which one who is to act shall be selected, and such person shall act accordingly until a President or Vice-President shall have qualified.

Sec. 4. The Congress may by law provide for the case of the death of any of the persons from whom the House of Representatives may choose a President whenever the right of choice shall have devolved upon them, and for the case of the death of any of the persons from whom the Senate may choose a Vice-President whenever the right of choice shall have devolved upon them.

Sec. 5. Sections 1 and 2 shall take effect on the 15th day of October following the ratification of this article.

Sec. 6. This article shall be inoperative unless it shall have been ratified as an amendment to the Constitution by the legislatures of three-fourths of the several States within seven years from the date of its submission.

Art. XXI
December 5, 1933

Sec. 1. The eighteenth article of amendment to the Constitution of the United States is hereby repealed . . .

Art. XXII
February 26, 1951

Sec. 1. No person shall be elected to the office of the President more than twice, and no person who has held the office of President, or acted as President for more than two years of a term to which some other person was elected President shall be elected to the office of the President more than once. But this Article shall not apply to any person holding the office of President when this Article was proposed by the Congress, and shall not prevent any person who may be holding the office of President, or acting as President, during the term within which this Article becomes operative from holding the office of President or acting as President during the remainder of such term.

Article XXIII
March 29, 1961

SEC. 1. The District constituting the seat of Government of the United States shall appoint in such manner as the Congress may direct:

A number of electors of President and Vice-President equal to the whole number of Senators and Representatives in Congress to which the District would be entitled if it were a State, but in no event more than the least populous state; they shall be in addition to those appointed by the states, but they shall be considered, for the purposes of the election of President and Vice-President, to be electors appointed by a state; and they shall meet in the District and perform such duties as provided by the twelfth article of amendment.

SEC. 2. The Congress shall have power to enforce this article by appropriate legislation.

Article XXIV
January 24, 1964

SEC. 1. The right of citizens of the United States to vote in any primary or other election for President or Vice-President, for electors for President or Vice-President, or for Senator or Representative in Congress, shall not be denied or abridged by the United States or any stateby reason of failure to pay any poll tax or other tax.

SEC. 2. The Congress shall have power to enforce this article by appropriate legislation.

Article XXV
February 23, 1967

SEC. 1. In case of the removal of the President from office or his death or resignation, the Vice-President shall become President.

SEC. 2. Whenever there is a vacancy in the office of the Vice-President, the President shall nominate a Vice-President who shall take the office upon confirmation by a majority vote of both houses of Congress.

SEC. 3. Whenever the President transmits to the President pro tempore of the Senate and the Speaker of the House of Representatives his written declaration that he is unable to discharge the powers and duties of his office, and until he transmits to them a written declaration to the contrary, such powers and duties shall be discharged by the Vice-President as Acting President.

SEC. 4. Whenever the Vice-President and a majority of either the principal officers of the executive departments, or of such other body as Congress may by law provide, transmit to the President pro tempore of the Senate and the Speaker of the House of Representatives their written declaration that the President is unable to discharge the powers and duties of his office, the Vice-President shall immediately assume the powers and duties of the office as Acting President.

Thereafter, when the President transmits to the President pro tempore of the Senate and the Speaker of the House of Representatives his written declaration that no inability exists, he shall resume the powers and duties of his office unless the Vice-President and a majority of either the principal officers of the executive department, or of such other body as Congress may by law provide, transmit within four days to the President pro tempore of the Senate and the Speaker of the House of Representatives their written declaration that the President is unable to discharge the powers and duties of his office. Thereupon Congress shall decide the issue, assembling within 48 hours for that purpose if not in session. If the Congress, within 21 days after receipt of the latter written declaration, or, if Congress is not in session, within 21 days after Congress is required to assemble, determines by two-thirds vote of both houses that the President is unable to discharge the powers and duties of his office, the Vice-President shall continue to discharge the same as Acting President; otherwise, the President shall resume the powers and duties of his office.

Article XXVI
July 7, 1971

Sec. 1. The right of citizens of the United States, who are eighteen years of age or older, to vote shall not be denied or abridged by the United States or by any State on account of age.

Sec. 2. The Congress shall have power to enforce this article by appropriate legislation.

Index

Page numbers in bold text indicate the primary article on a topic or court case. Page numbers in italics indicate illustrations.

A

Index

C

D

F

Index

G

Index

H

Index

K

L

M

Index

N

Index

Q

R

Index

S

T

U

V

Index

W

Supreme Court DRAMA

Cases That Changed America

Supreme Court DRAMA

Cases That Changed America

Daniel E. Brannen, &
Dr. Richard Clay Hanes
Elizabeth Shaw, Editor

VOLUME 3

AFFIRMATIVE ACTION
ASSISTED SUICIDE AND THE RIGHT TO DIE
CIVIL RIGHTS AND EQUAL PROTECTION
GENDER DISCRIMINATION
REPRODUCTIVE RIGHTS
RIGHTS OF IMMIGRANTS, GAYS, AND THE DISABLED
VOTING RIGHTS

U·X·L®
AN IMPRINT OF THE GALE GROUP
DETROIT · NEW YORK · SAN FRANCISCO
LONDON · BOSTON · WOODBRIDGE, CT

Supreme Court Drama: Cases That Changed America

DANIEL E. BRANNEN
RICHARD CLAY HANES

Staff

Elizabeth M. Shaw, U•X•L Editor
Carol DeKane Nagel, U•X•L Managing Editor
Thomas L. Romig, U•X•L Publisher

Shalice Shah-Caldwell, Permissions Associate (Pictures)
Maria Franklin, Permissions Manager
Robyn Young, Imaging and Multimedia Content Editor

Rita Wimberley, Senior Buyer
Evi Seoud, Assistant Manager, Composition Purchasing and Electronic Prepress
Dorothy Maki, Manufacturing Manager
Mary Beth Trimper, Production Director
Michelle DiMercurio, Senior Art Director

Pamela A. Reed, Imaging Coordinator
Randy Basset, Image Database Supervisor
Barbara Yarrow, Imaging and Multimedia Content Manager

Linda Mahoney, LM Design, Typesetting

Cover photographs: Reproduced by permission of the Library of Congress and the Supreme Court of the United States.

Library of Congress Cataloging-in-Publication Data

Brannen, Daniel E., 1968-
Supreme Court drama: cases that changed the nation / Daniel E. Brannen, Jr. and Richard Clay Hanes ; Elizabeth M. Shaw, editor.
p. cm.
Includes bibliographical references and index.
ISBN 0-7876-4877-9 (set) – ISBN 0-7876-4878-7 (v.1) – ISBN 0-7876-4879-5 (v.2) –ISBN 0-7876-4880-9 (v.3) – ISBN 0-7876-4881-7 (v.4)
1.Constitutional law–United States–Cases–Juvenile literature. 2. United States. Supreme Court–Juvenile Literature. [1. Constitutional law–United States–Cases. 2. United States. Supreme Court.] I. Hanes, Richard Clay, 1946- II. Shaw, Elizabeth M., 1973- III. Title.

KF4550.Z9 B73 2001
347.73'26'0264–dc21

00-056380

Printed in Canada

10 9 8 7 6 5 4 3 2

Contents

Contents

Contents

VOLUME 2: CRIMINAL JUSTICE AND FAMILY LAW

Contents

Contents

Contents

Trials Alphabetically

A

B

F

G

H

I

J

K

L

M

N

O

P

R

S

T

U

V

W

Trials Chronologically

Trials Chronologically

1831

1832

1833

1841

1842

1857

1858

1866

1875

1879

1883

1884

1886

1895

1896

1897

1905

1908

1911

1915

1918

1919

1925

1927

1931

1932

1934

1936

1937

1938

1940

1941

1942

1943

1944

1945

1947

1948

1951

1954

1955

1957

1958

1967

1968

1969

1970

1971

1972

1973

1974

1975

1976

1977

1978

1979

1980

1981

1982

1984

1985

1986

1987

1988

1989

1990

1991

1992

1993

1994

1995

1996

1997

1998

1999

2000

Reader's Guide

U.S. citizens take comfort and pride in living under the rule of law. Our elected representatives write and enforce the laws that cover everything from family relationships to the dealings of multi-billion-dollar corporations, from the quality of the air to the content of the programs broadcast through it. But it is the judicial system that interprets the meaning of the law and makes it real for the average citizen through the drama of trials and the force of court orders and judicial opinions.

The four volumes of *Supreme Court Drama: Cases that Changed America* profile approximately 150 cases that influenced the development of key aspects of law in the United States. The case profiles are grouped according to the legal principle on which they are based, with each volume covering one or two broad areas of the law as follows:

- **Volume : Individual Liberties** includes cases that have influenced such First Amendment issues as freedom of the press, religion, speech, and assembly. It also covers the right to privacy.
- **Volume 2: Criminal Justice and Family Law** covers many different areas of criminal law, such as capital punishment, crimnal procedure, family law, and juvenile law.
- **Volume 3: Equal Protection and Civil Rights** includes cases in the areas of affirmative action, reproductive rights segregation, and voting rights, as well as areas of special concern such as immigrants, the disabled, and gay and lesbian citizens. Sexual harassment and the right to die are also represented in this volume.

- **Volume 4: Business and Government Law** also encompasses two major spheres of the law. Monopolies, antitrust, and labor-related cases supplement the business fundamentals of corporate law. The government cases document the legal evolution of the branches of the federal government as well as the federal government's relation to state power. Separate topics address military issues, taxation, and legal history behind some Native American issues.
- **Appendixes** to all volumes also present the full text of the U.S. Constitution and its amendments and a chronological table of Supreme Court justices.

Coverage

Issue overviews, averaging 2,000 words in length provide the context for the case profiles that follow. Case discussions range from 750 to 2,000 words according, to their complexity and importance. Each provides the background of the case and issues involved, the main arguments presented by each side, and an explanation of the Supreme Court's decision, as well as the legal, political, and social impact of the decision. Excerpts from the Court's opinions are often included. Within each issue section, the cases are arranged from earliest to most recent.

When a single case could be covered under several different areas—the landmark reproductive rights decision in *Roe v. Wade,* for example, is also based upon an assertion of privacy rights—the case is placed with the issue with which it is most often associated. Users should consult the cumulative index that appears in each volume to find cases throughout the set that apply to a particular topic.

Additional Features

- The issues and proceedings featured in *Supreme Court Drama* are presented in language accessible to middle school users. Legal terms must sometimes be used for precision, however, so a Words to Know section of more than 300 words and phrases appears in each volume.
- A general essay providing a broad overview of the Supreme Court of the United States and the structure of the American legal system.
- **Bolded** cross-references within overview and case entries that point to cases that appear elsewhere in the set.

- Tables of contents to locate a particular case by name or in chronological order.
- A cumulative index at the end of each volume that includes the cases, people, events and subjects that appear throughout *Supreme Court Drama.*

Suggestions Are Welcome

We welcome your comments on *Supreme Court Drama: Cases That Changed America.* Please write, Editors, *Supreme Court Drama,* U•X•L, 27500 Drake Road, Farmington Hills, MI 48331-3535; call toll-free: 1-800-877-4253; fax to 248-414-5043; or send e-mail via http://www.galegroup.com.

Advisors

The editor is grateful for all the assistance and insight offered by the advisors to this product.

- Mary Alice Anderson, Media Specialist, Winona Middle School, Winona, Minnesota
- Sara Brooke, Librarian, Ellis School, Pittsburgh, Pennsylvania
- Marolynn Griffin, Librarian, Desert Ridge Middle School, Albuquerque, New Mexico
- Dr. E. Shane McKee, Instructor, The Putney School at Elm Lea Farm, Putney, Vermont

The editor and writers would also like to acknowledge the tireless review and copy editing work done by:

- Aaron Ford, The Ohio State University, Columbus, Ohio
- Kathleen Knisely, Franklin County Courts, Columbus, Ohio
- Courtney Mroch, Freelance Writer, Jacksonville, Florida
- Melynda Neal, Franklin County Courts, Columbus, Ohio
- Berna Rhodes-Ford, Franklin County Courts, Columbus, Ohio
- Gertrude Ring, Freelance Writer, Los Angeles, California
- Lauren Zupnic, Franklin County Courts, Columbus, Ohio

Guide to the Supreme Court of the United States

The United States Supreme Court is the highest court in the judicial branch of the federal government. That means the Supreme Court is equal in importance to the president, who heads the executive branch, and Congress, which heads the legislative branch. Congress makes laws, the president enforces them, and the Supreme Court interprets them to make sure they are properly enforced.

The Supreme Court's main job is to review federal (national) and state cases that involve rights or duties under the U.S. Constitution, the document outlining the laws and guidelines for lawmaking and enforcement in the United States. The Court does this to make sure that all federal and state governments are obeying the Constitution.

For example, if Congress passes a law that violates the First Amendment freedom of speech, the Supreme Court can strike the law down as unconstitutional. If the president violates the Fourth Amendment by having the Federal Bureau of Investigation search a person's home without a warrant, the Supreme Court can fix the violation. If a state court violates the Constitution by convicting someone of a crime in an unfair trial, the Supreme Court can reverse the conviction.

As the highest court in the United States government, the Supreme Court also has the job of interpreting federal law. Congress creates law to regulate crimes, drugs, taxes, and other important issues across the nation. When someone is accused of violating a federal law, a federal

court must interpret the law to decide whether the accused has broken the law. In this role, the Supreme Court makes the final decision about what a federal law means.

The Federal Court System

The Supreme Court was born in 1789, when the United States adopted the Constitution. Article III of the Constitution says, "The judicial Power of the United States, shall be vested in one supreme Court, and in such inferior Courts as the Congress may from time to time ordain and establish." With this sentence, the Constitution made the Supreme Court the highest Court in the judicial branch of the federal government. It also gave Congress the power to create lower courts.

Congress used that power to create a large judicial (court) system. The system has three levels. Trial courts, called federal district courts, are at the lowest level. There are ninety-four federal district courts covering different areas of the country. Each federal district court handles trials for cases in its area.

Federal district courts hold trials in both criminal and civil cases. Criminal trials involve cases by the government against a person who is accused of a crime, like murder. Civil trials involve cases between private parties, such as when one person accuses another of breaking a contract or agreement.

When a party loses a case in federal district court, she usually may appeal the decision to a U.S. court of appeals. Federal courts of appeals are the second level in the federal judicial system. There are twelve courts of appeals covering twelve areas, or circuits, of the country. For example, the district courts in Connecticut, New York, and Vermont are part of the Second Circuit. Appeals from district courts in those states go to the U.S. Court of Appeals for the Second Circuit.

During an appeal, the losing party asks the court of appeals to reverse or modify the trial court's decision. In essence, she argues that the trial court made an error when it ruled against her.

The party who loses before the court of appeals must decide whether to take her case to the U.S. Supreme Court. The Supreme Court is the third and highest level of the federal judicial system. The process of taking a case to the U.S. Supreme Court is described below.

State Court Systems

Most states have a judicial system that resembles the federal system. Trial courts hold trials in both criminal and civil cases. Most states also have special courts that hear only certain kinds of cases. Family, juvenile, and traffic courts are typical examples. There also are state courts, such as justices of the peace and small claims courts, that handle minor matters.

Appeals from all lower courts usually go to a court of appeals. The losing party there may take her case to the state's highest court, often called the state supreme court. When a case involves the U.S. Constitution or federal law, the losing party sometimes may take the case from the state supreme court to the U.S. Supreme Court.

Bringing a Case to the U.S. Supreme Court

There are three main ways that cases get to the U.S. Supreme Court. The most widely used method is to ask the Supreme Court to hear the case. This is called filing a petition for a writ of *certiorari.* The person who files the petition, usually the person who lost the case in the court of appeals, is called the petitioner. The person on the other side of the case is called the respondent. The Court only grants a small percentage of the writ petitions it receives each year. It usually tries to accept the cases that involve the most important legal issues.

The second main way to bring a case to the Supreme Court is by appeal. An appeal is possible only when the law that the case involves says the parties may appeal to the Supreme Court. The losing party who files the appeal is called the appellant, while the person on the other side of the case is a called the appellee.

The third main way to bring a case to the Supreme Court is by filing a petition for a writ of habeas corpus. This petition is mainly for people who have been imprisoned in violation of the U.S. Constitution. For example, if an accused criminal is convicted and jailed after the police beat him to get a confession (a police act that is illegal), the prisoner may ask the Supreme Court to release him by filing a petition for a writ of habeas corpus. The person who files the petition is called the petitioner, while the person holding the petitioner in jail is called the respondent.

The process of arguing and deciding a case in the Supreme Court is similar no matter how the case gets there. The parties file briefs that

explain why they think the lower court's decision in their case is either right or wrong. The Supreme Court reviews the briefs along with a record of the evidence presented during trial in the federal district court or state trial court. The Supreme Court also may allow the parties to engage in oral argument, which is a chance for the lawyers to explain their clients' cases. During oral argument, the Supreme Court justices can ask questions to help them make the right decision.

After the justices read the briefs, review the record, and hear oral argument, they meet privately in chambers to discuss the case. Eventually, the nine justices vote for the party they think should win the case. A party must receive votes from five of the nine justices to win the case. The justices who cast the votes for the winning party are called the majority, while the justices who vote for the losing party are called the minority.

After the justices vote, one justice in the majority writes an opinion to explain the Court's decision. Other justices in the majority may write concurring opinions that explain why they agree with the Court's decision. Justices in the minority may write dissenting opinions to explain why they think the Court's decision is wrong.

The Supreme Court's decision is the final word in a case. Parties who are unhappy with the result have no place to go to get a different ruling. The only way to change the effect of a Supreme Court decision is to have Congress change the law, have the entire nation change, or amend, the Constitution, or have the president appoint a different justice to the Court when one retires or dies. This is part of the federal government's system of checks and balances, which prevents one branch from becoming too strong.

Supreme Court Justices

Supreme Court justices are among the greatest legal minds in the country. Appointment to the job is usually the high point of a career that involved some combination of trial work as a lawyer, teaching as a professor, or service as a judge on a lower court.

Under the Constitution, the president appoints Supreme Court justices with the advice and consent of the Senate when one of the nine justices retires, dies, or is removed from office. Supreme Court justices cannot be removed from office except by impeachment and conviction by Congress for serious crimes. That means the process of appointing a new justice usually begins when one of the justices retires or dies.

The president begins the process by nominating someone to fill the empty seat on the Court. The president usually names someone who he thinks will interpret the Constitution favorably to his political party's wishes. In other words, democratic presidents typically nominate liberal justices, while republican presidents nominate conservative justices.

The next step in the process is for the Senate Judiciary Committee to review the president's recommendation. If the Senate is controlled by the president's political party, the review process usually results in Senate approval of the president's selection.

If the president's political opposition controls the Senate, the review process can be fierce and lengthy. The Judiciary Committee calls the nominee before it to answer questions. The Committee's goal is to determine whether the nominee is qualified to be a Supreme Court justice. The Committee also uses the investigation to try to figure out how the nominee will decide controversial cases, such as cases involving abortion. After its investigation, the Committee recommends whether the Senate should confirm or reject the president's nomination. Two-thirds of the senators must vote for the nominee to confirm him as a new Supreme Court justice.

The Supreme Court has changed greatly over the years. One of the Court's greatest liberal periods was when Chief Justice Earl Warren headed the Court from 1953 to 1969. In 1954, the Warren Court decided one of its most famous cases, *Brown v. Board of Education,* in which it forced public schools to end the practice of separating black and white students in different schools.

The Warren Court was followed by one of the Court's greatest conservative periods, under Chief Justice Warren E. Burger from 1969 to 1986, followed by Chief Justice William H. Rehnquist from 1986 onward. In one of the Rehnquist Court's most important decisions, *Clinton v. Jones* (1997), the Court said the president may be sued while in office for conduct unrelated to his official duties. The decision allowed Paula Jones to sue President William J. Clinton for sexual harassment.

Unfortunately, the justices on the highest court in a nation of diversity have not been very diverse themselves. Until 1916, all Supreme Court justices were white, Christian men. That year, Louis D. Brandeis became the first Jewish member of the Supreme Court. In 1967, Thurgood Marshall became the first African American justice. Clarence Thomas became just the second in 1991. In 1981, President Ronald Reagan nominated Sandra Day O'Connor to be the first woman on the Supreme Court. Ruth Bader Ginsburg joined her there in 1993.

Research and Activity Ideas

Activity 1: New School Rule

Assignment: Imagine that your school principal has just announced a new school rule for detention. Students who get detention are not allowed to explain themselves, even if they did nothing wrong. Instead, they must sit in the principal's office during lunch. They are not allowed to eat lunch, not allowed to talk at all, and must listen to Frank Sinatra music during the entire period. Your teacher has asked you to prepare a written report on whether this new rule violates the U.S. Constitution.

Preparation: Begin your research by reading the Bill of Rights, which contains the first ten amendments to the U.S. Constitution, along with the Fourteenth Amendment. These amendments contain many rights that might apply to the principal's new rule. Do you see any that might help? Continue your research by looking in *Supreme Court Drama: Cases That Changed America* for essays and cases on the freedom of speech, cruel and unusual punishment, and students' rights in school. Consult the library and Internet web sites for additional research material. Does it seem to matter whether you are in a public or private school?

Presentation: After you have gathered your information, prepare a report that explains what you found. Does the principal's new rule violate the Constitution? Why or why not? Explain your conclusions by referring to specific amendments from the Constitution and specific cases from *Supreme Court Drama.*

Activity 2: Taking a Case to Court

Assignment: Pretend you were in a bookstore that was being robbed. When the police arrived to arrest the criminal, they accidentally arrested you. During the arrest they treated you roughly and broke your arm. Your lawyer has informed you that you may sue the police to recover damages in either state or federal court. Before deciding which court system to use, you must do some research about both systems.

Preparation: Begin by reading the Introduction to *Supreme Court Drama: Cases That Changed America* so you can learn about the federal and state court systems in general. Continue with library and Internet research for more information about these systems. Then figure out which courts you need to use for your case. For the state system, use the library and Internet to find your local trial court for civil cases. Then find your state court of appeals and supreme courts in case you lose in the trial court. For the federal system, find the federal district court and U.S. court of appeals for your area. Write to the state supreme court and the U.S. court of appeals to find out what percentage of cases make it from those courts to the U.S. Supreme Court each year.

Presentation: Write a letter to your attorney explaining what you found. Tell her where you need to file your case if you choose the state system, and where you need to take appeals in that system. Do the same for the federal system. Tell her what your chances are of getting to the U.S. Supreme Court with your case.

Activity 3: Oral Argument

Activity: Imagine that a new religious group called Planterism has moved into your community. Planters are a group of men who worship trees, flowers, and other plant life. Once every week they hold an all-night ceremony during which they burn a tree as a sacrifice for all living plants. The ceremony disturbs neighbors who are trying to sleep and threatens to eliminate rare trees in your town.

Your mayor or other local leader decides he does not like Planters, so he enacts the following law:

> **Everyone in this town must follow Christianity, Judaism, or some other popular religion. Anyone who follows a false religion, including Planterism, is guilty of a felony. Anyone who burns a tree as a**

sacrifice during a religious ceremony is guilty of a felony. Anyone who disturbs the peace with a religious ceremony at night is guilty of a felony.

Violation of this law by men is punishable by life in prison without a trial. If the local police suspect a man is violating this law, they shall enter his house immediately without a warrant, arrest him, and take him to jail for imprisonment. Violation of this law by women is punishable by thirty days in jail only after a jury finds the woman guilty in a fair trial.

Your teacher has instructed the class to convene a Supreme Court to determine whether this law violates the U.S. Constitution.

Preparation: Select nine members of your class to be justices on the Court. The rest of your class should divide into three teams. One team will represent the mayor, who will argue in favor of the law. The second team will represent a group of Planters who want to challenge the law. The third team will represent a group of Christians, who want to burn palms on Palm Sunday, a religious holiday that happens once a year.

The justices and all three teams should begin by reading the Bill of Rights and the Fourteenth Amendment of the U.S. Constitution. Continue by reading *Supreme Court Drama: Cases That Changed America* for essays and cases on the freedom of religion, the establishment clause, search and seizure, cruel and unusual punishment, governmental power, due process of law, and gender discrimination. Supplement this with research from library materials and Internet web sites. You may want to assign small groups from each team to handle specific issues.

Presentation: When everyone has completed the research, all three teams should prepare to argue before the Supreme Court. The team representing the mayor should explain why the law should be upheld. The teams representing the Planters and the Christians should explain why the law should be struck down as unconstitutional. During the argument, the justices are allowed to ask questions of each team. After every team has made its argument, the justices should meet to discuss the case and to make a ruling. Is the law unconstitutional? Which parts are valid and which are not?

Words to Know

A

Accessory Aiding or contributing in a secondary way to a crime or assisting in or contributing to a crime.

Accomplice One who knowingly and voluntarily helps commit a crime.

Acquittal When a person who has been charged with committing a crime is found not guilty by the courts.

Admissible A term used to describe information that is allowed to be used as evidence or information in a court case.

Adultery Voluntary sexual relations between an individual who is married and someone who is not the individual's spouse.

Affidavit A written statement of facts voluntarily made by someone in front of an official or witness.

Affirmative action Employment programs required by the federal government designed to eliminate existing and continuing discrimination, to remedy lingering effects of past discrimination, and to create systems and procedures to prevent future discrimination; commonly based on population percentages of minority groups in a particular area. Factors considered are race, color, sex, creed (religious beliefs), and age.

Age of consent The age at which a person may marry without parental approval.

Words to Know

Age of majority The age at which a person, formerly a minor or an infant, is recognized by law to be an adult, capable of managing his or her own affairs and responsible for any legal obligations created by his or her actions.

Aggravated assault A person is guilty of aggravated assault if he or she tries to cause serious bodily injury to another or causes such injury purposely, knowingly, or recklessly without any concern for that person or without remorse.

Alien Foreign-born person who has not been naturalized to become a U.S. citizen under federal law and the Constitution.

Alimony Payment a family court may order one person in a couple to make to the other when the couple separates or divorces.

Amendment An addition, deletion, or change to an original item, such as the additions to the Constitution.

Amicus curiae Latin for "friend of the court"; a person with strong interest in, views on, or knowledge of the subject matter of a case, but is not a party to the case. A friend of the court may petition the court for permission to file a statement about the situation.

Amnesty The action of a government by which all persons or certain groups of persons who have committed a criminal offense—usually of a political nature that threatens the government (such as treason)—are granted immunity from prosecution.

Appeal Timely plea by an unsuccessful party in a lawsuit to an appropriate superior court that has the power to review a final decision on the grounds that the decision was made in error.

Appellate court A court having jurisdiction to review decisions of a lower court.

Apportionment The process by which legislative seats are distributed among those who are entitled to representation; determination of the number of representatives that each state, county, or other subdivision may send to a legislative body.

Arbitration Taking a dispute to an unbiased third person and agreeing in advance to comply with the decision made by that third person, after both parties have had a chance to argue their side of the issue.

Arraignment The formal proceeding where the defendant is brought before the trial court to hear the charges against him or her and to enter a plea of guilty, not guilty, or no contest.

Arrest The taking into custody of an individual for the purpose of answering the charges against him or her.

Arrest warrant A written order issued by an authority of the state and commanding that the person named be taken into custody.

Arson The malicious burning or exploding of a house, building, or property.

Assault Intentionally harming another person.

Attempt Unsuccessfully preparing and trying to carry out a deed.

B

Bail An amount of money the defendant needs to pay the court to be released while waiting for a trial.

Bankruptcy A federally authorized procedure by which an individual, corporation, or municipality is relieved of total liability for its debts by making arrangements for the partial repayment of those debts.

Battery An intentional, unpermitted act causing harmful or offensive contact with another person.

Beneficiary One who inherits something through the last will and testament (will) of another; also, a person who is entitled to profits, benefits, or advantage from a contract.

Bigamy The offense of willfully and knowingly entering into a second marriage while married to another person.

Bill A written declaration that one hopes to have made into a law.

Bill of rights The first ten amendments to the U.S. Constitution, ratified (adopted by the states) in 1791, which set forth and guaranteed certain fundamental rights and privileges of individuals, including freedom of religion, speech, press, and assembly; guarantee of a speedy jury trial in criminal cases; and protection against excessive bail and cruel and unusual punishment.

Black codes Laws, statutes, or rules that governed slavery and segregation of public places in the South prior to 1865.

Bona fide occupational qualification An essential requirement for performing a given job. The requirement may even be a physical condition beyond an individual's control, such as perfect vision, if it is absolutely necessary for performing a job.

Brief A summary of the important points of a longer document.

Burden of proof The duty of a party to convince a judge or jury of their position, and to prove wrong any evidence that damages the position of the party. In criminal cases the party must prove their case beyond a reasonable doubt.

Burglary The criminal offense of breaking and entering a building illegally for the purpose of committing a crime.

Bylaws The rules and regulations of an association or a corporation to provide a framework for its operation and management.

C

Capacity The ability, capability, or fitness to do something; a legal right, power, or competency to perform some act. An ability to comprehend both the nature and consequences of one's acts.

Capital punishment The lawful infliction of death as a punishment; the death penalty.

Cause A reason for an action or condition. A ground of a legal action.

Censorship The suppression of speech or writing that is deemed obscene, indecent, or controversial.

Certiorari Latin for "to be informed of"; an order commanding officers of inferior courts to allow a case pending before them to move up to a higher court to determine whether any irregularities or errors occurred that justify review of the case. A device by which the Supreme Court of the United States exercises its discretion in selecting the cases it will review.

Change of venue The removal of a lawsuit from one county or district to another for trial, often permitted in criminal cases in which the court finds that the defendant would not receive a fair trial in the first location because of negative publicity.

Charter A grant from the government of ownership rights of land to a person, a group of people, or an organization, such as a corporation.

Circumstantial evidence Information and testimony presented by a party in a civil or criminal case that allows conclusions to be drawn about certain facts without the party presenting concrete evidence to support their facts.

Citation A paper commonly used in various courts that is served upon an individual to notify him or her that he or she is required to appear at a specific time and place.

Citizens Those who, under the Constitution and laws of the United States, owe allegiance to the United States and are entitled to the enjoyment of all civil rights awarded to those living in the United States.

Civil law A body of rules that spell out the private rights of citizens and the remedies for governing disputes between individuals in such areas as contracts, property, and family law.

Civil liberties Freedom of speech, freedom of press, freedom from discrimination, and other rights guaranteed and protected by the Constitution, which were intended to place limits on government.

Civil rights Personal liberties that belong to an individual.

Class action A lawsuit that allows a large number of people with a common interest in a matter to sue or be sued as a group.

Clause A section, phrase, paragraph, or segment of a legal document, such as a contract, deed, will, or constitution, that relates to a particular point.

Closing argument The final factual and legal argument made by each attorney on all sides of a case in a trial prior to the verdict or judgment.

Code A collection of laws, rules, or regulations that are consolidated and classified according to subject matter.

Collective bargaining agreement The contractual agreement between an employer and a labor union that controls pay, hours, and working conditions for employees which can be enforced against both the employer and the union for failure to comply with its terms.

Commerce Clause The provision of the U.S. Constitution that gives Congress exclusive power over trade activities between the states and with foreign countries and Native American tribes.

Words to Know

Commercial speech The words used in advertisments by commercial companies and service providers. Commercial speech is protected under the First Amendment as long as it is not false or misleading.

Common law The principles and rules of action, embodied in case law rather than legislative enactments, applicable to the government and protection of persons and property, Common laws derive their authority from the community customs and traditions that evolved over the centuries as interpreted by judicial tribunals (types of courts).

Common-law marriage A union of two people not formalized in the customary manner but created by an agreement by the two people to consider themselves married followed by their living together.

Community property The materials and resources owned in common by a husband and wife.

Complaint The possible evidence that initiates a civil action; in criminal law, the document that sets in motion a person's being charged with an offense.

Concurring opinion An opinion by one or more judges that provides separate reasoning for reaching the same decision as the majority of the court.

Conditional Subject to change; dependent upon the occurrence of a future, uncertain event.

Confession A statement made by an individual that acknowledges his or her guilt of a crime.

Conflict of interest A term used to describe the situation in which a public official exploits his or her position for personal benefit.

Consent Voluntary agreement to the proposal of another; the act or result of reaching an agreement.

Conspiracy An agreement between two or more persons to engage in an unlawful or criminal act, or an act that is innocent in itself but becomes unlawful when done by those participating.

Constituent A person who gives another person permission to act on his or her behalf, such as an agent, an attorney in a court of law, or an elected official in government.

Constitution of the United States A document written by the founding fathers of the United States that has been added to by Congress over

the centuries that is held as the absolute rule of action and decision for all branches and offices of the government, and which all subsequent laws and ordinances must be in accordance. It is enforced by representatives of the people of the United States, and can be changed only by a constitutional amendment by the authority that created it.

Contempt An act of deliberate disobedience or disregard for the laws or regulations of a public authority, such as a court or legislative body.

Continuance The postponement of an action pending (waiting to be tried) in a court to a later date, granted by a court in response to a request made by one of the parties to a lawsuit.

Corporations Business entities that are treated much like human individuals under the law, having legally enforceable rights, the ability to acquire debt and pay out profits, the ability to hold and transfer property, the ability to enter into contracts, the requirement to pay taxes, and the ability to sue and be sued.

Counsel An attorney or lawyer.

Court of appeal An intermediate court of review that is found in thirteen judicial districts, called circuits, in the United States. A state court of appeal reviews a decision handed down by a lower court to determine whether that court made errors that warrant the reversal of its final decision.

Covenant An agreement, contract, or written promise between two individuals that frequently includes a pledge to do or refrain from doing something.

Criminal law A body of rules and statutes that defines behavior prohibited by the government because it threatens and/or harms public safety, and establishes the punishments to be given to those who commit such acts.

Cross-examination The questioning of a witness or party during a trial, hearing, or deposition by the opposing lawyer.

Cruel and unusual punishment Such punishment as would amount to torture or barbarity, any cruel and degrading punishment, or any fine, penalty, confinement, or treatment so disproportionate to the offense as to shock the moral sense of the community.

Custodial parent The parent to whom the court grants guardianship of the children after a divorce.

Words to Know

D

Death penalty See Capital punishment.

De facto Latin for "in fact"; in deed; actually.

Defamation Any intentional false communication, either written or spoken, that harms a person's reputation; decreases the respect, regard, or confidence in which a person is held; or causes hostile or disagreeable opinions or feelings against a person.

Defendant The person defending or denying; the party against whom recovery is sought in an action or suit, or the accused in a criminal case.

Defense The forcible reaction against an unlawful and violent attack, such as the defense of one's person, property, or country in time of war.

De jure Latin for "in law"; legitimate; lawful, as a matter of law. Having complied with all the requirements imposed by law.

Deliberate Willful; purposeful; determined after thoughtful evaluation of all relevant factors. To act with a particular intent, which is derived from a careful consideration of factors that influence the choice to be made.

Delinquent An individual who fails to fulfill an obligation or otherwise is guilty of a crime or offense.

Domestic partnership laws Legislation and regulations related to the legal recognition of nonmarital relationships between persons who are romantically involved with each other, have set up a joint residence, and have registered with cities recognizing said relationships.

Denaturalization To take away an individual's rights as a citizen.

Deportation Banishment to a foreign country, attended with confiscation of property and deprivation of civil rights.

Deposition The testimony of a party or witness in a civil or criminal proceeding taken before trial, usually in an attorney's office.

Desegregation Judicial mandate making illegal the practice of segregation.

Disclaimer The denial, refusal, or rejection of a right, power, or responsibility.

Discrimination The grant of particular privileges to a group randomly chosen from a large number of people in which no reasonable dif-

ference exists between the favored and disfavored groups. Federal laws prohibit discrimination in such areas as employment, housing, voting rights, education, access to public facilities, and on the bases of race, age, sex, nationality, disability, or religion.

Dismissal A discharge of an individual or corporation from employment.

Dissent A disagreement by one or more judges with the decision of the majority on a case before them.

Divorce A court decree that terminates a marriage; also known as marital dissolution.

Double jeopardy A second prosecution for the same offense after acquittal or conviction or multiple punishments for the same offense. The evil sought to be avoided by prohibiting double jeopardy is double trial and double conviction, not necessarily double punishment.

Draft A mandatory call of persons to serve in the military.

Due process of law A fundamental, constitutional guarantee that all legal proceedings will be fair and that one will be given notice of the proceedings and an opportunity to be heard before the government acts to take away one's life, liberty, or property. Also, a constitutional guarantee that a law shall not be unreasonable, random, or without consideration for general well-being.

Duress Unlawful pressure exerted upon a person to force that person to perform an act that he or she ordinarily would not perform.

E

Emancipation The act or process by which a person is liberated from the authority and control of another person.

Entrapment The act of government agents or officials that causes a person to commit a crime he or she would not have committed otherwise.

Equal Pay Act Federal law that commands the same pay for all persons who do the same work without regard to sex, age, race, or ability.

Equal protection The constitutional guarantee that no person or class of persons shall be denied the same protection of the laws that is enjoyed by other persons or other classes in like circumstances in their lives, liberty, property, and pursuit of happiness.

Words to Know

Establishment Clause The provision in the First Amendment that provides that there will be no laws created respecting the establishment of a religion, inhibiting the practice of a religion, or giving preference to any or all religions. It has been interpreted to also denounce the discouragement of any or all religions.

Euthanasia The merciful act or practice of terminating the life of an individual or individuals inflicted with incurable and distressing diseases in a relatively painless manner.

Exclusionary rule The principle based on federal constitutional law that evidence illegally seized by law enforcement officers in violation of a suspect's right to be free from unreasonable searches and seizures cannot be used against the suspect in a criminal prosecution.

Executive agreement An agreement made between the head of a foreign country and the president of the United States. This agreement does not have to be submitted to the Senate for consent, and it supersedes any contradicting state law.

Executive orders When the president uses some part of a law or the Constitution to enforce some action.

Executor The individual legally named by a deceased person to administer the provisions of his or her will.

Ex parte Latin for "on one side only"; done by, for, or on the application of one party alone.

Expert witness A witness, such as a psychological statistician or ballisticsexpert, who possesses special or superior knowledge concerning the subject of his or her testimony.

Ex post facto laws Latin for "after-the-fact laws"; laws that provide for the infliction of punishment upon a person for some prior act that, at the time it was committed, was not illegal.

Extradition The transfer of a person accused of a crime from one state or country to another state or country that seeks to place the accused on trial.

F

Family court A court that presides over cases involving: (1) child abuse and neglect; (2) support; (3) paternity; (4) termination of custody due to constant neglect; (5) juvenile delinquency; and (6) family offenses.

Federal Relating to a national government, as opposed to state or local governments.

Federal circuit courts The twelve circuit courts making up the U.S. Federal Circuit Court System. Decisions made by the federal district courts can be reviewed by the court of appeals in each circuit.

Federal district courts The first of three levels of the federal court system, which includes the U.S. Court of Appeals and the U.S. Supreme Court. If a participating party disagrees with the ruling of a federal district court in its case, it may petition for the case to be moved to the next level in the federal court system.

Felon An individual who commits a felony, a crime of a serious nature, such as burglary or murder.

Felony A serious crime, characterized under federal law and many state statutes as any offense punishable by death or imprisonment in excess of one year.

First degree murder Murder committed with deliberately premeditated thought and malice, or with extreme atrocity or cruelty. The difference between first and second degree murder is the presence of the specific intention to kill.

Fraud A false representation of a matter of fact—whether by words or by conduct, by false or misleading allegations, or by concealment of what should have been disclosed—that deceives and is intended to deceive another so that the individual will act upon it to her or his legal injury.

Freedom of assembly See Freedom of association.

Freedom of association The right to associate with others for the purpose of engaging in constitutionally protected activities, such as to peacefully assemble.

Freedom of religion The First Amendment right to individually believe and to practice or exercise one's religious belief.

Freedom of speech The right, guaranteed by the First Amendment to the U.S. Constitution, to express beliefs and ideas without unwarranted government restriction.

Freedom of the press The right, guaranteed by the First Amendment to the U.S. Constitution, to gather, publish, and distribute information and ideas without government restriction; this right encompasses

freedom from prior restraints on publication and freedom from censorship.

Fundamental rights Rights that derive, or are implied, from the terms of the U.S. Constitution, such as the Bill of Rights, the first ten amendments to the Constitution.

G

Gag rule A rule, regulation, or law that prohibits debate or discussion of a particular issue.

Grandfather clause A portion of a statute that provides that the law is not applicable in certain circumstances due to preexisting facts.

Grand jury A panel of citizens that is convened by a court to decide whether it is appropriate for the government to indict (proceed with a prosecution against) someone suspected of a crime.

Grand larceny A category of larceny—the offense of illegally taking the property of another—in which the value of the property taken is greater than that set for petit larceny.

Grounds The basis or foundation; reasons sufficient in law to justify relief.

Guardian A person lawfully invested with the power, and charged with the obligation, of taking care of and managing the property and rights of a person who, because of age, understanding, or lack of self-control, is considered incapable of administering his or her own affairs.

Guardian ad litem A guardian appointed by the court to represent the interests of infants, the unborn, or incompetent persons in legal actions.

H

Habeas corpus Latin for "you have the body"; a writ (court order) that commands an individual or a government official who has restrained another to produce the prisoner at a designated time and place so that the court can determine the legality of custody and decide whether to order the prisoner's release.

Hate crime A crime motivated by race, religion, gender, sexual orientation, or other prejudice.

Hearing A legal proceeding in which issues of law or fact are tried and evidence is presented to help determine the issue.

Hearsay A statement made out of court that is offered in court as evidence to prove the truth of the matter asserted.

Heir An individual who receives an interest in, or ownership of, land or tenements from an ancestor who died through the laws of descent and distribution. At common law, an heir was the individual appointed by law to succeed to the estate of an ancestor who died without a will. It is commonly used today in reference to any individual who succeeds to property, either by will or law.

Homicide The killing of one human being by another human being.

Hung jury A trial jury selected to make a decision in a criminal case regarding a defendant's guilt or innocence that is unable to reach a verdict due to a complete division in opinion.

I

Immunity Exemption from performing duties that the law generally requires other citizens to perform, or from a penalty or burden that the law generally places on other citizens.

Impeachment A process used to charge, try, and remove public officials for misconduct while in office.

Inalienable Not subject to sale or transfer; inseparable.

Incapacity The absence of legal ability, competence, or qualifications.

Income tax A charge imposed by government on the annual gains of a person, corporation, or other taxable unit derived through work, business pursuits, investments, property dealings, and other sources determined in accordance with the Internal Revenue Code or state law.

Indictment A written accusation charging that an individual named therein has committed an act or admitted to doing something that is punishable by law.

Indirect tax A tax upon some right, privilege, or corporation.

Words to Know

Individual rights Rights and privileges constitutionally guaranteed to the people as set forth by the Bill of Rights; the ability of a person to pursue life, liberty, and property.

Infant Persons who are under the age of the legal majority—at common law, twenty-one years, now generally eighteen years. According to the sense in which this term is used, it may denote the age of the person, the contractual disabilities that nonage entails, or his or her status with regard to other powers or relations.

Inherent rights Rights held within a person because he or she exists.

Inheritance Property received from a person who has died, either by will or through state laws if the deceased has failed to execute a valid will.

Injunction A court order by which an individual is required to perform or is restrained from performing a particular act. A writ framed according to the circumstances of the individual case.

In loco parentis Latin for "in the placeof a parent"; the legal doctrine under which an individual assumes parental rights, duties, and obligations without going through the formalities of legal adoption.

Insanity defense A defense asserted by an accused in a criminal prosecution to avoid responsibility for a crime because, at the time of the crime, the person did not comprehend the nature or wrongfulness of the act.

Insider Relating to the federal regulation of the purchase and sale of stocks and bonds, anyone who has knowledge of facts not available to the general public.

Insider trading The trading of stocks and bonds based on information gained from special private, privileged information affecting the value of the stocks and bonds.

Intent A determination to perform a particular act or to act in a particular manner for a specific reason; an aim or design; a resolution to use a certain means to reach an end.

Intermediate courts Courts with general ability or authority to hear a case (trial, appellate, or both) but are not the court of last resort within the jurisdiction.

Intestate The description of a person who dies without making a valid will.

Involuntary manslaughter The act of unlawfully killing another human being unintentionally.

Irrevocable Unable to cancel or recall; that which is unalterable or irreversible.

J

Judicial Relating to courts and the legal system.

Judicial discretion Sound judgment exercised by a judge in determining what is right and fair under the law.

Judicial review A court's authority to examine an executive or legislative act and to invalidate (cancel) that act if it opposes constitutional principles.

Jurisdiction The geographic area over which authority (such as a cout) extends; legal authority.

Jury In trials, a group of people selected and sworn to inquire into matters of fact and to reach a verdict on the basis of evidence presented to it.

Jury nullification The ability of a jury to acquit the defendant despite the amount of evidence against him or her in a criminal case.

Just cause A reasonable and lawful ground for action.

Justifiable homicide The killing of another in self-defense or in the lawful defense of one's property; killing of another when the law demands it, such as in execution for a capital crime.

Juvenile A young individual who has not reached the age whereby he or she would be treated as an adult in the area of criminal law. The age at which the young person attains the status of being a legal majority varies from state to state—as low as fourteen years old, as high as eighteen years old; however, the Juvenile Delinquency Act determines that a youthful person under the age of eighteen is a juvenile in cases involving federal jurisdiction.

Juvenile court The court presiding over cases in which young persons under a certain age, depending on the area of jurisdiction, are accused of criminal acts.

Juvenile delinquency The participation of a youthful individual, one who falls under the age at which he or she could be tried as an adult, in illegal behavior.

L

Larceny The unauthorized taking and removal of the personal property of another by a person who intends to permanently deprive the owner of it; a crime against the right of possession.

Legal defense A complete and acceptable response as to why the claims of the plaintiff should not be granted in a point of law.

Legal tender All U.S. coins and currencies—regardless of when coined or issued—including (in terms of the Federal Reserve System) Federal Reserve notes and circulating notes of Federal Reserve banks and national banking associations that are used for all public and private debts, public charges, taxes, duties, and dues.

Legislation Lawmaking; the preparation and enactment of laws by a legislative body.

Liability A comprehensive legal term that describes the condition of being actually or potentially subject to (responsible for) a legal obligation.

Libel and slander The communication of false information about a person, a group, or an entity, such as a corporation. Libel is any defamation that can be seen, such as in print or on a film or in a representation such as a statued. Slander is any defamation that is spoken and heard.

Litigation An action brought in court to enforce a particular right; the act or process of bringing a lawsuit in and of itself; a judicial contest; any dispute.

Living will A written document that allows a patient to give explicit instructions about medical treatment to be administered when the patient is terminally ill or permanently unconscious; also called an advance directive.

Lobbying The process of influencing public and government policy at all levels: federal, state, and local.

M

Magistrate Any individual who has the power of a public civil officer or inferior judicial officer, such as a justice of the peace.

Majority Full age; legal age; age at which a person is no longer a minor. The age at which, by law, a person is capable of being legally respon-

sible for all of his or her acts (i.e., contractual obligations) and is entitled to manage his or her own affairs and to the enjoy civic rights (i.e., right to vote). Also the status of a person who is a major in age.

Malice The intentional commission of a wrongful act, without justification, with the intent to cause harm to others; conscious violation of the law that injures another individual; a mental state indicating a disregard of social responsibility.

Malpractice When a professional, such as a doctor or lawyer, fails to carry out their job correctly and there are bad results.

Mandate A judicial command or order from a court.

Manslaughter The unjustifiable, inexcusable, and intentional killing of a human being without deliberation, premeditation, or malice.

Material Important; significant; substantial. A description of the quality of evidence that possesses such value as to establish the truth or falsity of a point in issue in a lawsuit.

Mediation Settling a dispute or controversy by setting up an independent person between the two parties to help them settle their disagreement.

Minor An infant or person who is under the age of legal competence. In most states, a person is no longer a minor after reaching the age of eighteen (though state laws might still prohibit certain acts until reaching a greater age; i.e., purchase of liquor).

Misdemeanor Offenses lower than felonies and generally those punishable by fine, penalty, or imprisonment other than in a penitentiary.

Mistrial A courtroom trial that has been ended prior to its normal conclusion. A mistrial has no legal effect and is considered an invalid trial. It differs from a new trial, which recognizes that a trial was completed but was set aside so that the issues could be tried again.

Mitigating circumstances Circumstances that may be considered by a court in determining responsibility of a defendant or the extent of damages to be awarded to a plaintiff. Mitigating circumstances do not justify or excuse an offense but may reduce the charge.

Monopoly An economic advantage held by one or more persons or companies because they hold the exclusive power to carry out a particular business or trade or to manufacture and sell a particular task or produce a particular product.

Moratorium A suspension (ending) of activity or an authorized period of delay or waiting. A moratorium is sometimes agreed upon by the interested parties, or it may be authorized or imposed by operation of law.

Motion A written or oral application made to a court or judge to obtain a ruling or order directing that some act be done in favor of the applicant.

Motive An idea, belief, or emotion that causes a person to act in a certain way, either good or bad.

Murder The unlawful killing of another human being without justification or excuse.

N

National origin The country in which a person was born or from which his or her ancestors came. One's national origin is typically calculated by employers to provide equal employment opportunity statistics in accordance with the provisions of the Civil Rights Act.

Naturalization A process by which a person gains nationality and becomes entitled to the privileges of citizenship. While groups of individuals have been naturalized in history by treaties or laws of Congress, such as in the case of Hawaii, typically naturalization occurs on the individual level upon the completion of a list of requirements.

Necessary and Proper Clause The statement contained in Article I, Section 8, Clause 18 of the U.S. Constitution that gives Congress the power to pass any laws that are necessary and proper to carrying out its specifically granted powers.

Negligence Conduct that falls below the standards of behavior established by law for the protection of others against unreasonable risk of harm.

Nonprofit A corporation or an association that conducts business for the benefit of the general public rather than to gain profits for itself.

Notary public A public official whose main powers include administering oaths and witnessing signatures, both important and effective ways to minimize fraud in legal documents.

O

Obscenity An act, spoken word, or item tending to offend public morals by its indecency or lewdness.

Ordinance A law, statute, or regulation enacted by a municipality.

P

Palimony The settlement awarded at the end of a non-marital relationship, where the couple lived together for a long period of time and where there was an agreement that one partner would support the other in return for the second making a home and performing domestic duties.

Pardon When a person in power, such as a president or governor, offers a formal statement of forgivenss for a crime and takes away the given punishment.

Parental liability A statute (law), enacted in some states, that makes parents responsible for damages caused by their children if it is found that the damages resulted from the parents' lack of control over the acts of the child.

Parole The release of a person convicted of a crime prior to the end of that person's term of imprisonment on the condition that they will follow certain strict rules for their conduct, and if they break any of those rules they will return to prison.

Patents Rights granted to inventors by the federal government that permit them to keep others from making, using, or selling their invention for a definite, or restricted, period of time.

Peremptory challenge The right to challenge the use of a juror in a trial without being required to give a reason for the challenge.

Perjury A crime that occurs when an individual willfully makes a false statement during a judicial proceeding, after he or she has taken an oath to speak the truth.

Petition A formal application made to a court in writing that requests action on a certain matter.

Petit larceny A form of larceny—the stealing of another's personal property—in which the value of the property that is taken is generally less than $50.

Words to Know

Plaintiff The party who sues in a civil action.

Plain view doctrine In the context of searches and seizures, the principle that provides that objects that an officer can easily see can be seized without a search warrant and are fair to use as evidence.

Plea The phase in a court case where the defendant has to declare whether they are guilty or not guilty.

Police power The authority that states to employ a police force and give them the power to enforce the laws and protect the community.

Poll tax A specified sum of money to be paid by each person who votes.

Polygamy The offense of having more than one wife or husband at the same time.

Precedent A court decision that is cited as an example to resolve similar questions of law in later cases.

Preponderance of evidence A rule that states that it is up to the plaintiff to convince the judge or the jury of their side of the case in or to win the case.

Prima facie [*Latin,* On the first appearance.]A fact presumed to be true unless it is disproved.

Prior restraint Government violating freedom of speech by not allowing something to be published.

Privacy In constitutional law, the right of people to make personal decisions regarding intimate matters; under the common law, the right of people to lead their lives in a manner that is reasonably secluded from public scrutiny, whether such scrutiny comes from a neighbor's prying eyes, an investigator's eavesdropping ears, or a news photographer's intrusive camera; and in statutory law, the right of people to be free from unwarranted drug testing and electronic surveillance.

Privilege An advantage or benefit possessed by an individual, company, or class beyond those held by others.

Privileges and immunities Concepts contained in the U.S. Constitution that place the citizens of each state on an equal basis with citizens of other states with respect to advantages resulting from citizenship in those states and citizenship in the United States.

Probable cause Apparent facts discovered through logical inquiry that would lead a reasonably intelligent person to believe that an accused person has committed a crime.

Probate court Called Surrogate or Orphan's Court in some states, the probate court presides over wills, the administration of estates, and, in some states, the appointment of guardians or approval of the adoption of minors.

Probation A sentence whereby a convict is released from confinement but is still under court supervision; a testing or a trial period. It can be given in lieu of a prison term or can suspend a prison sentence if the convict has consistently demonstrated good behavior.

Procedural due process The constitutional guarantee that one's liberty and property rights may not be affected unless reasonable notice and an opportunity to be heard in order to present a claim or defense are provided.

Property A thing or things owned either by government—public property—or owned by private individuals, groups, or companies—private property.

Prosecute To follow through; to commence and continue an action or judicial proceeding to its conclusion. To proceed against a defendant by charging that person with a crime and bringing him or her to trial.

Prosecution The proceedings carried out before a court to determine the guilt or innocence of a defendant. The term also refers to the government attorney charging and trying a criminal case.

Punitive damages Money awarded to an injured party that goes beyond that which is necessary to pay for the individual for losses and that is intended to punish the wrongdoer.

Q

Quorum A majority of an entire body; i.e., a quorum of a legislative assembly.

Quota The number of persons or things that must be used, or admitted, or hired in order to be following a rule or law.

R

Rape A criminal offense defined in most states as forcible sexual relations with a person against that person's will.

Ratification The confirmation or adoption of an act that has already been performed.

Reapportionment The realignment of voting districts done to fulfill the constitutional requirement of one person, one vote.

Referendum The right reserved to the people to approve or reject an act of the legislature, or the right of the people to approve or reject legislation that has been referred to them by the legislature.

Refugees Individuals who leave their native country for social, political, or religious reasons, or who are forced to leave as a result of any type of disaster, including war, political upheaval, and famine.

Rehabilitation Work to restore former rights, authority, or abilities.

Remand To send back.

Replevin A legal action to recover the possession of items of personal property.

Reprieve The temporary hold put on a death penalty for further review of the case.

Rescind To declare a contract void—of no legal force or binding effect—from its beginning and thereby restore the parties to the positions they would have been in had no contract ever been made.

Reservation A tract of land under the control of the Bureau of Indian Affairs to which a Native American tribe retains its original title of ownership, or that has been set aside from the public domain for use by a tribe.

Reserve Funds set aside to cover future expenses, losses, or claims. To retain; to keep in store for future or special use; to postpone to a future time.

Resolution The official expression of the opinion or will of a legislative body.

Retainer A contract between attorney and client specifying the nature of the services and the cost of the services.

Retribution Punishment or reward for an act. In criminal law, punishment is based upon the theory that every crime demands payment.

Reverse discrimination Discrimination against a group of people that is generally considered to be the majority, usually stemming from the enforcement of some affirmative action guidlelines.

Revocation The recall of some power or authority that has been granted.

Robbery The taking of money or goods in the possession of another, from his or her person or immediate presence, by force or intimidation.

S

Sabotage The willful destruction or impairment of war material or national defense material, or harm to war premises or war utilities. During a labor dispute, the willful and malicious destruction of an employer's property or interference with his or her normal operations.

Search warrant A court order authorizing the examination of a place for the purpose of discovering evidence of guilt to be used in the prosecution of a criminal action.

Second degree murder The unlawful taking of human life with malice, but without premeditated thought.

Sedition A revolt or an incitement to revolt against established authority, usually in the form of treason or defamation against government.

Seditious libel A written communication intended to incite the overthrow of the government by force or violence.

Segregation The act or process of separating a race, class, or ethnic group from a society's general population.

Self-defense The protection of one's person or property against some injury attempted by another.

Self-incrimination Giving testimony in a trial or other legal proceeding that could subject one to criminal prosecution.

Sentencing The post-conviction stage of a criminal justice process, in which the defendant is brought before the court for penalty.

Separate but equal The doctrine first accepted by the U.S. Supreme Court in *Plessy v. Ferguson* establishing that different facilities for blacks and whites was valid under the Equal Protection Clause of the Fourteenth Amendment as long as they were equal.

Separation of church and state The separation of religious and government interest to ensure that religion does not become corrupt by government and that government does not become corrupt by religious conflict. The principle prevents the government from supporting the practices of one religion over another. It also enables the government to do what is necessary to prevent one religious group from violating the rights of others.

Separation of powers The division of state and federal government into three independent branches.

Settlement The act of adjusting or determining the dealings or disputes between persons without pursuing the matter through a trial.

Sexual harassment Unwelcome sexual advances, requests for sexual favors, and other verbal or physical conduct of a sexual nature that tends to create a hostile or offensive work environment.

Share A portion or part of something that may be divided into components, such as a sum of money. A unit of stock that represents ownership in a corporation.

Shield laws Statutes that allow journalists not to disclose in legal proceedings confidential information or sources of information obtained in their professional capacities.

Statutes that restrict or prohibit the use of certain evidence in sexual offense cases, such as evidence regarding the lack of chastity of the victim.

Shoplifting Theft of merchandise from a store or business establishment.

Small claims court A special court that provides fast, informal, and inexpensive solutions for small claims.

Solicitation The criminal offense of urging someone to commit an unlawful act.

Statute An act of a legislature that declares, or commands something; a specific law, expressed in writing.

Statute of limitations A type of federal or state law that restricts the time within which legal proceedings may be brought.

Statutory law A law which is created by an act of the legislature.

Statutory rape Sexual intercourse by an adult with a person below a designated age.

Subpoena Latin for "under penalty"; a formal document that orders a named individual to appear before an officer of the court at a fixed time to give testimony.

Suffrage The right to vote at public elections.

Summons The paper that tells a defendant that he or she is being sued and asserts the power of the court to hear and determine the case. A form of legal process that commands the defendant to appear before the court on a specific day and to answer the complaint made by the plaintiff.

Supreme court The highest court in the U.S. judicial system.

Surrogate mother A woman who agrees under contract to bear a child for an infertile couple. The woman is paid to have a donated fertilized egg or the fertilized egg of the female partner in the couple (usually fertilized by the male partner of the couple) artificially placed into her uterus.

Suspended sentence A sentence that states that a criminal, in waiting for their trial, has already served enough time in prison.

Symbolic speech Nonverbal gestures and actions that are meant to communicate a message.

T

Testify To provide evidence as a witness in order to establish a particular fact or set of facts.

Testimony Oral evidence offered by a competent witness under oath, which is used to establish some fact or set of facts.

Trade secret Any valuable commercial information that provides a business with an advantage over competitors who do not have that information.

Trade union An organization of workers in the same skilled occupation or related skilled occupations who act together to secure for all members favorable wages, hours, and other working conditions.

Treason The betrayal of one's own country by waging war against it or by consciously or purposely acting to aid its enemies.

Treaty A compact made between two or more independent nations with a view to the public welfare.

Trespass An unlawful intrusion that interferes with one's person or property.

Trial A judicial examination and determination of facts and legal issues arising between parties to a civil or criminal action.

Trial court The court where civil actions or criminal proceedings are first heard.

Truancy The willful and unjustified failure to attend school by one required to do so.

Words to Know

U

Unenumerated rights Rights that are not expressly mentioned in the written text of a constitution but instead are inferred from the language, history, and structure of the constitution, or cases interpreting it.

Unconstitutional That which is not in agreement with the ideas and regulations of the Constitution.

Uniform commercial code A general and inclusive group of laws adopted, at least partially, by all of the states to further fair dealing in business.

V

Valid Binding; possessing legal force or strength; legally sufficient.

Vandalism The intentional and malicious destruction of or damage to the property of another.

Venue A place, such as a city or county, from which residents are selected to serve as jurors.

Verdict The formal decision or finding made by a jury concerning the questions submitted to it during a trial. The jury reports the verdict to the court, which generally accepts it.

Veto The refusal of an executive officer to approve a bill that has been created and approved by the legislature, thereby keeping the bill from becoming a law.

Voir dire Old French for "to speak the truth"; the preliminary examination of possible jurors to determine their qualifications and suitability to serve on a jury, in order to ensure the selection of a fair and impartial jury.

Voluntary manslaughter The unlawful killing of a person where there is no malice, premeditation or deliberate intent but too near to these standards to be classified as justifiable homicide.

W

Waive To intentionally or voluntarily give up a known right or engage in conduct that caused your rights to be taken away.

Ward A person, especially an infant or someone judged to be incompetent, placed by the court in the care of a guardian.

Warrant A written order issued by a judicial officer commanding a law enforcement officer to perform a duty. This usually includes searches, seizures and arrests.

White collar crime Term for nonviolent crimes that were committed in the course of the offender's occupation.

Will A document in which a person explains the management and distribution of his or her estate after his or her death.

Workers' compensation A system whereby an employer must pay, or provide insurance to pay, the lost wages and medical expenses of an employee who is injured on the job.

Writ An order issued by a court requiring that something be done.

Z

Zoning Assigning different areas within a city or county different uses, whereby one area cannot be used for any other purpose other than what it is designated. For example, if an area is assigned as residential, an office building could not be built there.

Racial and gender (sex) discrimination in the United States have a long history. Discrimination is defined as giving privileges to one group but not another. Throughout the eighteenth, nineteenth, and at least until the mid-twentieth century, racial and gender discrimination denied black Americans and women opportunities in the most basic aspects of their lives including work, education, and voting rights.

Following the American Civil War (1861–65), Congress passed and the states approved amendments to guarantee rights to former slaves. One of the amendments, the Fourteenth Amendment approved in 1868, made it unlawful to "deprive any person of life, liberty, or property" and promised "equal protection of the laws." Congress also found it necessary to pass laws to make sure the amendments were enforced. However, more often than not, the U.S. Supreme Court handed down rulings on these laws that allowed discrimination to continue. Blacks and women experienced little "equal protection of the laws."

Not until the 1950s and 1960s during the Civil Rights Movement did the Supreme Court begin to strike down laws that discriminated against individuals on the basis of race and sex. Through the Court's decisions in

Brown v. Board of Education (1954) and ***Reed v. Reed*** (1971), the Court ruled that black Americans and women must have equal protection rights as guaranteed by the Fourteenth Amendment. During the same time period Congress passed the Civil Rights Act of 1964 prohibiting discrimination on the basis of race, color, religion, sex, or national origin. The Supreme Court in ***Heart of Atlanta Motel v. United States*** (1964) ruled on the 1964 act. The Court upheld the act finding Congress has the constitutional power to promote equality of opportunity and to prevent discrimination. Black Americans and women finally had a law under which they could claim equal protection rights when they were discriminated against in such areas as education and employment.

How Could Negative Effects of Discrimination Be Overcome?

Although jubilant over the civil rights successes, forward thinking leaders for black Americans and women knew the successes would not be enough to overcome two and a half centuries of discrimination. Organizations such as the National Association for the Advancement of Colored People (NAACP) and the National Organization of Women (NOW) proposed programs to give a degree of preferential (preferred) treatment to individuals of groups long discriminated against. The name *affirmative action* was given to these programs. "Affirm" means in this case to support an individual's civil rights by taking positive "action" to protect individuals from the lasting effects of discrimination. The goals of these action programs are increased job opportunities, employment promotions, and increased admissions to universities.

As early as 1961, three years before the landmark Civil Rights Act, President John F. Kennedy seemed to already be aware of the need. Actually using the term "affirmative action," he signed Executive Order 10925 requiring federal contractors (private companies who do work for the government) to hire more minority employees. Likewise, President Lyndon Johnson believed that the scars caused by years of legal discrimination could not be easily erased. In a commencement speech he delivered at Howard University on June 4, 1965, President Johnson showed a wise understanding of the problem saying, "You do not take a person who, for years, has been hobbled by chains and liberate him, bring him up to the starting line of a race and then say, 'You're free to compete with all the others,' and justly believe that you have been completely fair."

Johnson asserted that simply freedom from discrimination was not enough, opportunity had be provided as well. Johnson continued, "not just equality as a right and a theory, but equality as a fact."

Backing up his words that same year, President Johnson signed Executive Order 11246 providing a practical way to carry out affirmative action plans. The order required federal contractors to file written affirmative action plans with the Office of Federal Contract Compliance Programs (OFCCP) under the Department of Labor.

U.S. presidents continued to support affirmative action programs. President Richard M. Nixon was the first to require specific number goals or quotas and timetables for hiring minorities and women. For example, a federal contractor might be required to hire at least twelve minority or women workers for every one hundred workers and to hire those twelve within six months. Government set-asides also appeared. Set-aside programs have a goal that a certain percentage, such as five percent, of all government contracts should be given to minority and women-owned businesses. In 1977 President Jimmy Carter supported affirmative action by signing the Public Works Employment Act. The act required that at least ten percent of federal funds in each grant awarded by the Department of Commerce to state or local governments for local public works projects must be used to contract for services or supplies from businesses owned by minorities.

Characteristics of Affirmative Action Programs

Affirmative action programs have four general characteristics. First, they may be begun and supported by either government agencies or set up voluntarily by private organizations such as private universities or vocational schools, businesses, or labor unions.

Second, when considering an individual for a job, promotion, or admission to a school, the program must look at personal factors such as race or gender. However, the individual must also be qualified for the job or education program they apply to. Therefore, the individual may not receive job or education opportunities based solely on their race or gender.

Third, a program must clearly be designed to make up for unfair treatment in the past of the race or gender group to which the individual belongs. Fourth, affirmative action plans are to be only temporary solutions and are not meant to continue forever.

Affirmative Action as a Jump Start

Supporters claim only with these positive action programs can black Americans and women achieve equality of opportunity. The reason, which President Johnson referred to in his Howard University speech, lies in the fact that both blacks and women were prevented by long term discrimination from gaining education and job skills, pushing them into and keeping them in the lowest levels of employment. Whether required by the government or voluntarily begun by private employers or schools, affirmative action programs are the best means to overcoming the negative outcomes of discrimination. In effect, they serve as a "jump start" to put the discriminated groups on a more level playing field with those who traditionally have not suffered discrimination. Affirmative action programs are widely established in government agencies, businesses, and schools.

But What About the Fourteenth Amendment?

By the late 1970s public sentiment was growing against affirmative action programs. Whatever happened to "equal protection of the laws" under the Fourteenth Amendment? Does it allow certain kinds of preferential treatment typical of affirmative action plans for specific groups of persons? Similarly, what about the Civil Rights Act of 1964 prohibiting discrimination on the basis of race, color, religion, sex, and national origin? Cries of reverse discrimination began to be heard. Reverse discrimination is the lessening of opportunity for a group of people not traditionally discriminated against, such as white adult males.

To many, there seemed to be conflict between civil rights laws and affirmative action. The civil rights laws basically forbid individuals and organizations, such as businesses and schools, to consider race and gender as factors for making decisions. Affirmative action policies, however, require that race and gender be taken into account when hiring or admitting to school individuals and that preference be given to minorities or women to make up for past discrimination. As affirmative action cases began to reach the Supreme Court in the mid-1970s, the Court wrestled with these questions of equal protection and fairness.

Affirmative action disputes eventually became the main form of civil rights cases before the Court. Between 1974 and 1987 the Court's record was mixed on affirmative action cases and in no case were more than six justices in agreement.

Cases Challenging Affirmative Action

The first case challenging affirmative action to be decided by the Supreme Court was ***Regents of the University of California v. Bakke*** in 1978. The case involved the charge of "reverse discrimination" in which a California university medical school had set aside sixteen slots out of one hundred solely for minority applicants. Allan Bakke, a non-minority applicant, was twice turned down by the medical school yet minorities with lower entrance scores were accepted. In reaction, Bakke charged he was discriminated against by the school in violation of the Fourteenth Amendment's Equal Protection Clause and Title VI of the 1964 Civil Rights Act. After hearing the arguments presented by Bakke and the University of California, the Court agreed with Bakke that the school had discriminated against him. The Court ruled that setting quotas (requiring that a predetermined number of openings be filled by minorities) was not an acceptable form of addressing past injustices. On the other hand, the Court also ruled that affirmative action programs could be appropriate under certain circumstances. Consideration of race would not violate the Equal Protection Clause if race is one of several factors considered, not the only factor considered. The Court said that for the government to treat citizens unequally the government must show a very important need, such as making up for past specific instances of discrimination, and that the program must be very carefully applied.

The Court's next affirmative action case was ***United Steelworkers v. Weber*** (1979). The case simply asked the question whether or not the Civil Rights Act prohibited an employer from voluntarily establishing a temporary affirmative action training program which favored blacks over whites. The Court decided to permit the program which would lead to better, more skilled jobs for black Americans in an industry which historically they had been under represented. Following the *United Steelworkers* case, ***Fullilove v. Klutznick*** (1980) led the Court to uphold the government set-aside program established by the 1977 Public Works Employment Act.

During the 1980s, President Ronald Reagan's administration was openly opposed to affirmative action and was pleased by two Supreme Court rulings. The Court determined in *Firefighters Local Union No.*

1784 v. Stotts (1984) and *Wygant v. Jackson Board of Education* (1986) that affirmative action policies could not be used by companies when laying off workers. Seniority, not race, should be a key factor in deciding who should be let go. But by 1987 the Court had established in *Johnson v. Transportation Agency* a firm stance in favor of affirmative action. The Court supported a county agency's action in promoting a woman ahead of a male with slightly higher test scores. Correcting the under representation of women in the agency was a suitable goal to justify the agency decision. In *United States v. Paradise* (1987) the Court upheld a temporary quota system to promote black state troopers in Alabama. The "one black, one white" promotion quota corrected employment discrimination long present in the Alabama state police.

Affirmative action cases continued into the 1990s. In *Adarand Constructors, Inc. v. Pena* (1995) the Court tightened requirements on affirmative action programs. Writing for the Court, Justice Sandra Day O'Connor commented, "Government may treat people differently because of their race only for the most compelling [very important] reasons." To ensure that all persons receive equal protection of the laws affirmative action programs could only be considered legal if they were designed to correct specific instances of past discrimination.

Becoming one of the most controversial social issues of the day, the affirmative action debate continued. President Bill Clinton delivered his "Mend it, but don't end it" speech in July of 1995. Summarizing the overall picture of affirmative action, he commented,

> **We had slavery for centuries before the passage of the Thirteenth, Fourteenth, and Fifteenth Amendments. We waited another hundred years for the civil rights legislation. Women have had the vote for less than a hundred years. We have always had difficulty with these things, as most societies do. But we are making more progress than many other nations. Since, based on the evidence, the job is not done, here is what I think we should do. We should reaffirm the principle of affirmative action and fix the practices.**

Despite the call to fix, not abandon affirmative action programs, in 1996 Californians voted to ban existing state government affirmative action programs. Supporters of the ban claimed that by eliminating preferences racial and gender equality under state law would be reestablished in education, contracting, and employment. Believing the initiative likely violated the Equal Protection Clause of the Fourteenth Amendment, a federal court judge stopped the ban from taking effect and allowed affirmative action programs to continue. A federal appeals court in 1997 reversed the judge's decision and allowed the ban to take effect.

To Be Fair and Equal—the Debate Continues

Fairness and equal protection are central questions in the affirmative action debate. White males and middle-class white females have strongly opposed affirmative action policies. White males commonly argue that they are being unfairly discriminated against for past injustices they had no personal responsibility for. Supporters of affirmative action, on the other hand, have contended that white males continue to directly benefit from past discrimination. They point to a 1995 study showing that white males still held 95 percent of top management positions in major companies and that men earned up to 45 percent more money than women or minorities. Critics of affirmative action also argue that the tradition of rewarding a job well done or hard work is lessened with a lessening in standards for hiring and promotion. Supporters counter that any influence in the reward system, if any, is minimal.

Aside from public debates, the courts have given their approval to affirmative action programs. However, the courts have sent a clear message that for a company to impose preferences to individuals based on their race or sex, they must be able to show the preferential treatment is directly related to making up for specific past discrimination. Likewise, government programs giving special consideration to previously disadvantaged groups must show their programs are very carefully designed and serve a compelling public purpose of making up for past injustices.

Suggestions for further reading

Chavez, Lydia. *The Color Bind: California's Battle to End Affirmative Action.* Berkeley: University of California Press, 1998.

Edley, Christopher, Jr. *Not All Black and White: Affirmative Action, Race, and American Values.* New York: Hill & Wang Pub., 1996.

Guernsey, Joan Bren. *Affirmative Action: A Problem or a Remedy?* (Pro/Con Series). Minneapolis, MN: Lerner Publications Co., 1997.

Regents of the University of California v. Bakke 1978

Petitioner: The University of California at Davis Medical School

Respondent: Allan Bakke

Petitioner's Claim: That the University of California Medical School's special admission affirmative action program violated Bakke's civil rights when he was denied admission.

Chief Lawyer for Petitioner: Archibald Cox, Paul J. Mishkin, Jack B. Owens, Donald L. Reidhaar

Chief Lawyer for Respondent: Reynold H. Colvin

Justices for the Court: Chief Justice Warren Burger, Lewis F. Powell, Jr., William H. Rehnquist, John Paul Stevens, Potter Stewart

Justices Dissenting: Harry A. Blackmun, William J. Brennan, Jr., Thurgood Marshall, Byron R. White

Date of Decision: June 28, 1978

Decision: Ruled in favor of Bakke by finding the school's special admissions program unconstitutional because of its use of quotas and that Bakke should be admitted.

Significance: The Court ruled that race could be one factor among several considered for admissions, but it could not be the only factor considered. Since race could be considered, the ruling was the first court approval of affirmative action.

On October 12, 1977 a long line wound its way up the marble staircase and between the towering columns of the U.S. Supreme Court building. Some had camped out all night to get a chance to hear the case to be argued that day, *Regents of the University of California v. Allan Bakke,* the first affirmative action case to reach the Supreme Court.

The courtroom was packed, yet most of the audience had obtained tickets through their connections to the court or through the parties to the case. Despite their special interest in the case, only a small number of people of color or women could be spotted in the select gathering. This alone was testimony (evidence) to the many years of gender (sex) exclusion in professional circles.

Demonstrators who marched in the streets that day were of a decidedly different makeup. Men and women of all colors marched not only outside the Court but from New York to Berkeley, California, raising banners and chanting slogans such as "We won't go back. We won't go back!" The crowds put the Court and world on notice that whatever the outcome in the case, the struggle to open the doors of universities to minorities would go on, never to return to the days when the same demonstrators' grandparents and parents could not gain admission. However, not all Americans supported these demonstrators. Many were opposed to giving increased opportunity at the expense of others through affirmative action programs.

What's All the Fuss About?

Affirmative action means making a special effort to provide opportunities in education and businesses for members of groups (people of color and women) that had been discriminated (giving privileges to one group but not to another) against in the past. In the mid-1970s, educational affirmative action programs often used "quotas." Quotas meant setting a goal that a certain number of minority students would be admitted.

The medical school at the Davis campus of the University of California had such a program in 1970. The program called for a quota of sixteen out of one hundred openings to be filled by disadvantaged students from minority groups. The medical school viewed minority groups as "Blacks," "Chicanos," "Asians," and "American Indians." Under special admission procedures, the minority applicants were evaluated by placing less focus on test scores and grade point average and more on the applicant's overall life and qualifications. The medical school did not

AFFIRMATIVE ACTION

rate or compare special applicants against students applying under regular admission requirements, but recommended special applicants for admission until the sixteen places were filled. This enabled sixteen minority students to join Davis' freshman class of one hundred students.

Allan Bakke

Allan Bakke, a white, thirty-seven year old engineer, wanted to be a medical doctor. He applied in 1973 and again in 1974 through the regular admission process to the University of California at Davis Medical School. Although each year he appeared more qualified than several students admitted through the affirmative action special admissions program, Bakke was rejected both years. As a result, Bakke sued for admission to the Davis medical school. He claimed the medical school's special admission policy denied admission to him solely on the basis of his race thus violating his rights under the Equal Protection Clause of the Fourteenth Amendment. The trial court agreed with Bakke and ruled the special admissions procedure unconstitutional (not following the intent of the U.S. Constitution). Yet, the court refused to order the school to admit

There were many protests surrounding the Bakke *decision.* Reproduced by permission of AP/Wide World Photos.

Bakke. In 1976, the California Supreme Court agreed with the trial court's judgement, but also ordered the school to admit Bakke. The university appealed to the U.S. Supreme Court which agreed to hear the case.

The Arguments

As demonstrators chanted outside, Archibald Cox for the university and Reynold Colvin, Bakke's lawyer, argued the case. Cox, a Harvard law professor who had appeared before the Court many times, defended the university's affirmative action special admissions program. He claimed it was a fair and constitutional way of making up for past discrimination against minority groups. The program gave new opportunity to members of groups which had not had these opportunities in the past.

Colvin, in his first Supreme Court appearance, made several claims against the university. He argued that the admission policy was in conflict with Title VI of the Civil Rights Act of 1964. Title VI prohibits discrimination based on race, color, or national origin in programs which receive federal funds. All state university programs, including the Davis medical school, receive such funds. Furthermore, Colvin argued if Title VI was violated, then the Equal Protection Clause of the Fourteenth Amendment guaranteeing "equal protection of the laws" was also violated. Therefore, the special admission policy was unconstitutional. Continuing in Bakke's defense, Colvin suggested the program went too far in offering increased opportunities for minority groups and seemed to be "reverse discrimination." Reverse discrimination is the lessening of opportunity for a group of people not traditionally discriminated against such as white males.

Two Majority Opinions

More than eight months would pass before the Supreme Court delivered its decision. The Court was as sharply divided over the affirmative action issue as the nation was. Two majority opinions were presented. Each of the opinions was agreed to by a different grouping of five justices. Justice Lewis F. Powell was key to the Bakke decision being the only justice in both majorities.

The two 5–4 majority opinions delivered by Justice Powell were:

(1) The special admissions program with a fixed quota or number of places available only to minorities violated Title VI of the Civil Rights

Act of 1964. Those places were denied to white applicants based only on their race. The university's policy was struck down and the university was ordered to admit Bakke.

(2) Admissions programs do not violate the Equal Protection Clause of the Fourteenth Amendment if they consider race as one of several factors used to decide admission. Therefore, race may be considered but it may not be the only factor considered.

Developing the Two Opinions

The two majority opinions developed in the following manner. In the first opinion four justices (John Paul Stevens, Warren Burger, Potter Stewart, and William Rehnquist) avoided completely the constitutional issue of Equal Protection and instead said it was "crystal clear" that the quota system violated Title VI of the Civil Rights Act. These four also agreed race could never be a factor in admissions. Although he reasoned differently, Justice Powell agreed the quota system violated Title VI. His agreement with the Title VI part added up to a five-justice majority, making quota systems illegal. However, he did not agree race could never be used in admission programs.

In the second opinion four different justices (William J. Brennan, Thurgood Marshall, Byron White, and Harry Blackmun) pointed out that "race conscious programs" do not violate the Equal Protection Clause as long as race was only one factor among many factors considered for admission to a program. Powell agreed, and his agreement made a five-justice majority on that point.

Allan Bakke was admitted to the medical school at the University of California Davis. He graduated in 1982.

Justice Marshall's Dissent

Justice Marshall, the first African American to serve on the Supreme Court and a strong supporter of affirmative action programs, commented in one of his most famous dissents,

> **The position of the Negro today in America is the tragic but inevitable (unavoidable) consequence of centuries of unequal treatment. Measured by any benchmark of comfort or achievement, meaningful equality remains a distant dream for the Negro. . .**

LEWIS FRANKLIN POWELL, JR.

Appointed by President Richard M. Nixon, Lewis Franklin Powell, Jr., served as an associate justice of the U.S. Supreme Court from 1972 until his retirement in 1987. Born into a distinguished Virginia family whose first American ancestor was an original settler of the Jamestown colony in 1607, Powell received his law degree from Washington and Lee University and his masters in law at Harvard in 1932. Powell became one of Virginia's most respected and honored lawyers as well as a strong community leader. While serving on the Richmond School Board and the Virginia State Board of Education, he oversaw the peaceful integration of the state's public schools in the late 1950s.

As an admired Supreme Court member, Powell generally held conservative views but was comfortable taking a middle stand. He often cast a deciding vote, or "swing vote," in cases where justices' opinions were split. Balancing the rights of a society against rights of individuals, Powell frequently cast decisive pro-civil rights votes. His most famous decisive vote came in *Regents of the University of California v. Bakke* (1978) where he prohibited quota systems in university admission policies but upheld the principle of "affirmative action."

Now, we have the Court again stepping in, this time to stop affirmative action programs of the type [quota system] used by the University of California.

Impact

Based on the ruling, quota systems used in affirmative action programs were out but race could be considered if other factors were also considered. This concession that race could be used as a factor was at least a partial victory for affirmative action and demonstrators who had filled the streets. As is often the case, the divided or split decision seemed to allow more room for differing applications across the country. For example, universities with strong affirmative action programs used the part that the race factor could continue to help them build strong multiracial communities. On the other hand, schools that had always been reluctant in racially integrating their campuses used the decision to abandon attempts at affirmative action.

Affirmative action continued to be a controversial topic in the 1990s. In 1995 demonstrators in California again took to the streets in support of affirmative action programs at the state universities. President Bill Clinton made his famous speech on affirmative action in July of 1995 saying to "mend it, but don't end it." However, in 1996 Californians voted to ban existing state government affirmative action programs. The issue remains controversial and complex.

Suggestions for further reading

Dreyfuss, Joel, and Charles Lawrence III. *The Bakke Case: The Politics of Inequality.* New York: Harcourt, Brace, Jovanovich, 1979.

Lawrence, Charles R., III, and Mari J. Matsuda. *We Won't Go Back: Making the Case for Affirmative Action.* Boston: Houghton Mifflin Company, 1997.

Welch, Susan, and John Gruhl. *Affirmative Action and Minority Enrollments in Medical and Law Schools.* Ann Arbor: University of Michigan Press, 1998.

United Steelworkers of America v. Weber 1979

Petitioner: United Steelworkers of America

Respondent: Brian Weber

Petitioner's Claim: That an affirmative action program started by Kaiser Aluminum, in voluntary partnership with the United Steelworkers, did not violate Title VII of the 1964 Civil Rights Act.

Chief Lawyers for Petitioner: Michael E. Gottesman

Chief Lawyers for Respondent: Michael R. Fontham

Justices for the Court: Harry A. Blackmun, William J. Brennan, Jr., Warren E. Burger, Thurgood Marshall, William H. Rehnquist, Potter Stewart, Byron R. White

Justices Dissenting: Warren E. Burger, William H. Rehnquist

Date of Decision: June 27, 1979

Decision: Ruled in favor of United Steelworkers and reversed the rulings of two lower courts by upholding the legality of the affirmative action plan.

Significance: The decision was the first Supreme Court ruling to address the issue of affirmative action in employment. Affirmative action programs were not in violation of Title VII of the Civil Rights Act as long as private parties entered into such programs voluntarily and on a temporary basis. The ruling encouraged private employers to experiment with affirmative action plans to open job opportunities for minorities.

AFFIRMATIVE ACTION

Between 1947 and 1962 the unemployment of black Americans compared to whites skyrocketed. In 1947 the non-white employment rate was 64 percent higher than the white rate. By 1962 it was 124 percent higher than the white rate. Determined to address long standing inequalities between blacks and whites in America and to help end discrimination (giving privileges to one group but not to another similar group) against blacks, Congress passed the Civil Rights Act of 1964. The act banned discrimination because of a person's color, race, national origin, or religion. Responding to questions like the one asked by Senator Hubert Humphrey, "What good does it do a Negro to be able to eat in a fine restaurant if he cannot afford to pay the bill?" Congress made sure the Civil Rights Act included sections dealing with employment. The language of subsection 703(a) of Title VII of the Civil Rights Act reads:

> **It shall be an unlawful employment practice for an employer (1) to fail to refuse to hire or to discharge [fire] any individual . . . because of such individual's race . . . or (2) to limit, segregate [separate into groups] or classify his employees or applicants for employment in any way which would deprive [take away] or tend to deprive any individual of equal opportunities . . . because of such individual's race. . .**

This wording was further supported in Section 703(d) which forbids employers, labor organizations, or any combination of the two to discriminate against any individual on the basis of race, color, religion, sex or national origin in apprenticeship (learning a craft or trade from an already skilled worker) or on-the-job training programs.

Despite the act's clear language, forward-thinking leaders in America believed more would be necessary to overcome two and a half centuries of discrimination and to promote equal opportunity. Together, black and political leaders began in the 1960s to fashion plans known as affirmative action plans. Affirmative action means making a special effort or taking a specific action to promote opportunities in education or employment for members of groups discriminated against in the past. The goals of these programs are increased job opportunities, employment promotions, and admissions to universities for minorities.

Kaiser's Affirmative Action Plan

In 1974 the United Steelworkers of America, a labor union, and Kaiser Aluminum and Chemical Company, a huge steel maker with fifteen plants nationwide, voluntarily agreed to set up an affirmative action plan. According to the plan, Kaiser would reserve 50 percent of the places in its craft-training (apprenticeship) programs for black workers. The plants would continue this policy until the percentage of black American craft workers in its plants was equal to the percentage of black Americans in the local population. The education provided in the craft-training programs turned unskilled workers into higher paid skilled workers.

At Kaiser's plant in Gramercy, Louisiana less than 2 percent of all skilled workers were black Americans despite the fact that 39 percent of the total labor force in the town was black. The low percentage of skilled black workers was a reflection of past discrimination. Black workers in the area had long been denied opportunities to become skilled craftworkers. The Gramercy plant's affirmative action plan, following the guidelines worked out between the steelworker's union and Kaiser, was to have approximately 39 percent of its skilled positions filled by black Americans. The plan was temporary and would be ended when they reached the goal.

Brian Weber, Man of Steel

Brian Weber was a white unskilled union worker at Kaiser in Gramercy. He applied for a position in the craft-training program but was rejected although he had more seniority than several of the blacks selected. Seniority is a status or rank that an individual has attained based on the amount of time the individual has spent on the job. A common labor practice is to give better jobs or job training placements to those with more seniority. Before the affirmative action plan, Kaiser used seniority to decide who was admitted to training programs. However, under the affirmative action plan, to keep the training program at 50 percent blacks and 50 percent whites, the company had to choose some blacks with less seniority than some whites.

Weber charged that since his rejection was due to his race, he had been discriminated against in violation of the Civil Rights Act Title VII, sections 703(a) and (d). He filed a class action suit (lawsuit brought by a number of persons with a common interest) in U.S. District Court. Weber's argument was simple. Under Title VII an employer may not discriminate on the basis of race or color. Weber claimed Kaiser's affirmative action plan did just that. The plan actually was "reverse discrimination," discrimination against a group which has not historically been discriminated against such as white males. The district court and the Court of Appeals of the Fifth Circuit agreed with Weber. The courts ruled that race-based employment practices, even those designed to fix past discrimination, were themselves discriminatory in violation of Title VII. The United Steelworkers of America Union appealed to the U.S. Supreme Court.

Court Gives History Lesson

The Supreme Court reversed the two lower courts' rulings in a 5-2 vote. Justice William J. Brennan, Jr., writing for the majority, delivered a history lesson on discrimination in the United States. He also illustrated how the Court must carefully consider America's past in order to shape its future more fairly for all. Justice Brennan identified the question as:

> **Whether Title VII forbids private employers and unions from voluntarily agreeing upon . . . affirmative action plans that accord [give] racial preferences in the manner and for the purpose provided in the Kaiser-USWA plan.**

Recognizing that Weber's argument was understandable and had merit (value), Brennan examined the concerns Congress had when it passed the Civil Rights Act of 1964. Extensively quoting Senator Humphry's speeches made in the Senate in 1963, Brennan noted "'the plight of the Negro in our economy'" and how "blacks were largely relegated [assigned to a low ranking job] to 'unskilled and semi-skilled jobs.' . . . As a consequence the 'position of the Negro worker [was] steadily worsening.'" Brennan continued, "it was to this problem that Title VII's prohibition against racial discrimination in employment was primarily addressed."

Given the legislative history of the Civil Rights Act, Brennan wrote that the Court could not agree with Weber. Congress had not meant to prohibit the private business sector from voluntarily taking steps designed to meet the goals of Title VII. Brennan commented that to interpret 703(a) and (d) as forbidding "all race-conscious affirmative action would bring about an end completely at variance with [opposite to] the purpose of the statute [law] and must be rejected." The Court held, "Title VII's prohibition in 703 (a) and (d) against racial discrimination does not condemn all private, voluntary, race-conscious affirmative action plans."

UNDERSTANDING LABOR UNIONS

Before labor unions were formed, wage earners had no voice in their pay, work hours, or working conditions. Newly established labor unions allowed workers to gain some control over their employment conditions. A labor union is an organization of employees whose purpose is to gain, through legal bargaining with an employer, better working conditions, pay, and benefits (health insurance, retirement plan, etc.).

Workers in the United States have formed three main kinds of unions: (1) craft unions limited to skilled tradesmen such as carpenters; (2) industrial unions open to skilled and unskilled workers in mass-producing industries such as the automobile and steel industries; and, (3) public employee unions such as city workers, fire fighters, and police.

Unions in trades such as steelmaking, bricklaying, and printing provide apprentice programs in cooperation with employers to train persons to become skilled trade workers. The training combines on-the-job experience with individual and classroom instruction.

Banding together in a group gives workers more power than they would have as individuals. Numerous lawsuits brought by unions on behalf of their workers have reached the U.S. Supreme Court.

Where Was Weber's Equal Protection?

The Equal Protection Clause of the Fourteenth Amendment, often used in charges against affirmative action plans, did not apply in this case. The reason was that the Equal Protection Clause guarantees that "equal protection of the laws" shall not be denied by any state. The keyword here is "state." Kaiser is a private company. A year before *Weber,* the Court ruled that the Equal Protection Clause did apply in the affirmative action case of ***University of California v. Bakke*** (1978) because it involved a state-funded university. The United Steelworkers of America was a private union and Kaiser a private business, hence the Equal Protection Clause could not be applied.

Suggestions for further reading

American Federation of Labor and Congress of Industrial Organization. [Online] Website: http://www.aflcio.org (Accessed July 31, 2000).

Lynch, Frederick R. *Invisible Victims: White Males and the Crisis of Affirmative Action.* New York: Praeger, 1991.

Mosley, Albert G., and Nicholas Capaldi. *Affirmative Action: Social Justice or Unfair Preference.* Lanham: Rowman & Littlefield Publishers, 1996.

Skrentny, John David. *The Ironies of Affirmative Action: Politics, Culture, and Justice in America.* Chicago: The University of Chicago Press, 1996.

Fullilove v. Klutznick
1980

Petitioner: H. Earl Fullilove and others

Respondent: Philip M. Klutznick, U.S. Secretary of Commerce

Petitioner's Claim: That a provision in the law requiring that 10 percent of all federal funds for local public works projects go to minority-owned businesses violates the U.S. Constitution.

Chief Lawyers for Petitioner: Robert G. Benisch and Robert J. Hickey

Chief Lawyers for Respondent: Drew S. Days III

Justices for the Court: Harry A. Blackmun, William J. Brennan, Jr., Warren E. Burger, Thurgood Marshall, Lewis F. Powell, Byron R. White

Justices Dissenting: William H. Rehnquist, John Paul Stevens, Potter Stewart

Date of Decision: July 2, 1980

Decision: Affirmed lower court rulings rejecting the petitioners' claim that minority "set-asides" were unconstitutional.

Significance: The decision clarified the Court's position on the constitutionality of minority set-aside programs. Plus many state and local governments adopted set-aside programs for minority-owned businesses.

Congress had long struggled with the fact that when various government agencies, including state and local governments, contracted for construction of public works projects rarely did they contract with minority-owned businesses. Public works projects are projects that receive money from the federal government for such things as construction of schools, courthouses, post offices, roads, bridges, dams, power projects, water systems, and waste treatment plants. Federal money received by governmental agencies to pay for the projects almost never reached minority business enterprises (companies).

In May of 1977, President Jimmy Carter signed the Public Works Emplyment Act, making it a law. Courtesy of the Library of Congress.

According to Representative Mitchell of Maryland, speaking on the floor of the House of Representatives on February 23, 1977, " . . . every agency of the Government has tried to figure out a way to avoid doing this very thing. Believe me, these bureaucracies can come up with 10,000 ways to avoid doing it."

Minority Business Enterprise Provision

Representative Mitchell pointed out that in 1976 less than one percent of federal funds for these projects found their way to minority companies, yet minorities made up 15-18 percent of the general population. Representative Mitchell's efforts ended with passage of the Public Works Employment Act of 1977. The act authorized an additional $4 billion for federal grants [money from the federal government for projects] to be awarded by the Secretary of Commerce to state and local governments for use in local public works projects. But there was a "catch" to these dollars. The catch was a section of the act, Section 103 (f) (2) called the "minority business enterprise" or MBE provision. The MBE provision required that,

> **. . . no grant shall be made under the Act for any local public works project unless the applicant gives satisfactory assurance to the secretary [of Commerce] that at least 10 per cent of the amount of each grant shall be expended [spent] for [services from] minority business enterprises.**

So 10 percent of the federal grant money provided for each project had to go to minority-owned businesses. This forced governments to contract with those businesses for at least some work on each project. Minority group members were defined as citizens of the United States who are "Negroes, Spanish-speaking, Orientals, Indians, Eskimos, and Aleuts."

Public Works Employment Act Challenged

Signed into law by President Jimmy Carter in May of 1977, the Public Works Employment Act was an affirmative action plan designed to increase opportunities for businesses owned by groups traditionally discriminated against in U.S. history. This plan was a "set-aside" program, that is, 10 percent of federal grant money directed to public works projects had to be "set-aside" and awarded to MBE's. This was the first federal law, since the mid-1800s, to establish a specific class of persons based on race to which special treatment was to be given.

As expected after only six months the act was challenged in court. H. Earl Fullilove and several associations of non-minority construction contractors filed suit against Philip M. Klutznick, U.S. Secretary of Commerce. They complained the 10 percent MBE requirement had hurt their companies incomes because of lost business—business which now went to the MBEs. They charged the MBE provision was unconstitutional (the law did not follow the intent of the U.S. Constitution) because it violated the Equal Protection Clause of the Fourteenth Amendment of the U.S. Constitution and also the equal protection promised under the Due Process Clause of the Fifth Amendment. The Equal Protection Clause guarantees that no person or class of persons will be denied the same protection of the laws enjoyed by other persons or classes in similar circumstances in their lives, liberty, property, and pursuit of happiness. Due process is also a constitutional guarantee that before the government acts to take away a person's life, liberty, or property fair legal proceedings must take place. They demanded that no more federal monies be given to minority contractors pending the outcome of their lawsuit.

First the district court and then the U.S. Court of Appeals for the Second Circuit ruled against Fullilove and affirmed (supported) the MBE program as constitutional. The court of appeals cited the many years of governmental attempts to remedy (fix) past racial and ethnic (groups of various races) discrimination. The Court found it "difficult to imagine" any other purpose for the MBE provision.

Fullilove's group appealed to their last avenue of hope, the U.S. Supreme Court who agreed to hear the case.

Congress Need Not Be Color-Blind

On July 2, 1980, the U.S. Supreme Court issued its 6-3 plurality ruling (a majority agrees on the decision but for different reasons). The justices again affirmed the constitutionality of the Public Works Employment Act and rejected Fullilove's claims. Chief Justice Warren Burger wrote that Congress had frequently used the Spending Power provision of Article I of the Constitution to hold back federal money until "governments or private parties [agreed] to cooperate voluntarily with federal policy." The Spending Power provision, the Court recognized, allowed Congress to "provide for the . . . general Welfare" and the MBE provision does that. Furthermore Justice Burger commented that in attempting to right past discrimination, Congress need not act in a wholly "color-blind" fashion. The set-asides were a "reasonably necessary means of furthering the compelling [important] governmental interest in redressing [to make up for] the discrimination, that affects minority contractors." Even though groups were receiving preferential treatment under the law, the Equal Protection Clause was not violated because the preferential treatment was necessary to boost the opportunities of those groups.

Chief Justice Burger also wrote that Due Process was not violated. While Congress, in debating passage of the act, had not actually held hearings on set-asides, they nevertheless had acted in a knowledgeable and reasonable manner to correct long recognized discrimination practices in the construction industry. Yet another reason for the plurality rul-

THE HOT CONTROVERSY OVER REVERSE OR BENIGN DISCRIMINATION

Affirmative action programs to correct past discrimination against minorities and women have led to a new form of discrimination known as reverse or benign (with good intentions) discrimination. White males generally are thought of as being the victims by losing jobs or educational opportunities to minorities or women.

Supporters of affirmative action say the programs were never suppose to be painless. The group which historically did not suffer but rather benefitted greatly from its privileged status must now suffer. Yet, supporters point to statistics showing white males are suffering little. Any setbacks suffered by white male reduced opportunities are more likely results of the U.S. economy and job markets. Critics say the cost to those who are being required to pay for historical wrongs are paying too much. They point to reverse discrimination in college admissions, scholarships, government contracts, and jobs in the private and public sectors.

The second main argument is over the idea of merit. Critics claim that better qualified candidates lose out as a result of affirmative action. They contend that only individual qualities should determine who is hired or granted admission. Supporters say those who question merit miss the point. Affirmative action merely gives a jump start and does not ignore merit. Besides, merit can not be precisely ranked in individuals. Additionally, there are many "no merit" situations in American society such as the children of the rich attend the best schools regardless of their qualifications

ing was the MBE, when highly scrutinized (examined by the Court), still passed as constitutional.

Burger concluded simply with, "The MBE provision of the Public Works Employment Act of 1977 does not violate the [U.S.] Constitution."

The act was reasonably debated then well written, had the honest and important goal to right past discriminations, and Congress had the constitutional power to enforce the set-asides.

Because of *Fullilove,* many state and local governments adopted set-aside programs for minority owned businesses. Some withstood court tests while less flexible ones did not. By the late 1980s the Court had reinforced its position in upholding affirmative action in three cases, *Local Number 28 of the Sheet Metal Workers' International v. Equal Employment Opportunity Commission* (1986); *Local Number 93, International Association of Firefighters, AFL-CIO C.L.C. v. City of Cleveland, et al.* (1986); and, *Johnson v. Transportation Agency* (1987).

Reverse Discrimination

Fullilove, along with ***University of California v. Bakke*** (1978) and ***United Steelworkers of America v. Weber*** (1979), all tested the problem of "reverse discrimination." Reverse discrimination is discrimination against a group not historically discriminated against as white males. With all three cases, the Court showed a tendency to protect affirmative action even at the expense of what appeared to be injustice to equally qualified white contractors, students or workers.

Suggestions for further reading

Mills, Nicolaus, ed. *Debating Affirmative Action: Race, Gender, Ethnicity, and the Politics of Inclusion.* New York: Dell Publishing, 1994.

Minority Business Development Agency. [Online] Website: http://www.mbda.gov (Accessed on July 31, 2000).

McWhiter, Darien A. *The End of Affirmative Action: Where Do We Go From Here?* New York: Carol Publishing Group, 1996.

Zelnick, Bob. *Backfire: A Reporter's Look at Affirmative Action.* Washington, DC: Regnery Publishing, Inc., 1996.

Metro Broadcasting, Inc. v. Federal Communications Commission 1990

Petitioner: Metro Broadcasting, Inc.

Respondent: Federal Communications Commission

Petitioner's Claim: That FCC programs designed to increase minority ownership of broadcast licenses violate the principle of equal protection.

Chief Lawyer for Petitioner: Gregory H. Guillot

Chief Lawyer for Respondent: Daniel M. Armstrong

Justices for the Court: Harry A. Blackmun, William J. Brennan, Jr., Thurgood Marshall, John Paul Stevens, Byron R. White

Justices Dissenting: Anthony M. Kennedy, Sandra Day O'Connor, Chief Justice William H. Rehnquist, Antonin Scalia

Date of Decision: June 27, 1990

Decision: Ruled in favor of the FCC by finding that its minority ownership policies did not violate equal protection.

Significance: For the first time the Court endorsed a federal program intended to promote increased minority participation, rather than merely remedy past racial discrimination. The opportunity to broadcast opinions of racial minorities benefits not only minorities, but the public in general.

Historically in the United States, the broadcasting or media communications industry (newspapers, radio, television) reflected the white American's world. For example, little appreciation or understanding of black American culture, thought, or history was communicated. A 1968 report by the National Advisory Commission on Civil Disorders noted, "The world that television and newspapers offer to their black audience is almost totally white." Minorities, including not only black Americans but also Hispanics, Orientals, and Native Americans, rarely saw their viewpoints expressed over the airways.

Policies of the FCC

In the Communication Act of 1934, Congress assigned authority to the Federal Communication Commission (FCC) to grant licenses to persons wishing to construct and operate radio broadcast stations in the United States. The act also encouraged the FCC to promote diversification (a variety of viewpoints representing all citizens) of programming. The FCC used various strategies to attract minority participation but little broadcast diversity resulted. To try harder, the FCC in 1978 adopted a "Statement of Policy on Minority Ownership of Broadcast Facilities." Intended to increase minority ownership of broadcast licenses, the statement outlined two FCC policies, known as the minority preference or ownership policies. First, in selecting companies applying for licenses, the FCC would give special consideration to radio or television stations owned or managed by minority groups. Race would be one of several factors looked at. Secondly, the FCC would permit a broadcaster in danger of losing its license, known as a "distressed" broadcaster, to transfer that license through a "distress sale" to an FCC-approved minority company thereby avoiding a FCC hearing on their suitability. The license sale price could not exceed 75 percent of its fair market value. Despite these FCC's efforts, by 1986 minorities still only owned just over 2 percent of the more than 11,000 radio and television stations. Many of these served limited geographic areas with relatively small audiences.

The FCC's minority preference policies were considered affirmative action policies. Affirmative action means making a special effort or taking a specific action to promote opportunities in business or education for members of groups historically discriminated against. The FCC policies were intended to increase opportunities in the broadcasting industry for minorities. Two cases challenging the constitutionality of the FCC's minority preference policies reached the U.S. Supreme Court in 1990.

Metro Broadcasting

Metro Broadcasting, Inc. and Rainbow Broadcasting each applied for a license to construct and operate a new television station in Orlando, Florida. Metro was a non-minority business, but Rainbow was 90 percent Hispanic-owned. In 1983, the license was granted Metro. However, the FCC reviewed the decision the following year and awarded the license to Rainbow instead. Metro appealed to the U.S. Court of Appeals for the District of Columbia Circuit which agreed with the FCC decision. Metro, challenging FCC's policy awarding preferences to minority-owned businesses, appealed to the U.S. Supreme Court. The Court agreed to hear the case.

Shurberg Broadcasting—Second Case

In 1980, the Faith Center, Inc., a licensee in Hartford, Connecticut, sought permission to transfer its license under the distress-sale policy. After several attempts to transfer to minority-owned companies fell through, Faith Center finally sold its license to Astroline Communications Company, a minority-owned business. Shurberg Broadcasting was also seeking a license but because it was a non-minority business, Shurberg could not buy Faith Center's license. Shurberg challenged the transfer to Astroline on several grounds including that the FCC's distress-sale policy violated its constitutional right to equal protection. Equal protection is a constitutional guarantee that no person or group of persons will be denied the same treatment of the laws as another person or group under similar circumstances. The FCC rejected Shurberg's challenge, but the U.S. Court of Appeals for the District of Columbia agreed with Shurberg. The FCC had violated its right of equal protection under the Fifth Amendment.

The case was examined under equal protection of the Fifth Amendment instead of under the Equal Protection Clause of the Fourteenth Amendment because the Fourteenth applies only to questions involving laws of state government. The Fifth applies to federal government laws and policies. The decision was appealed to the U.S. Supreme Court which agreed to hear the case.

To Promote Diversity

The Supreme Court combined the two cases and heard them at the same time since both considered whether or not the minority preference policies of the FCC were constitutional under the equal protection guarantee of the Fifth Amendment. Justice William J. Brennan, Jr. delivered the 5-4 decision of the Court ruling in favor of FCC in both cases. In making its decision, the Court considered several key factors.

First, the Court examined whether the policies were designed to make up for past specific acts of discrimination. Previous Court decisions on affirmative action policies strongly emphasized that preferential treatment had to remedy (make up for) specific past discrimination. For example, in ***United Steelworkers of America v. Weber*** (1979) Kaiser Aluminum's affirmative action policy was upheld. Kaiser's program specifically made up for the fact that throughout the company's history black Americans had been denied opportunities to become highly paid skilled workers. Kaiser's policy was designed to remedy or fix its past discrimination against blacks. The policy was "remedial." However, in a far-reaching conclusion, Brennan wrote in the FCC case,

> **Congress and the Commission [FCC] do not justify the minority ownership policies strictly as remedies for victims of this discrimination [under representation of minorities in broadcasting], however. Rather, Congress and the FCC have selected the minority ownership policies primarily to promote programming diversity, and they urge that such diversity is an important governmental objective [goal] that can serve as a constitutional basis for the preference policies. We agree.**

The key phrase is "to promote . . . diversity." With this statement, the Court for the first time upheld an affirmative action policy designed not to remedy specific past discrimination but to promote diversity.

An Important Governmental Objective

The Court found that program diversity is an important governmental objective because underrepresentation of minorities in broadcasting not only hurts minority audiences but also the entire viewing and listening public. The public has a right to receive a diversity of views and information over the airwaves, therefore the FCC had to encourage minorities to enter broadcasting. Justice Brennan wrote, "Minority viewpoint in programming serves not only needs and interests of minority but enriches and educates the non-minority audience." Justice Brennan concluded, "

FEDERAL COMMUNICATIONS COMMISSION

The Federal Communications Commission (FCC) is an independent U.S. government agency, established by the Communication Act of 1934. The FCC is directly responsible to Congress. It is charged with regulating interstate and international communication by radio, television, wire, satellite, and cable in the United States. The FCC's seven operating bureaus are Cable Services, Common Carrier, Consumer Information, Enforcement, International, Mass Media, and Wireless Communications. These bureaus are responsible for regulatory programs, processing licenses, aiding in emergency alerts, national defense, analyzing complaints, conducting investigations, and taking part in FCC hearings. As the United States entered the digital age, the FCC is committed to creating a competitive marketplace in Internet connections, phone service, and assuring choices in video entertainment.

The FCC is dedicated to making certain the "Information Age" technologies reach all Americans from business districts to the poorest neighborhoods. While controlling the access and flow of information has become increasingly vital to business success, only approximately 3 percent of commercial broadcast stations has minority ownership. In early 2000 the FCC announced one thousand new low-power non-commercial FM radio stations for community groups, churches, and educational organizations to aid in broadening the range of interests and ideas.

. . . the interest in enhancing broadcast diversity is, at the very least, an important governmental objective, and is therefore a sufficient basis for the Commission's [FCC's] minority ownership policies."

Will FCC's Policies Achieve the Objective?

If diversity of programming is the objective of the government, will increased minority ownership opportunities be, in fact, a good way to achieve diversity? First, Justice Brennan examined in detail the "historical evolution of current federal policy" regarding the broadcasting industry. Congress had required diversity since 1934 and the FCC had developed policies to carry out the requirement. But, previous approaches had not produced adequate diversity. Both Congress and the FCC after "long study, painstaking consideration of all available alternatives [programs tried] came to the conclusion that "minority ownership policies [best] advance the goal of diverse programming." The FCC's minority preference policies take direct aim "at the barriers that minorities face in entering the broadcasting industry." Similarly, the distress-sale policy addresses a common minority company problem of too little capital (money) with which to purchase licenses. It effectively lowers the sale price of existing stations plus provides an incentive for distressed stations to seek out minority buyers.

Turning Point

Justice Brennan summarized:

> **FCC policies do not violate equal protection . . . since they [the policies] bear the imprimatur [mark] of longstanding Congressional support and direction and are substantially related to the achievement of important governmental objectives [directly work to achieve the goal] of broadcasting diversity.**

More importantly, the ruling marked a turning point in American social history. With this decision the Court for the first time approved the constitutionality of affirmative action policies designed to promote minority diversity, rather than to just remedy past discrimination.

Suggestions for further reading

Federal Communications Commission. [Online] Website: http://www.fcc.gov (Accessed on July 31, 2000).

National Association of Broadcasters. [Online] Website: http://www.nab.org (Accessed on July 31, 2000).

Torres, Sasha, ed. *Living Color: Race and Television in the Unites States.* Duke University Press, 1998.

Death is the end of life and the process of dying involves choices and actions. By the end of the twentieth century not only has life become more complicated, but so has the process of dying. No longer do many Americans die early from infectious diseases (strep throat, pneumonia, etc.), but life expectancies run well into the seventies with heart disease and cancer being primary killers. Medical technology can keep terminally ill (dying) patients alive much longer than ever before. Patients who previously would have died quickly from an inability to eat and drink or other complications now can be sustained for days, weeks, even years. Intravenous (IV) feeding and hydration (watering), artificial blood circulating and respiratory systems, antibiotics, and chemotherapy (treatment for cancer) enable life to be prolonged.

Die Nobly and at the Right Time

The Roman's philosophy about dying was, "To live nobly also means to die nobly and at the right time." Figuring out what is the "right time" is the key problem, especially toward the end of the twentieth century. In the 1990s the courts wrestled with ethical (moral codes) and legal controversies. When should an artificial respirator or feeding tube be removed from a person in a coma? When should chemotherapy be discontinued for a cancer patient? Not only when, but who has the right to make the call? Patient's rights groups and physician's organizations as well as religious groups battle for control over decisions about how and when an individual dies. Laws and court decisions began to establish rules and standards to apply to the dying. For example, the right of an individual to refuse medical procedures—sometimes referred to as the right to die—has been affirmed. Before considering court decisions, the difference between right to die and assisted suicide must be clear.

The Right to Die

The right to die generally refers to allowing a patient to die by natural causes when life-sustaining treatment is taken away. The cause of death is considered, therefore, the illness. A competent person may refuse medical treatment. A competent patient is considered by the courts one who can give consent (agree) to be treated or not be treat. The ability to accept or refuse medical treatment is often referred to as bodily self-determination or patient autonomy (self-reliance). On the other hand, an incompetent patient does not have the ability to make such decisions.

A competent person, realizing that he may become incompetent as time passes, may leave instructions to others about desired medical decisions. These directions are called an advance directive or living will. Another option is for the person to appoint a trusted individual to make decisions when he becomes unable to do so. This individual would be called a proxy directive or durable power of attorney. In the 1990s most states had living will laws and all fifty had durable power-of-attorney laws. More people chose to use proxy directives or power-of-attorney than living wills.

Assisted Suicide

Assisted suicide, generally referred to as physical-assisted suicide, is when a doctor helps individuals take their own lives. Generally, the physician helps a patient to take his own life by prescribing a drug that the doctor knows will be used by the patient to commit suicide. The patient dies not by natural causes, but by human action. Assisted suicide is a felony offense in most states. Only in Oregon has physician-assisted suicide been legalized. Oregon voters approved the Oregon Death with

Dignity Act in November of 1994 and, in a repeat voter referendum in 1997, refused to repeal (cancel) the act. The Oregon law is crafted with many requirements and restrictions.

The most famous individual associated with physician-assisted suicide through the 1990s was Dr. Jack Kervorkian, also known as the "suicide doctor." With questionable screening procedures, the retired pathologist assisted in numerous suicides using a machine that allows the patient to decide when to deliver a lethal (killing) poison. Charged numerous times with murder, Kervorkian was found guilty in 1997 of second degree murder in a Michigan trial.

By the 1990s the difference in the meaning of the two terms, right to die and assisted suicide, became clouded in the general public's mind. This is because organizations promoting assisted-suicide legislation began to refer to their effort as the right-to-die movement.

The Controversy Over Assisted Suicide

Supporters of assisted suicide say it is not really different from withholding life supporting medical care and that it is a merciful and dignified option for individuals whose quality of life has become intolerable due to illness. It is a more visible and more easily regulated decision.

On the other side is the American Medical Association whose Code of Medical Ethics considers assisted suicide very different from removal of life sustaining medical care. Although accepting that removal of life support is sometimes necessary to honor a patient's wishes, it holds that assisted suicide is against professional ethics. Others in opposition see a "slippery slope" where legalizing assisted suicide could lead to abuses of the chronically ill, handicapped, and elderly. The Catholic Church, arguing that human life should not be destroyed for any reason, is one of many religious organizations opposed to assisted suicide.

Vital Decisions

Approximately fifteen years before most cases considering life-and-death medical decisions began working their way through the legal system, the 1975 case of Karen Ann Quinlan was decided in the New Jersey Supreme Court. For the first time Americans focused on the right to die. Quinlan, a twenty-one year old woman in a coma from apparent ingestion of tranquilizers and alcohol. She was on life support and her condition was considered hopeless. Her parents asked that life-sustaining medical care be stopped. In a unanimous decision, the New Jersey Supreme Court ruled that Quinlan had a constitutional right to privacy to refuse medical treatment. Under the circumstances, her father's decision to end care should be honored. The *Quinlan* decision established the first legal guidelines for withholding life supporting medical treatment.

In 1990 the U.S. Supreme Court jumped into the right to die argument with a decision in ***Cruzan v. Director, Missouri Department of Health.*** Nancy Cruzan, permanently unconscious from brain injuries sustained in an automobile accident, had previously made informal statements to her roommate about never wanting to be kept in a "vegetative" state. Her parents contended that these statements were enough to indicate her wishes and the life preserving medical treatment should stop. The Court ruled that when a competent person issues "clear and convincing" instructions as to medical care including food and water, it is their constitutional right to have those directions followed. The right has been rooted in common law for centuries. However, the Court decided Cruzan's statements to her roommate were not clear and convincing instructions. In the absence of "clear and convincing" instructions from what became an incompetent person, the Court recognized the state of Missouri's interest in protecting life and safeguarding against potential abuses. The Court refused to require Missouri to honor the "substituted judgement" of Cruzan's family as had been honored in the Quinlan case. The Court left it up to states to adopt "clear and convincing" evidence standards. A key result of the ruling was that it encouraged people to leave advance instructions since the courts will honor them. This ruling was an affirmation of an individual's control of their right to die. The Court, reflecting general public opinion, was comfortable in allowing a competent person to refuse treatment, even if it meant their death. However, that same level of comfort for many people and the courts has not been reached for assisted suicide.

Is Assisted Suicide a Right?

Justice Sandra Day O'Connor had commented in *Cruzan* that the country was only beginning to address questions of medical ethics and that the crafting of procedures should be left to the states. In ***Washington v. Glucksberg*** (1997) the Supreme Court was asked to review the constitutionality of a Washington state statute prohibiting physician-assisted suicide. The law made it a crime to assist, aid or cause the suicide of another person. Many other states have similar laws. Four physicians, three seriously ill patients, and a non-profit counseling organization asked that the law be negated claiming assisted suicide was a constitutional right. The Court in examining U.S. history, tradition, and legal practice and finding no support for assisted suicide as a fundamental right, upheld the Washington law. The Court commented that the state of Washington had a real interest in preserving life, preventing suicide, and safeguarding the poor, sick, and elderly from relatives that might encourage assisted suicide.

On the same day in 1997, the Court also released its decision in a similar case, ***Vacco v. Quill.*** A New York law prohibits helping another person commit suicide while allowing competent adult patients to terminate (stop) life sustaining measures. Three doctors and three terminally ill patients claimed this was inconsistent and in violation of "equal protection of the laws" guaranteed in the Fourteenth Amendment. The Court concluded that physician-assisted suicide is very different from refusing medical treatment. States may treat each practice differently without being in conflict with equal protection.

A Matter of States

Through *Washington v. Glucksberg* and *Vacco v. Quill* the Court rejected the idea that assisted suicide was a constitutional right and confirmed that states could draft laws banning assisted suicide.

Through 1999 no cases involving the Oregon Death With Dignity Act had reached the Supreme Court. However, the U.S. Senate was considering passage of the Pain Relief Promotion Act. This bill would prevent use of federally controlled medications in assisting suicide and, if passed, would in effect outlaw the procedures of the Oregon law.

Suggestions for further reading

Bender, David L., and Bruno Leone, eds. *Euthanasia: Opposing Viewpoints.* San Diego: Greenhaven Press, Inc., 1989.

Cox, Donald W. *Hemlock's Cup: The Struggle for Death with Dignity.* Buffalo, NY: Prometheus Books, 1993.

Delury, George E. *But What If She Wants to Die? A Husband's Diary.* New York: Carol Publishing Group, 1997.

Cruzan v. Director, Missouri Department of Health 1990

Petitioner: Nancy Beth Cruzan, by her parents and co-guardians

Respondent: Director, Missouri Department of Health

Petitioner's Claim: That the state of Missouri had no legal authority to interfere with parents' wish to remove a life-sustaining feeding tube from their daughter's comatose body.

Chief Lawyer for Petitioner: William H. Colby

Chief Lawyer for Respondent: Robert L. Presson, Attorney General of Missouri

Justices for the Court: Anthony Kennedy, Sandra Day O'Connor, Chief Justice William H. Rehnquist, Antonin Scalia, Byron R. White

Justices Dissenting: Harry A. Blackmun, William J. Brennan, Jr., Thurgood Marshall, John Paul Stevens

Date of Decision: June 25, 1990

Decision: Ruled in favor of Missouri by determining the state did not violate the Fourteenth Amendment guarantee of liberties of the comatose patient.

Significance: The case marked the first time the U.S. Supreme Court ruled in a right-to-die case. The Court ruled that rejection of life preserving medical treatment by a competent person is a liberty protected by the Constitution.

Right-to-die is a general term referring to a patient's right to die by natural causes when refusing life sustaining treatment. The refusal can be made by a competent (able to make decisions on their own) patient realizing that their decision may mean death.

Even before the birth of America, right-to-die had been considered a liberty in English common law (legal based on practices rather than laws). As under the U.S. Constitution, such liberties are fundamental freedoms in which a person may participate relatively free from government interference.

Right-to-die is quite different from assisted suicide which was prominent in news in the 1990s. Assisted suicide is when a doctor helps individuals to take their own lives. The patient dies not by natural causes, but by human action.

The first case involving right-to-die that come to the nation's attention was that of Karen Ann Quinlan in 1975. The case involved a young woman in a permanent vegetative state and her family's legal battle to remove life support from her. The case was decided in the New Jersey Supreme Court with a ruling to honor the family's wishes. Not until 1983 did a right-to-die case reach the U.S. Supreme Court.

An Accident on an Icy Missouri Road

Twenty-five year old Nancy Beth Cruzan, driving on an icy Missouri road in January of 1983, lost control of her car. The accident left Cruzan brain damaged and in what doctors described as a "permanent vegetative state." She could not move, speak, or communicate, and showed no indication of thinking abilities, but was able to breath on her own. About a month after the accident a feeding tube was inserted into her stomach through which she received all her nutrition and fluids (food and water). Doctors estimated with this life support she could be kept alive another thirty years.

Clear and Convincing Evidence

By 1988, Lester and Joyce Cruzan had lost all hope that their daughter could ever emerge from her vegetative state. They asked the Missouri state hospital to remove the feeding tube. Hospital officials refused, so the parents sought a court order to have the tube removed. The trial court ordered removal of the tube by finding that a person in Nancy's condition had a right to direct the removal of her life supporting feeding tube.

At issue with this decision was that Nancy could not actually relate her wishes. Before the accident as a healthy active, competent young woman, Nancy had neither made a living will nor appointed anyone to make health care decisions for her if she ever became incompetent (unable to make decisions on her own). However, she had apparently once remarked that she would not want to live in a "vegetative state." Similarly, she stated "that if she couldn't do things for herself 'even halfway, let alone not at all,' she wouldn't want to live that way." The trial court had decided these statements indicated Nancy would not desire to be kept in her vegetative condition and that her parent's wishes to remove the feeding tube should be honored.

The state of Missouri appealed to the Missouri Supreme Court which reversed (changed) the lower court's ruling. A majority of members of the Missouri Supreme Court believed Nancy's remarks about her future care were general and made in a casual way. For a parent or guardian to make a decision for an incompetent patient to remove life support, under Missouri law, the patient must have left "clear and con-

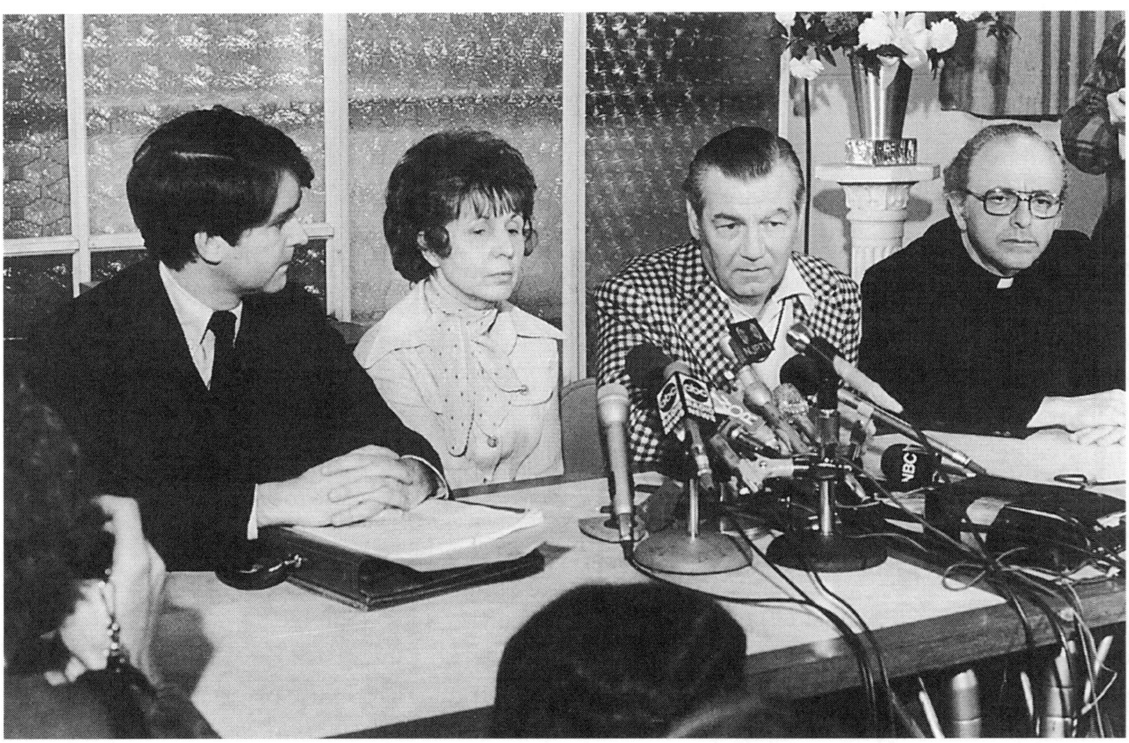

The first right to die case to gain national attention was that of Karen Ann Quinlan. Her parents, Joseph and Julia Quinlan, fought to remove her life support and won. Reproduced by permission of AP/Wide World Photos.

vincing . . . reliable evidence" of her wishes. The court concluded that such evidence was not available from Nancy.

The Cruzans appealed to the U.S. Supreme Court which agreed to hear the case.

The Arguments

Lawyers for the Cruzan family argued before the Supreme Court that "forced . . . medical treatment, and even . . . artificially-delivered food and water [as in the case of Nancy's feeding tube]" would be a violation of a competent person's liberty. Likewise, "an incompetent person should possess the same right in this respect as is possessed by a competent person." A "substituted judgement" of close family members must be accepted, they argued, even if no proof existed that their views reflected the views of the patient. The lawyers contended that Missouri's refusal to allow the parents to direct the removal of their incompetent daughter's feeding tube was in violation of Nancy's constitutional liberty.

The state of Missouri argued that in the interest of protecting an individual's liberty to have their wishes carried out, the State requires that "clear and convincing evidence" be available and that this "rule of decision" is not prohibited by the U.S. Constitution.

U.S. Supreme Court's First Right-to-Die Ruling

In a 5-4 ruling, Chief Justice Rehnquist wrote the opinion for the majority. Rehnquist first affirmed (supported) that "the right of a competent individual to refuse medical treatment" (the right-to-die) is a "constitutionally protected liberty interest" under the Fourteenth Amendment. [The] Fourteenth Amendment provides that no State shall "deprive any person of life, liberty, or property, without due process of law." The Court clearly agreed that to deny a person the right to refuse medical treatment resulting in prolonged misery would deprive the person of their constitutional liberty.

Rehnquist described the problem before the Court, "In this Court, the question is simply and starkly whether the United States Constitution prohibits Missouri from choosing the rule of decision [using the clear evidence rule]" in such instances. Rehnquist recognized that Missouri honestly sought to safeguard against potential abuses in such situations where persons are incompetent. The state worries that family members would not always make the decision that the incompetent person might make if they were competent. Rehnquist asked, "Does Missouri have the right to put state interests to protect life above all else when the choice between life and death is a deeply personal decision of obvious and overwhelming finality [the final ending]?"

The Supreme Court, agreeing with the Missouri Supreme Court, ruled that Missouri's law requiring clear evidence of a person's wishes for the removal of life-saving treatment was, in fact, not prohibited by the Constitution's Fourteenth Amendment. Lacking such clear wishes, the state had an honest interest in preserving human life at all costs.

Four Justices Disagree with the Majority

Justice William J. Brennan, Jr., wrote for the dissenting justices,

> **Dying is personal . . . For many, the thought of an ignoble end [not noble] steeped in decay, is abhorrent [horrible] . . . , no state interests could outweigh the rights of an individual in Nancy Cruzan's position. Whatever a state's possible interest in mandating [requiring] life-support treatment under other circumstances, there is no good to be obtained here by Missouri's insistence that Nancy Cruzan remain on life-support systems if it is indeed her wish not to do so.**

Further Explanation

Justice Sandra Day O'Connor, agreeing with the majority, expanded the meaning of the ruling. She pointed out that the Court considered both the advanced medical technology and simple food and water as the same. A person could refuse not only the complex treatment but the simple sustaining efforts. She wrote of the "difficult and sensitive" nature of right-to-die issues emphasizing that in this ruling the Court had only ruled that one state's, Missouri's, law did not violate the Constitution. However, O'Connor suggested the best place to develop "appropriate procedures for safeguarding incompetent's liberty interests is entrusted to the 'laboratory' of the states."

OREGON - LABORATORY FOR THE STATES

In the 1990s the hottest topic involving death and dying was physician-assisted suicide. U.S. Supreme Court decisions of the 1980s and 1990s showed an inclination to give states broad decision-making power to develop laws to aid a person to die with dignity. Oregon became the first state in the United States to approve an assisted-suicide law. Oregon's Death With Dignity Act legalized physician-assisted suicide took effect October 27, 1997.

The law, carefully developed with many safeguards such as psychological evaluation and a fifteen-day waiting period, allowed terminally-ill state residents to receive from a doctor a prescription for lethal drugs which the patient would use to end his life. Opponents feared that terminally-ill patients, guilt-ridden over expensive medical care, would rush to use the option. After the first year, only twenty-three patients had received prescriptions for lethal drugs. Fifteen of those actually used the drugs and died. None of the fifteen had expressed concern about medical financial problems. Instead, patients were most concerned about loss of personal autonomy (self-control) and control over the manner in which they died.

Ironically, the law has prompted improvements in health care. Hoping to avoid requests for assisted suicide, Oregon doctors showed increasing interest in relieving patient's suffering by offering seminars on improving care for the terminally ill. Also, although Oregon was already a leader in hospice care (care for the terminally ill), this type of care further expanded.

Impact

Although the Court's ruling went against the Cruzans' wishes because of Nancy's incompetency, it nevertheless did much to support patient's rights to influence medical decisions in their natural dying process. First, the Court affirmed as a constitutional right that a competent person may reject life-preserving medical treatment. Secondly, the Court ruled that a person could reject not only complex medical treatments but also food and water. Thirdly, the Court made it clear that the states are the most appropriate government bodies to best develop ways of protecting liberty interests of incompetent persons. The states could use either the "substituted judgement" of family or other means, such as clear evidence laws like Missouri.

Suggestions for further reading

Baird, Robert M., and Stuart E. Rosenbaum, eds. *Euthanasia: The Moral Issues.* Buffalo, NY: Prometheus Books, 1989.

Humphrey, Derek, and Mary Clement. *Freedom to Die: People, Politics, and the Right-to-Die Movement.* New York: St. Martin's Press, 1998.

McKhanna, Charles F. *A Time to Die: The Place for Physician Assistance.* New Haven: Yale University Press, 1999.

Vacco v. Quill
1997

Petitioners: Dennis C. Vacco, Attorney General of New York

Respondents: Timothy E. Quill, Samuel C. Klagsbrun, Howard A. Grossman

Petitioners' Claim: That New York's ban on physician-assisted suicide did not violate the Equal Protection Clause.

Chief Lawyers for Petitioners: Barbara Gott Billet, Daniel Smirlock, Michael S. Popkin

Chief Lawyers for Respondents: Laurence H. Tribe, David J. Burman, Carla A. Kerr, Peter J. Rubin, Kari Anne Smith, Kathryn L. Tucker

Justices for the Court: Stephen Breyer, Ruth Bader Ginsburg, Anthony M. Kennedy, Sandra Day O'Connor, Chief Justice William H. Rehnquist, Antonio Scalia, David H. Souter, John Paul Stevens, Clarence Thomas

Justices Dissenting: None

Date of Decision: June 26, 1997

Decision: Ruling in favor of New York state, the Court decided laws banning physician-assisted suicide do not violate the constitutional equal protection guarantees.

Significance: The ruling provided constitutional support to state laws banning physician-assisted suicide. The Court recognized a legal difference between ending life-prolonging treatment to terminally ill patients and assisted suicide.

Advances in medical science had greatly extended human life expectancy by the dawn of the twenty-first century. Although generally viewed as a desirable development, prolonging the lives of terminally ill (not expected to recover) patients can lead to great suffering. Desiring a quick and dignified death, terminal patients sometimes turned to others, especially physicians to help end their life. Many individuals sympathized with this need including a number of doctors (physicians) in the medical profession. Physician-assisted suicide, or simply assisted suicide, means that one individual, most often a doctor, helps another to take his own life. Generally, a physician does this by prescribing a lethal (deadly) dose of a drug which the patient may then use to commit suicide. The issue of physician-assisted suicide is hotly debated among the general public and in legislative activities.

"Right to Die," or "Death With Dignity"

The debate reached the U.S. Supreme Court in 1990 in ***Cruzan v. Director, Missouri Department of Health.*** In *Cruzan* the Court recognized the right of a competent (able to make decisions) adult to refuse unwanted medical treatment even if exercising that right would most likely result in death. The Court defined this right as a constitutional liberty protected under the Fourteenth Amendment. The Fourteenth Amendment provides that no state shall "deprive any person of life, *liberty,* or property, without due process of law [fair legal procedures]." To be ruled a constitutionally protected liberty, an activity must be supported by a long tradition. The Court's decision that refusing medical treatment is a protected liberty was based on an ancient common law (common practices of individuals carried on for centuries) tradition of protecting patients from unwanted medical treatment. In historical times this protective tradition was known as freedom from "unwanted touching."

In 1997 the Court tackled physician-assisted suicide in two cases, ***Washington et al. v. Glucksberg*** and ***Vacco v. Quill,*** both involving the Fourteenth Amendment. In *Washington et al.,* the Court found that physician-assisted suicide, unlike the right to refusing medical treatment, was not a constitutionally protected liberty and, therefore, not protected by Due Process Clause of the Fourteenth Amendment. The Court found that physician-assisted suicide was not rooted either in common law practices or in U.S. history. Rather, it has generally been considered a crime and prohibited in almost every state.

The Court took the opportunity in *Vacco v. Quill* (1997) to explain further the difference between refusing life sustaining support and assisted-suicide.

Dying in the State of New York

In 1965 New York passed laws prohibiting assisted suicide. By the early 1990s, New York laws allowed physicians to withhold life-prolonging treatment to terminally ill patients who did not wish to receive it. This did not mean the state endorsed physician-assisted suicide, however. New York carefully drew a line between "killing" and "letting die."

Three New York state physicians, Timothy E. Quill, Samuel C. Klagsbrun, and Howard A. Grossman, were sympathetic to patients wishing to end their lives. They were willing to prescribe lethal medication for competent, terminally-ill patients but could not because of the state's ban on assisted suicide. To challenge the ban, the three physicians and three terminally-ill patients sued the New York's attorney general, Dennis C. Vacco. The three physicians claimed New York's law violated the Equal Protection Clause of the Fourteenth Amendment. The physicians argued that terminally-ill patients receiving life-prolonging treatment could choose to die by ending the treatment, but those not receiving life-prolonging treatment could not choose to end their lives with medical assistance. They claimed refusing the treatment was essentially the same as physician-assisted suicide. Therefore, the New York law did not treat all terminally-ill competent persons wishing to end their life the same. It treated those on life support one way and those not on life support another way and, therefore, violated "equal protection under the laws."

The Equal Protection Clause commands that no state shall "deny to any person within its jurisdiction (geographical area over which it has control) the equal protection of the laws." Equal protection of the laws means individuals in like situations must be treated the same.

Upholding the state law, the District Court disagreed with the physicians but the Court of Appeals for the Second Circuit reversed (changing an earlier decision by a lower court) the district court's decision. The court of appeals viewed removal of life support and assisted suicide as like actions. Allowing those on life support to "hasten their deaths" by removing their support but not allowing those who happened not to be on life support to hasten death with prescribed drugs was unequal treatment or unequal protection under the New York law. New York appealed to the U.S. Supreme Court and the Court agreed to hear the case.

The Same or Different?

Determining whether refusing life supporting medical care and physician assisted suicide are the same or different activities was the key point on which the case turned. Agreeing with the earlier district court decision, the Supreme Court ruled that New York's assisted suicide ban did not violate the Equal Protection Clause of the Fourteenth Amendment. Chief Justice William H. Rehnquist wrote the opinion for the unanimous, 9-0, Court. Rehnquist rejected the Court of Appeals' conclusion that removal of life support and assisted suicide were the same:

> **When a patient refuses life-sustaining medical treatment, he dies from an underlying fatal disease . . . but if a patient ingests lethal medication prescribed by a physician he is killed by that medication.**

Rehnquist wrote that this distinction "has been widely recognized and endorsed in the medical profession, the state courts, and the overwhelming majority of state legislatures." Since the two actions are different, they can be dealt with differently without conflicting with equal protection. According to the Rehnquist, the Equal Protection Clause "embodies [contains] a general rule that States must treat like cases alike but may treat unlike cases accordingly [differently]." Rehnquist pointed out the Constitution does not require things that are different in fact or opinion to be treated by law as though they were the same.

Chief Justice Rehnquist listed New York's many important reasons for forbidding assisted suicide:

> **prohibiting intentional killing and preserving life; preventing suicide; maintaining physicians' role as their patients' healers; protecting vulnerable people . . . pressure to end their lives; and avoiding a possible slide toward euthanasia [assisted suicide].**

A Perplexing Issue

The Court announced its decision in *Vacco* on the same day it announced its decision in *Washington et al. v. Glucksberg. Vacco* and *Washington et al.* each ruled specifically on two state laws banning assisted suicide, New York's and Washington's. The rulings confirmed states could enact

JACK KEVORKIAN

Jack Kevorkian, known as "Dr. Death" or "the suicide doctor," was born in Pontiac, Michigan in 1928. Jack's parents were Armenian refugees who had many relatives murdered in what is referred to as the Armenian holocaust during World War I. Kevorkian graduated from the University of Michigan School of Medicine in 1952 and served in the medical profession as a pathologist, a doctor who performs autopsies. One of his experiences during medical school involved dealing with a terminally-ill cancer patient who seemed to be pleading for a quick death. At this time Kevorkian decided that assisted suicide was ethical, regardless of public opinion.

Beginning in the late 1950s and continuing until the late 1980s, Kevorkian engaged in controversial research and writing concerning such topics as the appearance of the eyes of dying patients and legalizing medical experiments on death-row inmates. Kevorkian was banished from the medical establishment and did not hold a hospital staff position after 1982. By 1989 he developed a suicide machine that would allow people to kill themselves by touching a button. During the 1990s Kevorkian admittedly assisted in 130 suicides. He was charged with murder several times but always acquitted until 1999 when he was found guilty of murdering Thomas York who suffered from Lou Gehrig's disease.

Kevorkian, assisted suicide's most visible advocate, became Inmate No. 284797 in a Michigan prison. However, supporters of assisted suicide as well as opponents say he sparked their debate and brought the issue to the forefront of American society.

such laws without violating either the Due Process Clause or the Equal Protection Clause of the Fourteenth Amendment. However, several justices wrote concurring opinions (agreeing but for different reasons) that applied to both cases and expanded discussions on how to treat "death with dignity" issues.

Justice Sandra Day O'Connor, joined by Justice Ruth Bader Ginsburg, stressed that finding a proper balance between the interests of terminally ill patients and the interests of society is best left to the states. Both Justice John Paul Stevens and Justice Stephen Breyer remained open to the possibility that death with dignity might include a competent patient's right to control the manner of death and degree of physician intervention. In certain situations the patient's interest in hastening death might outweigh a state's interest in preserving life.

In the year 2000 only Oregon allowed assisted suicide and no cases challenging the law had yet reached the courts. Americans continued their earnest debate about the legality and morality of physician-assisted suicide.

Suggestions for further reading

Humphrey, Derek, and Mary Clement. *Freedom to Die: People, Politics, and the Right-to-Die Movement.* New York: St. Martin's Press, 1998.

McKhanna, Charles F. *A Time to Die: The Place for Physician Assistance.* New Haven: Yale University Press, 1999.

Woodman, Sue. *Last Rights: The Struggle Over the Right to Die.* New York: Plenum Press, 1998.

Washington v. Glucksberg 1997

Petitioner: State of Washington

Respondent: Harold Glucksberg

Petitioner's Claim: That Washington's ban on assisting or aiding a suicide does not violate the Due Process Clause of the Fourteenth Amendment.

Chief Lawyer for Petitioner: William L. Williams

Chief Lawyer for Respondent: Kathryn L. Tucker

Justices for the Court: Stephen Breyer, Ruth Bader Ginsburg, Anthony M. Kennedy, Sandra Day O'Connor, Chief Justice William H. Rehnquist, Antonin Scalia, David H. Souter, John Paul Stevens, Clarence Thomas

Justices Dissenting: None

Date of Decision: June 26, 1997

Decision: Ruled that Washington's ban on assisted suicide is constitutional.

Significance: The Court ruled that assisted suicide is not a fundamental liberty protected by the Constitution. State laws prohibiting assisted suicide are, therefore, constitutional.

By the beginning of the twenty-first century the process of dying had become complicated, involving more choices and actions. Choices about artificial life support in determining how and when an individual dies were common. Historically, assisted suicide had not been one of those choices. Assisted suicide, frequently referred to as physician-assisted suicide, means that one individual, generally a doctor, helps another person take his own life. A physician does this by prescribing a lethal (deadly) dose of a drug that the doctor knows will be used by the patient to commit suicide. The patient dies by human action, not by natural causes.

Felony in Washington

Throughout U.S. history most states prohibited assisted suicide. For example, it has always been a felony (serious) crime to assist a suicide in the state of Washington. Washington's first Territorial Legislature in 1854 outlawed "assisting another in the commission of self murder."

In 1994 four medical physicians from the state of Washington, three gravely ill patients, and Compassion in Dying, a non-profit organization that counsels people considering physician-assisted suicide, decided to challenge the modern-day Washington state law prohibiting physician assisted suicide. The physicians, who occasionally treated terminally ill patients, had said they would assist these patients in ending their lives if

Dr. Jack Kevorkian has been a very vocal supporter and participant in the assisted suicide cause. Reproduced by permission of Archive Photos, Inc.

not for Washington's assisted suicide ban. The Washington law provides: "A person is guilty of promoting a suicide attempt when he knowingly causes or aids another person to attempt suicide." The plaintiffs (group bringing the suit) claimed there is "a liberty interest protected by the Fourteenth Amendment which extends to a personal choice by a mentally competent terminally ill adult to commit physician assisted suicide." The Fourteenth Amendment to the Constitution provides that a state may not deprive a person of life, *liberty,* or property without the *due process of law.* Due process means all legal proceedings will be fair. The Washington law, charged the plaintiffs, is unconstitutional (does not follow the intent of the U.S. Constitution) because it bans the liberty of assisted suicide which they claim is protected by the Fourteenth Amendment's Due Process Clause. Both the liberty in question and the due process which protects it are of a special legal nature.

Special Liberties and Due Process

The words "physician-assisted suicide" are certainly never mentioned in the Constitution or Bill of Rights. The type of liberty the plaintiffs referred to is an "unenumerated" liberty or right. Unenumerated liberties are not written into the text of the Constitution or Bill of Rights but come from common law (common practices of individuals carried on for centuries) and philosophy, and are deeply rooted in the U.S. legal system. Such liberties are fundamental (essential) freedoms in which a person may participate relatively free from government interference. A few examples of such liberties are a person's right to marry, have children, raise children, direct their child's education, marital privacy, and the right to refuse life saving medical treatment. These abstract fundamental liberty interests have been recognized by the U.S. Supreme Court in various cases and are considered protected by the Due Process Clause of the Fourteenth Amendment. This special type of due process protection is known as substantive due process. Substantive due process protects those unenumerated liberties which are generally beyond the reach of governmental interference. The government may not regulate these liberties even by the use of fair procedures.

Is assisted suicide an unenumerated fundamental liberty? If it is, it is protected as the plaintiffs claim. If it is not, it is not protected and the state of Washington may ban it without violating the Fourteenth Amendment.

Let the Courts Decide

The U.S. District Court for the Western District of Washington ruled assisted suicide a liberty protected by substantive due process and, ruling in favor of the plaintiffs, found the Washington law unconstitutional. The U.S. Court of Appeals for the Ninth Circuit agreed with the district court. The state of Washington next appealed to the U.S. Supreme Court who agreed to hear the case.

The U.S. Supreme Court, reversing the appeals court decision, ruled assisted suicide is not a fundamental liberty interest, therefore not protected by substantive due process. Chief Justice William H. Rehnquist wrote for the unanimous (9–0) court.

Determining a Liberty Interest

The Court applied a two-part test to determine what truly is a fundamental liberty interest. First, the fundamental liberty interest must be "deeply rooted in this Nation's history and tradition." On this first point Chief Justice Rehnquist wrote:

> **An examination of our Nation's history, legal traditions, and practices demonstrates that Anglo American common law has punished or otherwise disapproved of assisting suicide for over 700 years.**

Rehnquist continued that assisted suicide was certainly not rooted in U.S. history because it is considered a crime and prohibited in almost every state. The laws make no exception for those persons near death. Further, "the prohibitions have in recent years been reexamined and, for the most part reaffirmed in a number of States." In the year 2000 assisted suicide was legal only in Oregon. Thus, assisted suicide fails the first part of the test.

Second, the fundamental liberty interest must be carefully defined and described. Chief Justice Rehnquist lists the Ninth Circuit Court's various descriptions of the liberty interest as "right to die," "right to control one's final days," and "the liberty to shape death." The Court found that the Ninth Circuit Court did not properly describe the liberty interest. Redefining the liberty in dispute, Rehnquist wrote,

> **Since the Washington statute prohibits 'aid[ing], another person to attempt suicide,' the question**

> **before the Court is more properly characterized as whether the 'liberty' specially protected by the [Due Process] Clause includes a right to commit suicide which itself includes a right to assistance in doing so.**

Therefore, it also failed the second part of the test. The Court concluded, " . . . the respondents [plaintiffs] asserted [claimed] 'right' to assistance in committing suicide is not a fundamental liberty interest protected by the Due Process Clause."

Furthermore, the Court found that Washington's assisted suicide ban was rationally (reasonably) connected to many governmental interests. Some of "these interests include prohibiting intentional killing and preserving human life; preventing the serious public health problem of suicide, . . . maintaining physicians' role as their patients' healers," and protecting vulnerable (aged, mentally retarded, and seriously ill) groups from pressure to end their life.

Refusal of Treatment Versus Assisted Suicide

The Court made it clear that assisted suicide is far different from a competent person's right to refuse unwanted medical treatment, even if it means such refusal would hasten their death. Assisted suicide results in a death caused by another person. When a person dies because they have refused medical treatment, they have essentially died a natural death. Historically, a person has had the right to refuse medical treatment. In ***Cruzan v. Director, Missouri Department of Health*** (1990) the Court affirmed as a constitutional liberty the right to reject not only life preserving medical treatment but also life sustaining food and water.

An Earnest Debate

The justices did not entirely agree on the reasoning, but all nine agreed that no fundamental right exists to assisted suicide. The Washington law banning assisted suicide was upheld. The decision left it to each individual state to decide how to most appropriately deal with the assisted suicide issue. As the Court concluded,

HEMLOCK SOCIETY

By the beginning of the twenty-first century many organizations, both supporting and opposing assisted suicide, promoted their beliefs through the Internet, books, and various publications. Founded in 1980 by Derek Humphrey, The Hemlock Society is the oldest and largest pro-assisted suicide organization with more than 27,000 members in the United States. As do most pro-assisted suicide groups, The Hemlock Society refers to itself as a "right-to-die organization" involved in the "right-to-die movement." The society takes its name from a poisonous herb, hemlock. The Greek philosopher, Socrates, died by drinking a hemlock brew.

Hemlock believes "that people who wish to retain their dignity and choice at the end of life should have the option of a peaceful, gentle, certain and swift death in the company of their loved ones. The means to accomplish this with . . . medication . . . prescribed by the doctor and self-administered." Hemlock educates both citizens and physicians, advocates, legislates (helps change and design the laws), and litigates (takes court action). Hemlock strongly opposes suicide for reasons other than ending the suffering of dying.

The Patients' Rights Organization (PRO-USA) is Hemlock's legislative arm. Its funds go directly into legislative efforts to change laws through lobbying and to promote state ballot measures. It has supported legislation for physician-aided dying in more than twenty states.

Throughout the Nation, Americans are engaged in an earnest and profound debate about the morality, legality, and practicality of physician-assisted suicide. Our holding permits this debate to continue, as it should in a democratic society.

Assisted suicide was legalized in Oregon in 1997. However, no case challenging the law had reached the courts in its the first few years.

Suggestions for further reading

Longwood College of Virginia Library (A comprehensive guide to doctor assisted suicide websites and literature). [Online] Website: http://web.lwc.edu/administrative/library/suic.htm.

Ontario Consultants on Religious Tolerance (all viewpoints including religious). [Online] Website: http://www.religioustolerance.org/euthanas.htm (Accessed on July 31, 2000).

The Hemlock Society. [Online] Website: http://www.hemlock.org (Accessed on July 31, 2000).

Webb, Marilyn, et al. *The Good Death: The New American Search to Reshape the End of Life.* New York: Bantam Books, 1997.

Woodman, Sue. *Last Rights: The Struggle Over the Right to Die.* New York: Plenum Press, 1998.

CIVIL RIGHTS AND EQUAL PROTECTION

An American belief in fairness is basic to present-day U.S. society. Consequently, the use of personal traits such as race, gender (sex of the person), or nationality to legally set apart one group of people from others raises serious concerns over human equality. However, this notion of equality in the United States at the beginning of the twenty-first century is not the same as when America was very young. Although the 1776 Declaration of Independence proclaimed that "all Men are created equal" with certain basic rights including "Life, Liberty, and the Pursuit of Happiness," the goal of liberty from England was stronger than striving for equality among the colonists. As a result, some classes of people enjoyed more rights than others. For example, in the first years of the nation only white male adult citizens who owned property could vote. Excluded were women, people of color, and the poor who held no property to speak of. Slavery was recognized as an important part of the nation's economy. In fact, nowhere did the term equality appear in the U.S. Constitution adopted in 1789 or the Bill of Rights of 1791.

Following the American Civil War (1861–65), Congress passed three new amendments to the Constitution, the Thirteenth, Fourteenth, and Fifteenth amendments. Collectively known as the Civil Rights

Amendments, their main purpose was to abolish slavery, provide citizenship to the newly-freed slaves, and to guarantee their civil rights. Civil rights refers to the idea of participating free from discrimination (giving privileges to one group but not another) in public activities such as voting, staying in an inn, attending a theater performance, or seeking employment. The idea of equality under the law first appeared in the Constitution with the passage of the Fourteenth Amendment ratified (approval) in 1868. The amendment contained wording that people refer to as the Equal Protection Clause. The Equal Protection Clause declares that state governments can not "deprive any person of life, liberty, or property, without due process of the law (all legal proceedings must be fair); nor deny to any person within its jurisdiction (geographical area over which authority extends) the equal protection of the laws." Equal protection of the laws means no person or persons will be denied the same protection of the laws that is enjoyed by other persons or groups.

The Long Struggle Toward Equality

Equal treatment of America's diverse population, however, did not immediately follow. When cases involving equality issues were first brought before the federal courts including the U.S. Supreme Court, the courts consistently interpreted the Fourteenth Amendment narrowly (very limited in meaning). The first major interpretation came in the *Slaughterhouse Cases* (1873). The Supreme Court held that basic civil rights of individuals were primarily protected by state law. Federal government protection was limited to a narrow set of rights such as protection on the high seas and the right to travel to and from the nation's capital. A second example of narrow interpretation came in 1883 in the ***Civil Rights Cases*** involving the Civil Rights Act of 1875 passed by Congress to enforce the Civil War Amendments. This act sought to assure equal access to public transportation and public places such as inns and theaters. The Supreme Court ruled that the Fourteenth Amendment only applied to discrimination by state governments, not to discrimination by private persons such as owners of railroads, theaters or inns. The Court ruling largely overturned (negated) the 1875 act leaving the federal government virtually powerless to control discrimination against blacks by private persons. Taking advantage of this powerlessness, the governments of many Southern states created segregation (separation of groups by race) laws in the 1880s known as Jim Crow laws. Black supporters of racial justice, such as Frederick Douglass and Ida B. Wells-Barnett (see sidebar), crusaded against the often violent treatment of African Americans.

The next major setback to those seeking true equality in access to public facilities (places) was the ***Plessy v. Ferguson*** (1896) decision in which the Court established the "separate but equal" rule. The rule meant that violation of the Equal Protection Clause would not occur as long as African Americans had access to the same kind of facilities as whites, even if they were separate from those used by whites. This ruling led to African Americans and whites having separate water fountains, separate public restrooms, and separate schools. The ruling basically promoted racial segregation, and rarely were the separate facilities of equal quality.

Ironically, aliens (citizens from foreign countries) initially received more favorable treatment from the courts concerning equality than African Americans. In ***Yick Wo v. Hopkins*** (1886) the Supreme Court ruled in favor of a Chinese laundry owner. The owner claimed a San Francisco city ordinance (law) concerning business licenses, although containing no discriminatory wording, was intended to shut down Chinese laundry businesses in the city. *Yick Wo* was the only successful equal protection challenge among the first cases brought to the Supreme Court in the decades following the ratification of the Fourteenth Amendment. In fact, the Fourteenth Amendment's guarantee of equal protection seemed useless for seventy years after it became a part of the Constitution. During those decades the Court tended to view equality in terms of protection of property rights or business interests, not individual civil rights.

A Shift to Individual Civil Rights

The historically important shift in applying equal protection to individual civil rights began to occur in the late 1930s through efforts of the National Association for the Advancement of Colored People (NAACP) and other groups. The courts responded with favorable decisions for racial minorities suffering injustices. For example, in *Missouri ex rel. Gaines v. Canada* (1938) the Supreme Court ruled in favor of an individual denied entrance into a state law school. The Court found that a requirement based solely on race violated the Equal Protection Clause.

The Modern Civil Rights Era

Two major 1954 Court decisions introduced the modern civil rights era. In the epic case of ***Brown v. Board of Education,*** the Supreme Court struck down the "separate but equal" rule by finding that public school segregation was unconstitutional (not following the intent of the U.S.

Constitution). A civil rights revolution was begun. That same year in *Bolling v. Sharpe* the Court held that the Due Process Clause in the Fifth Amendment prohibited racial discrimination by the federal government just as the Equal Protection Clause of the Fourteenth Amendment prohibits discrimination by state governments. The door was opened to much broader protection of individuals' civil rights.

Still, progress in society recognizing individual civil rights following decades of discrimination was slow. Numerous protests followed often involving highly publicized acts of civil disobedience (peacefully disobeying laws considered unjust) under the leadership of Dr. Martin Luther King, Jr. and others. Eventually widespread violence erupted in the nation's cities.

The Federal government began responding to the growing social unrest in the mid-1960s with a series of laws designed to further recognize civil rights and equality under the law. The 1963 Equal Pay Act required that men and women receive similar pay for performing similar work. The landmark 1964 Civil Rights Act prohibited discrimination based on race, color, national origin, or religion at most privately-owned businesses that serve the public. The 1964 act also established equal opportunity in employment on the basis of race, religion, and sex. An important Court decision occurred in 1964 as well. In ***Reynolds v. Sims*** the Court extended equal protection to voters rights. The "one person, one vote" rule resulting from the decision was put into law by Congress the following year in the 1965 Voting Rights Act. Prohibited were state residency requirements, poll taxes (pay a tax before voting), and candidate filing fees that traditionally were used to discriminate against poorer minority voters. In 1967 the Court in ***Loving v. Virginia*** ruled that state law could not prohibit interracial marriages thus recognizing the right of individuals to select their own marriage partners. A fourth important law followed in 1968 with the Fair Housing Act prohibiting discrimination in housing.

The successes of the civil rights movement of the 1950s and 1960s, focused primarily on racial discrimination, began to influence concerns over other forms of inequality. In 1971, the Court in ***Reed v. Reed*** overturned a state law arbitrarily discriminating against women. This decision extended the Equal Protection Clause to apply to gender discrimination. Courts also found some laws discriminatory against illegitimate children (parents not married) and unwed fathers. In *Weber v. Aetna Casualty & Surety Co.* (1972) the Court ruled that illegitimate children should have the same rights as other children. They should not be penalized through life for their parents' actions over which they had no control. Through the 1980s and 1990s equal protection issues tackled new topics such as sexual harassment, gay rights, affirmative (vigorous encouragement of increased representation of women and minorities) action, and assisted suicide (right to choose when to die).

Standards of Scrutiny

The Equal Protection Clause does not require that all people be treated equally at all times. Discrimination is sometimes legally permitted, such as not allowing people under eighteen years of age to vote in elections. The key decision often before the courts is to determine when discrimination is justified.

Through the nineteenth and twentieth centuries the Supreme Court increasingly recognized that throughout America's history some groups tended to be inappropriately discriminated against more than other groups. For example, people of color and women are two groups who have been traditionally discriminated against more than white men. Over the last 150 years of Supreme Court debates and decisions, the Court determined that to properly defend these groups' civil rights, the cases involving them would have to be looked at very closely. At the beginning of the twenty-first century the Court used three different standards or levels of examination or inquiry, called scrutiny, to test a case for equal protection violations. A case receives the highest level of scrutiny or "strict scrutiny" if it involves racial issues, aliens, or issues of nationality. At the intermediate level of scrutiny are cases involving women or "illegitimate persons" (individuals whose parents were not married). All other cases involving equal protection considerations fall into what is called "rational basis" scrutiny.

Changing Government Roles

The role of government regarding civil rights and equal protection changed dramatically through the twentieth century. Originally, the government primarily sought to resolve conflicts between individuals or other parties and to protect a private individual's behavior from government restrictions unless the behavior was extreme or endangering others. By the end of the century the government had become more of a promoter of community general welfare. It became acceptable to limit the behavior or actions of some people in order to protect the rights of others. An example is a requirement that owners of restaurants, whether they want to or not, must serve all members of the public unless questions of safety or health arise. Many saw this change as a shift from emphasis on political liberty from government rules during the eighteenth century colonial period to ensuring equality for all in the later years of the twentieth century. The Equal Protection Clause has become the primary constitutional shield for protecting the civil rights of the many groups of people in the United States.

Suggestions for further reading

Barker, Lucius J., Mack H. Jones, and Katherine Tate. *African Americans and the American Political System.* Fourth Edition. Upper Saddle River, NJ: Prentice-Hall, 1999.

Clayton, Ed. *Martin Luther King: The Peaceful Warrior.* Englewood Cliffs: Prentice-Hall, 1996.

Duster, Alfreda M. *Crusade for Justice: The Autobiography of Ida B. Wells.* Chicago: University of Chicago Press, 1970.

Weber, Michael. *Causes and Consequences of the African American Civil Rights Movement.* Austin, TX: Raintree Steck-Vaughn Publishers, 1998.

United States v. Cinque
1841

Appellant: United States

Appellees: Joseph Cinque and forty-eight other African captives

Appellant's Claim: That the slaves aboard the *Amistad* were guilty of murder and piracy for taking over the ship on which they were being transported.

Chief Lawyer for Appellant: Harry D. Gilpin, U.S. Attorney General

Chief Lawyer for Appellees: John Quincy Adams, Roger S. Baldwin

Justices for the Court: Philip P. Barbour, John Catron, John McKinley, John McLean, Joseph Story, Smith Thompson, Chief Justice Roger B. Taney, James M. Wayne

Justices Dissenting: Henry Baldwin

Date of Decision: January 1841

Decision: Found Cinque and the other captive Africans not guilty of mutiny since they were held captive in violation of international slave trade laws.

Significance: Abolitionists seeking to end slavery in the United States hailed as a victory the decision not to convict slaves from the schooner *Amistad* for killing two of their captors in order to gain freedom. Though the ruling did not directly apply to slavery, it served to fuel increasing tensions in the United States over the slavery issue ultimately leading to the American Civil War.

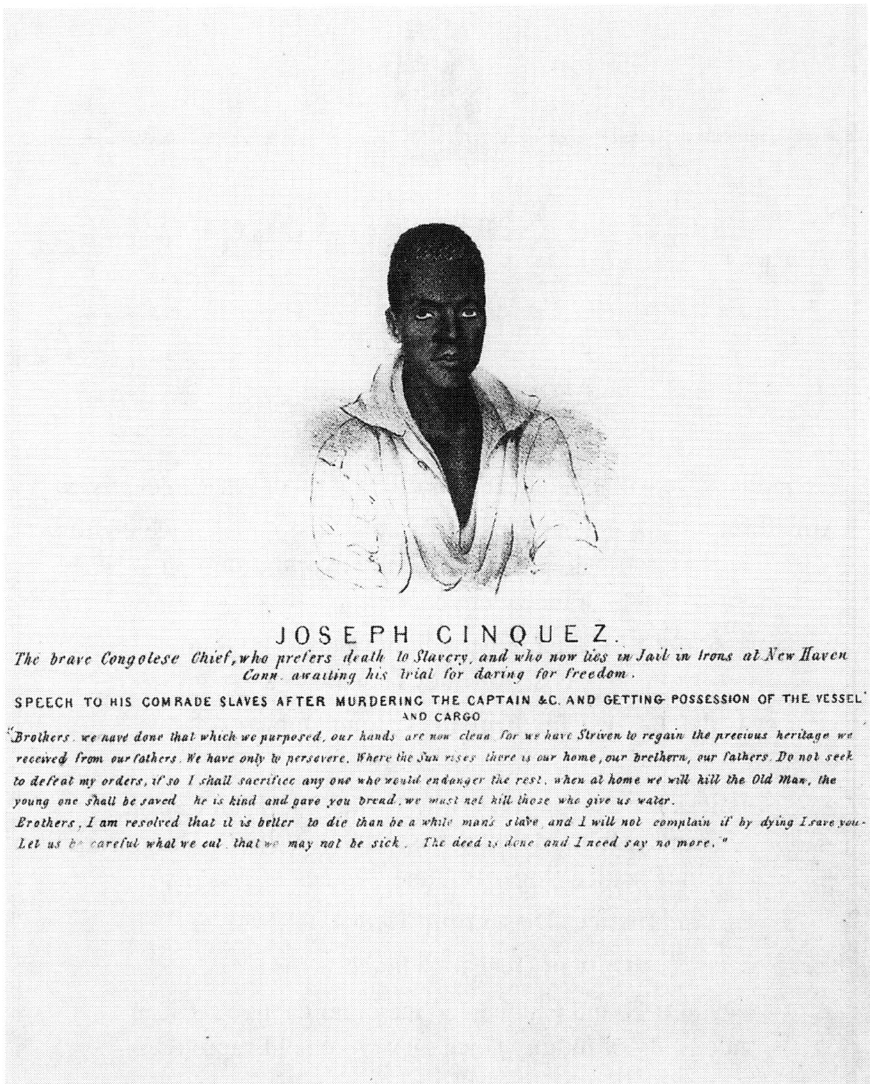

The verdict poster from the United States v. Cinque *case.*
Courtesy of the Library of Congress.

An extensive slave trade involving the shipping of captured Africans to the New World colonies grew in the seventeenth and eighteenth centuries. By the Revolutionary War (1776–83) over a half million black slaves lived in the American colonies. Given their importance to the economy of the Southern colonies, the U.S. Constitution did not address slavery. In fact, protection was provided to the Southern states, including a prohibition against Congress from passing legislation outlawing slavery until at least after 1808. In addition, fugitive slaves who escaped from Southern states to the North had to be returned when caught.

In 1808 Congress did begin to take action against slavery by banning the importation of new slaves into the country. With the growth throughout Europe and the United States of the abolitionist movement intent on abolishing (ending) slavery, most European nations had also outlawed the shipping of slaves to the New World by the 1830s. Among those was Spain which, under pressure from Great Britain, finally passed its own laws in 1835.

With its international power in decline, Spain was unable to enforce its restrictions. Wealthy landowners who dominated the Spanish colonies, including Cuba, needed a steady supply of slaves to work their large estates. They could not afford to obey the new Spanish law and wait for children of their existing slaves to grow up to meet their growing demand. Consequently, an illegal slave trade mushroomed despite international efforts to stop it. Slavers would capture healthy young black women and men in western Africa and ship them to Cuba for sale. Spanish colonial governmental authorities did nothing to stop this trade.

Joseph Cinque's Journey to America

In April of 1839, slavers brought yet another shipment of slaves to Havana, Cuba from what is now Sierra Leone on the West African coast. Among them was a black man known to the Spaniards as Joseph Cinque. In June, two Spaniards, Jose Ruiz and Pedro Montes, who owned estates in the Cuban town of Puerto Principe purchased fifty-three captured Africans, including Cinque. The slaves were loaded on the schooner *Amistad* under command of shipmaster Ramon Ferrer to sail along the Cuban coast from Havana to their estates.

Having left Havana on June 28 for Puerto Principe, the desperate Africans quickly saw their chance for freedom. On the night of July 1, the captives led by Cinque rebelled, killing Ferrer and a crew member, and gained control of the ship. Four of the Africans died. They spared the lives of Ruiz and Montes so they could steer the ship back home to Africa across the Atlantic Ocean.

By day the *Amistad* journeyed east and by night the two Spaniards secretly reversed their course back west. Finally, after meandering for almost two months, the winds and currents drove the schooner northward drifting along the coast of the United States. On August 26th the U.S.S. Washington spotted the *Amistad* anchored a half mile off the coast of Long Island, New York. The Americans seized the ship and crew, and brought them to New London, Connecticut. U.S. authorities placed the surviving forty-nine Africans in prison.

Upon arrival in New London, Ruiz and Montes pressed their claim for the ship and its cargo including the slaves. The minister to the United States from Spain also filed a claim requesting the release of the ship and its cargo to the two Spaniards in keeping with a 1795 international treaty between the United States and Spain. Spain requested return of the slaves unless U.S. authorities determined the Africans had been illegally captured and hence not Spanish property. Wishing to avoid diplomatic headaches with Spain, U.S. President Martin Van Buren, directed U.S. District Attorney William S. Holabird to charge Cinque and the other captives with murder and piracy aboard the *Amistad.* The United States sought their return to Spanish authorities in Cuba to face punishment.

The plight of the forty-nine Africans quickly became the subject of impassioned debate in the United States between pro-slavery and anti-slavery proponents for the next two years. Seizing the case as a major opportunity to combat slavery, abolitionist Lewis Tappan led an extensive campaign arousing public sympathy for the Africans.

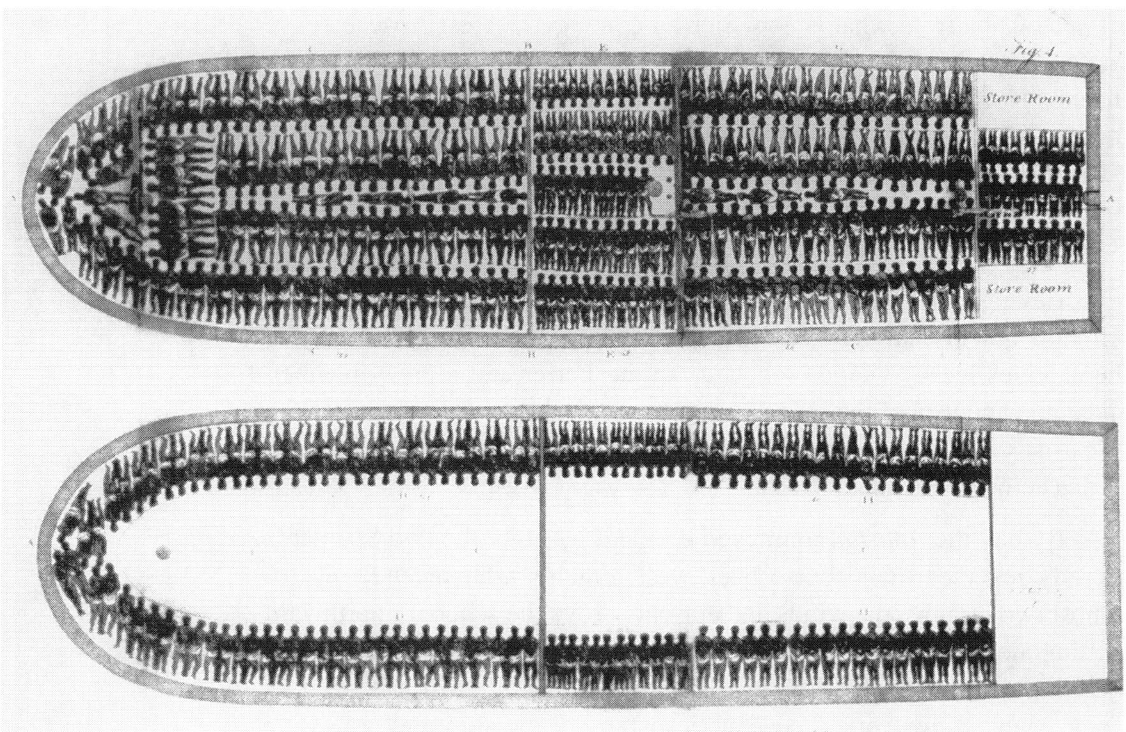

This diagram of a slave ship shows one example of how Africans were imprisoned in very tight quarters while being smuggled from their homelands. Courtesy of the Library of Congress.

The Captives Are Not Slaves

The Africans' case went to trial in September of 1839 in the U.S. District for Connecticut in Hartford. The district court judge Andrew T. Judson. Judson had a history of rulings against blacks. Representing Cinque and the other captives were defense lawyers recruited by abolitionists. Among them was future Senator Roger S. Baldwin and former U.S. President John Quincy Adams. The defense argued that Cinque and the others had been captured in violation of Spanish law, hence they were not legal slaves and not "property" of Ruiz and Montes. Consequently, they had a right to free themselves due to the horrible conditions they had been held under. In addition, they would meet almost certain death at the hands of the Spanish colonial authorities once returned to Cuba for their actions on the *Amistad.*

Key to the African's defense was a British official stationed in Havana, Dr. Richard R. Madden, who related his observations while traveling about Cuba. Describing the condition of Cuban slaves, Madden stated, " . . . so terrible were these atrocities [horrible treatment], so murderous the system of slavery, so transcendent [unspeakable] the evils I witnessed, over all I have ever heard or seen of the rigour [hardship] of slavery elsewhere, that at first I could hardly believe the evidence of my senses." Madden testified about the European laws banning slave trade and that the Africans had been illegally smuggled into Cuba. Consequently, they were not legal slave property.

On January 23, 1840, Judge Judson to the surprise of many including Van Buren ruled in favor of Cinque and the other Africans. Because they were attempting to free themselves from illegal capture, they were found not guilty of murder and piracy. The *Amistad* and its cargo not including the African captives would be returned to Ruiz and Montes. The United States appealed the decision to the U.S. Supreme Court.

Knowing the Supreme Court included five justices, including Chief Justice Roger B. Taney, from the South who had owned slaves, the defense for Cinque relied on the prestige of John Quincy Adams to present their case. Arguments were made on February 22, 1840. Less than a month later on March 9th, Justice Joseph Story presented the Court's decision. They voted 8-1 to uphold the lower court's decision in favor of Cinque. Cinque and the others were finally free, but no money was provided for their return to Africa. With donated private funds, the Africans finally were able to return home with two African American missionaries.

JOSEPH CINQUE

Despite having captured the imagination of the American public for three years, little is actually known about the life of the leader of the *Amistad* rebellion except for what court testimony revealed. A member of the Mende of Western Africa, his African name as translated in English was Sengbe Pieh, translated to Cinque by his Spanish captors. Cinque was from the town of Mani, about ten days walk from the African coast. Born around 1811, he was a rice farmer in his late twenties when captured in January of 1839 while walking on a trail near his home, as he recalled. He described his father as a Mende chief. He was married with three children.

Those who met Cinque during his brief stay in the United States described him as a very charismatic (influential) leader. He posed an aggressive intensity, even while in chains in an American prison. During the period between trials, Cinque traveled with abolitionist leaders giving anti-slavery speeches.

Upon returning to Africa, Cinque found that his family had been wiped out in slaving wars. Working with the American Mende Mission, Cinque traded goods along the coast and little was known of his later life. There were many rumors about his later life, including becoming a slaver himself, but no information has ever been found.

A Key Step

Though claimed a major victory by abolitionists, the decision of the Court was actually not so broadsweeping as to abolish slavery. It primarily held that Africans who were not considered slaves could not be considered property. However, the ruling was considered a major step on the road for total elimination of slavery which came over twenty years later. The story of Cinque and the *Amistad* became the subject of a major motion picture in 1997, *Amistad,* by famed director Steven Spielberg.

Suggestions for further reading

Cable, Mary. *Black Odyssey: The Case of the Slave Ship* Amistad. New York: Penguin Books, 1977.

Jones, Howard. *Mutiny on the* Amistad: *The Saga of a Slave Revolt and Its Impact on American Abolition, Law, and Diplomacy.* New York: Oxford University Press, 1987.

Martin, Christopher. *The* Amistad *Affair.* New York: Abelard-Schuman, 1970.

Owens, William A. *Black Mutiny: The Revolt on the Schooner* Amistad. Baltimore: Black Classic Press, 1997.

Prigg v. Pennsylvania 1842

Appellant: Edward Prigg

Appellee: Commonwealth of Pennsylvania

Appellant's Claim: That the Pennsylvania law under which he was convicted for returning a runaway slave to her master was unconstitutional.

Chief Lawyers for Appellant: Messrs. Meredith and Nelson

Chief Lawyer for Appellee: Mr. Johnson, Attorney General of Pennsylvania

Justices for the Court: Henry Baldwin, John Catron, Peter Vivian Daniel, John McKinley, Joseph Story, Roger Brooke Taney, Smith Thompson, James Moore Wayne

Justices Dissenting: John McLean

Date of Decision: March 1, 1942

Decision: The Supreme Court struck down Pennsylvania's law and reversed Prigg's conviction.

Significance: On one level, *Prigg* strengthened the federal government's power and weakened state power. On another level, the decision was a victory for slavery, which would divide the country in a civil war nineteen years later.

Margaret Morgan was an African American slave in Maryland in 1832. That year, Morgan escaped from her owner, Margaret Ashmore, and fled to Pennsylvania, which had abolished slavery. Morgan spent the next couple years in Pennsylvania raising her children, one of whom was born a free person in Pennsylvania.

When the United States wrote the Constitution in 1787, the states that allowed slavery wanted to make sure slaves could not escape to the free states. In Article IV of the Constitution, the framers said escaped slaves must be returned to their owners on demand. Six years later, Congress passed the first Fugitive Slave Act. The law said a slave owner could demand return of an escaped slave by getting a warrant from a federal or state judge or magistrate. The owner needed no evidence except his own word to prove that he owned an escaped slave.

In February 1837, Margaret Ashmore appointed attorney Edward Prigg as her agent to return Margaret Morgan. That month, Prigg went to see Thomas Henderson, a justice of the peace in York county, Pennsylvania, where Morgan was living. Prigg asked Henderson to arrest Morgan for delivery back to Ashmore. Henderson had the constable arrest Morgan and her children but then declined to take any more action.

Kidnapped

Prigg was determined to return Morgan to Ashmore. Using force and violence with help from three other men, Prigg captured Morgan on April 1, 1837 and took her to Maryland. There Morgan was forced back into slavery.

In March 1826, Pennsylvania had passed its own law about returning escaped slaves. The law made it a felony to kidnap a person and take her to captivity without following the proper procedures to prove she was a slave. To prove ownership, a slave owner had to present testimony from a neutral person. The purpose of the law was to make sure free people were not captured and taken to slavery in a Southern state on the strength of just the owner's word.

Pennsylvania arrested Prigg and charged him with violating the law by kidnapping Margaret Morgan. The trial court convicted Prigg and the Supreme Court of Pennsylvania affirmed. Prigg appealed to the U.S. Supreme Court.

At the time of Prigg's case, turmoil over slavery was just beginning to simmer in the United States. Northern states wanted the federal government to outlaw slavery in all new territories and states. Southern states did not think the federal government had such power. They believed each state should be free to decide for itself whether or not to allow slavery.

Associate Justice Joseph Story.
Reproduced by permission of Archive Photos, Inc.

When Prigg appealed his case to the Supreme Court, he based his argument on the issue of federal versus state power. Prigg said the U.S. Consti-tution required Penn-sylvania to return escaped slaves to their owners by following federal law. Pennsylvania was not free to enact its own law with its own procedures for returning escaped slaves. That made Pennsylvania's law unconstitutional. Because Pennsylvania convicted Prigg under an unconstitutional law, Prigg said his conviction must be overturned.

Federal Government Reigns Supreme

With an 8–1 decision, the Supreme Court ruled in favor of Prigg. Justice Joseph Story wrote the Court's opinion. Justice Story said the Constitution clearly said states must return escaped slaves to their owners on demand. Congress, then, necessarily had the power to enact legislation to enforce that part of the Constitution. Under the Constitution, fed-

JUSTICE JOSEPH STORY

Joseph Story was born in Marblehead, Massachusetts, on September 18, 1779. He was a child of the American Revolution whose father participated in the Boston Tea Party in 1773. In 1798, Story graduated second in his class from Harvard University and went to study law in Marblehead and then Salem, Massachusetts. Story was admitted to the bar in 1801 and practiced law in Salem for the next few years.

Story served in the Massachusetts legislature from 1805 to 1808, when he was elected to the U.S. House of Representatives. A member of Jefferson's Republican-Democratic party, Story fell into disfavor with the party and ended up back in the Massachusetts legislature as speaker of the house in 1811. Later that year, President James Madison appointed Story to the U.S. Supreme Court.

As an associate justice for thirty-four years, Story supported a strong national government. During his service on the Court he also taught law at Harvard University. While at Harvard, Story wrote a famous series of treatises on American law. Story died on September 10, 1845, after a sudden illness.

eral law is the "supreme Law of the land." States cannot interfere with federal law.

The ultimate question, then, was whether Congress and the states both could enact legislation on the subject. Story said only Congress could enact appropriate legislation. Otherwise different states might enact conflicting laws. That would make the process for returning escaped slaves different from state to state. It would allow some states to make it more difficult than others made it to return escaped slaves. The Court said that would be unworkable and unfair to the Southern states.

Pennsylvania, then, had no power to enact the 1826 law under which it convicted Prigg. The Court overturned Prigg's conviction and set him free. Margaret Morgan remained in captivity in Maryland.

Impact

Prigg was a victory for the states that allowed slavery. It forced the free states to follow the federal procedure for returning escaped slaves. *Prigg* also was a victory for the federal government. It gave the federal government power to prevent the states from passing legislation in areas that the Constitution reserved for the federal government. Nineteen years later, the issues of federal power, state power, and slavery would divide the United States in the American Civil War.

Suggestions for further reading

Adams, Judith. *The Tenth Amendment.* Englewood Cliffs: Silver Burdett Press, 1991.

Batchelor, John E. *States' Rights.* New York: Franklin Watts, 1986.

Bourgoin, Suzanne Michele, and Paula Kay Byers, eds. *Encyclopedia of World Biography.* Detroit: Gale Research, 1998.

Goode, Stephen. *The New Federalism: States' Rights in American History.* New York: Watts, 1983.

Witt, Elder, ed. *Congressional Quarterly's Guide to the U.S. Supreme Court.* District of Columbia: Congressional Quarterly Inc., 1990.

Ableman v. Booth
1859

Appellants: Stephen V.R. Ableman and the United States

Appellee: Sherman M. Booth

Appellant's Claim: That Booth, who had been freed from jail by the Supreme Court of Wisconsin, should serve the sentence imposed by a federal court for helping a slave escape.

Chief Lawyer for Appellants: Jeremiah S. Black, U.S. Attorney General

Chief Lawyer for Appellee: None

Justices for the Court: John Archibald Campbell, John Catron, Nathan Clifford, Peter Vivian Daniel, Robert Cooper Grier, John McLean, Samuel Nelson, Roger Brooke Taney, James Moore Wayne

Justices Dissenting: None

Date of Decision: March 7, 1859

Decision: A state court cannot free a prisoner from confinement by the United States government.

Significance: On one level, *Ableman* strengthened the federal government's power and weakened state power by declaring federal law supreme. On another level, the decision was a victory for slavery, which would divide the country in a civil war just two years later.

The *Ableman* cases were part of the turmoil that split the United States apart in the American Civil War. Just like the war, the cases concerned the issues of slavery, the supreme power of the federal government, and states' rights.

Joshua Glover was a slave on a farm in St. Louis, Missouri. In 1852, Glover escaped from his owner, Bennami S. Garland, and fled to the free state of Wisconsin. There Glover found work at a sawmill near Racine.

Article IV of the U.S. Constitution said escaped slaves must be returned to their owners. Under the Fugitive Slave Act of 1850, Congress set up a procedure to accomplish this. The law allowed slave owners to get a warrant from a federal commissioner to return an escaped slave to captivity. The commissioners were allowed to recruit people to help the slave owner capture the escaped slave.

On March 10, 1854, Glover was playing cards with two African American friends in a cabin on the outskirts of Racine. Garland appeared at the cabin with two U.S. deputy marshals and four other men to capture Glover. Garland and his men injured Glover during a struggle, handcuffed him, and took him to a jail in Milwaukee. At the time, the federal government used state and local jails because it did not have many of its own.

Escape

Abolitionists in Milwaukee soon learned of Glover's arrest. Abolitionists were people who wanted to get rid of, or abolish, slavery. Sherman M. Booth, one of their leaders, was the fiery editor of an abolitionist newspaper. Booth rode throughout the streets of Milwaukee shouting, "Freemen! To the rescue! Slave catchers are in our midst! Be at the courthouse at two o'clock!"

On the evening of March 11, a large crowd gathered outside the Milwaukee courthouse where Glover was imprisoned. Booth gave a passionate speech attacking the return of fugitive slaves. The crowd then broke down the courthouse door, took Glover out, and put him on a ship going to Canada.

On March 15, U.S. Marshal Stephen V.R. Ableman arrested Booth under a warrant issued by a commissioner under the Fugitive Slave Act of 1850. The commissioner charged Booth with violating the Fugitive Slave Act by helping Glover escape. The commissioner ordered Booth to

Chief Justice Roger Brooke Taney.
Courtesy of the Library of Congress.

be held in jail for trial in the U.S. District Court in Wisconsin.

Wisconsin Challenges the Federal Government

On May 27, Booth asked Associate Justice Abram D. Smith of the Supreme Court of Wisconsin for a writ of habeas corpus. A writ of habeas corpus is an order to free someone who is being jailed in violation of the U.S. Constitution. Booth said the Fugitive Slave Act, under which he was being held for trial, was unconstitutional because it did not give escaped slaves a fair trial.

Justice Smith agreed with Booth and ordered Ableman to set Booth free. Ableman did so but also asked the entire Supreme Court of Wisconsin to review the case. The court reviewed the case and affirmed Justice Smith's decision, so Ableman appealed to the U.S. Supreme Court.

In January 1855, before the Supreme Court had decided the case, Booth was arrested again under a new warrant from the U.S. District Court in Wisconsin. The new warrant charged Booth with the same violation as the commissioner had charged. This time, however, Booth faced a full trial and was convicted and sentenced to one month in jail and a $1,000 fine.

Once again, Booth asked the Supreme Court of Wisconsin for a writ of habeas corpus. On February 3, the court freed Booth a second time, ruling that the United States was holding him in prison under an unconstitutional law. The court said the state of Wisconsin had the power to protect its citizens from wrongful federal laws. The United States appealed this decision to the U.S. Supreme Court, which said it would decide both cases together.

Federal Courts Reign Supreme

With a unanimous decision, the Supreme Court ruled in favor of Ableman and the federal government. Writing for the Court, Chief Justice Roger Brooke Taney used the Supremacy Clause of the Constitution. That Clause says the Constitution and federal laws "shall be the supreme Law of the Land, and the judges in every State shall be bound thereby." Under this clause, states cannot interfere with federal law because federal law is supreme.

By setting Booth free, the Supreme Court of Wisconsin had disregarded federal law. It made federal law inferior instead of superior. Chief Justice Taney said if states were allowed to do that, the federal government could not survive. Each state would interpret federal law differently,

Often escaped slaves would set up group homes to support and aid one another in finding their way North and finding new homes. Courtesy of the Library of Congress.

FUGITIVE SLAVE ACT

In 1793, Congress passed the first Fugitive Slave Act. The law allowed slave owners to capture escaped slaves in free states and return them to slavery by getting a warrant from a federal or state judge or magistrate. The law gave slave owners the burden of capturing escaped slaves. It also made it difficult to get a warrant because there were few federal judges with that power in each state.

Southern states with slavery pressured Congress to enact a stricter law, which it did in 1850. The Fugitive Slave Act of 1850 allowed federal judges to appoint commissioners to hear slave cases. These commissioners also had power to recruit citizens to capture escaped slaves. If the commissioner decided in favor of the slave owner, he got a $10 fee. If he decided in favor of the accused slave, he only got a $5 fee. The new law obviously favored slave owners and slavery over humanity and the free states.

Northern states rebelled against the Fugitive Slave Act of 1850. Some called for repeal of the law. Many African Americans in the north left the United States for Canada. Lawyers challenged the new law in court. When those challenges failed, Northerners took to forcible resistance, fighting against slave catchers and hiding escaped slaves. Some states passed personal liberty laws to frustrate the Fugitive Slave Act.

Ableman v. Booth was one of the final victories for slave owners in the federal government. After Abraham Lincoln became president in 1860, the country split apart in a civil war over the issues of slavery and states' rights.

leading to conflict and confusion. The only solution was to require states governments and their courts to obey federal law and treat it as supreme.

Taney warned Wisconsin that it had no reason to be jealous of the federal government's power. Each state voluntarily joined the United States by agreeing to obey the U.S. Constitution. In return, the states received protection by the federal government from other states and foreign nations. The price of admittance, however, was to make state governments inferior to the federal government.

Because it decided that Wisconsin had no power to disregard federal law, the Supreme Court said it did not have to decide whether the Fugitive Slave Act was constitutional. Without explanation, however, the Court said the law was constitutional and the decisions by the Supreme Court of Wisconsin would have to be reversed.

Aftermath

The Supreme Court of Wisconsin ignored Chief Justice Taney's decision. The federal government, however, arrested Booth in March 1860 and put him in prison in the federal customs house in Milwaukee. A state court issued another writ of habeas corpus to release Booth, but the federal marshal ignored it. Because he would not pay his fine, Booth remained in prison until early 1861.

Suggestions for further reading

Adams, Judith. *The Tenth Amendment.* Englewood Cliffs: Silver Burdett Press, 1991.

Batchelor, John E. *States' Rights.* New York: Franklin Watts, 1986.

Brown, Thomas J., ed. *American Eras: 1850–1877.* Detroit: Gale Research, 1997.

Goode, Stephen. *The New Federalism: States' Rights in American History.* New York: Watts, 1983.

Civil Rights Cases
1883

Appellants: United States in four cases, Mr. and Mrs. Richard A. Robinson in one case

Appellees: Stanley, Ryan, Nichols, Singleton, Memphis & Charleston Railroad

Appellant's Claim: That their right of equal access to various publicly used facilities was violated.

Chief Lawyers for Appellants: U.S. Solicitor General Samuel F. Phillips; William M. Randolph for the Robinsons

Chief Lawyers for Appellees: William Y. C. Humes and David Postern

Justices for the Court: Samuel Blatchford, Joseph P. Bradley, Stephen Johnson Field, Horace Gray, Stanley Matthews, Samuel Freeman Miller, Chief Justice Morrison R. Waite, and William B. Woods.

Justices Dissenting: John Marshall Harlan I

Date of Decision: October 15, 1883

Decision: Found in favor of the appellees because the 1875 Civil Rights Act was unconstitutional.

Significance: The Court ruled 8–1 that Congress did not have the constitutional power to enforce civil rights requirements on private individuals or businesses. The decision greatly undermined the laws passed by Congress during the Reconstruction which were designed to grant equal rights to the newly freed African American slaves.

"They raise their voices in song and dance in the streets. I wish you could see these people as they step from slavery into freedom. Families, a long time broken up, are reunited and oh! such happiness. I am glad I am here." An unknown Union officer wrote these words to his wife in 1865 at the conclusion of the American Civil War (1861–65) as slaves throughout the South took their first cautious steps as freed people. Yet, the celebration would be short-lived. The joy of freedom gave way to a struggle for black American's civil rights (personal rights belonging to an individual as a resident of a particular country).

The civil right's struggle of black Americans included not only such sweeping issues as voting rights but also seemingly simple everyday activities like freely choosing what inn or hotel to stay at, admission to a theater, or where to sit in a railroad car. Even early Supreme Court rulings, rather than furthering the civil rights of the former slaves, would actually delay the freedom process for at least four decades following the Civil War.

An Uncertain Freedom

The economic effects of the Civil War on the South were devastating with small farms as well as plantations destroyed. African Americans, although finally freed, were uneducated, poor, and still largely remained at the mercy of the white population.

The United States government began to rebuild the South with a process known as Reconstruction lasting from 1865 to 1877. The South was put under military occupation which provided a temporary measure of protection for the ex-slaves. Realizing the former slaves' liberty was insecure, Congress approved and the states ratified (approved) three amendments between 1865 and 1870, known as the Civil Rights or Reconstruction Amendments. The Thirteenth, Fourteenth, and Fifteenth Amendments together were meant to guarantee blacks liberties outlined in the Bill of Rights and ensure equal protection of the laws. Equal protection means that no person or persons will be denied the same protection of the laws that is enjoyed by other persons or groups.

Civil Rights Amendments

The Thirteenth Amendment, ratified in 1865 just eight months after the end of the Civil War, prohibited slavery. Ratified in 1868, the Fourteenth Amendment made black persons citizens and stated:

> **No State shall make or enforce any law which shall abridge [take away] the privileges . . . of citizens of the United States; nor shall any State deprive [take from] any person of life, liberty or property, without due process of law [fair legal hearings]; nor deny to any person within its jurisdiction [geographic area] the equal protection of the laws.**

The Fifteenth Amendment, ratified in 1870, was designed to protect the voting rights of blacks. All three ended with a section stating that Congress could enforce the amendments by passing appropriate laws.

Public Accommodations and the Fourteenth Amendment

Opposition to ending slavery remained strong in Southern states and many whites refused to treat freed slaves equally. For example, former slaves were routinely denied the use of "public accommodations" including inns, theaters, restaurants, railroad cars, and other facilities whose services are available to the general population. These denials took away black Americans' privileges as citizens of the United States in defiance of the Fourteenth Amendment. Therefore, Congress found it necessary to pass laws ensuring the enforcement of the Civil Rights Amendments. One such law, based on both the Thirteenth and Fourteenth amendments, was the Civil Rights Act of 1875. The first section of the act addressed the accommodations problem by prohibiting discrimination (giving privileges to one group but not another) in public facilities.

Whites Only

Following passage of the 1875 Civil Rights Act, many cases came to courts claiming discrimination. Five reached the Supreme Court. All five were based upon the failure of blacks to be treated the same as whites. In four of the cases, the United States, representing the black Americans, was the party bringing suit against the offenders. Two cases, against individuals named Stanley and Nichols, resulted from the denial of inn or hotel accommodations to black persons. The other two cases, filed against people named Ryan and Singleton, involved denial of theater admission. Ryan, refused to seat a black person in a certain section of Maguire's theater in San Francisco. Singleton denied a black person a seat in the Grand

Opera House in New York. In the fifth case, Mr. and Mrs. Richard A. Robinson brought action against the Memphis and Charleston Railroad Company in Tennessee. A conductor on the line refused to allow Mrs. Robinson access to the ladies' car because she was of African descent. The Supreme Court combined the cases which became known as the *Civil Rights Cases.* All the cases, relying on the Civil Rights Act of 1875, claimed discrimination against African Americans by private individuals who denied the black persons access to public accommodations and that these denials were yet another form of slavery.

Questioning Constitutionality

Immediately, the Court identified the primary question in the *Civil Rights Cases* as whether or not the 1875 act was a constitutional law. To be constitutional a law must reflect what the U.S. Constitution and its amendment intended. If the Court found the law to be unconstitutional then none of the suits could stand. On October 15, 1883, the Court decided by an eight to one vote that neither the Thirteenth nor Fourteenth Amendment gave the United States government power to sue private persons for discrimination against black persons. Since no other basis but the Thirteenth and Fourteenth amendments were used to justify the law, the Court ruled the first and second sections of the Civil Rights Act of 1875 unconstitutional and void (no longer valid). The black Americans lost in all five cases.

Badge of Slavery

Writing the majority opinion, Justice Joseph Bradley commented the Fourteenth Amendment prohibited discriminatory actions by a state but not discrimination by private individuals. Therefore, if private business owners refused to serve or accommodate African Americans, Congress could not force them to do so. Bradley wrote, "Individual invasion of individual rights is not the subject-matter of the amendment." The Court also observed, "It [the Fourteenth Amendment] does not authorize Congress to create a code of municipal [local] law for the regulation of private rights."

Bradley also rejected the law based on the Thirteenth Amendment. Bradley stated the Thirteenth Amendment clearly allowed Congress "to enact all necessary and proper laws for the . . . prevention of slavery," but he refused to view racial discrimination as a "badge of slavery." Agreeing with the defense he observed,

JIM CROW LAWS

Following a series of Supreme Court decisions restricting Congress' power to enforce the Civil War Amendments, the Southern states in the 1880s began passing laws to keep white and black people separate in public and private places. These laws came to be known as Jim Crow laws. Named after a minstrel show character who sang a funny song which ended in the words "But everytime I turn around I jump Jim Crow." These laws made life very hard for black Americans. It seemed every time they turned around there was a strict new law.

By the early twentieth century the word segregation was used to describe the system of separating people on the basis of race. Racial segregation existed in hotels, transportation systems, parks, schools, and hospitals throughout the South for many decades.

Such an act of refusal has nothing to do with slavery or involuntary servitude. . . It would be running the slavery argument into the ground to make it apply to every act of discrimination which a person may see to make as to the guests he will entertain, or as to the people he will take into his coach or cab or car, or admit to his concert or theater.

The Lone Dissenter

Justice John Marshall Harlan I, a former slave owner, was the only justice to disagree with the majority. In a famous dissent, he argued that the spirit of the Thirteenth and Fourteenth Amendments was to guarantee equal rights to African Americans. The Civil Rights Act of 1875 had been passed with that intent in mind. Harlan pointed out that inns, theaters, and transportation vehicles, even though privately owned, are generally available to the public. Discrimination against African Americans in these accommodations was indeed a "badge of slavery." The amendments gave Congress the authority to outlaw all "badges and incidents" of slavery be they state or private actions.

Aftermath

Over the next eighty years the *Civil Rights Cases'* decision severely limited the federal government's power to guarantee the civil rights of black Americans. Following the decision, several northern and western states enacted their own bans on discriminatory practices in public places but other states, especially Southern states, did the opposite. They began writing racial discrimination and segregation (separation of groups by race) policies into laws that became known as Jim Crow laws. The laws segregated blacks from whites in hotels, theaters, and public transportation and persisted for many decades. Not until 1964 did Congress, referring to Justice Harlan's dissent, pass the landmark Civil Rights Act of the modern era. One of its sections prohibited discrimination in public accommodations. The 1964 act's constitutionality was quickly upheld by the Supreme Court's decision in ***Heart of Atlanta Motel, Inc. v. United States*** thus reversing the earlier ruling in *Civil Rights Cases.*

Suggestions for further reading

Hoobler, Dorothy, and Thomas Hoobler. *The African American Family Album.* New York: Oxford University Press, 1994.

Hughes, Langston, and Milton Meltzer. *A Pictorial History of the Negro in America.* Third Revised Edition. New York: Crown Publishers, Inc., 1968.

Liston, Robert. *Slavery in America: The Heritage of Slavery.* New York: McGraw-Hill Book Company, 1972.

Medearis, Angela Shelf. *Come This Far to Freedom: A History of African Americans.* New York: Atheneum, 1993.

Meltzer, Milton, ed. *In Their Own Words: A History of the American Negro, 1865–1916.* New York: Thomas Y. Crowell Company, 1965.

Meltzer, Milton, ed. *The Black Americans: A History in Their Own Words, 1619–1983.* New York: Thomas Y. Crowell, 1984.

Myers, Walter D. *Now is Your Time! The African-American Struggle for Freedom.* New York: HarperTrophy, 1991.

Time-Life Books. *African Americans Voices of Triumph: Perseverance.* Alexandria, VA: Time-Life Books, 1993.

Yick Wo v. Hopkins 1886

Petitioner: Yick Wo

Respondent: Peter Hopkins, San Francisco Sheriff

Petitioner's Claim: That San Francisco was enforcing an ordinance (city law) in a discriminatory manner against Chinese persons.

Chief Lawyers for Petitioner: Hall McAllister, D.L. Smoot, L.H. Van Schaick

Chief Lawyers for Respondent: Alfred Clarke, H.G. Sieberst

Justices for the Court: Samuel Blatchford, Joseph P. Bradley, Stephen Johnson Field, Horace Gray, John Marshall Harlan I, Stanley Matthews, Samuel Freeman Miller, Chief Justice Morrison R. Waite, and William B. Woods

Justices Dissenting: None

Date of Decision: May 10, 1886

Decision: The earlier conviction of Yick Wo for violating the ordinance was unconstitutional.

Significance: The Court ruled that even if a law is written in a non-discriminatory way, enforcing the law in a discriminatory manner is still unconstitutional. The Court also ruled that the Equal Protection Clause of the Fourteenth Amendment applies to non-U.S. citizens as well as citizens in the country. Importantly, the case represented an early step by the Court to protect individual's civil rights.

For Chinese men and boys who had never been more than a few miles from home, starting out on a 7,000 mile journey across the Pacific could be terrifying. Yet with hope and courage, beginning in 1849 they crowded in the holds of ships, then suffered eight long weeks of ocean voyage to arrive in America, the land they called *Gum Sahn* or Gold Mountain. The first immigrants came to work in the mines during the California gold rush of 1849. Thousands more arrived in the 1860s to help build the Central Pacific Railroad, part of the first transcontinental railroad system in the United States.

Between 1850 and 1880 the Chinese immigrant population in the United States grew from 7,000 to more than 100,000. Approximately 75,000 settled in California, which amounted to ten percent of that state's population. Half of those 75,000 lived in San Francisco. During the 1870s the hardworking Chinese became essential to the important industries of cigar making, shoemaking, woolen mills, and laundering.

Anti-Chinese Feelings

Chinese immigrants in America often faced prejudice (hateful attitudes against a group) and lived in segregated (separated by race) neighborhoods, called "Chinatowns." Not only were their customs and language very different from those of Americans, but they were willing to work for low wages. Whites feared losing their jobs to the Chinese. California experienced an economic depression (decrease in business activity with fewer jobs) in the 1870s suffering widespread unemployment and bank failures. Many unemployed workers blamed their troubles on Chinese laborers. Anti-Chinese riots took place in San Francisco in 1877. Through the 1870s the city of San Francisco passed several ordinances (city laws) to discourage Chinese settlement.

The Laundry Ordinance

By 1880 Chinese owned most laundries in San Francisco, commonly operated in wooden buildings. On May 26, 1880, during the height of white Californians' concern over the Chinese, San Francisco passed an ordinance requiring all laundries to be in brick or stone buildings. To stay in business, owners of laundries in wooden buildings had to obtain a laundry operating license issued by the city's Board of Supervisors. Failure to obtain a license while continuing to operate a laundry in a

Many immigrants found themselves working long hours in tough conditions. Reproduced by permission of the Corbis Corporation.

wooden building could lead to a misdemeanor (less serious crime) conviction, a thousand dollar fine, and jail term of up to six months. The city had a compelling interest (important need) to pass the ordinance, to minimize fire danger. As written, the ordinance made no distinction (did not mention any difference) between laundries run by Chinese immigrants and those run by whites. Therefore, the ordinance seemed to not concern itself with the race of the laundries' operators.

However, since almost all Chinese laundries were located in wooden buildings the ordinance seemed to take aim at Chinese businesses. Additionally, the Board of Supervisors routinely approved all white applications to run laundries in wooden buildings. Yet, in 1885 the Board denied all but one of 200 Chinese applications even though their laundries had previously passed city inspections. The only Chinese owner given a license had probably not been identified as Chinese by the Board.

Yick Wo

Yick Wo, a Chinese resident of San Francisco, had lived in California since 1861 and operated a laundry for twenty-two years. In 1884 his laundry which was located in a wooden structure passed an inspection by local fire and health authorities. However, in 1885 the Board of Supervisors denied his application for a license to continue running his laundry. Wo discovered that all the owners of wooden Chinese laundries with one exception were also denied licenses.

Highly suspicious of discriminatory (giving privileges to one group but not another) practices, Wo decided to legally challenge the ordinance. He continued to operate his laundry and was arrested, convicted in police court, and ordered to pay a fine of $10. Refusing to pay the fine, he was ordered to jail for ten days. When the California Supreme Court refused to hear his case, Wo appealed to the U.S. Supreme Court which did agree to hear the case. Wo named San Francisco Sheriff Peter Hopkins, who locally enforced the ordinance, in the suit.

Homework Done, Argument Ready

Wo's lawyers argued before the U.S. Supreme Court that the ordinance was being unfairly enforced in an obviously discriminatory manner. Having done his homework, Wo supported his charge by producing statistics showing that eighty laundries located in wooden structures were legally operating under the Board of Supervisor's licensing requirements. Of those, seventy-nine were owned by non-Chinese and only one by a Chinese. Reminding the Court nearly two hundred Chinese laundries located in similar structures had been denied licenses by the San Francisco Board of Supervisors, Wo proceeded to charge the Board with seeking to wipe out the city's Chinese laundry business. Wo continued that he and the other Chinese business owners were being denied equal protection under the law, a right guaranteed to them by the Fourteenth Amendment. The amendment reads, "No State shall . . . deny to any person within its jurisdiction [geographic area over which a government has authority] the equal protection of the laws." That is, no person or persons shall be denied the same protection of the laws that is enjoyed by other persons or groups.

The city of San Francisco argued that the Fourteenth Amendment could not interfere with police powers granted by the U.S. Constitution to cities and states to enforce local laws concerning use of property.

Pledge of Equal Protection

Supreme Court Justice Stanley Matthews observed the laundry ordinance seemed to be written without intending to discriminate against anyone, legally described as "neutral on its face," and for a compelling reason, fire safety. However the ordinance was enforced in such a way to show flagrant (extreme) discrimination to one class, the Chinese. Matthews, writing for the unanimous (all members in agreement) court, penned:

"Though the law itself be fair on its face [as written] and impartial [fair] in appearance, yet, if it is applied and administered by public authority [enforced by supervisors and police] with an evil eye and an unequal hand, so as to make unjust and illegal discriminations between persons. . . "

Pointing out the clearly unjust manner with which enforcement was carried out, Matthews continued:

"While this consent [licenses granted] of the supervisors is withheld from them [the Chinese] and from two hundred others who also petitioned [applied], all of whom happen to be Chinese subjects, eighty others, not Chinese subjects, are permitted to carry on the same business under similar conditions. The fact of this discrimination is admitted. . . No reason for it exists except hostility to the race and nationality to which the petitioners belong, and which in the eye of the law is not justified."

CHINATOWNS

Upon arriving in America, Chinese banded together to live in distinct communities. The first Chinatown grew up in San Francisco in the early 1850s. With not enough timber available to supply the building needs, entire structures were often shipped from China and put back together in San Francisco. The people dressed in native costumes and kept stores as they would in China. Most Chinatown businesses were small with their street front open, vegetables and groceries overflowing on the sidewalks. Cigar stands, shoe cobblers, pharmacies with herbal medicines, fortune tellers, and gambling and opium dens shared spaces up and down a system of streets, alleys, and passages. A stranger easily could become hopelessly lost in the maze.

As anti-Chinese feelings increased, some sought new homes eastward. By 1920 thousands of Chinese lived in communities in Boston, New York, and Chicago. Only in Chinatowns did Chinese live a freer, more humane life among family and friends, creating the illusion that Chinatown was really China.

Matthews agreed with Wo that equal protection under the law granted by the Fourteenth Amendment was denied to Wo and the other Chinese businessmen.

"The discrimination is therefore, illegal, and the public administration which enforces it is a denial of the equal protection of the laws and a violation of the Fourteenth Amendment of the Constitution."

Justice Matthews also addressed the fact that Wo was an alien, a citizen of a foreign country living in the United States. He wrote the equal protection of the Fourteenth Amendment applies "to all persons within the territorial jurisdiction [geographical area of a government's authority], without regard to any differences of race, of color, or of nationality, and the equal protection of the laws is a pledge of the protection of equal laws."

With that, the Supreme Court found in favor of Yick Wo, ordered him discharged, and struck down the ordinance.

Yick Wo v. Hopkins pioneered three key ideas. First, the Fourteenth Amendment protected all persons living in the United States, not just citizens. Second, if a law has a discriminatory purpose or is enforced unfairly, even though it is neutral on its face, the courts will apply the equal protection pledge of the Fourteenth Amendment and strike down the law. Third, the case began a process of more carefully looking at laws affecting groups of people which through American history had been persistently discriminated against. However, building on the ideas proved to be a slow process. Eventually, the *Yick Wo* case became a central part of the civil rights law but not until the mid-twentieth century.

Suggestions for further reading

Chen, Jack. *The Chinese of America.* San Francisco: Harper & Row, 1980.

Chin, Frank. *Donald Duk.* Minneapolis, MN: Coffee House Press, 1991.

Hoobler, Dorothy, and Thomas Hoobler. *The Chinese American Family Album.* New York: Oxford University Press, 1994.

Jones, Claire. *The Chinese in America.* Minneapolis, MN: Lerner Publications Company, 1972.

McCunn, Ruthanne L. *Chinese American Portraits: Personal Histories, 1828–1988.* San Francisco: Chronicle Books, 1988.

See, Lisa. *On Gold Mountain.* New York: St. Martin's Press, 1995.

Wilson, John. *Chinese Americans.* Vero Beach, FL: Rourke Corporation, Inc., 1991.

Wu, Dana Ying-Hui, and Jeffrey Dao-Sheng Tung. *Coming to America: The Chinese American Experience.* Brookfield, CT: The Millbrook Press, 1993.

Korematsu v. United States 1944

Petitioner: Toyosaburo Korematsu

Respondent: United States

Petitioner's Claim: That convicting him for refusing to leave the West coast during World War II violated the U.S. Constitution.

Chief Lawyers for Petitioner: Wayne M. Collins and Charles A. Horsky

Chief Lawyer for Respondent: Charles Fahy, U.S. Solicitor General

Justices for the Court: Hugo Lafayette Black, William O. Douglas, Felix Frankfurter, Stanley Forman Reed, Wiley Blount Rutledge, Harlan Fiske Stone

Justices Dissenting: Robert H. Jackson, Frank Murphy, Owen Josephus Roberts

Date of Decision: December 18, 1944

Decision: The Supreme Court said Korematsu's conviction was constitutional.

Significance: In *Korematsu,* the Supreme Court tacitly approved laws and military orders that sent Japanese Americans into confinement during World War II.

On December 7, 1941, Japan brought the United States into World War II by attacking the American Pacific fleet at Pearl Harbor, Hawaii. Japan killed 2,043 Americans during the surprise attack and destroyed American warships and aircraft. The next day, Congress declared war on Japan.

After being surprised at Pearl Harbor, the United States feared Japan would attack or invade along the Pacific coast. In February 1942, President Franklin D. Roosevelt issued Executive Order 9066. President Roosevelt said wartime success depended on protecting the United States from espionage and sabotage. In his executive order, the president gave the military authority to define and take control over vulnerable areas of the country.

Lieutenant General DeWitt was in charge of the U.S. military in the westernmost part of the nation. On 27 March 1942, General Dewitt issued an order preventing persons of Japanese descent from leaving the West coast region. On May 3, 1942, General DeWitt issued another order forcing Japanese Americans to leave the West coast region through a Civil Control Station. The combined effect of both orders was to allow the United States to round up Japanese Americans for confinement in internment camps during the war. The purpose of confinement was to prevent Japanese Americans from helping the Japanese Empire in its war against the United States. The United States made no effort to distinguish between loyal and disloyal Japanese Americans.

Civil Disobedience

Toyosaburo Korematsu, who went by the name of Fred, was an American citizen of Japanese descent. Korematsu lived in San Leandro, California, near San Francisco. Korematsu was rejected for military service for health reasons but had a good job in the defense industry. Korematsu was a loyal, law-abiding American citizen in every way.

Korematsu did not think it was right for the United States to force Japanese Americans into internment camps. Instead of obeying the military orders, he fled from the San Francisco Bay area. Determined to escape confinement, Korematsu had some minor facial surgery, changed his name, and pretended to be a Mexican American. Eventually, however, he was arrested and charged with disobeying the military order to leave the West coast.

CIVIL RIGHTS AND EQUAL PROTECTION

Korematsu pleaded not guilty and fought the government's case. He said the United States had no power to send an entire race of Americans into confinement when they had done nothing wrong. The court, however, convicted Korematsu and put him on probation for five years. The military then seized Korematsu, sent him to an Assembly Center, and eventually confined him in an internment camp in Topaz, Utah. Meanwhile, Korematsu took his case to the U.S. Supreme Court.

Military Orders Reign Supreme

With a 6–3 decision, the Supreme Court ruled in favor of the United States. Justice Hugo Lafayette Black wrote the Court's opinion. Justice Black said the government needs an extremely good reason for any law that limits the civil rights of an entire racial group. Sadly, the Court found a good reason in the federal government's military powers.

The U.S. Constitution gives the president and Congress certain war powers. Congress has the power to declare war and to provide for the defense of the United States. The president is the commander-in-chief of

This young girl is waiting for her family to be checked into a internment camp. Courtesy of the Library of Congress.

the military forces. Under their constitutional powers, the president and the military may do anything that is reasonable to conduct a war.

Justice Black said it was reasonable for the military to order all Japanese Americans to leave the West coast. Although not all Japanese Americans were disloyal, some were. During investigations after the relocation, five thousand Japanese Americans refused to swear unqualified allegiance to the United States or to renounce allegiance to the Japanese Emperor. Several thousand even asked to be sent back to Japan.

Justice Black said that under the war emergency that existed after Japan bombed Pearl Harbor, the government did not have time to separate the loyal from the disloyal. It was reasonable, then, to order all Japanese Americans to leave the vulnerable area of the West coast. By refusing to obey that order, Korematsu had violated federal law and his conviction was constitutional.

To the dismay of many, the Court refused to decide whether it was legal to confine Japanese Americans in internment camps. Korematsu had only been convicted for refusing to leave San Leandro to report to a Civil Control Station. He was not convicted for refusing to report to an

Many Japanese Americans were held at the Manzanar Internment Camp in Independence, California. Reproduced by permission of the Corbis Corporation.

JAPANESE AMERICAN RELOCATION DURING WORLD WAR II

During World War II, the United States of America, the land of the free, forced 112,000 people of Japanese ancestry to leave their homes in the West coast region. Around 70,000 of those people were American citizens. Many of them spent time in ten internment camps located in California, Arizona, Wyoming, Colorado, Utah, and Arkansas. Some who were certified as "loyal" were allowed to go free to settle in the Midwest or the East.

As they left the West coast, Japanese Americans were allowed to take only what they could carry. This forced them to sell their homes and belongings, often at unfairly low prices. A 1983 study estimated that Japanese Americans lost as much as $2 billion in property during this time to arson, theft, and vandalism. Once in the internment camps, Japanese Americans lived like prisoners. They received the barest essentials needed for survival and could not leave the camps on their own.

On December 18, 1944, the United States announced that it would close the internment camps by the end of 1945. It was not until 1988, however, that Congress apologized to Japanese Americans for their confinement. That year it passed a law giving $20,000 to each confinee who was still alive.

internment camp. Nonetheless, the Court's decision was a tacit approval of the internment of Japanese Americans during the war.

Concentration Camps

Justices Robert H. Jackson, Frank Murphy, and Owen Josephus Roberts dissented, which means they disagreed with the Court's decision. These justices thought it was unfair for the Court to avoid the question of whether internment was legal. After all, the only reason for requiring Korematsu to report to a Civil Control Station was to send him to an Assembly Center for delivery to an internment camp.

The internment of Japanese Americans deeply disturbed the dissenting justices. Justice Roberts called it a "case of convicting a citizen as a punishment for not submitting to imprisonment in a concentration camp, based on his ancestry, and solely because of his ancestry." Justice Murphy called the relocation racial discrimination that deprived Americans of their right to live, work, and move about freely. Justice Jackson warned that the Court's decision would be a "loaded weapon ready for the hand of any authority" that decided to imprison an entire race of Americans in the future.

Suggestions for further reading

Alonso, Karen. *Korematsu v. United States: Japanese-American Internment Camps.* Enslow Publishers, Inc., 1998.

Bondi, Victor, ed. *American Decades: 1940–1949.* Detroit: Gale Research Inc., 1995.

Chin, Steven A. *When Justice Failed: The Fred Korematsu Story.* Raintree/Steck-Vaughn, 1995.

Davis, Daniel S. *Behind Barbed Wire: The Imprisonment of Japanese Americans during World War II.* New York: Dutton, 1982.

Dictionary of American History. Vol. III. New York: Charles Scribner's Sons, 1976.

Fremon, David K. *Japanese-American Internment in American History.* Enslow Publishers, Inc., 1996.

Sinnott, Susan. *Our Burden of Shame: The Japanese-American Internment during World War II.* New York: Franklin Watts, Inc., 1995.

Stanley, Jerry. *I Am an American: A True Story of Japanese Internment.* New York: Crown Publishers, 1994.

Tunnell, Michael O., and George W. Chilcoat. *The Children of Topaz: The Story of a Japanese-American Internment Camp Based on a Classroom Diary.* Holiday House, 1996.

Boynton v. Virginia
1960

Petitioner: Bruce Boynton

Respondent: Commonwealth of Virginia

Petitioner's Claim: That arresting a black interstate bus passenger for refusing to leave a whites-only section of a bus station restaurant violated the Interstate Commerce Act and the Equal Protection Clause of the U.S. Constitution.

Chief Lawyer for Petitioner: Thurgood Marshall

Chief Lawyer for Respondent: Walter E. Rogers

Justices for the Court: William J. Brennan, Jr., Tom C. Clark, William O. Douglas, Felix Frankfurter, John Marshall Harlan II, Potter Stewart, Chief Justice Earl Warren

Justices Dissenting: Hugo L. Black, Charles E. Whittaker

Date of Decision: December 5, 1960

Decision: Ruled in favor of Boynton by finding that restaurant facilities in bus terminals that primarily exist to serve interstate bus passengers can not discriminate based on race according to the Interstate Commerce Act.

Significance: The decision supporting federal government actions in desegregating certain public facilities paved the way for further civil rights activism. Resistance to the ruling by many Southerners led to the Freedom Rides on interstate buses by young activists the following summer. The Rides in addition to other protest activities the next two years led to the 1964 Civil Rights Act banning racial discrimination in all public facilities.

Businesses known as "common carriers" are transportation companies that advertise to the public to carry passengers for a fee. States regulate carriers that operate solely within their borders, but the federal government through authority in the Commerce Clause of the U.S. Constitution regulate carriers involved in interstate (traveling from one state to another) or foreign travel.

To regulate various aspects of business between states Congress passed the landmark Interstate Commerce Act in 1887 and amended it through later years. As stated in Section 203, the act applied to "all vehicles . . . together with all facilities and property operated or controlled by any such carrier or carriers, and used in the transportation of passengers or property in interstate or foreign commerce." Further, Section 216(d) of Part II of the act states,

> **It shall be unlawful for any common carrier [using a] motor vehicle engaged in interstate . . . commerce to make, give, or cause any undue or unreasonable preference [favorite choice] or advantage to any particular person . . . in any respect whatsoever; or to subject any particular person . . . to any unjust discrimination [treating individuals in similar situations differently] or any unjust or unreasonable prejudice [bias] or disadvantage in any respect whatsoever. . .**

Based on the act, the U.S. Supreme Court ruled in *Mitchell v. United States* (1941) that if a railroad provides dining cars, then passengers must be treated equally by the dining car service. Later in *Henderson v. United States* (1950) the Court further affirmed that service to passengers in railroad dining cars could not be separated according to race (racial segregation) by curtains or even signs.

Bruce Boynton

In 1958 Bruce Boynton, a black student at Howard University Law School in Washington, D.C., boarded a Trailways bus in Washington bound for his home in Montgomery, Alabama. Leaving Washington at 8:00 PM, the bus stopped at about 10:40 PM at the Trailways Bus Terminal in Richmond, Virginia. Given a forty minute stopover, Boynton got off the bus to eat a bite at the Bus Terminal Restaurant located in the terminal building. The restaurant was racially segregated (keeping racial

CIVIL RIGHTS AND EQUAL PROTECTION

groups from mixing), divided into sections for whites and blacks. Boynton proceeded to sit down on a stool in the white section and ordered a sandwich and tea. After refusing to move to the colored section at the request of the waitress, the assistant manager appeared and ordered Boynton to move to the other section. He insisted he was an interstate bus passenger protected by federal desegregation laws (prohibiting the practice of separating races) and did not have to move. As a result, a local police officer arrested Boynton charging him with misdemeanor trespassing. The Police Justice's Court of Richmond found Boynton guilty of violating Virginia state trespass law and fined him ten dollars.

Boynton appealed his conviction to the Hustings Court of Richmond asserting that "he had a federal right . . . to be served without discrimination by this restaurant used by the bus carrier for the accommodation of its interstate passengers." He was on the property with "authority of law." He argued that since the restaurant "was an integral part of the bus service for interstate passengers" the use of the Virginia trespass law violated the Interstate Commerce Act as well as various parts of the U.S. Constitution including the Fourteenth Amendment. The amendment reads, "nor shall any State . . . deny any person within its

Freedom Riders, following the Boynton *decision, were protected at every bus stop.* Reproduced by permission of Magnum Photos.

jurisdiction the equal protection of the laws." Nevertheless, Hustings Court confirmed his conviction.

Appeal to the Virginia Supreme Court led to the same results. With the assistance of lawyers from the National Association for the Advancement of Colored People (NAACP), Boynton next took his constitutional arguments to the U.S. Supreme Court which agreed to hear his case.

A Part of Bus Service

Presenting arguments for Boynton in October of 1960 was the future first black Supreme Court justice Thurgood Marshall. Marshall had played a key role in the earlier landmark victory in ***Brown v. Board of Education*** (1954) involving discrimination in public schools. Marshall pressed the issue of constitutional violations including the Fourteenth Amendment's Equal Protection Clause. The U.S. Justice Department also joined the case on behalf of Boynton raising the issue that Boynton faced "unjust discrimination" in violation of the Interstate Commerce Act. In an unusual move, the Supreme Court decided to not hear the case based on Boynton's charges of constitutional violations, but instead chose to rule on the conflict between the Interstate Commerce Act and the Virginia state law in this case.

The state of Virginia argued that the Bus Terminal Restaurant of Richmond, Inc., was neither owned nor operated by the bus company. In fact, the restaurant served the general public as well as bus passengers. Being a private company, it was not subject to the same federal law restrictions as the interstate carrier, they argued.

Justice Hugo L. Black wrote the decision of the Court. Justice Black recalled the earlier *Mitchell* and *Henderson* decisions asserting that those decisions readily applied to all transportation services in terminals and terminal restaurants provided for passengers by interstate carriers. In fact, Black stated that the facilities did not even have to be owned or operated by the carrier, but simply "an integral [important] part of transportation" that they provide. Black commented, "Interstate passengers have to eat, and they have a right to expect that this essential . . . food service . . . would be rendered [provided] without discrimination prohibited by the Interstate Commerce Act."

To address in more detail the restaurant's arguments, Black explored the relationship between Trailways bus line and the restaurant.

He claimed the contract between the two clearly showed that, though the restaurant was open to the general public, clearly its primary purpose was to serve bus passengers. The bus line owned the building in which it leased space to the restaurant company and the restaurant paid $30,000 annually to the bus line plus a percentage of profits. Black concluded it had "a single purpose . . . to serve passengers of one or more bus companies. . . " Trailways used the restaurant facilities regularly as if it owned it thus providing "continuous cooperative transportation services between the terminal, the restaurant and buses like Trailways."

Black wrote,

> **. . . if the bus carrier has volunteered to make terminal and restaurant facilities and services available to its interstate passengers as a regular part of their transportation, and the terminal and restaurant have acquiesced [agreed] and cooperated in this undertaking, the terminal and restaurant must perform these services without discriminations prohibited by the Act.**

Ella Josephine Baker was one of the founding forces behind the Freedom Rides. Reproduced by permission of AP/Wide World Photos.

ELLA JOSEPHINE BAKER AND SNICK

The *Boynton* ruling was among many events fueling the civil rights movement of the 1950s and 1960s. One key black organizer during this period was Ella Josephine Baker. Born in Norfolk, Virginia, Baker quickly became involved in political activities concerning social justice and equality by the later 1920s. In the 1930s Baker joined the National Association for the Advancement of Colored People (NAACP) as an assistant field secretary working to increase its Southern membership. In 1957 she was a founding member of the Southern Christian Leadership Conference (SCLC) as was Dr. Martin Luther King, Jr.

To better organize the rising tide of nonviolent protests by black Americans in the 1950s, Baker founded the Student Nonviolent Coordinating Committee (SNCC), popularly known as Snick. Under Ella's direction, Snick quickly developed an aggressive approach to protests. Following the *Boynton* decision banning segregation of interstate bus facilities, Snick along with other organizations promoted the Freedom Rides of 1961. The Rides challenged segregationist policies along bus routes from Washington, D.C. to Jackson, Mississippi. After the Freedom Rides, Baker pursued voter registration efforts in the South in 1963. Later, Baker led Snick in protests against the Viet Nam War and pursued civil rights for blacks in Africa and Latin America. Ella Baker died in New York City at the age of eighty-three.

Therefore, Boynton "had a federal right to remain in the white portion of the restaurant. He was there under 'authority of law'—the Interstate Commerce Act. . . "

Black added that this decision did not mean that all independent roadside restaurants that a bus might stop at would need to comply with the anti-discrimination measures in the act, only those restaurants that "operate as an integral part of the . . . bus carrier's transportation service for interstate passengers." The Court, voting 7-2, reversed the trespass conviction and sent the case back to Virginia.

Freedom Riders

Angered by the *Boynton* decision many whites in the South ignored the ruling and continued segregationist policies for public facilities. In reaction to the Southern resistance, the "Freedom Rides" occurred in 1961. The Rides consisted of seven black and six white students riding two buses from Washington, D.C. destined for New Orleans, Louisiana. The students purposefully violated segregation policies on buses, public restrooms, terminal waiting areas, and restaurants along the way. Faced with violent reactions along the route, including one bus being firebombed, they ended their rides early at Jackson, Mississippi under guard of U.S. Marshalls. The Rides caught the attention of the public and Congress leading to passage of the 1964 Civil Rights Act banning racial segregation in all public facilities including restaurants and hotels.

Suggestions for further reading

Cashman, Sean D. *African Americans and the Quest for Civil Rights, 1900-1990.* New York: New York University Press, 1991.

Levine, Michael L. *African Americans and Civil Rights: From 1619 to the Present.* Phoenix, AZ: Oryx Press, 1996.

Steinhorn, Leonard, and Barbara Diggs-Brown. *By the Color of Our Skin: The Illusion of Integration and the Reality of Race.* New York: E.P. Dutton, 1999.

Thermstrom, Stephan, and Abigail Thermstrom. *America in Black and White: One Nation, Indivisible.* New York: Simon & Schuster, 1999.

Monroe v. Pape
1961

Petitioners: Mr. Monroe and his family members

Respondents: Detective Pape, the City of Chicago, and twelve other city police officers

Petitioners' Claim: That a warrantless search of a private residence conducted in a humiliating manner by police violated the families' civil rights under the 1871 Civil Rights Act.

Chief Lawyer for Petitioners: Donald P. Moore

Chief Lawyer for Respondents: Sydney R. Drebin

Justices for the Court: Hugo L. Black, William J. Brennan, Jr., Tom C. Clark, John Marshall Harlan II, William O. Douglas, Felix Frankfurter, Potter Stewart, Chief Justice Earl Warren, Charles E. Whittaker

Justices Dissenting: None

Date of Decision: February 20, 1961

Decision: Ruled in favor of Monroe by finding that Monroe could sue individual policeman, but not the city of Chicago.

Significance: The decision upheld the rights of individuals to seek compensation (payment) for abuses of their civil rights by state or local government authorities. Though excluding cities from liability (responsibility) in this case, the Court later extended liability to city and state governments in a 1978 ruling.

CIVIL RIGHTS AND EQUAL PROTECTION

Immediately after the American Civil War (1861–65), the U.S. government began rebuilding the South's society and devastated economy through a program known as Reconstruction. The program included placing the South under military occupation to provide some protection for ex-slaves. Knowing well how insecure liberty was for the former slaves, three U.S. constitutional amendments were adopted between 1865 and 1870, known as the Civil Rights Amendments. Together, the Thirteenth, Fourteenth, and Fifteenth amendments guaranteed blacks individual rights provided for in the Bill of Rights in addition to other rights. For example, the Fourteenth Amendment reads,

> **No State shall make or enforce any law which shall abridge [take away] the privileges . . . of citizens of the United States; nor shall any State deprive [take from] any person of life, liberty or property, without due process of law [fair legal hearings]; nor deny to any person within its jurisdiction [geographic area] the equal protection of the laws.**

Despite these national efforts, conditions for the former slaves improved little as many whites refused to treat freed slaves equally. A Southern white backlash rose. White supremacist (those believing one race is superior than all others) organizations, including the Ku Klux Klan established in 1866, increasingly turned to terrorist activities directed against blacks involving murder, bombings, and lynching. Often these activities were conducted with the approval if not active support of local officials and law enforcement. In other situations, local white police, juries, and judges were pressured to not protect black Americans or enforce laws. Consequently, local and state courts were often not effective in prosecuting the Klansmen.

The Ku Klux Klan Act

As violence against blacks continued to escalate, President Ulysses S. Grant urged Congress to take action. In a 1871 note to Congress, Grant wrote that in some states life and property were no longer safe and that "the power to correct these evils is beyond the control of State authorities I do not doubt." In response, Congress passed the Civil Rights Act of 1871 to enforce the Fourteenth Amendment's equal protection and due process of the laws. The act was also known as the Ku Klux Klan Act since its purpose was to protect blacks from Klan intimidation (threats of violence) and from government authorities either sympathetic to Klan goals or intimidated by Klan threats as well.

The Klan Act declared that any state or local government official, such as a police officer enforcing the law, treating a citizen in a way that denies them their constitutional rights could be held responsible to pay the wronged person for damages. The act opened the door for individuals who experienced improper police behavior, such as unreasonable searches or seizures prohibited by the U.S. Constitution's Fourth Amendment, to sue those officers for their actions. Police "search and seizure" is the inspection of a place or person for evidence related to an investigation and taking the evidence, if found, to court. To avoid Klan-influenced state or local courts, the act also gave victims the choice of going directly to federal courts concerning their charges where they might receive a fairer trial.

However, for ninety years following the law's passage courts applied it in very few instances. Courts still relied on early English legal traditions in which a person's right to sue governmental officials was very limited, a concept known as "official immunity [safe from lawsuit]." Consequently, black Americans received little protection under the 1871 act until the 1960s.

The Monroe Household Ransacked

Early in the morning of October 29, 1958 at 5:45 AM while investigating a murder case, twelve Chicago police officers led by Deputy Chief of Detectives Pape broke through two doors into the Monroe family home to conduct a search. They had obtained no search warrants beforehand. At gunpoint, the police forced all members of the family out of bed, including six children and both parents. They were forcefully led to the middle of their living room where they stood together naked. According to the Monroes' complaint, Pape struck Mr. Monroe several times with a flashlight while calling him "nigger" and "black boy." Mrs. Monroe and several of the children were pushed and kicked. The police aggressively searched the house dumping out the contents of drawers and closets on the floors and ripping mattresses open. After finding no evidence, Pape took Mr. Monroe to the police station and held him for ten hours. Pape neither brought specific charges against him nor did he bring Mr. Monroe before a judge when first arriving at the police station as legally required. Monroe was not allowed to contact an attorney as well.

Not wanting to let matters die after their ordeal, the Monroes filed a lawsuit against the city of Chicago and the thirteen police officers in the local district court charging them in violation of the Ku Klux Klan Act. Claiming they were merely performing their duties in a potentially hazardous situation, the city and police sought a dismissal of charges and received it. The Monroes appealed but the court of appeals upheld the district court's actions. Not receiving satisfactory results locally, the Monroes decided to take their case directly to the U.S. Supreme Court. The Court agreed to hear it.

The Court Overrules

Before the Court in November of 1961, the city of Chicago and the police officers argued that federal courts had no jurisdiction (proper authority to hear the case) in such disputes between local authorities and citizens. Local courts and state laws were quite sufficient to resolve such complaints. The Monroes argued that they were denied due process under the Fourteenth Amendment because of the illegal search and seizure. In response, the Court ruled unanimously in favor of the Monroes. They could legally sue the individual police officers for damages. However, the Court upheld the lower court decisions regarding the city of Chicago. City governments were not open to lawsuit under the 1871 act.

Justice William O. Douglas, writing the Court's opinion, first asserted that the federal courts did have jurisdiction in this case. The Fourth Amendment of the Constitution prohibits unreasonable search and seizures and these prohibitions apply to states through the Due Process Clause of the Fourteenth Amendment. Regarding the Monroes' charges, Douglas affirmed that the 1871 act requires states to enforce their laws fairly for all their citizens.

Douglas wrote, "Congress has the power to enforce provisions of the Fourteenth Amendment against those who carry a badge of authority of a State and represent it in some capacity, whether they act in accordance with their authority or misuse it."

The Right to Sue Cities, Too

The *Monroe* decision brought the long neglected Ku Klux Klan Act into full effect as Congress had originally intended. The ruling allowed citizens to sue state or local authorities for damages when the authorities

THE KU KLUX KLAN

Following the American Civil War (1861–65), resentment among white Southerners quickly grew as the U.S. government introduced policies designed to restructure Southern society to include newly freed black slaves. Seeking to reestablish political control by Southern whites, a group of former Confederate soldiers in Tennessee founded the Ku Klux Klan in 1866. A secret fraternal organization opposed to the granting of civil rights to black Americans, it was not specifically created for terrorism. However, the Klan quickly became involved in violent activities, including the lynching of blacks, murders, rapes, and bombings. The goal was to scare blacks into continued social oppression. The Klan's trademark was the wearing of white robes and hoods, reportedly representing the ghosts of Confederate dead but also useful for concealing individual identities and enhancing their menacing behavior.

Membership quickly grew to several hundred thousand by 1870. As Southern whites began to regain political power in the later 1870s, the Klan's membership and influence sharply declined. However, its peak years came later in the 1920s as anit-racial sentiment flared in the cities. Klan numbers grew to three or four million and its substantial political influence extended to states outside the South. The Klan helped elect to state and national positions many candidates who agreed with their cause. Faced with a public backlash by 1930, the Klan's popularity once again declined. Another smaller rise in Klan activity occurred in the 1960s in reaction to the Civil Rights Movement as the Klan became associated with several highly publicized violent acts against civil rights activists. By the 1990s Klan membership fell below 10,000 as white supremacists splintered into several organizations, including the Aryan Nations. Besides opposing civil rights for blacks, through its history the Klan has also fought against the rights of Jews, Catholics, foreign immigrants, and unions.

behaved improperly while carrying out their official duties. However, the Court's decision that a city could not be sued still restricted the ability of victims to seek damages when city authorities had violated their civil rights. The Court later recognized the individual's right to sue cities in *Monell v. Department of Social Services* (1978). Importantly, the *Monroe* decision also affirmed that for cases involving federal civil rights violations, citizens did not have to go to possibly unsympathetic state or local courts before taking their complaints to federal courts.

Suggestions for further reading

Collins, Allyson. *Shielded From Justice: Police Brutality and Accountability in the United States.* Washington, DC: Human Rights Watch, 1998.

Horowitz, David A. *Inside the Klavern: The Secret History of a Ku Klux Klan of the 1920s.* Carbondale, IL: Southern Illinois University Press, 1999.

Jackson, Kenneth T. *The Ku Klux Klan in the City, 1915-1930.* Chicago: I. R. Dee, 1992.

Washington, Linn. *The Beating Goes On: Police Brutality in America.* Belfast, ME: Common Courage Press, 2000.

Heart of Atlanta Motel v. United States 1964

Appellant: Heart of Atlanta Motel, Inc.

Appellee: United States

Appellant's Claim: That Title II of the Civil Rights Act of 1964, requiring hotel and motel owners to provide accommodations to black Americans, cannot be enforced against privately owned establishments.

Chief Lawyer for Appellant: Moreton Rolleston, Jr.

Chief Lawyer for Appellee: Archibald Cox, U.S. Solicitor General

Justices for the Court: Hugo L. Black, William J. Brennan, Jr., Tom C. Clark, William O. Douglas, Arthur Goldberg, John Marshall Harlan II, Potter Steward, Chief Justice Earl Warren, Byron R. White

Justices Dissenting: None

Date of Decision: December 14, 1964

Decision: Ruled in favor of the United States by upholding Title II of the Civil Rights Act of 1964.

Significance: In the first major test of the landmark Civil Rights Act of 1964, the Court unanimously upheld the act. The decision greatly aided black Americans in their civil rights struggle. The Commerce Clause of the U.S. Constitution proved to be a powerful tool in the battle to end racial discrimination.

CIVIL RIGHTS AND EQUAL PROTECTION

More often than not, black Americans in the early 1960s had to rely on rented rooms in private homes or the hospitality of friends if they were to travel far from their home. Hotels and motels dotted along highways and in towns provided comfortable accommodations for white Americans but black Americans had no access to these establishments.

Discrimination in Accommodations

The accommodation problem was recognized as early as the 1870s when Congress passed the Civil Rights Act of 1875. The act prohibited discrimination (giving privileges to one group, but not to another similar group) in facilities such as inns and theaters which were privately owned but commonly open to the public. Yet, in ***Civil Rights Cases*** (1883) the U.S. Supreme Court struck down the act. Saying that discrimination prohibitions applied only to government actions, the Court ruled the act could not apply to the discriminatory actions of private persons. The government remained powerless to stop discrimination by private persons for the next eighty years.

President Lyndon B. Johnson signing the Civil Rights Act of 1964. Courtesy of the Library of Congress.

Decades of discrimination led to the civil rights movement of the 1950s and 1960s. Civil rights are a person's individual rights set by law. Black Americans, denied their civil rights, protested in the streets. Congress responded to the social unrest by passing comprehensive civil rights legislation, the Civil Rights Act of 1964. Title II of this act prohibited discrimination based on race, color religion, or national origin in public accommodations that were in any way involved in interstate commerce. Examples of public accommodations are privately owned inns, hotels, motels, and restaurants which are open to the general public. Interstate commerce means any business or trade carried on between different states. Inns, hotels, and motels do business with guests traveling between states by providing them lodging. Therefore, they are part of interstate commerce.

Article I, Section 8 of the Constitution, known as the Commerce Clause, grants Congress the power to regulate all interstate commerce. Does Congress have the power to regulate discriminatory practices by private individuals such as owners of motels that affect interstate commerce? It had tried to do just that with passage of Title II of the Civil Rights Act of 1964. The first case challenging the constitutionality of the landmark act reached the Supreme Court within the year.

The Heart of Atlanta Motel

The Heart of Atlanta Motel, located near interstate and state highways, had 216 rooms available to guests. The motel advertised extensively outside the state of Georgia through national media and magazines with national circulation. It also accepted convention trade from outside Georgia. Approximately 75 percent of its registered guests were from out of state. Before passage of the Civil Rights Act of 1964 the motel followed the common practice of refusing to rent rooms to black Americans. They fully intended to continue the practice. The motel's owner filed a lawsuit contending that Congress had exceeded its power under the Commerce Clause by passing Title II of the act to regulate local private businesses such as his hotel. Second, the owner claimed that the act violated "the Fifth Amendment because appellant [the owner] is deprived of the right to choose its customers and operate its business as it wishes, resulting in a taking of its liberty and property without due process of law." The Fifth Amendment says that no person shall be "deprived of life, liberty, or property, without due process of law."

The U.S. government countered by claiming the "unavailability to Negroes of adequate accommodations interferes significantly with interstate travel" hence interferes with interstate commerce. Therefore, under the Commerce Clause Congress had not exceeded its power and could regulate "such obstructions" to interstate commerce. Furthermore, the Fifth Amendment allows "reasonable regulation" and neither the appellant's liberty nor due process was violated.

The District Court upheld Title II of the act and ordered the motel owner to stop "refusing to accept Negroes as guests in the motel by reason of their race or color." The hotel operators appealed to the U.S. Supreme Court which agreed to hear the case.

The Civil Rights Act of 1964 Upheld

Writing for a unanimous (9-0) Court which found against Heart of Atlanta Motel, Justice Tom C. Clark delivered the decision upholding Title II of the Civil Rights Act of 1964. Justice Clark wrote that in researching Congress' debate over the Civil Rights Act of 1964 the evidence was clear the difficulties black Americans encountered in their attempts to find accommodations "had the effect of discouraging travel on the part of a substantial [large] portion of the Negro community." The evidence was "overwhelming . . . that discrimination by hotels and motels impedes [interferes with] interstate travel" and, therefore, obstructs interstate commerce. Justice Clark quoting from *Caminetti v. United States* (1917) wrote "the transportation of passengers in interstate commerce, it has long been settled, is within the regulatory powers of Congress, under the commerce clause of the constitution and the authority of Congress to keep the channels of interstate commerce free . . . is no longer open to question."

Next, Justice Clark wrote that not only did the Commerce Clause authorize Congress to regulate interstate commerce but allowed it to regulate activities within a state that had a "harmful effect" on interstate commerce. Because of its harmful effect on interstate commerce, "racial discrimination by motels serving travelers, however 'local' their operations may appear" could be regulated by Congress. Although the Heart of Atlanta Motel claimed its operation was local, the Court decided that the effects of its policies and practices reached far beyond Atlanta and the state border. Congress' regulation of racial discrimination in accommodations through Title II of the Civil Rights Act of 1964 was a constitutional approach which also contributed to correcting a "moral and social wrong."

COMMERCE CLAUSE

Article I, Section 8, Clause 3 of the U.S. Constitution gives solely to Congress the power to regulate commerce between states and with foreign countries and Indian tribes. As used by the Constitution, the term commerce means all business or trade in any form between citizens. Interstate commerce is business between citizens across state lines. Sale and transportation of a product by persons in Florida to persons in Texas would be interstate commerce. In contrast, intrastate commerce is business conducted within one state only and subject to state control only.

The Commerce Clause empowers Congress to pass laws to regulate the flow of interstate commerce in order to keep interstate transactions free from local restrictions imposed by the states. If Congress finds that intrastate activities influence business between different states, it may regulate that area of intrastate commerce. For example, access to lodgings and restaurants located in each state allow persons to travel and do business from state to state. Therefore, they fall under interstate commerce regulation.

Other examples of federally regulated interstate commerce are transportation of goods between states and transmission of information across state lines by telephone, radio, television, or mail.

Turning to the issue of whether or not the Fifth Amendment rights of the owner of Heart of Atlanta Motel had been violated by Title II, the Court rejected the charge. Justice Clark found "a long line of cases" where the Court had denied the claim that "prohibition of racial discrimination in public accommodations interferes with personal liberty."

The Commerce Clause—A Powerful Tool

Heart of Atlanta Motel was the first legal challenge to the Civil Rights Act of 1964. The U.S. Supreme Court promptly and unanimously upheld the act. This outcome was far different than the decision in the *Civil Rights Cases* (1883) which left the Civil Rights Act of 1875 useless. The Commerce Clause became a powerful tool for combating racial discrimination. It gave Congress the constitutional backing to pass legislation promoting equal rights for black Americans. In a case decided the same day, *Katzenbach v. McClung* (1964), the Court reasoned in a similar manner as in *Heart of Atlanta Motel. Katzenbach* involved a small restaurant which did not serve blacks. Its customers were mostly local, but the restaurant did purchase some supplies which originally came from out of state. Because of the purchases of these supplies, the restaurant's activities were part of interstate commerce. Therefore, the government could regulate the restaurant and require it to serve blacks. Taken together, *Heart of Atlanta Motel* and *Katzenbach* demonstrated that Congress had found an effective constitutional pathway for combating racism in America.

Suggestions for further reading

Chideya, Farai. *The Color of Our Future: Our Multiracial Future.* New York: William Morrow & Co., 1999.

Griffin, John H. *Black Like Me.* New York: Signet, 1996.

Steinhorn, Leonard, and Barbara Diggs-Brown. *By the Color of Our Skin.* New York: E.P. Dutton, 1999.

Loving v. Virginia 1967

Appellants: Mildred Jeter Loving, Richard Perry Loving

Appellee: Commonwealth of Virginia

Appellant's Claim: That Virginia state laws prohibiting interracial marriages violate the Fourteenth Amendment's equal protection and due process clauses.

Chief Lawyer for Appellants: Bernard S. Cohen

Chief Lawyer for Appellee: R.D. McIlwaine III

Justices for the Court: Hugo L. Black, William J. Brennan, Jr., William O. Douglas, Abe Fortas, John Marshall Harlan II, Potter Stewart, Chief Justice Earl Warren, Byron R. White

Justices Dissenting: None (Justice Thurgood Marshall did not participate)

Date of Decision: June 12, 1967

Decision: Ruled in favor of the Lovings by finding Virginia's laws banning interracial marriage unconstitutional.

Significance: The Court emphasized that all racial classifications are suspect and subject to strict scrutiny by the courts. Protecting an individual's freedom to choose a marriage partner, the ruling outlawed all state laws prohibiting interracial marriage.

CIVIL RIGHTS AND EQUAL PROTECTION

In the United States at the beginning of the twenty-first century, Americans considered the freedom to choose a marriage partner a fundamental right. The idea that government could interfere with that choice was unthinkable. Yet, as late as 1967 laws prohibiting "miscegenation" were on the books in sixteen states. Miscegenation refers to marriage between a Caucasian (white) and a member of any other race. It was not until June of 1967 that the U.S. Supreme Court finally declared such laws unconstitutional in *Loving v. Virginia.*

Interracial Marriage in Virginia

Virginia was one of the sixteen states with miscegenation laws in 1967. Three laws applied: (1) Provision 20-57 of the Virginia Code automatically voided all marriages between "a white person and a colored person" without any legal hearings; (2) 20-58 made it a crime for any white person and colored person to leave Virginia to be married and then return to live in Virginia; and, (3) 20-59 provided punishment by declaring interracial marriages a felony leading to a prison sentence of not less than one nor more than five years for each individual involved. Although

Richard and Mildred Loving fought all the way to the Supreme Court for their right to be married in any state. Reproduced by permission of AP/Wide World Photos.

penalties for miscegenation had been common in Virginia since slavery times, Virginia's codes were based on the Racial Integrity Act of 1924. This act absolutely prohibited a white person from marrying anyone other than another white person. Virginia passed the act following World War I in a time of distrust for anyone not Caucasian. The miscegenation codes were still actively enforced into the 1960s.

Mildred Jeter and Richard Loving

In June of 1958, two Virginia residents, Mildred Jeter, a black American woman, and Richard Loving, a white man, married in the District of Columbia according to its laws. Shortly after their marriage, the Lovings returned to Caroline County, Virginia where they established their home. In October of 1958 a grand jury for the Circuit Court of Caroline County issued an indictment (charge) against the Lovings for violating Virginia's codes banning interracial (between different races) marriage. The Lovings pleaded guilty to the charge and were sentenced to one year in jail. The trial judge suspended the sentence on the condition the Lovings leave Virginia and not return together for twenty-five years. In his opinion, the trial judge stated,

> **Almighty God created the races white, black, yellow, . . . and red, and he placed them on separate continents. And, but for the interference with his arrangement, there would be no cause for such marriage. The fact that he separated the races shows that he did not intend for the races to mix.**

After their convictions, the Lovings moved to the District of Columbia. They requested a state trial court to vacate (to set aside or make void) the judgement against them on the ground that the Virginia miscegenation laws violated the Fourteenth Amendment. The Fourteenth Amendment declares that no state shall "deprive any person of life, liberty, or property, without due process of law [Due Process Clause]; nor deny to any person within its jurisdiction [geographical area over which a government has authority] the equal protection of the laws [Equal Protection Clause]." Due process of law means fair legal hearings must take place. Equal protection of the laws means persons or groups of persons in similar situations must be treated equally by the laws. The Lovings' request was denied in January of 1965 but their case moved onto the Virginia Supreme Court of Appeals the following month.

The appeals court upheld the constitutionality of the miscegenation laws and affirmed the Lovings' convictions. The court referred to its 1955 decision in *Naim v. Naim* where it concluded that Virginia had legitimate (honest) purposes for the miscegenation laws. Those purposes were "to preserve the racial integrity of its citizens," and to prevent "the corruption of blood," and "a mongrel breed of citizens." Furthermore, the appeals court asserted that for a law "containing" racial classifications (groupings of people based on some selected factor) all the Equal Protection Clause required was that both the white and black participants be punished equally thus avoiding discrimination (treating individuals in similar situations differently) claims. This equal punishment idea was known as "equal application." If both were punished equally, as was the case with the Lovings, then no violation of the Equal Protection Clause existed and, likewise, no "invidious [objectionable, intent to harm] discrimination against race." The state found support for "equal application" theory in the U.S. Supreme Court case of *Pace v. Alabama* (1883).

The Lovings next appealed to the U.S. Supreme Court which agreed to hear the case.

To the U.S. Supreme Court

In a 8–0 decision, the Court disagreed with the lower courts' decisions and reversed the Lovings' convictions. Justice Thurgood Marshall did not participate. Delivering the Court's opinion, Chief Justice Earl Warren wrote,

> **This case presents a constitutional question never addressed by this Court: whether a statutory [law] . . . to prevent marriages between persons solely on the basis of racial classifications violates the Equal Protection and Due Process Clauses of the Fourteenth Amendment.**

The Court answered the question in a two-part decision.

Race Classification Is Always Suspicious

First, the Court rejected the Virginia Supreme Court of Appeals' finding that because of "equal application," or equal punishment, there was no racial discrimination. The Court pointed out that the *Pace v. Alabama* (1883) decision had not survived later decisions by the Court. The "equal application" concept was no longer valid.

Chief Justice Warren wrote, "The clear and central purpose of the Fourteenth Amendment was to eliminate all official state sources of invidious racial discrimination." Warren continued that the Equal Protection Clause of the Fourteenth Amendment "demands" that any law based on racial classification is "suspect" (suspicious) and must be examined with rigid scrutiny (strict, intense examination). In other words, the Court automatically viewed racial classification as suspicious and would assume that it probably violated the Equal Protection Clause. A law with suspect classification would normally be judged unconstitutional unless the government could justify it with a compelling (extremely important) reason for its need. A law that's purpose is racial discrimination or antagonism can never be found constitutional.

Chief Justice Warren stated that "there can be no question" Virginia's miscegenation laws were clearly based solely on classification of people according to race. The Court, applying strict scrutiny, found no compelling (overwhelming need for) reason for Virginia's action. Therefore, Warren wrote, "There can be no doubt that restricting the freedom to marry solely because of racial classifications violates the central meaning of the Equal Protection Clause."

The Fundamental Freedom to Marry

Secondly, the Court identified marriage as one of the "basic civil rights of man."

Restricting the freedom to marry was in direct violation of the Due Process Clause of the Fourteenth Amendment. Chief Justice Warren eloquently explained,

> **to deny this fundamental freedom on so unsupportable a basis as the racial classifications [in the Virginia law], . . . classifications so directly subversive of the principle of equality at the heart of the Fourteenth Amendment is sure to deprive all the State's citizens liberty without due process of law. The Fourteenth Amendment requires that the freedom of choice to marry not be restricted by invidious racial discrimination. Under our Constitution, the freedom to marry, or not marry, a person of another race resides with the individual and cannot be infringed [restricted] by the State.**

INTERRACIAL MARRIAGES

By 1990 there were four times as many interracial marriages as in 1960 but the overall number remained small. Considering only black-white marriages, in 1991 just 0.4 percent of total marriages were black-white couples.

With a further decline in social prejudices in the 1990s, surveys indicated young Americans were more open to the idea of interracial union. Experts predicted an increase of cross-cultural marriages involving not only black and white Americans but many other races. Between 1980 and 1996 the number of total married couples in the United States increased 10 percent to 54,664,000, but the number of interracial marriages had almost doubled to 1,260,000.

Interestingly, however, by the late 1990s many black women began to oppose the idea of interracial marriage. Instead, they preferred black to black marriages for racial strength and stabilization of the black family.

In *Loving* the Court held that all racial classifications are suspect classifications subject to strict scrutiny. It struck down all laws prohibiting interracial marriage.

Suggestions for further reading

Funderburg, Lise. *Black, White, Other: Biracial Americans Talk About Race and Identity.* New York: W. Morrow and Co., 1994.

Higginbotham, A. Leon. *Shades of Freedom: Racial Politics and Presumptions of the American Legal Press.* New York: Oxford University Press, 1996.

Kaeser, Gigi. *Of Many Colors: Portraits of Multiracial Families.* Amherst: University of Massachusetts Press, 1997.

McDonald, Laughlin, and John A. Powell. *The Rights of Racial Minorities* (ACLU Handbooks for Young Americans). New York:

Reed v. Reed
1971

Appellant: Sally Reed

Appellee: Cecil Reed

Appellant's Claim: That a Idaho law favoring the appointment of a man, merely because he was male, over a woman to be administrator of a deceased person's estate violates the Equal Protection Clause of the Fourteenth Amendment.

Chief Lawyers for Appellant: Allen R. Derr, Ruth Bader Ginsburg

Chief Lawyers for Appellee: Charles S. Stout, Myron E. Anderson

Justices for the Court: Hugo L. Black, Harry A. Blackmun, William J. Brennan, Jr., Chief Justice Warren E. Burger, William O. Douglas, John Marshall Harlan II, Thurgood Marshall, Potter Stewart, Byron R. White

Justices Dissenting: None

Date of Decision: November 22, 1971

Decision: Ruled in favor of Sally Reed by finding that Idaho's probate law discriminated against women.

Significance: This decision was the first time in the Fourteenth Amendment's 103-year history that the Supreme Court ruled that its Equal Protection Clause protected women's rights. The ruling formed the basis for protecting women's and men's rights in gender discrimination claims in many situations over the next thirty years.

CIVIL RIGHTS AND EQUAL PROTECTION

The Fourteenth Amendment of the U.S. Constitution reads, "No State shall make or enforce any law which shall abridge [lessen] the privileges . . . of citizens of the United States . . . nor deny to any person within its jurisdiction [geographical area over which a government has control] the equal protection of the laws." Equal protection of the laws means persons or groups of persons in similar situations must be treated equally by the laws. Although the Fourteenth Amendment was adopted in 1868, it was 103 years before the U.S. Supreme Court applied this constitutional guarantee of equal protection to women. The Court did so with *Reed v. Reed* in 1971. Lawyer in the case and future Supreme Court Justice Ruth Bader Ginsburg labeled Reed a "turning point case." The Court for the first time held a state law invalid because it discriminated (unfairly giving privileges to one group but not to another similar group) against women.

The Reeds of Idaho

The case had its beginning on March 29, 1967 in Ada County, Idaho when nineteen-year-old Richard Lynn Reed, using his father's rifle, committed suicide. Richard's adoptive parents, Sally and Cecil Reed, had

Associate Justice Ruth Bader Ginsburg. Courtesy of the Supreme Court of the United States.

separated sometime prior to his death. Richard's early childhood was spent in the custody (the legal right to make key decisions for another) of Sally, but once he reached his teenage years custody was transferred to his father. Ginsburg recalled that Sally had opposed the custody change and later believed part of the responsibility for her son's death rested with Cecil.

Probate Court

Richard died without a will, so Sally filed a petition in the Probate Court of Ada County to be administrator (director) of Richard's estate (all that a person owns), valued at less than one thousand dollars. Probate courts oversee the administration of deceased persons' estates. Cecil Reed filed a competing petition seeking to have himself appointed as the administrator of his son's estate.

Following a hearing on the two petitions, the Probate Court appointed Cecil the administrator. In deciding who would be administrator, the court did not consider the capabilities of each parent but went strictly by Idaho's mandatory (required) probate code. Section 15-312 of the code reads:

> **Administrator of the estate of a person dying intestate [to die without a valid will] must be granted to some one . . . in the following order: (1) the surviving husband or wife or . . . ; (2) the children; (3) the father or mother. . .**

Under this section "father" and "mother" were equal in being entitled (authorized) to administer the will. However, Section 15-314 provided, "Of several persons claiming and equally entitled to administer, males must be preferred to females and relatives of whole to those of the half blood."

Apparently, the probate judge considered himself bound by Section 15-314 to choose the male, Cecil, over the female, Sally, since the two were otherwise "equally entitled."

Mixed Signals

Sally appealed the Probate Court's decision to the District Court of the Fourth Judicial District. Sally's lawyer, Allen R. Derr, argued that Idaho's law violated Sally's constitutional rights of equal protection of the laws guaranteed in the Fourteenth Amendment. The District Court agreed, held the challenged section of the law unconstitutional, and ordered the case back to the Probate Court to determine which parent was better qualified, regardless of sex, to be administrator. However, the order was not carried out since Cecil immediately appealed to the Idaho Supreme Court.

The Idaho Supreme Court rejected the District Court's ruling and reestablished Cecil, since he was male, as administrator of his son's estate. In reaching their decision, the Idaho Supreme Court looked at why the Idaho legislature had passed Section 15-314 in the first place. They found that Idaho's legislature "evidently concluded that in general men are better qualified to act as an administrator than women." Also, they found that the workload of the Probate Court would be lessened if it was not required to have a hearing every time two or more relatives petitioned to be administrator. Therefore, the Idaho Supreme Court found it neither unreasonable nor arbitrary (dictatorial, not open to other opinions) but an easy convenience for the courts to decide simply on the basis of being male or female. Sally appealed to the U.S. Supreme Court which agreed to hear the case.

Equal Protection for Women, Too

Ginsburg along with others associated with the Women's Rights Project of the American Civil Liberties Union (ACLU) joined Derr to represent Sally before the U.S. Supreme Court. Derr's team argued, as women's rights advocates had since the 1870s, that women's rights were protected under the Fourteenth Amendment's Equal Protection Clause. Cecil's lawyers argued that the Idaho law provided a reasonable way of cutting Probate Court's heavy workload.

The Court, in a unanimous (9–0) decision, ruled that the Idaho probate law violated the Fourteenth Amendment. Chief Justice Warren E. Burger, in delivering the opinion of the Court, wrote:

> **Having examined the record and considered the briefs [summaries written by the lawyers] and oral arguments of the parties, we have concluded that the arbitrary preference established in favor of males by 15-314 of the Idaho Code cannot stand in the face of the Fourteenth Amendment's command that no State deny the equal protection of the laws to any person within its jurisdiction.**

RUTH BADER GINSBURG

Born in Brooklyn, New York in 1933, Ruth Bader Ginsburg graduated Phi Beta Kappa (with high honors) in 1954 from Cornell University. She married, gave birth to her first child, then entered Harvard University Law School by 1956. As editor of the highly respected *Harvard Law Review,* she gained the nickname "Ruthless Ruthie." When her husband began work with a New York law firm, she transferred to Columbia Law School where she received her law degree in 1959, tied for first in her class.

Although an accomplished scholar, when Ginsburg sought employment she ran into the traditional stereotyping (fixed impression) of female lawyers which limited opportunities in a male-dominated profession. In addition to being female, she was also Jewish and a mother. Ginsburg persevered, eventually becoming a law professor at Rutgers University School of Law from 1963 to 1972. She then taught at Columbia Law School from 1972 to 1980, becoming the first female faculty member to earn tenure (permanent staff position).

During her time at Columbia, she was also an attorney for the American Civil Liberties Union where she founded the Women's Rights Project. Championing the rights of women, she argued six cases before the U.S. Supreme Court between 1973 and 1976 and won five of them. Ginsburg demanded equal protection be applied to gender issues and the end of discrimination along gender lines. President Jimmy Carter appointed Ginsburg in 1980 to the U.S. Court of Appeals for the District of Columbia Circuit where she served until 1993 when President Bill Clinton nominated her for Associate Justice on the U.S. Supreme Court. The Senate confirmed Ginsburg by a vote of 96-3. As a justice, Ginsburg became a tireless supporter of equal rights and equal treatment for all.

Although the Court pointed out that at times the Fourteenth Amendment allows persons or a group of persons to be put into classifications (groupings of people based on some selected factor) and treated differently, those classifications "must be reasonable, not arbitrary" and must honestly relate to a state objective (goal). The Idaho Supreme Court had found Section 15-314's objective was to reduce workload; however, the U.S. Supreme Court found:

> **The crucial question . . . is whether 15-314 advances that objective in a manner consistent with the command of the Equal Protection Clause. We hold that it does not. To give a mandatory preference to members of either sex over members of the other, merely to accomplish the elimination of hearings . . . is to make the very kind of arbitrary legislative choice forbidden by the Equal Protection Clause of the Fourteenth Amendment; and . . . the choice . . . may not lawfully be mandated solely on the basis of sex.**

Sally Reed and her lawyers had won what women had sought in the courts for a century—Fourteenth Amendment protection of women's equal rights under the laws.

A Cornerstone for Future Cases

Reed v. Reed was the first ruling by the U.S. Supreme Court that concluded laws arbitrarily requiring gender (based on the sex of the person) discrimination were violations of the Equal Protection Clause of the Fourteenth Amendment. During the following decades, the Court used this decision as a basis to strike down many laws discriminating against women. Men also benefitted from the ruling since it prevents courts from basing opinions on generalizations about either gender.

Suggestions for further reading

American Civil Liberties Union. [Online] Website: http://www.aclu.org (Accessed on July 31, 2000).

Cullen-DuPont, Kathryn. *The Encyclopedia of Women's History in America.* New York: Facts on File, 2000.

Davis, Flora. *Moving the Mountain: The Women's Movement in America Since 1960.* Chicago: University of Illinois Press, 1999.

Ross, Susan D., Lisabelle K. Pingler, Deborah A. Ellis, and Kary L. Moss. *The Rights of Women: The Basic ACLU Guide to Women's Rights.* 3rd Edition. Carbondale: Southern Illinois University Press, 1993.

Gender discrimination, or sex discrimination, may be described as the unfair treatment of a person because of that person's sex. Historically, females have been discriminated against in the United States based solely on their gender. The Supreme Court did not consider women under the Fourteenth Amendment's guarantee of "equal protection of the laws" until the 1970s. By the late twentieth century, civil rights laws prohibiting sex discrimination were being applied to the protection of males as well.

Fatherly Protection

Paternalism is defined as the protective behavior of a father toward his child. Like the general public's view toward women at the time, the Supreme Court's attitude toward women and their role in American society in the nineteenth century was one of paternalism. Women, they believed, belonged at home to care for their families and were much too delicate to have occupations or deal with issues outside of the home. This philosophy was used repeatedly from the 1870s until the 1960s to justify ignoring the Fourteenth Amendment's "equal protection of the laws" when issues concerning unfair treatment of women arose. Equal protection was intended to be a constitutional guarantee that no person or persons would be denied protection of the laws that is enjoyed by other persons or groups.

An early example of this disregard for the Fourteenth Amendment came in *Bradwell v. Illinois* (1873). Based completely on gender, a state refused to issue a woman a license to practice law, an apparent clear violation of "equal protection of the laws." However, the Court agreed with the state and justified their decision with a paternalistic explanation. Justice Joseph P. Bradley wrote that women's "natural . . . delicacy" made them unfit "for many of the occupations of civil life [such as being a lawyer]." Continuing, he observed that "divine ordinance [God's laws]" and the very "nature of things" indicated that a woman must remain within her home circle.

Likewise, the Court ruled in ***Minor v. Happersett*** (1875), that the Fourteenth Amendment did not require state governments to allow women to vote. The *Minor* decision was not erased until 1920, when the Nineteenth Amendment to the U.S. Constitution giving women the right to vote was adopted. Concerning jury duty, the Court in ***Strauder v. West Virginia*** (1880) decided that state governments could prohibit women from serving on juries. Concerned about women's health and morals, the Court in *Cronin v. Adams* (1904) upheld a Denver law barring the sale of liquor to women and prohibiting them to work in bars or stores where liquor was sold. The Court with the same fatherly attitude also addressed and upheld state laws setting maximum working hours for women in ***Muller v. Oregon*** (1908). However, for men, setting similar limitations on working hours was considered a violation of their right to work. This protective attitude was still alive in 1961 with the ruling in *Hoyt v. Florida.* In that case, the Court again upheld an exemption (free of a duty) for women from jury duty commenting, "Woman is still regarded as the center of home and family life."

Civil Rights Era of the 1950s and 1960s

Despite paternalistic views, the mid-twentieth century found many women working outside the home to support themselves and their families. Because women had traditionally been expected to remain at home with limited access to colleges, they were less educated, and thus, left with only low paying, low skill jobs. Women frequently received less pay than a man for the same job. This was based on the idea that women's earnings were less important than a man's when looking at support of families.

The civil rights movement of the 1950s and 1960s made more people aware of all types of discrimination, including gender discrimination. The fact that women were suffering from discrimination that was traditionally rooted in the nation's paternalistic attitudes became apparent to many, including members of Congress. Congress began passing legislation with the intention of fixing this unjust situation. They passed the Equal Pay Act in 1963, followed by the monumental Civil Rights Act of 1964.

Title VII of the Civil Rights Act of 1964 makes it "an unlawful employment practice for an employer . . . to discriminate against any individual with respect to his compensation [pay], terms, conditions, or privileges of employment, because of such individual's race, color, religion, sex, or national origin." Interestingly, Title VII was originally drafted to prohibit discrimination on the basis of "race, color, religion, or national origin," not sex. In a move to defeat the proposed bill, Southern conservatives added sex to the Title VII wording. The conservatives believed this addition was so outrageous that the entire bill would fail. The strategy, however, back-fired and the bill passed. President Lyndon Johnson signed the bill into law without raising any issue with the new wording prohibiting discrimination based on sex. The act also established the Equal Employment Opportunity Commission (EEOC), whose job was to create regulations to enforce the law.

Success in the 1970s

Beginning in the 1970s, women successfully challenged discrimination based on sex in the courts. With the passage of the Civil Rights Act of 1964, women finally had a law under which they could seek equal protection. The Supreme Court's first ruling that struck down a state law that unfairly discriminated against women was in *Reed v. Reed* (1971). In that case, an Idaho law gave men automatic preference over women to administer (to have charge over) the estate (all possessions) of someone who died without a will. In 1975 in ***Taylor v. Louisiana,*** the Court overturned the 1880 *Strauder* decision by ruling that states could not exclude women from jury duty based on sex alone. During this period, Congress continued to pass laws barring gender-based discrimination. For example, the Education Amendments of 1972 prohibited sex discrimination in all educational programs receiving federal aid. In 1973 Congress approved a bill prohibiting the denial of financial credit based on sex.

Men also sought equal protection from gender discrimination. In *Frontiero v. Richardson* (1973) the Court ruled on a military regulation that required husbands, in order to receive certain benefits, to prove they were dependents or relied on their military wife for support. A wife of a military man never had to prove dependency. Therefore, the law was based purely on gender and was struck down. Likewise, the Court struck down in *Craig v. Boren* (1976) an Oklahoma law permitting the sale of low-alcohol beer to women at the age of eighteen, but to men at the age of twenty-one.

Gender discrimination in educational programs

Title IX of the Education Amendments of 1972 prohibits gender discrimination in federally funded education programs, including athletic activities. Title IX has prompted legal action by female athletes, who claim they are not provided the same benefits, treatments, services, and opportunities as their male peers.

In 1982 the Court in ***Mississippi University for Women v. Hogan*** struck down a women-only admissions policy at a state university school of nursing. In yet another strike against the paternalistic view toward women, the Supreme Court in ***United States v. Virginia*** (1996) found a male-only admission policy practiced by Virginia Military Institute (VMI) unconstitutional (does not follow the intent of the Constitution).

Sexual harassment defined

Although great strides in fighting gender discrimination were taken in the 1970s, largely due to the Civil Rights Act of 1964, abuses falling within the category of sexual harassment generally were not addressed. Finally, in 1980 due to pressure from women's groups, the EEOC wrote and released guidelines (instructions) which defined sexual harassment. They described it as one form of sex discrimination prohibited by the 1964 act. EEOC guidelines define sexual harassment in the following way:

> **Unwelcome sexual advances, requests for sexual favors, and other verbal or physical conducts of a sexual nature constitute (are) sexual harassment when: (1) submission to (agree to) . . . or rejection of such conduct by an individual is used as the basis for employment decisions affecting such indi-**

viduals, or (2) such conduct has the purpose or effect of unreasonably interfering with an individual's work performance or creating an intimidating, hostile (threatening), or offensive working environment.

The first key word in the definition is "unwelcome." Unwelcome or uninvited sexual communication or conduct is prohibited. A court will review the whole circumstance of a reported situation to determine if the conduct was unwelcome. The next key words in the definition are sexual advances or favors. Verbal advances or favors might include oral or written requests for dates or sex, comments about the victim's body, jokes, or whistles. Physical advances or favors might include hugging, kissing, grabbing, staring, or standing very close. Cartoons or pictures of a sexual nature may also be considered advances.

Next, the EEOC guidelines distinguish between two types of sexual harassment. The first type is referred to as "quid pro quo," giving one valuable thing to receive another valuable thing. In familiar terms, this is called a "sex for jobs" situation. An example of sexual harassment that would be considered "quid pro quo" is when a supervisor seeks sex from an employee in exchange for a pay raise, a promotion, or even continuation of the employee's job. The second type of sexual harassment is referred to as "hostile working environment." An example of "hostile working environment" sexual harassment is when the repeated sexual conduct or communication of a supervisor or co-worker creates a threatening work environment for an employee. The employee's salary or job security may not be involved. However, the offensive actions have poisoned the work environment making it difficult or unpleasant for an employee to do his or her job.

Supreme Court begins to speak

The Supreme Court did not address the issue of sexual harassment until the 1986 case of ***Meritor Savings Bank v. Vinson*** The ruling in *Meritor* became a turning point for sexual harassment cases. The Court used the EEOC's guidelines to unanimously (all justices in agreement) decide that sexual harassment in the workplace is illegal and protected under Title VII of the Civil Rights Act of 1964. After 1986, both state courts and the Supreme Court continued to clarify (make clearer) what constituted sexual harassment.

Damages or monetary awards for victims

In 1991, the U.S. Senate held confirmation hearings on Clarence Thomas' appointment to a justice position on the Supreme Court. During the hearings Anita Hill testified that she had been sexually harassed by Thomas. Although Justice Thomas' appointment was not blocked, the hearings did bring sexual harassment to the attention of the entire nation. Partly due to this increased visibility, Congress passed the 1991 Civil Rights Act allowing for monetary payments (damages) to be paid to victims of sexual harassment.

Supreme Court adds further insights

In *Harris v. Forklift* (1993) the Court ruled that a victim has to suffer psychological damage in order to prove a hostile work environment. The Court ruled in *Burlington Industries, Inc. v. Ellerth* (1997) that a quid pro quo case could come from a single incident, but a hostile work environment generally develops over time and the victim must show "severe or pervasive (persistent over time)" conduct. Also in *Burlington Industries,* the Court outlined important steps employers could take to help them avoid liability (employer held responsible for an employees conduct), such as putting policies in place to prevent and correct sexually harassing behavior. *Faragher v. Boca Raton* (1998) provided yet another wake-up call to large employers. The Court asserted that companies must establish policies against sexual harassment by describing ways to investigate and correct wrongdoings. They must also clearly communicate these policies to their employees. Failing to communicate with employees could result in employer liability for the offensive behavior of its supervisors.

In ***Oncale v. Sundowner Offshore Services Incorporated et al.*** (1998), the Court dealt with "same sex" offenses. The Court ruled that an employee can seek damages from his employer even when the victim is sexually harassed by another employee of the same sex.

Sexual harassment in schools

Sexual harassment is prohibited in all federally funded schools under Title IX of the Education Amendments of 1972. Schools must have a policy prohibiting sexual discrimination including sexual harassment, and must inform students, employees, and parents of the policy. Similar categories of quid pro quo and hostile work environment exist under

Title IX. For example, a situation in which a teacher or coach makes sex a requirement for a passing grade would be considered quid pro quo harassment. Hostile environment, on the other hand, applies when a student is subjected to "unwelcome" and "pervasive" actions. In the academic setting, the party claiming harassment must report the incident to authorities who have the power to correct the situation within the system. In *Gebser et al. v. Lago Vista Independent School District* (1998), the Court held that a student could not recover damages for sexual harassment because school officials were never notified of the alleged harassment. Therefore, the school had no opportunity to resolve the situation.

Sexual harassment in the U.S. Military

Sexual harassment is prohibited in all branches of the military. In 1994, Secretary of Defense, William Perry, created the military's version of the EEOC, the Defense Equal Opportunity Council Task Force on Discrimination and Sexual Harassment (DEOC). The DEOC was created to investigate the procedures used by the military to register complaints and to suggest means of improving the procedures. Sexual harassment in the military can be particularly harmful to a victim's life. Victims and offenders may often live close together, and a superior in the military has great power to influence a subordinate's (soldier) future life path. Despite attempts to prevent sexual harassment in the military, top officials admitted that sexual harassment persisted within all ranks, genders, and racial groups at the end of the twentieth century.

Prevention of sexual harassment

The Supreme Court and state courts have clearly shown that they will apply EEOC guidelines in sexual harassment cases. EEOC guidelines include directions for employers on how to prevent, recognize, investigate, and resolve sexual harassment within businesses. As a result, many organizations established steps to follow with complaints. Complaints may be filed within the business or directly with the EEOC or state or local agencies responsible for fair employment practices. In severe or unresolved cases, lawsuits may be filed seeking damages (monetary payments). The ongoing battle of eliminating sexual harassment depends on constant vigilance (watchfulness) in the workplace, educational system, and the military.

Suggestions for Further Reading

Chaiet, Donna. *Staying Safe at School.* New York: Rosen Publishing Group, 1995.

O'Shea, Tracy, and Jane LaLonde. *Sexual Harassment: A Practical Guide to the Law, Your Rights, and Your Options for Taking Action.* New York: St. Martin's Griffin, 1998.

Petrocelli, William, and Barbara Kate Repa. *Sexual Harassment on the Job.* Berkeley, CA: Nolo Press, 1994.

Segrave, Kerry. *The Sexual Harassment of Women in the Workplace, 1600 to 1993.* Jefferson, NC: McFarland & Company, Inc., 1994.

Minor v. Happersett
1875

Appellant: Virginia Minor

Appellee: Reese Happersett

Appellant's Claim: That Missouri violated the U.S. Constitution by refusing to let women vote.

Chief Lawyer for Appellant: Francis Minor

Chief Lawyer for Appellee: None

Justices for the Court: Joseph P. Bradley, Nathan Clifford, David Davis, Stephen Johnson Field, Ward Hunt, Samuel Freeman Miller, William Strong, Noah Haynes Swayne, Morrison Remick Waite

Justices Dissenting: None

Date of Decision: March 29, 1875

Decision: The Supreme Court said Missouri did not violate the Constitution.

Significance: With *Minor,* the Supreme Court said voting is not a privilege of citizenship. Women did not get the right to vote nationwide until the United States adopted the Nineteenth Amendment in 1920.

The fight for women's suffrage generated many interesting and witty posters. Courtesy of the Library of Congress.

Many Americans consider the right to vote to be a privilege of citizenship. When the United States was born in 1776, however, voting was reserved almost exclusively for white men. Women and black men had to fight for the right to vote, which is called suffrage.

When the American Civil War ended in 1865, the United States ended slavery with the Thirteenth Amendment. Three years later in 1868, it adopted the Fourteenth Amendment to prevent states from giving black Americans fewer rights than white Americans received. The Fourteenth

Amendment says, "No State shall make or enforce any law which shall abridge [limit] the privileges and immunities of citizens of the United States." In 1870, African American men received the right to vote under the Fifteenth Amendment.

Women's Suffrage

When the United States adopted the Fourteenth Amendment, Virginia Minor was president of the Woman Suffrage Association of Missouri. At the time, Missouri's constitution said only men could vote. Minor decided to challenge the law. On October 15, 1872, Minor went to register to vote in the November 1872 presidential election. Reese Happersett, the registrar of voters, refused to register Minor because she was a woman.

With help from her husband, attorney Francis Minor, Virginia Minor filed a lawsuit against Happersett in the Circuit Court of St. Louis. Minor said Happersett violated the U.S. Constitution by refusing to register her to vote. Minor's main argument was that voting was a right of citizenship. She said the Fourteenth Amendment made it illegal for Missouri to take the right to vote away from any citizens, including women. She also said Missouri's constitution violated many other parts of the U.S. Constitution, such as the guarantee of a republican form of government.

All or Nothing at All

The Circuit Court of St. Louis and the Supreme Court of Missouri ruled in favor of Happersett. Determined to succeed, Minor appealed to the U.S. Supreme Court. She told the nation's highest court, "There can be no half-way citizenship. Woman, as a citizen of the United States, is entitled to all the benefits of that position, and liable to all its obligations, or to none."

With a unanimous decision, however, the Supreme Court ruled in favor of Happersett. Writing for the Court, Chief Justice Morrison Remick Waite said, "There is no doubt that women may be citizens." In fact, he said, women had been citizens of the United States from the very beginning, well before adoption of the Fourteenth Amendment. The question was whether all citizens are entitled to be voters.

Women marched, petitioned and picketed for their right to vote. Reproduced by permission of Archive Photos, Inc.

It took many dedicated and devoted volunteers to win the vote for women. Reproduced by permission of Culver Photos.

The Constitution does not define the "privileges and immunities" of citizens. To decide if the right to vote was a privilege of citizenship, Waite looked to the American colonies. When the original thirteen colonies adopted the U.S. Constitution, women could not vote anywhere except in New Jersey. Since ratification of the Constitution in 1790, no state that had been admitted to the Union allowed women to vote. Chief Justice Waite said that meant the right to vote was not a privilege of citizenship. Since suffrage was not a

THE NINETEENTH AMENDMENT

When the United States declared independence in 1776, New Jersey was the only colony that allowed women to vote. It took 144 years for the United States to give women the right to vote nationwide with the Nineteenth Amendment in 1920.

The Nineteenth Amendment was the achievement of the women's suffrage movement that began at the Seneca Falls Convention of 1848. Elizabeth Cady Stanton started the movement there by writing the Seneca Falls Declaration of Rights and Sentiments. Over the next seven decades, women fought for suffrage through groups such as the National Woman Suffrage Association, the American Woman Suffrage Association, the National American Woman Suffrage Association, and the Congressional Union for Woman Suffrage.

In 1866, Democratic Representative James Brooks of New York offered the first women's suffrage amendment in Congress. Congressmen offered similar amendments on a regular basis beginning in 1880, only to be defeated time after time. In May 1919, President Woodrow Wilson called a special session of Congress to consider the Nineteenth Amendment. The Senate finally passed it that month and the United States ratified, or approved, it in August 1920.

privilege of citizenship, the Fourteenth Amendment did not prevent states from denying the right to women.

Impact

At the end of his opinion, Chief Justice Waite said, "Our province is to decide what the law is, not to declare what it should be. … If the law is wrong, it ought to be changed; but the power for that is not with us." The power, of course, was with the people of the United States through their representatives in Congress and state government. It was not until 1920, forty-five years after *Minor v. Happersett,* that the United States gave the right to vote to women and men alike.

Suggestions for further reading

Baughman, Judith S., ed. *American Decades: 1920–1929.* Detroit: Gale Research Inc., 1996.

Brill, Marlene Targ. *Let Women Vote.* Millbrook Press, 1995.

Frost, Elizabeth, and Kathryn Cullen-DuPont. *Women's Suffrage in America: An Eyewitness History.* New York: Facts on File, 1992.

Grote, Joann A. *Women Win the Vote.* Barbour & Co., 1998.

Harvey, Miles. *Women's Voting Rights.* Children's Press, 1998.

Meyers, Madeleine. *Forward into the Light: The Struggle for Women's Suffrage.* Lowell: Discovery Enterprises, 1994.

Nash, Carol Rust. *The Fight for Women's Right to Vote in American History.* Enslow Publishers, Inc., 1998.

Pascoe, Elaine. *The Right to Vote.* Millbrook Press, 2000.

Vile, John R., ed. *Encyclopedia of Constitutional Amendments, Proposed Amendments, and Amending Issues.* Santa Barbara: ABC-CLIO, Inc., 1996.

Michael M. v. Superior Court of Sonoma County 1981

Petitioner: Michael M.

Respondent: Superior Court of Sonoma County

Petitioner's Claim: That the California "statutory rape" statute unlawfully discriminated on the basis of gender.

Chief Lawyer for Petitioner: Gregory F. Jilka

Chief Lawyer for Respondent: Sandy R. Kriegler

Justices for the Court: Harry A. Blackmun, Chief Justice Warren E. Burger, Lewis F. Powell, Jr., William H. Rehnquist, Potter Stewart

Justices Dissenting: William J. Brennan, Jr., Thurgood Marshall, John Paul Stevens, Byron R. White

Date of Decision: March 23, 1981

Decision: Ruled in favor of the state of California, upholding its statutory rape law.

Significance: Using intermediate scrutiny, the Court upheld a gender-based distinction in criminal law because it addressed an important state goal.

On the summer evening of June 3, 1978, three males including a seventeen-year-old male named Michael M. approached a sixteen-year-old female, Sharon, and her sister. Michael and Sharon, although they had not known each other previously, left the group. Sharon recalled what happened next in a preliminary hearing.

> **We were drinking at the railroad tracks and we walked over to this bush and he started kissing me and stuff, and I was kissing him back, too, at first. Then I was telling him to stop . . . and I was telling him to slow down and stop. He said, 'Okay, okay.' But then he just kept doing it . . . he asked me if I wanted to walk him over to the park; so we walked over to the park and we sat down on a bench and then he started kissing me again and we were laying on the bench. And he told me to take my pants off . . . I said, 'No,' and I was trying to get up and he hit me back down on the bench and then I just said to myself, 'Forget it,' and I let him do what he wanted to do. . .**

Sharon then had sexual intercourse with Michael.

Statutory Rape

A criminal charge was filed in the Municipal Court of Sonoma County, California, claiming that Michael M. had unlawful sexual intercourse with a woman under the age of eighteen. This action violated California's "statutory rape" law. Statutory rape is the crime of having sexual intercourse with a female under an age set by statute (law passed by a legislature), regardless of whether or not she consents (agrees) to the act. Under California's statutory rape law, when two people between the ages of fourteen and seventeen had sexual intercourse and they were not married, the male was guilty of statutory rape but the female was not.

In his defense, Michael M. challenged the constitutionality of California's statutory rape law on the basis of "equal protection of the laws," a civil rights guarantee of the Fourteenth Amendment. To be constitutional, a law must follow the intent of the Constitution. Michael M. claimed the law discriminated (giving privileges to one group but not to another similar group) on the basis of gender (the sex of the person) since males alone could be charged under the law. He charged this was unequal protection of the laws and, therefore, unconstitutional. The California Supreme Court ruled against Michael, and upheld (gave support to) the law. Appeal was taken to the U.S. Supreme Court.

U.S. Supreme Court Decides

The U.S. Supreme Court in a 5-4 vote, upheld California's statutory rape law. The Court stated that the law did not violate the Equal Protection Clause of the Fourteenth Amendment. A majority of justices agreed on the result but could not agree on the reasons for so ruling. Therefore, the Court's opinion, delivered by Justice William H. Rehnquist, is called a plurality opinion. Justice Rehnquist's opinion explained the various arguments in favor of the law.

Preventing Underage Pregnancy

First, the Court recognized that the California law discriminated against a certain group of persons, males, based on gender alone. Under scrutiny (close examination) standards set by the Court, increased scrutiny must be given to cases involving discrimination based on gender. The scrutiny level used in gender cases is intermediate scrutiny as was established in ***Mississippi University for Women v. Hogan.*** Under intermediate scrutiny, the law in question must address an "important" interest of the state and if written so that it is "substantially [strongly] related" to that state interest. In other words, the state must have a very important reason to write the law in the first place and the law must be written so that it strongly and directly addresses the issue. The Court ruled that the state's important reason was to prevent underage pregnancy. Rehnquist commented,

> **We are satisfied not only that the prevention of illegitimate [teenage] pregnancy is at least one of the 'purposes' of the statute, but that the State has a strong interest in preventing such pregnancy.**

Consequences Fall to the Female

Equal protection of the laws historically has not been interpreted by the courts to mean that all persons in a state must be equally affected by each law all the time. For instance, persons in state prisons will not have the same equal protection of the laws granted persons who are not in prison. Groups of persons must be in similar circumstances or situations to receive equal protection. The courts call this "similarly situated."

The Court reasoned that males and females are not "similarly situated" with regard to the burdens of pregnancy. For example, pregnancy poses a health risk to young women, but does not pose such a risk to men. As long as the law being applied to one gender and not the other is based on realistic sex differences, it can be seen as constitutional. Rehnquist wrote,

> **Because virtually all of the significant harmful . . . consequences of teenage pregnancy fall on the young female, a legislature acts well within its authority when it elects to punish only the participant [the male] who, by nature, suffers few of the consequences of his conduct. . . Moreover, the risk of pregnancy itself constitutes a substantial [strong] deterrence [prevent from acting] to young females. [A] criminal sanction [control] imposed solely on males thus serves to roughly 'equalize' the deterrents on the sexes.**

Thus, the Court saw the law as equalizing consequences and deterrence for males and females.

Would a Gender-Neutral Law Be Better?

Michael M.'s defense argued that a gender-neutral law would serve California just as well in preventing teenage pregnancies. A gender-neutral law would hold both male and female equally criminally responsible. However, the plurality of justices were convinced by California's argument that a gender-neutral statute rape law would be harder to enforce. The state argued it would reduce the likelihood of a woman reporting a violation if she herself might be subject to prosecution.

Dissenting Justices

The dissenting justices also used the intermediate-scrutiny test but found the California law failed to pass the test. They argued that there was not enough evidence to prove that the law as written strongly addressed the problem of teenage pregnancy. They said that California had not proved that the gender-based discriminatory law prevents underage women from having sexual intercourse or that there are fewer teenage pregnancies under the law than their would be under a gender-neutral law. They pointed out that thirty-seven states have gender-neutral statutory rape laws. These laws, they believed, are potentially greater preventatives for underage sexual activity since two persons instead of one could be punished.

DATE RAPE

According to the National Victim Center, one out of every eight adult women has been raped and eighty-four percent of rape victims are under the age of twenty-four. The typical rapist is not a stranger. A troubling statistic is four out of five rape victims knew their attackers, according to the FBI. Date rape or acquaintance rape most often is carried out not only by people a victim knows but, much worse, a person they trust. The typical rapist shames, threatens, or intimidates the female into having sex with him. Some victims of date rape become overwhelmed with guilt, especially if they made a bad judgement call about becoming physically involved with the male in the first place. It is common for victims of date rape to feel like they somehow "asked for it." Studies estimate as many as eighty-five percent of rapes go unreported.

Impact

The decision showed that a state can apply laws to males and females differently and be considered constitutionally correct by the courts when the state can show an important reason for doing so. The decision, however, raised unanswered questions for the future about determining when males and females are or are not legally similarly situated when issues arise.

Suggestions for further reading

Miklowitz, Gloria D. *Past Forgiving.* New York: Simon & Schuster Books for Young Readers, 1995.

Parrot, Andrea. *Coping with Date Rape and Acquaintance Rape.* New York: Rosen Publishing Group, 1999.

Warshaw, Robin. *I Never Called It Rape: The Ms. Report on Recognizing, Fighting, and Surviving Date and Acquaintance Rape.* New York: Harper Perennial, 1994.

Williams, Mary E., ed. *Date Rape.* San Diego, CA: Greenhaven Press, 1998.

Mississippi University for Women v. Hogan 1982

Petitioner: Mississippi University for Women

Respondent: Joe Hogan

Petitioner's Claim: That the state supported school's nursing program did not violate gender discrimination laws because its single-sex admission policy was a form of affirmative action.

Chief Lawyer for Petitioner: Hunter M. Gholson

Chief Lawyer for Respondent: Wilbur O. Colom

Justices for the Court: William J. Brennan, Jr., Thurgood Marshall, Sandra Day O'Connor, John Paul Stevens, Byron R. White

Justices Dissenting: Harry A. Blackmun, Chief Justice Warren E. Burger, Lewis F. Powell, Jr., William H. Rehnquist

Date of Decision: July 1, 1982

Decision: That the Mississippi University for Women had violated Hogan's constitutional right to equal protection of the law guaranteed by the Fourteenth Amendment by barring his admission to its nursing school.

Significance: The Court found that men as well as women are constitutionally protected against gender discrimination. A new level of scrutiny, intermediate scrutiny, is applied in gender discrimination cases. The case lead to the end of publicly funded single-sex schools.

GENDER DISCRIMINATION AND SEXUAL HARASSMENT

The Mississippi University for Women had a long history of quality, single-sex education. Reproduced by permission of the Mississippi University for Women.

In 1979 Joe Hogan was a surgical nurse and nursing supervisor in a medical center in Columbia, Mississippi. Through various two- and three-year programs, it was possible to have a nursing career without obtaining a four-year university degree. However, as in the case of many careers, a four-year degree meant a higher skill level which also meant a higher salary. Desiring to complete his four-year degree, Hogan applied to a university in his hometown of Columbus. The problem he ran into was reflected in the name of the school, Mississippi University for Women.

The Fourteenth Amendment to the U.S. Constitution, approved in 1868, guaranteed "equal protection of the laws" to "any person" within a state. However, it would take the passage of the 1964 Civil Rights Act almost a century later to begin correcting gender (sex) discrimination. Gender discrimination is the unfair treatment of a person or group because of their sex. Traditionally, in the thoughts of most Americans and in reality, gender discrimination meant discrimination against women. However, "any person" in the Fourteenth Amendment certainly referred to both women and men. Increasingly in the 1970s cases involving discrimination against men began to reach the U.S. Supreme Court.

Males Need Not Apply

Although men were allowed to audit (to attend without receiving formal credit) courses, the Mississippi University for Women was a single-sex school and its nursing program was only open to women. Founded in 1884 as the Mississippi Industrial Institute and College for the Education of White Girls of the State of Mississippi, it was one of the country's first public state-supported, single-sex universities for women. Many single-sex private colleges also existed. The nursing school was founded in 1971 and had been offering a four-year degree in nursing since 1974. Since the nearest co-educational (for both men and women) nursing program was 147 miles away, Hogan applied to Mississippi University for Women and was rejected only on the basis of his gender. The school suggested he audit courses but he decided to turn to the courts for help.

Hogan filed a lawsuit in U.S. District Court claiming the school policy violated his constitutional freedom of equal protection of the laws under the Fourteenth Amendment. Hogan, determined to make a change in his community, requested that the university's women-only admissions policy be changed. Eventually, Hogan's suit made not only a change in his community but changed the way equal protection cases are examined when it appears a person has been discriminated against because of gender.

Standards of Examination in Equal Protection Cases

The U.S. Supreme Court, to be certain it looks at cases fairly, develops standards to follow. These standards are applied in the same manner to cases asking similar questions. In equal protection cases courts look especially in depth when it appears an individual or a group of people is being discriminated against simply because they belong to a certain race or nationality. This in-depth look is called strict scrutiny (examination). For example an equal protection case involving a black American or an Irish American would be looked at with strict scrutiny to be sure the person was not unfairly singled out by the policy or law because of race or nationality. If it is determined by the court that an individual or group is being unfairly treated due to race, nationality, or alienage (a person living in the United States but a citizen of another country), then the court will next apply a test called "compelling" state interest. A state would be required to prove that no other way existed to accomplish the goal of the law and that the law was essential to the interest or operation of the state. Few laws survive the strict scrutiny examination. Most are struck down.

Until the 1970s if the equal protection case did not involve race, nationality, or alienage, then a low-level scrutiny was applied. Gender cases were included in the low-level scrutiny. This low-level scrutiny was called "rational basis." The state only had to prove the law in question was based on a "legitimate" (honest) interest of the state. For example, a state discriminates against persons under sixteen years of age by having a law which prevents them from driving a car. The court recognizes that this law applies to all persons under sixteen, not just persons of a certain race, so strict scrutiny is not applied. Instead, rational-basis scrutiny is applied. Therefore, the state must simply prove it has a legitimate interest to allow this law. The legitimate interest is safety of the public roads. The court agrees this is an honest interest of the state and the law stands.

In Joe Hogan's case the U.S. Supreme Court confirmed a new mid-way standard between strict scrutiny and low-level rational basis, called intermediate scrutiny, to use in gender cases. This mid-way standard was first introduced by Justice William J. Brennan, Jr., in *Craig v. Boren* (1976) but became much better defined with Justice Sandra Day O'Connor's opinion in *Mississippi University for Women v. Hogan.*

You Take the Low Road, I'll Take the High Road

Earlier in Hogan's case, the U.S. District Court for the Northern District of Mississippi took the low-level rational basis road by applying only "minimal" scrutiny. Deciding against Hogan, the court ruled that the state had a legitimate interest in providing a female-only nursing program.

The appeals court, rejecting the district court decision, said the low-level "minimal" scrutiny was not enough examination and needed a higher level of scrutiny. The appeals court noted that gender discrimination had long been a problem and found no differences between men and women to rationalize separate educational facilities for nursing. The court ruled that the admissions policies of Mississippi University for Women as a whole were discriminatory and, indeed, unconstitutional. The appeals court declared Hogan should be admitted. To resolve the two conflicting lower court opinions, the U.S. Supreme Court agreed to hear the case.

Affirmative Action Meets Equal Protection

Arguing its case before the Supreme Court, Mississippi University claimed that its single-sex nursing school was a form of "affirmative action." Affirmative action programs, begun in the 1960s, were widespread in government agencies and educational institutions by the 1970s. The programs sought to correct past discrimination by providing preferential treatment to women and blacks. In defending its rejection of Mr. Hogan, the university argued that (1) having a school for women only made up for past gender discrimination, and (2) the presence of men would hurt female students' performance.

In a 5-4 decision, the Court upheld the appeals court ruling in favor of Hogan. Justice Sandra Day O'Connor, writing her first opinion for the Court, begun by deciding which level of scrutiny to use. Obviously, a gender problem does not fall in strict scrutiny reserved for race, nationality, or alienage. However, low-level rational basis scrutiny did not give enough examination to the historic gender discrimination problem. O'Connor chose an intermediate-level scrutiny for gender cases. She wrote that the state must show "important governmental objectives [goals]" for the law or policy.

Using intermediate scrutiny, O'Connor concluded Mississippi University for Women's goal of correcting past discrimination against women with their women-only policy was unimportant. Noting that 98.6 percent of all nursing degrees in the United States are earned by women, she reasoned there was no discrimination against women in their pursuit of a nursing degree. In fact, restricting the program to women tended to further the stereotype (fixed mental picture) of nursing as "woman's work."

GENDER AND REVERSE DISCRIMINATION

Women have long fought for equal rights in areas of compensation that range from pay to benefits; but cases such as *Mississippi University for Women v. Hogan* signify a countertrend, that of reverse-discrimination lawsuits. The most famous of these was *University of California v. Bakke* (1978), which challenged reverse discrimination on the basis of race; but challenges on the basis of gender have been viewed differently by the Supreme Court. This is perhaps because gender, unlike race, was not a factor in the drafting or the passage of the Fourteenth Amendment.

Part of what makes questions about reverse discrimination difficult is the fact that they can be approached on many different levels. There is, for instance, the political or legal level, based on the Constitution, statutes, and general beliefs about fairness. But there are also viewpoints based on tradition or on actual practices. Thus for instance, alimony laws, which have tended to favor women, are written that way because past experience—at least, prior to the 1970s—showed that women were more likely than men to be financially hurt in a divorce settlement.

In answer to the university's second argument, O'Connor observed that men already sit in on classes with no negative effect on the female students' performance.

Therefore, the O'Connor agreed with the court of appeals' ruling. The Court found the gender-discrimination policies of Mississippi University for Women unconstitutional in violation of the Fourteenth Amendment's "equal protection of the laws."

The End of Public Single-Sex Schools

Dissenting (not agreeing with majority opinion) justices argued that single-sex educational facilities were historically an important part of the American educational scene. The dissenters feared this decision would lead to the elimination of publicly supported colleges exclusively for women, which is what happened.

Despite later public pressure to raise the standard to strict scrutiny for gender issues, the intermediate-scrutiny level as used in the *Mississippi University for Women* case continued to be applied by courts in the late 1990s. In ***United States v. Virginia*** (1996), the Court used intermediate scrutiny in striking down Virginia Military Institute's policy excluding women as students. By the end of the twentieth century, the only single-sex universities still operating were private institutions.

Suggestions for further reading

Beckwith, Francis J., and Todd E. Jones, eds. *Affirmative Action: Social Justice or Reverse Discrimination?* Amherst, NY: Prometheus Books, 1997.

Nerad, Maresi. *The Academic Kitchen: A Social History of Gender Stratification at the University of California, Berkeley.* Albany: State University of New York Press, 1999.

Streitmatter, Janice L. *For Girls Only: Making a Case for Single-Sex Schooling.* Albany: State University of New York Press, 1999.

Meritor Savings Bank v. Vinson 1986

Petitioner: Meritor Savings Bank

Respondent: Mechelle Vinson

Petitioner's Claim: That under the Civil Rights Act of 1964 businesses are responsible for sexual discrimination in the workplace only when resulting in economic loss to the victim.

Chief Lawyer for Petitioner: F. Robert Troll, Jr.

Chief Lawyer for Respondent: Patricia J. Barry

Justices for the Court: Harry A. Blackmun, William J. Brennan, Jr., Chief Justice Warren E. Burger, Thurgood Marshall, Sandra Day O'Connor, Lewis F. Powell, Jr., William H. Rehnquist, John Paul Stevens, Byron R. White

Justices Dissenting: None

Date of Decision: June 19, 1986

Decision: Ruled in favor of Mechelle Vinson

Significance: This case became the cornerstone for answering sexual harassment questions raised under Title VII of the Civil Rights Act of 1964. The Court, using Equal Employment Opportunities Commission guidelines, established that hostile environment is a form of sexual harassment even when the victim suffers no economic losses.

Testifying at the 1991 Senate hearings on the confirmation of Clarence Thomas to the U.S. Supreme Court, Ellen Wells talked about a form of gender or sex discrimination (unequal treatment of a person because of that person's sex) known as sexual harassment:

> **You blame yourself. Perhaps its the perfume I have on. . . And so you try to change your behavior because you think it must be me. . . And then I think you perhaps start to get angry and frustrated. But there's always that sense of powerlessness. And you're also ashamed. . . What did you do? And so you keep it in. You don't say anything. And if someone says to you: You should go forward, you have to think: How am I going to pay the phone bill if I do that? . . . So you're quiet. And you're ashamed. And you sit there and you take it.**

Although Wells said this in the 1990s, history indicates that sexual harassment is not new. For example, the following quote from *A History of Women in America,* by C. Hymowitz and M. Weissman (1978), describes the plight of women factory workers in the early twentieth century.

> **Wherever they worked, women were sexually harassed by male workers, foremen and bosses. Learning to 'put up' with this abuse was one of the first lessons on the job. . . It was common practice at the factories for male employers to demand sexual favors from women workers in exchange for a job, a raise, or better position.**

The Fourteenth Amendment, approved in 1868, guaranteed "equal protection of the laws" to all persons living in America. That is, no person or persons shall be denied the same protection of the laws that is enjoyed by other persons or groups. However, equal protection rights were not extended to women until almost a century later.

Congress Takes Action

By the 1950s and 1960s various forms of discrimination including racial and gender discrimination, had become a focus of the nation. To help remedy (correct) various forms of discrimination, Congress passed the

GENDER DISCRIMINATION AND SEXUAL HARASSMENT

Civil Rights Act of 1964. Title VII of the act prohibited discrimination on the basis of race, color, religion, sex, or national origin in employment matters. The act also created the Equal Employment Opportunities Commission (EEOC) to enforce Title VII. However, not until 1980 did the EEOC define sexual harassment as a form of sex discrimination prohibited by the 1964 act.

Associate Justice Clarence Thomas was questioned about accusations of sexual harassment at his nomination hearings.
Reproduced by permission of AP/Wide World Photos.

The EEOC developed guidelines which women could use to finally gain equal protection rights in sexual harassment matters. The guidelines defined sexual harassment as unwelcome sexual advances of either a verbal or physical nature. Examples of verbal or physical advances could include requests for dates or sex, comments about a person's body, whistles, hugging, kissing, or grabbing. For unwelcome sexual advances to be considered harassment they must be associated with at least one of the two following situations. First, the "agreement to" or "reflection of" the advances is tied to the targeted person's job. "Agreement to" could mean promise of promotions, raises or simply keeping the job. "Rejection of" could have the opposite effects. This type of sexual harassment is referred to as "quid pro quo," Latin for "you have to do 'this' to get 'that.'" In familiar terms this is called sex-for-jobs. The second type of harassment, referred to as hostile environment, occurs when the advances make a workplace so unpleasant or difficult that targeted persons have trouble doing their jobs.

The Story of Mechelle Vinson

Mr. Sidney Taylor, vice president and branch manager of Meritor Savings Bank, hired Ms. Mechelle Vinson as a teller trainee in September of 1974. She steadily rose from teller to head teller to assistant branch manager on merit (her abilities). After four years working at the same branch, Vinson informed Taylor in September of 1978 that she was taking sick leave for an unknown period of time. After two months the bank fired her for using too much leave.

Vinson sued both Taylor and the bank under Title VII. She claimed that Taylor had constantly subjected her to sexual harassment during her four years at the bank. Vinson alleged (claimed) Taylor improperly touched her, exposed himself to her, and had sex with her. Fearing the loss of her job, Vinson never told the bank of Taylor's behavior nor had she submitted a complaint to the EEOC. Taylor, contending Vinson's charges resulted from a work dispute, denied all charges. Meritor Savings pointed out Vinson had suffered no economic loss, therefore no quid pro quo harassment existed, and also the bank claimed no liability (responsibility) since it was never notified of the behavior.

Conflicting Lower Court Decisions

At the first trial, a district court concluded Vinson was not the victim of sexual harassment because the sexual relationship with Taylor was "voluntary" and had no impact on her continued employment. No quid pro quo harassment existed. Also, the court agreed with the bank that it had no liability for its supervisor's actions since Vinson had never formally complained through its grievance (complaint) procedures.

Vinson appealed the court's decision. The court of appeals disagreed with the district court and reversed (changed) the decision. The appeals court ruled that it did not matter that Vinson's employment was not affected. What did matter was that a hostile environment "existed for years and that environment was a type of sexual harassment prohibited under Title VII." The court also questioned the "voluntary" nature of the Vinson-Taylor relationship. Considering the liability issue the appeals court ruled that businesses are always responsible for sexual harassment committed by their supervisors. Meritor Savings then appealed to the U.S. Supreme Court.

At Last, a Sexual Harassment Case Reaches Supreme Court

Agreeing to hear the case, the Supreme Court considered three questions most important: (1) is a hostile working environment created by unwelcome sexual behavior a form of employment discrimination prohibited under Title VII when no economic loss or quid pro quo harassment exists; (2) does a Title VII violation exist when the relationship is "voluntary"; and, (3) is a business liable for a hostile working environment if it is not aware of the misconduct?

Supreme Court's Opinion

Justice William H. Rehnquist, writing for the unanimous court (all justices in agreement) and following the EEOC guidelines, answered the three questions.

(1) The Court rejected the bank's argument that Title VII prohibits only quid pro quo harassment. EEOC guidelines state that hostile environ-

Women's organizations found Anita Hill to be a strong spokesperson for the issue of sexual harassment in the workplace. Reproduced by permission of AP/Wide World Photos.

CLARENCE THOMAS–ANITA HILL HEARINGS

The issue of sexual harassment exploded into the living rooms of Americans the weekend of October 11 to October 13, 1991, preempting everything network television had to offer. Black conservative Clarence Thomas, a Supreme Court nominee, seemed on his way to a Senate confirmation. Then on October 6, a story broke through the news media that Anita Hill, a black law professor, had revealed to the Senate Judiciary Committee investigating Thomas' nomination that she had been sexually harassed by Thomas in the early 1980s as they worked together. Thomas' confirmation was thrown in doubt.

Amid public pressure, the Senate Judiciary Committee held a fully televised hearing to air Hill's complaint and Thomas' defense. Some of the most extraordinary public testimony ever given to a congressional committee began. Both Hill and Thomas spoke convincingly and with great emotion. Hill spent seven hours describing Thomas' sexual advances. Thomas denied all charges describing the hearing as a "high-tech lynching." In the end the Senate voted to confirm Thomas, but the controversy continued. Some critics accused Hill of being part of a liberal political or feminist move to defeat Thomas. Hill supporters, outraged at the committee's treatment of her, flooded women's organizations with calls and letters. The nature of sexual harassment in the workplace had come to the forefront of American discussion.

ment is a type of sexual discrimination prohibited in the workplace. The Court found Vinson's charges sufficient to claim hostile environment sexual harassment. The Court did write that hostile environment harassment must be severe or pervasive (happened again and again) to support a claim.

(2) The Court also asserted that whether a sexual relationship was "voluntary" is not important, the key is whether or not the advances were unwelcome. A person, out of fear of losing a job, might well voluntarily

cooperate even if the conduct was unwelcome. Therefore, to determine if the conduct was unwelcome the Court must look at all aspects of the case.

(3) The Court did not specifically define employer liability, but did disagree with both the district and appeals court decisions. The Court stated that the "absence of notice to an employer does not necessarily insulate (protect) that employer from liability." At the same time, employers are not always automatically liable for sexual harassment by their supervisors. The Court went along with EEOC suggestions which said liability issues require careful examination of the role of the supervisor in the company and whether or not an appropriate complaint procedure which employees knew about was in place.

Building on Meritor

After 1986, both state courts and the Supreme Court continued to clarify (make clearer) what constituted sexual harassment. For example, (1) damages (money payments) paid to the victim may be allowed, (2) psychological damage does not need to occur to claim a hostile work environment, (3) companies must have sexual harassment policies, and (4) harassment can occur even if the offender and victim are of the same sex.

Suggestions for further reading

Eskenazi, Martin, and David Gallen. *Sexual Harassment: Know Your Rights!* New York: Carroll & Graf Publishers, Inc., 1992.

Nash, Carol R. *Sexual Harassment: What Teens Should Know.* Springfield, NJ: Enslow Publishers, 1996.

Petrocelli, William, and Barbara Kate Repa. *Sexual Harassment on the Job.* Berkeley, CA: Nolo Press, 1994.

Swisher, Karin L. *Sexual Harassment.* San Diego, CA: Greenhaven Press, Inc., 1992.

Automobile Workers v. Johnson Controls 1991

Petitioners: International Union, United Automobile, Aerospace, and Agricultural Implement Workers of America, and others

Respondent: Johnson Controls, Inc.

Petitioner's Claim: That Johnson Controls' fetal protection policy discriminates against women in violation of Title VII of the 1964 Civil Rights Act as amended by the Pregnancy Discrimination Act (PDA).

Chief Lawyer for Petitioners: Marsha S. Berzon

Chief Lawyer for Respondent: Stanley S. Jaspan

Justices for the Court: Harry A. Blackmun, Anthony Kennedy, Thurgood Marshall, Sandra Day O'Connor, Chief Justice William H. Rehnquist, Antonin Scalia, David H. Souter, John Paul Stevens, Byron R. White

Justices Dissenting: None

Date of Decision: March 20, 1991

Decision: Ruled against Johnson Controls, Inc. by finding that their fetal protection policy violated Title VII of the Civil Rights Act of 1964 as amended by the PDA

Significance: The ruling prohibited any discrimination based on a worker's ability to have children. The Court recognized a woman's right to make her own decisions about pregnancy, during potentially harmful work, and the economic needs of her family.

Sex (gender) discrimination, the unfair treatment of a person or group of persons because of their sex, was common in the American workplace until passage of the Civil Rights Act of 1964. Title VII (Equal Employment Opportunity), Section 703, parts (a)(2) of the act read,

> **It shall be an unlawful employment practice for an employer . . . to limit, segregate [separate out] or classify his employees in any way which would deprive [take away] or tend to deprive any individual of employment opportunities . . . because of such individual's race, color, religion, sex, or national origin.**

Although the act clearly prohibited discrimination based on sex in the workplace, nowhere did it address the issue of pregnant workers. Fetal (referring to the unborn child) protection policies barring fertile women (capable of bearing children) from certain jobs out of fear that those jobs could cause harm to a fetus (unborn child) carried by the women became widespread in the 1970s. Given the fact that only women can become pregnant, these policies quickly became controversial. Women's rights advocates believed the policies violated Title VII of the Civil Rights Act of 1964 by depriving women workers certain employment opportunities. In response, Congress amended (changed or add to make clearer) Title VII with the Pregnancy Discrimination Act (PDA) in 1978. The part of the PDA which amended Title VII stated that unless pregnant employees differ from others "in their ability or inability to work" they must be "treated the same" as other employees "for all employment-related purposes." In other words, a woman could not be discriminated against merely for her potential to become pregnant or for her actual pregnancy unless it affected her ability to do the job. Nevertheless, fetal protection policies continued in many companies into the 1980s. Not until this case did the U.S. Supreme Court rule in this area.

Johnson Controls, Inc. - Battery Manufacturer

Johnson Controls manufactured batteries. The battery manufacturing process used lead as a main ingredient. Lead exposure (come in contact with) in both men and women may cause health problems such as fertility problems and possibly birth defects in children born to workers.

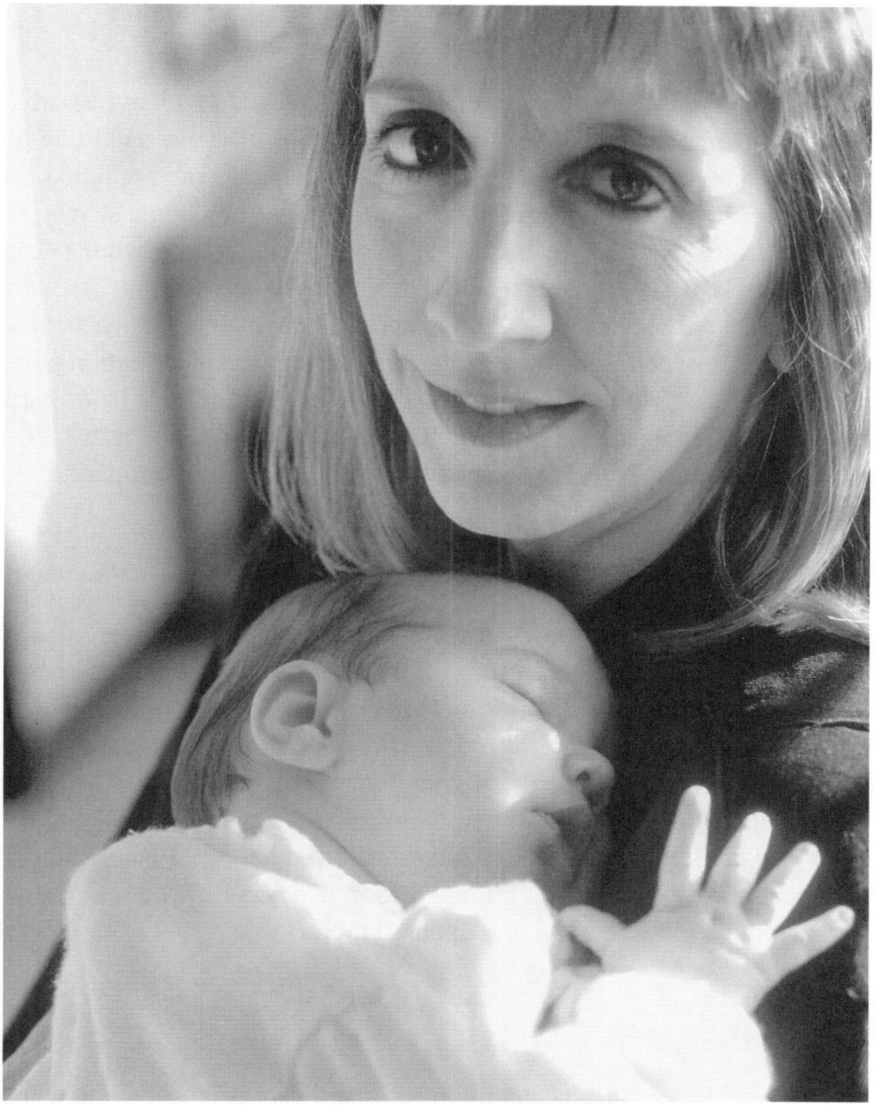

The Court decided that companies could not discriminate against a worker based on their ability to have children. Reproduced by permission of Robert J. Huffman.

Originally Johnson Controls only hired males but after passage of the 1964 Civil Rights Act the business began hiring women. As women began working in its plants, Johnson Controls developed and issued an official policy concerning employment of women in lead-exposure work which read,

> **Since not all women who can become mothers wish to become mothers, (or will become mothers), it would appear to be illegal discrimination to treat**

all who are capable of pregnancy as though they will become pregnant.

By adopting this policy, Johnson Controls hoped to avoid discrimination problems since it stopped short of excluding all women capable of becoming pregnant from lead exposure jobs. The company required any woman wishing to work where lead exposure existed to sign a statement stating that she had been advised of the risk of having a child while being exposed to lead. Over the next five years, eight women employees with high lead blood levels became pregnant. Although none of the babies suffered defects, Johnson Controls developed a new fetal protection policy banning all "women . . . capable of bearing children" from lead exposed jobs. "Capable of bearing children" was defined as "all women except those whose inability to bear children is medically documented."

Class-action Lawsuit

A class-action lawsuit is one which is brought by a large number of people as a group. These people all have a common interest. Various labor unions brought a class-action lawsuit in Wisconsin against Johnson Controls, claiming its fetal protection policy was sex discrimination prohibited by Title VII of the Civil Rights Act as amended by the PDA. Two individuals included in the suit were Mary Craig and Elsie Nason. Mary Craig had chosen to be sterilized rather than lose her job. Elsie Nason, a fifty-year-old divorcee, had suffered a loss of pay when she was transferred out of a job where she was exposed to lead.

A Business Necessity

The local district court decided in favor of Johnson Controls. The court stressed the likelihood that exposure to lead put a fetus, as well as the reproductive abilities of would-be parents, at risk. Neither the union nor employees had previously offered an acceptable alternative way to protect the fetus. The court found the company's policy to be a "business necessity." The suing groups appealed.

The Court of Appeals next also ruled in favor of Johnson Controls. Not only did the Court of Appeals decide Johnson's policy was a business necessity but decided that such policies could exclude women without being called discrimination under "a bona fide occupational qualification" (BFOQ) clause found in Title VII, section 703, part (e)(1) of the

Civil Rights Act. No other court of appeals had applied BFOQ in similar cases. Use of the BFOQ caught the U.S. Supreme Court's attention and the Court decided to hear the case.

Outright Sex Discrimination

Justice Harry A. Blackmun delivered the opinion of the Court in a close 5-4 decision. After noting that "we are concerned with an employer's gender-based fetal-protection policy" he asked,"May an employer exclude a fertile female employee from certain jobs because of its concern for the health of the fetus the woman might conceive [become pregnant]?"

Ruling against Johnson Controls, the opinion of the Court was that Johnson clearly had discriminated against women. Blackmun wrote,

> **The bias (prejudiced view) in Johnson Controls policy is obvious. Fertile men, but not fertile women are given a choice as to whether they wish to risk their reproductive health for a particular job. Section 703(a) of the Civil Rights Act of 1964 . . . as amended [by PDA] . . . prohibits sex-based classification in terms and conditions of employment. . .**

The Court also held that Johnson's policy was outright sex discrimination. The lower courts discussion of business necessity, they asserted, was a mistake and not at all appropriate. Using BFOQ consideration was a better way to approach the issue.

Don't Let the Plane Crash

BFOQ consideration permits an employer to discriminate only when it is necessary to the normal operation of that particular business or as interpreted by the courts, when a severe safety problem would be created. For example, in *Western Airlines, Inc. v. Criswell* (1985), one type of discrimination was allowed, age discrimination. It was determined that a flight engineer over the age of sixty might not perform all tasks assigned causing a "safety emergency." For the safety of the passengers, planes must not crash. This fact was "indispensable" to the operation of the airline business and age discrimination was allowed. In the case of Johnson Controls, sex or pregnancy did not actually interfere with the employees ability to perform the job.

Blackmun wrote,

> **We have no difficulty concluding that Johnson Controls cannot establish a BFOQ. Fertile women as far as appears in the record, participate in the manufacture of batteries as efficiently as anyone else.**

Strictly a Family Affair

Blackmun further commented that "danger to a woman herself does not justify discrimination." It is her business to decide if she will take the risk. Likewise, the risks a pregnant woman assumes for her fetus are not her employer's concern. Such decisions, Blackmun wrote,

> **Must be left to the parents . . . rather than the employers. . . Title VII and the PDA simply do not allow a woman's dismissal because of her failure to submit to sterilization [or because she may become pregnant].**

Company Liability (Responsibility)

Blackmun commented that although forty states permitted lawsuits to recover money for injuries to a fetus, the cases were always based on negligence (carelessness). If the company complies with basic national safety standards and fully informs the woman of the risk, as Johnson Controls did, then the employer has not been negligent and will not be liable for injury.

Fearful of a Mixed Reaction

Anticipating a mixed reaction from the general public to the Court's finding, Blackmun, giving powerful reasons for the ruling, wrote,

> **Our holding today . . . is neither remarkable nor unprecedented [a new idea or occurrence]. Concern for a woman's existing or potential offspring historically has been the excuse for denying women equal employment opportunities. . . It is no more appropriate for the courts than it is for individual employers to decide whether a woman's reproductive role is more important to herself and**

her family than her economic role. Congress has left this choice to the woman as hers to make.

Suggestions for further reading

Blank, Robert H. *Fetal Protection in the Workplace: Women's Rights, Business Interests, and the Unborn.* New York: Columbia University Press, 1993.

Daniels, Cynthia R. *At Women's Expense: State Power and the Politics of Fetal Rights.* Cambridge, MA: Harvard University Press, 1993.

Morgan, Lynn M., and Meredith W. Michaels, eds. *Fetal Subjects, Feminist Positions.* Philadelphia: University of Pennsylvania Press, 1999.

Samuels, Suzanne Uttaro. *Fetal Rights, Women's Rights: Gender Equality in the Workplace.* Madison, WI: University of Wisconsin Press, 1995.

United States v. Virginia
1996

Petitioner: United States

Respondents: Commonwealth of Virginia, Governor Lawrence Douglas Wilder, Virginia Military Institute, et al.

Petitioner's Claim: That the Virginia Military Institute's refusal to admit female students violated the Fourteenth Amendment

Chief Lawyer for Petitioner: Paul Bender, U.S. Deputy Solicitor General

Chief Lawyer for Respondent: Theodore B. Olsen

Justices for the Court: Stephen Breyer, Ruth Bader Ginsburg, Anthony M. Kennedy, Sandra Day O'Connor, William H. Rehnquist, David H. Souter, John Paul Stevens

Justices Dissenting: Antonin Scalia (Clarence Thomas did not participate)

Date of Decision: June 26, 1996

Decision: Excluding women from state-funded schools violates the Fourteenth Amendment.

Significance: America's last two state-funded all-male colleges were forced to admit women or give up state funding.

The Equal Protection Clause of the Fourteenth Amendment of the U.S. Constitution protects citizens from discrimination by state governments. (Discrimination is unequal treatment of people in the same situation.) States and organizations that receive state funding must obey the Equal Protection Clause. Governments use the Equal Protection Clause to end discrimination based on race, religion, and sex or gender. In 1996 the U.S. Supreme Court used it to force an all-male, state-funded military college in Virginia to accept female students.

The Virginia Military Institute (VMI) is a state-funded military college that opened in Lexington, Virginia, in 1839. Around 1990 a female high school student complained to the U.S. Department of Justice that VMI would not accept female students. (The U.S. Department of Justice is the branch of the federal government that enforces federal law by prosecuting people who violate the law.) In 1990 the Justice Department filed a case accusing Virginia and VMI of violating the Equal Protection Clause by refusing to accept women at VMI. In the two years before the lawsuit, VMI ignored requests from more than 300 women about attending college there.

When the case went to trial in a federal court, VMI said that its long tradition of excluding women was important to its goal of producing citizen-soldiers. According to VMI, citizen-soldiers are men who can be military leaders during war and leaders in society during peacetime. Students at VMI receive a military-style education that includes tough physical training and cramped living quarters. VMI said admitting women would prevent it from providing this education to men.

After a six-day trial, Judge Jackson L. Kiser ruled that VMI could continue to exclude women. Kiser agreed that the all-male school served Virginia's substantial interest in giving men a military-style education.

The U.S. Department of Justice appealed to the U.S. Court of Appeals for the Fourth Circuit. Writing for the court on October 5, 1992, Judge Paul V. Niemeyer agreed that Virginia had a substantial interest in providing a military education to its citizens. But Judge Niemeyer also said that providing that education to men only violated the Equal Protection Clause. Judge Niemeyer ruled that Virginia must either admit women to VMI, open a separate military school for women, or stop giving money to VMI. (A school that does not get money from the state or federal government does not have to obey the Equal Protection Clause.) Niemeyer ordered Virginia to choose an option and to ask Judge Kiser to approve the plan.

Separate but equal?

Virginia and VMI responded by creating Virginia Women's Institute for Leadership (VWIL), an all-female program at Mary Baldwin College in Virginia. VWIL shared VMI's goal of producing citizen-soldiers, but it did not have the same military-style features. VWIL cadets lived separately instead of together and had more classroom instruction than physical training. VWIL also had fewer academic programs, received less state funding, and had fewer Ph.D. professors than VMI. Finally, VWIL could not offer the reputation VMI had earned over 150 years of providing education.

After reviewing VWIL's program, Judge Kiser ruled that it satisfied the Equal Protection Clause. When the Justice Department appealed this time, the Fourth Circuit Court of Appeals approved Judge Kiser's decision. It said that although VMI and VWIL were not identical, they were close enough to provide both men and women with a military-style education in Virginia.

Reversing discrimination

The Justice Department appealed to the U.S. Supreme Court. On June 26, 1996, the Supreme Court voted 7–1 that VMI must either give up state funding or admit women. Justice Ruth Bader Ginsburg, the second woman to serve on the Supreme Court, wrote the opinion for the Court. (Justice Clarence Thomas did not participate in the decision because his son was attending VMI.)

In her opinion, Justice Ginsburg said that under the Equal Protection Clause, sex discrimination is allowed only if it serves a substantial state interest. A substantial state interest is one that is important enough to make sex discrimination acceptable, such as creating jobs for women. According to Ginsburg, the state interest being served may not rely on old ideas that women are less talented than men. It also may not "create or perpetuate [continue] the legal, social, and economic inferiority of women."

Ginsburg decided that VMI's all-male program did not serve a substantial state interest in Virginia. She said the goal of producing citizen-soldiers with a military education does not require excluding women, and that women are able to succeed at VMI and would not ruin the quality of its program. Ginsburg said, "Women's successful entry into the Federal military academies, and their participation in the nation's military forces, indicate that Virginia's fear for the future of VMI may not be solidly grounded."

FIRST WOMAN AT THE CITADEL

It took a legal battle for Shannon R. Faulkner to become the first female cadet at the Citadel, a previously all-male military college in Charleston, South Carolina. The Citadel accepted Faulkner's application in 1993 only because she failed to say she was female. The Citadel refused to admit Faulkner when it learned her gender. Faulkner filed a lawsuit, and on July 22, 1994, a federal trial court ruled that the Citadel violated the Equal Protection Clause. The Fourth Circuit Court of Appeals agreed, ruling in April 1995 that South Carolina either had to admit women to the Citadel or create a military school for women.

Faulkner joined the Citadel's Corps of Cadets on August 14, 1995. On her first day of training, she suffered heat exhaustion and received treatment at the school's medical facility, where four male cadets also were treated. Faulkner returned to classes four days later, but then left the Citadel. Observers said that it was difficult for Faulkner to be the only woman at a school that did not want to accept her. Thirty-four male cadets from her group, however, also quit during the first week. Faulkner's failure to complete the Citadel's program did not harm the example she set for women.

Ginsburg also addressed the idea that VWIL provided a separate but equal education for women. After looking at the two programs, Ginsburg decided that VWIL was a "pale shadow" of VMI's famous program. "Women seeking and fit for a VMI quality education cannot be offered anything less under the State's obligation to afford the genuinely equal protection," she wrote.

Justice Antonin Scalia wrote a dissenting opinion, disagreeing with the Supreme Court's decision. Justice Scalia believed that single-gender education was an important option for students, and that the Court's decision would destroy that option. Scalia wrote, "I do not think any of us, women included, will be better off for its destruction."

A few good women

The Supreme Court's decision opened the doors for women at both VMI and the Citadel in South Carolina, the United States's last two state-funded, all-male military colleges. Although officials at both colleges were disappointed by the decision, they promised to obey it with honor. On May 15, 1999, Melissa K. Graham and Chih-Yuan Ho became the first women to graduate from VMI.

Suggestions for further reading

Hanmer, Trudy J. *Sexism and Sex Discrimination.* New York, NY: Franklin Watts, 1990.

The World Book Encyclopedia, 1997 ed., entries on "Education," "Coeducation." Chicago, IL: World Book, 1997.

Oncale v. Sundowner Offshore Services Incorporated et al. 1998

Petitioner: Joseph Oncale

Respondent: Sundowner Onshore Services Incorporated, John Lyons, Danny Pippen, and Brandon Johnson

Petitioner's Claim: That on-the-job sexual harassment by coworkers of the same sex is still sexual discrimination.

Chief Lawyers for Petitioner: Nicholas Canaday III

Chief Lawyers for Respondent: Harry M. Reasoner

Justices for the Court: Stephen Breyer, Ruth Bader Ginsburg, Anthony M. Kennedy, Sandra Day O'Connor, Chief Justice William H. Rehnquist, Antonin Scalia, David H. Souter, John Paul Stevens, Clarence Thomas

Justices Dissenting: None

Date of Decision: March 4, 1998

Decision: Ruled in favor of Oncale by finding that one person harassing another person of the same sex is sex discrimination prohibited by federal law.

Significance: The ruling recognized the right of individuals to claim sexual harassment even when the threatening individual and the victim are of the same sex. The Court found that Title VII applies to all sexual harassment situations which affect a person's employment.

GENDER DISCRIMINATION AND SEXUAL HARASSMENT

Sex discrimination involves the selection of one person over another for a job or for promotion purely on the basis of their gender (sex). Discrimination against women in the workplace had a long history in the United States. Women were routinely paid less than male workers doing the same work, not considered for management positions, and barred from certain professions, such as lawyers and even serving on juries. To correct this longstanding bias against women, Congress passed Section VII of the Civil Rights Act of 1964 that prohibited sex discrimination in employment. Title VII made it "an unlawful employment practice for an employer . . . to discriminate against any individual with respect to his compensation [pay], terms, conditions, or privileges of employment, because of such individual's race, color, religion, sex, or national origin." Discrimination against men by women was hardly considered an issue, not to mention sex discrimination between two women or two men. In fact, not until 1973 in *Frontiero v. Richardson* did the Court even recognize that men could be victims of sex discrimination.

A new kind of gender issue grew in the 1980s called sexual harassment. Sexual harassment usually meant that a person at work was demanding sex from another person in an harassing way. Often a supervisor would be demanding sexual favors in exchange for some favorable employment action, such as a promotion or even keeping a job. Less clearly sexual harassment could occur simply through constant workplace threats, insults, or ridicule, creating what is known as a "hostile work environment." In ***Meritor Savings Bank v. Vinson*** (1986) the Supreme Court ruled for the first time that these types of sexual harassment were a form of legally prohibited sex discrimination. Sexual harassment was a federal offense covered by the Civil Rights Act.

Before long cases of alleged sexual harassment between individuals of the same sex began to make it to the courts. The resulting court rulings were very inconsistent. Often the courts stated that same-sex sexual harassment would have to include some form of demands for sex, such as between a homosexual employer and an employee of the same sex. A district court decision in *Garcia v. Elf Atochem* (1994) ruled that there could be no same-sex sexual harassment. Another district court in *Baskerville v. Culligan International Co.* (1995) disagreed, ruling that same-sex claims could be covered by Title VII. And a third in 1996 ruled that same-sex harassment could not be responsible for a hostile work environment. The Supreme Court had yet to be clearly heard on the subject.

The Plight of Joseph Oncale

In August of 1991 twenty-one-year-old Joseph Oncale was hired by Sundowner Offshore Services in Houma, Louisiana to be a roustabout. Roustabouts are unskilled laborers working in an oilfield. Oncale was part of an eight-man crew working on a Chevron USA oil platform in the Gulf of Mexico. The crew included John Lyons, Danny Pippen, and Brandon Johnson. Pippen and Lyons were supervisors over Oncale. After a few weeks of work, Oncale began to be the target of a series of threatening and humiliating actions by Lyons, Pippen, and Johnson, often in front of co-workers. In one instance, while on a small boat going from one oil platform to another, the three men physically assailed him in a sexual manner. The assaults continued with threats of rape over the next several weeks.

Desperate, Oncale complained to company officials. However, when the officials approached the workers about the complaints they denied Oncale's charges. The company, claiming only horseplay had taken place, took no action, not even an investigation. Oncale, fearing what would eventually happen to him, quit in November, only four months after being hired.

Oncale Goes to Court

After leaving, Oncale filed a sex discrimination lawsuit with the Fifth Circuit Court of Appeals in New Orleans, Louisiana. The suit sought payment for damages from Sundowner and the three men who had threatened and accosted him. He had lost his job because of the embarrassing behavior of the co-workers and lack of response by the company to his pleas.

Based on the recent *Garcia* decision, the district court dismissed the case claiming that no federal laws recognized same-sex sexual discrimination. Oncale appealed the decision, but the appeals court promptly agreed with the first opinion. Upon the appeals court decision, the U.S. Department of Justice decided to help Oncale take his case to the Supreme Court, which agreed to hear it.

The Supreme Court

Before the Supreme Court, Oncale's and the government's lawyers argued that Title VII of the Civil Rights Act was written simply in sex-neutral terms. It did not mention harassment only in terms of men harassing women. Sex discrimination is prohibited regardless of the gender of the people involved. On the other hand, Sundowner argued that same-sex harassment was not even in the minds of legislators when the act was passed. According to Sundowner, the law was clearly intended to protect females. Applying it to a case like Oncale's, they argued, would be a great misuse of the law, making it more of a code for decent behavior rather than a discrimination law. Rowdy behavior would be confused with sexual harassment.

In an unanimous (all nine justices agreeing) decision, the Court ruled in favor of Oncale thus reversing the two lower court decisions. Justice Antonin Scalia, writing for the Court, presented a forceful response. Though he noted that no doubt same-sex harassment was not the primary problem Congress had in mind when writing the law, he emphasized that the harm from same-sex harassment was no less serious than if the two people were of different sexes. Therefore, any form of sexual harassment in the workplace directly affecting a person's employment clearly violated Title VII of the Civil Rights Act. As Scalia noted, the law was intended "to strike at the entire spectrum [variation] of disparate [unequal] treatment of men and women in employment." The law is violated when "discriminatory intimidation, ridicule, and insult" becomes so overwhelming that an abusive work environment is created.

Scalia further noted that "harassing conduct need not be motivated by sexual desire to support an inference [idea] of discrimination on the basis of sex." In conclusion, Scalia wrote that routine interaction between employees should not be affected by the Court's ruling. Only behavior "so . . . offensive as to alter 'conditions' of the victim's employment" would be prohibited. Determining when sexual harassment had indeed occurred would be tricky. The situation in which the actions occur is all-important in deciding if harassment in fact occurred. As Scalia noted, a pat on the rear of a football player by his coach on the field is quite different than the same action toward the coach's secretary in the office. The "surrounding circumstances, expectations, and relationships" would have to be closely examined for each case using common sense.

By the time of the Supreme Court decision, Oncale was twenty-seven years old, married, and had two children. The Court returned his case to the district court so that he might have a trial to try to prove that the actions by his co-workers constituted sexual harassment in the workplace.

The *Oncale* decision finally made clear the legal status of same-sex sexual harassment. Two other Supreme Court decisions in 1998 further broadened employers' legal responsibilities for protecting their workers

RESOLVING SEXUAL HARASSMENT DISPUTES

In a series of rulings in the 1990s including *Oncale,* the Supreme Court clarified and broadened employer responsibilities. Faced with potentially expensive lawsuits and costly damage payments to victims of on-the-job sexual harassment by the employers, both public agencies and private businesses began educating their employees on how to avoid sexual harassment situations. It also became apparent that quick resolution of disputes was needed. Training materials described what sexual harassment is, what rights employees have to correct an unwanted situation, and penalties employees faced for violating the rules.

The bigger organizations also adopted in-house procedures for resolving sexual harassment claims before they could reach the courts. The usual goal is to resolve the dispute as quickly and informally as possible to save money, time, and workplace disruptions. These procedures commonly involve the harassed employee contacting a counselor designated by the company, a person to whom an employee could file a complaint, different from the employee's supervisor, within a certain time period after the incident, often within 45 days. The counselor normally (1) advises the employee of their rights, (2) helps define the dispute, (3) offers a solution, usually within a required time span such as 30 days, and (4) takes the dispute resolution to managers for acceptance. The counselors also keep company managers aware of troublesome patterns related to discrimination or harassment so as to avoid disputes. If this informal process fails, the employee can then proceed with a formal complaint possibly leading to more formal investigations by the company or outside parties. Courts have normally recognized these kinds of informal resolution processes and will not accept cases if the alleged victim has not followed company policies in making complaints.

from on-the-job sexual harassment. For instance, hostile actions based on the sex of the victim could justify sexual harassment claims, even without involvement of sexual desire. If sex or gender was not a key factor in the incidents, then the hostile actions would not be considered sexual harassment and would not necessarily violate federal law. The actions would be considered assault under state laws. Employers in the late 1990s began more diligently developing company policies and guidelines for their employees, giving training, providing handbooks to each employee, and informing employees of their rights.

Suggestions for further reading

Baridon, Andrea P., and David R. Eyler. *Working Together: New Rules and Realities for Managing Men and Women at Work.* New York: McGraw-Hill, 1994.

Eskenazi, Martin, and David Gallen. *Sexual Harassment: Know Your Rights.* New York: Carroll & Graf Publishers, Inc., 1992.

Petrocelli, William, and Barbara Kate Repa. *Sexual Harassment on the Job.* Berkeley, CA: Nolo Press, 1994.

The right of a woman to determine when and how she will give birth, commonly known as reproductive rights, was not legally recognized until the last half of the twentieth century. Reproductive rights includes not only the highly controversial issue of abortion, but also a wide range of other related topics including contraception (preventing pregnancy), sex education, surrogate (substitute) motherhood, in-vitro fertilization ("test tube babies"), condom availability, and sterilization (making incapable of reproduction). Public acceptance of birth control and other measures associated with reproductive choices have changed dramatically through the years in the United States.

Changing Attitudes in the Nineteenth Century

In the early nineteenth century, the average white American woman gave birth to seven children. As the nineteenth century progressed, the American economy changed from a predominately agricultural society with families living and working together on farms to growth of industrial centers involving factory work for husbands. The economic need for large families declined. As a result, scientific information on birth control began to be distributed by social reformers. In addition, few criminal laws existed banning abortion (ending a pregnancy before childbirth by removing the unborn child) and abortion was legal under common law (following common practices rather than laws passed by legislatures). Abortions were commonly associated with disposing of fetuses (unborn child) resulting from rape or conception out of wedlock. They normally were performed in the first four or five months of pregnancy. Abortions, however, were very dangerous to the woman with many left unable to bear children later, or actually dying from the procedure.

As the number of abortions began to significantly increase in the mid-nineteenth century, particularly among white middle-class women, conservatives rallied in opposition to birth control and abortion. They lobbied Congress for laws banning such activities. As a result, Congress passed the Comstock Law in 1873. The law prohibited the distribution of information that promoted methods of preventing pregnancy or that supported abortion. States also began passing laws prohibiting the use of contraceptives. Established in 1847, the American Medical Association (AMA) was interested in driving out of business unlicensed people performing abortions. Joined by religious leaders, they successfully led a campaign outlawing abortion. By the 1880s all states had passed laws banning abortion based on their police powers to regulate public health and safety. All had criminal penalties for persons performing abortions and some even adopted penalties for the women who had the abortions. Abortions were only legal when needed to save the mother's life. These restrictions changed little until the 1960s.

The Long Struggle for Reproductive Rights

Those supportive of birth control options for women began an active campaign in the early twentieth century to end the many prohibitions (forbidden by law) established in the late nineteenth century. Guided by reformer Margaret Sanger, a national movement developed leading eventually to establishment of Planned Parenthood Federation of America in 1942. By the 1960s birth control was legalized in almost all states though the actual distribution of birth control information was still commonly illegal. Many states also loosened their abortion laws to allow abortions when pregnancies resulted from rape or when the fetus likely had a serious birth defect.

The first major U.S. Supreme Court case recognizing reproductive rights came in 1965 in ***Griswold v. Connecticut.*** The Court, in recognizing a basic constitutional right to privacy, struck down a Connecticut state law prohibiting married couples from using contraceptives. Seven years later in 1972 the Court extended the right to use contraceptives to unmarried people as well in ***Eisenstadt v. Baird.*** Later in 1977 the Court in *Carey v. Population Services International* extended the right to contraceptive use to minors. The decisions opened the door for providing information to school students in sex education programs and even providing contraceptives.

The landmark Supreme Court ruling in reproductive rights however came in 1973. In the famous ***Roe v. Wade*** decision, the Court extended the right to privacy to include the right to abortions as well. A Texas law had prohibited abortions during the first trimester (first three months) of pregnancy except in situations where the mother's life was threatened. The Court ruled this prohibition violated the Equal Protection Clause of the Fourteenth Amendment. In a major determination, the Court wrote that a fetus was not a viable human being (capable of meaningful life after birth) until the third trimester (last three months of pregnancy). Therefore, prohibitions on abortions were not legally appropriate until after that time in a pregnancy. Even at that late point in the pregnancy the state must still make allowance for abortions when necessary to save the mother's life or protect her health.

By recognizing reproductive rights of women, many believed the Court had helped women gain some social and economic equality with men through their ability to control their reproductive processes. Women could pursue professions, like men, largely free of unexpected or unwanted disruptions of child birth or tending to children.

The Abortion Battle Continues in the Courts

The next major ruling in reproductive rights came in ***Planned Parenthood of Central Missouri v. Danforth*** in 1976. State law had required minors to obtain written permission from at least one parent and required a wife to obtain permission from a husband before having an abortion. The Court ruled these requirements unconstitutional (not following the intent of the constitution).

After suffering these major defeats in the courts, opponents to abortion adopted a new strategy to combat abortions. Also, many organizations were created opposing such sweeping reproduction rights. Pressing for legislation banning the use of public funds to pay for abortions, they succeeded in having Congress pass a law in 1976 prohibiting the use of federal monies for almost all abortions. The new law was immediately challenged, but the Supreme Court in a series of 1977 rulings held the law as constitutional. Public funds could only be used in situations of clear medical need. In a much bolder move, a constitutional amendment banning abortions was attempted but fell just short of adoption in 1983.

The debate over parental involvement in abortions for minors also continued in the courts. In 1979 in *Bellotti v. Baird II* the Court further strengthened the 1976 *Danforth* ruling that had prohibited parental consent requirements in state laws. However, anti-abortion advocates made some gains in 1990 in *Hodgson v. Minnesota* and *Ohio v. Akron Center for Reproductive Health.* In these cases the Supreme Court upheld state laws requiring some forms of parental notification prior to obtaining an abortion, but not requiring parental approval. Most states soon passed laws adopting the parental notification requirements.

Since the *Roe v. Wade* decision, the debate over abortion rights has continued, even involving several U.S. Presidents encouraging the Supreme Court to reverse its 1973 ruling. In 1989 in *Webster v. Reproductive Health Services* the Court expanded the right of states to regulate abortions. The ruling upheld a Missouri law prohibiting use of publically funded facilities or personnel to perform abortions and created certain other requirements of the attending doctors. In 1992 the Court accepted another reproductive rights case which many anticipated would lead to a reversal of the *Roe* decision. However, much to the surprise of many, the Court did not overturn *Roe,* but did give states more flexibility to regulate abortions. In ***Planned Parenthood of Southeastern Pennsylvania v. Casey*** the Court ruled that states could regulate abortions prior to fetus viability, but they must not place "undue burdens" on the mother seeking an abortion. A new, weaker standard was created to judge the appropriateness of restrictions on abortions. In sum, since the *Roe* decision in 1973 the Court has steadily increased restrictions on reproductive rights regarding abortions.

War in the Streets

Violence against abortion clinics escalated in the 1990s involving blockades, arson, bombings, vandalism, and shootings. The anti-abortion organization, Operation Rescue, organized mass demonstrations outside abortion clinics, blocking their entrances and harassing women seeking abortions. Court injunctions (orders) against such activities led to a Supreme Court decision. In *Schenck v. Pro-Choice Network of Western New York* (1997) the justices identified the types of restrictions lower court judges could apply to anti-abortion protesters. The Court was attempting to balance free speech rights of the protesters with public safety, property rights, and reproductive rights of those seeking and giving abortions.

In reaction to the violent disruption of legal abortions, Congress passed the Freedom of Access to Clinic Entrances Act in 1994 prohibiting physical threats, blockades, and property damage. Congress also addressed other aspects of abortions. In 1997 it passed the Partial Birth Abortion Ban to prohibit certain types of abortions. But the bill was vetoed by President Bill Clinton over concerns that it did not adequately take into account the mother's safety and health. Abortion rights continued to be a hot topic in Congress.

Artificial Insemination, In Vitro Fertilization, and Surrogacy

Advances in medical technology late in the twentieth century brought new ways of creating pregnancy and with it new legal issues regarding reproductive rights. Artificial insemination involves the sperm of a donor father being medically placed in a woman. This technique not only extended reproductive rights to a woman whose husband may be sterile and cannot produce sufficient sperm, but also to lesbian couples. In vitro fertilization came to the public's attention in 1978 with the birth of the first "test tube child" conceived through the technique. This procedure involves fertilization of a human egg outside the womb and then medically placing the resulting embryo in a woman.

These new forms of conception brought the use of surrogate (substitute) motherhood. The surrogate mother could either be artificially inseminated with sperm from a donor father, or with the fertilized egg cell inserted in her. The surrogate mother then would give custody of the child to the intended parents upon birth. Though initially surrogate mothers were close friends or relatives of the intended parents, by the 1980s contracts with previous strangers became more common.

The first case addressing disputes involving surrogacy came to the courts in 1986 in *In re Baby M.* William and Dr. Elizabeth Stern had arranged for Mary Beth Whitehead to be a surrogate mother. Whitehead was medically inseminated with Stern's sperm and agreed to give the resulting child to the Sterns after birth. She was to be paid $10,000 in addition to medical expenses. However, upon birth of the baby, Whitehead refused to turn custody of the baby to the Sterns. The New Jersey Supreme Court ruled that such contracts were inappropriate and against the public good. Reproductive rights did not include the right to establish such contracts. Surrogacy by contract, the court asserted, was another form of illegal child selling. However, in the best interest of the child in this instance, the court awarded custody to Mr. Sterns and gave Whitehead visitation rights.

The 1990s brought other complex legal disputes over surrogacy. Determining the true legal parents is one complex issue resulting from the expanded reproductive rights. The California Supreme Court in *Johnson v. Calvert* (1993) affirmed the California Uniform Parentage Act in which both the intended mother and the surrogate mother could be identified as the legal mother. Also, the intended father could be a legal father. Implications of such rights came up in California a short time later. John and Luanne Buzzanca had anonymous (unknown contributor) egg and sperm implanted in the mother's womb. However, the Buzzanca's divorced shortly before birth of the child and Luanne sued John for child support. John Buzzanca resisted, claiming the child was not a biological product of their marriage. In 1999 in *In re Marriage of Buzzanca* a California appellate court ruled that Luanne and John were indeed both the legal parents and John was responsible to provide financial child support. Because of the numerous complexities that can result from all different types of parent relationships, the courts have sought to resolve disputes on a case by case basis rather than broad sweeping rulings.

As the twenty-first century began, other complex family law issues faced the courts. Issues involving rights to frozen sperm and eggs, often associated with divorce cases and death of donors, began to occur. Family law appeared to still have plenty of potential for great expansion as reproductive technologies continued to evolve.

Suggestions for further reading

Butler, Douglas J., ed. *Abortion and Reproductive Rights.* CD-ROM, J. Douglas Butler, Inc., 1997.

Currie, Stephen. *Abortion.* San Diego: Greenhaven Press, 2000.

Ginsburg, Faye D. *Contested Lives: The Abortion Debate in an American Community.* Berkeley, CA: University of California Press, 1988.

National Abortion & Reproductive Rights Action League. [Online] Website: http://www.naral.org (Accessed on July 31, 2000).

Olasky, Marvin. *Abortion Rites: A Social History of Abortion in America.* Washington, DC: Regnery Publishing, Inc., 1995.

Stevens, Leonard A. *The Case of Roe v. Wade.* New York: Putnam and Sons, 1996.

Buck v. Bell
1927

Appellant: Carrie Buck

Appellee: Dr. J. H. Bell

Appellant's Claim: That Virginia's eugenic sterilization law violated Carrie Buck's right to equal protection of the laws and due process provided by the U.S. Constitution's Fourteenth Amendment.

Chief Lawyers for Appellant: Irving Whitehead

Chief Lawyers for Appellee: Aubrey E. Strode

Justices for the Court: Louis D. Brandeis, Oliver Wendell Holmes, James Clark McReynolds, Edward T. Sanford, Harlan F. Stone, George Sutherland, William H. Taft, Willis Van Devanter

Justices Dissenting: Pierce Butler

Date of Decision: May 2, 1927

Decision: Upheld as constitutional Virginia's compulsory sterilization of young women considered "unfit [to] continue their kind."

Significance: Virginia's law served as a model for similar laws in thirty states, under which 50,000 U.S. citizens were sterilized without their consent. During the Nuremberg war trials following World War II (1939–45) , German lawyers cited the decision as a precedent for the sterilization of two million people in its "Rassenhygiene" (race hygiene) program. U.S. sterilization programs continued into the 1970s.

Sterilization of "Mental Defectives"

In a 1927 letter written shortly after the *Buck v. Bell* decision, Supreme Court justice Oliver Wendell Holmes said, "One decision . . . gave me pleasure, establishing the constitutionality of a law permitting the sterilization [to make incapable of producing children] of imbeciles." "Imbeciles," "feebleminded," and "mental defectives" were harsh terms frequently used during the nineteenth and early twentieth centuries when referring to persons with mental retardation (MR). A fear of allowing persons with MR to have children grew from the eugenics movement in the late nineteenth century. Based on newly developing scientific theories concerning heredity, the movement sought to control mating and reproduction to improve both physical and mental qualities of the general human population. By the 1910s a scientific foundation for eugenics had accumulated data based on studies of generations of "mental defectives." Experts called for sterilization of the "feebleminded" as the best way to stop future generations of "mental defectives."

Consequently, personal decisions of the mentally retarded about becoming parents and raising children became increasingly subjected to government regulation. State laws were passed directing others to make these choices for them. Several state asylums (institutions housing persons with MR and other mental problems) began sterilizing their patients. By 1917 twelve states passed sterilization laws.

Dr. Albert Priddy

Central to the drive for population improvement through the eugenics movement and sterilization was Dr. Albert Priddy, superintendent of the State Colony for Epileptics and Feeble-Minded at Lynchburg, Virginia. During the 1910s, with encouragement of the colony's board of directors, Priddy sterilized some seventy-five to one hundred young women without their consent. However, the Virginia legislature had not clearly endorsed sterilization and Priddy discontinued the operations in 1918. Priddy, his friend Aubrey Strode who was a state legislator and chief administrator of the colony, and the eugenical community pressured the legislature for a clear sterilization law. With the state experiencing budget problems, Priddy's group proposed a law that provided for release after sterilization of individuals who otherwise might require permanent costly stays at the Colony.

REPRODUCTIVE RIGHTS

In 1924 the Virginia Assembly enacted a law permitting forced sterilization of "feebleminded" or "socially inadequate person[s]." The law outlined the process to be followed including appointing a guardian, hearings, and court appeals. Three generations of the Buck family living in Virginia soon became entangled in this legal web.

The Bucks

Emma Buck, the widowed mother of three small children, supported her children through prostitution and charity until they were finally taken from her. Three year-old Carrie Buck, Emma's daughter, went to live with J. T. and Alice Dobbs. Carrie progressed normally through five years of school before being taken out so she could assume more household duties. The Dobbs were completely satisfied with Carrie until at age seventeen she claimed she had been raped by the Dobbs' son and became pregnant. A Binet-Simon I. Q. test revealed Carrie's mental age as nine. As soon as Carrie's baby, Vivian, was born the Dobbs had Carrie committed to the Colony for the Epileptic and

Carrie Buck Eagle and her husband, William Eagle. Courtesy of the Library of Congress.

Feebleminded in 1924. Only four years earlier, Carrie's mother had been found to have a mental age of eight and was confined at the same institution.

Concluding Carrie had inherited her feeblemindedness from her mother and that baby Vivian had no doubt inherited the same condition, Dr. Priddy saw Carrie as a perfect test case for Virginia's new sterilization law. He recommended she be sterilized because she was feebleminded and a "moral delinquent."

The Perfect Test Case

Dr. Priddy's recommendation met with the Colony board's approval. They hired Aubrey Strode to represent the Colony and Irving Whitehead, former Colony board member and friend of Strode, to represent Carrie.

In November of 1924, *Buck v. Priddy* was argued before the Circuit Court of Amherst. Strode called eight witnesses and presented one expert's written testimony. Carrie was characterized as having inherited her feeblemindedness from her mother. Although Carries's baby, Vivian, was only eight months old, she was likewise described as "not quite a normal baby." Carrie, already having one illegitimate child, was described as the "potential parent of [more] socially inadequate offspring." Dr. Priddy testified that Carrie, "would cease to be a charge on society if sterilized. It would remove one potential source" of more feebleminded offspring.

Whitehead made no defense for Carrie neglecting to point out her church attendance and normal school record. Although he would be required to argue for Carrie in the higher courts, Whitehead really sought the same result as Priddy and Strode. They intended to appeal the case through all the courts hoping to receive total support for the sterilization law.

The Circuit Court upheld the law and ordered the sterilization of Carrie Buck. Whitehead appealed in 1925 to the Supreme Court of Appeals of the State of Virginia which upheld the Circuit Court decision. The case was now *Buck v. Bell* because Dr. Priddy had died and Dr. J. H. Bell had taken his place at the Colony. Whitehead next appealed the case to the U.S. Supreme Court.

"Three generations of imbeciles are enough."

In the brief (a summary outlining the essential information) he submitted to the Supreme Court, Whitehead claimed that the Virginia law was void (should no longer be law) because it denied Carrie due process of law and equal protection of the laws, rights guaranteed by the Fourteenth Amendment. The Fourteenth Amendment states that no state shall "deprive any person of life, liberty or property without due process of law; nor deny to any person . . . equal protection of the laws." Due process means a person must have fair legal proceedings. Equal protection means persons or groups of persons in similar situations must be treated equally by the laws.

Strode's brief countered that Carrie had been given a great deal of due process and that the state could make sterilization decisions for people like Carrie without violating equal protection. Justice Oliver Wendell Holmes delivered the 8-1 opinion upholding the Virginia sterilization law.

After reviewing the long process the law requires a superintendent of a hospital or colony to follow before carrying out sterilization, Holmes concluded due process was not violated. Holmes wrote,

> **There can be no doubt that so far as procedure is concerned the rights of the patient are most carefully considered, and . . . every step in this case was taken in scrupulous compliance with the statute [followed exactly the procedures outlined by the law].**

Holmes similarly rejected the claim of equal protection violation saying the law treated all persons in similar situations as Carrie.

Agreeing with the philosophy of eugenics, Justice Holmes proclaimed that society must be protected from "being swamped with incompetence." He wrote, "It is better for all the world, if instead of waiting to execute offspring for crime, or to let them starve for their imbecility, society can prevent those who are manifestly unfit from continuing their kind . . . three generations of imbeciles are enough [referring to the three Bucks]."

What Became of Carrie Buck?

Dr. Bell sterilized Carrie Buck in October of 1927 and then released her from the Colony. She married William Davis Eagle in 1932 and, after his

EUGENICS

Eugenics is a science theory developed in the late nineteenth century concerned with improving hereditary qualities of the human population by encouraging persons who are considered above average mentally and physically to have more children and discouraging offspring from parents of lesser mental and physical abilities. Francis Galton began using the term in 1883 which is Greek meaning good birth. Charles Darwin's theory of natural selection introduced in 1859 provided the basic concepts behind eugenics. Galton reasoned that society's sympathy and caring for the weak stopped proper natural selection in mankind. This allowed "inferior" humans to live and reproduce when they otherwise would have been selected against and eliminated. Therefore, eugenics is a replacement of natural selection with conscious, controlled selection of desirable characteristics and the elimination of undesirable ones.

By 1931 eugenicists had convinced American states to pass sterilization laws barring "flawed" individuals from reproducing. Worldwide, by the mid-1930s Norway, Sweden, Denmark, Switzerland, and Germany followed suit. In 1933 Germany had passed the Hereditary Health Law. In the name of eugenics, Germany's Adolf Hitler sterilized and murdered millions in the 1930s and 1940s.

While sterilizations were no longer practiced, eugenic organizations still exist in the United States at the beginning of the twenty-first century. New forms of selecting hereditary traits appeared such as the widely accepted practice of aborting a fetus (unborn child) if found to have a disability and through sperm selection from sperm donor banks for methods of artificial conception.

death, married Charlie Detamore. Later recollections of her minister, neighbors, friends, and health care providers plus letters she wrote to the Virginia colony seeking custody of her mother all suggest Carrie was truly not "feebleminded."

At least twenty-seven other states and several countries passed laws similar to Virginia's resulting in forced sterilization of thousands of people. By the mid-twentieth century Americans had become more sensitive to and educated about the needs of persons with MR. By the 1960s people with MR began to mainstream into a more normal everyday life in schools and with their families. Sterilization of persons with MR still continued in the United States until the mid-1970s. However, by the close of the twentieth century the *Buck v. Bell* decision had not yet been overturned.

Suggestions for further reading

Brantlinger, Ellen A. *Sterilization of People with Mental Disabilities.* Westport, CT: Auburn House Publications, 1995.

Eugenics Watch. [Online] Website: http://www.africa2000.com/ENDX/endx.htm (Accessed on July 31, 2000).

Field, Martha A., and Valerie A. Sanchez. *Equal Treatment for People with Mental Retardation: Having and Raising Children.* Boston: Harvard University Press, 2000.

Future Generations. [Online] Website: http://www.eugenics.net (Accessed on July 31, 2000).

Smith, J. David, and K. Ray Nelson. *The Sterilization of Carrie Buck.* Far Hills, NJ: New Horizon Press, 1989.

Eisenstadt v. Baird
1972

Appellant: Thomas Eisenstadt, Sheriff of Suffolk County, Massachusetts

Appellee: William R. Baird, Jr.

Appellant's Claim: That the Massachusetts Supreme Judicial Court erred in overturning Baird's conviction on charges of distributing contraceptives without a proper liscense.

Chief Lawyers for Appellant: Joseph R. Nolan

Chief Lawyers for Appellee: Joseph D. Tydings

Justices for the Court: Harry A. Blackmun, William J. Brennan, Jr., William O. Douglas, Thurgood Marshall, Potter Stewart, Byron R. White

Justices Dissenting: Chief Justice Warren E. Burger (Lewis F. Powell, Jr., and William H. Rehnquist did not participate)

Date of Decision: March 22, 1972

Decision: Ruling in favor of Baird, the Court upheld the Massachusetts Supreme Judicial Court decision that the state law was unconstitutional because it denied unmarried and married persons equal protection in violation the Fourteenth Amendment.

Significance: The decision expanded the right of privacy to unmarried people and made contraceptives legally available to them throughout the United States. Importantly, the decision broadened the constitutional right of privacy in a way that foreshadowed the Court's landmark finding the following year that the right to privacy protects a woman's right to have an abortion.

REPRODUCTIVE RIGHTS

In 1873 U.S. Congress passed of a federal law, commonly known as the Comstock Act, prohibiting the distribution of birth control devices as well as information about birth control methods. Most states also had laws banning the sale, distribution, and advertising of contraceptives (birth control devices). One state law, Connecticut's, completely banned the use of contraceptives for anyone anywhere. In spite of the laws, the need for birth control resulted in the growth of birth control advocacy (support, in favor of) groups. In 1916 Margaret Sanger opened a birth control clinic in New York City and, continuing her role of reforming attitudes toward birth control, founded the organization Planned Parenthood in 1942.

Opened in 1961, the Planned Parenthood League of Connecticut, directed by Estelle Griswold, provided information to married people about the use of birth control methods to prevent pregnancy. Soon, Griswold faced charges of violating Connecticut's 1879 law banning the use of contraceptives. The U.S. Supreme Court struck down the law in ***Griswold v. Connecticut*** (1964) as an unconstitutional invasion of an

TYPES OF CONTRACEPTIVES

Effectiveness	*Predicted (%)*	*Actual (%)*
Birth control pills	99.9	97
Condoms	98	88
Depo Provera	99.7	99.7
Diaphragm	94	82
IUDs	99.2	97
Norplant	99.7	99.7
Tubal sterilization	99.8	99.6
Spermicides	97	79
Vasectomy	99.9	99.9

Source: Adapted from Trousel et al, *Obstetrics and Gynecology,* 76 1990: 558.

The effectiveness of different kinds of contraception. Reproduced by permission of Stanley Publishing.

individual's right to privacy in relationships between married adults. The Court ruled that contraceptives could not be banned for married adults. However, furnishing contraceptives to unmarried people remained illegal in many states. In Massachusetts a birth control law made it a felony (serious crime),

> **for anyone to give away a drug, medicine, instrument or article for the prevention of conception [pregnancy] except in the case of (1) a registered [licensed] physician administering or prescribing it for a married person or (2) an active registered pharmacist furnishing it to a married person presenting a registered physician's prescription.**

William R. Baird, Jr., Arrested for Lecture

In 1967, birth control activist William R. Baird, Jr. came to the campus of Boston University to give a lecture to students on birth control methods and to distribute birth control devices to interested coeds. Pointing out that over ten thousand women had died from illegal abortions in 1966, he condemned laws making contraceptives available only to married women under a doctor's care. He intended to "test this law in Massachusetts. . . No group, no law, no individual can dictate to a woman what goes on in her own body." Baird was neither a licensed physician nor licensed pharmacist. Between 1500 to 2000 people attended his lecture on contraception and at the end he gave a woman a package of contraceptive foam directly violating the law. Baird was immediately arrested.

Baird Convicted

Baird was not arrested for distributing the contraceptive foam to an unmarried person. No proof was actually ever offered that the woman was unmarried. Instead, Baird was charged under the law with having no license and, therefore, no authority to distribute to anyone. The Massachusetts Superior Court found Baird guilty of violating the law as did the Massachusetts Supreme Judicial Court. The Supreme Judicial Court saw the law as a health measure designed to prevent "dangerous physical consequences" by allowing only a licensed physician or pharmacist to legally distribute contraceptives. Baird was neither a licensed physician nor pharmacist, therefore not authorized to distribute the contraceptive. Hence, he violated the law.

Almost three years after his first conviction, the First Circuit Court of Appeals ruled in July of 1970 that the Massachusetts birth control law was unconstitutional and reversed Baird's conviction. The appeals court interpreted the law as actually a prohibition on contraception which the *Griswold* decision outlawed when it struck down Connecticut's prohibition against the use of contraceptives by married couples. Sheriff Thomas Eisenstadt of Suffolk County, Massachusetts appealed to the U.S. Supreme Court. The Supreme Court agreed to hear the case.

Equal Protection Violation

Baird's chief argument for the Court was simple, the law was unconstitutional because it treated two similar groups (married and unmarried persons) unequally and the state did not have a compelling (very important) reason or purpose to do so. Justice William J. Brennan, Jr., delivered the opinion of the Court, a 6–1 vote as two justices did not take part.

After accepting that Baird could indeed speak for unmarried persons who had been denied access to contraceptives, the Court examined

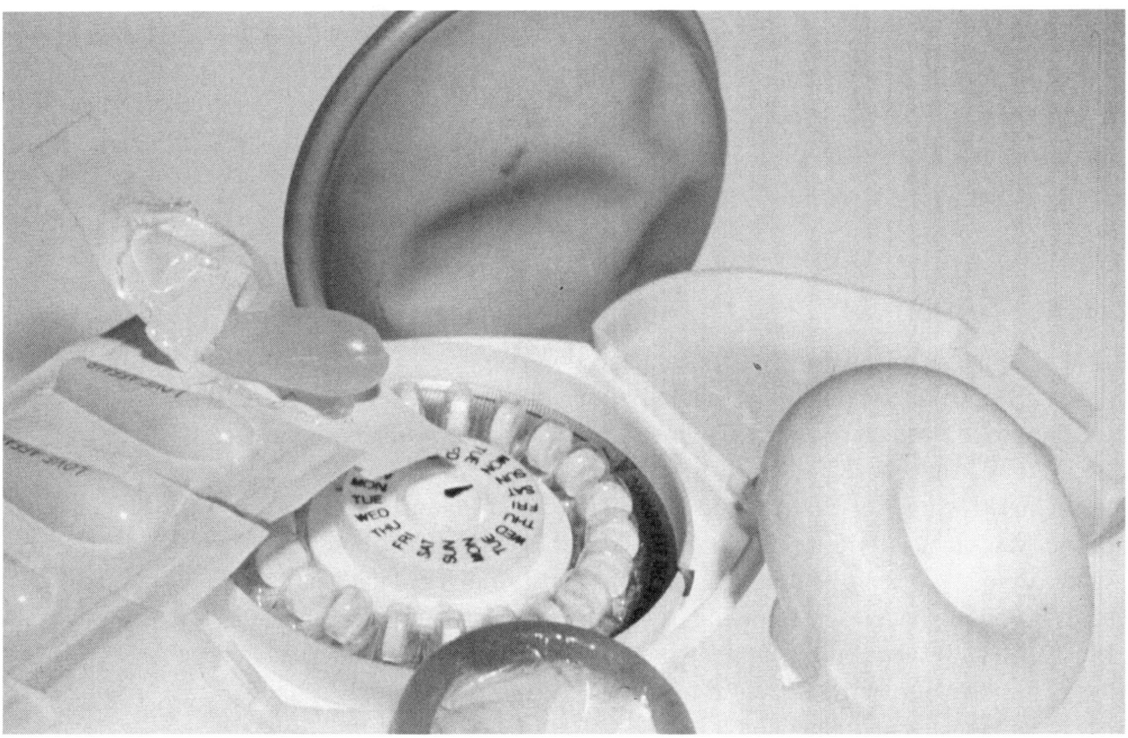

Contraceptives come in many different forms. Reproduced by permission of the Gamma Liaison Network.

the Massachusetts law to see if it violated the Equal Protection Clause of the Fourteenth Amendment. The Equal Protection Clause says that a state shall not deny equal protection of the laws to any person. The Massachusetts law, obviously, treated unmarried persons and married persons unequally in their access to contraceptive. If it did violate equal protection, the Court would then have to find a compelling purpose for the state to need the law or it could not stand. The Court considered three points before coming to their conclusion.

First, the Court inspected the law to see if the state's purpose could legitimately be to discourage premarital sexual intercourse, called "fornication" in legal matters. Brennan wrote, "the statute [law] is riddled with exceptions making contraceptives freely available for use in premarital sexual relations [under various circumstances]." Because of the many exceptions or holes in the law, Brennan noted deterring fornication could not reasonably be considered as the key purpose of the ban on distribution of contraceptives to unmarried persons.

Secondly, the Court, continuing to look for a compelling state aim, explored the Massachusetts Supreme Judicial Court's decision. The purpose of the law was, according to that court, to protect "the health needs of the community by regulating the distribution of potentially harmful articles [some types of contraceptives]." The Court found that when the law was first written by the Massachusetts legislature, its purpose had nothing to do with health, but was directed at preserving morals. Besides, this law would still be "discriminatory against the unmarried, and was overbroad [reach too far]." There were other laws to prohibit distribution of harmful drugs. Justice Brennan rejected health as the law's purpose.

Thirdly, Justice Brennan asked, "If the Massachusetts statute cannot be upheld as a deterrent to fornication or as a health measure, may it, nevertheless, be sustained simply as a prohibition on contraception?" Agreeing with the First Circuit Court of Appeals, Brennan wrote,

> **whatever the rights of the individual to access . . . contraceptives may be, the rights must be the same for the unmarried and married alike. If under *Griswold* the distribution of contraceptives to married persons cannot be prohibited, a ban on distribution to unmarried persons would be equally impermissible [not permitted].**

Next came Justice Brennan's famous and memorable reasoning,

REPRODUCTIVE RIGHTS

> **It is true that in *Griswold* the right of privacy in question inhered [exists in] in the marital relationship. Yet the marital couple is not an independent entity [body] with a mind and heart of its own, but an association of two individuals each with a separate intellectual and emotional makeup. If the right of privacy means anything, it is the right of the individual, married or single, to be free from unwarranted governmental intrusion into matters so fundamentally affecting a person as the decision whether to bear or beget [create] a child.**

With that the Court held the Massachusetts laws clearly violated the Equal Protection Clause by treating married and unmarried persons unequally. It further found that Massachusetts had no compelling reason to have the law. The Court affirmed the First Circuit Court of Appeals ruling that the law was unconstitutional and overturned Baird's conviction.

Many schools and community centers have started handing out contraceptives and health information as a way of keeping teens safe and informed. Reproduced by permission of AP/Wide World Photos.

PLANNED PARENTHOOD FEDERATION/WESTERN HEMISPHERE REGION (IPPF/WHR)

IPPF/WHR was founded in New York City in 1954 and is one of six regions that make up the International Planned Parenthood Federation. The IPPF/WHR region covers forty-six countries throughout Latin America, the Caribbean, the United States, and Canada. The IPPF/WHR serves more than eight million people each year through over 40,000 service clinics. Their mission is to "Promote and defend the right of women and men, including young people, to decide freely the number and spacing of their children, and the right to the highest possible level of sexual and reproductive health."

IPPF/WHR focuses especially on advancing the family planning movement in traditionally underserved areas and emphasizes mother and child health. Through information, support, and providing access to family planning services, IPPF/WHR works to eliminate unsafe abortions.

Expanding Privacy

The Supreme Court established a broader view of privacy in *Eisenstadt,* stating that all individuals married or single, enjoy the liberty to make certain personal decisions free from government interference. This clearly included the decision whether or not to have a baby. This reasoning would foreshadow the Court's 1973 finding in ***Roe v. Wade*** that the right to privacy protected a woman's right to have an abortion. Four years later the Supreme Court also cited *Eisenstadt* in ruling in *Carey v. Population Services International* (1977) that states could not prohibit the distribution of contraceptives to minors.

Suggestions for further reading

Benson, Michael D. *Coping with Birth Control.* New York: Rosen Publishing Group, 1998.

International Planned Parenthood Federation, Western Hemisphere Region, Inc. [Online] Website: http://www.ippfwhr.org (Accessed July 31, 2000).

Jacobs, Thomas A. *What Are My Rights?: 95 Questions and Answers About Teens and the Law.* Minneapolis, MN: Free Spirit Publishing, Inc., 1997.

Roe v. Wade
1973

Plaintiff: Norma McCorvey (known as Jane Roe)

Defendant: Henry B. Wade, Texas District Attorney

Plaintiff's Claim: That a 1859 Texas abortion law violated women's constitutional right to have an abortion.

Chief Lawyers for Plaintiff: Sarah Weddington and Linda Coffee

Chief Lawyers for Defendant: Jay Floyd and Robert Flowers

Justices for the Court: Harry A. Blackmun, William J. Brennan, Jr., Chief Justice Warren E. Burger, William O. Douglas, Thurgood Marshall, Lewis F. Powell, Potter Stewart

Justices Dissenting: William H. Rehnquist, Byron R. White

Date of Decision: January 22, 1973

Decision: Ruled in favor of Roe and struck down the Texas abortion law as unconstitutional.

Significance: The decision legalized abortion. The ruling included three key ideas. First, the ruling recognized the right of women to choose to have an abortion during the stage of pregnancy (one to six months) when the fetus has little chance of survival outside the womb and to obtain the abortion without unreasonable interference from the state. Secondly, the ruling confirmed a state's power to restrict abortions, except to protect a woman's life or health, at the stage (seven to nine months) when a fetus could live outside the womb. Third, the ruling confirmed the principle that the state has interests in both the health of the woman and the life of the fetus.

"My name is Norma McCorvey, but you know me as 'Jane Roe.' Twenty-one years ago, when I was poor and alone and pregnant, I was the plaintiff in *Roe v. Wade,* the Supreme Court decision that gave American women the right to choose abortion, to control their . . . own bodies, lives, and destinies" (from *I Am Roe* [1994], an autobiography by Norma McCorvey).

For years after the *Roe v. Wade* decision McCorvey remained anonymous. But in the early 1990s she began to emerge as a public figure. She worked as a telephone counselor in an abortion clinic and later as a cleaning woman, but when time allowed she would travel to various parts of the country to speak at colleges and to women's groups. People reacted to McCorvey in different ways. Some saw her as a famous woman whose name appears in many publications. Others think of her as a "heavy-duty feminist theorist or even a politician," characterizations she laughed at in her autobiography. Those opposed to abortion often called her a "demon" or "baby-killer." But in her own words, "Actually, Norma McCorvey is none of these women. I'm just a regular woman who like so many other regular women, got pregnant and didn't know what to do. . . "

Perhaps more than any other U.S. Supreme Court decision in history, the *Roe v. Wade* ruling, legalizing abortion, aroused passion and controversy. The 1973 decision touched off a battle between supporters of the Pro-Life movement seeking to overturn the ruling and the Pro-Choice supporters working to prevent the decision from being reversed or weakened. The Pro-Life group viewed abortion as murder. The Pro-Choice group was completely convinced that denying a woman the "right to choose" whether or not to have an abortion was an unacceptable government invasion of her freedom and privacy.

A look back at the history of abortion legislation in the United States reveals the stage that was set for *Roe v. Wade.*

Abortion Legal History

No abortion laws existed in the United States until the nineteenth century. The American Medical Association (AMA), established in 1847, became interested in driving out of business unlicensed persons performing abortions. Joined by religious leaders, the AMA successfully lead campaigns to outlaw abortions. By the 1880s all states had laws banning abortions except those performed to save the mother's life. In the 1960s two inci-

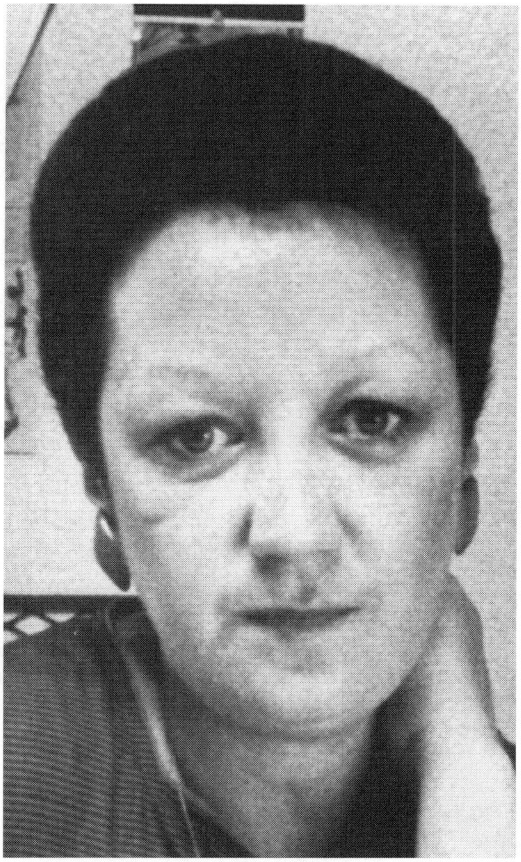

Norma McCorvey decided she was going to support the anti-abortion cause in the 1990s.
Reproduced by permission of the Corbis Corporation.

dents influenced a reexamination of abortion laws: (1) the discovery that thalidomide, a drug commonly prescribed for the nausea of early pregnancy, caused birth defects and (2) the 1962 to 1965 German measles epidemic. Both resulted in thousands of children born with often severe defects. Pregnant women affected by the incidents could not seek abortions due to the strict laws.

Influenced by the 1960s civil rights movement seeking equality for black Americans, women's rights organizations began to see abortion reform as an important step in the quest for equality of the sexes. Women, they reasoned, needed control of their bodies if they were to have control of their lives. Under the banner of reproductive freedom, they demanded outright repeal (cancellation) of state abortion laws. Soon, courts began to attack the most strict state laws. At the same time, the U.S. Supreme Court was developing a concept of the right to privacy in a person's sexual matters. Into this setting entered three women, Norma McCorvey, Sarah Weddington, and Linda Coffee.

Three Women From Texas

Twenty-one year old Norma McCorvey's marriage had ended, and her five year old daughter was being raised by her mother. In 1969 McCorvey, working as a traveling carnival ticket seller, became pregnant

REPRODUCTIVE RIGHTS

again. McCorvey first sought an illegal abortion but became terrified by what she discovered and decided against it. Although illegal abortions were fairly common, many women were permanently injured or died because of the unsanitary conditions under which the abortions were performed. The Texas anti-abortion law, adopted in 1859, prohibited abortions except when considered necessary to save the mother's life. Women who could afford it traveled to other states where abortion laws were less strict or where they could find a doctor who would certify that their abortion was necessary to protect their health. However, McCorvey was poor and, more often than not, poor women got the bad abortions.

Sarah Weddington and Linda Coffee were two of five women in the freshman law school class of 1965 at the University of Texas. Like many women of their generation, both of them became involved in the women's civil rights movement. With the doors to traditional law practices still largely closed to women at the time of their graduation, Weddington and Coffee decided to test the Texas abortion law. They began actively looking for a suitable case. Soon, Coffee learned of Norma McCorvey's plight. Although McCorvey's pregnancy would come to a conclusion before any lawsuit could successfully work its way through the courts,

The abortion struggle has shown little evidence of changing over the years.
Reproduced by permission of the Corbis Corporation.

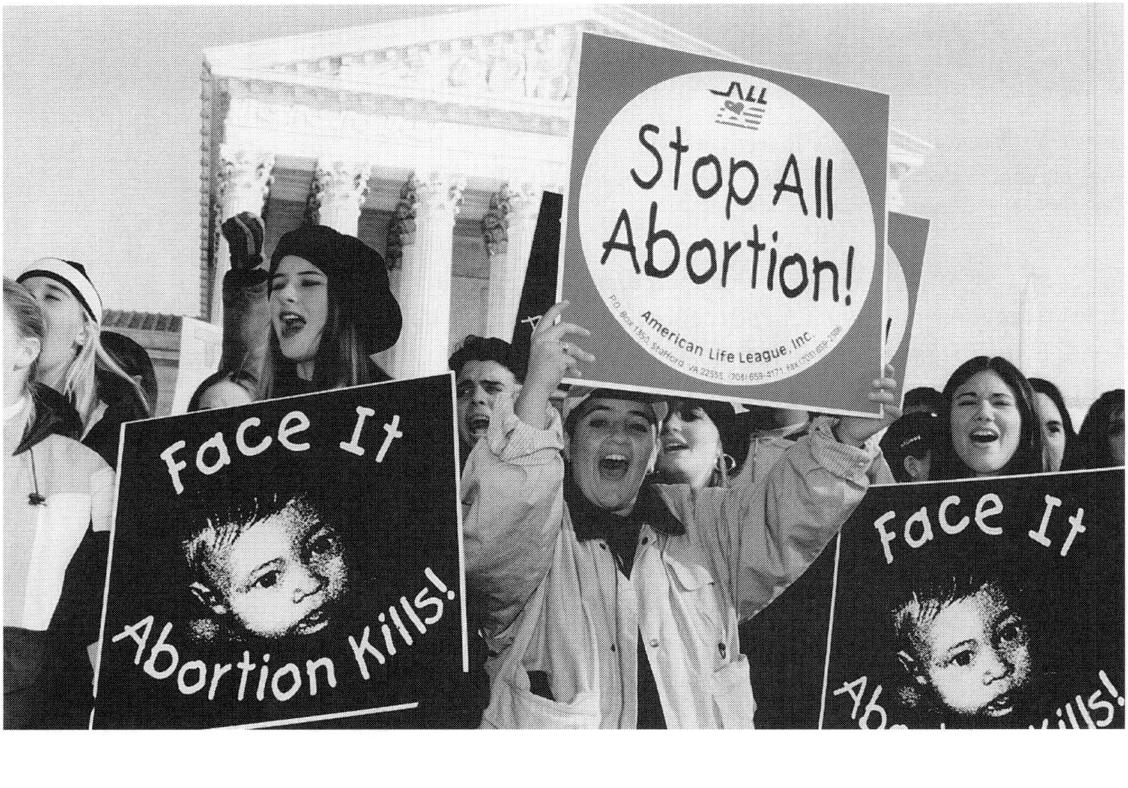

she agreed to be the plaintiff (the party that sues) in Coffee's and Weddington's test case. McCorvey would be known as "Jane Roe" to protect her real identity. Later, Coffee and Weddington both admitted they were too young and inexperienced to fully understand what they were taking on but both knew the case would be an important one.

A Jammed Dallas Courtroom

The case was first argued before three judges of the Fifth Circuit Court in Dallas on May 23, 1970. Coffee and Weddington had restructured their case to a class-action suit (a lawsuit representing a large number of people with a common interest) so that McCorvey would represent not just herself but all pregnant women.

Coffee and Weddington wanted a decision on whether or not a pregnant woman had the right to decide for herself if an abortion was necessary. They based their arguments on the Ninth and Fourteenth amendments to the U.S. Constitution. The Ninth Amendment stated that even though certain rights were not specifically named in the Constitution, they could still be held by the people. The Fourteenth Amendment prohibited states from denying citizens life, liberty, or property without due process of law (fair legal hearings). In 1965 the U.S. Supreme Court case ***Griswold v. Connecticut*** had clearly established a constitutional right to privacy found in and protected by the Ninth and Fourteenth amendments. In their case, Coffee and Weddington believed the right or liberty denied Roe by the Texas law was this right to privacy. The Texas law was, they stated, unconstitutional, violating privacy protections the Court found in both amendments. They reasoned this right to privacy should certainly protect the right of a woman to decide whether or not to become a mother.

District Attorney Henry Wade chose John Tolles to defend the enforcement of the Texas abortion law. The Texas Attorney General chose Jay Floyd to defend the law itself. The state prepared its case primarily on the basis that a fetus had legal rights which must be protected by the Constitution.

For the defense, Floyd first claimed that, since Roe's pregnancy had reached a point by that time where an abortion would certainly be unsafe, there was no case. Tolles followed by stating the position "that the right of the child to life is superior to that of a woman's right to privacy."

The three judges disagreed with Floyd and Tolles. They ruled that the Texas law violated Roe's right to privacy found in the Ninth and

Fourteenth Amendment. A woman did have the right to terminate her pregnancy. The case proceeded to the U.S. Supreme Court.

A Landmark Decision

The case generated intense interest from all over the nation. Forty-two *amici curiae* or "friend of the court" briefs (summary of the beliefs of a certain group about the case) supporting a woman's right to choose an abortion were filed with the Court.

Standing before the Court on December 13, 1971, Coffee, Weddington, Floyd, and Tolles argued the case. However, only seven judges were present and, after hearing the arguments, they decided the case so important that it should be re-argued when the two newly appointed justices, William Rehnquist and Lewis Powell, had joined the Court. The four lawyers did so on October 10, 1972, repeating their arguments.

Justice Harry A. Blackmun wrote the majority opinion for the 7-2 Court which found in favor of Roe. On January 22, 1973, Justice

Sarah Weddington was one of the lawyers arguing Norma McCorvey's case in front of the Supreme Court. Reproduced by permission of the Corbis Corporation.

Blackmun, acknowledging the extreme "sensitive and emotional nature of the abortion controversy," read his majority opinion in the Court chamber filled with reporters.

Rooted in Common Law

The Court first had to decide if the right to choose to terminate pregnancy was indeed a fundamental liberty protected by the Ninth and Fourteenth Amendment. Traditionally, the Court refuses to recognize new fundamental liberties unless they had historically been a right in English common law (based on common practices of a people through time) dating back sometimes as far as the twelfth and thirteenth centuries. Blackmun related the findings of the Court's research. Until the mid-nineteenth century, common law basically relied on the concept of "quickening." Quickening is the first recognizable movement of the fetus within the mother's womb, generally in the fourth to sixth months of pregnancy. Before quickening, the fetus (unborn child) was regarded as part of the mother rather than a separate person. Its destruction was allowed and not considered a crime. Even after quickening, early common law generally viewed termination of the pregnancy not as a crime, certainly not murder. Therefore, the termination of pregnancy *was* indeed rooted in common law. Laws strictly prohibiting abortion did not appear until in the mid-nineteenth century apparently to protect women's health from the then dangerous abortion procedure. Justice Blackmun concluded that abortion, allowed throughout common law, could be considered a protected liberty, and since medical advances had made abortion safe when properly carried out, no reason existed to continue the abortion laws.

Right of Privacy

Next, Justice Blackmun established that the right to an abortion fell within the right of privacy. Delivering the crucial point of the decision, Blackmun wrote,

> **The right of privacy, whether it be founded in the Fourteenth Amendment's concept of personal liberty and restrictions on state action . . . or . . . in the Ninth Amendment's reservation of rights to the people is broad enough to encompass [include] a woman's decision to terminate her pregnancy.**

Continuing, Justice Blackmun disagreed with Texas' claim that the law protected "prenatal life [before birth]." He explained that "the word 'person' as used in the Fourteenth Amendment, does not include the unborn."

However, Blackmun said that neither the woman's right to privacy in abortion nor the fetus' lack of a right to the state's protection was unlimited. He wrote,

> **The State does have an important and legitimate [honest] interest in preserving and protecting the health of the pregnant woman . . . and . . . it has still another important and legitimate interest in protecting the potentiality of human life [the not yet but soon to be born] . . . as the woman approaches term [ninth month of pregnancy]. . .**

Roughly following the quickening concept in common law, Justice Blackmun offered the states a formula to balance these competing interests. During the first trimester (first three months of pregnancy) the decision to abort would be the mother's and her physician. During the second trimester (months 4-6; the stage when quickening occurs), a state might regulate the abortion "in ways that are reasonably related to maternal [mother's] health." This meant that the state, recognizing several medical procedures existed to carry out abortion, must encourage the procedures which are safest for the mother's health. The fetus, at this stage, most likely could not live outside the mother's womb, so the mother's health is the primary concern. In the last trimester (months 7-9) until birth, a state might "regulate," even prohibit, abortion except to preserve the life or health of the mother. By this stage of pregnancy the fetus could likely live outside the womb, therefore emphasis should be shifted to protection of the unborn child. Hence, abortion may be prohibited.

The Texas abortion law was found unconstitutional and struck down.

In Dissent

Justices Rehnquist and Byron R. White dissented. Rehnquist disagreed that a medical abortion fell under the right of privacy. White believed the Court had wrongly considered a mother's convenience or whim over the "life or potential life of the fetus."

SARAH WEDDINGTON

Sarah Ragle Weddington was born in Abilene, Texas to a Methodist minister father and a mother who taught school. Excelling in her studies, she graduated from high school early and earned a college degree from McMurray College in 1965. Working at various jobs in the Texas legislature in the state capitol of Austin, Weddington quickly became interested in a law career. She, consequently, earned a law degree from the University of Texas in 1967 and began a law practice in Austin. Soon, she along with Linda Coffee, became the chief lawyers challenging Texas' abortion law in Roe v. Wade. In 1972 at age twenty-seven, Sarah presented legal arguments for the case before the Supreme Court justices. She also served in the Texas House of Representatives from 1972 to 1977.

Following success in the landmark abortion case, Sarah became a national figure. President Jimmy Carter appointed her to several key positions including special presidential assistant on various matters including women's rights. In 1977 Weddington was also appointed as a lawyer for the U.S. Department of Agriculture in Washington, D.C. In 1980 Weddington represented the United States at the World Conference of Women in Copenhagen, Denmark. Sarah later returned to Austin and the University of Texas as instructor and public speaker. In 1992 she published a book, *A Question of Choice,* on abortion rights and other women's issues.

Pro-Life v. Pro-Choice

Following the decision in *Roe v. Wade,* nineteen states needed to rework their abortion laws while thirty-one, including Texas, saw their strict anti-abortion laws entirely struck down. Immediately, *Roe* opponents, "Pro-Life" groups, began their assault on the decision. Several constitutional amendments prohibiting abortions were introduced in Congress. When these failed, *Roe*'s opponents tried to organize the required thirty-four state legislatures to call for a constitutional convention but this also failed by the mid-1980s.

By the early 1980s the Republican Party adopted the Pro-Life position, gaining support of many religious leaders' but losing much support among women. Both Republican presidents, Ronald Reagan and President George Bush, asked the Supreme Court to overturn *Roe.* The Democratic Party, which supported *Roe,* benefitted from the women's vote as Bill Clinton, a supporter of a woman's right to choose, was elected president in 1992 and 1996.

By 1999, Gallup polls showed that 45 percent of Americans fell into the Pro-Choice camp, believing an abortion decision must be left to the woman and her physician. Forty-two percent considered themselves Pro-Life supporters. Pro-Lifers were well-organized, well-funded, and on occasion radical elements turned violent.

Following the *Roe* decision, many of the Supreme Court's more liberal members retired in the 1980s and 1990s. The more conservative Court steadily allowed the states more flexibility in regulating abortion and indicated a willingness to re-examine the *Roe* decision. Many predicted ***Planned Parenthood of Southeastern Pennsylvania v. Casey*** (1992) would overturn *Roe,* but the Court upheld *Roe.* In the year 2000, the basic decision still stood.

Suggestions for further reading

Faux, Marian. *Roe v. Wade: The Untold Story of the Landmark Supreme Court Decision That Made Abortion Legal.* New York: Macmillan Publishing Company, 1988.

McCorvey, Norma. *I Am Roe: My Life, Roe v. Wade, and Freedom of Choice.* New York: HarperCollins Publishers, Inc., 1994.

Stevens, Leonard A. *The Case of Roe v. Wade.* New York: G. P. Putnam's Sons, 1996.

Weddington, Sarah. *A Question of Choice.* New York: Putnam, 1992.

Planned Parenthood of Central Missouri v. Danforth 1976

Appellants: Planned Parenthood of Central Missouri, David Hall, M.D., and Michael Freiman, M.D.

Appellee: John C. Danforth, Attorney General of Missouri

Appellants' Claim: That a Missouri abortion law was too restrictive on many aspects of the abortion process thus violating the patients' constitutional rights.

Chief Lawyers for Appellants: Frank Susman

Chief Lawyers for Appellees: John C. Danforth

Justices of the Court: Harry A. Blackmun, William J. Brennan, Jr., Thurgood Marshall, Lewis F. Powell, Jr.

Justices Dissenting: Chief Justice Warren E. Burger, William H. Rehnquist, John Paul Stevens, Byron R. White

Date of Decision: July 1, 1976

Decision: Ruled in favor of Danforth on some state requirements including provisions defining viability of the fetus, requiring a written consent by the pregnant women before an abortion, and keeping detailed medical records by abortion clinics. On other parts of the law, the Court ruled in favor of Planned Parenthood striking down Missouri's requirement for a husband's consent and, for unmarried minors, parental consent before receiving an abortion, prohibition of the saline amniocentesis abortion procedure, and requirement for physicians to preserve the fetus' life after an abortion.

Planned Parenthood of Central Missouri v. Danforth was just the sort of case the Supreme Court expected on the heels of the landmark *Roe v. Wade* decision legalizing abortion. The case presented many "logical [reasonable]" questions following the earlier ruling.

Decided in 1973 ***Roe v. Wade*** had been the most important and controversial legal victory for women since achieving the right to vote. *Roe* established a "right to privacy" involving "a woman's decision whether or not to terminate [end] her pregnancy." However, in *Roe* the Supreme Court "emphatically rejected" the idea that "the woman's right is absolute [unlimited] and that she is entitled to terminate her pregnancy at whatever time in whatever way and for whatever reason she alone chooses." Instead, the Court sought to balance a woman's privacy rights against a state's interest in protecting life, in this case the unborn child. The Court provided in *Roe* a balancing formula of acceptable action based on the three stages of pregnancy: (1) during the first three stages of pregnancy the state could not interfere at all in a decision to abort; (2) the next three months of pregnancy (fourth through the sixth month) the state could reasonably regulate the way abortions are done to protect maternal [the mother's] health; and, (3) the last three months of pregnancy (seventh through the ninth month), a stage when the fetus (unborn child) is viable (able to live on its own or with medical help), the state may greatly restrict the mother's decision to have an abortion unless it is necessary "for the life or health of the mother."

Missouri Tackles Abortion Procedures

With the *Roe* decision, strict anti-abortion laws in many states quickly became unconstitutional, including a 1969 Missouri abortion law. However, with the Court recognizing through its balancing formula that states still held an interest in protecting an unborn child, many states began enacting new, revised abortion laws. These new laws, while not directly violating the decisions in Roe, attempted to place some restrictions on abortion. In June of 1974 the Missouri General Assembly passed a new abortion act, House Bill 1211, and the governor signed it into law. The new Missouri law placed a number of requirements on the abortion procedure, and outlawed certain practices.

Within three days of House Bill 1211's passage, Planned Parenthood of Central Missouri and two physicians who regularly performed abortions, David Hall and Michael Freiman, challenged the law in the U.S. Court for the Eastern District of Missouri. The action was

Many public figures lend their voices to the pro-choice cause, such as Cybil Shephard, Whoopi Goldberg, and Marlowe Thomas. Reproduced by permission of the Corbis Corporation.

brought on behalf of all licensed physicians involved with abortions and their patients desiring to terminate pregnancy within Missouri. John C. Danforth, Attorney General of Missouri, argued the case for the state of Missouri in support of the new abortion law. Being contested in the suit was the constitutionality of several provisions (parts or sections of the law). The provisions concerned various issues including the definition of viability, required consent before an abortion, use of a procedure called saline amniocentesis, record keeping by clinics, and the professional care given to an aborted fetus.

The District Court found in favor of the state of Missouri in all but one of the contested issues. Planned Parenthood and the two doctors then took their case to the U.S. Supreme Court. The Court agreed to hear the case so it could clear up questions concerning abortion procedures.

A Complex Ruling

Justice Harry A. Blackmun, who had written the Court's decision in *Roe v. Wade,* again delivered the Court's opinion, this time in a complex eight-part decision. The Court upheld some parts of the Missouri law but struck down others.

First, the Court dismissed one part that declared if an infant survived the abortion it would be taken from its parents and made a state ward. Blackmun pointed out that neither Planned Parenthood nor the two suing physicians really had anything to do with such a situation and, therefore, could not appropriately challenge that part of the law.

Next, Blackmun turned to the law's definition of viability, "that stage of fetal development when the life of the unborn child may be con-

Supporters on both side of the abortion issue find it to be a very emotional struggle. Reproduced by permission of the Corbis Corporation.

tinued indefinitely outside the womb by natural or artificial life-supportive systems." In *Roe* he had loosely defined "viable" as the point where the fetus could possibly live outside the mother's womb, using artificial aid if necessary. While stating that neither legislatures nor the courts should try to define what is essentially a technical medical concept, Blackmun nevertheless concluded Missouri's definition of viability was consistent with Roe and upheld the state's definition.

Three Consent Issues

Blackmun next tackled three separate consent issues in the Missouri law. First, Blackmun found constitutional the requirement that a woman must provide written consent (agreement) to the abortion before undergoing it. Blackmun reasoned abortion was a very stressful operation. Requiring written consent from the woman showed she was in control of the decision.

Secondly, Blackmun ruled that spousal consent (husband must agree to the abortion) was unconstitutional. When it comes to making the final decision about having an abortion, Blackmun concluded that "the woman who physically bears the child" should be the one to decide.

Thirdly, Blackmun found unconstitutional the requirement of parental consent for an unmarried minor's (under eighteen years of age) abortion during the first twelve weeks of pregnancy. Blackmun reasoned that constitutional rights do not "magically" appear when one turns eighteen. Furthermore, Blackmun believed the parent consent requirement "providing the parent with absolute power" would not necessarily "serve to strengthen the family unit" as argued by the state.

Three More Issues

The Missouri law prohibited use of saline amniocentesis, the injection of a saline (salt solution) fluid into the sac surrounding the fetus. The fluid causes the fetus to be almost immediately rejected by the mother's body. Blackmun denied this restriction because the procedure was the most commonly used abortion procedure and provided a high degree of safety for the mother. Blackmun stressed that termination of pregnancy by other available means was "more dangerous to the woman's health than the method outlawed."

Two sections of the law required detailed record keeping of all abortions performed. The law required these records be kept seven years.

HOW THE ABORTION DEBATE HAS CHANGED

At the beginning of the twenty-first century, the 1973 decision of *Roe v. Wade* legalizing abortion in the early stages of pregnancy before the unborn fetus could likely survive outside the womb still stood. Abortion debates remained as passionate as ever but generally concerned a "grab bag" of secondary issues and efforts by states to whittle away at a woman's access to abortion. The various issues at the state level included: requiring waiting periods and counseling for women seeking abortions, requiring parental consent, providing money for contraceptive education and family planning, and setting rules for protestors who attempt to blockade abortion clinics. Possibly the most emotional of all was the banning of "partial-birth abortion" which makes illegal certain abortion procedures performed during the last six months of pregnancy.

Congress likewise passed legislation prohibiting federal funding for abortions for various groups such as poor women enrolled in Medicaid, Native American women covered by Indian Health Services, and women in federal prisons, the military, and the Peace Corps. Meanwhile, technological developments have entered the abortion debates. For example, the new French-developed drug RU-486 with the scientific name of mifepristone, also known as the "morning after pill," induces abortion without surgical procedure. The Feminist Majority Foundation waged a nationwide campaign urging its approval. U.S. clinics began testing the drug by 1998.

Blackmun agreed that these requirements were "reasonably directed to the preservation of maternal [the mother's] health. . . " He, therefore, allowed both.

Lastly, Blackmun declared unconstitutional the law's requirement that physicians provide professional care to the fetus as if it was "intended to be born and not aborted" or face manslaughter charges.

Building on Abortion Law

Looking at many facets of abortion procedures, the Court found constitutional the provisions of the law dealing with the term viability, written consent of the woman having the abortion, and extensive record keeping by clinics. The Court decided four other parts were unconstitutional: (1) requirements for husband consent; (2) requirements for parental consent of an unmarried minor; (3) prohibition of the saline amniocentesis medical procedure; and, (4) requiring professional care of the aborted fetus under the threat of manslaughter against the doctor.

Most important was the decisions concerning consent. The Court's position on parental consent later shifted some. In *Belotti v. Baird* (1979) the Court again struck down a state law requiring consent of both parents or the court. The Court found the law unconstitutional because it took away a minor's ability to choose regardless of her best interests, or ability to make informed decisions. But, in *H.L.V. Matheson* (1981) and *Hodgson v. Minnesota* (1990), the Court upheld laws requiring a physician to notify parents of a minor before performing an abortion. The Court reasoned the laws required only notification rather than consent and were in the best interest of the minor.

In ***Planned Parenthood of Southeastern Pennsylvania v. Casey*** (1992) the Court placed strong restrictions on minors by requiring that they obtain informed consent from at least one parent or a court before receiving an abortion. In *Casey,* the Court still refused to require husband notification.

Suggestions for further reading

Boyle, Mary. *Re-Thinking Abortion: Psychology, Gender, Power, and the Law.* New York: Routledge, 1997.

Graber, Mark A. *Rethinking Abortion: Equal Choice, the Constitution and Reproductive Politics.* Princeton, NJ: Princeton University Press, 1999.

Rein, Mei Ling, Siegel, Mark A., and Nancy R. Jacobs, eds. *Abortion: An Eternal Social and Moral Issue.* Buffalo, NY: Information Plus, 1998.

Planned Parenthood of Southeastern Pennsylvania v. Casey 1992

Petitioner: Planned Parenthood of Southeastern Pennsylvania

Respondent: Robert P. Casey, Governor of Pennsylvania, and others

Petitioner's Claim: That restrictions on abortion in a Pennsylvania abortion law violated the Due Process Clause.

Chief Lawyer for Petitioner: Kathryn Kolbert

Chief Lawyer for Respondent: Ernest D. Preate, Jr., Attorney General of Pennsylvania

Justices for the Court: Harry A. Blackmun, Anthony M. Kennedy, Sandra Day O'Connor, David H. Souter, John Paul Stevens

Justices Dissenting: Chief Justice William H. Rehnquist, Antonin Scalia, Clarence Thomas, Byron R. White

Date of Decision: June 29, 1992

Decision: While reaffirming the earlier *Roe v. Wade* decision, the Court also declared Pennsylvania's Abortion Control Act law largely constitutional with some exceptions.

Significance: The decision resolved a national dispute over abortion by upholding the essentials of *Roe v. Wade* while permitting Pennsylvania to regulate abortions so long as the state did not place an undue burden on women.

Through the 1980s the U.S. Supreme Court, took on a decidedly more conservative viewpoint toward the abortion issue than the 1970s court that had decided ***Roe v. Wade*** legalizing abortion. President Ronald Reagan had appointed justices Sandra Day O'Connor, Antonin Scalia, and Anthony Kennedy to the Court and promoted William Rehnquist to Chief Justice. The changed Court was willing to allow states more authority to regulate abortion. In 1988 Justice Harry A. Blackmun, the author of the *Roe v. Wade* decision, shocked a University of Arkansas audience by bluntly asking, "Will *Roe v. Wade* go down the drain?" He answered his own question with a prediction. "There's a very distinct possibility that it will. . . You can count votes [of the current justices]."

An "Undue Burden"

In 1989, anticipated by Blackmun's words, the Supreme Court in *Webster v. Reproductive Health Services* came within one vote of overturning *Roe v. Wade.* In *Webster* the Court upheld Missouri's right to prohibit using public facilities for abortions, and to require doctors to test for fetal viability (if the unborn child had a possibility of living outside the womb). More importantly four justices, Rehnquist, Kennedy, Scalia, and Byron R. White, voted to completely overturn *Roe v. Wade.* O'Connor was most likely to be the fifth and deciding vote to overturn *Roe.* Yet, she cast her vote to uphold *Roe* suggesting another case would likely come along to more appropriately test *Roe.* However, O'Connor did present a new idea or standard, called "undue burden." She found that Missouri's law was not an "undue burden" (did not create major obstacles) on the right to choose an abortion and was, therefore, constitutionally acceptable.

Testing the Limits

With this new "undue burden" standard left largely undefined and with *Roe v. Wade* having come close to being overturned, *Webster* served as an invitation to state legislators to test just how far the Supreme Court would let them go in regulating abortions. Between 1989 and 1992 more than 700 bills regulating abortion in various ways were introduced across the country. The bills included requirements involving parental consent, husband consent, clinic abortion reporting, and clinic licensing. All were designed to push the limits of the Court's most recent abortion ruling. Some states, such as Louisiana, even attempted to make all abortions illegal, but without success.

Pennsylvania became the first in this wave to approve new abortion restrictions when it amended the Abortion Control Act originally enacted in 1982. Governor Robert P. Casey signed the amendment in November of 1989, only four months after the *Webster* decision. Provisions (parts) of the amended Abortion Control Act, which immediately came under fire by Pro-Choice groups (supporting abortion rights), required:

(1) a woman seeking an abortion to give her consent and be provided with state-written information twenty-four hours before the abortion;

(2) a minor to obtain consent from one of her parents or a court;

(3) a married woman to notify her husband of her intended abortion;

(5) reporting requirements for abortion clinics.

To Court

Before any of these provisions took effect, five abortion clinics, a physician representing himself, and a class of physicians who provided abortion services went to court to have the law declared unconstitutional. They contended the law violated a woman's right to choose an abortion

Both sides of the abortion argument express themselves with marches and demonstrations. Reproduced by permission of the Corbis Corporation.

free from state interference. All parties were combined into one case, *Planned Parenthood of Southeastern Pennsylvania v. Casey.*

The District Court ruled that all provisions being challenged were unconstitutional and stopped Pennsylvania from enforcing them. The Court of Appeals for the Third Circuit went almost entirely toward the opposite direction, upholding all the provisions except for the husband notification requirement. The stage was set for the U.S. Supreme Court to hear the case.

To The Heart of Roe v. Wade

Oral arguments began on April 22, 1992 bringing hundreds of thousands of Pro-Choice and Pro-Life (opposing abortions and *Roe v. Wade* decision) women and men to Washington, D.C. As demonstrators rallied outside, lawyers inside took their arguments straight to the heart of *Roe v. Wade.*

Attorneys challenging the Pennsylvania law took the dramatic position that *Roe v. Wade* must be upheld and the law struckdown. Kathryn Holbert, an experienced American Civil Liberties Union (ACLU) lawyer, explained the fundamental issue,

> **[Does] . . . government [have] the power to force a woman to continue or to end pregnancy against her will? Since . . . *Roe v. Wade*, a generation of American women [have been] . . . secure in the knowledge . . . their child-bearing decisions [are protected]. This landmark decision . . . not only protects rights of bodily integrity and autonomy [control over one's own body], but has enabled millions of women to participate fully and equally in society.**

On the other side, attorneys arguing for the Pennsylvania law joined by representatives of President George Bush's administration desired an overthrow of *Roe v. Wade.*

A Surprise Behind Closed Doors

Assuming that a majority of the other justices agreed with him, Chief Justice Rehnquist began to draft the Court's opinion to overturn *Roe.* Rehnquist knew he had Scalia, Clarence Thomas, and White with him. He assumed he also could count on Kennedy and most likely O'Connor.

REPRODUCTIVE RIGHTS

Marches occur all around the country both in support and against abortion. Reproduced by permission of the Corbis Corporation.

However, behind closed doors in a far corner of the Supreme Court building, Justice David H. Souter met with Kennedy and O'Connor. Unexpectedly, Kennedy changed his mind and in a compromise with O'Connor and Souter, the three fashioned an opinion leaving *Roe* intact while upholding the Pennsylvania law. Their private compromise derailed Rehnquist's work. According to *New York Times* reports, Rehnquist and Scalia "were stunned." They failed to gather the five votes needed to overthrow *Roe.* Souter, Kennedy, and O'Connor along with Blackmun and Justice John Paul Stevens voted to uphold the landmark decision.

The Essence of Roe

On Monday morning of June 29, 1992, observers, believing *Roe* would be overturned, were completely unprepared for the decision. The conservative-dominated Court defied all predictions. O'Connor, Kennedy, and Souter delivered the Court's opinion upholding "*Roe*'s essential holding," recognizing a woman's right to choose an abortion. The three thoroughly reviewed the *Roe* decision (see *Roe v. Wade*) and the principles it was based on. The justices affirmed [supported] that the right to have an abortion is indeed a liberty protected by the Due Process Clause of the Fourteenth Amendment. Souter stated, "No state shall 'deprive any person of life, liberty, or property, without due process of law.' The controlling word . . . is 'liberty'."

In a memorable quote, the three justices stated, "It is a promise of the Constitution that there is a realm of personal liberty which the government may not enter."

In Affirming Roe

O'Connor, Kennedy, and Souter used the doctrine of *stare decisis,* meaning courts respect precedents. They are slow to interfere with principles announced in former decisions. Their opinion referred to many former cases which collectively defined liberties not specifically written in the Constitution or Bill of Rights.

The justices rejected "*Roe*'s rigid trimester [based on stages of pregnancy] framework. . . " Instead, the "undue burden standard should be employed. An undue burden exists, and therefore a provision of law is invalid [unlawful], if its purpose or effect is to place substantial obstacles in the path of a woman seeking an abortion before the fetus [unborn child] attains viability."

Since *Roe* recognized a state's interest in the potential life of the fetus, the justices wrote that a state may impose requirements without causing an undue burden on the woman, such as a rquired waiting period during which the woman would receive further information on the process of abortion. With this, the justices upheld all of the provisions of the Pennsylvania Abortion Control Act except requiring the woman to notify her husband of the intended abortion. The Court considered this requirement an undue burden.

AMERICAN ATTITUDES ON ABORTION

Two questions asked by the Gallup Poll show how Americans's attitudes toward abortion have changed over the years. "With respect to the abortion issue, would you consider yourself to be pro-choice or pro-life?" In September of 1997, 56 percent of Americans regarded themselves as pro-choice and 33 percent pro-life. By Spring of 1999 the gap had closed to 48 percent pro-choice and 42 per cent pro-life.

"Do you think abortions should be legal under any circumstances, legal only under certain circumstances, or illegal in all circumstances?" In April of 1975, 21 percent of Americans answered yes to legal under any circumstance. Fifty-four percent chose legal only under certain circumstances while 22 percent answered illegal in all circumstances. By January of 2000, twenty-seven years after *Roe v. Wade,* the breakdown was 26 percent, 56 percent, and 15 percent. These percentages reflect a small increase in the number of persons supporting abortion under any circumstances.

In all, the Court reaffirmed the essential principles of *Roe* while also allowing states to impose requirements on the abortion process just so long as they do not *cause* an undue burden on the woman.

Reactions

Politically, both sides, Pro-Choice and Pro-Life, declared defeat. Pro-Choice asserted that state regulations such as mandatory waiting periods and parental consent would work together to weaken *Roe.* Furthermore, Pro-Choice groups realized they were only one vote away from seeing *Roe* overturned. On the other side, Pro-Life groups had clearly failed to have abortion made illegal.

For years after the *Casey* decision, the case was widely believed to be the most important abortion decision since *Roe.* It was viewed as a case where justices put respect for earlier Court decisions ahead of political pressures. Because the decision came from a court thought to be conservative, a woman's right to an abortion appeared to rest on somewhat firmer ground.

Suggestions for further reading

The Gallup Poll. [Online] http://www.gallup.com/poll/indicators/ind-abortion.asp (Accessed on July 31, 2000).

The National Abortion and Reproductive Rights Action League Foundation (NARAL). [Online] Website: http://www.naral.org (Accessed on July 31, 2000).

National Right to Life Committee, Inc. [Online] Website: http://www.nrlc.org (Accessed on July 31, 2000).

"Roe v. Wade," A Reader. *Belmont, CA: Wadsworth Publications, 1998.*

Rein, Mei Ling, Siegel, Mark A., and Nancy R. Jacobs, eds. *Abortion: An Eternal Social and Moral Issue.* Buffalo, NY: Information Plus, 1998.

The Fourteenth Amendment to the U.S. Constitution has been key to the protection of the civil rights of immigrants, gays and lesbians, and the disabled. The amendment provides that no state shall deny "any person within its jurisdiction [geographical area over which it has authority] the equal protection of the law." This is the Equal Protection Clause. Likewise, the Fourteenth Amendment provides that no state shall deprive any person of life, liberty, or prosperity "without due process of law." Due process means an individual, if charged with a crime, must have fair legal hearings. Many legal actions involving immigrants, gays and lesbians, and the disabled are brought under the Fourteenth Amendment. Resulting court decisions reflect the morals and always changing social standards of a diverse nation.

Immigrant's Rights

"Give us your tired, your poor, your huddled masses yearning to breathe free." Invitation on the Statute of Liberty in New York City.

According to the American Civil Liberties Union (ACLU), some fifty-five million immigrants have come to America from its birth to the end of the twentieth century. Except for Native Americans, all people in the United States have immigrant ancestors, or are present-day immigrants. The United States has been shaped by immigrants and the inscription on the Statute of Liberty testifies to the country's commitment to immigration.

Aliens are foreign born individuals who have not become U.S. citizens through naturalization, the process by which a person becomes a U.S. citizen. Aliens are classified in several ways including non-immigrant and immigrant, and documented (legal alien) and undocumented (illegal alien). Non-immigrants do not intend to settle permanently in the United States. Examples are students, vacationers, and foreign government personnel. Persons granted immigrant status, on the other hand, intend to live and work in the United States and become U.S. citizens.

Immigrants are entitled to many of the same rights as those enjoyed by native-born U.S. citizens. Although they cannot vote or hold federal elective office until they become citizens, the Constitution and Bill of Rights generally apply. The Equal Protection Clause of the Fourteenth Amendments guarantees "equal protection of the laws" to any person living in the United States, citizen or not. States have often passed laws and regulations that violate immigrants' rights and the Equal Protection Clause generally has protected immigrants from these laws.

Even undocumented or illegal aliens (those who have not entered the country legally), once on American soil have some rights under the Constitution. To enter the country illegally is a crime punishable by deportation (forced to leave the country). However, the U.S. Supreme Court, as early as 1903 in *Yamataya v. Fisher* has ruled repeatedly that illegal immigrants may have the right to a hearing that satisfies the Due Process Clause of the Fourteenth Amendment.

Immigration Law

All immigrants are subject to federal immigration law which serves as the nation's gate keeper: who enters, for how long, who may stay, and who may leave. The U.S. Congress has total authority over all immigration law. Although this authority has a long controversial history dating back to the second half of the nineteenth century, the authority was solidified in 1952 with the passage of the Immigration and Nationality Act (INA). INA became the basic source of immigration law. The INA was amended many times as Congress' preferences evolved into a patchwork of regulations reflecting who was wanted and who was not.

Beginning in 1986 Congress passed major new legislation which followed two lines of thought: (1) the need to stop illegal immigration, and (2) the need to make laws more fair for legal immigrants. The Immigration Reform and Control Act (IRCA) of 1986 set up requirements aimed at controlling the entry of illegal immigrants. The Illegal Immigration Reform and Immigrant Responsibility Act of 1996 contained measures to prevent illegal immigration from increasing and to speed up deportation of those illegal immigrants caught. On the other hand the Immigration Act of 1990 dealt with establishing limits on the number of legal immigrants admitted each year and created ways to admit more immigrants from underrepresented countries.

U.S. Supreme Court Cases and Immigrants

Many U.S. Supreme Court cases have protected immigrants from discriminatory state and local laws and enforced the idea that only Congress can enact immigrant law. In ***Yick Wo v. Hopkins*** (1886), the Court ruled that the Fourteenth Amendment's equal protection of the laws applied to immigrants as well as citizens. The decision rejected a San Francisco law clearly discriminating against Chinese. In 1915 in ***Truax v. Raich,*** the Court overruled an Arizona law and established the right to earn a living as a basic freedom that could not be denied to immigrants.

The Court's stance changed a bit in the late 1970s and 1980s. The Court upheld New York's restrictive policies denying teacher credentials to alien immigrants in *Ambach v. Norwick* (1979). It then upheld a California law preventing alien immigrants from serving as probation officers in *Cabell v. Chavey-Salido* (1982). On the other hand, the Court ruled in a 1982 Texas case, *Plyler v. Doe,* that children of illegal aliens have the right to attend public schools.

The mid- to late-1990s saw more state attempts to limit immigrants' rights as California voters passed the controversial Proposition 187 in 1994. Proposition 187 restricted public services, such as public school education and non-emergency health care, to illegal aliens, and required immigrant students to learn English. Congress itself passed legislation to cut social benefits such as Medicaid (health insurance) and Supplementary Security Income (additional income payments) in 1996. However, the Court took steps in *League of United Latin American Citizens v. Pete Wilson* (1997) and *Sutich v. Callahan* (1997) to restore such services.

Rights of the Disabled

Roughly forty-three million people in the United States possess one or more physical or mental disabilities. Disability was first defined in Section 504 of the Rehabilitation Act of 1973 as, "any person who has a physical or mental impairment which substantially limits one or more major life activities."

A major life activity is a basic function which the average person can perform with little or no difficulty, such as caring for oneself, walking, seeing, hearing, speaking, learning, and working. Examples of physical impairments are deafness, blindness, speech impairments, and crippling conditions. It also includes such diseases such as cancer, arthritis, and heart disease which have progressed to a point to limit a person's basic functioning. In *Bragdon v. Abbott* (1998) the U.S. Supreme Court ruled that infection with HIV virus (AIDS) constitutes a disability. Mental impairments include mental illness, severe emotional disturbances, traumatic brain injury, and specific learning disabilities, such as the condition commonly known as dyslexia. In every case, the disability must limit an individual's major life activity.

Society has often isolated and restricted persons with disabilities. Disabled individuals have a long history of unequal treatment and occupy an inferior status in society due to characteristics beyond their control. Disabled persons are often politically powerless and unable to pursue legal avenues to counter the discrimination. Rights of disabled persons were established in the second half of the twentieth century though Congressional legislation and in the courts.

Cases and Laws—Laws and Cases

Case decisions and legislative acts (laws) mixed together to develop the rights of disabled persons. Education of the disabled was often a driving force behind cases and laws. In 1971, *Pennsylvania Association for Retarded Citizens (PARC) v. The Commonwealth of Pennsylvania* established the right to a free public education for all children with mental retardation. *Mills v. Board of Education of the District of Columbia* established the right of every child to an education full of equal opportunities. Lack of funds was not an acceptable excuse for lack of educational opportunity. A landmark law extending civil rights to people with disabilities is the Rehabilitation Act of 1973. Section 504 of this law states, "no otherwise qualified handicapped individual shall, solely by reason of his handicap, be excluded from the participation in, be denied the benefits of, or be subjected to discrimination in any program or activity receiving federal financial assistance (monetary funds)." The court orders of the cases decided in 1971 and 1972 are basically contained in Section 504, the name by which the law is commonly referred to. This law, worded almost identically to the Civil Rights Act of 1964 which prohibited discrimination on the basis of race, color, or national origin, expanded opportunities for children and adults with disabilities in education and employment.

Closely following Section 504 was Education for All Handicapped Children Act (EHA) in 1975. This law required a free and appropriate public education for ALL children regardless of their disability. Categories of disability under EHA include specific learning disabilities making up over fifty percent of students identified as having a disability, speech impairments, mental retardation, serious emotional disturbances, and all physical impairments.

Various cases, such as *Board of Education v. Rowley* (1982), heard in the U.S. Supreme Court, further defined an "appropriate" education. Also, persons with mental retardation recorded victories in ***O'Connor v. Donaldson*** (1975), *Youngberg v. Rome* (1982), and ***City of Cleburne v. Cleburne Living Center*** (1985). The first two cases established that persons with mental retardation indeed have constitutional rights. In *City of Cleburne* the Court ruled that communities cannot use a discriminatory residential zoning law to prevent establishment of group homes for persons with mental retardation.

Two major pieces of legislation were passed in 1990. The Education of the Handicapped Act Amendments of 1990 changed the name of EHA to Individuals with Disabilities Education Act (IDEA). IDEA was a common term used throughout educational circles at the end of the twentieth century. This act, in addition to expanding services for the disabled, added autism and traumatic brain injury to the list of disabling conditions. In 1999 Attention Deficit Hyperactive Disorder (ADHD) was added as a disabling condition.

The second major piece of 1990 legislation was the sweeping Americans with Disabilities Act (ADA). Congress passed ADA to provide a clear and comprehensive national order for elimination of discrimination against individuals with disabilities. It was built on the foundation of Section 504 and extended coverage into the private employment sector not previously subject to federal law. ADA also extended civil rights protection into to all public services, public accommodations, transportation, and telecommunications.

Major provisions of ADA include: (a) private employers with fifteen or more employees may not refuse to hire or promote a person because of his disability alone; (b) all new vehicles, such as buses purchased by public services, must have handicapped access; (c) public accommodations such as hotels, restaurants, and malls, must be accessible and must not refuse service to persons with disabilities; and, (d) telephone companies must offer services for the deaf.

Gay and Lesbian Rights

Gay and lesbian organizations seek legal and social equality for gay men and lesbians in the United States. The terms gay and lesbian refer to people who are sexually attracted to and sexually prefer people of the same sex. The sexual preference of an individual for one sex or the other is called a person's sexual orientation. "Sexual orientation" is the phrase generally used when crafting legislation or making claims of discrimination concerning gay and lesbian rights. While the term gay can refer to either male or female, gay is generally used to refer to men. Lesbian always refers to women. Homosexual is a term which refers to either gay men or lesbians.

In the United States, through the 1950s gay men and lesbians kept their sexual orientation a secret as homosexual behavior has a long history of being considered a crime. Hiding their sexual orientation was described by the phrase "in the closet." Encouraged by the 1960s Civil Rights Movement involving black Americans and women and spurred in 1969 by a violent incident in New York City known as Stonewall, the homosexual culture began to come out of the closet and openly work for equality. The gay right movement was born.

Sexual Activity as a Crime

Since the eighteenth century colonial period, sodomy (the sexual acts of homosexuals) has been a crime, generally a felony (serious crime). Until 1961 all states outlawed sodomy. The gay rights movement made the repeal (abolishment) of sodomy laws a primary goal.

Handing the movement a setback, in 1986 the U.S. Supreme Court ruled in ***Bowers v. Hardwicks*** that homosexuals have no right to engage in sodomy even when it is performed in private and between consenting (willing) adults. The Court found state laws prohibiting such activity do not violate constitutional rights to privacy. Although controversial, the ruling would be the Court's only statement on gay and lesbian rights for almost a decade.

Serving in the Military

Gay men and lesbians fought legal battles in the 1980s and 1990s to serve in the nation's armed forces from which they had traditionally been banned. Historically, the disclosure of homosexual orientation led to discharge. Defense Department data from 1980 to 1990 showed that the various service branches discharged approximately 1500 people each year due to sexual orientation. In 1993 the newly elected President Bill Clinton, determined to keep a campaign pledge, attempted to remove the military ban against gays. However, many senior military officials strongly objected to Clinton's proposal. Clinton developed a compromise plan known as "don't ask, don't tell." Congress wrote the policy into law in September of 1993. "Don't ask, don't tell" prohibits the military from asking about the sexual orientation of its military persons without a specific reason. Two 1994 Court cases dealt with the issue of discharging personnel when they made known their sexual orientation, *Meinhold v. United States Department of Defense* and *Cammermeyer v. Aspin.* The first case to test the constitutionality of the "don't ask, don't tell" policy was *McVeigh v. Cohen* (1998). In each case the courts ruled to reinstate the discharged individuals.

Legalizing Gay and Lesbian Relationships

A major concern of many gay men and lesbians is the legal recognition of their relationships. A same-sex marriage is not treated the same legally as a marriage between a man and a woman. Examples of legal benefits which do not extend to same-sex relationship are survivor benefits when one partner dies, health insurance, and custody of children. The AIDS epidemic makes health insurance a vital issue to the gay and lesbian groups.

Recognition of same-sex marriage has been rejected by the courts until 1996 in *Baehr v. Miike.* The First Circuit Court of Hawaii ruled that denial of a marriage contract to same-sex partners violated the Equal Protection Clause of the Hawaii Constitution. The U.S. Congress, believing that same-sex marriages would soon become legal in Hawaii moved quickly to pass the Defense of Marriage Act (DOMA) in 1996. DOMA defines "marriage" and "spouse" to include only partners of the opposite sex and permits states to bar legal recognition of same-sex marriages performed in other states. A major breakthrough came late in 1999 when the Vermont Supreme Court ruled that same-sex couples should have the same state constitutional protections and rights as traditional marriages.

Issues at State and Local Levels

Gay and lesbian organizations have worked for legislation at the state and local level to ban discrimination based on sexual orientation in housing, banking, and employment. In 1998 ten states had such laws. They are California, Connecticut, Hawaii, Massachusetts, Minnesota, New Hampshire, New Jersey, Rhode Island, Vermont, and Wisconsin.

Despite these successes for gay men and lesbians, those opposed to the social and legal equality for homosexuals created a political backlash in various states during the 1990s. Calling homosexuality abnormal and perverse, the Oregon Citizens Alliance placed a voter referendum (proposed law) on the 1992 Oregon ballot. The referendum would have prohibited civil rights protections for gays and lesbians and required local governments and schools to discourage homosexuality. The referendum was defeated with fifty-seven voting against it.

In Colorado, the state legislature took steps to ban what they saw as a growing legal tolerance of homosexuals. They passed an amendment to the state constitution prohibiting the state or any local government from passing laws to protect the civil rights of gays and lesbians. In the first gay rights case to reach the U.S. Supreme Court since *Bowers* in 1986, the Court found in ***Romer v. Evans*** (1996) the amendment unconstitutional. Writing for the Court, Justice Anthony M. Kennedy commented the only purpose of the Colorado amendment was to make homosexuals "unequal to everyone else. This Colorado cannot do." The decision caused emotional debate predicting future legal battles over gay and lesbian rights.

Future Rights Issues

As time passes, different groups and different issues concerning the groups discussed above will continuously come to the attention of the public, legislatures, and the courts.

Suggestions for further reading

Clendinen, Dudley, and Adam Nagourney. *Out of Good: The Struggle to Build a Gay Rights Movement in America.* New York: Simon & Schuster, 1999.

Cozic, Charles P. *Illegal Immigration: Opposing Viewpoints.* San Diego, CA: Greenhaven Press, Inc., 1997.

Lambda Legal Defense and Educational Fund. [Online] Website: http://www.lambdalegal.org (Accessed on July 31, 2000).

National Gay & Lesbian Task Force. [Online] Website: http://www.ngltf.org (Accessed on July 31, 2000).

The International Dyslexia Association (formerly the Orton Dyslexia Society). [Online] Website: http://www.interdys.org (Accessed on July 31, 2000).

Truax v. Raich
1915

Appellants: William Truax, Sr., Wiley E. Jones, W.G. Gilmore

Appellee: Mike Raich

Appellants' Claim: That an alien had no legal right to sue the state of Arizona or prevent enforcement of Arizona's Anti Alien Act.

Chief Lawyers for Appellants: Wiley E. Jones, Leslie C. Hardy, George W. Harben

Chief Lawyers for Appellee: Alexander Britton, Evans Browne, Francis W. Clements

Justices for the Court: Louis D. Brandeis, William Rufus Day, Oliver Wendell Holmes, Charles E. Hughes, Joseph McKenna, Mahlon Pitney, Willis Van Devanter, Edward D. White

Justices Dissenting: James C. McReynolds

Date of Decision: November 1, 1915

Decision: Ruled in favor of Raich by finding that Arizona's law denied him his Fourteenth Amendment right to equal protection of the laws and was therefore unconstitutional and unenforceable.

Significance: By declaring Arizona's law unconstitutional, the Supreme Court identified the right to earn a living as a basic freedom protected by the Fourteenth Amendment. The decision reaffirmed the Yick Wo decision that the Equal Protection Clause applied to any person, citizen or alien, living within the United States and that only the U.S. Congress could enact immigration law.

Between 1870 and 1920, twenty-six million people arrived at immigration stations in New York City. Ships as far as the eye could see would be lined up for days in New York Harbor until a space to dock opened at the immigrant processing center on Ellis Island. After leaving Ellis Island many headed for New York but others bought tickets for Chicago, Cleveland, St. Louis, and other cities throughout the United States. All were searching for jobs and a new better life in America.

Equal Protection for Immigrants

Only the U.S. Congress has the authority to determine who may enter the United States. Once an immigrant is admitted to the United States, he or she is entitled to equal protection of the law. The Equal Protection Clause is found in the Fourteenth Amendment to the U.S. Constitution and provides that no state shall "deprive any person of life, liberty, or property, without due process of law [fair legal proceedings]; nor deny to any person within its jurisdiction [geographical area over which a government has authority] the equal protection of the laws." Equal protection means that persons or groups of persons in similar situations must be treated equally by the laws.

Extension of equal protection to new immigrants or aliens (citizen or subject of a foreign country living in the United States) was firmly established in the Supreme Court case ***Yick Wo v. Hopkins*** (1886). The Court ruled that Equal Protection Clause applied "to all persons within the territorial jurisdiction, without regard to any differences of race, of color, or of nationality [referring to country where a person was born]." Beginning with *Yick Wo* the Court generally required states to show a very important reason or need for any law which applied one way to aliens and a different way to citizens. If no important reason was shown, the law would be found unconstitutional.

Also, in *Yick Wo* the Court described a person's right to earn a living as "essential to the enjoyment of life" and protected by the Fourteenth Amendment. Thirty years later the Court again showed support for the *Yick Wo* decision in the 1915 case of *Truax v. Raich.*

Mike Raich and Arizona's Anti-Alien Employment Act

In December of 1914 Mike Raich, an Austrian native living in Arizona, was in danger of losing his job as a restaurant cook. A state-wide vote by

Arizona citizens had led to the adoption of "an Act to Protect the Citizens of the United States in Their Employment Against Noncitizens of the United States, in Arizona, and to Provide Penalties and Punishment for the Violation Thereof." Shortened to the Anti-Alien Employment Act, the act required all businesses with five or more employees to hire a workforce at least 80 percent native-born American. Penalties subjected violators to not less than a $100 fine and thirty days imprisonment.

Restaurant owner, William Truax, Sr., had nine employees, including Raich. Seven of them were not native-born Americans. Fearing the penalties, Truax informed Raich that he would be fired as soon as the Anti-Alien Act became law. His firing would happen solely because he was an alien.

On December 15, 1914 the act was signed into law. A day later Raich filed a suit in Arizona's U.S. District Court against Arizona Attorney General Wiley E. Jones, Cochise County Attorney W.G. Gilmore, and Truax. Raich charged the act denied his Fourteenth Amendment right to equal protection under the law. The court issued a temporary order preventing Truax from firing Raich.

Many hopeful immigrants spent weeks on ships to reach the shores of America and the promise of better lives. Courtesy of the Library of Congress.

Gilmore, Jones, and Truax asked for dismissal of Raich's suit against them. But on January 7, 1915 a federal district court in San Francisco ruled Arizona's Anti Alien Act unconstitutional and, therefore, unenforceable. Gilmore, Jones, and Truax appealed to the U.S. Supreme Court which agreed to hear the case.

A Direct Violation

Justice Charles Evans Hughes, writing for the majority in an 8–1 decision, focused on whether or not the act violated the Fourteenth Amendment. Hughes explained that Raich, being a lawful inhabitant of Arizona, was "entitled under the Fourteenth Amendment to the equal protection of its laws." Furthermore, referring to the due process and equal protection clauses of the Fourteenth Amendment and quoting from the *Yick Wo v. Hopkins ruling,* Hughes wrote,

> **The description, 'any person within its jurisdiction,' as it has frequently been held, includes aliens. 'These provisions [clauses] . . . are universal in their application, to all persons within the territorial jurisdiction, without regard to any differences of race, of color, or of nationality; and the equal protection of the laws is a pledge of the protection of equal laws.**

Hughes noted that the Arizona act plainly described its purpose in its lengthy title, "an act to protect the citizens of the United States in their employment against noncitizens [aliens] of the United States, in Arizona." The act clearly separated citizens and aliens into two groups and applied the law differently to each. Raich was forced out of his job "as a cook in a restaurant, simply because he is an alien." The firing directly violated the Fourteenth Amendment's equal protections which extend to aliens.

Clearly, Hughes stated, "It requires no argument to show that the right to work for a living in the common occupations of the community is of the very essence of the personal freedom and opportunity that it was the purpose of the [Fourteenth] Amendment to secure. If this could be refused solely upon the ground of race or nationality, the [Fourteenth Amendment's guarantee of] equal protection of the laws would be a barren form of words [meaningless]."

Hughes continued that a person "cannot live where they cannot work" because work is essential to their livelihood. Therefore, the act

RIGHTS OF IMMIGRANTS, GAYS AND LESBIANS, AND THE DISABLED

was also invalid because it dictated where aliens may or may not live by denying them opportunities to work in the state of Arizona. Only Congress, not states, may regulate where aliens may live and enact immigration law.

A See Saw Court

The *Truax* ruling had a rocky road ahead as suspicions and prejudice against immigrants grew during and after World War I. In 1927 the Court appeared to abandon its 1915 *Truax* decision in the *Clarke v. Deckebach* ruling. While the Court still prohibited "plainly irrational discrimination against aliens," the Court ruled that some instances could occur when a state would have a good reason to deny rights to aliens. In *Clarke,* the Court allowed Cincinnati to prohibit aliens from operating pool halls because the aliens might operate them in an unacceptable manner.

Approximately twenty years later in *Takaahashi v. Fish and Game Commission* (1948) the Court returned to its position that earning a living was a liberty that could not be denied an individual just because he was an alien. Supporting aliens' rights further in 1971, *Graham v. Richardson*

Many immigrants found work in the agricultural industry in the early 1900s. Reproduced by permission of the Corbis Corporation.

DO IMMIGRANTS TAKE JOBS AWAY FROM AMERICANS?

Persons granted legal immigrant status intend to live and work in the United States and become U.S. citizens. A common concern among the U.S. public is that these newly arrived immigrants are taking jobs away from existing U.S. citizens. However, by the end of the twentieth century many studies such as those by the Rand Corporation, the Council of Economic Advisors, the National Research Council, and the Urban Institute concluded that immigrants do not have a negative effect on earnings or the employment opportunities of native-born Americans. In fact, immigrants create more jobs than they fill. The studies show that immigrants are more likely to be self-employed than native Americans and start new businesses. Eighteen percent of new small businesses, which account for 80 percent of new jobs available each year in the United States, are started by immigrants. Immigrants also raise the productivity of already established businesses, invest capital (money) in businesses, and spend dollars on consumer goods. Therefore, there is a strong argument that immigrants are good for the U.S. job market and all Americans benefit from their arrival.

signaled that equal protection cases involving aliens would be subjected to the same thorough review that racial discrimination cases receive.

However, the Court has viewed some occupations as requiring that employees be citizens. In *Ambach v. Norwick* (1979) the Court, in a 5-4 decision, upheld a New York law prohibiting aliens who refused to apply for U.S. citizenship from teaching in public schools. Likewise, in *Cabell v. Chavez* (1982), another 5-4 Court decision upheld a California requirement that all law enforcement personnel be U.S. citizens.

Suggestions for further reading

American Civil Liberties Union. [Online] Website: http://www.aclu.org (Accessed July 31, 2000).

American Immigration Lawyers Association. [Online] Website: http://www.aila.org (Accessed July 31, 2000).

Fiss, Owen M. *A Community of Equals: The Constitutional Protection of New Americans.* Boston: Beacon Press, 1999.

U.S. Immigration and Naturalization Service. [Online] Website: http://www.ins.usdoj.gov (Accessed July 31, 2000).

O'Connor v. Donaldson 1975

Petitioner: Dr. J. B. O'Connor

Respondent: Kenneth Donaldson

Petitioner's Claim: That O'Connor, representing the Florida State Hospital at Chattahoochee, had violated Donaldson's constitutional rights by keeping him in custody for a supposed mental illness against his will for nearly fifteen years.

Chief Lawyer for Petitioner: Raymond W. Gearney

Chief Lawyer for Respondent: Bruce J. Ennis, Jr.

Justices for the Court: Harry A. Blackmun, William J. Brennan, Jr., Chief Justice Warren E. Burger, William O. Douglas, Thurgood Marshall, Lewis F. Powell, Jr., William H. Rehnquist, Potter Stewart, Byron R. White

Justices Dissenting: None

Date of Decision: June 26, 1975

Decision: Ruled that Donaldson possessed certain constitutional rights which had been violated, and that he could gather damages from those individuals who had violated his rights.

Significance: The decision affirmed that mentally ill persons have constitutional rights which must be protected. This recognition paved the way for people with mental illness to live in their communities rather than institutions.

Society has often isolated and confined persons with mental illness. Likewise, the U.S. mental health system has a long history of unequal treatment of mentally ill individuals. Occupying an inferior status in U.S. culture due to personal characteristics beyond their control, they have commonly been politically powerless, unable to pursue legal paths to establish their own rights. Many persons with mental illness had been subjected to a system which often warehoused them in state mental institutions for years, frequently offering no psychiatric therapy. Non-dangerous persons were likely to be housed with the dangerous in overcrowded conditions. Many were committed (ordered confinement for a mentally ill or incompetent person) to institutions against their will for an indefinite (no specific end) time period and denied basic constitutional civil rights (rights given and defined by laws). An early advocate (one who defends or argues for a cause for another person) for the rights of the mentally ill, Bruce Ennis, Jr., commented in 1973 in "The Legal Rights of the Mentally Handicapped" that mentally-ill individuals were "our country's most profoundly victimized [severely cheated] minorities."

During the 1960s and 1970s many minority groups began to fight for their civil rights. Black Americans, women, and gays and lesbians all worked to halt the discrimination they had faced daily. In response, Congress passed America's most significant law to ban discrimination, the Civil Rights Act of 1964. Within this social activist period, advocates for the mentally ill and those mentally-ill persons who were able began to challenge the mental health system. Just as other minority groups had done, they chose to use the courts to improve the mental health system and to protect their civil rights. Amid a flurry of lawsuits was the case of Kenneth Donaldson, a case that would make it all the way to the U.S. Supreme Court.

The Long Commitment of Kenneth Donaldson

A forty-eight year old man from Philadelphia, Kenneth Donaldson traveled in 1956 to Florida to visit his aging parents. In conversation with his parents, he mentioned that he believed one of his neighbors in Philadelphia might be poisoning his food. Worried that his son suffered from paranoid delusions (a tendency of a person toward excessive suspiciousness or distrustfulness), Donaldson's father asked the court for a sanity hearing. Sanity hearings are held to determine if a person is mentally

Bruce Ennis, Jr., represented Kenneth Donaldson in front of the Supreme Court.
Reproduced by permission of AP/Wide World Photos.

healthy. Upon evaluation, Donaldson was diagnosed with "paranoid schizophrenia" (disorders in feelings, thoughts, and conduct). The court committed Donaldson, who was not represented by legal council at his commitment hearing, to the Florida mental health facility at Chattahoochee. This commitment was involuntary and of a civil (no criminal action involved) nature.

Even though Donaldson had never been dangerous to himself or others, he was placed with dangerous criminals at the Florida hospital. To make matters worse his ward, with over one thousand males, was severely understaffed. There was only one doctor, who happened to be an obstetrician (delivers babies), one nurse to hand out medications, and no psychiatrists or counselors. Donaldson never received any treatment except what the hospital called "milieu therapy." Milieu therapy in Donaldson's case translated into being kept in a room with sixty criminally committed patients. Donaldson's confinement would last fourteen and a half years.

Beginning immediately upon confinement, Donaldson, on his own behalf, fought to speak to a lawyer and demand to have his case reheard. Believing he should be freed, Donaldson argued that he did not have a lawyer at his commitment hearing; that he was neither mentally ill nor dangerous; and, that if he was in fact mentally ill, he was not offered any treatment. Later, Donaldson would argue that he had not been released even when two different sources promised to take responsibility for his care.

First, an old college friend had sought to have the state release Donaldson to his care and, later in 1963, a half-way home for the mentally ill in Minnesota had agreed to assume responsibility for him. Apparently for no cause, the hospital rejected both offers. Although the hospital staff had the power to release a patient such as Donaldson, Dr. J. B. O'Connor, the hospital's superintendent during most of this period, refused the release. O'Connor stated that Donaldson would have been unable to make a "successful adjustment outside the institution," although at the eventual trial O'Connor could not recall the basis for that conclusion. It was a few months after O'Connor's retirement that Donaldson finally gained his release.

Released!

Immediately upon his release Donaldson found a responsible job as a hotel clerk. He had no problem keeping his job or living on his own. In February of 1971, almost fifteen years after first being committed, Donaldson brought a lawsuit in the U.S. District Court for the Northern District of Florida against O'Connor and other hospital staff. Donaldson charged "that they had intentionally [on purpose] and maliciously [intent of committing an unlawful act] deprived him of his constitutional right to liberty [freedom]." The Fourteenth Amendment states that no state may "deprive any person of life, liberty, or property, without due process of law [fair legal hearing]." Dr. O'Connor's defense was that he acted in good faith in confining Donaldson since a Florida state law, which had since been repealed, had "authorized indefinite custodial [to protect and maintain confinement] of the 'sick' even if they were not treated and their release would not be harmful. . . " The court found in favor of Donaldson, awarding him monetary damages (money payment for wrongs against an individual). The Court of Appeals for the Fifth Circuit affirmed the ruling. O'Connor appealed to the U.S. Supreme Court which agreed to hear the case. The advocate Bruce Ennis, Jr. represented Donaldson.

Justice At Last

In a unanimous (9-0) decision, the Supreme Court ruled that Donaldson possessed certain rights and that he could be awarded damages from individuals who had taken those rights away. Justice Potter Stewart, writing for the Court, viewed the case as raising a "single, relatively simple, but nonetheless important question concerning every man's constitutional right to liberty" guaranteed by the Fourteenth Amendment.

COMMITMENT

Commitment of mentally ill or incompetent persons against their will (involuntary) has long involved weighing the person's civil rights with the rights of society to be protected from possibly dangerous individuals. Each state has its own laws for involuntary commitment. These laws define the types of mental illnesses and conditions that can lead to institutional commitment and those that can not. Those conditions generally excluded are drug or alcohol addition, mental retardation, and epilepsy.

In most states "dangerousness" to oneself or others is one key factor to consider. But there usually must be other closely related factors as well such as a persistently disabling condition which prevents responsible decisions. Also, hospitalization must not restrain the individual's liberties more than is really needed.

Involuntary commitment of persons convicted of a crime raise many constitutional problems. If a person is acquitted (found not guilty) of a crime by reason of insanity, his length of commitment for treatment is normally determined by the rate of his recovery. Many times this could lead to much longer confinement than if found guilty and sentenced in the first place. Cases of persons convicted of sex-related crimes are especially difficult. Courts have ruled that possibility of future crimes is not a reason to take away a person's freedom. However, under public pressure, state have passed laws allowing commitment of sexually dangerous persons if they seem likely to commit future criminal acts. Challenges are sure to follow.

First, the Court ruled on the authority of the state to hospitalize mentally ill persons. Ruling that diagnosis of mental illness does not alone justify confining individuals against their will for an indefinite period of time, Justice Stewart wrote,

> **A State cannot constitutionally confine . . . a non-dangerous individual who is capable of surviving safely in freedom by himself or with the help of willing and responsible family members or friends.**

The ruling applied only to involuntarily civilly committed patients who were not a danger to themselves or others.

Secondly, the Court held that state hospital officials could be held liable (responsible for) for damages if their actions were carried out "maliciously . . . or oppressively [unreasonably severe]" and with the knowledge that their actions violated a person's constitutional rights.

Third and most significantly, the Court decision recognized the necessity of protecting the rights of mentally ill individuals. However, the Court left unsettled the issue of whether a person has a constitutional right to treatment if they are hospitalized for mental illness. Future cases would have to resolve that issue.

The *O'Connor* ruling encouraged others to challenge the mental health system when the civil rights of the mentally ill were abused. The decision also paved the way for many individuals suffering from mental illness to be able to remain within their local communities rather than being institutionalized.

Suggestions for further reading

Melton, Gary B., Philip M. Lyons, and Willis J. Spaulding. *No Place to Go: The Civil Commitment of Minors (Children and Law).* Lincoln, NE: University of Nebraska Press, 1998.

National Alliance for the Mentally Ill. [Online] Website: http://www.nami.org (Accessed on July 31, 2000).

Winick, Bruce, Jr. *The Right to Refuse Mental Health Treatment (Law & Public Policy: Psychology and the Social Sciences).* American Psychological Association, 1997.

Plyler v. Doe
1982

Appellants: J. and R. Doe, certain named and unnamed undocumented alien children

Appellees: James L. Plyler and others

Appellants' Claim: That a Texas law withholding public funds from local school districts for educating children not legally present in the United States and encouraging school districts to deny these children enrollment is constitutionally valid.

Chief Lawyers for Appellants: Peter D. Roos, Peter A. Schey

Chief Lawyers for Appellees: John C. Hardy, Richard L. Arnett

Justices for the Court: Harry A. Blackmun, William J. Brennan, Jr., Thurgood Marshall, Lewis F. Powell, Jr., John Paul Stevens

Justices Dissenting: Chief Justice Warren E. Burger, Sandra Day O'Connor, William Rehnquist, Byron R. White

Date of Decision: June 15, 1982

Decision: Ruled in favor of Doe (the illegal alien children) by finding that the Texas law violated the Fourteenth Amendment's Equal Protection Clause and struck it down.

Significance: With this decision, states could no longer deny public education to children only because they were illegal aliens. The Court's opinion provided an important statement on the importance of education to American society.

The school on the Texas-Mexico border is known as a "gate school." Behind the playground is a chain-link fence dividing the United States from Mexico. From the playground children and teachers can see a Border Patrol jeep, its officer continuously peering through binoculars down along the border and school grounds. The officer is waiting and watching for yet another individual or family, desperate for a better way of life, to attempt to illegally (without permission) cross the border into Texas. Of the predominately Hispanic children at the gate school, the principal says it is difficult to tell who is documented (legal) or undocumented (illegal). To the principal it does not matter. She believes that a school should educate all children living within the United States boundaries and she intends to do just that. She is supported by the landmark U.S. Supreme Court ruling of *Plyler v. Doe* (1982) which ended years of controversy by ruling that states have the responsibility to educate children of undocumented aliens.

Equally Protected

Although the United States has restricted entry of foreigners into its borders since the late nineteenth century, countless individuals and families have illegally made their way into America. Border states like Texas, New Mexico, Arizona, and California have seen the largest arrival of "illegal aliens." Illegal aliens are citizens of a foreign country living in America without permission. Illegal entry into the United States is a crime and persons who unlawfully enter are subject to deportation (sending an alien back to the country from which he came). However, once in the United States illegal aliens share some of the same rights as any legal alien or U.S. citizen. One of these rights is equal protection of the laws provided in the Fourteenth Amendment's Equal Protection Clause. The Equal Protection Clause provides that no state shall "deny to any person within its jurisdiction [geographical area over which a government has authority] the equal protection of the laws." Equal protection means that persons or groups of persons in similar situations must be treated equally by the laws. The Court first recognized in ***Yick Wo v. Hopkins*** (1886) that these rights extended to all persons, not just citizens, living within U.S. boundaries.

Tyler School District

With growing numbers of illegal aliens in the state, the Texas legislature in May of 1975 decided to change its education laws. The new law would withhold from local school districts any state funds used to educate children of illegal aliens. The 1975 change also authorized local school districts to deny enrollment in their public school to children of illegal aliens. Though the Tyler Independent School District continued to allow children of doubtful legal status to attend their schools, in July of 1977 they announced these children must begin paying a "tuition fee" in order to enroll.

In reaction, a class action lawsuit (lawsuit brought on behalf of a large group with a common interest) was filed in the U.S. District Court for the Eastern District of Texas. The lawsuit was on behalf of all school-age children of Mexican origin living in Smith County, Texas, who could not prove they had legally entered the United States. The suit charged that this group of children was being unfairly denied a free public education. The suit named as defendants the Superintendent and members of the Board of Trustees of Tyler Independent School District.

After conducting a thorough hearing, in December of 1977 the district court found that barring undocumented children from the schools might eventually save public money but the quality of education would "not necessarily" improve. Furthermore, these children might become the legal citizens of the future but, without an education, they would be locked into a "subclass" at the lowest economic level. Therefore, the district court found the Texas laws violated the Fourteenth Amendment's Equal Protection Clause which protects illegal aliens from unequal treatment by the laws.

The Court of Appeals for the Fifth Circuit affirmed all the essential points of the district court's analysis and ruling. The case then moved to the U.S. Supreme Court.

Public Education in America

The Supreme Court decision in the *Plyler* case was a 5-4 split in favor of illegal alien children. The debate over the issues ran deep among the justices. Even the justices of the majority who agreed on the final decision had different reasons. Together, the concurring (agreeing with the decision) and dissenting (disagreeing with the decision) opinions provided a powerful look into the justices' beliefs about the importance of public education in American society.

Justice William J. Brennan, Jr., writing for the majority, identified that "the question presented . . . is whether, consistent [carrying out the intention of] with the Equal Protection Clause of the Fourteenth Amendment, Texas may deny to undocumented school-age children the free public education that it provides to children who are citizens of the United States or legally admitted aliens."

The school board argued that equal protection did not apply to those who entered the country illegally. The Court rejected their argument by emphasizing the decision of *Yick Wo* which declared all persons "within its [a government's] jurisdiction" came under Fourteenth Amendment protection. Deciding that illegal aliens came under the Equal Protection Clause was easy. The more difficult question was if Texas law violated equal protection.

A "Pivotal Role"

In arriving at their decision, the justices addressed the relationship between public education, the U.S. Constitution, and the importance of public education in American social order. Justice Brennan affirmed that education was not a right granted by the Constitution but added that education was more than "merely some government 'benefit' indistinguishable [cannot tell the difference] from other forms of social welfare legislation." Education was different because it plays a "fundamental" or "pivotal role" in maintaining our society. He added, "we cannot ignore the significant social costs borne by our Nation when select groups are denied the means to absorb the values and skills upon which our social order rests." Denial of a free public education to the children of illegal aliens places a lifetime hardship on them, for "illiteracy (inability to read) will mark them for the rest of their lives." Brennan found no reason for a state to cause such hardship on any individual. For these reasons the Court concluded the Equal Protection Clause required the Texas law be struck down.

In a concurring opinion, Justice Harry Blackmun stated that to provide an education to some but deny it to others "immediately and inevitably [always] creates class distinctions [differences]" inconsistent with the purposes of the Equal Protection Clause. Blackmun observed "an uneducated child is denied even the opportunity to achieve." Likewise, Justice Thurgood Marshall concurred that denying public education based on class is "utterly incompatible" with the Equal Protection Clause. Justice Lewis Powell pointed out that the Texas law "assigned a legal status [to the children] due to a violation of law by their parents." These children "should not be left on the streets uneducated" as a consequence of their parents' actions over which they had no control.

RIGHT TO A PUBLIC EDUCATION

"American people have always regarded education and [the] acquisition of knowledge as matters of supreme importance." *Meyer v. Nebraska* (1923).

" . . . public schools [are] most vital . . . for the preservation of a democratic system of government." *Abington School District v. Schempp* (1963).

These quotes from earlier Supreme Court decisions were used again in the *Plyler v. Doe* (1982) case. Yet, the Constitution makes no mention of education and the Court has never acknowledged it as a fundamental right. According to the Tenth Amendment, powers not given to the federal government are reserved to the states. Educating children in the United States has long been a responsibility of individual states which assign to local school systems. However, since the ***Brown v. Board of Education*** (1954) decision the Court has insisted that public education be equally available to all children. Through a combination of various laws and Supreme Court interpretations of the Fourteenth Amendments' Equal Protection Clause, schools have ever increasing responsibilities to provide equal opportunities to groups or classes previously barred from equal access. These opportunities extend to children of all races, to the physically and mentally disabled, to non-English speaking children, and to children of illegal aliens.

A State Matter

The dissenting opinion, written by Chief Justice Warren Burger, pointed out that the majority opinion, while denying education was a constitutionally protected right nevertheless did not make it clear just where education fell. Though Burger did not deny education's importance, the fact of its importance "does not elevate it to the status of a 'fundamental right.'" Burger observed that the solution of the issue should have been left to the state legislature even as disagreeable "as that may be to some."

The Role of Schools

The Court, in striking down the Texas law, addressed the role of schools in a democratic society and decided it was central to the American culture. The *Plyler* decision added a new responsibility for public schools. Public schools are obliged (required) to provide tuition-free education not only to American citizens and lawful alien children but also to children of illegal aliens.

Public resistance persisted, however. In 1994 California voters passed Proposition 187 restricting public school education for children of illegal aliens. In September of 1999 a U.S. District Court judge ruled that no child in California would be denied an education because of their place of birth.

Suggestions for further reading

Atkin, S. Beth. *Voices From the Field: Children of Migrant Farmworkers Tell Their Stories.* Boston: Joy Street Books, 1993.

Chavez, Leo R. *Shadowed Lives: Undocumented Immigrants in American Society.* Fort Worth, TX: Harcourt Brace College Publications, 1998.

Conover, Ted. *Coyotes: A Journey Through the Secret World of America's Illegal Aliens.* New York: Vintage Books, 1987.

Kellough, Patrick H., and Jean L. Kellough. *Public Education and the Children of Illegal Aliens.* Monticello, IL: Vance Bibliographie, 1985.

Cleburne v. Cleburne Living Center 1985

Petitioner: City of Cleburne, Texas

Respondent: Cleburne Living Center

Petitioner's Claim: That the decision to deny the Cleburne Living Center a special use zoning permit served a legitimate government need and the zoning ordinance was constitutional.

Chief Lawyer for Petitioner: Earl Luna, Robert T. Miller, Jr., Mary Milford

Chief Lawyer for Respondent: Renea Hicks, Diane Shisk, Caryl Oberman

Justices for the Court: Harry A. Blackmun, Chief Justice Warren E. Burger, Sandra Day O'Connor, Lewis F. Powell, Jr., William H. Rehnquist, Byron R. White

Justices Dissenting: William J. Brennan, Jr., Thurgood Marshall, John Paul Stevens

Date of Decision: July 1, 1985

Decision: Ruled in favor of Cleburne Living Center by finding that the denial of a permit was based on prejudice against persons with mental retardation. The zoning ordinance was declared unconstitutional.

Significance: No more groups were added to the intermediate scrutiny list. The ruling helped eliminate housing discrimination against the disabled and encouraged group homes.

Society has often isolated and restricted persons with mental retardation (MR) within institutions and hospitals. The American Association on Mental Retardation defines mental retardation as significantly below average intellectual functioning combined with problems in carrying out everyday life activities. However, people with MR range from those with disabilities hardly noticeable to others needing constant care.

By the 1960s group homes became a desirable living arrangement option. The homes allowed persons with MR to lead normal lives as much as possible by residing in a regular community setting. Twenty-four hour supervision and support was provided. However, controversy grew between organizations trying to establish group homes and existing neighbors. Neighbors' arguments against the homes varied widely from safety fears to potential economic effects on their property values. This scene played out in Cleburne, Texas.

The Feathersone Group Home

Cleburne Living Center (CLC) sought to lease a house at 201 Featherstone Street to establish a group home for the mentally retarded. The home would house thirteen men and women with MR. They would be under constant supervision of the CLC staff. The city of Cleburne identified the group home as a "hospital for the feeble-minded" requiring a special use permit. The zoning ordinance (assigns particular uses to certain areas of a city) for the area required special use permits for construction of "hospitals for the insane or feeble-minded, or alcoholic [sic] or drug addicts or penal or correctional institutions." After a public hearing on CLC's application, the City Council voted three to one to deny CLC a special use permit.

CLC filed suit in Federal District Court charging the city's zoning ordinance was unconstitutional and, therefore, invalid (not legal). It discriminated, they claimed, against persons with MR in violation of the Fourteenth Amendment's Equal Protection Clause in the U.S. Constitution. The Equal Protection Clause states that no state shall "deny to any person within its jurisdiction [geographic area over which a government has authority] the equal protection of the laws." Equal protection means that all people in similar situations must be treated the same under the law.

Was Fear Important?

The District Court found that the Council's decision was based mainly on the fact that the group home's residents would be persons with MR. Nevertheless, the court found the zoning ordinance constitutional. The court applied only the lowest level of scrutiny (examination) required in equal protection cases and found that the city had a legitimate (honest) interest to respect the fears of residents in the immediate neighborhood.

Upon appeal by the CLC, the Court of Appeals for the Fifth Circuit disagreed with the district court and, ruling in favor of CLC, reversed the decision. The Court of Appeals applied an intermediate level of scrutiny to the zoning ordinance. The intermediate level requires that the government, in this case the city of Cleburne, have not just a legitimate reason but an important reason to discriminate against a certain group. Ruling the ordinance unconstitutional and therefore invalid, the Court of Appeal found that the city had no important reason or interest making it necessary to direct discrimination against persons with MR. Cleburne appealed to the U.S. Supreme Court which agreed to hear the case.

In a 6-3 decision, the Supreme Court decided Cleburne's zoning ordinance was unconstitutional and violated the Equal Protection Clause. The Court disagreed with the Court of Appeals on the scrutiny level issue, but, nevertheless, agreed on the end result that invalidated Cleburne's zoning ordinance.

When Is Intermediate Scrutiny Necessary?

Writing for the Court, Justice Byron R. White analyzed the two major points of the case. First, the Court turned its attention to the scrutiny issue. The Court held that the Court of Appeals erred in applying the intermediate level of scrutiny. The Court refused to allow persons with MR to be elevated to a heightened level of scrutiny. White explained that the Court had devised three levels of scrutiny for equal protection cases. The levels assess the constitutionality of different kinds of state and local legislation that affected certain groups or classes of individuals who had been traditionally and purposefully discriminated against through America's history. The highest level of scrutiny applies to laws that classify groups by race, alienage (a person living in the United States but a citizen of a foreign country), or national origin. The next level of scrutiny, intermediate, applies to women and illegitimate children (born out of wedlock). If any of these groups are singled out for particular treatment in a law, the law may be found unconstitutional unless the law serves either a "compelling" (very important) or important interest to the government. If the law does not single out any of these groups, it must only have a rational (reasonable) or legitimate basis for treating groups differently.

As a group persons with MR are neither a certain race, alienage, national origin, all female, or illegitimate. Therefore, they do not automatically fall into the top or intermediate levels of scrutiny. The Court of Appeals was mistaken in trying to elevate them into one of these higher levels. Citing several major pieces of legislation specifically designed to outlaw discrimination against the mentally retarded, White showed that persons with MR have neither been traditionally nor purposefully treated unequally by the laws. White also pointed out that persons with MR have a "reduced ability to cope with and function in the everyday world. . . They are thus different. . . Legislators, guided by qualified professionals . . . " are better able to address their needs than are the courts. A degree of different treatment would indeed be expected to best serve persons with MR. Therefore, the government has a rational basis to enact legislation that treats persons with MR differently. White concluded the lowest level of scrutiny with the rational basis requirement is sufficient protection for persons with MR. The Court reasoned to elevate persons with MR to the intermediate scrutiny level would also require they elevate all persons with disabilities to that level and they were not willing to do so.

Pure Prejudice

Having addressed the scrutiny issue, White next turned to the specific question of whether Cleburne's zoning ordinance requiring special permits for "hospitals" for the "feeble-minded" was constitutional. White stated, "We inquire . . . whether requiring a special use permit for the Featherston home in the circumstances here deprives respondents [CLC] of the equal protection of the laws."

White first wrote,

> **The city does not require a special use permit . . . for apartment houses, multiple-dwellings, boarding . . . houses . . . nursing homes [etc.]. . . It does, however, insist on a special permit for the Featherston home, and it does so . . . because it**

ZONING ORDINANCES

Zoning ordinances divide a village, town, city, or county into residential (single family and multi-family), commercial or retail, and industrial (light or heavy manufacturing) districts. Ordinances must be part of a comprehensive plan for the entire area. Ordinances generally require certain building features or architecture, limit density, provide for parking areas, schools, parks, and may establish historical areas or buildings.

Ordinances must promote the common welfare of all people of the community rather than promoting a particular group's desires. The zoning ordinances must be reasonable because by their nature they limit use of property by the owners and they may not be used arbitrarily by governments. With the use of maps, ordinances must be clear and specific in describing districts. Only persons wronged by the regulations may challenge them.

The goals are to maintain the area's characteristics important to the residents, control population density, and create healthful and attractive areas. They must look to the future and strive to bring about orderly growth and development by considering practicalities such as adequate streets, walkways, and drainage sewers.

Municipalities have some flexibility to impose restrictions they otherwise might not be able to require such as requiring special use permits in specific situations. These permits must have reasonable goals before they may be imposed

would be a facility for the mentally retarded. May the city require the permit for this facility when other care and multiple-dwelling facilities are freely permitted?

White looked for a rational basis (all that is required at the lowest scrutiny level) for the city ordinance to treat persons with MR unequally. The City Council argued that the majority of property owners located within 200 feet of the Featherstone facility had negative attitudes toward or fear of the facility. The Court responded, "mere negative attitudes, or fear, . . . are not permissible bases for treating a home for the mentally retarded differently from apartment houses, multiple dwellings, and the like." The Council argued that the facility was across the street from a junior high school and students might harass the Featherstone residents. The Court countered that thirty mentally retarded students attend the junior high suggesting students are already used to persons with MR. The Council put forth several more concerns such as the home's location on a "five hundred year flood plain." The Court reasoned that none of these concerns set the Featherstone home apart. All of the concerns could also apply to any of the other buildings in the area not required to a have a special permit. The Court found no rational basis or reason to treat the mentally retarded differently. White concluded, "The short of it is that requiring the permit in this case appears to us to rest on an irrational prejudice against the mentally retarded." The Court found the ordinance unconstitutional and therefore invalid.

The Cleburne decision closed the door to more groups being added to the heightened scrutiny list. At the same time, it helped eliminate one form of housing discrimination, discrimination against the disabled. The decision opened wider the opportunity for persons with mental retardation to live within "normal" communities.

Suggestions for further reading

American Association on Mental Retardation. [Online] Website: http://www.aamr.org (Accessed on July 31, 2000).

The Arc of the United States (national organization of and for people with mental retardation). [Online] Website: http://www.arc.org (Accessed on July 31, 2000).

Meyer, Donald, ed. *Views From Our Shoes: Growing Up with a Brother or Sister with Special Needs.* Bethesda, MD: Woodbine House, 1997.

Bowers v. Hardwick
1986

Appellant: Michael J. Bowers, Attorney General of Georgia

Appellee: Michael Hardwick

Appellant's Claim: That state laws making sodomy a criminal offense do not violate the constitutionally protected right to privacy.

Chief Lawyer for Appellant: Michael E. Hobs

Chief Lawyer for Appellee: Laurence Tribe

Justices for the Court: Chief Justice Warren E. Burger, Sandra Day O'Connor, Lewis F. Powell, Jr., William H. Rehnquist, Byron R. White

Justices Dissenting: Harry A. Blackmun, William J. Brennan, Jr., Thurgood Marshall, John Paul Stevens

Date of Decision: June 30, 1986

Decision: The ruling upheld the Georgia law by reasoning that no fundamental right has been granted to homosexuals to engage in sodomy and, therefore, the law did not violate the right of privacy guaranteed under due process.

Significance: The decision left existing state sodomy laws intact. The ruling dealt a major setback to the gay and lesbian civil rights movement since their opponents could argue that granting civil rights to persons who regularly commit the criminal act of sodomy could not be justified.

In 1986 half a million gay men and lesbians marched in Washington, D. C. protesting the U.S. Supreme Court decision in *Bowers v. Hardwick* (1986), the Court's first ruling on gay rights. The decision upheld a Georgia law forbidding sodomy and was considered a major setback to the gay rights movement. Sodomy is sexual activity common among gays and lesbians. The terms gay and lesbian refer to people sexually attracted to persons of their same sex. The term gay usually refers to men and lesbian always refers to women. Homosexual is a term which refers to either gay men or lesbians.

Sodomy had long been considered a criminal offense in state and local law. Since criminal sodomy laws were aimed at homosexuals, gay men and lesbians kept their sexual orientation (the sexual preference of an individual for one sex or the other) a secret. This secret existence in which homosexuals found themselves was referred to as being "in the closet." Encouraged by successes of black Americans and women during the 1960s' Civil Rights Movement and outraged by an incident, known as Stonewall, at a New York bar in 1969, homosexuals began to "come out." This meant identifying themselves as gay or lesbians and openly working for legal and social equality. The gay rights movement made the repeal (to abolish) of sodomy laws a primary goal.

Michael Hardwick's Private Affairs

Michael Hardwick was a gay bartender living in Atlanta, Georgia. When Hardwick failed to pay a fine for drinking in public, a police officer came to his home to serve a warrant (a written order) against him. The officer gained entrance to the home by another tenant who did not know if Hardwick was home. The officer entered Hardwick's bedroom where he found him having sex with his partner. Hardwick was arrested and charged with committing sodomy with a consenting (willing) male.

Hardwick brought suit in Federal District Court challenging the constitutionality of the Georgia sodomy law. The District Court dismissed the suit without a trial. Hardwick then appealed to the U.S. Court of Appeals for the Eleventh Circuit. The court of appeals found the law violated Hardwick's fundamental right to privacy protected by both the Ninth Amendment and the Due Process Clause of the Fourteenth Amendment. The Ninth Amendment provides that even though certain rights are not specifically named in the U.S. Constitution, they could still be considered fundamental rights held by the people. The Fourteenth Amendment prohibits states from denying citizens "life, liberty or property, without due process of law [fair legal proceedings]." In 1965 the U.S. Supreme Court case, ***Griswold v. Connecticut,*** dealing with birth control or contraception, had clearly established a constitutional right to privacy as part of the fundamental rights in the Ninth Amendment. The right to privacy was protected by the Due Process Clause of the Fourteenth Amendment. This right in private matters was again stated in ***Roe v. Wade*** (1973) which dealt with abortion. The court of appeals agreed with Hardwick that the Georgia law violated his fundamental rights because his homosexual actions were in the privacy of his own home and, therefore, beyond the reach of any state interference. In this light, the court of appeals returned the case to the district court, ordering it to try the case.

Before the trial could begin, Michael Bowers, the Georgia attorney general, appealed to the U.S. Supreme Court for a review of the court of appeals' ruling. The Supreme Court agreed to hear the case.

A Fundamental Right?

Justice Byron R. White, writing the Court's opinion, stated the question before the Court,

> **The issue presented is whether the Federal Constitution confers a fundamental right upon homosexuals to engage in sodomy and hence invalidates the laws of the many States that still make such conduct illegal and have done so for a very long time.**

In a 5-4 decision in favor of Georgia, the Court rejected the thinking of the court of appeals. First, the Court dismissed the idea that its previous rulings on the privacy issues of contraception and abortion had anything to do with this case. In fact, White drew a sharp distinction between the previous cases and homosexual activity:

> **Accepting the decisions in these cases . . . we think it evident [clear] that none of the rights announced in those cases bears any resemblance to the claimed constitutional right of homosexuals to engage in acts of sodomy. . . No connection between family, marriage, or procreation [to have a baby] on the one hand and homosexual activity on the other hand has been demonstrated.**

White next rejected the argument that engaging in homosexual activity was a fundamental right protected by the Due Process Clause. Justice White wrote that fundamental rights or liberties are deeply rooted in U.S. history and tradition. If they did not exist, justice would not exist. He found that sodomy was never rooted in this Nation's history. Quite the opposite, it had long been prohibited by the states. According to White,

> **Sodomy was a criminal offense at common law and was forbidden by the laws of the original 13 States when they ratified the Bill of Rights. In 1868, when the Fourteenth Amendment was ratified, all but 5 of the 37 States in the Union had criminal sodomy laws. In fact, until 1961, all 50 States outlawed sodomy, and today [1986], 24 States and the District of Columbia continue to provide criminal penalties for sodomy performed in private between consenting [willing] adults.**

Likewise, certainly justice and order would still exist even if sodomy did not. White observed, for the Court to declare sodomy a fundamental constitutionally protected right and negate all the state laws would be taking on the role of the legislative branch. Making decisions on how to govern the country is constitutionally a legislative activity in which the Court may not engage.

Don't Go Down That Road

White further addressed the issue that Hardwick's homosexual conduct was carried out in the privacy of his home. White stated that not all acts just because they are done in private are legal. For example, White wrote, " . . . the possession and use of illegal drugs, do not escape the law where they are committed at home." White explained the homosexual conduct could not be allowed "while leaving exposed to prosecution adultery, incest, and other sexual crimes even though they are committed in the home. We are unwilling to start down that road."

A Bitter Dissent

In a bitter dissent, Justice Harry A. Blackmun, the principle author of *Roe v. Wade,* commented the Court's decision "makes for a short opinion, but it does little to make for a persuasive one." He stated that this case was not so much "about a fundamental right to engage in homosexual

SODOMY LAWS

Sodomy laws generally prohibit certain sexual acts, even between willing adults in the privacy of their homes. Punishment ranges from $200 fines to twenty years imprisonment. Once all fifty states and Puerto Rico had sodomy laws but many have been repealed or struck down in the courts. In 1999 thirteen states and Puerto Rico still had sodomy laws which applied to both same-sex (homosexual) and opposite-sex (heterosexual) activities. Five states, Arkansas, Kansas, Missouri, Oklahoma, and Texas, had sodomy laws targeting only homosexuals.

Sodomy laws have frequently been used to deny gay men and lesbians their civil rights. For example, some courts under the laws have justified removing children from gay or lesbian parents. Occasionally, cities have used the laws to arrest gay individuals for merely discussing sex in conversations, conversations which heterosexuals have daily.

In November of 1998, the Georgia Supreme Court struck down its 182-year-old sodomy law, the same law the U.S. Supreme Court upheld in the 1986 case of *Bowers v. Hardwick.* The Georgia court ruled the law violated the right to privacy protected by the state's constitution. Chief Justice Robert Benham wrote, "We cannot think of any other activity that reasonable persons would rank as more private and more deserving of protection from governmental interference than consensual [willing], private, adult sexual activity."

sodomy" but instead about the most prized right of civilized man, " . . . namely, the right to be let alone." Blackmun eloquently wrote:

> **individuals define themselves in a significant way through their intimate sexual relationships with others suggests, in a Nation as diverse as ours, that there may be many right ways of conducting those relationships, and that much of the richness of a relationship will come from the freedom an indi-**

vidual has to choose the form and nature of these intensely personal bonds.

A Mistake

Justice Lewis F. Powell held the swing vote in the decision. At first Powell had been in favor of striking down the Georgia law as it carried a prison sentence with conviction. This he reasoned would violate the Eighth Amendment as "cruel and unusual punishment." However, because Hardwick had not actually even been tried, "much less convicted and sentenced," Powell could not justify overturning the state law. Powell, therefore, became the fifth justice to vote against striking down the Georgia law. He later publicly confessed that changing his vote in Bowers had probably been a mistake.

Quest For Civil Rights Derailed

Deciding that private homosexual activities did not fall under the right of privacy guaranteed under due process dealt a severe blow to the gay and lesbian rights movement and their quest for civil rights. Gay rights opponents began to charge that it was ridiculous to think about granting civil rights to persons who regularly practiced criminal acts. The Supreme Court would not face gay rights issues again until 1996 in ***Romer v. Evans*** when the decision would be different. In *Romer* the Court granted constitutional protection against government or private discrimination based on sexual orientation. It was hailed as the first key victory in the struggle for gay and lesbian civil rights. The decisions in *Bowers* and then in *Romer* reflected America's changing standards toward the gay and lesbian communities.

Suggestions for further reading

American Civil Liberties Union. [Online] Website: http://www.aclu.org (Accessed on July 31, 2000).

Lambda Legal Defense and Educational Fund. [Online] Website: http://www.lambdalegal.org (Accessed on July 31, 2000).

National Gay and Lesbian Task Force. [Online] Website: http://www.ngltf.org (Accessed on July 31, 2000).

Richards, David A. J. *Women, Gays, and the Constitution: The Grounds for Feminism and Gay Rights in Culture and Law.* Chicago: University of Chicago Press, 1998.

Romer v. Evans
1996

Petitioner: Roy Romer, Governor of Colorado, and others

Respondent: Richard G. Evans and others

Petitioner's Claim: That the Colorado Supreme Court erred in striking down a state constitutional amendment prohibiting any government efforts to protect homosexuals against discrimination.

Chief Lawyers for Petitioner: Timothy M. Tymkovich

Chief Lawyers for Respondent: Jean E. Dubofsky

Justices for the Court: Stephen Breyer, Ruth Bader Ginsburg, Anthony M. Kennedy, Sandra Day O'Connor, David H. Souter, John Paul Stevens

Justices Dissenting: Chief Justice William H. Rehnquist, Antonin Scalia, Clarence Thomas

Date of Decision: May 20, 1996

Decision: Agreeing with the Colorado Supreme Court, ruled in favor of Evans that the state amendment prohibiting protections of gay and lesbian rights was unconstitutional.

Significance: First victory of gay and lesbian civil rights in the U.S. Supreme Court. The Court gave homosexuals constitutional protection against government or private discrimination.

Gay men and lesbians number in the millions and are found in every sector of American society—doctors, nurses, computer whizzes, musicians, athletes, teachers, construction workers, dads, moms, and teenagers. The terms gay and lesbian refer to people who are sexually attracted to and prefer persons of the same sex. Though the term gay can refer to either men or women, gay usually is used in referring to men and lesbian always refers to women. Homosexual is another term which refers to both gay men and lesbians.

Throughout most of America's history, homosexuals have kept their sexual orientation (the sexual preference of an individual for one sex or the other) a secret or "in the closet." Secrecy was important because homosexuality has been considered a criminal offense in state and local laws, and religious organizations condemned the behavior. However, a fight in a New York bar in 1969 marked the beginning of a nationwide "coming out."

The Coming Out

"Coming out" is the name gay and lesbians give the process of identifying, accepting, and then disclosing their sexual orientation. On June 27,

The first National March on Washington for Lesbian and Gay Rights occurred in October of 1979. Reproduced by permission of Joan E. Biren.

1969 in New York, police raided the Stonewall Inn, a gay bar located in Greenwich Village. Raiding gay bars was not an uncommon police activity all across America. However, this time the people inside the bar resisted arrest and clashed with the city police. For three nights New York gays rioted, releasing years of suppressed frustration over the discrimination they experienced daily. Especially for younger gay men and women, Stonewall became a symbol of a new attitude of openly "coming out." Resisting negative stereotyping (fixed mental picture or a fixed attitude toward something) and legal and social discrimination suddenly became more common.

Gay Rights Movement is Born

Every year after the Stonewall riots, homosexuals marched in New York City to remember the event. Gay men and lesbians began to seek legal and social equality in America. The federal government had moved to prohibit discrimination on the basis of race, religion, and national origin, but had yet to take a stand on sexual orientation. The movement, which had become known as the gay rights movement, grew during the 1970s and 1980s. Demanding fair legal treatment, between 25,000 and 40,000 gay rights activists marched in San Francisco in November of 1978 and 75,000 strong marched in Washington, D.C. in October of 1979, the first National March on Washington for Lesbian and Gay Rights.

Despite some gains by the movement, in 1986 the U.S. Supreme Court dealt it a major setback. In ***Bowers v. Hardwick,*** the Court refused to grant a constitutional right of privacy for homosexual acts carried out in private homes. State laws thus continued to criminalize such acts. In response, over half-a-million gay men and lesbians rallied in Washington, D.C. in 1987 in another National March on Washington.

In the 1990s, homosexuals and their lifestyle faced growing opposition from some religious groups and conservatives concerned about the nation's moral values. A decade after *Bowers* the Supreme Court would face gay rights issues again in *Romer v. Evans* (1996). This time the legal battleground was set in the state of Colorado.

Amendment 2—No Civil Rights for Gays

In support of gay rights, several communities in Colorado, including Denver, Aspen, and Boulder, passed local laws banning discrimination in employment, housing, and education on the basis of sexual orientation. By 1992 a group, Colorado for Family Values, concerned that the growing acceptance of homosexual lifestyles would harm American traditions and morals, led an effort against the communities' anti-discrimination laws. They proposed a state constitutional amendment to repeal (cancel) the laws and stop any future efforts to legally protect homosexuals. Following a petition drive, the amendment was placed on the November ballot in 1992.

The ballot measure, known as Amendment 2, passed and became part of the Colorado state constitution. Amendment 2 prohibited all state and local governments and courts to take any action designed to protect persons based on their "homosexual, lesbian, or bisexual [sexually oriented to both males and females] orientation, conduct, practices or relationships." As originally intended, it required the immediate repeal (to abolish) of all existing laws barring discrimination based on sexual preference and allowed discrimination against gay and lesbians in areas such as employment, insurance, housing, and welfare services.

Immediately, eight individuals, including gay municipal worker Richard Evans, and the cities of Denver, Boulder, and Aspen, which had their gay rights laws repealed, challenged Amendment 2 in the state courts. Finally, in 1994 the Colorado Supreme Court ruled that Amendment 2 could not be enforced. It found Amendment 2 prevented one "class" of persons with non-traditional sexual orientations composed of gays, lesbians, and bisexuals from using normal political procedures to protect themselves from discrimination. One normal procedure which all other groups could follow would be to seek passage of a law to correct injustices. Now this named group of persons would have to amend the state constitution before such corrective laws could even be considered, not a normal procedure. The amendment would effectively end any civil rights for gays. Furthermore, the state supreme court could find no compelling (very important) reason demonstrating the government's need for Amendment 2. Colorado, whose governor was Roy Romer, appealed the ruling to the U.S. Supreme Court which agreed to hear the case.

"This Colorado Cannot Do"

Before the U.S. Supreme Court, Colorado argued that Amendment 2 merely took away the "special rights" or a special protection the local laws had granted to homosexuals. The Court in a 6-3 decision strongly disagreed with the state of Colorado. Though following a different line of

Governor Roy Romer worked to deny gays and lesbians special protections under the law. Reproduced by permission of the Corbis Corporation.

reasoning than the Colorado Supreme Court, the Court upheld the previous decision that Amendment 2 was unconstitutional (does not follow the intent of the U.S. Constitution) and, therefore, unenforceable.

Justice Anthony M. Kennedy wrote the powerfully worded majority opinion. Addressing the so-called "special protections" argument, Kennedy concluded the special protections were not special at all but merely "the safeguards that others enjoy. . . These are protection taken for granted by most people either because they already have them or do not need them. . . " Instead, Kennedy pointed out these safeguards "are protections against exclusion from an almost limitless number of transactions and endeavors [such as employment and housing] that constitute ordinary civic life [life as a citizen] in a free society." In other words, these safeguards are protection against discrimination and to take them away from gay people "imposes a special disability upon those persons alone.

Kennedy identified the real question before the Court. Did Amendment 2 violate the Fourteenth Amendment's Equal Protection Clause that guarantees that no state shall deny to any person the "equal protection of the laws?" The Court found that Amendment 2 did indeed violate the clause. The violation was such a sweeping, across the board denial of gay peoples' rights of protection. The court concluded that it could only have been passed with the goal of harming a politically unpopular group. The Court could identify no "legitimate" (honest) gov-

NATIONAL GAY AND LESBIAN ORGANIZATIONS

Lambda Legal Defense and Education Fund, founded in 1972, is dedicated to achieving full recognition of the civil rights of gay men, lesbians, and people with HIV/AIDS. Lambda's legal staff of attorneys together with a network of volunteer Cooperating Attorneys, combat discrimination based on sexual orientation. Working on an average of fifty cases at any one time, issues include a wide variety of topics such as discrimination in employment, housing, the military; HIV/AIDS-related cases, equal marriage rights, parenting, "sodomy" laws, and anti-gay ballot initiatives. Lambda also provides legal services to homosexuals and encourages homosexuals to join the legal profession.

The National Gay and Lesbian Task Force (NGLTF), founded in 1973, supports local communities in organizing advocacy groups for gays and lesbians. The NGLTF strengthens gay and lesbian movements at the state and local levels at the same time connecting these activities to a national scene. At the national level it works to promote legislation to enhance gay and lesbian civil rights. Headquartered in Washington, D.C., it serves as a national resource center.

ernment need or reason for its passage. Amendment 2 is unconstitutional, Kennedy commented, because any law that makes it "more difficult for one group of citizens than all others to seek aid from the government is itself a denial of equal protection of the laws in the most literal [real or concrete] sense."

Kennedy forcefully ended by stating, "We must conclude that Amendment 2 classifies homosexuals not to further a proper legislative end but to make then unequal to everyone else. This Colorado cannot do. A state cannot so deem a class of persons a stranger to its laws."

Homosexual organizations applauded and cheered the decision saying it was the most important victory ever in the struggle for gay men and lesbians' civil rights. Finally, the U.S. Supreme Court had given constitutional protection against government or private discrimination based on sexual orientation. Groups opposed to gay rights, bitterly disappointed with the ruling, said it would greatly heighten tension between those for and against gay rights.

Suggestions for further reading

Cohen, Susan, and Daniel Cohen. *When Someone You Know Is Gay.* New York: Laurel-Leaf Books, 1989.

Lambda Legal Defense and Educational Fund. [Online] Website: http://www.lambdalegal.org (Accessed on July 31, 2000).

National Gay & Lesbian Task Force. [Online] Website: http://www.ngltf.org (Accessed on July 31, 2000).

Nava, Michael, and Robert Dawidoff. *Created Equal: Why Gay Rights Matter to America.* New York: St. Martin's Press, 1994.

Robson, Ruthann. *Gay Men, Lesbians, and the Law.* New York: Chelsea House Publishers, 1997.

Through the early period of American history, races (groups of people normally identified by their skin color) were kept separate by social custom. White business owners simply refused to serve blacks. Slavery of black Americans was recognized as economically crucial to the Southern region. Political and legal liberties were not shared equally. For instance, only white male adults with property could vote in public elections. Boston's segregated (keeping races separate) public school system was affirmed by the Massachusetts Supreme Court in 1850.

First Efforts of Desegregation

The Emancipation Proclamation issued by President Abraham Lincoln in 1863 represented a first step to end these segregationist social customs. Immediately following the end of the American Civil War (1861–65) a series of three constitutional amendments, known as the Civil Rights Amendments were adopted to end such social customs and further racial integration (mixing of the races). The Thirteenth Amendment outlawed slavery. The Fourteenth and Fifteenth Amendments protected the constitutional civil rights of the newly freed slaves. Specifically, the Fourteenth Amendment extended "equal protection of the laws" to all Americans. It also maintained that everyone through the "due process" clause would be subject to the same legal processes. The Fifteenth Amendment extended voting rights to black males.

In spite of the new amendments, efforts to establish desegregation (abolishing segregation) social policies was met with severe resistance, particularly among the Southern states. State laws were passed restricting the freedom of black Americans, such as where blacks could sit on railroad cars and what public schools they could attend. The laws, known as Jim Crow Laws, sought to legally enforce racial segregation. Congress responded with federal laws supporting equal rights among all races. Civil Rights Acts were passed in 1866 and 1870 to enforce the civil rights amendments. With access to public facilities still being denied to many Americans on account of race and skin color, Congress passed another Civil Rights Act in 1875 making public facilities including railroads and hotels accessible to black Americans.

Severely hindering desegregation, Supreme Court decisions involving disputes over these rights commonly sided with the states during this period. The Court greatly limited the federal government's power to enforce the civil rights amendments. For example, in ***Civil Rights Cases*** (1883), a combination of three separate lower court cases involving similar civil rights disputes, the Supreme Court ruled application of the 1875 Civil Rights Act to private individuals or businesses unconstitutional (not following the intent of the U.S. Constitution and its amendments). The government could not force private businesses, such as hotels, restaurants, and railroad cars to integrate. As a result, by 1890 black Americans had few civil rights, particularly in the South.

"Separate But Equal"

The biggest blow against desegregation of public facilities came in the ***Plessy v. Ferguson*** (1896) ruling. By upholding a Louisiana law segregating access to railway cars between black and white Americans, a concept known as "separate but equal" was established. The decision maintained that segregation did not violate the equal protection clause of the Fourteenth Amendment if black and white Americans were given access to separate but equal facilities. The decision essentially gave approval to all laws requiring racial segregation.

Following the *Plessy* ruling, Jim Crow laws greatly expanded, particularly in the South where ninety percent of black Americans resided. Racial segregation was introduced into almost every aspect of American life in the fifteen Southern states plus West Virginia and Oklahoma. Other states allowed segregation but did not require it. Many of these laws were designed to keep black Americans from voting, causing segregation in access to political power. Other early laws focused on segregation of trains, both railway car seating and train station waiting rooms. State and local laws soon focused on public drinking fountains and restrooms, schools, hospitals, jails, streetcars, theaters, and amusement parks. There were white drinking fountains and black drinking fountains, white restrooms and black restrooms. Though separate, the facilities were rarely equal. The quality of facilities available to black Americans were normally far inferior to those available to white Americans. In 1915 it was revealed South Carolina was spending twelve times more public funds per student on white schools in comparison to schools for black Americans. Segregation was also enforced in the military where duties were given often on the basis of race. Segregated regiments were used in World War I (1914–18) and again in World War II (1939–45) until 1948 when desegregation was commanded by Presidential order.

With segregation practices more prevalent in the South, between 1900 and 1910 over 300,000 black Americans fled to the North and West seeking a better life. This movement, called the Great Migration, continued through the rest of the twentieth century. However, reception of these new residents in the North was not always friendly. Race riots broke out in 1917. Again in 1919 violence erupted in Chicago where many were killed when four black Americans attempted to enter a beach reserved for white Americans.

The Struggle Again For Desegregation

Organized opposition to segregation laws steadily grew. The National Urban League was formed in 1909 to assist black Americans readjusting from the rural South to the urban North. In 1910 the National Association for the Advancement of Colored People (NAACP) was established. The NAACP focused on lobbying federal and state governments for changes. The organization also began initiating lawsuits challenging segregation policies. Through their actions the Supreme Court ruled in *Buchanan v. Warley* (1917) that segregation of residential areas was unconstitutional. A Louisville, Kentucky city ordinance had prohibited black Americans from living on the same streets as white Americans. The right to serve on juries was upheld in *State v. Young* (1919).

While the NAACP took avenues toward lawsuits and legislation, others seeking desegregation took different approaches. For example, Booker T. Washington, a black educator, believed desegregation would result from becoming more economically equal. He established the Tuskegee Institute to provide industrial job training for black Americans to economically improve themselves.

Despite these efforts racism raged on with violent Ku Klux Klan terrorism peaking in the 1920s. Founded in the late nineteenth century, the Klan was a militant white racist organization with almost five million segregationists were members by 1929.

Limited progress at desegregation was made during the 1930s as the nation, especially black Americans, suffered through the Great Depression (1929–38). Yet, progress was made in some areas. Through continued pressure from the NAACP and others, Philadelphia public schools were desegregated. In 1936, the Supreme Court in *Murray v. Maryland* required desegregation at Maryland law schools.

Separate Is Unequal

The major break finally came in a 1954 Kansas case. A black father, Oliver Brown, refused to send his daughter to a black school which was further from his home than a white school. When the close-by Topeka school refused to enroll his daughter, the NAACP Legal Defense Fund led by future Supreme Court justice Thurgood Marshall took Brown's case to the Supreme Court. In ***Brown v. Board of Education*** (1954), the Court reversed the earlier *Plessy* decision and struck down the "separate but equal" standard. As the Court asserted, "separate educational facilities are inherently unequal." Racial segregation denied blacks equal protection of the laws under the Fourteenth Amendment, the Court declared. Federal district courts across the nation were given the command to desegregate public schools "with all deliberate speed." In this sweeping and historic decision, the Court reversed decades of legally forced racial segregation.

Rather than actually resolving the issue racial segregation, however, the *Brown* decision led to increased frustrations and violence. Many Southern states and school districts refused to comply with desegregation court orders. Various "freedom of choice" plans were created to preserve segregated schools. These plans allowed families to send their children to the school of their choice. Naturally, white families chose their predominately white neighborhood schools which they had been using while black families stayed in predominately black schools out of fear. Federal troops and law enforcement agents were called to enforce some local court orders. U.S. Marshalls forced integration at a Little Rock, Arkansas high school in 1957. Federal troops were called into action in 1963 at the University of Alabama and University of Mississippi to enforce desegregation and restore peace.

Besides at schools, desegregation was also ordered by the courts in transportation facilities, public housing, voting booths, and other public places like department stores, theaters, beaches, parks, libraries, and restaurants. Continued resistence to desegregation, particularly in the South, led to organized protests by blacks. Often led by Dr. Martin Luther King, Jr., of the Southern Christian Leadership Conference, many non-violent techniques were employed including "sit-ins," picketing, and boycotts. One of the most noted events was the 1955 boycott of the Montgomery, Alabama buses in reaction to the arrest of Rosa Parks, a black woman, for sitting in the white section of a public bus.

The Civil Rights Movement Peaks

By the early 1960s the civil rights movement had become a major national freedom effort. Many white American college students from the North began to get involved in support of black Americans. In 1961 black and white American students conducted Freedom Rides on public buses and stayed at hotels testing desegregation laws along their traveled routes. Violence by Southern white supremacists (those who believe white Americans are superior over black Americans) grew. A leader of the NAACP, Medgar Evers, was shot and killed in 1963 in Mississippi. Four black American young girls were murdered in a Ku Klux Klan church bombing in Birmingham, Alabama. Also in Mississippi, three white students teaching blacks how to register to vote were murdered. Southern law enforcement attacked peaceful black protesters with fire hoses, dogs, and clubs. Dr. King, frequently arrested for various minor charges by Southern authorities in efforts to diffuse the civil rights movement, wrote a famous letter known as "Letter from Birmingham City Jail" in 1963. In it he defended use of civil disobedience (refusing to obey a law to demonstrate against its unfairness) tactics in combating unjust laws. Civil disobedience refers to peacefully not obeying laws considered socially unjust. In an epic civil rights event in 1963, Dr. King led a march of 250,000 people to Washington, D.C. demanding an end to discrimination and segregation.

Congress responded to growing public pressure by passing the landmark Civil Rights Act of 1964, which forbids discrimination on the basis of race, color, religion, and national origin. The act prohibited segregation in all privately owned public facilities associated, however remotely, with interstate commerce. The act also prohibited discrimination in education and employment. The Supreme Court immediately defended the act as constitutional in ***Heart of Atlanta Motel v. United States*** (1964). Following a 1965 march in Selma, Alabama led by King in protest of voting restrictions on blacks that led to violent police attacks on the protesters, Congress passed the Voting Rights Act of 1965. Soon Congress also passed the Fair Housing Act in 1968 prohibiting discrimination in renting and purchasing homes. Desegregation of neighborhoods was further supported in 1968 in ***Jones v. Alfred H. Mayer Co.*** when the Court ruled it illegal to refuse to sell or rent to a person because of skin color.

Segregation and discrimination still persisted and frustrations further mounted. Race riots erupted in the Watts section of Los Angeles in 1965. Violence spread through thirty American cities in 1967 causing extensive death, injury, and property damage. In 1968 Dr. King was assassinated, a major blow to the desegregation movement.

The Continued Struggle for Desegregation

Some successes in desegregation continued. Implementing school desegregation orders of the Brown decision continued to be a problem. In ***Swann v. Charlotte-Mecklenburg Board of Education*** (1971), the Court supported local busing plans. Busing often involved transporting black school children from the inner city largely black schools to the mostly white schools of the suburbs. Busing continued to be a highly controversial desegregation strategy through the end of the twentieth century.

Another face to desegregation efforts came in the form of affirmative action programs in the 1970s. Minorities were given preferences in hiring for employment or admissions to schools in an attempt to further integrate the workforce and student bodies.

Despite major gains in desegregation following the 1950s in education, public places, employment, and transportation, segregation was still a dominant feature of American society. Residential neighborhood patterns and growth of private schools have particularly continued the segregated way of life in America. The workforce and university student bodies saw the most change.

At the end of the twentieth century, old arguments remained alive in American thought. Some continued to oppose governmental desegregation efforts claiming the Fourteenth Amendment only banned discrimination, not segregation. Conversely, others claimed to segregate is to unfairly discriminate.

Suggestions for further reading

Holliday, Laurel. *Children of the Dream: Our Own Stories of Growing Up Black in America.* New York: Pocket Books, 1999.

Lewis, John. *Walking with the Wind: A Memoir of the Movement.* New York: Simon & Schuster, 1998.

Williams, Juan. *Eyes on the Prize: America's Civil Rights Years, 1954–1965.* New York: Viking Penguin, Inc., 1987.

Wolters, Raymond. *The Burden of Brown: Thirty Years of School Desegregation.* Knoxville, TN: The University of Tennessee Press, 1984.

Plessy v. Ferguson 1896

Petitioner: Homer A. Plessy

Respondent: J. H. Ferguson, New Orleans Criminal District Court Judge

Petitioner's Claim: That Louisiana's law requiring blacks and whites to ride in separate railway cars violated Plessy's right to equal protection under the law.

Chief Lawyers for Petitioner: F. D. McKenney, S. F. Phillips

Chief Lawyer for Respondent: M. J. Cunningham, Louisiana Attorney General

Justices for the Court: Henry B. Brown, Stephen J. Field, Melville W. Fuller, Horace Gray, Rufus W. Peckham, George Shiras, Jr., Edward Douglas White

Justices Dissenting: John Marshall Harlan I (David Josiah Brewer did not participate)

Date of Decision: May 18, 1896

Decision: Ruled in favor of Ferguson by finding that Louisiana's law providing for "separate but equal" treatment for blacks and whites was constitutionally valid.

Significance: The decision was a major setback for minorities seeking equality in the United States. The ruling further paved the way for numerous state laws throughout the country making segregation which resulted in discrimination legal in almost all parts of daily life. The "separate but equal" standard lasted until the 1950s when the Supreme Court finally reversed this decision.

In 1900, Theodore Roosevelt was quoted as saying: "As a race . . . the [blacks] are altogether inferior to the whites . . . [and] can never rise to a very high place. . . I do not believe that the average Negro . . . is as yet in any way fit to take care of himself and others. . . If he were . . . there would be no Negro race problems." (from *In Their Own Words: A History of the American Negro* [1965], edited by Milton Meltzer.

Such were the misguided perceptions of many white Americans in the late nineteenth and early twentieth centuries. Despite efforts by Congress and the federal government in the wake of the American Civil War (1861–65) to abolish slavery and extend the same basic civil rights enjoyed by white Americans to black Americans, prejudice against blacks remained strong. The U.S. Supreme Court consistently delivered decisions greatly limiting how much the government could do to protect the rights of blacks. Southern states increasingly passed laws, known as Jim Crow laws, keeping whites and blacks separated. State-ordered segregation [keeping races from mixing] continued a way of life in the South well established from earlier slavery days.

In 1890, Louisiana passed a law known as the Separate Car Law requiring railroads to provide "equal but separate accommodations for the white and colored races." The law barred anyone from sitting in a railway car not designated for their own race. The law was not only poorly received by Louisiana's black population, but also by the railway companies because of the extra expense needed to provide separate cars.

Homer Adolph Plessy

As soon as the Separate Car Law was passed, black leaders in Louisiana became determined to challenge the law. They formed a Citizen's Committee to develop a strategy to test its constitutionality. Acting on their behalf, Homer A. Plessy, a shoemaker, bought a first class ticket on June 7, 1892 on the East Louisiana Railroad to ride from New Orleans to his home in Covington, Louisiana. Plessy, only one-eighth black, had light colored features and mostly appeared white. Under Louisiana law he was still considered black. When questioned by a railway conductor after finding a seat in the whites-only railroad car, he responded that he was colored. The conductor ordered Plessy to the colored-only car. Refusing to move, Plessy was arrested by Detective Chris Cain, removed from the train, and taken to the New Orleans city jail.

A Badge of Inferiority

Plessy and the Citizen's Committee immediately filed a lawsuit in the District Court of Orleans Parish claiming the Louisiana law denied him "equal protection of the laws" as guaranteed by the Fourteenth Amendment. The amendment states, "No State shall make or enforce any law which shall abridge [lessen] the privileges . . . of citizens of the United States . . . nor deny to any person within its jurisdiction [geographical area over which a government has authority] the equal protection of the laws." Equal protection of the laws means persons or groups of persons in similar situations must be treated equally by the laws. In addition, Plessy charged the restrictions, in a sense, reintroduced slavery by denying equality. Thus, the law also violated the Thirteenth Amendment's ban on slavery. Plessy argued that the state law "stamps the colored race with a badge of inferiority."

Judge John H. Ferguson, relying on several legal precedents (principles of former decisions), found Plessy guilty and sentenced him to either pay a twenty-five dollar fine or spend twenty days in jail. Plessy appealed to the Louisiana Supreme Court which upheld the conviction. Plessy next appealed to the U.S. Supreme Court for a court order forbidding Ferguson from carrying out the conviction. The Court accepted the case, but due to the large number of cases waiting to be decided by the Court, almost four years passed before it was heard.

Separate But Equal

Finally, on April 13, 1896 Plessy argued his case in Court. The state responded that the Louisiana law merely made a distinction between blacks and whites, but did not actually treat one as inferior to the other. Less than a month later, on May 18, the Court issued its 7-1 decision in accepting the state's arguments. Justice Henry B. Brown, delivering the Court's decision, wrote,

> **A statute [law] which implies [expresses] merely a legal distinction between the white and colored races—a distinction which is found in the color of the two races, and which must always exist so long as white men are distinguished from the other race by color—has no tendency to destroy the legal equality of the two races.**

The Court reaffirmed Plessy's conviction by finding that the Louisiana's law did not violate either the Thirteenth or Fourteenth Amendments. Brown stated that the equal protection clause of the Fourteenth Amendment "could not have been intended to abolish distinctions based upon color, or to enforce social . . . equality." Segregation did not violate equal protection, according to Brown. The state had properly used its police powers in a "reasonable" way to promote the public good by keeping peace between the races. As Brown commented, "If the two races are to meet upon terms of social equality, it must be the result of voluntary consent of the individuals." With that finding, Brown gave Supreme Court approval to the "separate but equal" concept.

A Color-Blind Constitution

In a historically important and emotional dissent, Justice John Marshall Harlan, a native Kentuckian and former slaveholder, boldly wrote,

> **Our Constitution is color-blind, and neither knows nor tolerates classes among citizens. . . In my opinion, the judgement this rendered will, in time, prove to be . . . [harmful]. . . The present decision . . . will not only stimulate aggressions . . . brutal and irritating, on the admitted rights of colored citizens, but will encourage the belief that it is possible, by means of state enactments [laws], to defeat the beneficent [valuable] purposes . . . which the people of the United States had in view when they adopted the recent [Thirteenth and Fourteenth] amendments of the Constitution.**

Agreeing with Plessy's arguments, Harlan charged that segregation created a "badge of servitude" likening it to slavery.

Separate And Unequal

The ruling, that gave constitutional approval to racial segregation, presented a major setback to black Americans and others seeking equality between the races. It would greatly influence social customs in the United States for most of the next six decades. The Court did not address that separate facilities would deny blacks access to the same quality of accommodations as whites. Rarely would separate facilities be as good,

HENRY BILLINGS BROWN

Supreme Court Justice Henry Billings Brown delivered the Court opinion in *Plessy v. Ferguson* (1896) essentially condemning black Americans to extensive racial discrimination for at least the next sixty years. Born in South Lee, Massachusetts in 1836, Brown was the son of a prosperous New England businessman. He was a graduate of Yale University with some limited training in law at Yale and Harvard. After moving to Michigan, Brown married the daughter of a wealthy Detroit lumber trader and, consequently, became independently wealthy. Brown established a successful law practice and taught law. In 1875 he was appointed to the U.S. District Court for the Eastern District of Michigan and in 1890 was appointed by President Benjamin Harrison to the U.S. Supreme Court.

Many considered Brown to be wise and fair during his time and warmly amiable in character. However, Brown largely opposed government regulation of business and recognition of individual civil rights, focusing instead on protecting property rights and free enterprise. Brown was a social elitist [higher social standing than most] who held many of the prejudices prominent during his time toward blacks, women, Jews, and immigrants. He did not believe laws should require changes in social custom when strong public sentiments were against it. Though he was relatively popular at the time, his decision in *Plessy* upholding state-required segregation later greatly affected his reputation. Due to failing eyesight, Brown retired from the Court in 1906 and later died in New York City in 1913 at the age of seventy-seven.

and because of the lengthy history of discrimination in America, blacks held little political power to make sure separate facilities would become equal in quality.

The phrase "separate but equal" became symbolic of forced racial segregation in the nation invading almost every aspect of American society, including restaurants, railroads, streetcars, waiting rooms, parks, cemeteries, churches, hospitals, prisons, elevators, theaters, schools, public restrooms, water fountains, and even public telephones. Not until 1954 in ***Brown v. Board of Education*** did the Court finally act to overturn the "separate but equal" doctrine, three generations after the fateful *Plessy* decision.

Suggestions for further reading

Fireside, Harvey. Plessy v. Ferguson: *Separate But Equal?* Enslow Publishers, Inc., 1997.

Howard, John R. *The Shifting Wind: The Supreme Court and Civil Rights from Reconstruction to* Brown. Albany, NY: State University of New York Press, 1999.

Lofgren, Charles A. *The* Plessy *case: a legal-historical interpretation.* New York: Oxford University Press, 1987.

Olsen, Otto H. *The Thin Disguise: Turning Point in Negro History,* Plessy v. Ferguson, *1864–1896.* New York: Humanities Press 1967.

Shelley v. Kraemer 1948

Petitioner: J.D. Shelley

Respondent: Louis Kraemer

Petitioner's Claim: That contracts preventing African Americans from purchasing homes violate the Fourteenth Amendment.

Chief Lawyers for Petitioner: George L. Vaughn and Herman Willer

Chief Lawyer for Respondent: Gerald L. Seegers

Justices for the Court: Hugo Lafayette Black, Harold Burton, William O. Douglas, Felix Frankfurter, Frank Murphy, Frederick Moore Vinson

Justices Dissenting: None (Robert H. Jackson, Stanley Forman Reed, and Wiley Blount Rutledge did not participate)

Date of Decision: May 3, 1948

Decision: The Supreme Court said the Fourteenth Amendment prevents courts from enforcing race discrimination in real estate contracts.

Significance: *Shelley* ended a powerful form of race discrimination in housing.

When the American Civil War ended in 1865, the United States ended slavery with the Thirteenth Amendment. Three years later in 1868, it adopted the Fourteenth Amendment. The Equal Protection Clause of the

Fourteenth Amendment says a state may not "deny to any person within its jurisdiction the equal protection of the laws." The main purpose of the Equal Protection Clause was to prevent states from discriminating against African Americans.

The Fourteenth Amendment only applies to the states. It does not prevent race discrimination by individual people. After 1868, racial prejudice led many people to continue race discrimination on their own.

Whites Only

In 1911 there was a neighborhood in St. Louis, Missouri, where thirty-nine people owned fifty-seven parcels of land. In February of that year, thirty of the owners signed an agreement not to rent or sell their property to African Americans or Asian Americans. Such an agreement is called a restrictive covenant. The owners who signed the restrictive covenant had forty-seven of the fifty-seven parcels in the neighborhood.

In August 1945, J.D. Shelley and his wife, who were African Americans, bought a parcel of land in the neighborhood from someone named Fitzgerald. The Shelleys were unaware of the restrictive covenant. Louis Kraemer and his wife, who owned another parcel in the neighborhood, sued the Shelleys in the Circuit Court of St. Louis. The Kraemers asked the court to take the Shelleys' land away and give it back to Fitzgerald.

The court ruled in favor of the Shelleys because the restrictive covenant did not have the proper signatures. On appeal, however, the Supreme Court of Missouri reversed and ruled in favor of the Kraemers. The court said the restrictive covenant was legal and ordered the Shelleys to leave their land. Determined to stay, the Shelleys took the case to the U.S. Supreme Court.

Race Discrimination Unenforceable

With a 6–0 decision, the Supreme Court reversed again and ruled in favor of the Shelleys. Chief Justice Frederick Moore Vinson wrote the opinion for the Court. Chief Justice Vinson said the right to own property is one of the rights protected by the Fourteenth Amendment. That means a state would not be allowed to create a restrictive covenant that discriminated against people because of their race.

Real estate covenants worked to keep minority families from buying houses in nicer neighborhoods. Reproduced by permission of Ken Estell.

Missouri, of course, did not create the restrictive covenant that applied to the Shelleys' land. Private owners created it in 1911. That meant the restrictive covenant itself did not violate the Fourteenth Amendment. The only way to enforce the covenant, however, was to go to court, as the Kraemers had done.

Chief Justice Vinson said the Fourteenth Amendment made it illegal for state courts to enforce restrictive covenants that discriminate against people because of their race. Vinson said, "freedom from discrimination by the States in the enjoyment of property rights was among

CHIEF JUSTICE FREDERICK MOORE VINSON

Frederick Moore Vinson was born in Louisa, Kentucky, on January 22, 1890. Vinson worked his way through Centre College in Kentucky, earning an undergraduate degree in 1909 and a law degree in 1911. He then practiced law in his hometown until 1923, serving briefly during that time as city attorney and commonwealth attorney.

In 1923, Vinson was elected to the U.S. House of Representatives. He served there from 1924 to 1929 and again from 1931 to 1938. In between he practiced law in Ashland, Kentucky. In 1938 Vinson became a judge on the U.S. Court of Appeals for the District of Columbia. After working as a judge for five years, Vinson pursued a career in the executive branch of the federal government. He worked for presidents Roosevelt and Truman, serving under Truman as Secretary of the Treasury.

When Chief Justice Harlan Fiske Stone died in 1946, President Truman appointed Vinson to replace Stone. From Vinson's years of loyal service to American presidents, Truman knew Vinson would protect presidential power from the Supreme Court. During his seven years on the Supreme Court, Vinson voted regularly in favor of governmental power over individual rights. ***Shelley v. Kraemer*** was a rare exception to that tendency. Vinson died from a heart attack on September 8, 1953.

the basic objectives sought … by the framers of the Fourteenth Amendment. … The Fourteenth Amendment declares that all persons, whether colored or white, shall stand equal before the laws of the States."

In the end, then, the Kraemers were not allowed to take the Shelleys' land away. The decision was an early victory for African Americans, who were struggling to protect their civil rights. Six years later, the Court would order public schools to stop segregation, the practice of separating blacks and whites in different schools. Such decisions gave Americans the chance to live and go to school together in the melting pot of the United States.

Suggestions for further reading

Bourgoin, Suzanne Michele, and Paula Kay Byers, eds. *Encyclopedia of World Biography.* Detroit: Gale Research, 1998.

Gillam, Scott. Discrimination: Prejudice in Action. Enslow Publishers, Inc., 1995.

McKissack, Pat. Taking a Stand against Racism and Racial Discrimination. New York: Franklin Watts, 1990.

Phillips, Angela. Discrimination. New Discovery Books, 2000.

Wilson, Anna. African Americans Struggle for Equality. Vero Beach: Rourke, 1992.

Witt, Elder, ed. *Congressional Quarterly's Guide to the U.S. Supreme Court.* District of Columbia: Congressional Quarterly Inc., 1990.

Brown v. Board of Education 1954

Appellants: Oliver Brown and several other parents of black schoolchildren

Appellee: Board of Education of Topeka, Kansas

Appellant's Claim: That racial segregation of public schools denied black schoolchildren equal protection of the law as guaranteed by the Fourteenth Amendment.

Chief Lawyer for Appellants: Robert L. Carter, Thurgood Marshall, Spottswood W. Robinson, Charles S. Scott

Chief Lawyer for Appellee: Harold R. Fatzer, Paul E. Wilson

Justices for the Court: Hugo L. Black, Harold Burton, Tom C. Clark, William O. Douglas, Felix Frankfurter, Robert H. Jackson, Sherman Minton, Stanley Forman Reed, Chief Justice Earl Warren

Justices Dissenting: None

Date of Decision: May 17, 1954

Decision: Ruled in favor of Brown by finding that racial segregation in public schools was unconstitutional.

Significance: The decision was an historic ruling regarding segregation of public places. In ending segregation of public schools, the decision overturned *Plessy*'s "separate but equal" doctrine and paved the way for desegregation of other types of public places in the next two decades.

SEGREGATION AND DESEGREGATION

Immediately following the end of the American Civil War (1861–65), the U.S. government took a number of measures to recognize and protect the civil rights of black Americans. Three new constitutional amendments were adopted between 1865 and 1870 banning slavery, extending basic rights to blacks, and granting citizenship. From approximately 1865 to 1877, the U.S. military occupied the former Confederate states to enforce social and political changes in Southern society. In addition, Congress passed civil rights laws to protect black Americans from discrimination in public places. However, resistance by many Southern whites to social change remained strong. Finally, by the mid-1870s government efforts to force social change had weakened and Southern whites began to gain political control of the South again. The Southern states and local governments began to pass laws to keep blacks politically and economically inferior to whites. Many of the laws, known as Jim Crow laws, forced public racial segregation (keeping the races from mixing).

The U.S. Supreme Court handed down rulings which greatly hindered black's drive for social justice. First, in ***Civil Rights Cases*** (1883) the Court ruled that constitutional protections did not extend to privately owned public places, such as restaurants, inns, and theaters. Therefore, private owners of such establishments could keep blacks from entering. Then, in 1896 the Court ruled in ***Plessy v. Ferguson*** that keeping races separated was constitutionally valid as long as facilities for blacks were equal to those for whites. This decision establishing the "separate but equal" doctrine added further support to Jim Crow laws. State-required segregation invaded every aspect of public social life in schools, transportation, and housing, particularly in the South.

Greatly disappointed with the Court decisions and not accepting that the Constitution allows racial discrimination, a group of black and white proponents of social justice came together in 1909 to form the National Association for the Advancement of Colored People (NAACP). The NAACP was dedicated to fighting segregation and the Jim Crow laws in the courts. After achieving some courtroom victories, the NAACP began to focus in the 1930s on segregation in public schools. By 1939, future Supreme Court justice Thurgood Marshall assumed leadership of the NAACP's legal department, known as the NAACP Legal Defense Fund.

Following World War II (1939–45), Marshall and the NAACP gained two victories in school segregation. The Court in *Sweatt v. Painter* (1950) ruled that a separate law school for blacks in Texas could not provide the same opportunities as the long established University of Texas Law School. In *McLaurin v. Oklahoma State Regents* (1950) the Court ruled that a separate library and lecture hall seat for a black graduate student were not constitutional. However, the NAACP had not directly addressed the "separate but equal" doctrine or school segregation in general. They began searching for the perfect cases to challenge those social policies.

Oliver Brown's Daughter, Linda

Like many states, Kansas had passed a law giving school districts the choice of segregating their schools. The Topeka school district chose to do just that. By the early 1950s twenty-two public elementary schools existed in town, eighteen for white schoolchildren and four for black schoolchildren.

Born in 1919, Oliver Brown was a railroad welder, a war veteran, and assistant pastor at his church. He had no reputation as a social activist, quietly living in his community. Living close to his work, his neighborhood bordered a railroad switching yard. He and his wife had three daughters. Though they lived only seven blocks from the nearest elementary school, it was for whites only. His children had to walk through the dangerous switching yard to the nearest black school about a mile away. Oliver did not want to have his eight year-old daughter walk through the switchyards to school simply because she was black. Brown learned of the NAACP looking for test cases to challenge school segregation policies and agreed to join the effort in addition to several other parents of black schoolchildren in Topeka. In September of 1950, Oliver took his daughter Linda to the nearby white school to enroll in the third grade. The school's principal refused to admit her.

In March of 1951 Brown aided by NAACP lawyers filed a lawsuit against the Topeka Board of Education in the U.S. District Court for the District of Kansas requesting a court order to prohibit continuation of the segregated school system.

The District Court tried the case in late June. Among witness supporting Brown were experts testifying that segregated schools were automatically unequal despite their quality because the separation gave black children a feeling of inferiority. Such a system could not possibly prepare them for their adult lives. The school board responded that because almost all aspects of public life were racially segregated even restaurants and bathrooms, segregated schools were actually preparing the children for the realities of adult life. The board did not see segregation as an undesirable way to live. The Board pointed to some famous black Americans as examples that segregation did not keep blacks from success. Brown countered that exceptions always exist, but for most children segregation significantly reduces opportunities later in life. People tend to live up to what is expected of them, and segregation sends a clear message of lower expectations.

In August of 1951 the District Court issued its ruling. Despite agreeing with Brown's arguments concerning the bad effects of school segregation on black schoolchildren, the court stated that because of the Supreme Court ruling in *Plessy* it had no choice but to rule in favor of the Board of Education. No constitutional violations existed.

Oliver Brown Goes to Washington

Brown appealed the court decision to the U.S. Supreme Court. The Court accepted the case and in June of 1952 combined it with four other cases challenging school segregation policies elsewhere in the nation. On December 9, 1952, the two sides presented their arguments before the Court. Brown argued that the school segregation policy violated his family's equal protection of the law under the Fourteenth Amendment. The amendment declares, "No state shall . . . deny to any person within its jurisdiction [geographic area over which the government has authority] the equal protection of the laws." John W. Davis, a presidential candidate earlier in 1924, presented the Board of Education's arguments. He claimed that the Fourteenth Amendment never intended to prevent segregation of schools. Besides, he claimed, "the happiness, the progress and the welfare of these children is best promoted in segregated schools." He further added the courts did not even have constitutional authority to direct how local school districts would be operated.

With only eight members of the Court present instead of the usual nine, a stalemate was reached after hearing arguments. The Court requested the two sides to come back and reargue the case again. The Court further requested that for the second hearing, the two sides should focus on some specific issues, including the Fourteenth Amendment's Equal Protection Clause. The Court wanted to explore more about the amendment's intent toward school segregation at the time of adoption. Though disappointed with the Court's decision to rehear the case, Brown and the NAACP lawyers saw it as an indication the Court was considering overturning *Plessy.*

Mr. Brown Returns to Washington

While the parties were away preparing their new arguments, Chief Justice Fred M. Vinson died and Earl Warren was appointed in his place. Arguments on the points the Court had requested were held almost exactly one year later on December 8, 1953. Research by the parties indicated that school segregation was not really considered when the Fourteenth Amendment was written and adopted. In fact, required school attendance essentially did not exist in the 1860s. Consequently, effects of the amendment on public education was not a major concern at the time.

On May 17, 1954, the Court delivered its unanimous (9-0) ruling with a fairly brief written opinion for such an important case. The Court found in favor of Brown and the NAACP by agreeing segregation is automatically unequal regardless if the black children had the same quality of facilities, teachers, and books. New Chief Justice Earl Warren, writing for the Court, emphasized that education had become a much more important part of American life since the 1890s when the *Plessy* decision had been made. As Warren wrote,

> **Today, education is perhaps the most important function of the state and local governments. . . It is required in the performance of our most basic public responsibilities. . . It is the very foundation of good citizenship. Today it is a principal instrument in awakening the child to cultural values, in preparing him for later professional training, and in helping him to adjust normally to his environment. . . Such an opportunity . . . is a right which must be made available to all on equal terms.**

Building on its 1950 decisions in *Sweatt* and *McLaurin,* Warren wrote,

> **We conclude that in the field of public education the doctrine of 'separate but equal' has no place. Separate educational facilities are inherently [undeniably] unequal. Therefore, we hold that the [Browns] and others similarly situated . . . by reason of the segregation complained of, [are] deprived of the equal protection of the laws guaranteed by the Fourteenth Amendment.**

The "separate but equal' doctrine allowing the separation of children by race into different schools violated the Fourteenth Amendment. Relying on the results of seven sociological studies on the harmful effects of racial segregation, he added that segregation gave black schoolchildren "a feeling of inferiority [feeling less worthy than others] as to their status [place] in the community that may affect their hearts and minds in a way unlikely to ever be undone." Not only were their lives harmed, but the general welfare of American society as well.

The Court remanded (returned) Brown's and the other four cases back to the local courts to determine if the local schools were doing enough to move desegregation (outlawing segregation) along.

The Court also requested the NAACP lawyers to come back yet again the following year with suggestions on how school desegregation should be carried out. In 1955 the Court unanimously ruled that all school districts must desegregate "with all deliberate speed." The Court established guidelines giving local school officials the main responsibility for desegregation, but gave the federal district courts responsibility to watch over how the schools were doing. The courts were to consider unique local factors hindering desegregation progress.

Slow Change

The Brown decision introduced fundamental changes in U.S. society. But, just as it took nearly sixty years to reverse legalized discrimination as supported by the *Plessy* decision, another twenty years would pass before school desegregation in America would be accomplished. Resistance to the *Brown* decision contributed to the growth of the civil rights movement in the 1950s. Considerable social unrest and violence followed in the 1960s. Oliver Brown died in 1961, not to see the ultimate results of his efforts to simply have children attend the public school closest to their home. One by one the government took resistant local school districts to court to force desegregation. Finally, by the early 1970s school segregation policies had been largely eliminated.

The *Brown* ruling also set the stage for desegregation in other phases of public life as well, from bus stations to public libraries to restrooms. However, the racial mix in public schools still was an issue by the close of the twentieth century. White flight to the suburbs in the 1960s and growth of private schools still left a largely segregated system with black urban schools and white suburban schools. Still, the *Brown*

THURGOOD MARSHALL

Thurgood Marshall, one of the chief lawyers for Oliver Brown in his case against the Topeka Board of Education, later became the first black American Supreme Court justice. Marshall was born in Baltimore, Maryland on July 2, 1908 and named after his grandfather, a former slave. His father, William, was a railroad dining car waiter and later chief waiter at a private club. His mother, Norma, taught school at a segregated black elementary school. Young Marshall grew up experiencing first hand the widespread racial discrimination of early twentieth century America. He attended Lincoln University in Pennsylvania, the oldest black college in the United States and there displayed strong speaking skills while leading a successful debate team. Unable to attend the University of Maryland Law School because it was white-only, Marshall graduated first in his class in law from Howard University.

Dedicated to combating social injustice, Marshall quickly attracted the attention of the National Association for the Advancement of Colored People (NAACP) which was recruiting lawyers to fight segregation laws. One of his first successful cases was ending the segregation policies of the University of Maryland Law School. At age thirty, Marshall became chief lawyer for the NAACP. He successfully argued twenty-nine cases before the U.S. Supreme Court, becoming known as "Mr. Civil Rights."

In 1961 President John F. Kennedy appointed Marshall to a federal judge position and in 1965 he became Solicitor General of the United States under President Lyndon B. Johnson. In 1967, Johnson nominated him to the Supreme Court where he served until 1991. Thurgood Marshall died of heart failure two years later at age eighty-four. Widely respected for his lifelong fight for individual rights, thousands of mourners waited hours in winter weather to pay their last respects as his body lay in state in the Supreme Court building.

ruling is regarded as one of the most important Supreme Court decisions in the nation's history.

Suggestions for further reading

Fireside, Harvey, and Sarah B. Fuller. Brown v. Board of Education: *Equal Schooling for All.* Hillside, NJ: Enslow Publishers, Inc., 1994.

Howard, John R. *The Shifting Wind: The Supreme Court and Civil Rights from Reconstruction to* Brown. Albany, NY: State University of New York Press, 1999.

Thomas, Bettye C., and V. P. Franklin. *My Soul Is a Witness: A Chronology of the Civil Rights Era, 1954-1965.* New York: Henry Holt and Company, 1999.

Ware, Leland. *Thurgood Marshall: Freedom's Defender.* Alexandria, VA: Time Life Education, 1999.

Williams, Juan. *Thurgood Marshall: American Revolutionary.* New York: Time Books, 1998.

Swann v. Charlotte-Mecklenburg Board of Education 1971

Appellant: James E. Swann

Appellee: Charlotte-Mecklenburg Board of Education

Appellant's Claim: That the local public school desegregation plan was inadequate to achieve integration and protect the civil rights of its students.

Chief Lawyers for Appellant: Julius LeVonne Chambers, James M. Nabritt III

Chief Lawyers for Appellee: William J. Waggoner, Benjamin S. Horack

Justices for the Court: Hugo L. Black, Harry A. Blackmun, William J. Brennan, Jr., Chief Justice Warren E. Burger, William O. Douglas, John Marshall Harlan II, Thurgood Marshall, Potter Stewart, Byron R. White

Justices Dissenting: None

Date of Decision: April 20, 1971

Decision: Ruled in favor of Swann by upholding the federal district court's ambitious desegregation plan designed to fully integrate the district's public schools.

Significance: The ruling affirmed the role of federal district courts in overseeing operations of local school districts.

SEGREGATION AND DESEGREGATION

Following the landmark Supreme Court decision in ***Brown v. Board of Education*** (1954) ending legally enforced racial segregation (keeping races apart) in public schools, progress toward racial integration (mixing of the races) continued to be slow. The tradition of having separate schools for black and white children was well established in American culture.

A Southern Resistance

The Southern states in particular immediately began thinking of ways to avoid obeying the Court's desegregation (ban segregation) directions given in *Brown*. In reaction, the Court in *Brown v. Board of Education II* (1955) directed the lower federal district courts to develop plans to force desegregation. Resistance persisted. One Virginia school board even closed its public schools to avoid integrating them. Tuition monies were granted to students to attend segregated private schools. In reaction, the Supreme Court in *Griffin v. County School Board* (1964) ordered the public schools to open again. "Freedom of choice" plans were also introduced in which children could choose which school to attend, white or black. The Court in *Green v. County School Board* (1968) ruled this approach was not strong enough to truly achieve integration. The Court held that the student bodies of each school should be similar in mix of races as the population in the area in general.

As white Americans fled the trouble-ridden cities to suburbs and predominately white schools, the distinct courts decided the primary way to swiftly integrate schools was through busing. Busing involved carrying students long distances on a daily basis to create more racially-mixed schools.

The Charlotte-Mecklenburg School District

The Charlotte-Mecklenburg School District of North Carolina was large, including both the city of Charlotte as well as the rural region of Mecklenburg County. The district included 101 schools scattered across some 550 square miles. Twenty-nine percent of the 84,000 school-age children in the area were black and most of them lived in one particular section of Charlotte. A desegregation plan was created in 1965 to integrate the public schools. The plan had redrawn school attendance zones and allowed students freedom of choice regarding which school they wished to attend. Almost 30,000 students were bused to distant schools under the plan. However, little integration resulted as over half of the black students remained in all-black schools. The schools remained generally the same as before.

Swann Applies Green

Inspired by the Court's decision in *Green,* James Swann and other residents of the school district finally filed a lawsuit in 1968 claiming the integration plan was not effective. Unlike previous court cases, however, that focused primarily on rural school districts, this case involved urban (city) schools. For example, the school district involved in the Green decision was a small rural school district. Charlotte-Mecklenburg, on the other hand, was what is known as a large "unified" school district including various communities.

Swann won his suit in federal district court. Overseeing a new Charlotte-Mecklenburg plan, the court created a much more ambitious and expensive plan in 1970 involving increased school busing. The plan stated that twenty-nine percent of each public school should consist of

The police were often forced to monitor the bussing of African American students into white schools for the students' protection. Reproduced by permission of the Corbis Corporation.

black students, reflecting the percentage of black students in the entire school district. An additional 13,000 students would need to be bused. To begin applying the plan the district had to buy one hundred new buses. The plan would cost a half million dollars a year in addition to one million dollars to get started. Not surprisingly, the new plan met considerable resistance from the school board.

The school board appealed the plan to the Fourth Circuit Court of Appeals. The appeals court, agreeing with the board, reversed part of the plan claiming it placed an unreasonable burden on the board. In response to Swann's defeat in the appeals court, the Legal Defense Fund of the National Association for the Advancement of Colored People (NAACP) appealed the decision to the U.S. Supreme Court which agreed to hear the case.

To the Supreme Court

Challenged in the Supreme Court, the Court in 1971 unanimously ruled in favor of Swann and the NAACP. The more extensive desegregation plan developed by the district court was to be followed. Chief Justice Warren E. Burger, writing for the Court, recognized that busing, though not necessarily a desirable means, may be the only means to begin the school integration process. Freedom of choice in deciding which school a child would like to attend could not adequately solve the segregation issue. As Burger stated,

> **In these circumstances, we find no basis for holding that the local school authorities may not be required to employ bus transportation as one tool of school desegregation. Desegregation plans cannot be limited to the walk-in [close-by] school.**

Chief Justice Burger supplied broad guidelines to district court judges still dealing with segregated school systems. The mathematical ratios imposed on Charlotte-Mecklenburg, in which twenty-nine out of every one hundred students in each school would be black, was one approach meeting the Court's approval. Another tool was redesign of school attendance boundaries to include residential areas of both races.

Courts in Charge of Schools

The Court once again approved supervision of public school districts by federal district court judges. The Court commanded that district courts

SCHOOL BUSING

The Court decision in *Swann v. Charlotte Mecklenburg Board of Education* (1971) firmly established that lower federal district courts could force school districts to adopt school busing plans to achieve racial integration. School busing, itself, was not new to students at the time. Almost forty percent of American schoolchildren in the 1960s rode buses to schools. But the nature of busing changed. Instead of riding to the nearest community school, now children began riding to distant schools in unfamiliar places. For example, in *Evans v. Buchanan* (1977) a massive desegregation busing plan was created in Delaware combining many school districts into one that held forty percent of all the state's school students.

Opposition to such busing was immediately strong from both white and black Americans. Though a number of children received improved educational opportunities in better supported suburban schools, many believed busing placed unnecessary hardships on the schoolchildren. The reasons were many. Often the rides were long, it was more difficult for many parents to participate in their children's education, participating in after-school activities was difficult, bused children lost their sense of community, some children became even more alienated (withdrawn) from school, and limited school funds were being used for busing rather than for education. Often children still tended to socialize with their own race in their new schools. This led to segregation within schools and sometimes actually increasing interracial hostilities and tensions of the community.

Through the 1980s opposition to busing grew steadily. Finally, in 1991 the Court essentially ended the forced-school busing era by ruling in *Board of Education of Oklahoma City Public Schools v. Dowell* that busing was intended only to be a temporary measure. Some school busing programs did continue, largely voluntarily under supervision of local school boards.

were to "make every effort to achieve the greatest possible degree of actual desegregation." The severity of the constitutional violation, Burger wrote, should determine the extent of the forced integration measures. In a later ruling the Court added that such fixes could be discontinued when integration was accomplished.

The Court's support of the Charlotte plan led to extensive busing programs in many parts of the United States during the 1970s, including Boston, Los Angeles, Cleveland, and other major cities. Busing became one of the most controversial social issues of the decade. The mood of the Supreme Court toward forced desegregation, particularly through busing, began to change by the 1980s with five new justices appointed. The Court became less supportive of such sweeping district court desegregation plans as approved in Charlotte-Mecklenburg. In fact, the 1971 *Swann* decision was the last unanimous ruling (all nine justices agreeing) by the Supreme Court in school desegregation cases, a remarkable trend that had started with the *Brown* decision in 1954.

Busing continued to spark controversy through the end of the century. Busing was highly unpopular among black Americans because of the distances their children were being taken and fears of safety in predominately white schools. Resistance was most pronounced in the North, perhaps less accustomed to long-distance busing than the largely rural South. Such court-ordered desegregation plans as adopted by Charlotte-Mecklenburg led to very mixed results in achieving integration through the years. Despite extensive busing, many schools still remained racially segregated to a large degree. The rise of largely white private schools and the trend of white families moving out of the cities to new school districts in the suburbs where few minorities lived were key reasons.

Suggestions for further reading

Belknap, Michel R. *Desegregation of Public Education.* New York: Garland Press, 1991.

Leone, Bruno. Racism: *Opposing Viewpoints.* 2nd Edition. St. Paul, MN: Greenhaven Press, 1986.

Schwartz, Bernard. *Swann's Way: The School Busing Case and the Supreme Court.* New York: Oxford University Press, 1986.

Watras, Joseph. *Politics, Race, and Schools: Racial Integration, 1954-1994.* New York: Garland Publications, 1997.

The American governmental system is a representative democracy with a key fundamental element—the right or privilege to vote. The system operates by peaceable argument. People take sides, debate (argue their views), and vote to reach a decision. Just because a decision is reached does not suggest the arguments are over. The decision only means voters will abide by the decision of the majority for a specific amount of time until the next vote is taken. Consequently, in the United States, government by the people never means full consent (everyone agreeing on one way). At any given time many citizens may be opposed to who is in power or may be against what the government is doing.

But even the smallest minorities, by participating actively, may influence a democracy. A democracy undergoes constant change in responding to the needs and concerns of its people. Voting provides the means to change.

Historical Perspective

At the beginning of the twenty-first century most Americans think of the right to vote as one of the most basic rights of U.S. citizenship. However, citizenship and voting have not always been directly related. From the signing of the U.S. Constitution in 1787 until 1971, large numbers of American citizens could not vote.

The Framers of the Constitution feared giving too much political power to the people would encourage mob rule. In 1776 John Adams, a respected advocate for American liberty who would become America's second president, warned that granting the vote to everyone would bring political disaster. In 1787 Alexander Hamilton told the constitutional convention that "the people seldom judge or determine right." The Framers believed voting should be limited to white landowning men. Owning property, they believed, gave men a stake in society and made them more responsible citizens.

As originally adopted, the U.S. Constitution allowed those eligible to vote to only elect members of the House of Representatives. To check the power of the people, the President and senators were elected by state legislators. The Framers also left to the states the power to decide which of their citizens should have the right to vote. As they hoped, most states enacted laws requiring some kind of property or wealth—usually a certain amount of land—before allowing men to vote. The common man who owned no property or lacked a fixed amount of wealth could not vote at all. Congress did reserve for itself in Article I of the Constitution the power to control the time and place of elections.

The property requirements became increasingly unpopular. Beginning in Ohio in 1802, state after state passed laws giving the vote to all white men whether they owned property or not. By the late 1820s only Virginia still had the property requirement. Male citizens also won the right to vote in presidential elections and to choose senators by direct vote when the Seventeenth Amendment was ratified in 1913.

Yet, most adult citizens still could not vote simply because they were female, black, or young. The struggle for the right to vote would continue as a peoples' fight, battling step by step, to turn America into a nation truly "of the people."

Women Gain the Right to Vote

The extraordinary letter by Abigail Adams illustrated that even before the Constitution was penned a few women were not content to be voiceless in the new nation. But the thought of women voting seemed ridiculous to many men and women. Most women accepted the idea of leaving decisions of government, like those of the family, to males. Yet, in July of 1848 five women in the village of Seneca Falls, New York called a meeting that started a fight to secure the woman's right to vote. Lead by Elizabeth Stanton, the group presented a resolution declaring, "we insist that [women] have immediate admission to all rights and privileges which belong to them as citizens of the United States . . . it is the duty of the women of this country to secure to themselves the right of elective franchise [the right to vote]." Suffrage (right to vote) associations concerned with women's rights began to appear around the nation. Victories were small at first but on December 10, 1869 the women of Wyoming became the first to win an unlimited right to vote.

The Supreme Court did not help the suffrage cause. In 1875, in ***Minor v. Happersett,*** the Court ruled that granting voting rights only to men in a state constitution was legal since the U.S. Constitution left the choice of who was qualified to vote to the states.

At the time, many considered petitions to Congress for a nationwide constitutional amendment granting women the right to vote laughable. However, in 1878 Susan B. Anthony managed a senate committee hearing on an amendment which simply declared, "The right of citizens of the United States to vote shall not be denied or abridged by the United States or any State on account of sex."

By 1890 a more united front emerged with the National American Women's Suffrage Association (NAWSA). By 1910 eleven states had granted women the right to vote. The campaign grew and by 1914 all major women's groups had joined the suffrage campaign with some groups, such as the National Women's Party, becoming militant.

Finally, in 1919 following World War I (1914–18) in which women admirably worked on the home front in support of military efforts, Congress passed a constitutional amendment giving women nationwide the right to vote. By 1920 the Nineteenth Amendment was ratified and became law with wording exactly as Anthony crafted in 1878. Little legal resistance to women's suffrage occurred following adoption of the amendment.

Black Americans Gain the Right to Vote

Ratified in 1870, fifty years before the Nineteenth Amendment, the Fifteenth Amendment stated "The right of citizens of the United States to vote shall not be denied or abridged by the United States or by any State on account of race, color, or previous condition of servitude." Although passed and ratified to assure black Americans the right to vote, blacks would not be able to freely exercise their voting rights until 1965.

Following the end of the American Civil War (1861–65), many people, particularly in the South, were determined to keep newly freed blacks as close to servitude as possible. Yet, by the end of 1867, under federal army rule, about 700,000 Southern black males had become registered voters. Under military protection, they joined in choosing delegates to form new state governments and electing officials to run them.

White Republicans from the North and the new black Republican leaders, primarily controlled the resulting governments. This outraged the Southern population, long a stronghold of the Democratic Party and white supremacy.

Realizing the importance of the right to vote, segregationists (those intent on keeping blacks and whites separate) used any means possible to keep black men from voting. Even with military protection, many black voters had been intimidated (threatened) and cheated of their votes. The intimidation grew violent and that violence became organized with such groups as the Ku Klux Klan. The Klan's hooded midnight riders terrorized their victims by burning their homes, barns, and crops, and whipping, clubbing, and murdering.

Recognizing the Fifteenth Amendment was ineffective, Congress in the 1870s passed laws banning terrorist groups and imposing stiff penalties for interfering with black voters. However, the Supreme Court persisted in a narrow view that only states could define who could vote, consequently taking the teeth out of the laws. Federal enforcement lessened. Furthermore, the Court viewed acts of private individuals denying the voting rights of others as outside the reach of federal government power. By 1900 all eleven former Confederate states had made it virtually impossible for blacks to vote.

Southern states carefully worded their voting requirements to avoid obvious constitutional violations. As long as the states' requirements did not appear to discriminate on the basis of "race, color, or previous condition of servitude" they were not considered in violation of the Fifteenth Amendment. Though written to appear as applying equally to all men, in reality their requirements were directed solely against persons of color. The exclusion strategies included grandfather clauses, literacy tests, white primaries, and the poll tax. These requirements, in their various forms, successfully excluded blacks from political participation until the mid-1960s. Whites completely dominated all levels of government in Southern states.

Grandfather Clauses and Literacy Tests

A "grandfather clause" required all voters to show that their ancestors could vote in 1866, before the post-Civil War Reconstruction era, or pass a literacy (able to read) test. First enacted in Mississippi in 1890, this strategy spread rapidly throughout the Southern states. Most whites were exempted from the literacy test, whether they could read or not, by the grandfather clause because typically most white men had ancestors eligible to vote in 1866. On the other hand, blacks in 1890 had no ancestors who were eligible to vote in 1866. In Mississippi by 1892 black voter registration dropped from approximately 70 percent of black adult males to under 6 percent. When tested in courts, states contended the Fifteenth Amendment was not violated because all voter applicants were required to pass the clause or test. In 1915 the Supreme Court struck down grandfather clauses as unconstitutional in *Guinn v. United States.* However, literacy tests were not suspended.

White Primaries

If a black American somehow managed to get past all the barriers and gain the right to vote, his vote was usually insignificant anyway due to the white-only primaries. Under laws adopted by most Southern states, political parties could set their own rules for membership in their party. While the Republican Party was non-existent, the Democratic Party organized as private clubs in each state excluding all blacks. Only members of the Democratic Party could vote for candidates in its primaries. Since the Democratic Party was overwhelmingly dominate, whoever won the all-white primary would win the general election. The black vote cast in the general election, therefore, was meaningless.

Cases challenging the practice began reaching the Supreme Court. In *Grovey v. Townsend* (1935) the Court unanimously decided the political party was a private club of volunteers, not part of the state government. Therefore, its actions were not restricted by the Constitution. However, in *United States v. Classic* (1941) the Court recognized the primary was becoming a key part of the state election process. Three years later in the landmark case of *Smith v. Allwright* (1944), the Court held that voting in primary elections was "a right secured by the

Constitution." Private all-white primaries were unconstitutional. The decision was later reaffirmed in *Terry v. Adams* (1953) finally ending white-only primaries.

Poll Tax

Another common barrier to black voters and to poor whites was the poll tax. The poll tax was simply a fee charged at the polling (voting) place. When the Constitution was written, the poll tax was considered a legitimate way to raise revenue, but by the 1850s poll taxes had disappeared. They returned in some states in the early twentieth century as a means to exclude blacks from the political process since many could not afford to pay the tax. The Court in *Breedlove v. Suttles* (1937) upheld the poll tax because it was applied to both black and white voters. Public opinion grew against the tax in the 1940s. But, it was not until 1964 that Congress was finally able to pass and the states ratify the Twenty-Fourth Amendment to the Constitution, abolishing the poll tax in federal elections. States still imposed poll taxes for state and local elections until the Court in *Harper v. Virginia State Board of Elections* (1966) finally struck down all poll taxes.

Voting Rights Act of 1965

The Civil Rights Movement of the 1950s and 1960s greatly raised public awareness of racial discrimination in America. Following the historic voting freedom march of 3,200 black protestors and white sympathizers from Selma to Montgomery, Alabama led by Dr. Martin Luther King, the Voting Rights Act of 1965 was signed into law by President Lyndon B. Johnson. Urging the passage of the act, Johnson had spoken to a joint session of Congress in March 1965, "Unless the right to vote be secured and undenied, all other rights are insecure and subject to denial for all citizens. The challenge of this right is a challenge to America itself."

The act prohibited any voting qualification requirements such as literacy tests in federal, state, local, general, and primary elections in any state or county where less than half the voting age residents were registered to vote. It applied to any type of qualification that denied the right of a U.S. citizen to vote because of race, color, or membership in a language minority group. In certain counties, registration would be taken over by federal examiners to ensure fairness in determining voter eligibility. The act also required seven states to obtain federal approval before making any changes to their election systems such as relocating polling sites, changing ballot forms, and altering election districts.

The act was immediately challenged in *South Carolina v. Katzenbach* (1966), but the Supreme Court ruled the act consistent with Congress' power to eliminate racial discrimination in voting. Within only a few years the rise in black voter registration was dramatic. In Mississippi alone black registration rose again to almost 60 percent by 1968. The act was amended in 1970 to suspend literacy tests nationwide. This suspension was upheld by the Court in ***Oregon v. Mitchell*** (1970).

One More Group—the Young

A still later group of Americans to achieve the right to vote were men and women aged eighteen to twenty. From ancient English common law, the age when a boy became a man was generally considered twenty-one. By the time the Fourteenth Amendment was ratified in 1868, twenty-one had become the standard age adopted by states to first vote. The amendment did not actually say anyone had to be that old to vote, but it did penalize states "when the right to vote . . . is denied to any of the male inhabitants of such State being twenty-one years of age. . . "

Attempts to lower the voting age to eighteen grew during World War I (1914–18) and World War II (1939–45). If young people were old enough to pay taxes and be sent to war, many believed, they should be able to vote. However, opponents argued that brawn to fight did not mean maturity to vote. By the 1950s opinion polls showed most Americans favored lowering the age, but Congress was unable to pass an amendment until March of 1971. The states took only two months to ratify the Twenty-sixth Amendment. As of 1971, virtually all American citizens age eighteen and older, regardless of race or sex, were eligible to vote.

Redistricting and Representation

A key issue related to voting rights and repeatedly brought before the courts is representation of minorities in the government in proportion to their numbers in the general population. Following passage of the Voting Rights Act, blacks made substantial political gains but were still under represented in proportion to their numbers. In 1975 only fifteen blacks were among the 435 members of the U.S. House of Representatives. By 1989 there were only twenty-five. If blacks were represented proportionately to the number of black Americans in the nation, there should be between forty and fifty members.

A key to fair representation from city to national levels is the way boundaries of political voting districts are drawn. Every ten years after a new national census is taken, state legislatures must redraw district boundaries to reflect population change, a process known as "redistricting" or "reapportionment." The political party in power in the state legislature controls the process. Unfortunately, drawing of boundaries often has more to do with political self-interest than fairness. "Gerrymandering" or the unfair drawing of district lines has frequently been at issue. If Republicans controlled the state legislature they would shape boundaries to create secure Republican districts. Democrats would do the same if they held power. Also, if boundaries split an area of black voters between three or four districts, their chance of electing a black is less. In reaction, black leaders demanded boundaries be drawn in a way to improve chances of electing black legislators.

In *Colegrove v. Green* (1946) the Court expressed reluctance about becoming involved in redistricting issues. Finally in ***Baker v. Carr*** (1962) the Court ruled federal courts could indeed address problems of unequal distribution of voters in legislative districts. In ***Reynolds v. Sims*** (1964) the Court applied the "one person, one vote" redistricting rule originally established in *Gray v. Sanders* (1963). The issue leading to the "one person, one vote" decision was the problem of rural district boundaries drawn many years ago. As city populations grew through the 1950s, rural districts with small populations would often have the same legislative representation as city districts containing many more residents. Because the practice violated the Equal Protection Clause of the Fourteenth Amendment, the Court sought to have districts redrawn to better correspond with population size. In *Wesberry v. Sanders* (1964) the Court urged states to make an honest effort to draw congressional districts with as nearly equal populations as possible.

The Road to a Fully Representative Government

By 2000 Americans had been shaping their right to vote for over two hundred years. Expansion of the right to vote came in response to the demands of the people for equality and fairness in the voting process. By consistently enlarging the number of eligible voters, Americans have enlarged their entire base of government through participation of more people. Voting decisions gradually came to represent a diversity of groups having a meaningful voice.

Suggestions for further reading

Severn, Bill. *The Right To Vote.* New York: Ives Washburn, Inc., 1972.

Thernstrom, Stephan, and Abigail Thernstrom. *America in Black and White: One Nation, Indivisible.* New York: Simon & Schuster, 1997.

Baker v. Carr
1962

Appellants: Charles W. Baker and others

Appellees: Joe E. Carr and others

Appellants' Claim: That voting districts drawn in a way that produces unequal political representation violates the Fourteenth Amendment's Equal Protection Clause.

Chief Lawyers for Appellants: Charles S. Rhyme, Z.T. Osborn, Jr.

Chief Lawyer for Appellees: Jack Wilson, Assistant Attorney General of Tennessee

Justices for the Court: Hugo L. Black, William J. Brennan, Jr., Tom C. Clark, William O. Douglas, Potter Stewart, Chief Justice Earl Warren

Justices Dissenting: Felix Frankfurter, John Marshall Harlan II (Charles Evans Whittaker did not participate)

Date of Decision: March 26, 1962

Decision: Ruled in favor of Baker by finding that constitutional challenges to apportionment could be addressed by federal courts.

Significance: This decision opened the door for under represented voters to have their voting districts redrawn under the direction of federal courts. The ruling initiated a decade of lawsuits eventually resulting in a redrawing of the nation's political map. The decision represented a major shift in the Court's position on the relationship of voting districts and constitutional protections.

The purpose of voting in America is to give citizens the opportunity to determine who will be making governmental decisions. Those elected are expected to represent the interests of the people in their district when crafting laws and policies. The way boundaries of voting districts are drawn and the number of voters contained within each district largely determines how fairly people are represented by that process.

For example, electing members to the U.S. House of Representatives is based on population figures. Congress limits the number of House members to a total of 435 nationwide. The number of representatives from each state is subject to change every ten years depending on population changes recorded by the U.S. census, a count of people and where they live. States gaining or losing population between the 1990 census and 2000, must redraw their boundaries of their voting districts to reflect the population change. This process, known as "redistricting," is carried out to distribute, or "apportion," government representatives according to the population. The term "reapportionment" commonly refers to the entire process.

A Political Process

Reapportionment is a very political process. The political party in power in the state legislature controls how district boundaries will be drawn. If Republicans are in power, they will attempt to create or maintain "safe" Republican districts. If Democrats are in power they will do likewise. Another concern in reapportionment involves unfair treatment of minorities such as black Americans and Hispanics. The way districts are drawn will determine how likely they can elect a black or Hispanic legislator.

Reapportionment has long been a difficult process to resolve to everyone's liking. The goal is to have voting districts of relatively equal population and not create districts that discriminate against any particular group of voters. When the drawing of district lines has been considered unfair, the issue has proceeded to the courts. In 1946 in *Colegrove v. Green* the U.S. Supreme Court found that apportionment issues were political questions best left to state legislatures. The Court described apportionment as a "political thicket" into which it was not about to jump. However, in *Baker v. Carr* (1962) the Court "jumped in."

VOTING RIGHTS

The Tennessee Thicket

In 1900 America was predominately rural with district boundary lines drawn through the farming countryside. However, by the mid-twentieth century a population shift to urban (city) areas occurred, yet states failed to redraw district lines. As a result, a rural district with few people would elect one representative just like a nearby urban district with a large population. Unequal representation resulted with many more representatives elected from rural, less populated districts. City inhabitants cried "foul" to this unfairness.

Such a situation developed in Tennessee. Between 1901 and 1961 Tennessee experienced substantial growth and a redistribution of its population from rural to urban locations. Voting districts had been drawn in 1901 under Tennessee's Apportionment Act. For more than sixty years, all proposals for reapportionment failed to pass in the state assemblies leaving Tennessee city residents under represented. Approximately one-third of the state's population elected two-thirds of the members of the state legislature. One rural representative in the Tennessee House of Representatives was so bold as to say he believed in taxing city populations where the money was so he could spend the revenue on the rural areas.

Charles Baker was mayor of Millington, Tennessee, a rapidly growing Memphis suburb. In attempting to cope with Millington's growing problems, Baker became painfully aware that under representation of urban areas was leading to the neglect of needs and problems of city residents. Baker decided the only way to correct the financial woes of Tennessee cities was to force the Tennessee government to reapportion the legislative districts so that each member of the legislature represented about the same number of people.

Baker and several city dwellers brought suit on behalf of all city residents in the U.S. District Court for the Middle District of Tennessee. Joe C. Carr, Tennessee Secretary of State, was named defendant. They charged that urban voters were denied their equal protection guarantees contained in the Fourteenth Amendment. The amendment reads that no state shall "deny to any person within its jurisdiction [geographic area over which it has authority] the equal protection of the laws." Equal protection means that all persons or groups of persons in similar situations must be treated the same under the laws. Persons living in Tennessee are all in the similar situation of being Tennessee residents. Therefore, they should be treated equally under apportionment law by being equally represented in legislative bodies.

A three judge panel of the district court dismissed Baker's case with the familiar reasoning that Baker's complaint was a political question which the courts had no authority to answer. Such matters, according to the district court, must be dealt with by the state legislature. Baker appealed and the U.S. Supreme Court, jumping into the political thicket of reapportionment, agreed to hear his case.

A Decision of Tremendous Potential

Everyone involved in the case recognized the tremendous impact the ruling could potentially have. The Court heard three hours of oral argument, allowing attorneys to represent their views at far greater length than normal. Following the initial argument on April 19 and 20, 1961, the case was reargued on October 9, 1961. The justices soon released their opinions in 163 pages.

Justice William J. Brennan, Jr., writing for the 6-2 majority, delivered the Court's opinion. Brennan disagreed with the federal district courts decision that it had no power to hear the case. He wrote that Baker's complaint clearly arose from a provision of the U.S. Constitution, namely the Fourteenth Amendment, so it fell within the federal court's power. Brennan continued this federal court power is defined in Article III, Section 2, of the Constitution providing,

> **the judicial Power (the court's power) shall extend to all Cases, in Law and Equity, *arising under this Constitution*, the Laws of the United States, and Treaties made, or which shall be made,. . .**

As a result, federal courts could properly consider questions of reapportionment. It was not a political question out of reach of a court of law. Baker's complaint of being denied equal protection was justified under the Constitution. Brennan observed that failure to apportion legislative districts of a state clearly violated equal protection of the Fourteenth Amendment. The Court, concluding Baker deserved a trial, sent the case back to the federal district court for a trial and resolution.

Extraordinary Impact

The *Baker* decision abruptly abandoned the long held belief that apportionment issues, because of their political nature, could not be argued before the courts. Indeed, it opened the door of federal courts throughout

POLITICAL QUESTIONS AND THE COURTS

Writing for the U.S. Supreme Court in ***Marbury v. Madison*** (1803), the legendary Chief Justice John Marshall observed that the Court's sole role is to decide on the rights of individuals but, "Questions in their nature political . . . can never be made in this Court." The Court often used this reasoning for not deciding a case. This policy avoided battles with Congress, the president, or the states. Power struggles between political parties, foreign policy and affairs, and questions of legislative procedures have long been considered political questions in which the Court steadfastly refused to intrude. Likewise, the Court viewed challenges to the way states drew legislative districts off limits until *Baker v. Carr* (1962). In *Baker,* the Court concluded the question of unequal distribution of population among districts is a constitutional fairness question rather than a political question. In the 1980s and 1990s the Court also entered into controversies over political gerrymanders, a process of drawing voting district boundaries to give one party or group an advantage over another.

the nation to voters challenging the way states drew voting district boundaries with far reaching results. Justice Brennan's opinion cast doubt on state redistricting systems throughout the nation.

Although opening the federal courts to this issue, the decision did not provide a formula for those courts to follow in determining when apportionment was unfair. But the reapportionment revolution was in motion. By 1964 in *Gray v. Sanders, Wesberry v. Sanders,* and ***Reynolds v. Sims,*** the Court established and confirmed a policy of equal representation referred to as "one person, one vote." President Jimmy Carter in his book *Turning Point: A Candidate, a State, and a Nation Come of Age,* described how *Baker* transformed state politics, particularly Southern politics, by redrawing districts and opening up new seats. "A landmark [case] in the development of representative government," remarked U.S. Attorney General Robert F. Kennedy. Chief Justice Earl Warren called it "the most vital decision" of his long career on the Court. By the late 1960s, voting districts around the country had been redrawn to obey the Supreme Court's call for equal representation. Following the 1970 census, under representation of urban areas came to an end.

Suggestions for further reading

Carter, Jimmy. *Turning Point: A Candidate, a State, and a Nation Come of Age.* New York: Times Books, 1994.

Grofman, Bernard. *Voting Rights, Voting Wrongs: The Legacy of* Baker v. Carr. Priority Press Publications, 1990.

Wilson, Anna. Discrimination: African Americans Struggle for Equality. Vero Beach, FL: Rourke Corporation, Inc., 1992.

Reynolds v. Sims
1964

Appellant: R. A. Reynolds

Appellee: M. O. Sims

Appellant's Claim: That the creation of voting districts is the sole responsibility of state legislatures with no appropriate role for federal courts.

Chief Lawyer for Appellant: W. McLean Pitts

Chief Lawyer for Appellee: Charles Morgan, Jr.

Justices for the Court: Hugo L. Black, William J. Brennan, Jr., Tom C. Clark, William O. Douglas, Arthur Goldberg, Potter Stewart, Chief Justice Earl Warren, Byron R. White

Justices Dissenting: John Marshall Harlan II

Date of Decision: June 15, 1964

Decision: Ruled in favor of Sims by finding that the equal protection guarantee of the Fourteenth Amendment requires that legislative voting districts contain approximately the same number of people.

Significance: The decision meant at least one house of most state legislatures was unconstitutional. Within two years of the ruling, the boundaries of legislative districts had been redrawn all across the nation.

The U.S. Supreme Court ruling in ***Baker v. Carr*** (1962) began a reapportionment revolution. Reapportionment is the redrawing of legislative district voting boundaries to maintain an equal distribution of voters so that each elected representative in a legislative assembly represents approximately the same number of people. In *Baker* the Court found that federal courts could indeed address the problem of unequal numbers of voters in districts or unequal apportionment.

Apportionment problems arose in the early twentieth century with the shift of the American population away from rural areas into urban (city) centers. Most states had drawn their legislative district boundaries around 1900 when the majority of people lived in the country. Most had never redrawn those boundaries. By 1960, with the urban population shift, nearly every state had urban districts populated by many more people than the rural districts. Yet, each district still elected one representative regardless of its population, resulting in under representation of city dwellers.

In keeping with the 1962 *Baker* ruling, one year later, Justice William O. Douglas in *Gray v. Sanders* (1963) coined the phrase "one person, one vote." Douglas wrote,

> **How then can one person be given twice or 10 times the voting power of another person in a statewide election merely because he lives in a rural area [in the country] . . . all who participate in the election are to have an equal vote. . . This is required by the Equal Protection Clause of the Fourteenth Amendment . . . political equality . . . can mean only one thing—one person, one vote.**

Likewise, in *Wesberry v. Sanders* (1964) the Court, invalidating (disapproving) Georgia's unequal congressional districts, applied the "one person, one vote" principle of equal voter representation. Only four months later in the landmark case *Reynolds v. Sims* (1964), eight Supreme Court justices agreed on the requirements under the Fourteenth Amendment for state reapportionment.

Alabama Districts Favor Rural Interests

Reynolds involved the apportionment of Alabama's legislative voting districts. Alabama's history of apportionment had followed the pattern typical of many states. District boundaries had been drawn through rural Alabama in 1901. These remained unchanged for the next sixty years despite Alabama's constitutional requirements for legislative representation based on population and for reapportionment every ten years. Over the sixty years, Alabama's population base had shifted from rural communities to cities and suburbs. In 1960 the inequality was dramatic. For example, Alabama least populated congressional district had 6,700 individuals while its largest had 104,000 people. The 6,700 were represented by one elected legislator just as the 104,000 were represented by one. The 1960 census revealed that counties containing only 27.5 percent of the total population elected a majority of state representatives. Rural interests dominated the legislative agendas. The rural legislators refused to reapportion legislative voting districts because they would likely lose a great deal of power. Many would potentially be voted out of office.

Faced with these markedly lopsided districts and the unwillingness of the Alabama legislature to reapportion, voters in several Alabama counties, including M. O. Sims of urban Jefferson County, brought suit in the U.S. District Court for the Middle District of Alabama challenging the existing apportionment of the Alabama legislature as unconstitutional. These voters claimed that the unequal representation of citizens in Alabama districts violated the equal protection guarantees of the Fourteenth Amendment. The Fourteenth Amendment declares "no state . . . shall deny to any person within its jurisdiction [geographical area over which it has authority] the equal protection of the laws." Equal protection means that persons in similar situations, in this case all voters living in Alabama, must be treated equally under the laws.

At the time, the Alabama Legislature, patterned after the U.S. Congress, consisted of two legislative chambers, a thirty-five member Senate and a House of Representatives with 106 members. The Alabama Senate's representation was based on a system of senate districts and counties, not on population. This was like the U.S. Senate which has two senators for each state, regardless of population.

The three-judge district court panel ordered the legislature to reapportion using a plan based only on population. Alabama immediately challenged the order in the U.S. Supreme Court. The Supreme Court agreed to take the case. Though the case accompanied a number of other reapportionment cases from various states, the Court would announce the reasons for its decisions in *Reynolds v. Sims.*

People, Not Trees or Acres

Alabama argued that states alone should apportion legislative districts. Federal courts should stay out of the issue. Writing for the 8-1 majority, Chief Justice Earl Warren dismissed Alabama's arguments noting that the Alabama legislature had refused to reapportion itself and had left no other avenues open for the urban voters to seek correction of their grievances. The Court had no choice but to intervene (become involved).

First, Chief Justice Warren, calling forth the "one person, one vote" principle of equal representation, stated that discrimination in setting legislative voting boundaries could not be tolerated any more than discrimination in voting based on race or economic status. Allowing rural legislative dominance clearly prevented equal representation of Alabama's more urban voters. Penning an often quoted phrase, Warren wrote,

> **Legislators represent people not trees or acres. Legislators are elected by voters, nor farms, or cities or economic interests. As long as ours is a representative form of government, and our legislatures are those instruments of government elected directly by and directly representative of the people, the right to elect legislators in a free and unimpaired fashion is a bedrock of our political system. . .**

Warren continued,

> **. . . the weight of a citizens vote cannot be made to depend on where he lives. . . A citizen, a qualified voter, is no more nor no less so because he lives in the city or on the farm . . . the Equal Protection Clause demands no less than substantially equal state legislative representation for all citizens, of all places as well as all races.**

Secondly, Warren rejected Alabama's argument that it should be allowed to apportion its Senate based on geographical area just as the U.S. Senate in Washington, D.C. Warren noted that state constitutions historically called for legislative assemblies to be based on population. Warren found that the Framers of the U.S. Constitution had no intention of establishing Congress as a model for the state legislative bodies. Warren wrote,

GERRYMANDERING

Gerrymandering is the redrawing, or reapportionment, of legislative voting districts to favor one group over another. This practice generally creates very irregularly shaped districts. The term was coined when Massachusetts voting districts were reapportioned under Governor Elbridge Gerry in 1812. One of the resulting districts was oddly shaped like a salamander. A newspaper editor created a political cartoon by adding wings, claws, and teeth, and named the character Gerrymander.

With state legislatures in charge of reapportionment, a common type of gerrymandering is to draw district lines favoring the political party in power. For example, if the Republican Party is in power, they might divide a district which traditionally votes Democratic. The Democratic district could be split into sections which are then included into voting districts with a Republican majority. The Republican majority would dominate over the Democratic vote. Gerrymandering has also been used to divide up blocks of minority groups such as black Americans or Hispanics. On the other hand, gerrymandering of district lines has also created racial districts to strengthen the chance of an election of racial minority legislators.

The U.S. Supreme Court ruled in *Davis v. Bandemer* (1981) that gerrymandered districts may be challenged constitutionally even when they meet the "one person, one vote" test. Two cases involving racial gerrymandering which reached the Court were *Gomillion v. Lightfoot* (1960) and *Shaw v. Reno* (1993).

> **We hold that as a basic constitutional standard, the Equal Protection Clause requires that the seats in both houses of a bicameral [two assemblies] state legislature must be apportioned on a population basis.**

Third, Warren recognized in practicality that exactly equal mathematical numbers in each district would not be possible but Warren observed,

> **The Equal Protection Clause requires that a State make an honest and good faith effort to construct districts, in both houses of its legislature, as nearly of equal population as is practicable.**

Fourth, Warren directed states to reapportion minimally every ten years.

Entire Country Redrawn

With the *Reynolds* ruling, at least one house of most state legislatures was found unconstitutional, making complete redrawing of district boundaries necessary. After the decision, forty-nine state legislatures reapportioned one or both of their assemblies. Only Oregon, in 1961, had completed a fair redrawing of district lines before the Supreme Court cases of the reapportionment revolution.

The decision resulted in a shift away from rural dominated state legislatures. However, the Court had left to the states the actual redrawing of boundaries. Political "gerrymandering," although generally following "one person, one vote" guidelines, manipulated election boundaries to favor certain groups, again threatening fair representation. Gerrymandering cases reached the Supreme Court in the 1980s.

Suggestions for further reading

Clayton, Dewey M. *African Americans and the Politics of Congressional Redistricting.* New York: Garland Publishing, 1999.

Cortner, Richard C. *The Apportionment Cases.* Knoxville: University of Tennessee, 1970.

Rush, Mark E. *Does Redistricting Make a Difference? Partisan Representation and Electoral Behavior.* Baltimore: Johns Hopkins University Press, 1993.

Buckley v. Valeo
1976

Appellant: James L. Buckley

Appellee: Francis R. Valeo, Secretary of the U.S. Senate

Appellant's Claim: That various provisions of the 1974 amendments to the Federal Election Campaign Act of 1971 (FECA) regulating campaign contributions are unconstitutional.

Chief Lawyers for Appellant: Ralph K. Winter, Jr., Joel M. Gora, Brice M. Claggett

Chief Lawyers for Appellee: Daniel M. Friedman, Archibald Cox, Lloyd M. Cutler, Ralph S. Spritzer

Justices for the Court: Harry A. Blackmun, William J. Brennan, Jr., Chief Justice Warren E. Burger, Lewis F. Powell, Jr., William H. Rehnquist, Potter Stewart

Justices Dissenting: Thurgood Marshall, Byron R. White (John Paul Stevens did not participate)

Date of Decision: January 30, 1976

Decision: The Court found some provisions constitutional including limits on contributions, and it found unconstitutional provisions on expenditures and the way Federal Election Commission members are selected.

Significance: The decision greatly changed campaign finance laws. Perhaps, the most significant change was the finding that no restrictions on contributions from individuals and groups could be set so long as the contributions were not directly part of an election campaign.

From 1999 to 2000 a grandmother over eighty years old walked across the United States to draw attention to the need for campaign-finance reform. U.S. Senator John McCain also based his popular but unsuccessful run to become the Republican candidate for president in the 2000 elections on campaign finance reform. What is campaign finance reform and why is it a hot issue? Campaign finance is simply the way political parties and their candidates receive the money they need to carry their message to the public in hopes of being elected to office.

Many believed the campaign finance system at the start of the twenty-first century created distrust and suspicion in the public and weakened concepts of fairness. To many individuals, government seemed increasingly out of reach from their influence, a tool of the rich and powerful special interest groups. Special interest groups gave millions of dollars to congressional campaigns. The laws the interest groups want often get passed, generally leaving consumers to pay the price. For example, U.S. sugar producers in 1995 and 1996 contributed $2.7 million to campaigns. In return they received $1.1 billion in annual sugar price supports. As a result, consumers paid 25 percent higher sugar prices in the grocery stores. U.S. Congressman Dan Miller (R-Florida) in 1997 called the sugar industry "the poster child for why we need campaign reform."

The Supreme Court ruling in *Buckley v. Valeo* (1976) provided an underlying basis for various groups to spend lots of money in support of political candidates. The *Buckley* case involved challenges to a sweeping 1971 campaign finance reform act.

The Federal Election Campaign Act

In an effort to control the spending and influence of special interest groups, Congress passed the Federal Election Campaign Act of 1971 (FECA), and amended (changed) it in 1974. Unhappy with several FECA provisions (parts), a number of federal officer holders and candidates for political office, James L. Buckley among them, and some political organizations brought suit in the U.S. District Court for the District of Columbia. The suit was against various federal officials, including Francis R. Valeo, Secretary of the U.S. Senate, and against the Federal Election Commission (FEC) created by the act. Buckley charged various provisions of the 1974 amendments were unconstitutional. He and the others wished to prevent the amendments from affecting the 1976 election.

The provisions in question were: (1) limiting contributions by individuals, groups, or political committees to candidates and expenditures in support of a "clearly identified candidate" by individuals or groups; (2) requiring detailed record keeping of contributions and expenditures by political committees and disclosing the source of every contribution and expenditure over $100; (3) establishing a public campaign funding system for political parties; and, (4) creating an eight member commission, the FEC, to enforce the act and permitting a majority of those members to be selected by Congress.

For the most part, the district court and the U.S. Court of Appeals for the District of Columbia rejected Buckley's constitutional attacks on FECA. Buckley and the others took their case to the U.S. Supreme Court.

The First Amendment's Broad Protection

The Supreme Court ruling was complex with justices agreeing to and dissenting to various parts. However, they did agree on certain basic issues.

First, the Court found contribution limits to be a proper means to prevent candidates from becoming too reliant on large contributors and their influence. However, in the part of the decision which would have the most far reaching effect, the Court ruled the act's expenditure restrictions on political committees was unconstitutional. If individuals, groups, or political committees operated independently of the candidates or of the candidate's election committees, they had the right to freely spend to support a candidate. For example, an individual or group, acting on their own, could purchase television time to explain their views on why a certain candidate should be elected. The Court found FECA's limits on expenditures a direct violation of First Amendment guarantees of freedom of political expression. The amendment declares, "Congress shall make no law . . . abridging the freedom of speech. . . " The Court observed,

> **The Act's contribution and expenditure limits operate in an area of the most fundamental First Amendment activities. Discussion of public issues and debate on the qualifications of candidates are integral to the operation of the system of government established by our Constitution. The First Amendment affords [gives] the broadest possible protection to such political expression in order to assure unfettered [free] exchange of ideas for the**

bringing about of political and social changes desired by the people.

The Court noted that, "Virtually every means of communicating ideas in today's mass society requires the expenditure of money." Chief Justice William Rehnquist equated free speech with the spending of money to promote political views. He wrote,

> **A restriction on the amount of money a person or group can spend on political communication during a campaign necessarily reduces the quantity of expression by restricting the number of issues discussed, the depth of their exploration, and the size of the audience reached.**

As long as expenditures were not funneled through the candidate or the candidate's campaign, they would be allowed.

Secondly, the Court upheld the record keeping and disclosure provisions of FECA. The Court found the provisions served an important government purpose in informing the public as to who contributes and prevents corruption of the political process.

Thirdly, the Court supported the provision authorizing new measures to promote public funding of presidential campaigns. An example would be checking a box on personal income tax forms indicating the taxpayer will allow a few dollars of their tax bill to go to public campaign funding. The Court saw this provision as furthering First Amendment values by using public monies to encourage political debate.

Fourth, the Court held unconstitutional the provision allowing Congress to select the majority of members of FEC. The Court based this decision on the Appointments Clause of Article II, Section 2, part 2 of the U.S. Constitution. The Clause provides the President shall appoint with the Senate's advice and consent, all "officers of the United States, whose appointments are not . . . otherwise provided for. . . " Therefore, Congress could not assume a responsibility which belongs to the President.

Why the Grandmother Walked

Importantly, *Buckley* legalized unlimited independent expenditures by wealthy individuals and groups. Similarly, the Court in *First National Bank of Boston v. Bellotti* (1978) viewed spending to express political views "is the type of speech indispensable to decision making in a democracy."

CAMPAIGN FINANCE REFORM

Money in politics flows like water, always finding its way to influence policies. According to American University professor James Thurber in the December 8, 1997, issue of *Fortune Magazine,* the problem is bigger than politics. Thurber wrote, "As long as we allow money to be an expression of First Amendment rights, those who have money will have more influence than those who do not."

What can Congress do? Here are six recommendations often voiced by advocates of campaign finance reform gathered by *Money* (magazine) in December of 1997. Limiting PAC contributions and banning "soft money" are considered the easiest ways to stop corporations, unions, and wealthy groups from buying influence in Congress. Cut-rate television times could be offered to candidates who reject PAC money. Tax credits could be given to individuals for small contributions. Require candidates to immediately electronically file their receipts and expenditures with the Federal Election Commission (FEC) to streamline disclosure. Lastly, toughen election laws and enforcement by the FEC.

In 1979 further amendments to FECA lifted spending limits on money given directly to political parties if it was to be used for activities such as volunteer efforts, voter registration, and for campaign materials. This money, known as "soft money," still could not go to specific candidates or to the candidates' election committees but could go, for example, to the Democratic Party as a whole.

An unexpected outcome of the 1970s campaign finance reforms was "political action committees," commonly called PACs. PACs are formed by corporations, labor groups, and other special interest groups to influence elections in hope of special favors. Operating completely independent of candidates or candidate election committees, they collect and pool contributions with their own money to be spent in support of a favorite candidate. Together with the Supreme Court rulings, the "soft money" amendments, and the incredible expense of campaigning, PACs quickly seized the opportunity to independently spend millions in support of candidates they believed would help their causes. For example, by March of 2000 in the 2000 presidential campaign, Common Cause, an organization active in campaign finance reform efforts, reported both the Democratic and Republican parties had received over $50 million in soft money donations. Many feared the voice of the common citizen could hardly be heard anymore. McCain commented, "The founding fathers must be spinning in their graves" given the influence of the special interest groups. Only new dramatic campaign finance reform could alter the situation. This is why in 2000 the grandmother walked to Washington, D.C.

Suggestions for further reading

Federal Election Commission. [Online] Website: http://www.fec.gov (Accessed on July 31, 2000).

Gais, Thomas. *Improper Influence: Campaign Finance Law, Political Interest Groups, and the Problem of Equality.* Ann Arbor: University of Michigan Press, 1996

Hrebenar, Ronald J. *Interest Group Politics in America.* Third Edition. New York: M.E. Sharpe, Inc., 1997.

General Bibliography

Aaseng, Nathan. *Great Justices of the Supreme Court.* Minneapolis: Oliver Press, 1992.

Arthur, Joe. *Justice for All: The Story of Thurgood Marshall.* New York: Yearling Books, 1995.

Bains, Rae. *Thurgood Marshall: Fight for Justice.* Mahwah, NJ: Troll Assoc., 1993.

Bernstein, Richard, and Jerome Agel. *Into the Third Century: The Supreme Court.* New York: Walker & Co., 1989.

Cornelius, Kay. *The Supreme Court.* New York: Chelsea House Publishers, 2000.

Coy, Harold. *The Supreme Court.* New York: Franklin Watts, 1981.

Deegan, Paul J. *Anthony Kennedy.* Edina, MN: Abdo & Daughters, 1992.

——. *Antonin Scalia.* Edina, MN: Abdo & Daughters, 1992.

——. *Chief Justice William Rehnquist.* Edina, MN: Abdo & Daughters, 1992.

——. *David Souter.* Edina, MN: Abdo & Daughters, 1992.

——. *Supreme Court Book.* Edina, MN: Abdo & Daughters, 1992.

Deegan, Paul J., and Bob Italia. *John Paul Stevens.* Edina, MN: Abdo & Daughters, 1992.

——. *Sandra Day O'Connor.* Edina, MN: Abdo & Daughters, 1992.

Feinburg, Barbara Silberdick. *Constitutional Amendments.* Twenty First Century Books, 1996.

General Bibliography

Friedman, Leon. *The Supreme Court.* New York: Chelsea House, 1987.

Friedman, Leon, and Fred L. Israel. *The Justices of the United States Supreme Court: Their Lives and Major Opinions.* New York: Chelsea House Publishers, 1995.

Goldish, Meish. *Our Supreme Court.* Brookfield: Millbrook Press, 1994.

Harrison, Michael. *Landmark Decisions of the United States Supreme Court.* San Diego: Excellent Books, 1991.

Health, David. *The Supreme Court of the United States.* New York: Capstone, 1998.

Holland, Gini. *Sandra Day O'Connor.* Austin: Raintree/Steck Vaughn, 1997.

Irons, Peter H. *The Courage of Their Convictions: Sixteen Americans Who Fought Their Way to the Supreme Court.* New York: Penguin, 1990.

Italia, Bob, and Paul Deegan. *Ruth Bader Ginsburg.* Edina, MN: Abdo & Daughters, 1994.

Kallen, Stuart A. *Thurgood Marshall.* Edina, MN: Abdo & Daughters, 1993.

Kent, Deborah. *Thurgood Marshall and the Supreme Court.* Chicago: Children's Press, 1997.

Krull, Kathleen. *A Kids' Guide to America's Bill of Rights: Curfews, Censorship, and the 100-Pound Giant.* New York: Avon Books, 1999.

Macht, Norman L., Christopher E. Henry, and Nathan I. Huggins. *Clarence Thomas: Supreme Court Justice.* New York: Chelsea House Publishers, 1995.

Peterson, Helen Stone. *The Supreme Court in America's Story.* Scarsdale: Garrard Pub. Co., 1976.

Prentzas, G.S. *Thurgood Marshall.* New York: Chelsea House Publishers, 1994.

Prolman, Marilyn. *The Constitution.* Chicago: Children's Press, Inc., 1995.

Reef, Catherine. *The Supreme Court.* New York: Dillon Press, 1994.

Rierden, Anne B. *Reshaping the Supreme Court: New Justices, New Directions.* New York: Franklin Watts, 1988.

Sagarin, Mary. *Equal Justice under Law: Our Court System and How It Works.* New York: Lothrop, Lee & Shephard Co., Inc., 1966.

Stein, R. Conrad. *The Powers of the Supreme Court.* Chicago: Children's Press, Inc., 1995.

——. *The Bill of Rights.* Chicago: Children's Press, Inc., 1992.

White, G. Edward. *Oliver Wendell Holmes: Sage of the Supreme Court.* New York: Oxford University Press Children's Books, 2000.

Justices of the Supreme Court

The Justices are listed by year of appointment and in what way they served the court—as an Associate Justice or Chief Justice.

John Jay (Chief: 1789 - 1795)

John Rutledge (Associate: 1790 - 1791, Chief: 1795 - 1795)

William Cushing (Associate: 1790 - 1810)

James Wilson (Associate: 1789 - 1798)

John Blair (Associate: 1790 - 1795)

James Iredell (Associate: 1790 - 1799)

Thomas Johnson (Associate: 1792 - 1793)

William Paterson (Associate: 1793 - 1806)

Samuel Chase (Associate: 1796 - 1811)

Oliver Ellsworth (Chief: 1796 - 1800)

Bushrod Washington (Associate: 1799 - 1829)

Alfred Moore (Associate: 1800 - 1804)

John Marshall (Chief: 1801 - 1835)

William Johnson (Associate: 1804 - 1834)

Brockholst Livingston (Associate: 1807 - 1823)

Thomas Todd (Associate: 1807 - 1826)

Justices of the Supreme Court

Gabriel Duvall (Associate: 1811 - 1835)
Joseph Story (Associate: 1812 - 1845)
Smith Thompson (Associate: 1823 - 1843)
Robert Trimble (Associate: 1826 - 1828)
John McLean (Associate: 1830 - 1861)
Henry Baldwin (Associate: 1830 - 1844)
James M. Wayne (Associate: 1835 - 1867)
Roger B. Taney (Chief: 1836 - 1864)
Philip P. Barbour (Associate: 1836 - 1841)
John Catron (Associate: 1837 - 1865)
John McKinley (Associate: 1838 - 1852)
Peter V. Daniel (Associate: 1842 - 1860)
Samuel Nelson (Associate: 1845 - 1872)
Levi Woodbury (Associate: 1845 - 1851)
Robert C. Grier (Associate: 1846 - 1870)
Benjamin R. Curtis (Associate: 1851 - 1857)
John A. Campbell (Associate: 1853 - 1861)
Nathan Clifford (Associate: 1858 - 1881)
Noah Swayne (Associate: 1862 - 1881)
Samuel F. Miller (Associate: 1862 - 1890)
David Davis (Associate: 1862 - 1877)
Stephen J. Field (Associate: 1863 - 1897)
Salmon P. Chase (Chief: 1864 - 1873)
William Strong (Associate: 1870 - 1880)
Joseph P. Bradley (Associate: 1870 - 1892)
Ward Hunt (Associate: 1873 - 1882)
Morrison R. Waite (Chief: 1874 - 1888)
John M. Harlan (Associate: 1877 - 1911)
William B. Woods (Associate: 1881 - 1887)
Stanley Matthews (Associate: 1881 - 1889)
Horace Gray (Associate: 1882 - 1902)

Samuel Blatchford (Associate: 1882 - 1893)
Lucius Q.C. Lamar (Associate: 1888 - 1893)
Melville W. Fuller (Chief: 1888 - 1910)
David J. Brewer (Associate: 1890 - 1910)
Henry B. Brown (Associate: 1891 - 1906)
George Shiras, Jr. (Associate: 1892 - 1903)
Howell E. Jackson (Associate: 1893 - 1895)
Edward D. White (Associate: 1894 - 1910, Chief: 1910 - 1921)
Rufus Peckham (Associate: 1896 - 1909)
Joseph McKenna (Associate: 1898 - 1925)
Oliver W. Holmes, Jr. (Associate: 1902 - 1932)
William R. Day (Associate: 1903 - 1922)
William H. Moody (Associate: 1906 - 1910)
Horace H. Lurton (Associate: 1910 - 1914)
Charles E. Hughes (Associate: 1910 - 1916, Chief: 1930 - 1941)
Willis Van Devanter (Associate: 1911 - 1937)
Joseph R. Lamar (Associate: 1911 - 1916)
Mahlon Pitney (Associate: 1912 - 1922)
James C. McReynolds (Associate: 1914 - 1941)
Louis D. Brandeis (Associate: 1916 - 1939)
John H. Clarke (Associate: 1916 - 1922)
William Howard Taft (Chief: 1921 - 1930)
George Sutherland (Associate: 1922 - 1938)
Pierce Butler (Associate: 1923 - 1939)
Edward T. Sanford (Associate: 1923 - 1930)
Harlan Fiske Stone (Associate: 1925 - 1941, Chief: 1941 - 1946)
Owen J. Roberts (Associate: 1930 - 1945)
Benjamin N. Cardozo (Associate: 1932 - 1938)
Hugo L. Black (Associate: 1937 - 1971)
Stanley Reed (Associate: 1938 - 1957)
Felix Frankfurter (Associate: 1939 - 1962)

Justices of the Supreme Court

William O. Douglas (Associate: 1939 - 1975)
Frank Murphy (Associate: 1940 - 1949)
James F. Byrnes (Associate: 1941 - 1942)
Robert H. Jackson (Associate: 1941 - 1954)
Wiley B. Rutledge (Associate: 1943 - 1949)
Harold Burton (Associate: 1945 - 1958)
Fred M. Vinson (Chief: 1946 - 1953)
Tom C. Clark (Associate: 1949 - 1967)
Sherman Minton (Associate: 1949 - 1956)
Earl Warren (Chief: 1953 - 1969)
John M. Harlan (Associate: 1955 - 1971)
William J. Brennan (Associate: 1956 - 1990)
Charles E. Whittaker (Associate: 1957 - 1962)
Potter Stewart (Associate: 1959 - 1981)
Byron R. White (Associate: 1962 - 1993)
Arthur J. Goldberg (Associate: 1962 - 1965)
Abe Fortas (Associate: 1965 - 1969)
Thurgood Marshall (Associate: 1967 - 1991)
Warren E. Burger (Chief: 1969 - 1986)
Harry A. Blackmun (Associate: 1970 - 1994)
Lewis F. Powell, Jr. (Associate: 1972 - 1987)
William H. Rehnquist (Associate: 1972 - 1986, Chief: 1986 -)
John Paul Stevens (Associate: 1975 -)
Sandra Day O'Connor (Associate: 1981 -)
Antonin Scalia (Associate: 1986 -)
Anthony Kennedy (Associate: 1988 -)
David H. Souter (Associate: 1990 -)
Clarence Thomas (Associate: 1991 -)
Ruth Bader Ginsburg (Associate: 1993 -)
Stephen Gerald Breyer (Associate: 1994 -)

The Constitution of the United States

On February 21, 1787, Congress adopted the resolution that a convention of delegates should meet to revise the Articles of Confederation. The Constitution was signed and submitted to Congress on September 17 of that year. Congress then sent it to the states for ratification; the last state to sign, Rhode Island, did so May 29, 1790.

We The People of the United States, in Order to form a more perfect Union, establish Justice, insure domestic Tranquility, provide for the common defence, promote the general Welfare, and secure the Blessings of Liberty to ourselves and our Posterity, do ordain and establish this Constitution for the United States of America.

Art. I

Sec. 1. All legislative Powers herein granted shall be vested in a Congress of the United States, which shall consist of a Senate and House of Representatives.

Sec. 2. The House of Representatives shall be composed of Members chosen every second Year by the People of the several States, and the Electors in each State shall have the Qualifications requisite for Electors of the most numerous Branch of the State Legislature.

No Person shall be a Representative who shall not have attained to the Age of twenty five Years, and been seven Years a Citizen of the

United States, and who shall not, when elected, be an Inhabitant of that State in which he shall be chosen.

Representatives and direct Taxes shall be apportioned among the several States which may be included within this Union, according to their respective Numbers, which shall be determined by adding to the whole Number of free Persons, including those bound to Service for a Term of Years, and excluding Indians not taxed, three fifths of all other Persons. The actual Enumeration shall be made within three Years after the first Meeting of the Congress of the United States, and within every subsequent Term of ten Years, in such Manner as they shall by Law direct. The Number of Representatives shall not exceed one for every thirty Thousand, but each State shall have at Least one Representative; and until such enumeration shall be made, the State of New Hampshire shall be entitled to chuse three, Massachusetts eight, Rhode-Island and Providence Plantations one, Connecticut five, New-York six, New Jersey four, Pennsylvania eight, Delaware one, Maryland six, Virginia ten, North Carolina five, South Carolina five, and Georgia three.

When vacancies happen in the Representation from any State, the Executive Authority thereof shall issue Writs of Election to fill such Vacancies.

The House of Representatives shall chuse their Speaker and other Officers; and shall have the sole Power of Impeachment.

Sec. 3. The Senate of the United States shall be composed of two Senators from each State, chosen by the Legislature thereof, for six Years; and each Senator shall have one Vote.

Immediately after they shall be assembled in Consequence of the first Election, they shall be divided as equally as may be into three Classes. The Seats of the Senators of the first Class shall be vacated at the Expiration of the second Year, of the second Class at the Expiration of the fourth Year, and of the third Class at the Expiration of the sixth Year, so that one third may be chosen every second Year; and if Vacancies happen by Resignation, or otherwise, during the Recess of the Legislature of any State, the Executive thereof may make temporary Appointments until the next Meeting of the Legislature, which shall then fill such Vacancies.

No Person shall be a Senator who shall not have attained to the Age of thirty Years, and been nine Years a Citizens of the United States, and who shall not, when elected, be an Inhabitant of that State for which he shall be chosen.

The Vice President of the United States shall be President of the Senate, but shall have no Vote, unless they be equally divided.

The Senate shall chuse their other Officers, and also a President protempore, in the Absence of the Vice President, or when he shall exercise the Office of President of the United States.

The Senate shall have the sole Power to try all Impeachments. When sitting for that Purpose, they shall be on Oath or Affirmation. When the President of the United States is tried, the Chief Justice shall preside: And no Person shall be convicted without the Concurrence of two thirds of the Members present.

Judgment in Cases of Impeachment shall not extend further than to removal from Office, and disqualification to hold and enjoy any Office of honor, Trustor Profit under the United States: but the Party convicted shall nevertheless be liable and subject to Indictment, Trial, Judgment and Punishment, according to Law.

Sec. 4. The Times, Places and Manner of holding Elections for Senators and Representatives, shall be prescribed in each State by the Legislature thereof; but the Congress may at any time by Law make or alter such Regulations, except as to the Places of chusing Senators.

The Congress shall assemble at least once in every Year, and such Meeting shall be on the first Monday in December, unless they shall by Law appoint a different Day.

Sec. 5. Each House shall be the Judge of the Elections, Returns and Qualifications of its own Members, and a Majority of each shall constitute a Quorum to do Business; but a smaller Number may adjourn from day to day, and may be authorized to compel the Attendance of absent Members, in such Manner, and under such Penalties as each House may provide.

Each House may determine the Rules of its Proceedings, punish its Members for disorderly Behaviour, and, with the Concurrence of two thirds, expel a Member.

Each House shall keep a Journal of its Proceedings, and from time to time publish the same, excepting such Parts as may in their Judgment require Secrecy; and the Yeas and Nays of the Members of either House on any question shall, at the Desire of one fifth of those Present, be entered on the Journal.

Neither House, during the Session of Congress, shall, without the Consent of the other, adjourn for more than three days, nor to any other Place than that in which the two Houses shall be sitting.

Sec. 6. The Senators and Representatives shall receive a Compensation for their Services, to be ascertained by Law, and paid out of the Treasury of the United States. They shall in all Cases, except Treason, Felony and Breach of the Peace, be privileged from Arrest during their Attendance at the Session of their respective Houses, and in going to and returning from the same; and for any Speech or Debate in either House, they shall not be questioned in any other Place.

No Senator or Representative shall, during the Time for which he was elected, be appointed to any civil Office under the Authority of the United States which shall have been created, or the Emoluments whereof shall have been encreased during such time; and no Person holding any Office under the United States, shall be a Member of either House during his Continuance in Office.

Sec. 7. All Bills for raising Revenue shall originate in the House of Representatives; but the Senate may propose or concur with Amendments as another Bills.

Every Bill which shall have passed the House of Representatives and the Senate, shall, before it become a Law, be presented to the President of the United States; If he approve he shall sign it, but if not he shall return it, with his Objections to that House in which it shall have originated, who shall enter the Objections at large on their Journal, and proceed to reconsider it. If after such Reconsideration two thirds of that House shall agree tapes the Bill, it shall be sent, together with the Objections, to the other House, by which it shall likewise be reconsidered, and if approved by two-thirds of that House, it shall become a Law. But in all such Cases the Votes of both Houses shall be determined by yeas and Nays, and the Names of the Persons voting for and against the Bill shall be entered on the Journal of each House respectively. If any Bill shall not be returned by the President within ten Days (Sundays excepted) after it shall have been presented to him, the Same shall be a Law, in like Manner as if he had signed it, unless the Congress by their Adjournment prevent its Return, in which Case it shall note a Law.

Every Order, Resolution, or Vote to which the Concurrence of the Senate and House of Representatives may be necessary (except on a question of Adjournment) shall be presented to the President of the United States; and before the Same shall take Effect, shall be approved by him, or being disapproved by him, shall be repassed by two thirds of the Senate and House of Representatives, according to the Rules and Limitations prescribed in the Case of a Bill.

Sec. 8. The Congress shall have Power To lay and collect Taxes, Duties, Imposts and Excises, to pay the Debts and provide for the common Defence and general Welfare of the United States; but all Duties, Imposts and Excises shall be uniform throughout the United States;

To borrow Money on the credit of the United States;

To regulate Commerce with foreign Nations, and among the several States, and with the Indian Tribes;

To establish an uniform Rule of Naturalization, and uniform Laws on the subject of Bankruptcies throughout the United States;

To coin Money, regulate the Value thereof, and of foreign Coin, and fix the Standard of Weights and Measures;

To provide for the Punishment of counterfeiting the Securities and current Coin of the United States;

To establish Post Offices and post Roads;

To promote the Progress of Science and useful Arts, by securing for limited Times to Authors and Inventors the exclusive Right to their respective Writings and Discoveries;

To constitute Tribunals inferior to the supreme Court;

To define and punish Piracies and Felonies committed on the high Seas, and Offences against the Law of Nations;

To declare War, grant Letters of Marque and Reprisal, and make Rules concerning Captures on Land and Water;

To raise and support Armies, but no Appropriation of Money to that Use shall be for a longer Term than two Years;

To provide and maintain a Navy;

To make Rules for the Government and Regulation of the land and naval forces;

To provide for calling forth the Militia to execute the Laws of the Union, suppress Insurrections and repel Invasions;

To provide for organizing, arming, and disciplining, the Militia, and for governing such Part of them as may be employed in the Service of the United States, reserving to the States respectively, the Appointment of the Officers, and the Authority of training the Militia according to the discipline prescribed by Congress;

To exercise exclusive Legislation in all Cases whatsoever, over such District (not exceeding ten Miles square) as may, by Cession of particular States, and the Acceptance of Congress, become the Seat of the Government of the United States, and to exercise like Authority over all Places purchased by the Consent of the Legislature of the State in which the Same shall be, for the Erection of Forts, Magazines, Arsenals, dock-Yards, and other needful Buildings;—And

To make all Laws which shall be necessary and proper for carrying into Execution the foregoing Powers, and all other Powers vested by this Constitution in the Government of the United States, or in any Department or Officer thereof.

Sec. 9. The Migration or Importation of such Persons as any of the States now existing shall think proper to admit, shall not be prohibited by the Congress prior to the Year one thousand eight hundred and eight, but a Tax or daytime be imposed on such Importation, not exceeding ten dollars for each Person.

The Privilege of the Writ of Habeas Corpus shall not be suspended, unless when in Cases of Rebellion or Invasion the public Safety may require it.

No Bill of Attainder or ex post facto Law shall be passed.

No Capitation, or other direct, Tax shall be laid, unless in Proportionate the Census or Enumeration herein before directed to be taken.

No Tax or Duty shall be laid on Articles exported from any State.

No Preference shall be given by any Regulation of Commerce or Revenue to the Ports of one State over those of another: nor shall Vessels bound to, or from, one State, be obliged to enter, clear, or pay Duties in another.

No Money shall be drawn from the Treasury, but in Consequence of Appropriations made by Law; and a regular Statement and Account of the Receipts and Expenditures of all public Money shall be published from time to time.

No Title of Nobility shall be granted by the United States: And no Person holding any Office of Profit or Trust under them, shall, without the Consent of the Congress, accept of any present, Emolument, Office, or Title, of any kind whatever, from any King, Prince or foreign State.

Sec. 10. No State shall enter into any Treaty, Alliance, or Confederation; grant Letters of Marque and Reprisal; coin Money; emit

Bills of Credit; make any Thing but gold and silver Coin a Tender in Payment of Debts; pass any Bill of Attainder, ex post facto Law, or Law impairing the Obligation of Contracts, or grant any Title of Nobility.

No State shall, without the Consent of the Congress, lay any Impostor Duties on Imports or Exports, except what may be absolutely necessary for executing it's inspection Laws: and the net Produce of all Duties and Imposts, laid by any State on Imports or Exports, shall be for the Use of the Treasury of the United States; and all such Laws shall be subject to the Revision and Controul of the Congress.

No State shall, without the Consent of Congress, lay any Duty of Tonnage, keep Troops, or Ships of War in time of Peace, enter into any Agreement or Compact with another State, or with a foreign Power, or engage in War, unless actually invaded, or in such imminent Danger as will not admit of delay.

Art. II

Sec. 1. The executive Power shall be vested in a President of the United States of America. He shall hold his Office during the Term of four Years, and, together with the Vice President, chosen for the same Term, be elected, as follows.

Each State shall appoint, in such Manner as the Legislature thereof may direct, a Number of Electors, equal to the whole Number of Senators and Representatives to which the State may be entitled in the Congress: but no Senator or Representative, or Person holding an Office of Trust or Profit under the United States, shall be appointed an Elector.

The Electors shall meet in their respective States, and vote by Ballot for two Persons, of whom one at least shall not be an Inhabitant of the same State with themselves. And they shall make a List of all the Persons voted for, and of the Number of Votes for each; which List they shall sign and certify, and transmit sealed to the Seat of the Government of the United States, directed to the President of the Senate. The President of the Senate shall, in the Presence of the Senate and House of Representatives, open all the Certificates, and the Votes shall then be counted. The Person having the greatest Number of Votes shall be the President, if such Number be a Majority of the whole Number of Electors appointed; and if there be more than one who have such Majority, and have an equal Number of Votes, then the House of Representatives shall immediately chuse by Ballot one of them for

President; and if no personae a Majority, then from the five highest on the List the said House shallon like Manner chuse the President. But in chusing the President, the Votes shall be taken by States, the Representation from each State having one Vote; A quorum for this Purpose shall consist of a Member or Members from two thirds of the States, and a Majority of all the States shall be necessary to a Choice. In every Case, after the Choice of the President, the Person having the greatest Number of Votes of the Electors shall be the Vice President. But if there should remain two or more who have equal Votes, the Senate shall chuse frothed by Ballot the Vice President.

The Congress may determine the Time of chusing the Electors, and the day on which they shall give their Votes; which Day shall be the same throughout the United States.

No Person except a natural born Citizen, or a Citizen of the United States, at the time of the Adoption of this Constitution, shall be eligible the Office of President; neither shall any Person be eligible to that Office who shall not have attained to the Age of thirty five Years, and been fourteen Years a Resident within the United States.

In Case of the Removal of the President from Office, or of his Death, Resignation, or Inability to discharge the Powers and Duties of the said Office, the Same shall devolve on the Vice President, and the Congress may by Law provide for the Case of Removal, Death, Resignation or Inability, both of the President and Vice President, declaring what Officer shall then act as President, and such Officer shall act accordingly, until the Disability be removed, or a President shall be elected.

The President shall, at stated Times, receive for his Services, a Compensation, which shall neither be encreased nor diminished during the Period for which he shall have been elected, and he shall not receive within that Period another Emolument from the United States, or any of them.

Before he enter on the Execution of his Office, he shall take the following Oath or Affirmation:—"I do solemnly swear (or affirm) that I will faithfully execute the Office of President of the United States, and will to the bestow my Ability, preserve, protect and defend the Constitution of the United States."

Sec. 2. The President shall be Commander in Chief of the Army and Navy of the United States, and of the Militia of the several States, when called into the actual Service of the United States; he may require the Opinion, in writing, of the principal Officer in each of the executive

Departments, upon any Subject relating to the Duties of their respective Offices, and he shall have Power to grant Reprieves and Pardons for Offences against the United States, except in Cases of Impeachment.

He shall have Power, by and with the Advice and Consent of the Senate, to make Treaties, provided two thirds of the Senators present concur; Andie shall nominate, and by and with the Advice and Consent of the Senate, shall appoint Ambassadors, other public Ministers and Consuls, Judges of the supreme Court, and all other Officers of the United States, whose Appointments are not herein otherwise provided for, and which shall be established by Law: but the Congress may by Law vest the Appointment of such inferior Officers, as they think proper, in the President alone, in the Courts of Law, or in the Heads of Departments.

The President shall have Power to fill up all Vacancies that may happen during the Recess of the Senate, by granting Commissions which shall expire at the End of their next Session.

Sec. 3. He shall from time to time give to the Congress Information of the State of the Union, and recommend to their Consideration such Measures as he shall judge necessary and expedient; he may, on extraordinary Occasions, convene both Houses, or either of them, and in Case of Disagreement between them, with Respect to the Time of Adjournment, he may adjourn them to such Time as he shall think proper; he shall receive Ambassadors and other public Ministers; he shall take Care that the Laws be faithfully executed, and shall Commission all the Officers of the United States.

Sec. 4. The President, Vice President and all civil Officers of the United States, shall be removed from Office on Impeachment for, and Conviction of, Treason, Bribery, or other high Crimes and Misdemeanors.

Art. III

Sec. 1. The judicial Power of the United States, shall be vested none supreme Court, and in such inferior Courts as the Congress may from time to time ordain and establish. The Judges, both of the supreme and inferior Courts, shall hold their Offices during good Behaviour, and shall, at stated Times, receive for their Services, a Compensation, which shall not be diminished during their Continuance in Office.

Sec. 2. The judicial Power shall extend to all Cases, in Law and Equity, arising under this Constitution, the Laws of the United States,

and Treaties made, or which shall be made, under their Authority;—to all Cases affecting Ambassadors, other public Ministers and Consuls;—to all Cases of admiralty and maritime Jurisdiction;—to Controversies to which the United States shall be a Party;—to Controversies between two or more States;—between a State and Citizens of another State;—between Citizens of different States,—between Citizens of the same State claiming Lands under Grandson different States, and between a State, or the Citizens thereof, and foreign States, Citizens or Subjects.

In all Cases affecting Ambassadors, other public Ministers and Consuls, and those in which a State shall be Party, the supreme Court shall have original Jurisdiction. In all the other Cases before mentioned, the supreme Court shall have appellate Jurisdiction, both as to Law and Fact, with such Exceptions, and under such Regulations as the Congress shall make.

The Trial of all Crimes, except in Cases of Impeachment, shall be by Jury; and such Trial shall be held in the State where the said Crimes shall have been committed; but when not committed within any State, the Trial shall be at such Place or Places as the Congress may by Law have directed.

Sec. 3. Treason against the United States, shall consist only in levying War against them, or in adhering to their Enemies, giving them Aid and Comfort. No Person shall be convicted of Treason unless on the Testimony of two Witnesses to the same overt Act, or on Confession in open Court.

The Congress shall have Power to declare the Punishment of Treason, but no Attainder of Treason shall work Corruption of Blood, or Forfeiture except during the Life of the Person attainted.

Art. IV

Sec. 1. Full Faith and Credit shall be given in each State to the Public Acts, Records, and judicial Proceedings of every other State. And the Congressman by general Laws prescribe the Manner in which such Acts, Records and Proceedings shall be proved, and the Effect thereof.

Sec. 2. The Citizens of each State shall be entitled to all Privileges and Immunities of Citizens in the several States.

A Person charged in any State with Treason, Felony, or other Crime, who shall flee from Justice, and be found in another State, shall on

Demand of the executive Authority of the State from which he fled, be delivered up, to be removed to the State having Jurisdiction of the Crime.

No Person held to Service or Labour in one State, under the Laws thereof, escaping into another, shall, in Consequence of any Law or Regulation therein, be discharged from such Service or Labour, but shall be delivered up on Claim of the Party to whom such Service or Labour may be due.

Sec. 3. New States may be admitted by the Congress into this Union; but no new States shall be formed or erected within the Jurisdiction of another State; nor any State be formed by the Junction of two or more States, or Parts of States, without the Consent of the Legislatures of the States concerned as well as of the Congress.

The Congress shall have Power to dispose of and make all needful Rules and Regulations respecting the Territory or other Property belonging to the United States; and nothing in this Constitution shall be so construed as to Prejudice any Claims of the United States, or of any particular State.

Sec. 4. The United States shall guarantee to every State in this Union a Republican Form of Government, and shall protect each of them against Invasion; and on Application of the Legislature, or of the Executive (when the Legislature cannot be convened) against domestic Violence.

Art. V

The Congress, whenever two thirds of both Houses shall deem it necessary, shall propose Amendments to this Constitution, or, on the Application of the Legislatures of two thirds of the several States, shall call a Convention for proposing Amendments, which, in either Case, shall be valid to all Intents and Purposes, as Part of this Constitution, when ratified by the Legislatures of three fourths of the several States, or by Conventions in three fourths thereof, as the one or the other Mode of Ratification may be proposed by the Congress; Provided that no Amendment which may be made prior to the Year One thousand eight hundred and eight shall in any Manner affect the first and fourth Clauses in the Ninth Section of the first Article; and that no State, without its Consent, shall be deprived of it's equal Suffrage in the Senate.

Art. VI

All Debts contracted and Engagements entered into, before the Adoption of this Constitution, shall be as valid against the United States under this Constitution, as under the Confederation.

This Constitution, and the Laws of the United States which shall be made in Pursuance thereof; and all Treaties made, or which shall be made, under the Authority of the United States, shall be the supreme Law of the Land; and the Judges in every State shall be bound thereby, any Thing in the Constitution or Laws of any State to the Contrary notwithstanding.

The Senators and Representatives before mentioned, and the Members of the several State Legislatures, and all executive and judicial Officers, both of the United States and of the several States, shall be bound by Oath or Affirmation, to support this Constitution; but no religious Test shall ever be required as a Qualification to any Office or public Trust under the United States.

Art. VII

The Ratification of the Conventions of nine States, shall be sufficient for the Establishment of this Constitution between the States so ratifying the Same.

The Bill of Rights

Articles in addition to, and Amendment of the Constitution of the United States of America, proposed by Congress, and ratified by the Legislatures of the several States, pursuant to the fifth Article of the original Constitution.

[The first ten amendments went into effect November 3, 1791.]

Art. I

Congress shall make no law respecting an establishment of religion, or prohibiting the free exercise thereof; or abridging the freedom of speech, or of the press; or the right of the people peaceably to assemble, and to petition the government for a redress of grievances.

Art. II

A well regulated Militia, being necessary to the security of a free State, the right of the people to keep and bear Arms, shall not be infringed.

Art. III

No Soldier shall, in time of peace be quartered in any house, without the consent of the Owner, nor in time of war, but in a manner to be prescribed by law.

Art. IV

The right of the people to be secure in their persons, houses, papers, and effects, against unreasonable searches and seizures, shall not be violated, and no Warrants shall issue, but upon probable cause, supported by Oath or affirmation, and particularly describing the place to be searched, and the persons or things to be seized.

Art. V

No person shall be held to answer for a capital, or otherwise infamous crime, unless on a presentment or indictment of a Grand Jury, except in cases arising in the land or naval forces, or in the Militia, when in actual service in time of War or public danger; nor shall any person be subject for the same offence to be twice put in jeopardy of life or limb; nor shall be compelled in any criminal case to be a witness against himself, nor be deprived of life, liberty, or property, without due process of law; nor shall private property be taken for public use, without just compensation.

Art. VI

In all criminal prosecutions, the accused shall enjoy the right to a speedy and public trial, by an impartial jury of the State and district wherein the crime shall have been committed, which district shall have been previously ascertained by law, and to be informed of the nature and cause of the accusation; to be confronted with the witnesses against him; to have compulsory process for obtaining witnesses in his favor, and to have the Assistance of Counsel for his defence.

Art. VII

In Suits at common law, where the value in controversy shall exceed twenty dollars, the right of trial by jury shall be preserved, and no fact tried by a jury, shall be otherwise re-examined in any Court of the United States, than according to the rules of the common law.

Art. VIII

Excessive bail shall not be required, nor excessive fines imposed, nor cruel and unusual punishments inflicted.

Art. IX

The enumeration in the Constitution, of certain rights, shall not be construed to deny or disparage others retained by the people.

Art. X

The powers not delegated to the United States by the Constitution, nor prohibited by it to the States, are reserved to the States respectively, or to the people.

Further Amendments to the Constitution

Art. XI
Jan. 8, 1798

The Judicial power of the United States shall not be construed to extend to any suit in law or equity, commenced or prosecuted against one of the United States by Citizens of another State, or by Citizens or Subjects of any Foreign State.

Art. XII
Sept. 25, 1804

The Electors shall meet in their respective states, and vote by ballot for President and Vice-President, one of whom, at least, shall not be an inhabitant of the same state with themselves; they shall name in their ballots the person voted for as President, and in distinct ballots the person voted for as Vice-President, and they shall make distinct lists of all persons voted for as President, and of all persons voted for as Vice-

President, and of the number of votes for each, which lists they shall sign and certify, and transmit sealed to the seat of the government of the United States, directed to the President of the Senate;—The President of the Senate shall, in the presence of the Senate and House of Representatives, open all the certificates and the votes shall then be counted;—The person having the greatest number of votes for President, shall be the President, if such number be a majority of the whole number of Electors appointed; and if no person have such majority, then from the persons having the highest numbers not exceeding three on the list of those voted for as President, the House of Representatives shall choose immediately, by ballot, the President. But in choosing the President, the votes shall be taken by states, the representation from each state having one vote; a quorum for this purpose shall consist of a member or members from two-thirds of the states, and a majority of all the states shall be necessary to a choice. And if the House of Representatives shall not choose a President whenever the right of choice shall devolve upon them, before the fourth day of March next following, then the Vice-President shall act as President, as in the case of the death or other constitutional disability of the President.—The person having the greatest number of votes as Vice-President, shall be the Vice-President, if such number be a majority of the whole number of Electors appointed, and if no person have a majority, then from the two highest numbers on the list, the Senate shall choose the Vice-President; a quorum for the purpose shall consist of two-thirds of the whole number of Senators, and a majority of the whole number shall be necessary to a choice. But no person constitutionally ineligible to the office of President shall be eligible to that of Vice-President of the United States.

Art. XIII
Dec. 18, 1865

Sec. 1. Neither slavery nor involuntary servitude, except as a punishment for crime whereof the party shall have been duly convicted, shall exist within the United States, or any place subject to their jurisdiction.

Sec. 2. Congress shall have power to enforce this article by appropriate legislation.

Art. XIV
July 28, 1868

Sec. 1. All persons born or naturalized in the United States, and subject to the jurisdiction thereof, are citizens of the United States and of the State wherein they reside. No State shall make or enforce any law which shall abridge the privileges or immunities of citizens of the United States; nor shall any State deprive any person of life, liberty, or property, without due process of law; nor deny to any person within its jurisdiction the equal protection of the laws.

Sec. 2. Representatives shall be apportioned among the several States according to their respective numbers, counting the whole number of persons in each State, excluding Indians not taxed. But when the right to vote at any election for the choice of electors for President and Vice President of the United States, Representatives in Congress, the Executive and Judicial officers of a State, or the members of the Legislature thereof, is denied to any of the male inhabitants of such State, being twenty-one years of age, and citizens of the United States, or in any way abridged, except for participation in rebellion, or other crime, the basis of representation therein shall be reduced in the proportion which the number of such male citizens shall bear to the whole number of male citizens twenty-one years of age in such State.

Sec. 3. No person shall be a Senator or Representative in Congress, or elector of President and Vice President, or hold any office, civil or military, under the United States, or under any State, who, having previously taken an oath, as a member of Congress, or as an officer of the United States, or as a member of any State legislature, or as an executive or judicial officer of any State, to support the Constitution of the United States, shall have engaged in insurrection or rebellion against the same, or given aid or comfort to the enemies thereof. But Congress may by a vote of two-thirds of each House, remove such disability.

Sec. 4. The validity of the public debt of the United States, authorized by law, including debts incurred for payment of pensions and bounties for services in suppressing insurrection or rebellion, shall not be questioned. But neither the United States nor any State shall assume or pay any debt or obligation incurred in aid of insurrection or rebellion against the United States, or any claim for the loss or emancipation of any slave; but all such debts, obligations and claims shall be held illegal and void.

Sec. 5. The Congress shall have power to enforce, by appropriate legislation, the provisions of this article.

Art. XV
March 30, 1870

Sec. 1. The right of citizens of the United States to vote shall not be denied or abridged by the United States or by any State on account of race, color, or previous condition of servitude.

Sec. 2. The Congress shall have power to enforce this article by appropriate legislation.

Art. XVI
February 25, 1913

The Congress shall have power to lay and collect taxes on incomes, from whatever source derived, without apportionment among the several States and without regard to any census or enumeration.

Art. XVII
May 31, 1913

The Senate of the United States shall be composed of two senators from each State, elected by the people thereof, for six years; and each Senator shall have one vote. The electors in each State shall have the qualifications requisite for electors of the most numerous branch of the State legislature.

When vacancies happen in the representation of any State in the Senate, the executive authority of such State shall issue writs of election to fill such vacancies: *Provided*, That the legislature of any State may empower the executive thereof to make temporary appointments until the people fill the vacancies by election as the legislature may direct.

This amendment shall not be so construed as to affect the election or term of any senator chosen before it becomes valid as part of the Constitution.

Art. XVIII
January 29, 1919

After one year from the ratification of this article, the manufacture, sale, or transportation of intoxicating liquors within, the importation thereof into, or the exportation thereof from the United States and all territory subject to the jurisdiction thereof for beverage purposes is hereby prohibited.

The Congress and the several States shall have concurrent power to enforce this article by appropriate legislation.

This article shall be inoperative unless it shall have been ratified as an amendment to the Constitution by the legislatures of the several States, as provided in the Constitution, within seven years from the date of the submission thereof to the States by Congress.

Art. XIX
August 26, 1920

The right of citizens of the United States to vote shall not be denied or abridged by the United States or by any States on account of sex.

The Congress shall have power by appropriate legislation to enforce the provisions of this article.

Art. XX
February 6, 1933

Sec. 1. The terms of the President and Vice-President shall end at noon on the twentieth day of January, and the terms of Senators and Representatives at noon on the third day of January, of the years in which such terms would have ended if this article had not been ratified; and the terms of their successors shall then begin.

Sec. 2. The Congress shall assemble at least once in every year, and such meeting shall begin at noon on the third day of January, unless they shall by law appoint a different day.

Sec. 3. If, at the time fixed for the beginning of the term of the President, the President-elect shall have died, the Vice-President-elect shall become President. If a President shall not have been chosen before

the time fixed for the beginning of his term, or if the President-elect shall have failed to qualify, then the Vice-President-elect shall act as President until a President shall have qualified; and the Congress may by law provide for the case wherein neither a President-elect nor a Vice-President-elect shall have qualified, declaring who shall then act as President, or the manner in which one who is to act shall be selected, and such person shall act accordingly until a President or Vice-President shall have qualified.

Sec. 4. The Congress may by law provide for the case of the death of any of the persons from whom the House of Representatives may choose a President whenever the right of choice shall have devolved upon them, and for the case of the death of any of the persons from whom the Senate may choose a Vice-President whenever the right of choice shall have devolved upon them.

Sec. 5. Sections 1 and 2 shall take effect on the 15th day of October following the ratification of this article.

Sec. 6. This article shall be inoperative unless it shall have been ratified as an amendment to the Constitution by the legislatures of three-fourths of the several States within seven years from the date of its submission.

Art. XXI
December 5, 1933

Sec. 1. The eighteenth article of amendment to the Constitution of the United States is hereby repealed . . .

Art. XXII
February 26, 1951

Sec. 1. No person shall be elected to the office of the President more than twice, and no person who has held the office of President, or acted as President for more than two years of a term to which some other person was elected President shall be elected to the office of the President more than once. But this Article shall not apply to any person holding the office of President when this Article was proposed by the Congress, and shall not prevent any person who may be holding the office of President, or acting as President, during the term within which this Article becomes operative from holding the office of President or acting as President during the remainder of such term.

Article XXIII
March 29, 1961

SEC. 1. The District constituting the seat of Government of the United States shall appoint in such manner as the Congress may direct:

A number of electors of President and Vice-President equal to the whole number of Senators and Representatives in Congress to which the District would be entitled if it were a State, but in no event more than the least populous state; they shall be in addition to those appointed by the states, but they shall be considered, for the purposes of the election of President and Vice-President, to be electors appointed by a state; and they shall meet in the District and perform such duties as provided by the twelfth article of amendment.

SEC. 2. The Congress shall have power to enforce this article by appropriate legislation.

Article XXIV
January 24, 1964

SEC. 1. The right of citizens of the United States to vote in any primary or other election for President or Vice-President, for electors for President or Vice-President, or for Senator or Representative in Congress, shall not be denied or abridged by the United States or any stateby reason of failure to pay any poll tax or other tax.

SEC. 2. The Congress shall have power to enforce this article by appropriate legislation.

Article XXV
February 23, 1967

SEC. 1. In case of the removal of the President from office or his death or resignation, the Vice-President shall become President.

SEC. 2. Whenever there is a vacancy in the office of the Vice-President, the President shall nominate a Vice-President who shall take the office upon confirmation by a majority vote of both houses of Congress.

SEC. 3. Whenever the President transmits to the President pro tempore of the Senate and the Speaker of the House of Representatives his written declaration that he is unable to discharge the powers and duties of his office, and until he transmits to them a written declaration to the contrary, such powers and duties shall be discharged by the Vice-President as Acting President.

SEC. 4. Whenever the Vice-President and a majority of either the principal officers of the executive departments, or of such other body as Congress may by law provide, transmit to the President pro tempore of the Senate and the Speaker of the House of Representatives their written declaration that the President is unable to discharge the powers and duties of his office, the Vice-President shall immediately assume the powers and duties of the office as Acting President.

Thereafter, when the President transmits to the President pro tempore of the Senate and the Speaker of the House of Representatives his written declaration that no inability exists, he shall resume the powers and duties of his office unless the Vice-President and a majority of either the principal officers of the executive department, or of such other body as Congress may by law provide, transmit within four days to the President pro tempore of the Senate and the Speaker of the House of Representatives their written declaration that the President is unable to discharge the powers and duties of his office. Thereupon Congress shall decide the issue, assembling within 48 hours for that purpose if not in session. If the Congress, within 21 days after receipt of the latter written declaration, or, if Congress is not in session, within 21 days after Congress is required to assemble, determines by two-thirds vote of both houses that the President is unable to discharge the powers and duties of his office, the Vice-President shall continue to discharge the same as Acting President; otherwise, the President shall resume the powers and duties of his office.

Article XXVI
July 7, 1971

Sec. 1. The right of citizens of the United States, who are eighteen years of age or older, to vote shall not be denied or abridged by the United States or by any State on account of age.

Sec. 2. The Congress shall have power to enforce this article by appropriate legislation.

Index

Page numbers in bold text indicate the primary article on a topic or court case. Page numbers in italics indicate illustrations.

A

Index

D

F

G

H

I

Index

K

L

M

N

Q

R

Index

S

T

Y

Z

Supreme Court DRAMA

Cases That Changed America

Supreme Court DRAMA

Cases That Changed America

Daniel E. Brannen, &
Dr. Richard Clay Hanes
Elizabeth Shaw, Editor

VOLUME 4

BUSINESS LAW
FEDERAL POWERS AND SEPARATION OF POWERS
FEDERALISM AND STATE POWERS
LABOR AND LABOR PRACTICES
MILITARY LAW
NATIVE AMERICANS
TAXATION

U·X·L®
AN IMPRINT OF THE GALE GROUP
DETROIT · NEW YORK · SAN FRANCISCO
LONDON · BOSTON · WOODBRIDGE, CT

Supreme Court Drama: Cases That Changed America

DANIEL E. BRANNEN
RICHARD CLAY HANES

Staff

Elizabeth M. Shaw, U•X•L Editor
Carol DeKane Nagel, U•X•L Managing Editor
Thomas L. Romig, U•X•L Publisher

Shalice Shah-Caldwell, Permissions Associate (Pictures)
Maria Franklin, Permissions Manager
Robyn Young, Imaging and Multimedia Content Editor

Rita Wimberley, Senior Buyer
Evi Seoud, Assistant Manager, Composition Purchasing and Electronic Prepress
Dorothy Maki, Manufacturing Manager
Mary Beth Trimper, Production Director
Michelle DiMercurio, Senior Art Director

Pamela A. Reed, Imaging Coordinator
Randy Basset, Image Database Supervisor
Barbara Yarrow, Imaging and Multimedia Content Manager

Linda Mahoney, LM Design, Typesetting

Cover photographs: Reproduced by permission of the Library of Congress and the Supreme Court of the United States.

Library of Congress Cataloging-in-Publication Data

Brannen, Daniel E., 1968-
Supreme Court drama: cases that changed the nation / Daniel E. Brannen, Jr. and Richard Clay Hanes ; Elizabeth M. Shaw, editor.
p. cm.
Includes bibliographical references and index.
ISBN 0-7876-4877-9 (set) – ISBN 0-7876-4878-7 (v.1) – ISBN 0-7876-4879-5 (v.2) –ISBN 0-7876-4880-9 (v.3) – ISBN 0-7876-4881-7 (v.4)
1.Constitutional law–United States–Cases–Juvenile literature. 2. United States. Supreme Court–Juvenile Literature. [1. Constitutional law–United States–Cases. 2. United States. Supreme Court.] I. Hanes, Richard Clay, 1946- II. Shaw, Elizabeth M., 1973- III. Title.

KF4550.Z9 B73 2001
347.73'26'0264–dc21

00-056380

Printed in Canada

10 9 8 7 6 5 4 3 2

Contents

Contents

Contents

VOLUME 2: CRIMINAL JUSTICE AND FAMILY LAW

Contents

CAPITAL PUNISHMENT

CRIMINAL LAW AND PROCEDURE

Contents

Contents

Contents

Contents

Contents

Contents

Trials Alphabetically

A

B

F

G

H

I

J

K

L

M

N

O

P

R

S

T

U

V

W

Y

Trials Chronologically

Trials Chronologically

1879

1883

1884

1886

1895

1896

1897

1905

1908

Trials Chronologically

1936

1937

1938

1940

1941

1942

1943

Trials Chronologically

1944

1945

1947

1948

1951

1954

1955

1957

1958

1960

1961

1962

1963

1964

1965

1966

Trials Chronologically

1967

1968

1969

1970

1971

1972

1973

1974

1975

1976

1977

1978

Trials Chronologically

1986

1987

1988

1989

1990

Trials Chronologically

1991

1992

1993

1994

1995

1996

1997

1998

1999

2000

Reader's Guide

U.S. citizens take comfort and pride in living under the rule of law. Our elected representatives write and enforce the laws that cover everything from family relationships to the dealings of multi-billion-dollar corporations, from the quality of the air to the content of the programs broadcast through it. But it is the judicial system that interprets the meaning of the law and makes it real for the average citizen through the drama of trials and the force of court orders and judicial opinions.

The four volumes of *Supreme Court Drama: Cases that Changed America* profile approximately 150 cases that influenced the development of key aspects of law in the United States. The case profiles are grouped according to the legal principle on which they are based, with each volume covering one or two broad areas of the law as follows:

- **Volume : Individual Liberties** includes cases that have influenced such First Amendment issues as freedom of the press, religion, speech, and assembly. It also covers the right to privacy.
- **Volume 2: Criminal Justice and Family Law** covers many different areas of criminal law, such as capital punishment, crimnal procedure, family law, and juvenile law.
- **Volume 3: Equal Protection and Civil Rights** includes cases in the areas of affirmative action, reproductive rights segregation, and voting rights, as well as areas of special concern such as immigrants, the disabled, and gay and lesbian citizens. Sexual harassment and the right to die are also represented in this volume.

- **Volume 4: Business and Government Law** also encompasses two major spheres of the law. Monopolies, antitrust, and labor-related cases supplement the business fundamentals of corporate law. The government cases document the legal evolution of the branches of the federal government as well as the federal government's relation to state power. Separate topics address military issues, taxation, and legal history behind some Native American issues.
- **Appendixes** to all volumes also present the full text of the U.S. Constitution and its amendments and a chronological table of Supreme Court justices.

Coverage

Issue overviews, averaging 2,000 words in length provide the context for the case profiles that follow. Case discussions range from 750 to 2,000 words according, to their complexity and importance. Each provides the background of the case and issues involved, the main arguments presented by each side, and an explanation of the Supreme Court's decision, as well as the legal, political, and social impact of the decision. Excerpts from the Court's opinions are often included. Within each issue section, the cases are arranged from earliest to most recent.

When a single case could be covered under several different areas—the landmark reproductive rights decision in *Roe v. Wade,* for example, is also based upon an assertion of privacy rights—the case is placed with the issue with which it is most often associated. Users should consult the cumulative index that appears in each volume to find cases throughout the set that apply to a particular topic.

Additional Features

- The issues and proceedings featured in *Supreme Court Drama* are presented in language accessible to middle school users. Legal terms must sometimes be used for precision, however, so a Words to Know section of more than 300 words and phrases appears in each volume.
- A general essay providing a broad overview of the Supreme Court of the United States and the structure of the American legal system.
- **Bolded** cross-references within overview and case entries that point to cases that appear elsewhere in the set.

- Tables of contents to locate a particular case by name or in chronological order.
- A cumulative index at the end of each volume that includes the cases, people, events and subjects that appear throughout *Supreme Court Drama.*

Suggestions Are Welcome

We welcome your comments on *Supreme Court Drama: Cases That Changed America.* Please write, Editors, *Supreme Court Drama,* U•X•L, 27500 Drake Road, Farmington Hills, MI 48331-3535; call toll-free: 1-800-877-4253; fax to 248-414-5043; or send e-mail via http://www.galegroup.com.

Advisors

The editor is grateful for all the assistance and insight offered by the advisors to this product.

- Mary Alice Anderson, Media Specialist, Winona Middle School, Winona, Minnesota
- Sara Brooke, Librarian, Ellis School, Pittsburgh, Pennsylvania
- Marolynn Griffin, Librarian, Desert Ridge Middle School, Albuquerque, New Mexico
- Dr. E. Shane McKee, Instructor, The Putney School at Elm Lea Farm, Putney, Vermont

The editor and writers would also like to acknowledge the tireless review and copy editing work done by:

- Aaron Ford, The Ohio State University, Columbus, Ohio
- Kathleen Knisely, Franklin County Courts, Columbus, Ohio
- Courtney Mroch, Freelance Writer, Jacksonville, Florida
- Melynda Neal, Franklin County Courts, Columbus, Ohio
- Berna Rhodes-Ford, Franklin County Courts, Columbus, Ohio
- Gertrude Ring, Freelance Writer, Los Angeles, California
- Lauren Zupnic, Franklin County Courts, Columbus, Ohio

Guide to the Supreme Court of the United States

The United States Supreme Court is the highest court in the judicial branch of the federal government. That means the Supreme Court is equal in importance to the president, who heads the executive branch, and Congress, which heads the legislative branch. Congress makes laws, the president enforces them, and the Supreme Court interprets them to make sure they are properly enforced.

The Supreme Court's main job is to review federal (national) and state cases that involve rights or duties under the U.S. Constitution, the document outlining the laws and guidelines for lawmaking and enforcement in the United States. The Court does this to make sure that all federal and state governments are obeying the Constitution.

For example, if Congress passes a law that violates the First Amendment freedom of speech, the Supreme Court can strike the law down as unconstitutional. If the president violates the Fourth Amendment by having the Federal Bureau of Investigation search a person's home without a warrant, the Supreme Court can fix the violation. If a state court violates the Constitution by convicting someone of a crime in an unfair trial, the Supreme Court can reverse the conviction.

As the highest court in the United States government, the Supreme Court also has the job of interpreting federal law. Congress creates law to regulate crimes, drugs, taxes, and other important issues across the nation. When someone is accused of violating a federal law, a federal

court must interpret the law to decide whether the accused has broken the law. In this role, the Supreme Court makes the final decision about what a federal law means.

The Federal Court System

The Supreme Court was born in 1789, when the United States adopted the Constitution. Article III of the Constitution says, "The judicial Power of the United States, shall be vested in one supreme Court, and in such inferior Courts as the Congress may from time to time ordain and establish." With this sentence, the Constitution made the Supreme Court the highest Court in the judicial branch of the federal government. It also gave Congress the power to create lower courts.

Congress used that power to create a large judicial (court) system. The system has three levels. Trial courts, called federal district courts, are at the lowest level. There are ninety-four federal district courts covering different areas of the country. Each federal district court handles trials for cases in its area.

Federal district courts hold trials in both criminal and civil cases. Criminal trials involve cases by the government against a person who is accused of a crime, like murder. Civil trials involve cases between private parties, such as when one person accuses another of breaking a contract or agreement.

When a party loses a case in federal district court, she usually may appeal the decision to a U.S. court of appeals. Federal courts of appeals are the second level in the federal judicial system. There are twelve courts of appeals covering twelve areas, or circuits, of the country. For example, the district courts in Connecticut, New York, and Vermont are part of the Second Circuit. Appeals from district courts in those states go to the U.S. Court of Appeals for the Second Circuit.

During an appeal, the losing party asks the court of appeals to reverse or modify the trial court's decision. In essence, she argues that the trial court made an error when it ruled against her.

The party who loses before the court of appeals must decide whether to take her case to the U.S. Supreme Court. The Supreme Court is the third and highest level of the federal judicial system. The process of taking a case to the U.S. Supreme Court is described below.

State Court Systems

Most states have a judicial system that resembles the federal system. Trial courts hold trials in both criminal and civil cases. Most states also have special courts that hear only certain kinds of cases. Family, juvenile, and traffic courts are typical examples. There also are state courts, such as justices of the peace and small claims courts, that handle minor matters.

Appeals from all lower courts usually go to a court of appeals. The losing party there may take her case to the state's highest court, often called the state supreme court. When a case involves the U.S. Constitution or federal law, the losing party sometimes may take the case from the state supreme court to the U.S. Supreme Court.

Bringing a Case to the U.S. Supreme Court

There are three main ways that cases get to the U.S. Supreme Court. The most widely used method is to ask the Supreme Court to hear the case. This is called filing a petition for a writ of *certiorari.* The person who files the petition, usually the person who lost the case in the court of appeals, is called the petitioner. The person on the other side of the case is called the respondent. The Court only grants a small percentage of the writ petitions it receives each year. It usually tries to accept the cases that involve the most important legal issues.

The second main way to bring a case to the Supreme Court is by appeal. An appeal is possible only when the law that the case involves says the parties may appeal to the Supreme Court. The losing party who files the appeal is called the appellant, while the person on the other side of the case is a called the appellee.

The third main way to bring a case to the Supreme Court is by filing a petition for a writ of habeas corpus. This petition is mainly for people who have been imprisoned in violation of the U.S. Constitution. For example, if an accused criminal is convicted and jailed after the police beat him to get a confession (a police act that is illegal), the prisoner may ask the Supreme Court to release him by filing a petition for a writ of habeas corpus. The person who files the petition is called the petitioner, while the person holding the petitioner in jail is called the respondent.

The process of arguing and deciding a case in the Supreme Court is similar no matter how the case gets there. The parties file briefs that

explain why they think the lower court's decision in their case is either right or wrong. The Supreme Court reviews the briefs along with a record of the evidence presented during trial in the federal district court or state trial court. The Supreme Court also may allow the parties to engage in oral argument, which is a chance for the lawyers to explain their clients' cases. During oral argument, the Supreme Court justices can ask questions to help them make the right decision.

After the justices read the briefs, review the record, and hear oral argument, they meet privately in chambers to discuss the case. Eventually, the nine justices vote for the party they think should win the case. A party must receive votes from five of the nine justices to win the case. The justices who cast the votes for the winning party are called the majority, while the justices who vote for the losing party are called the minority.

After the justices vote, one justice in the majority writes an opinion to explain the Court's decision. Other justices in the majority may write concurring opinions that explain why they agree with the Court's decision. Justices in the minority may write dissenting opinions to explain why they think the Court's decision is wrong.

The Supreme Court's decision is the final word in a case. Parties who are unhappy with the result have no place to go to get a different ruling. The only way to change the effect of a Supreme Court decision is to have Congress change the law, have the entire nation change, or amend, the Constitution, or have the president appoint a different justice to the Court when one retires or dies. This is part of the federal government's system of checks and balances, which prevents one branch from becoming too strong.

Supreme Court Justices

Supreme Court justices are among the greatest legal minds in the country. Appointment to the job is usually the high point of a career that involved some combination of trial work as a lawyer, teaching as a professor, or service as a judge on a lower court.

Under the Constitution, the president appoints Supreme Court justices with the advice and consent of the Senate when one of the nine justices retires, dies, or is removed from office. Supreme Court justices cannot be removed from office except by impeachment and conviction by Congress for serious crimes. That means the process of appointing a new justice usually begins when one of the justices retires or dies.

The president begins the process by nominating someone to fill the empty seat on the Court. The president usually names someone who he thinks will interpret the Constitution favorably to his political party's wishes. In other words, democratic presidents typically nominate liberal justices, while republican presidents nominate conservative justices.

The next step in the process is for the Senate Judiciary Committee to review the president's recommendation. If the Senate is controlled by the president's political party, the review process usually results in Senate approval of the president's selection.

If the president's political opposition controls the Senate, the review process can be fierce and lengthy. The Judiciary Committee calls the nominee before it to answer questions. The Committee's goal is to determine whether the nominee is qualified to be a Supreme Court justice. The Committee also uses the investigation to try to figure out how the nominee will decide controversial cases, such as cases involving abortion. After its investigation, the Committee recommends whether the Senate should confirm or reject the president's nomination. Two-thirds of the senators must vote for the nominee to confirm him as a new Supreme Court justice.

The Supreme Court has changed greatly over the years. One of the Court's greatest liberal periods was when Chief Justice Earl Warren headed the Court from 1953 to 1969. In 1954, the Warren Court decided one of its most famous cases, *Brown v. Board of Education,* in which it forced public schools to end the practice of separating black and white students in different schools.

The Warren Court was followed by one of the Court's greatest conservative periods, under Chief Justice Warren E. Burger from 1969 to 1986, followed by Chief Justice William H. Rehnquist from 1986 onward. In one of the Rehnquist Court's most important decisions, *Clinton v. Jones* (1997), the Court said the president may be sued while in office for conduct unrelated to his official duties. The decision allowed Paula Jones to sue President William J. Clinton for sexual harassment.

Unfortunately, the justices on the highest court in a nation of diversity have not been very diverse themselves. Until 1916, all Supreme Court justices were white, Christian men. That year, Louis D. Brandeis became the first Jewish member of the Supreme Court. In 1967, Thurgood Marshall became the first African American justice. Clarence Thomas became just the second in 1991. In 1981, President Ronald Reagan nominated Sandra Day O'Connor to be the first woman on the Supreme Court. Ruth Bader Ginsburg joined her there in 1993.

Research and Activity Ideas

Activity 1: New School Rule

Assignment: Imagine that your school principal has just announced a new school rule for detention. Students who get detention are not allowed to explain themselves, even if they did nothing wrong. Instead, they must sit in the principal's office during lunch. They are not allowed to eat lunch, not allowed to talk at all, and must listen to Frank Sinatra music during the entire period. Your teacher has asked you to prepare a written report on whether this new rule violates the U.S. Constitution.

Preparation: Begin your research by reading the Bill of Rights, which contains the first ten amendments to the U.S. Constitution, along with the Fourteenth Amendment. These amendments contain many rights that might apply to the principal's new rule. Do you see any that might help? Continue your research by looking in *Supreme Court Drama: Cases That Changed America* for essays and cases on the freedom of speech, cruel and unusual punishment, and students' rights in school. Consult the library and Internet web sites for additional research material. Does it seem to matter whether you are in a public or private school?

Presentation: After you have gathered your information, prepare a report that explains what you found. Does the principal's new rule violate the Constitution? Why or why not? Explain your conclusions by referring to specific amendments from the Constitution and specific cases from *Supreme Court Drama.*

Research and Activity Ideas

Activity 2: Taking a Case to Court

Assignment: Pretend you were in a bookstore that was being robbed. When the police arrived to arrest the criminal, they accidentally arrested you. During the arrest they treated you roughly and broke your arm. Your lawyer has informed you that you may sue the police to recover damages in either state or federal court. Before deciding which court system to use, you must do some research about both systems.

Preparation: Begin by reading the Introduction to *Supreme Court Drama: Cases That Changed America* so you can learn about the federal and state court systems in general. Continue with library and Internet research for more information about these systems. Then figure out which courts you need to use for your case. For the state system, use the library and Internet to find your local trial court for civil cases. Then find your state court of appeals and supreme courts in case you lose in the trial court. For the federal system, find the federal district court and U.S. court of appeals for your area. Write to the state supreme court and the U.S. court of appeals to find out what percentage of cases make it from those courts to the U.S. Supreme Court each year.

Presentation: Write a letter to your attorney explaining what you found. Tell her where you need to file your case if you choose the state system, and where you need to take appeals in that system. Do the same for the federal system. Tell her what your chances are of getting to the U.S. Supreme Court with your case.

Activity 3: Oral Argument

Activity: Imagine that a new religious group called Planterism has moved into your community. Planters are a group of men who worship trees, flowers, and other plant life. Once every week they hold an all-night ceremony during which they burn a tree as a sacrifice for all living plants. The ceremony disturbs neighbors who are trying to sleep and threatens to eliminate rare trees in your town.

Your mayor or other local leader decides he does not like Planters, so he enacts the following law:

> **Everyone in this town must follow Christianity, Judaism, or some other popular religion. Anyone who follows a false religion, including Planterism, is guilty of a felony. Anyone who burns a tree as a**

> **sacrifice during a religious ceremony is guilty of a felony. Anyone who disturbs the peace with a religious ceremony at night is guilty of a felony.**
>
> **Violation of this law by men is punishable by life in prison without a trial. If the local police suspect a man is violating this law, they shall enter his house immediately without a warrant, arrest him, and take him to jail for imprisonment. Violation of this law by women is punishable by thirty days in jail only after a jury finds the woman guilty in a fair trial.**

Your teacher has instructed the class to convene a Supreme Court to determine whether this law violates the U.S. Constitution.

Preparation: Select nine members of your class to be justices on the Court. The rest of your class should divide into three teams. One team will represent the mayor, who will argue in favor of the law. The second team will represent a group of Planters who want to challenge the law. The third team will represent a group of Christians, who want to burn palms on Palm Sunday, a religious holiday that happens once a year.

The justices and all three teams should begin by reading the Bill of Rights and the Fourteenth Amendment of the U.S. Constitution. Continue by reading *Supreme Court Drama: Cases That Changed America* for essays and cases on the freedom of religion, the establishment clause, search and seizure, cruel and unusual punishment, governmental power, due process of law, and gender discrimination. Supplement this with research from library materials and Internet web sites. You may want to assign small groups from each team to handle specific issues.

Presentation: When everyone has completed the research, all three teams should prepare to argue before the Supreme Court. The team representing the mayor should explain why the law should be upheld. The teams representing the Planters and the Christians should explain why the law should be struck down as unconstitutional. During the argument, the justices are allowed to ask questions of each team. After every team has made its argument, the justices should meet to discuss the case and to make a ruling. Is the law unconstitutional? Which parts are valid and which are not?

Words to Know

A

Accessory Aiding or contributing in a secondary way to a crime or assisting in or contributing to a crime.

Accomplice One who knowingly and voluntarily helps commit a crime.

Acquittal When a person who has been charged with committing a crime is found not guilty by the courts.

Admissible A term used to describe information that is allowed to be used as evidence or information in a court case.

Adultery Voluntary sexual relations between an individual who is married and someone who is not the individual's spouse.

Affidavit A written statement of facts voluntarily made by someone in front of an official or witness.

Affirmative action Employment programs required by the federal government designed to eliminate existing and continuing discrimination, to remedy lingering effects of past discrimination, and to create systems and procedures to prevent future discrimination; commonly based on population percentages of minority groups in a particular area. Factors considered are race, color, sex, creed (religious beliefs), and age.

Age of consent The age at which a person may marry without parental approval.

Words to Know

Age of majority The age at which a person, formerly a minor or an infant, is recognized by law to be an adult, capable of managing his or her own affairs and responsible for any legal obligations created by his or her actions.

Aggravated assault A person is guilty of aggravated assault if he or she tries to cause serious bodily injury to another or causes such injury purposely, knowingly, or recklessly without any concern for that person or without remorse.

Alien Foreign-born person who has not been naturalized to become a U.S. citizen under federal law and the Constitution.

Alimony Payment a family court may order one person in a couple to make to the other when the couple separates or divorces.

Amendment An addition, deletion, or change to an original item, such as the additions to the Constitution.

Amicus curiae Latin for "friend of the court"; a person with strong interest in, views on, or knowledge of the subject matter of a case, but is not a party to the case. A friend of the court may petition the court for permission to file a statement about the situation.

Amnesty The action of a government by which all persons or certain groups of persons who have committed a criminal offense—usually of a political nature that threatens the government (such as treason)—are granted immunity from prosecution.

Appeal Timely plea by an unsuccessful party in a lawsuit to an appropriate superior court that has the power to review a final decision on the grounds that the decision was made in error.

Appellate court A court having jurisdiction to review decisions of a lower court.

Apportionment The process by which legislative seats are distributed among those who are entitled to representation; determination of the number of representatives that each state, county, or other subdivision may send to a legislative body.

Arbitration Taking a dispute to an unbiased third person and agreeing in advance to comply with the decision made by that third person, after both parties have had a chance to argue their side of the issue.

Arraignment The formal proceeding where the defendant is brought before the trial court to hear the charges against him or her and to enter a plea of guilty, not guilty, or no contest.

Arrest The taking into custody of an individual for the purpose of answering the charges against him or her.

Arrest warrant A written order issued by an authority of the state and commanding that the person named be taken into custody.

Arson The malicious burning or exploding of a house, building, or property.

Assault Intentionally harming another person.

Attempt Unsuccessfully preparing and trying to carry out a deed.

B

Bail An amount of money the defendant needs to pay the court to be released while waiting for a trial.

Bankruptcy A federally authorized procedure by which an individual, corporation, or municipality is relieved of total liability for its debts by making arrangements for the partial repayment of those debts.

Battery An intentional, unpermitted act causing harmful or offensive contact with another person.

Beneficiary One who inherits something through the last will and testament (will) of another; also, a person who is entitled to profits, benefits, or advantage from a contract.

Bigamy The offense of willfully and knowingly entering into a second marriage while married to another person.

Bill A written declaration that one hopes to have made into a law.

Bill of rights The first ten amendments to the U.S. Constitution, ratified (adopted by the states) in 1791, which set forth and guaranteed certain fundamental rights and privileges of individuals, including freedom of religion, speech, press, and assembly; guarantee of a speedy jury trial in criminal cases; and protection against excessive bail and cruel and unusual punishment.

Black codes Laws, statutes, or rules that governed slavery and segregation of public places in the South prior to 1865.

Bona fide occupational qualification An essential requirement for performing a given job. The requirement may even be a physical condition beyond an individual's control, such as perfect vision, if it is absolutely necessary for performing a job.

Brief A summary of the important points of a longer document.

Burden of proof The duty of a party to convince a judge or jury of their position, and to prove wrong any evidence that damages the position of the party. In criminal cases the party must prove their case beyond a reasonable doubt.

Burglary The criminal offense of breaking and entering a building illegally for the purpose of committing a crime.

Bylaws The rules and regulations of an association or a corporation to provide a framework for its operation and management.

C

Capacity The ability, capability, or fitness to do something; a legal right, power, or competency to perform some act. An ability to comprehend both the nature and consequences of one's acts.

Capital punishment The lawful infliction of death as a punishment; the death penalty.

Cause A reason for an action or condition. A ground of a legal action.

Censorship The suppression of speech or writing that is deemed obscene, indecent, or controversial.

Certiorari Latin for "to be informed of"; an order commanding officers of inferior courts to allow a case pending before them to move up to a higher court to determine whether any irregularities or errors occurred that justify review of the case. A device by which the Supreme Court of the United States exercises its discretion in selecting the cases it will review.

Change of venue The removal of a lawsuit from one county or district to another for trial, often permitted in criminal cases in which the court finds that the defendant would not receive a fair trial in the first location because of negative publicity.

Charter A grant from the government of ownership rights of land to a person, a group of people, or an organization, such as a corporation.

Circumstantial evidence Information and testimony presented by a party in a civil or criminal case that allows conclusions to be drawn about certain facts without the party presenting concrete evidence to support their facts.

Citation A paper commonly used in various courts that is served upon an individual to notify him or her that he or she is required to appear at a specific time and place.

Citizens Those who, under the Constitution and laws of the United States, owe allegiance to the United States and are entitled to the enjoyment of all civil rights awarded to those living in the United States.

Civil law A body of rules that spell out the private rights of citizens and the remedies for governing disputes between individuals in such areas as contracts, property, and family law.

Civil liberties Freedom of speech, freedom of press, freedom from discrimination, and other rights guaranteed and protected by the Constitution, which were intended to place limits on government.

Civil rights Personal liberties that belong to an individual.

Class action A lawsuit that allows a large number of people with a common interest in a matter to sue or be sued as a group.

Clause A section, phrase, paragraph, or segment of a legal document, such as a contract, deed, will, or constitution, that relates to a particular point.

Closing argument The final factual and legal argument made by each attorney on all sides of a case in a trial prior to the verdict or judgment.

Code A collection of laws, rules, or regulations that are consolidated and classified according to subject matter.

Collective bargaining agreement The contractual agreement between an employer and a labor union that controls pay, hours, and working conditions for employees which can be enforced against both the employer and the union for failure to comply with its terms.

Commerce Clause The provision of the U.S. Constitution that gives Congress exclusive power over trade activities between the states and with foreign countries and Native American tribes.

Words to Know

Commercial speech The words used in advertisments by commercial companies and service providers. Commercial speech is protected under the First Amendment as long as it is not false or misleading.

Common law The principles and rules of action, embodied in case law rather than legislative enactments, applicable to the government and protection of persons and property, Common laws derive their authority from the community customs and traditions that evolved over the centuries as interpreted by judicial tribunals (types of courts).

Common-law marriage A union of two people not formalized in the customary manner but created by an agreement by the two people to consider themselves married followed by their living together.

Community property The materials and resources owned in common by a husband and wife.

Complaint The possible evidence that initiates a civil action; in criminal law, the document that sets in motion a person's being charged with an offense.

Concurring opinion An opinion by one or more judges that provides separate reasoning for reaching the same decision as the majority of the court.

Conditional Subject to change; dependent upon the occurrence of a future, uncertain event.

Confession A statement made by an individual that acknowledges his or her guilt of a crime.

Conflict of interest A term used to describe the situation in which a public official exploits his or her position for personal benefit.

Consent Voluntary agreement to the proposal of another; the act or result of reaching an agreement.

Conspiracy An agreement between two or more persons to engage in an unlawful or criminal act, or an act that is innocent in itself but becomes unlawful when done by those participating.

Constituent A person who gives another person permission to act on his or her behalf, such as an agent, an attorney in a court of law, or an elected official in government.

Constitution of the United States A document written by the founding fathers of the United States that has been added to by Congress over

the centuries that is held as the absolute rule of action and decision for all branches and offices of the government, and which all subsequent laws and ordinances must be in accordance. It is enforced by representatives of the people of the United States, and can be changed only by a constitutional amendment by the authority that created it.

Contempt An act of deliberate disobedience or disregard for the laws or regulations of a public authority, such as a court or legislative body.

Continuance The postponement of an action pending (waiting to be tried) in a court to a later date, granted by a court in response to a request made by one of the parties to a lawsuit.

Corporations Business entities that are treated much like human individuals under the law, having legally enforceable rights, the ability to acquire debt and pay out profits, the ability to hold and transfer property, the ability to enter into contracts, the requirement to pay taxes, and the ability to sue and be sued.

Counsel An attorney or lawyer.

Court of appeal An intermediate court of review that is found in thirteen judicial districts, called circuits, in the United States. A state court of appeal reviews a decision handed down by a lower court to determine whether that court made errors that warrant the reversal of its final decision.

Covenant An agreement, contract, or written promise between two individuals that frequently includes a pledge to do or refrain from doing something.

Criminal law A body of rules and statutes that defines behavior prohibited by the government because it threatens and/or harms public safety, and establishes the punishments to be given to those who commit such acts.

Cross-examination The questioning of a witness or party during a trial, hearing, or deposition by the opposing lawyer.

Cruel and unusual punishment Such punishment as would amount to torture or barbarity, any cruel and degrading punishment, or any fine, penalty, confinement, or treatment so disproportionate to the offense as to shock the moral sense of the community.

Custodial parent The parent to whom the court grants guardianship of the children after a divorce.

Words to Know

D

Death penalty See Capital punishment.

De facto Latin for "in fact"; in deed; actually.

Defamation Any intentional false communication, either written or spoken, that harms a person's reputation; decreases the respect, regard, or confidence in which a person is held; or causes hostile or disagreeable opinions or feelings against a person.

Defendant The person defending or denying; the party against whom recovery is sought in an action or suit, or the accused in a criminal case.

Defense The forcible reaction against an unlawful and violent attack, such as the defense of one's person, property, or country in time of war.

De jure Latin for "in law"; legitimate; lawful, as a matter of law. Having complied with all the requirements imposed by law.

Deliberate Willful; purposeful; determined after thoughtful evaluation of all relevant factors. To act with a particular intent, which is derived from a careful consideration of factors that influence the choice to be made.

Delinquent An individual who fails to fulfill an obligation or otherwise is guilty of a crime or offense.

Domestic partnership laws Legislation and regulations related to the legal recognition of nonmarital relationships between persons who are romantically involved with each other, have set up a joint residence, and have registered with cities recognizing said relationships.

Denaturalization To take away an individual's rights as a citizen.

Deportation Banishment to a foreign country, attended with confiscation of property and deprivation of civil rights.

Deposition The testimony of a party or witness in a civil or criminal proceeding taken before trial, usually in an attorney's office.

Desegregation Judicial mandate making illegal the practice of segregation.

Disclaimer The denial, refusal, or rejection of a right, power, or responsibility.

Discrimination The grant of particular privileges to a group randomly chosen from a large number of people in which no reasonable dif-

ference exists between the favored and disfavored groups. Federal laws prohibit discrimination in such areas as employment, housing, voting rights, education, access to public facilities, and on the bases of race, age, sex, nationality, disability, or religion.

Dismissal A discharge of an individual or corporation from employment.

Dissent A disagreement by one or more judges with the decision of the majority on a case before them.

Divorce A court decree that terminates a marriage; also known as marital dissolution.

Double jeopardy A second prosecution for the same offense after acquittal or conviction or multiple punishments for the same offense. The evil sought to be avoided by prohibiting double jeopardy is double trial and double conviction, not necessarily double punishment.

Draft A mandatory call of persons to serve in the military.

Due process of law A fundamental, constitutional guarantee that all legal proceedings will be fair and that one will be given notice of the proceedings and an opportunity to be heard before the government acts to take away one's life, liberty, or property. Also, a constitutional guarantee that a law shall not be unreasonable, random, or without consideration for general well-being.

Duress Unlawful pressure exerted upon a person to force that person to perform an act that he or she ordinarily would not perform.

E

Emancipation The act or process by which a person is liberated from the authority and control of another person.

Entrapment The act of government agents or officials that causes a person to commit a crime he or she would not have committed otherwise.

Equal Pay Act Federal law that commands the same pay for all persons who do the same work without regard to sex, age, race, or ability.

Equal protection The constitutional guarantee that no person or class of persons shall be denied the same protection of the laws that is enjoyed by other persons or other classes in like circumstances in their lives, liberty, property, and pursuit of happiness.

Words to Know

Establishment Clause The provision in the First Amendment that provides that there will be no laws created respecting the establishment of a religion, inhibiting the practice of a religion, or giving preference to any or all religions. It has been interpreted to also denounce the discouragement of any or all religions.

Euthanasia The merciful act or practice of terminating the life of an individual or individuals inflicted with incurable and distressing diseases in a relatively painless manner.

Exclusionary rule The principle based on federal constitutional law that evidence illegally seized by law enforcement officers in violation of a suspect's right to be free from unreasonable searches and seizures cannot be used against the suspect in a criminal prosecution.

Executive agreement An agreement made between the head of a foreign country and the president of the United States. This agreement does not have to be submitted to the Senate for consent, and it supersedes any contradicting state law.

Executive orders When the president uses some part of a law or the Constitution to enforce some action.

Executor The individual legally named by a deceased person to administer the provisions of his or her will.

Ex parte Latin for "on one side only"; done by, for, or on the application of one party alone.

Expert witness A witness, such as a psychological statistician or ballisticsexpert, who possesses special or superior knowledge concerning the subject of his or her testimony.

Ex post facto laws Latin for "after-the-fact laws"; laws that provide for the infliction of punishment upon a person for some prior act that, at the time it was committed, was not illegal.

Extradition The transfer of a person accused of a crime from one state or country to another state or country that seeks to place the accused on trial.

F

Family court A court that presides over cases involving: (1) child abuse and neglect; (2) support; (3) paternity; (4) termination of custody due to constant neglect; (5) juvenile delinquency; and (6) family offenses.

Federal Relating to a national government, as opposed to state or local governments.

Federal circuit courts The twelve circuit courts making up the U.S. Federal Circuit Court System. Decisions made by the federal district courts can be reviewed by the court of appeals in each circuit.

Federal district courts The first of three levels of the federal court system, which includes the U.S. Court of Appeals and the U.S. Supreme Court. If a participating party disagrees with the ruling of a federal district court in its case, it may petition for the case to be moved to the next level in the federal court system.

Felon An individual who commits a felony, a crime of a serious nature, such as burglary or murder.

Felony A serious crime, characterized under federal law and many state statutes as any offense punishable by death or imprisonment in excess of one year.

First degree murder Murder committed with deliberately premeditated thought and malice, or with extreme atrocity or cruelty. The difference between first and second degree murder is the presence of the specific intention to kill.

Fraud A false representation of a matter of fact—whether by words or by conduct, by false or misleading allegations, or by concealment of what should have been disclosed—that deceives and is intended to deceive another so that the individual will act upon it to her or his legal injury.

Freedom of assembly See Freedom of association.

Freedom of association The right to associate with others for the purpose of engaging in constitutionally protected activities, such as to peacefully assemble.

Freedom of religion The First Amendment right to individually believe and to practice or exercise one's religious belief.

Freedom of speech The right, guaranteed by the First Amendment to the U.S. Constitution, to express beliefs and ideas without unwarranted government restriction.

Freedom of the press The right, guaranteed by the First Amendment to the U.S. Constitution, to gather, publish, and distribute information and ideas without government restriction; this right encompasses

freedom from prior restraints on publication and freedom from censorship.

Fundamental rights Rights that derive, or are implied, from the terms of the U.S. Constitution, such as the Bill of Rights, the first ten amendments to the Constitution.

G

Gag rule A rule, regulation, or law that prohibits debate or discussion of a particular issue.

Grandfather clause A portion of a statute that provides that the law is not applicable in certain circumstances due to preexisting facts.

Grand jury A panel of citizens that is convened by a court to decide whether it is appropriate for the government to indict (proceed with a prosecution against) someone suspected of a crime.

Grand larceny A category of larceny—the offense of illegally taking the property of another—in which the value of the property taken is greater than that set for petit larceny.

Grounds The basis or foundation; reasons sufficient in law to justify relief.

Guardian A person lawfully invested with the power, and charged with the obligation, of taking care of and managing the property and rights of a person who, because of age, understanding, or lack of self-control, is considered incapable of administering his or her own affairs.

Guardian ad litem A guardian appointed by the court to represent the interests of infants, the unborn, or incompetent persons in legal actions.

H

Habeas corpus Latin for "you have the body"; a writ (court order) that commands an individual or a government official who has restrained another to produce the prisoner at a designated time and place so that the court can determine the legality of custody and decide whether to order the prisoner's release.

Hate crime A crime motivated by race, religion, gender, sexual orientation, or other prejudice.

Hearing A legal proceeding in which issues of law or fact are tried and evidence is presented to help determine the issue.

Hearsay A statement made out of court that is offered in court as evidence to prove the truth of the matter asserted.

Heir An individual who receives an interest in, or ownership of, land or tenements from an ancestor who died through the laws of descent and distribution. At common law, an heir was the individual appointed by law to succeed to the estate of an ancestor who died without a will. It is commonly used today in reference to any individual who succeeds to property, either by will or law.

Homicide The killing of one human being by another human being.

Hung jury A trial jury selected to make a decision in a criminal case regarding a defendant's guilt or innocence that is unable to reach a verdict due to a complete division in opinion.

I

Immunity Exemption from performing duties that the law generally requires other citizens to perform, or from a penalty or burden that the law generally places on other citizens.

Impeachment A process used to charge, try, and remove public officials for misconduct while in office.

Inalienable Not subject to sale or transfer; inseparable.

Incapacity The absence of legal ability, competence, or qualifications.

Income tax A charge imposed by government on the annual gains of a person, corporation, or other taxable unit derived through work, business pursuits, investments, property dealings, and other sources determined in accordance with the Internal Revenue Code or state law.

Indictment A written accusation charging that an individual named therein has committed an act or admitted to doing something that is punishable by law.

Indirect tax A tax upon some right, privilege, or corporation.

Words to Know

Individual rights Rights and privileges constitutionally guaranteed to the people as set forth by the Bill of Rights; the ability of a person to pursue life, liberty, and property.

Infant Persons who are under the age of the legal majority—at common law, twenty-one years, now generally eighteen years. According to the sense in which this term is used, it may denote the age of the person, the contractual disabilities that nonage entails, or his or her status with regard to other powers or relations.

Inherent rights Rights held within a person because he or she exists.

Inheritance Property received from a person who has died, either by will or through state laws if the deceased has failed to execute a valid will.

Injunction A court order by which an individual is required to perform or is restrained from performing a particular act. A writ framed according to the circumstances of the individual case.

In loco parentis Latin for "in the placeof a parent"; the legal doctrine under which an individual assumes parental rights, duties, and obligations without going through the formalities of legal adoption.

Insanity defense A defense asserted by an accused in a criminal prosecution to avoid responsibility for a crime because, at the time of the crime, the person did not comprehend the nature or wrongfulness of the act.

Insider Relating to the federal regulation of the purchase and sale of stocks and bonds, anyone who has knowledge of facts not available to the general public.

Insider trading The trading of stocks and bonds based on information gained from special private, privileged information affecting the value of the stocks and bonds.

Intent A determination to perform a particular act or to act in a particular manner for a specific reason; an aim or design; a resolution to use a certain means to reach an end.

Intermediate courts Courts with general ability or authority to hear a case (trial, appellate, or both) but are not the court of last resort within the jurisdiction.

Intestate The description of a person who dies without making a valid will.

Involuntary manslaughter The act of unlawfully killing another human being unintentionally.

Irrevocable Unable to cancel or recall; that which is unalterable or irreversible.

J

Judicial Relating to courts and the legal system.

Judicial discretion Sound judgment exercised by a judge in determining what is right and fair under the law.

Judicial review A court's authority to examine an executive or legislative act and to invalidate (cancel) that act if it opposes constitutional principles.

Jurisdiction The geographic area over which authority (such as a cout) extends; legal authority.

Jury In trials, a group of people selected and sworn to inquire into matters of fact and to reach a verdict on the basis of evidence presented to it.

Jury nullification The ability of a jury to acquit the defendant despite the amount of evidence against him or her in a criminal case.

Just cause A reasonable and lawful ground for action.

Justifiable homicide The killing of another in self-defense or in the lawful defense of one's property; killing of another when the law demands it, such as in execution for a capital crime.

Juvenile A young individual who has not reached the age whereby he or she would be treated as an adult in the area of criminal law. The age at which the young person attains the status of being a legal majority varies from state to state—as low as fourteen years old, as high as eighteen years old; however, the Juvenile Delinquency Act determines that a youthful person under the age of eighteen is a juvenile in cases involving federal jurisdiction.

Juvenile court The court presiding over cases in which young persons under a certain age, depending on the area of jurisdiction, are accused of criminal acts.

Juvenile delinquency The participation of a youthful individual, one who falls under the age at which he or she could be tried as an adult, in illegal behavior.

L

Larceny The unauthorized taking and removal of the personal property of another by a person who intends to permanently deprive the owner of it; a crime against the right of possession.

Legal defense A complete and acceptable response as to why the claims of the plaintiff should not be granted in a point of law.

Legal tender All U.S. coins and currencies—regardless of when coined or issued—including (in terms of the Federal Reserve System) Federal Reserve notes and circulating notes of Federal Reserve banks and national banking associations that are used for all public and private debts, public charges, taxes, duties, and dues.

Legislation Lawmaking; the preparation and enactment of laws by a legislative body.

Liability A comprehensive legal term that describes the condition of being actually or potentially subject to (responsible for) a legal obligation.

Libel and slander The communication of false information about a person, a group, or an entity, such as a corporation. Libel is any defamation that can be seen, such as in print or on a film or in a representation such as a statued. Slander is any defamation that is spoken and heard.

Litigation An action brought in court to enforce a particular right; the act or process of bringing a lawsuit in and of itself; a judicial contest; any dispute.

Living will A written document that allows a patient to give explicit instructions about medical treatment to be administered when the patient is terminally ill or permanently unconscious; also called an advance directive.

Lobbying The process of influencing public and government policy at all levels: federal, state, and local.

M

Magistrate Any individual who has the power of a public civil officer or inferior judicial officer, such as a justice of the peace.

Majority Full age; legal age; age at which a person is no longer a minor. The age at which, by law, a person is capable of being legally respon-

sible for all of his or her acts (i.e., contractual obligations) and is entitled to manage his or her own affairs and to the enjoy civic rights (i.e., right to vote). Also the status of a person who is a major in age.

Malice The intentional commission of a wrongful act, without justification, with the intent to cause harm to others; conscious violation of the law that injures another individual; a mental state indicating a disregard of social responsibility.

Malpractice When a professional, such as a doctor or lawyer, fails to carry out their job correctly and there are bad results.

Mandate A judicial command or order from a court.

Manslaughter The unjustifiable, inexcusable, and intentional killing of a human being without deliberation, premeditation, or malice.

Material Important; significant; substantial. A description of the quality of evidence that possesses such value as to establish the truth or falsity of a point in issue in a lawsuit.

Mediation Settling a dispute or controversy by setting up an independent person between the two parties to help them settle their disagreement.

Minor An infant or person who is under the age of legal competence. In most states, a person is no longer a minor after reaching the age of eighteen (though state laws might still prohibit certain acts until reaching a greater age; i.e., purchase of liquor).

Misdemeanor Offenses lower than felonies and generally those punishable by fine, penalty, or imprisonment other than in a penitentiary.

Mistrial A courtroom trial that has been ended prior to its normal conclusion. A mistrial has no legal effect and is considered an invalid trial. It differs from a new trial, which recognizes that a trial was completed but was set aside so that the issues could be tried again.

Mitigating circumstances Circumstances that may be considered by a court in determining responsibility of a defendant or the extent of damages to be awarded to a plaintiff. Mitigating circumstances do not justify or excuse an offense but may reduce the charge.

Monopoly An economic advantage held by one or more persons or companies because they hold the exclusive power to carry out a particular business or trade or to manufacture and sell a particular task or produce a particular product.

Words to Know

Moratorium A suspension (ending) of activity or an authorized period of delay or waiting. A moratorium is sometimes agreed upon by the interested parties, or it may be authorized or imposed by operation of law.

Motion A written or oral application made to a court or judge to obtain a ruling or order directing that some act be done in favor of the applicant.

Motive An idea, belief, or emotion that causes a person to act in a certain way, either good or bad.

Murder The unlawful killing of another human being without justification or excuse.

N

National origin The country in which a person was born or from which his or her ancestors came. One's national origin is typically calculated by employers to provide equal employment opportunity statistics in accordance with the provisions of the Civil Rights Act.

Naturalization A process by which a person gains nationality and becomes entitled to the privileges of citizenship. While groups of individuals have been naturalized in history by treaties or laws of Congress, such as in the case of Hawaii, typically naturalization occurs on the individual level upon the completion of a list of requirements.

Necessary and Proper Clause The statement contained in Article I, Section 8, Clause 18 of the U.S. Constitution that gives Congress the power to pass any laws that are necessary and proper to carrying out its specifically granted powers.

Negligence Conduct that falls below the standards of behavior established by law for the protection of others against unreasonable risk of harm.

Nonprofit A corporation or an association that conducts business for the benefit of the general public rather than to gain profits for itself.

Notary public A public official whose main powers include administering oaths and witnessing signatures, both important and effective ways to minimize fraud in legal documents.

O

Obscenity An act, spoken word, or item tending to offend public morals by its indecency or lewdness.

Ordinance A law, statute, or regulation enacted by a municipality.

P

Palimony The settlement awarded at the end of a non-marital relationship, where the couple lived together for a long period of time and where there was an agreement that one partner would support the other in return for the second making a home and performing domestic duties.

Pardon When a person in power, such as a president or governor, offers a formal statement of forgivenss for a crime and takes away the given punishment.

Parental liability A statute (law), enacted in some states, that makes parents responsible for damages caused by their children if it is found that the damages resulted from the parents' lack of control over the acts of the child.

Parole The release of a person convicted of a crime prior to the end of that person's term of imprisonment on the condition that they will follow certain strict rules for their conduct, and if they break any of those rules they will return to prison.

Patents Rights granted to inventors by the federal government that permit them to keep others from making, using, or selling their invention for a definite, or restricted, period of time.

Peremptory challenge The right to challenge the use of a juror in a trial without being required to give a reason for the challenge.

Perjury A crime that occurs when an individual willfully makes a false statement during a judicial proceeding, after he or she has taken an oath to speak the truth.

Petition A formal application made to a court in writing that requests action on a certain matter.

Petit larceny A form of larceny—the stealing of another's personal property—in which the value of the property that is taken is generally less than $50.

Words to Know

Plaintiff The party who sues in a civil action.

Plain view doctrine In the context of searches and seizures, the principle that provides that objects that an officer can easily see can be seized without a search warrant and are fair to use as evidence.

Plea The phase in a court case where the defendant has to declare whether they are guilty or not guilty.

Police power The authority that states to employ a police force and give them the power to enforce the laws and protect the community.

Poll tax A specified sum of money to be paid by each person who votes.

Polygamy The offense of having more than one wife or husband at the same time.

Precedent A court decision that is cited as an example to resolve similar questions of law in later cases.

Preponderance of evidence A rule that states that it is up to the plaintiff to convince the judge or the jury of their side of the case in or to win the case.

Prima facie [*Latin,* On the first appearance.]A fact presumed to be true unless it is disproved.

Prior restraint Government violating freedom of speech by not allowing something to be published.

Privacy In constitutional law, the right of people to make personal decisions regarding intimate matters; under the common law, the right of people to lead their lives in a manner that is reasonably secluded from public scrutiny, whether such scrutiny comes from a neighbor's prying eyes, an investigator's eavesdropping ears, or a news photographer's intrusive camera; and in statutory law, the right of people to be free from unwarranted drug testing and electronic surveillance.

Privilege An advantage or benefit possessed by an individual, company, or class beyond those held by others.

Privileges and immunities Concepts contained in the U.S. Constitution that place the citizens of each state on an equal basis with citizens of other states with respect to advantages resulting from citizenship in those states and citizenship in the United States.

Probable cause Apparent facts discovered through logical inquiry that would lead a reasonably intelligent person to believe that an accused person has committed a crime.

Probate court Called Surrogate or Orphan's Court in some states, the probate court presides over wills, the administration of estates, and, in some states, the appointment of guardians or approval of the adoption of minors.

Probation A sentence whereby a convict is released from confinement but is still under court supervision; a testing or a trial period. It can be given in lieu of a prison term or can suspend a prison sentence if the convict has consistently demonstrated good behavior.

Procedural due process The constitutional guarantee that one's liberty and property rights may not be affected unless reasonable notice and an opportunity to be heard in order to present a claim or defense are provided.

Property A thing or things owned either by government—public property—or owned by private individuals, groups, or companies—private property.

Prosecute To follow through; to commence and continue an action or judicial proceeding to its conclusion. To proceed against a defendant by charging that person with a crime and bringing him or her to trial.

Prosecution The proceedings carried out before a court to determine the guilt or innocence of a defendant. The term also refers to the government attorney charging and trying a criminal case.

Punitive damages Money awarded to an injured party that goes beyond that which is necessary to pay for the individual for losses and that is intended to punish the wrongdoer.

Q

Quorum A majority of an entire body; i.e., a quorum of a legislative assembly.

Quota The number of persons or things that must be used, or admitted, or hired in order to be following a rule or law.

R

Rape A criminal offense defined in most states as forcible sexual relations with a person against that person's will.

Ratification The confirmation or adoption of an act that has already been performed.

Reapportionment The realignment of voting districts done to fulfill the constitutional requirement of one person, one vote.

Referendum The right reserved to the people to approve or reject an act of the legislature, or the right of the people to approve or reject legislation that has been referred to them by the legislature.

Refugees Individuals who leave their native country for social, political, or religious reasons, or who are forced to leave as a result of any type of disaster, including war, political upheaval, and famine.

Rehabilitation Work to restore former rights, authority, or abilities.

Remand To send back.

Replevin A legal action to recover the possession of items of personal property.

Reprieve The temporary hold put on a death penalty for further review of the case.

Rescind To declare a contract void—of no legal force or binding effect—from its beginning and thereby restore the parties to the positions they would have been in had no contract ever been made.

Reservation A tract of land under the control of the Bureau of Indian Affairs to which a Native American tribe retains its original title of ownership, or that has been set aside from the public domain for use by a tribe.

Reserve Funds set aside to cover future expenses, losses, or claims. To retain; to keep in store for future or special use; to postpone to a future time.

Resolution The official expression of the opinion or will of a legislative body.

Retainer A contract between attorney and client specifying the nature of the services and the cost of the services.

Retribution Punishment or reward for an act. In criminal law, punishment is based upon the theory that every crime demands payment.

Reverse discrimination Discrimination against a group of people that is generally considered to be the majority, usually stemming from the enforcement of some affirmative action guidlelines.

Revocation The recall of some power or authority that has been granted.

Robbery The taking of money or goods in the possession of another, from his or her person or immediate presence, by force or intimidation.

S

Sabotage The willful destruction or impairment of war material or national defense material, or harm to war premises or war utilities. During a labor dispute, the willful and malicious destruction of an employer's property or interference with his or her normal operations.

Search warrant A court order authorizing the examination of a place for the purpose of discovering evidence of guilt to be used in the prosecution of a criminal action.

Second degree murder The unlawful taking of human life with malice, but without premeditated thought.

Sedition A revolt or an incitement to revolt against established authority, usually in the form of treason or defamation against government.

Seditious libel A written communication intended to incite the overthrow of the government by force or violence.

Segregation The act or process of separating a race, class, or ethnic group from a society's general population.

Self-defense The protection of one's person or property against some injury attempted by another.

Self-incrimination Giving testimony in a trial or other legal proceeding that could subject one to criminal prosecution.

Sentencing The post-conviction stage of a criminal justice process, in which the defendant is brought before the court for penalty.

Separate but equal The doctrine first accepted by the U.S. Supreme Court in *Plessy v. Ferguson* establishing that different facilities for blacks and whites was valid under the Equal Protection Clause of the Fourteenth Amendment as long as they were equal.

Separation of church and state The separation of religious and government interest to ensure that religion does not become corrupt by government and that government does not become corrupt by religious conflict. The principle prevents the government from supporting the practices of one religion over another. It also enables the government to do what is necessary to prevent one religious group from violating the rights of others.

Separation of powers The division of state and federal government into three independent branches.

Settlement The act of adjusting or determining the dealings or disputes between persons without pursuing the matter through a trial.

Sexual harassment Unwelcome sexual advances, requests for sexual favors, and other verbal or physical conduct of a sexual nature that tends to create a hostile or offensive work environment.

Share A portion or part of something that may be divided into components, such as a sum of money. A unit of stock that represents ownership in a corporation.

Shield laws Statutes that allow journalists not to disclose in legal proceedings confidential information or sources of information obtained in their professional capacities.

Statutes that restrict or prohibit the use of certain evidence in sexual offense cases, such as evidence regarding the lack of chastity of the victim.

Shoplifting Theft of merchandise from a store or business establishment.

Small claims court A special court that provides fast, informal, and inexpensive solutions for small claims.

Solicitation The criminal offense of urging someone to commit an unlawful act.

Statute An act of a legislature that declares, or commands something; a specific law, expressed in writing.

Statute of limitations A type of federal or state law that restricts the time within which legal proceedings may be brought.

Statutory law A law which is created by an act of the legislature.

Statutory rape Sexual intercourse by an adult with a person below a designated age.

Subpoena Latin for "under penalty"; a formal document that orders a named individual to appear before an officer of the court at a fixed time to give testimony.

Suffrage The right to vote at public elections.

Summons The paper that tells a defendant that he or she is being sued and asserts the power of the court to hear and determine the case. A form of legal process that commands the defendant to appear before the court on a specific day and to answer the complaint made by the plaintiff.

Supreme court The highest court in the U.S. judicial system.

Surrogate mother A woman who agrees under contract to bear a child for an infertile couple. The woman is paid to have a donated fertilized egg or the fertilized egg of the female partner in the couple (usually fertilized by the male partner of the couple) artificially placed into her uterus.

Suspended sentence A sentence that states that a criminal, in waiting for their trial, has already served enough time in prison.

Symbolic speech Nonverbal gestures and actions that are meant to communicate a message.

T

Testify To provide evidence as a witness in order to establish a particular fact or set of facts.

Testimony Oral evidence offered by a competent witness under oath, which is used to establish some fact or set of facts.

Trade secret Any valuable commercial information that provides a business with an advantage over competitors who do not have that information.

Trade union An organization of workers in the same skilled occupation or related skilled occupations who act together to secure for all members favorable wages, hours, and other working conditions.

Treason The betrayal of one's own country by waging war against it or by consciously or purposely acting to aid its enemies.

Treaty A compact made between two or more independent nations with a view to the public welfare.

Trespass An unlawful intrusion that interferes with one's person or property.

Trial A judicial examination and determination of facts and legal issues arising between parties to a civil or criminal action.

Trial court The court where civil actions or criminal proceedings are first heard.

Truancy The willful and unjustified failure to attend school by one required to do so.

U

Unenumerated rights Rights that are not expressly mentioned in the written text of a constitution but instead are inferred from the language, history, and structure of the constitution, or cases interpreting it.

Unconstitutional That which is not in agreement with the ideas and regulations of the Constitution.

Uniform commercial code A general and inclusive group of laws adopted, at least partially, by all of the states to further fair dealing in business.

V

Valid Binding; possessing legal force or strength; legally sufficient.

Vandalism The intentional and malicious destruction of or damage to the property of another.

Venue A place, such as a city or county, from which residents are selected to serve as jurors.

Verdict The formal decision or finding made by a jury concerning the questions submitted to it during a trial. The jury reports the verdict to the court, which generally accepts it.

Veto The refusal of an executive officer to approve a bill that has been created and approved by the legislature, thereby keeping the bill from becoming a law.

Voir dire Old French for "to speak the truth"; the preliminary examination of possible jurors to determine their qualifications and suitability to serve on a jury, in order to ensure the selection of a fair and impartial jury.

Voluntary manslaughter The unlawful killing of a person where there is no malice, premeditation or deliberate intent but too near to these standards to be classified as justifiable homicide.

W

Waive To intentionally or voluntarily give up a known right or engage in conduct that caused your rights to be taken away.

Ward A person, especially an infant or someone judged to be incompetent, placed by the court in the care of a guardian.

Warrant A written order issued by a judicial officer commanding a law enforcement officer to perform a duty. This usually includes searches, seizures and arrests.

White collar crime Term for nonviolent crimes that were committed in the course of the offender's occupation.

Will A document in which a person explains the management and distribution of his or her estate after his or her death.

Workers' compensation A system whereby an employer must pay, or provide insurance to pay, the lost wages and medical expenses of an employee who is injured on the job.

Writ An order issued by a court requiring that something be done.

Z

Zoning Assigning different areas within a city or county different uses, whereby one area cannot be used for any other purpose other than what it is designated. For example, if an area is assigned as residential, an office building could not be built there.

ANTITRUST, BUSINESS, CORPORATE AND CONTRACT LAW

Law that addresses business activities cover a broad range of economic topics including laws related to contracts, corporations, and trusts and monopolies. Responsibility for governmental oversight has greatly changed through time and is split between various governmental parts. For example, the Supreme Court has had relatively little affect on contract and corporate law where states have the primary responsibility for oversight. The federal government has responsibility in certain situations, such as interstate commerce.

Early History of Corporation and Contract Law

One of the most common types of business worldwide is the corporation. A corporation is a business that has been formally chartered (grant of ownership rights) by a state. It gains its own identity apart from the owners and investors. Chartering corporations has a long history. In the sixteenth century English merchants faced the dangers of the high seas both from weather and pirates. The shipping businesses sought protection from financial responsibility for cargo losses. As a result, early corporate charters granted by the English monarchy limited liability (financial responsibility) for any losses of corporate property. Many of these early corporations were also given monopoly (one company dominates a particular market) powers over territories and industries that the crown considered critical to English interests. In fact, English law had granted monopolies to specific trade and craft guild organizations by decree even in the Middle Ages. Some of the best known early English corporations in the eighteenth century were the East Indian Company and Hudson's Bay Company. The American colonies, with settlement beginning in the seventeenth century, were also chartered corporations. However, drafted in 1787, the U.S. Constitution makes no mention of corporations. They were primarily subject to state regulation. By 1800 the states had granted about 200 corporate charters.

To enforce business agreements including contracts, the English Parliament passed the Statute of Frauds in 1677. The law established standards for settling legal disputes over contracts. Later after American independence, all U.S. states adopted various forms of the English act establishing the basis for U.S. contract law. The only mention of contracts in the Constitution was the Contract Clause of Article I which reads, "No State shall . . . make any . . . Law impairing the Obligation [responsibility] of Contracts." Early in U.S. history, the Supreme Court applied the Contract Clause in ruling a state law unconstitutional in ***Fletcher v. Peck*** (1810). The Court gave a broad definition to what a contract is. Thus, employers were quite free to contract for labor with their employees and establish agreements with other businesses. Cases involving the Contract Clause were numerous in the nation's early years.

In 1819 the Court in *Dartmouth College v. Woodward* first recognized private profit-making corporations by extending protection of the Contract Clause to corporate charters. The Court considered the corporate charter a form of contract between the state and the private corporation. Protection of corporations by the Clause from unreasonable state regulation provided assurance to individuals to invest money in corporations and spur economic growth of the nation. In *Charles River Bridge v. Warren Bridge* (1837) the Court further defined a balance between a state interest in regulating corporations and protecting corporations from arbitrary (inconsistent) laws.

Freedom to Trade

Efforts by businesses to restrain trade by blocking activities of competitors in some way is as old as profit-making business itself. Early English and later U.S. efforts at restricting such anti-competitive behavior in business was largely based on common law principles dealing with contracts and conspiracies. Approaches varied greatly among the states. The Court ruled in *Swift v. Tyson* (1842) that federal courts should decide business disputes including accusations of restraint of competition using a "rule of reason." The rule of reason worked in the following manner. If state law applied restrictions broadly, the restrictions were often considered illegal. If more limited in time or geographic extent, the restraints might be allowed.

Congress held constitutional powers to regulate interstate commerce (trade or business across state lines) in the Commerce Clause in Article I, Section 8, of the Constitution. The Clause states that Congress could "regulate Commerce . . . among the several states." But the Court long interpreted the clause very narrowly and the federal government had little means to address unfair business practices. The courts through the nineteenth century were very protective of business interests shielding them from most forms of government interference. They supported a *laissez-faire* economy believing the marketplace, not government regulation, should primarily guide economic growth.

Rise of Trusts

Following the Civil War (1861–1865) the rise of industrialization greatly increased the output of U.S. manufacturers, as a result big business expanded rapidly. As the nation's economy changed from agriculture to industry. At the same time, construction of a national railroad system provided cheaper transportation for the increased supply of goods, greatly expanding markets.

As competition heightened because the supply of goods soon exceeded the demand, businesses sought means of protecting profits. However, state corporate laws strictly controlled mergers, forbidding companies to own stock in other companies. An alternative was for businesses to simply join with their competitors to set prices and control production. Therefore, given few legal restrictions over the rules of business competition, companies began to join together forming trusts to protect themselves from competition.

Trusts involved creating one corporation to manage the stocks of the cooperating corporations. Standard Oil became the first trust in 1882. Trusts began accumulating great economic power which they used to fix prices and drive out new competitors through price wars. Such business combinations in various industries, such as oil, steel, mining, tobacco, beef, whiskey, and sugar, led to concentration of capital (available money) and control by only a few people. Trust became a general term applied to national monopolies. Consumers, farmers, and small business owners became powerless. In addition, railroads often gave special treatment in the form of lower rates to their larger customers, the trusts. Yet, even more protections were extended to businesses rather than consumers. The Court ruled in *Santa Clara County v. Southern Pacific Railroad* (1886) that private corporations are "persons" under the Equal Protection Clause of the Fourteenth Amendment. This decision meant that corporations were protected by the Bill of Rights including freedom of speech.

Public demand for government intervention into trusts and unfair business practices that posed a threat to free market competition rose dramatically through the 1880's. In response, states began adopting various laws, but these proved inconsistent and did not apply to interstate commerce which was federal responsibility. Congress responded with two landmark pieces of federal legislation. First, Congress passed the Interstate Commerce Act of 1887 requiring railroads to maintain fair rates and stop their discriminatory practices against smaller customers.

In 1890 Congress passed the Sherman Antitrust Act, the first major national legislation addressing business practices. For the first time, national consistency existed for business regulation. Adopting the notion that competitive decisions made by businesses acting independently is the best guide for the American economy, the act prohibited trusts and other forms of cooperation which could potentially restrain interstate or international trade. In other words, the more independent companies competing with each other the better. Basically, all restraint of trade through cooperation is unacceptable. The act allowed for both criminal and civil prosecution of violators. The act also targeted actions of individual companies acting as monopolies.

Though strongly worded, the act was vague concerning enforcement leaving decisions to the courts and executive branch of government. Enforcement of antitrust law has been heatedly debated since. For example, President Grover Cleveland (1893–1897) did not favor enforcement believing trusts were a natural result of technological advances and actually kept the nation's economy stable by eliminating waste. Applying the narrow view of commerce, the Supreme Court even ruled in *United States v. E.C. Knight* (1895) that manufacturing was not considered interstate commerce although the goods produced were shipped throughout the United States. Consequently, despite the Sherman Antitrust Act, many key industries were left free to continue operating under trusts out of reach of government regulation. In this business climate, a major wave of mergers resulted in the late 1890s and early 1900s.

Antitrust Movements—A Zig-Zag Process

Bt the start of the twentieth century there was still no coordinated broad structure to the nation's economy. Neither a federal government tax collection system nor a safely regulated stock market existed. Britain remained the dominant player in the world economy and American business was largely controlled by wealthy industrialists. A few hundred large companies controlled almost half of U.S. manufacturing and greatly influenced almost all key industries. In 1901 J.P. Morgan and John D. Rockefeller together controlled 112 corporations consisting of over $22 billion in assets under the trust, Northern Securities Corporation of New Jersey.

Public concern lead to more federal antitrust enforcement efforts. The trustbusting movement took off in 1904 with the Supreme Court's decision in *Northern Securities Co. v. United States* (1904) breaking up a railroad trust. Over forty antitrust lawsuits were filed under President Theodore Roosevelt (1901–1909). Though best known as the "trustbuster," Roosevelt actually sought a middle ground in government oversight of corporate activities not intending to end all corporate mergers, just those causing hardships on consumers. Roosevelt believed the courts were favoring powerful business leaders and that some regulation was needed.

Another important victory for recognizing federal authority came in the ***Swift & Co. v. United States*** (1905) ruling. The Court reversed the previous *Knight* ruling and adopted a "stream of commerce" doctrine. The doctrine significantly broadened the Court's interpretation of congressional powers under the Commerce Clause. All business, including manufacturing, that may have an affect on interstate commerce was subject to congressional regulation.

However, other barriers to regulation of economic matters quickly came forward. The Due Process Clause in the Fifth and Fourteenth amendments states "No person shall be . . . deprived of life, liberty, or property, without due process of law." The courts looked at businesses and pursuit of business success as property and liberty protected from government control under those amendments. The Court began striking down state laws regulating work conditions such as hours and wages as in ***Lochner v. New York*** (1905) using the Due Process Clause to protect freedom of contract. Use of the Due Process Clause in the Fourteenth Amendment largely took the place of the Contract Clause in Article I to negate state laws regulating business activities and the Fifth Amendment blocked federal government regulations.

Nevertheless, antitrust law remained effective. Major Supreme Court decisions in 1911 ordered the break-up of Standard Oil in *Standard Oil Co. of New Jersey v. United States,* a corporate giant controlling railroads, sugar, and oil, and the tobacco trust in *United States v. American Tobacco Co.* These were the two largest industrial combinations in existence. Though the decisions supported the federal government's role in overseeing marketplace economics, they also reaffirmed the Court's use of the "rule of reason" in determining when regulations are too restrictive for specific business practices being questioned.

The continued unpredictability of antitrust rulings led, yet again, to public pressure for more effective trustbusting laws. Congress responded with the 1914 Clayton Act. The act more clearly described prohibited business practices that significantly limited competition or created a monopoly. Under that act companies could not charge different buyers different prices for the same products, or force buyers to sign contracts restricting them from doing business with competitors. It also restricted business mergers between competing companies and companies from buying stock in competing companies. Importantly, the act prohibited application of antitrust law against unions. Congress also passed the 1914 Federal Trade Commission Act creating the Federal Trade Commission (FTC) to tackle unfair business practices. Congress gave the FTC legal powers to issue cease-and-desist orders to combat unfair business activities.

With the economic boom years of the 1920s, political desire to protect business by freeing them from regulations increased. Protection of the freedom of contract rose to its height with decisions such as *Adkins v. Children's Hospital* (1923) overturning a minimum wage law, therefore allowing businesses to set their own wages in contracts with employees.

Given a relatively free hand in dealing with employees, unions, and consumers, corporations flourished in the 1920s but came to a crashing halt in 1929.

Dramatic Shift to Regulation

The stock market crash of 1929 resulted in the collapse of the American economy. Public confidence in business leaders dwindled in the early 1930's during the Great Depression. Federal regulation of business activity expanded considerably with passage of the Securities Exchange Act of 1934 placing securities (documents representing a right held in something, like stocks) under strict oversight. The public wanted greater reliability in what they actually were purchasing interest in, including protection from fraud in common stocks. In 1936 Congress passed the Robinson-Patman Act. Designed to protect small businesses from larger competitors, the act prohibited price discrimination in which companies favor one business over others through the prices they charge. Coupled with President Franklin D. Roosevelt's (1933–1945) attack on monopolies in the late 1930s trustbusting had returned. Eighty antitrust suits were filed in 1940.

In the late 1930s the Court and the nation made a dramatic shift away from emphasizing protection of business to accepting substantial government regulation of economic matters. Passage of the National Labor Relations Act of 1935 promoting labor unions and the landmark ruling in *National Labor Relations Board v. Jones & Laughlin* (1937) marked that transition. The liberty of contract doctrine under the Due Process Clause came to an end, as did use of the Contract Clause by the Court in recognizing states power to regulate private business. The Fair Labor Standards Act of 1938 established wage and hour regulations for all businesses involved in interstate commerce.

Following World War II, two key court decisions came in 1945. In ***International Shoe Co. v. State of Washington*** the Court recognized state authority to regulate out-of-state corporations operating within their boundaries. A lower court in *United States v. Aluminum Company of America* recognized the social, as well as economic, importance of antitrust law. With the Clayton Act ban on mergers rarely applied in courts, in 1950 Congress passed the last trustbusting law, the Celler-Kefauver Antimerger Act, closing some Clayton Act loopholes. Through the 1970s, demand grew for extensive and uniform regulation in the form of a body of federal corporate law. However, the Court in *Santa Fe*

Industries v. Green (1977) reaffirmed the states' primary role in regulating corporations except in matters concerning securities.

Trustbusting continued with the FTC decreasing the Xerox Company's control of the photocopy industry and the break-up of American Telephone and Telegraph (AT&T), accused of restricting competition in long-distance telephone service and telecommunications equipment. AT&T lost control over Western Electric, the manufacturing part of the company, and various regional operating telephone companies. Courts were skeptical of any cooperation between competitors and of mergers.

With the President Ronald Reagan (1981–1989) administration in power, the 1980s brought a major change in acceptance of government oversight. Reagan reduced the FTC budget as a historic wave of corporate mergers occurred in the mid-1980s. By 1990 states began picking up the slack as they increasingly challenged mergers. By the early 1990s federal interest grew again to examine anticompetitive practices. President Bill Clinton (1993–) increased the budgets of the Justice Department's Antitrust Division as 33 lawsuits were filed in 1994. The most publicized antitrust case involved the Microsoft Corporation, one of the most successful companies of the late twentieth century, accused of various monopolistic activities. Yet, another wave of mergers swept the United States in the late 1990s.

The Global Scene

With the end of World War II (1939–1945) in sight, forty-four nations met in New Hampshire to plan ahead for a new global economy. The meeting led to establishment of three important international organizations as special agencies to the United Nations: the International Bank for Reconstruction and Development more commonly known as the World Bank; the International Monetary Fund (IMF), and the General Agreement on Tariffs and Trade (GATT). Other arrangements followed In 1993 the United States, Canada, and Mexico signed the North American Free Trade Agreement (NAFTA) to share labor and resources. In 1995 the World Trade Organization (WTO) was created by GATT for enforcement of international trade and commerce agreements.

By the beginning of the twenty-first century, the age-old question still persisted as to how much government should limit corporate power and activities. Public opinion was mixed as it had been throughout much of history. In addition, the various international agreements and organizations greatly altered trade and commerce in general. Business issues and disputes became increasingly global in nature. Given increased international competition, public support for government regulation declined. Antitrust concerns also began changing in recognition of new kinds of corporate structures brought on by the transition from a manufacturing to information economy. New technologies challenged past notions of market domination. Ironically, recognition that mergers served to actually increase competitiveness in some global markets rose. Potential economic benefits to the nation and to business efficiency became much more important factors weighed in court decisions concerning both government and private interests.

Suggestions for further reading

Brands, H.W. *Master of Enterprise: Giants of American Business From John Jacob Astor and J.P. Morgan to Bill Gates and Oprah Winfrey.* New York: Free Press, 1999.

Friedman, Milton, and Rose Friedman. *Free to Choose.* New York: Harcourt Brace Jovanovich, 1980.

Heynes, Paul T. *The Economic Way of Thinking.* Seventh Edition. New York: Macmillan, 1994.

Sharp, Ansel M., Charles A. Register, and Richard Leftwich. *The Economics of Public Issues.* Eleventh Edition. Burr Ridge, IL: Irwin, 1994.

Fletcher v. Peck 1810

Appellant: Robert Fletcher

Appellee: John Peck

Appellant's Claim: That a 1796 act passed by the Georgia legislature could not take away property rights gained by land companies under the Yazoo Land Act of 1795.

Chief Lawyer for Appellant: Luther Martin

Chief Lawyers for Appellee: John Quincy Adams, Robert G. Harper, Joseph Story

Justices for the Court: Samuel Chase, William Cushing, William Johnson, Henry B. Livingston, Chief Justice John Marshall, Thomas Todd, Bushrod Washington

Justices Dissenting: None

Date of Decision: March 16, 1810

Decision: Ruled in favor of Fletcher by finding that a legislature could repeal or amend its previous acts, but could not undo actions that legally occurred under the previous act.

Significance: The ruling marked the first time that a state law had been overturned by the U.S. Supreme Court. The case was also the first affirming the Contract Clause of the U.S. Constitution. The solid legal standing of state land grants established by the Supreme Court reassured the public about purchasing lands as they became available as the United States expanded westward.

North America had long been settled by Native Americans before arrival of the first European colonists on the East Coast in the sixteenth century. Through conquest and agreements, the colonies increasingly assumed control of Indian lands. As part of this westward push, the state of Georgia took from the Indians a large thirty-five million acre region to its west in the Yazoo River area. Known as the Yazoo Lands, much later it became the states of Alabama and Mississippi. But in 1795 the Georgia legislature divided the area into four tracts and sold them to four land companies for a modest total price of only $500,000, or only one-and-a-half cents an acre. This was a good deal for the companies even at 1790s prices. The Georgia legislature overwhelmingly approved this land grant (a transfer of property to another), known as the Yazoo Land Act of 1795. Only one legislator voted against it. The four land companies then began dividing their lands into smaller tracts to sell at considerably higher prices for a substantial profit.

Public outrage erupted when stories of secret deals and partnerships soon came to light. Some of the legislators had been stockholders of the four land companies. In addition, almost every state legislator, two U.S. senators, and a number of judges including Supreme Court Justice James Wilson, had received bribes from the companies including a promised share of the expected large profits. A copy of the act was publicly burned and evidence of the law was erased from public records. The public ousted the corrupt legislature and voted in a new one.

Responding to the public outrage over the fraud and corruption, the new legislature passed a bill in 1796 canceling all property rights gained from the original sale and seeking to regain the lands. Refunds at the original purchase price were offered, but the new owners refused to return the land.

Meanwhile, parcels of the land were being sold and resold to others not involved in the scandal. Questions about the legality of the sales continued to grow. Because of the 1796 act, did the new owners hold legal rights to the lands they had purchased? Because many of the new owners lived far from Georgia in New England, it became a national issue and subject of debates in Congress.

John Peck's Property

One piece of the property of about 15,000 acres passed through several hands in the late 1790s until John Peck of Massachusetts acquired it in

1800. Three years later Peck sold the property for $3,000 to Robert Fletcher, a citizen of New Hampshire. With the 1796 act in mind, Peck wrote in the sales contract that all previous sales were legal. The contract read,

> **[T]he title to the premises [lands] as conveyed [sold] by the state of Georgia, and finally vested in [owned by] . . . Peck, has been in no way constitutionally or legally impaired [limited] by virtue of any subsequent [later] act of any subsequent legislature of the . . . state of Georgia.**

This section meant that despite the 1796 act, Peck still claimed a legal right to sell the land to Fletcher.

Fletcher became increasingly uncomfortable with the sale. Fearing losing both the land and his money, he filed suit in Circuit Court against Peck to challenge the 1796 act. Fletcher claimed that either the contract was not valid or the 1796 act canceling the original sale of the Yazoo tract was unconstitutional. If the act was constitutional, then it was not Peck's land to sell.

Arguments focused on a major issue of which principle should take priority: the state legislature's and public's desire to reverse the land deal, or protection of individual property rights. The Circuit Court ruled in favor of Peck that the sale was valid. Fletcher appealed the decision to the U.S. Supreme Court. The arguments were presented to the Court on February 15, 1810. One of Peck's lawyers was thirty-year-old Massachusetts attorney Joseph Story who, two years later, would become the youngest nominee in the Supreme Court's history.

Recognition of Contracts

The legendary Chief Justice John Marshall (1755–1835), writing for the Court on March 16, stated that the main question was if the 1796 law could negate all property rights established under the 1795 act. Marshall, although deploring the extensive corruption in the earlier state legislature, wrote that contracts signed under the original law must be accepted as valid. Motives of the legislators could not be formally considered by the Court and certainly were not the responsibility of those buyers who were following the law. Regarding the effect of the 1796 act on the 1795 act, Marshall first accepted the general principle that "one legislature is competent to repeal any act which a former legislature was competent to pass." However, it was clearly a different matter about a legislature undoing actions of people taken under the previous act while it was valid.

Importantly, Marshall considered the original land grant a type of contract. Therefore, the U.S. Constitution's Contract Clause found in Article I, section 10 applied. The section reads, "No State shall . . . pass any . . . ex post facto law [see sidebar], or Law impairing the Obligation [responsibility] of Contracts . . . " This clause, according to Marshall, applied to all parties, including states and individuals.

The right to land ownership created by a contract cannot be so readily taken away. The government could not seize property honestly acquired without just compensation (fair payment) for the loss of property. The intent of the Contract Clause, wrote Marshall, was to restrict state power over the property of its citizens. The 1796 law was an unconstitutional *ex post facto* law for penalizing one person "for a crime not committed by himself, but by those from whom he purchases." In spite of the profits dishonestly made by the land speculators, states could not negate the later contracts of sale. Political corruption charges were more a matter for the state government, not the Supreme Court.

A Historic Ruling

Peckham, coming out of one of the biggest scandals in Georgia history, was historically important for at least five reasons. First, it was the first Supreme Court ruling to strike down a state law. Secondly, the ruling established a protective attitude to commercial interests (businesses) by the courts. Thirdly, the Court recognized the Contract Clause as a key tool to limit state regulation of economic matters involving contracts and property rights. Federal protection of property rights, often using the Contract Clause, led to overturning numerous state laws through the next century. Fourth, the importance of contracts in American life was established. Lastly, the ruling also established that grants, such as state land grants, are the same under the law as contracts between private individuals.

The decision was considered a major defeat to those advocating stronger state power. The concept of contracts and their importance to property rights was further developed almost a decade later in *Trustees of Dartmouth College v. Woodward* (1819). With the public assured of federal protection of individual property rights and contracts including state land grants, large scale economic development across the nation proceeded as the nation spread across the West for the next half century.

EX POST FACTO LAWS

The term "ex post facto" comes from Latin meaning "after the fact." *Ex post facto* laws are, therefore, laws making certain actions a crime after the actions had already occurred. They have been historically considered unfair. *Ex post facto* laws are prohibited by the U.S. Constitution in Section 9 of Article 1 against federal actions and Section 10 against state actions. In other words, a legislature does not have the power to punish a person after an act has been committed if it was not illegal at the time. Similarly, laws cannot increase the penalties for crimes already committed. It is also illegal to change the rules of evidence to make it easier to convict a person for a crime committed prior to the new law.

For example, laws making parole requirements for convicts tougher for certain crimes cannot be applied to persons who had already committed the crime. Similarly, the creation of war crimes laws after World War II to try German leaders for actions during the war led to considerable legal opposition.

A broader view of the liberty to contract came later in the nineteenth century in other Court decisions which further limited state regulation of economic matters. Use of the contract clause and other constitutional clauses to limit state regulation ended by the 1930s. By 2000, federal and state regulation of contracts was rarely limited by the courts.

Suggestions for further reading

Coleman, Kennth, ed. *A History of Georgia.* Second Edition. Athens: University of Georgia Press, 1991.

Magrath, Peter C. *Yazoo: Law and Politics in the New Republic, the Case of* Fletcher v. Peck. Providence, RI: Brown University, 1966.

Merk, Frederick. *Manifest Destiny and Mission in American History: A Reinterpretation.*Cambridge, MS: Harvard University Press, 1995.

Allgeyer v. Louisiana 1897

Petitioner: E. Allgeyer & Co.

Respondent: State of Louisiana

Petitioner's Claim: That states restricting the right of companies to contract with whom they choose violates the Fourteenth Amendment's Due Process Clause.

Chief Lawyer for Petitioner: Branch K. Miller

Chief Lawyer for Respondent: M. J. Cunningham

Justices for the Court: David J. Brewer, Henry B. Brown, William R. Day, Chief Justice Melville W. Fuller, Horace Gray, John Marshall Harlan I, Rufus W. Peckham, George Shiras, Jr., Edward D. White

Justices Dissenting: None

Date of Decision: March 1, 1897

Decision: Ruled in favor of Allgeyer and reversed a lower court ruling by finding that the Due Process Clause includes an unwritten liberty of contract that cannot be restricted by state law.

Significance: The decision created a new liberty under the Fourteenth Amendment, the liberty of contract. For the first time, the Court ruled a state law unconstitutional because it denied a person the right to make a contract. States were largely blocked from passing laws protecting their citizens and the general public from unfair or unsafe business practices for the next forty years until the Court shifted philosophy in 1937.

ANTITRUST, BUSINESS, CORPORATE AND CONTRACT LAW

Through much of the nineteenth century, the federal government allowed states to freely regulate business activities within their borders. When laws were struck down by the U.S. Supreme Court for being unreasonable interference with business activities, it commonly used the Constitution's Commerce Clause or the Contracts Clause to justify its action. Regarding the Contract Clause, Article I, Section 10, Clause 3 of the U.S. Constitution states that "No state shall . . . pass any . . . law impairing the obligation of [responsibility to honor] contracts." The Commerce Clause is located in Article I, Section 8 and states that "The Congress shall have Power . . . To regulate Commerce [business activity] . . . among the several States . . . "

Toward the end of the nineteenth century trade and industry were greatly expanding across the nation. As the states began passing more laws to protect their citizens and businesses, the courts became interested in protecting the economic and property interests of the new industries and related business. These interests included the right of employers and employees in determining the work conditions and their employment relationship to one another.

To protect insurance companies in the port of New Orleans from outside competition, the Louisiana legislature in 1894 passed Act No. 66. The act made it illegal for individuals and companies to sign insurance contracts by mail with companies operating outside the state of Louisiana. The act stated,

> **Be it enacted by the general assembly of the state of Louisiana, that any person, firm or corporation who shall fill up, sign or issue in this state any certificate of insurance under an open marine policy . . . for . . . insurance on property . . . in this state [with] . . . any marine insurance company which has not complied in all respects with the laws of this state, shall be subject to a fine of one thousand dollars for each offense . . . for the benefit of the charity hospitals.**

Cotton for Europe

E. Allgeyer & Co. was a New Orleans cotton exporter that shipped cotton across the Atlantic Ocean to ports in Great Britain and other European countries. In 1894 Allgeyer purchased $200,000 of insurance coverage from the Atlantic Mutual Insurance Company of New York to guard against possible losses while shipping cotton. Atlantic Marine had no agent or place of business actually located in Louisiana. The contract was signed in New York. In preparation for shipping a hundred bales of cotton to Europe, Allgeyer mailed a notification to Atlantic Marine as the insurance contract required. In reaction, the state of Louisiana filed suit against Allgeyer in December of 1894 charging it had violated Act No. 66. Claiming that three violations had occurred, the state sought a $3,000 fine.

Allgeyer, in defense, claimed that the act was unconstitutional, depriving them of property without due process of law. Allgeyer asserted that since its business partner, Atlantic Mutual, was a New York company with offices in New York, then the insurance contract was actually a New York contract, not Louisiana. Further, Allgeyer claimed the Constitution protected the right to make contracts in other states.

The district court, although not necessarily agreeing with Allgeyer's arguments, nevertheless ruled against Louisiana. The court made several observations before issuing its decision. First, it did not deny that the state had authority to regulate companies conducting business within its boundaries. Furthermore, it recognized the validity of Article 236 of the Louisiana Constitution. The article prohibited insurance companies from other states doing business in Louisiana unless they had an actual place of business and authorized agent in the state. Regarding Allgeyer's contract, the court asserted that once it was signed in New Orleans, it became valid contract under New York law, even with the cotton still in Louisiana. But, to be legal in Louisiana, Atlantic Mutual must have purchased a license of the state and employed an agent in the state. Despite the uncertain nature of Allgeyer's insurance contract, the authority of the state, and the state's constitution, the court concluded the act violated Allgeyer's constitutional rights and overturned it.

Louisiana appealed the decision to the Louisiana Supreme Court which overturned the district court's decision. The court ruled that in violation of Act No. 66, Allgeyer, a Louisiana company, had indeed contracted for insurance for cotton located within Louisiana with an out-of-state company. The court found Allgeyer guilty of one violation of Act No. 66 and fined it $1,000. Allgeyer appealed the decision to the U.S. Supreme Court.

Liberty of Contract

In a unanimous decision, the Court reversed the Louisiana Supreme Court's decision and ruled Act No. 66 unconstitutional. Justice Rufus Peckham, in delivering the Court's ruling, defined a broad new unwritten right protected by the Due Process Clause of the Fourteenth Amendment, the liberty of contract. Peckham wrote,

> **the 'liberty' mentioned in that amendment . . . is deemed to embrace the right of the citizen to be free in the enjoyment of all his faculties; to be free to use them in all lawful ways; to live and work where he will; to earn his livelihood by any lawful calling; to pursue any livelihood or avocation [hobby]; and for that purpose to enter into all contracts which may be proper, necessary, and essential.**

In regard to the specific facts of this case, Peckham noted,

> **The contract in this case was . . . a valid contract, made outside of the state [in New York], to be performed outside of the state [on the Atlantic Ocean], although the subject was property temporarily within the state [Louisiana]. As the contract was valid in the place where made and where it was to be performed, the party to the contract . . . must have the liberty to do that act and to give that notification within the limits of the state [of Louisiana].**

Because Allgeyer had not actually signed the contract in Louisiana, the company had not violated Act No. 66. Only a notification had actually been sent in the mail from New Orleans. Furthermore, neither Allgeyer nor Atlantic Mutual had violated the state constitution because Atlantic Mutual had not conducted business in Louisiana. Nonetheless, Peckham held the act was unconstitutional because it inappropriately interfered with Allgeyer's liberty to sign a contract to insure its cotton shipment with whomever it chose. Peckham concluded, "In the privilege of pursuing an ordinary calling or trade, and of acquiring, holding, and selling property, must be embraced [accepted] the right to make all proper contracts in relation thereto . . . "

RUFUS WHEELER PECKHAM

Rufus Wheeler Peckham (1838–1909) was born in Albany, New York to a prominent family of lawyers and judges. His law training was by studying in his father's law firm. Peckham received an honorary degree from Columbia University in 1866. His public career in law began in 1869 as the district attorney for three years for Albany County, New York. After over a decade of private practice, in 1883 he was elected to the New York Supreme Court and in 1886 to the New York Court of Appeals. Peckham was nominated to the U.S. Supreme Court by President Grover Cleveland (1885–1889; 1893–1897) in 1895. His brother, Wheeler H. Peckham had been nominated the previous year, but was not approved by the U.S. Senate. Rufus Peckham, however, was readily approved.

With many corporate clients in his private practice, Peckham became well known for favoring property rights and contract rights on the Court. His two opinions for the majority in *Allgeyer v. Louisiana* (1895) and ***Lochner v. New York*** (1905) gained reputation through the years as substantial misinterpretations of the Fourteenth Amendment. Promoting an economic liberty, the rulings had far-reaching implications by leaving businesses essentially free to treat their employees as they desired. Peckham served on the Court until his death in October of 1909.

A Decline in State Powers

The *Allgeyer* decision marked a significant decrease in the power of states to regulate business activities within their boundaries. It also increased federal oversight of state government activities through the courts. The Due Process Clause for the first time was expanded to protect business activities from government regulation. Rather than protecting individual rights as intended when the Fourteenth Amendment was adopted in 1868 following the American Civil War (1861–1865), it now replaced the Commerce and Contract Clauses in protecting commercial activity. The decision was further developed in *Lochner v. New York*

(1905) which struck down a New York law setting maximum bakers hours and setting sanitation standards.

Legislation regulating economic activities and protecting workers was discouraged for the next four decades until 1937 when the Court changed course again becoming much less protective of contract and business rights.

Suggestions for further reading

Covington, Robert N., and Kurt H. Decker. *Individual Employee Rights in a Nutshell.* St. Paul, MN: West Information Publishing Group, 1995.

Fick, Barbara J. *American Bar Association Guide to Workplace Law: Everything You Need to Know About Your Rights as an Employee or Employer.* New York: Times Books, 1997.

Swift and Co. v. United States 1905

Appellant: Swift and Company

Appellee: United States

Appellant's Claim: That the Sherman Anti-trust Act of 1890 was vague and did not apply to businesses operating solely within a single state

Chief Lawyers for Appellant: John S. Miler and Merritt Starr

Chief Lawyers for Appellee: William H. Moody, U.S. Attorney General, and William A. Day

Justices for the Court: David J. Brewer, Henry B. Brown, William R. Day, Melville W. Fuller, John Marshall Harlan I, Oliver Wendell Holmes, Joseph McKenna, Rufus W. Peckham, Edward D. White

Justices Dissenting: None

Date of Decision: January 30, 1905

Decision: Ruled in favor of the United States by finding that the actions of Swift and Company affected interstate commerce and were an integral part of a larger interstate meat-packing industry.

Significance: This decision greatly expanded federal power under the Commerce Clause of the U.S. Constitution. The ruling held that even locally operating businesses that made products eventually sold in interstate markets could be subject to federal regulation.

Before the birth of the United States, English common law restricted business activity very little. By the mid-nineteenth century. Congress and the courts began restricting certain business efforts, known as restraint of trade, which limited competition. But, if specific trade restraints were limited in the time they were used or carried out in a small area, they were often allowed. A *laissez-faire* approach to business conduct persisted meaning that little governmental interference existed over business practices.

The Rise of Trusts

A rapidly expanding national railroad network spurred increased industrialization (growth of large businesses manufacturing goods) in the 1870s and 1880s. Prospects of ever-increasing profits led many businesses to join together in business combinations with the intent of forcing other, usually smaller, competitors out of business. These businesses combinations were called trusts. The public considered many actions of the trusts unfair. Trusts rose to dominate certain industries including sugar, oil, steel, meat-packing, and tobacco.

To many, trusts threatened the idea of free-enterprise in which businesses freely compete with one another. Public demand for government intervention into trusts dramatically increased through the 1880's. States tried adopting various laws to control trust activities, but these proved inconsistent and could not apply to interstate commerce (business activity between states) in which the trusts largely operated. The Commerce Clause of the U.S. Constitution reserves the responsibility to regulate interstate commerce to Congress, not the states. Congress, responding to the public outcry against the power of trusts, passed the Sherman Antitrust Act in 1890. The act, the first major national legislation addressing business practices, prohibited every "contract, combination in the form of trust . . . or conspiracy, in restraint of trade or commerce among the several states, or with foreign nations."

Though strongly worded by prohibiting all restraint of trade through business cooperation, the act was vague leaving enforcement to the courts and executive branch of government. President Grover Cleveland (1885–1889; 1893–1897), believing trusts were a natural result of technological advances and good for eliminating waste, was not inclined to enforce the act. Likewise, the very conservative U.S. Supreme Court of the time preferred not to inhibit business activities of employers. The first ruling involving the Sherman Act, *United States v. E.C. Knight Co.* (1895), provided a very narrow interpretation of what the court considered interstate commerce. Manufacturing was not considered interstate commerce thus leaving many key industries free to continue operating under trusts.

Swift Meat Packers

One meat packing company in operation at the beginning of the twentieth century was Swift and Co. Though Swift had slaughterhouses in various states including Illinois, Nebraska, Minnesota, and Missouri, they did not consider themselves an interstate business since each plant operated independently of other Swift plants. Strategically located at major railway terminal locations, each plant purchased livestock at the local stockyards, slaughtered the purchased stock in its facility, then sold the meat products to local purchasers. An interstate character to the process existed, however. The livestock was normally shipped thousands of miles from distant states to the stockyards where Swift would purchase them. Also, the local purchasers of Swift products would sell to wholesale meat companies, often located in other states, thus shipping the fresh meat on interstate railroads.

Swift and Co. had become very successful in the meat-packing industry, controlling about 60 percent of the national fresh meat market. Some of its methods to achieve that success were dishonest, however. For example, forming a beef trust through extensive agreements with other meat-packing houses they would manipulate (fix to their satisfaction) the interstate price of livestock. For example, they would send several buyers to a livestock auction and appear to compete against each other for the price. Though sometimes trying to manipulate low prices, other times they tried to make prices appear high for livestock. When word would get out to other livestock companies that high prices were being bid in a certain town, they would ship their livestock there to get higher profits, often flooding a particular market with livestock. The beef trust would then let the prices fall sharply allowing them to purchase the livestock at a bargain price. As a result, Swift and the beef trust would get much of its livestock at artificially-reduced prices, then sell its products at regular prices for a big profit. Through this means, they controlled livestock and meat prices in many stockyards and slaughterhouses around the nation.

Upon discovering Swift's auction practices, the United States filed charges of conspiracy to restrain trade under the Sherman Antitrust Act. The case was first heard in federal district court which ruled in favor of the United States. Swift then appealed to the U.S. Supreme Court.

A Stream of Commerce

Arguments were presented before the Court on January 6 and 7 of 1905. Swift argued that the Sherman Antitrust Act was too vague. How could companies know what activities could be considered illegal? Besides, all of its business activities of purchasing, processing, and selling was local. Only a few miles distance separated the stockyards from its slaughterhouses and meat-packing plants. Consequently, it was not interstate commerce and the federal government had no authority to regulate it. Regarding the bidding practices, Swift argued that livestock sellers always had the option of either not selling or accepting the sometimes artificially high bids. The government argued that even though Swift was intrastate (within a single state) in operation, its effects on the nation's economy were interstate in character.

Justice Oliver Wendell Holmes, Jr., writing for a 9–0 unanimous Court, presented the opinion on January 30. Holmes ruled that clearly Swift was trying to create a monopoly of the meat-packing industry through unfair means. The livestock Swift purchased had to be shipped interstate to supply Swift plants with meat, and Swift had to rely on meat markets in other states to sell its products. Acknowledging the vagueness of the Sherman Antitrust Act, Holmes sought to more clearly define through the ruling the kinds of actions considered illegal restraint of trade. Holmes sought a more "practical" concept of interstate commerce than the courts had previously offered. Holmes wrote,

> **When cattle are sent for sale from a place in one state, with the expectation that they will end their transit [trip], after purchase, in another, and when in effect they do so, with only the interruption necessary to find a purchaser at the stock yards, and when this is a typical constantly recurring course, the current thus existing is a current of commerce among the states, and the purchase of the cattle is a part . . . of such commerce.**

The doctrine (idea) of "stream of commerce" was thus applied for the first time. From the time livestock was purchased until the meat products were sold, Swift was part of a larger stream of commerce that involved interstate business. The meat-packing industry clearly relied on a flowing interstate process, regardless if some of its parts might only operate in a single state. Congress, Holmes asserted, has authority to regulate business any where along that stream.

TEDDY ROOSEVELT AND TRUSTBUSTING

By the time Theodore Roosevelt (1901–1909) first became President, only a few hundred large companies controlled almost half of U.S. manufacturing. Forming large trusts, they greatly influenced almost all key industries. The "trustbusting" movement briefly took off in 1904 with the Supreme Court's decision in *Northern Securities Co. v. United States* breaking up a railroad trust. Quickly, over forty more antitrust lawsuits were filed under Roosevelt. Though gaining the reputation as "trustbuster," Roosevelt actually sought a middle ground in government oversight of corporate activities. He, as did his successor President William Howard Taft (1909–1913), used the Sherman Act to force greater social accountability by businesses. Roosevelt did not intend to end all business combinations, only to regulate those considered grossly unresponsive to consumer needs.

The 1905 *Swift* decision came as Roosevelt was trying to shift emphasis from trustbusting to regulation of industry. As a result, the ruling was not applied often to other cases until the late 1930s when the Court began supporting broad federal powers under President Franklin D. Roosevelt's economic recovery program.

Regarding the manipulation of meat market prices, the temporary artificial rise followed by a sharp drop of prices clearly effected interstate commerce. Such manipulation of the free market price of livestock directly restrained trade.

Commerce Clause Expanded

Swift was the most important case concerning the beef trust ever heard by the Court. Abandoning its previous narrow interpretation of interstate commerce, the stream of commerce doctrine became the basic idea later used for expanding federal power under the Commerce Clause. Congress could regulate businesses involved to any degree in interstate commerce. Yet, for the economic boom years of World War I (1914–1918) and the

1920's, political interest in regulating business greatly diminished. President Franklin D. Roosevelt's (1933–1945) New Deal programs of the early 1930's actually encouraged industrial collaboration to boost economic recovery from the Great Depression. Not until Congress passed the Robinson-Patman Act in 1936 was the federal attack on monopolies and trusts renewed. As was the issue in *Swift,* the act was designed to protect small businesses from larger competitors.

Suggestions for further reading

Freyer, Tony Allan. *Regulating Big Business: Antitrust in Great Britain and America, 1880-1990.* New York: Cambridge University Press, 1992.

Gould, Lewis L. *The Presidency of Theodore Roosevelt.* Lawrence, KS: University Press of Kansas, 1991.

Miller, Nathan. *Theodore Roosevelt: A Life.* New York: William Morrow & Co., 1994.

Sullivan, E. Thomas, ed. *The Political Economy of the Sherman Act: The First One Hundred Years.* New York: Oxford University Press, 1991.

Standard Oil v. United States 1911

Plaintiff: Standard Oil of New Jersey

Defendant: United States

Plaintiff's Claim: That Standard Oil was not in violation of the Sherman Anti-trust Act by conspiring to restrain trade.

Chief Lawyer for Plaintiff: John G. Milburn

Chief Lawyer for Defendant: Frank B. Kellogg

Justices for the Court: Rufus R. Day, John Marshall Harlan I, Oliver Wendell Holmes, Charles E. Hughes, Joseph R. Lamar, Horace H. Lurton, Joseph McKenna, Willis Van Devanter, Chief Justice Edward D. White

Justices Dissenting: None

Date of Decision: May 15, 1911

Decision: Ruled in favor of the United States by affirming a lower court order that Standard Oil be broken apart.

Significance: Although supporting the break up of Standard Oil, the Court through the "rule of reason" left open the possibility that some cooperation in restraining trade among companies may be legal. The question of the government's role and power in restricting private economic activities continued into the twenty-first century with the issue of Microsoft business practices making headlines in the year 2000.

ANTITRUST, BUSINESS, CORPORATE AND CONTRACT LAW

Following the American Civil War (1861–1865), industrialization (growth of large businesses manufacturing goods) increased at a rapid pace. Construction of a national railroad system created cheaper transportation which greatly expanded markets allowing industrial productivity (ability to make more goods) to grow. As competition became more intense, companies sought ways to protect or expand profits. State laws in the late nineteenth century largely restricted economic growth through company mergers. Therefore, one of the more attractive means available for companies to expand profits was to simply collaborate (cooperate) with competitors to set prices and control production. These cooperative relationships often involved creating trusts in which a company would be created to oversee management of the cooperating companies. In 1882 Standard Oil of New Jersey became the first such trust. Trusts would fix prices and drive out new competition through price wars. Trusts in various industries, such as tobacco, beef, whiskey, and sugar, led to major concentrations of capital (money) within those trusts. Eventually, trust became a general term applied to national monopolies where only a few people controlled a major portion of the U.S. economy. Legislatures and the courts focused on protection of new businesses trying to enter markets. The freedom to contract dominated all legal considerations, not individual civil rights or consumer protection.

Standard Oil

Public concern over the practices of Standard Oil grew in the 1880s and continued to swell following passage of the Sherman Antitrust Act of 1890. The act prohibited unfair business practices designed to drive out competition but the government and courts were not willing to apply it very aggressively. By 1906 Standard Oil had become a monopoly, controlling over 80 percent of oil production in the United States. Majority ownership of the company was led by John D. Rockefeller (1839–1937). A $70 million dollar investment, establishing the company in the early 1880s, earned $700 million of profits in only fifteen years.

With little competition for some products, such as kerosene, Standard Oil charged excessive prices leading to remarkable profits. For products where competition did exist, Standard Oil could afford to drastically cut prices driving the smaller companies out of business. In addition, Standard Oil offered rebates (money refunds) to oil producing companies, enticing them to ship their oil only through Standard Oil pipelines. All of these practices are unfair restrictions on interstate commerce (conducting economic trade or business across state lines). A phrase often applied to these practices is "restraint of trade."

Although evidence was uncovered describing the unfair practices Standard Oil used in restricting competition, the U.S. government long refused to act. Finally, under President Theodore Roosevelt's (1901–1909) second term of office, public pressure resulted in an investigation of Standard Oil's practices and a lawsuit. The government charged that Standard Oil violated the Sherman Antitrust Act by illegally restricting interstate commerce. Standard Oil responded that many of the individual companies controlled by Standard Oil were actually competitive on their own, relatively free of the overarching trust company. Roosevelt's successor as President, William Howard Taft (1909–1913), inherited the case and kept pursuing prosecution.

Argued for eight months in St. Louis Federal Circuit Court, a decision was issued on November 20, 1909. Judge Walter Henry Sanborn ruled that indeed Standard Oil acted inappropriately to restrict interstate commerce. Although Standard Oil's individual companies might be capable of independent competition, actually they were sufficiently controlled by the Standard Oil trust company to prevent competition. Through this control, Standard Oil had tried to monopolize the petroleum industry. Sanborn wrote that "the combination and conspiracy in restraint of trade and its continued execution which have been found to exist, constitute illegal means by which the conspiring defendants combined, and still combine and conspire to monopolize a part of interstate and international commerce."

The penalty posed by Sanborn, however, was far from damaging for those holding the economic power in Standard. Standard Oil's controlling interest over the various companies was broken up, but that interest was merely shifted to Standard Oil's small group of primary stockholders. Consequently, little actually changed.

Rule of Reason

Standard Oil appealed the decision to the U.S. Supreme Court. Chief Justice Edward D. White, delivered the Court's 9–0 lengthy unanimous opinion in favor of the United States upholding the lower court's decision. White first found that the vagueness of the Antitrust Act "necessarily called for the exercise of judgement." White then proceeded to introduce a standard to be used in outlawing specific monopolies. This soon-to-be-controversial standard was called the "rule of reason" in outlawing specific monopolies. In a previous case involving the Sherman Antitrust Act, *Northern Securities Co. v. United States* (1904), White and three other dissenting justices had tried to introduce the rule of reason, but the majority of five in the case held that the act prohibited all restraints of trade. White had claimed it only prohibited trade restraints considered unreasonable.

In ***Standard Oil,*** White asserted the rule had long been part of English common law. The rule stated that if the company could justify a restraint of trade as a necessary part of a business transaction, and it was considered reasonable by the participating companies and the general public, then it would not be considered illegal. It would be up to the courts to decide on each case. White added that to ban all restraints of trade would cripple the U.S. economy and that restraint of trade was a key element of most business combinations.

Though agreeing with the decision against Standard Oil, Justice John Marshall Harlan opposed White's rule of reason. Harlan believed the rule would be difficult to apply in future cases consistently. As a result, companies and the public would be left confused about what was considered legally right or wrong in business. Harlan, still believing that all restraint of trade was illegal under the Sherman Act, wrote,

> **the Court has now read into the act of Congress words which are not to be found there, and has thereby done that which it [had judged] . . . could not be done without violating the Constitution, namely, by interpretation of a statute, changed a public policy declared by the legislative department.**

The Ongoing Debate of Monopolies

The individual companies resulting from the break-up of Standard Oil included such major gasoline suppliers as Exxon, Amoco, Mobil, Chevron, and Standard of California. Another trust broken up by a Supreme Court decision in 1911 was the American Tobacco Company. The decisions affirmed (supported) the federal government's role to oversee marketplace economics by determining when trusts restrict competition and restrain trade.

Ironically, although the decision went against Standard Oil, the rule of reason actually opened the door in following years for other large cor-

TRUSTBUSTING IN THE LATE TWENTIETH CENTURY

Public concern over trusts mounted again following World War II (1939–1945). From the 1950's into the 1970's, the federal government aggressively pursued the issue of powerful trusts. An example was the Federal Trade Commission's successful efforts at decreasing the Xerox Company's control of the photocopy industry. Trustbusting in the 1980's and 1990's shifted focus to policing bad conduct of companies rather than actually breaking up monopolies. Some notable trustbusting, however, included the break-up of American Telephone and Telegraph (AT&T). Charged with restricting competition in long-distance telephone service and production of telecommunications equipment, AT&T lost control over Western Electric, the manufacturing part of the company, and various regional telephone companies.

Opposed to government restriction of business activities, President Ronald Reagan (1981–1989) reduced trustbusting efforts as a historic wave of corporate mergers occurred in the mid-1980's. By 1990 the tide again shifted. States began to increasingly address monopolistic mergers and soon federal interest grew again in examining competitive practices. President Bill Clinton (1993–) once again increased federal antitrust efforts as thirty-three lawsuits were filed in 1994. The most important antitrust case of the 1990's involved the computer software company, Microsoft, accused of various monopolistic activities. As another wave of mergers once again swept the United States in the late 1990s, the age-old question still lingered, does government have a legal right to limit commercial power. The American public continued holding conflicting attitudes over business combinations as it had since the nineteenth century.

porate monopolies to continue operating, just as predicted by Justice Harlan. In 1913 the Court, using the rule, held that a combination of shoemaking manufacturers controlling over 80 percent of the market was not illegal. The Court reasoned that the trust was simply introducing greater efficiency in the industry.

The obvious unpredictability that the rule of reason posed for future court rulings led to public pressure to pass more effective trustbusting laws. Congress responded with the 1914 Clayton Act prohibiting companies from: (1) charging different buyers different prices for the same products; (2) forcing other companies to sign contracts restricting them from doing business with their competitors; (3) prohibiting mergers between competing companies; and, (4) restricting companies from buying stock in competing companies. Associated with the Clayton Act was the 1914 Federal Trade Commission Act creating the Federal Trade Commission (FTC) to combat unfair business practices.

Suggestions for further reading

Binghurst, Bruce. *Antitrust and the Oil Monopoly: The Standard Oil Cases, 1890-1911.* Westport, CT: Greenwood Press, 1979.

Nash, Gerald P. *United States Oil Policy, 1890-1914.* Pittsburgh: University of Pittsburgh Press, 1968.

Wallace, James. *Overdrive: Bill Gates and the Race to Control Cyberspace.* New York: J. Wiley, 1997.

Wickard v. Filburn
1942

Appellant: Claude R. Wickard, U.S. Secretary of Agriculture

Appellee: Rosco C. Filburn

Appellant's Claim: That the federal government has constitutional authority provided in the Commerce Clause to regulate wheat production, regardless if the particular crops were intended for sale in the market.

Chief Lawyers for Appellant: Francis Biddle, U.S. Attorney General, and Charles Fahy, U.S. Solicitor General

Chief Lawyer for Appellee: Webb R. Clark

Justices for the Court: Hugo L. Black, William O. Douglas, Felix Frankfurter, Robert H. Jackson, Frank Murphy, Stanley F. Reed, Owen J. Roberts, Chief Justice Harlan F. Stone

Justices Dissenting: None (James Francis Byrnes did not participate)

Date of Decision: November 9, 1942

Decision: Ruled in favor of Wickard in that the federal government has broad powers under the Commerce Clause to regulate all activities that remotely may affect interstate commerce.

Significance: The ruling established an exceptionally broad interpretation of the federal government's powers under the Commerce Clause. Congress could regulate agricultural production that might affect interstate commerce, even if it is not for sale. Federal and state regulation affecting nearly all forms of agricultural production and trade in the United States grew through the next several decades.

Agricultural production in the United States, largely involving small family-owned farms, enjoyed good economic times following the American Civil War (1861–1865) through World War I (1914–1918). The 1920s saw the rise of mass productivity inspired by the industrial revolution leading to increased production. With the greater supply of farm produce, prices began to substantially decline by the end of the decade. Many family farms folded due to inadequate profits. With the stock market crash of October of 1929 and the following Great Depression through the 1930s, economic hardships for farmers further increased. Much of the public was no longer able to afford farm produce and prices fell dramatically. Without sufficient profits, foreclosures (ending a property right to pay a debt) on farms whose owners could no longer to pay their mortgages increased sharply.

In reaction to the desperate trends, farmers began organizing to save their livelihoods. Some withheld food from markets to force prices back up. Violence erupted as efforts were made to keep some farmers from delivering their produce to market. Agitation against the government for lack of support increased. Some states began passing laws making it more difficult for banks for foreclose on farms. With a national farmer strike planned for May 13, 1933, newly elected President Franklin D. Roosevelt (1933–1945) signed the Agricultural Adjustment Act on May 12 to head off the protests. The act provided payments to farmers who voluntarily reduced their production. The act was part of Roosevelt's New Deal program to bring social and economic change to a struggling country.

However, like many laws passed by Congress at that time to spur economic recovery from the depression, the very conservative Supreme Court ruled the act unconstitutional in 1936. The Court held the federal government had no authority to become involved in what they considered local matters to be resolved by the states. In fact, the Court viewed agriculture as largely out of the realm of federal business regulation.

Beginning in 1935, Roosevelt renewed his efforts at social and economic reform with a second New Deal program. By this time, the makeup of the Supreme Court began to change. Some justices retired under political pressure from Roosevelt who sought to have a Court that would support his programs. Included in the renewed effort was the Agricultural Adjustment Act of 1938. The act provided for increased federal control of farm production, loans to farms, farm insurance, and soil conservation to maintain farm productivity. Unlike the earlier act which paid farmers to produce less of certain crops, the second act established market quotas (limits set on something) for various farm products. Those farmers exceeding the amounts set for them by the government could be fined.

The act was immediately the subject of a Supreme Court challenge in *Mulford v. Smith* (1938). The revamped Court supported it by ruling in favor of tobacco-growing quotas.

Filburn's Farm

Roscoe C. Filburn was a small-time Ohio farmer raising poultry and producing dairy products. He also grew a small crop of winter wheat. Under the act, the Department of Agriculture had designated eleven acres of Filburn's land for growing wheat. A particular yield for that acreage was also set. In defiance of the set levels, in 1941 Filburn planted wheat on twelve additional acres and exceeded his yield limits. The extra planting produced 249 bushels of wheat. The department fined Filburn $117. He refused to pay and the department put a lien (the property is subject to sale to pay debts) on his wheat.

In reaction, Filburn filed a lawsuit in federal district court against U.S. Secretary of Agriculture Claude R. Wickard. Filburn sought to overturn his wheat production restrictions. He claimed that limitations on crop production was outside the federal government's power to restrict agriculture. In his defense, Filburn also claimed his excess wheat was only for use on the farm to feed animals and would not be sold at the market. The district court decided in favor of Filburn by ruling that the federal government did not have authority to fine him. Wickard appealed the decision to the Supreme Court.

A Stronger Commerce Clause

By the time the case came before the Court for arguments on May 4, 1942, only one justice, Owen Roberts, remained from the earlier group which had staunchly opposed increased federal regulation proposed by Roosevelt and Congress in the New Deal programs. The Court ruled unanimously in favor of Wickard, overturning the lower court's ruling. Justice Robert H. Jackson, writing for the Court, wrote that even excess agricultural produce not intended to be sold at commercial markets could still affected interstate commerce. Jackson wrote that even though the amount of Filburn's excess wheat was itself small, taken in combination with other wheat farmers there could be a significant impact on interstate commerce. If Filburn grew his own wheat, then he would not need wheat from the open market. This would hurt other farmers by causing the demand and prices for wheat to go down. Jackson wrote,

> **The maintenance by government regulation of a price for wheat undoubtedly can be accomplished as effectively by sustaining or increasing the demand as by limiting the supply . . . That [Filburn's] own contribution to the demand for wheat may be trivial [very small] by itself is not enough to remove him from the scope of federal regulation where, as here, taken together with that of many others similarly situated, is far from trivial . . . Home-grown wheat in this sense competes with wheat in commerce . . . Congress may properly have considered that wheat consumed on the farm where grown if wholly outside the scheme of regulation would have a substantial effect in defeating and obstructing [the act's] purpose to stimulate trade . . . at increased prices.**

The Commerce Clause in Article 1, Section 8 of the U.S. Constitution states that Congress may "regulate Commerce . . . among the several States." The Court had long debated whether federal commerce power authorized the federal government to only be able to control actual goods and produce being shipped between states, or if it applied to the actual production and how the kind and level of production could influence commerce. Jackson decided the difference between production and sales did not really matter,

> **Whether the subject of the regulation in question was 'production,' 'consumption,' or 'marketing' is . . . not material for purposes of deciding the question of federal power . . . But even if [Filburn's] activity be local and though it may not be regarded as commerce, it may still, whatever its nature, be reached by Congress if it exerts a substantial economic effect on interstate commerce.**

The use of wheat quotas, even on crops not to be sold at market, was upheld by the Court.

COMMERCE CLAUSE AND THE TENTH AMENDMENT

With fear of centralized power brought by British rule, initially the states held almost total control over commercial activities under the Articles of Confederation, drawn up in 1781. However, much confusion resulted as each state established different regulations, often engaged in economic rivalries among themselves. Merchants were obviously reluctant to take economic risks in such an unpredictable and chaotic setting. Great agreement could be found to establish federal control over interstate and foreign trade when the Framers of the Constitution went to work in 1787 at the Constitutional Convention. As a result, creation of the Commerce Clause in Article 1, Section 8 of the Constitution drew little debate. Congress held power to "regulate Commerce with foreign Nations, and among the several States" under the Clause.

In 1791, the Tenth Amendment was ratified which recognizes states' powers. The amendment reads, "The powers not delegated to the United States by the Constitution, nor prohibited by it to the States, are reserved to the States . . . " The U.S. Supreme Court gave Congress broadly interpreted powers in the first case involving the Commerce Clause in ***Gibbons v. Ogden*** (1824). However, little developed from that power as often conflicting court opinions followed. With some exceptions, such as the railroads in the 1880s, respect for states' rights to regulate business under the Tenth Amendment dominated for over a century. In ***NLRB v. Jones & Laughlin Steel Corp.*** (1937) the Court dramatically changed course. For decades following 1937 the Tenth Amendment was much less emphasized and federal regulations grew to address almost every aspect of economic activities that even remotely affected interstate commerce.

Growth of Agricultural Law

The decision in *Wickard* represented the greatest expansion of federal regulatory power through the Commerce Clause by the courts. Any effect on interstate commerce, even activity seemingly distant from actual commerce, fell within the scope of federal control. The important use of the Commerce Clause later involved race discrimination cases. In ***Heart of Atlanta Motel v. United States*** (1964) the Court affirmed the 1964 Civil Rights Act and access by people of all races to commercial places used by interstate travelers.

Within this broad scope of authority, the field of agricultural law developed by the late twentieth century to stabilize and promote production of the national food supply and other farm products. Federal regulation, addressing cultivation of various crops and raising of livestock, continued under the oversight of the Secretary of Agriculture.

Suggestions for further reading

Albertson, Dean. *Roosevelt's Farmer: Claude R. Wickard in the New Deal.* New York: Columbia University Press, 1961.

Hamilton, David E. *From New Day to New Deal: American Farm Policy from Hoover to Roosevelt, 1928-1933.* Chapel Hill: University of North Carolina Press, 1991.

Romasco, Albert U. *The Politics of Recovery: Roosevelt's New Deal.* New York: Oxford University Press, 1983.

FEDERAL POWERS AND SEPARATION OF POWERS

Through the eighteenth century Great Britain sought to make its American colonies a key source of revenue by applying an economic concept known as mercantilism. The colonies were to send to Britain raw materials such as food, timber, and furs at low prices while importing British finished products at high prices. To make mercantilism most effective for Britain the colonies were also prohibited from trading with other countries. In reaction to Britain's heavy hand, the colonists refused to fully cooperate. Often, in defiance, taxes were not paid and trade with other countries occurred.

At the conclusion of the French and Indian War in 1763, England had doubled its North American territory but also found itself with a huge war debt. The British government believed the colonies should help pay this debt and enacted a series of strict financial control measures. The most hated of these attempts to raise money for the British was the Stamp Act of 1765. The act required colonists to buy a revenue stamp each time they registered a legal document or bought such items as newspapers, almanacs, liquor licenses, or even playing cards. In 1767 Parliament passed the Townshend Acts which taxed paint, glass, lead, paper, and tea. Eventually, the tea tax lead to the "Boston Tea Party." To punish the colonists, the British passed more measures which the colonists labeled the Intolerable Acts of 1774. At this time tensions reached the breaking point.

In September of 1774, the colonists assembled the First Continental Congress which drafted a message to Britain claiming they would no longer tolerate being deprived of their life, liberty, and property. Open rebellion leading to the Revolutionary War (1775–1783) followed. During the war, the Second Continental Congress met in 1781 to create a new government. But fearful of strong central governments as Great Britain's, the colonial leaders created the Articles of Confederation which established a weak union of strong state governments. The new national government was given few powers. The national legislature consisted of only one house in which each state had one vote. No federal courts existed.

Following the end of the war in 1783, the new union experienced major difficulties. The weak central government had no tax powers to raise money, and each state coined its own money, regulated commerce (business and trade) as it saw fit, and had state courts hearing cases involving federal law. A Constitutional Convention was called in May of 1787 to revise the Articles of Confederation and solve the problems it created. Debate focused on the role and structure of the federal government. Federalists wanted a strong central government. Antifederalists, states' rights advocates, wanted most power to remain with the states. A compromise led to division of political power between federal and state governments. The leaders, rather than fixing the Articles of Confederation, drafted the U.S. Constitution. Those leaders, known as the Framers, created a stronger federal government consisting of three branches, the legislature, the executive, and the courts. This idea for a separation of governmental powers was largely credited to James Madison (1751–1836) who was influenced by the writings of eighteenth century French philosopher Baron Montesquieu (1689–1755). Montesquieu had contended that tyranny (political oppression) would usually result when a government, like Great Britain, had all of its power concentrated in one body.

The Framers of the U.S. Constitution sought "to form a more perfect union, establish justice, insure domestic tranquility [peace], provide for the common defense, promote the general welfare, and secure the blessings of liberty" for the nation's citizens. The Constitution consisted of several main sections, called Articles. The first three articles divides powers among the three branches. Article I defined the powers of the legislature, Congress, Article II the role of the executive branch, the president, and Article III the powers of the Supreme Court, the judicial branch. The legislative branch makes laws, the executive branch carries out the laws, and the judicial branch interprets the laws and decides legal disputes. The remaining articles described other aspects of government.

The Legislative Branch

The legislative branch was considered the heart of the new nation with major governing powers. Therefore, the structure of Congress drew considerable debate. One proposal, known as the Virginia plan, called for a legislature composed of two houses, called a bicameral legislature. Representatives in both houses would be elected by the states based on their individual populations. As a result, the states with more people would have greater representation. In response, another plan, the New Jersey Plan, proposed a one-house legislature, unicameral. All states would have equal representation. Therefore, less populated states would have an equal voice with the more populated states. After much debate, a compromise was reached known as the Connecticut Compromise. The Framers of the Constitution decided on a bicameral legislature consisting of a Senate with each state equally represented and a House of Representatives with membership based on the population size of each state. The House was originally the only part of federal government elected by the people, hence considered the most important in representing people's views.

In modern times, the Senate contains 100 members with two from each of the fifty states. Though originally elected by the state legislatures, Senators are now elected directly by the people for six-year terms. A third of the Senate comes up for reelection every two years. Regarding the House, in 1929 Congress set the total number of representatives at 435. The national census taken every ten years determines how many representatives each state can have and those representatives are elected every two years.

Remembering the oppressive British central government and determined to avoid a legislature which could abuse its power, the Framers were more detailed about Congress' powers than for the other two branches of government. Congress received powers to tax and spend, approve treaties, regulate interstate and foreign commerce, conduct foreign affairs, raise an army and navy, coin money, and declare war. The supremacy of the federal government over state governments was established in two clauses. The Necessary and Proper Clause in Article I gave Congress broad powers to pass any laws that it can reasonably justify to carry out its powers. The Supremacy Clause in Article VI simply states that such laws passed by Congress, in addition to the Constitution itself and treaties approved by Congress, are the supreme law of the land. Whenever a conflict between a federal law and a state law occurs, the federal law always takes priority. Exercising its duty to interpret the Constitution, the Supreme Court recognized in ***McCulloch v. Maryland*** (1819) that Congress has implied powers not specifically mentioned in the Constitution, powers that come to all independent sovereign governments.

Some restrictions on Congress were included, such as prohibition against passing laws singling out specific individuals for punishment in *ex post facto* (after the fact) laws. Though the main body of the Constitution contains some restrictions on congressional power, the Bill of Rights added as the first ten amendments to the Constitution offers far more restrictions. Adopted in 1791 to appease states' rights advocates who feared the new central government would have too much power, the Bill of Rights protects various individual rights from federal actions, including freedom of speech, religion, and the press, the right to assemble in groups, and protections from certain search and seizures. Also included was the Tenth Amendment which limited the power of the federal government. The amendment reads that "the powers not delegated to the United States by the Constitution, nor prohibited by it to the States, are reserved to the States respectively, or to the people." However, the precise line between federal and state powers was not drawn leaving an ongoing debate between federalists and states' rights advocates.

A constant problem in separation of powers has been Congress' power "to declare War." Repeatedly through history, presidents have committed troops to armed conflict in foreign countries without first obtaining a declaration of war from Congress. President Abraham Lincoln did this when ordering blockades of Southern seaports in the Civil War (1861–1865), and the sending of troops a century later to the Vietnam war (1964–1975) was another example. Though presidents have been challenged in court on several occasions, the Supreme Court has largely stayed out of the issue leaving it to Congress to take whatever action it chooses which normally has been none.

Another issue involving separation of powers between the legislative and executive branches has been the frequent delegation of congressional powers to the president through laws passed. Usually this delegation happens when Congress passes laws to regulate some activity, such as creation of the Interstate Commerce Act of 1887 to regulate interstate commerce. The Court in *J.W. Hampton v. United States* (1928) gave support to such transfers of power as long as Congress establishes guidelines for the executive branch to follow in carrying out the duties.

The Executive Branch

Article II of the Constitution gives the President of the United States power to enforce the laws. The president must be a natural born citizen, at least thirty-five years of age, and have resided in the United States for at least fourteen years. The president serves a four-year term and is limited to two terms.

Perhaps fearing the concentration of power in a single person as with the late eighteenth century English monarchy of King George III, few powers are granted the executive. Roles and responsibilities are only very generally described. Nonetheless, through time the position has become recognized as the most powerful in the world and presidential powers have steadily grown largely unchecked. The courts have generally recognized broad presidential powers issuing few decisions restricting it. Though a civilian, the president as the commander-in-chief of the armed forces has ultimate control over the military. This power likely came from fear that the military might gain power over the civilian government. The president also has power to make treaties, with the advice and consent of the Senate, and to terminate treaties as recognized in *Goldwater v. Carter* (1979). The president holds broad foreign affairs powers as recognized by the Court in ***United States v. Curtiss-Wright Export Corp.*** (1936).

The president's key responsibility to "take care that the laws be faithfully executed" has been largely delegated to federal agencies of the executive branch, such as the departments of justice, interior, and agriculture. Heads of these various departments are members of the president's cabinet. The president may also propose legislation to Congress including the national budget.

Through executive powers that are largely concentrated in one person, the president can influence public opinion far more than the other two branches. The presidents through time have held widely varying ideas of how to use this power. Beginning with President Theodore Roosevelt (1901–1909), many presidents have expanded on how to use this unique power of persuasion and influence.

The Judicial Branch

Article III of the Constitution established only "one Supreme Court" but gave Congress power to create "such inferior [lower] courts as the Congress may from time to time ordain and establish." Congress exercised its authority to create a three level judicial system with the Supreme Court at the top, courts of appeal in the middle, and district courts at the bottom. The nation was divided into eleven judicial regions in which a court of appeals is in each. Federal district courts are located in each state.

The Constitution states that federal courts may only hear cases involving constitutional questions, federal law, treaties, maritime (activities on the oceans), when the United States is a party, and between two or more states, between a state and citizen of a different state, and between citizens of different states. Only cases involving ambassadors, other public ministers and consuls, and when a state is a party may come directly to the Supreme Court without first going through the lower courts. Federal courts may also issue *writs of habeas corpus* when questions about the legality of an individual's detention by authorities are raised and *writs of mandamus* which force government officials to carry out their public duties. The federal courts can issue arrest and search warrants and hear both criminal and civil cases.

The most important constitutional limitation on the federal court system is that only cases involving actual disputes can be heard. The courts cannot be asked to rule on the constitutionality of a law without an actual incident occurring. Still, the judiciary remains the last word on division of powers among the three branches.

Checks and Balances

To guard against one of the branches becoming too powerful or abusing its powers, the Framers constructed a complex series of checks and balances in which each branch watches over the other two. The Framers were more concerned about abuse of powers than government efficiency in making decisions. In reality, the three branches are more interrelated than they are actually separate. The president can veto laws passed by Congress or simply not carry out duties assigned to him by congressional acts. Congress can override a presidential veto with a vote by two-thirds of both houses. Congress can also determine the executive branch's budget and must confirm presidential appointees to various posts, including cabinet members and judges. Congress can also impeach the president, or other members of the executive branch. No one can be a member of the legislative and executive branches at the same time.

The president can keep check on the courts by appointing all federal judges including the Supreme Court justices. Because judges serve for life, presidents can exert an influence on U.S. policies well beyond their term of office. Life tenure also protects judges from the whims of public opinion. No Supreme Court justice has ever been removed from office by impeachment, but Congress has the power to do so. If Congress so desired, it could eliminate all federal courts except the Supreme Court. More realistically, Congress has the responsibility to confirm all judicial nominees.

In practicality, the Supreme Court is the least-checked branch of government. Because of their life time appointments, the judicial branch is least accountable to the public through the election process. The federal courts have power to declare unconstitutional acts of Congress or actions by the executive. As stated by Chief Justice John Marshall in the landmark ***Marbury v. Madison*** (1803) case establishing the concept of judicial review, "It is, emphatically, the province and duty of the judicial department to say what the law is." The judicial power has been well dramatized in numerous decisions, such as striking down the federal income tax in *Pollack v. Farmers' Loan and Trust Co.* (1895) and federal child labor laws in ***Hammer v. Dagenhart*** (1918). Having the power of judicial review as recognized in *Marbury,* the courts can review presidential actions and agency activities for their constitutionality and rule them void if found unconstitutional. Only four times in U.S. history have Supreme Court decisions been overridden by constitutional amendments which have been passed by Congress and ratified (adopted) by the states.

Although never mentioned in the Constitution, two established doctrines, executive immunity and executive privilege, shield the president to a certain degree from interference by the other branches. Executive immunity protects the president from judicial interference. A court cannot order the president to take, or to stop taking, action to carry out his executive duties. Executive immunity was recognized by the Court in ***Mississippi v. Johnson*** (1867) and later expanded in ***Nixon v. Fitzgerald*** (1982). Executive privilege refers to the president's ability to withhold information, documents or testimony of aides from congressional or judicial probes. The Supreme Court recognized the existence to at least a limited privilege in ***United States v. Nixon*** (1974).

In the slow-paced society in which the Framers lived in the late eighteenth century, concern over government abuse of power outweighed interest in government efficiency. The separation of powers was designed with that in mind. But, as the general pace of American life increased dramatically through the twentieth century, concerns over government efficiency grew. Yet, the idea of separation of powers has remained strong though their specific nature has changed with the Supreme Court having the final say in what it means at any particular time for any particular occasion.

Suggestions for further reading

Fisher, Louis. *The Politics of Shared Power: Congress and the Executive.* Third Edition. Washington, DC: Congressional Quarterly Press, 1993.

Fisher, Louis. *Constitutional Conflicts Between Congress and the President.* Fourth Edition. Lawrence: University of Kansas Press, 1997.

Jones, Charles O. *Separate But Equal Branches: Congress and the Presidency.* Chatham, NJ: Chatham House Publishers, Inc., 1995.

Sanford, William R., and Carl R. Green. *Basic Principles of American Government.* New York: Amsco School Publications, Inc., 1983.

Weissberg, Robert. *Understanding American Government.* New York: Holt, Rinehart and Winston, 1980.

Marbury v. Madison
1803

Plaintiffs: William Marbury, William Harper, Robert R. Hooe, Dennis Ramsay

Defendant: James Madison, U.S. Secretary of State

Plaintiff's Claim: That U.S. Secretary of State James Madison must deliver judicial commissions issued by his predecessor to their rightful recipients.

Chief Lawyer of Plaintiffs: Charles Lee

Chief Lawyer for Defendant: Levi Lincoln, U.S. Attorney General

Justices for the Court: Samuel Chase, William Cushing, Chief Justice John Marshall, William Paterson, Bushrod Washington

Justices Dissenting: None (Alfred Moore did not participate)

Date of Decision: February 24, 1803

Decision: Ruled in favor of Madison by finding that the Judiciary Act of 1789 giving legal authority to federal courts to order government officials to act was unconstitutional.

Significance: The ruling is considered by many the most important decision in American legal history. The Court established the guiding principles of judicial review which recognized the federal courts' role in reviewing acts of Congress and states regarding their constitutionality. The Supreme Court thus became a significantly powerful part of the American governmental system.

"It is, emphatically, the province [within court's power] and duty of the judicial department [the courts] to say what the law is." This dramatic and often quoted statement was made by Chief Justice John Marshall in *Marbury v. Madison* (1803). Often called the single most important decision in the history of the U.S. Supreme Court. *Marbury* established the power of judicial review. Judicial review allows federal courts to review laws enacted by Congress and to declare a law invalid if it is found to violate the Constitution. However, the Court may not invalidate (overturn) just any law merely because it violates the Constitution. Such a decision by the Court may be made only when a specific lawsuit is brought before the Court requiring a determination that a law is constitutional. Additionally, judicial review allows federal courts to see that government officials, including the president, act in accordance with constitutional principles.

An Active, Living Constitution

Unlike many constitutions of countries around the world, the Constitution of the United States is more than just a description of the existing governmental system. It is also an active, living instrument in which is found the source of power and limits of power among the three governmental branches.

Chief Justice Marshall viewed the Constitution as a broad outline describing important goals. The details of how to carry out those goals, of how to fill in the outline, was left to the working government. But, which part of government would have the ultimate responsibility to guard the written terms of the Constitution and to see that the power of each branch of government was properly limited? This question was first debated at length in the Philadelphia Constitutional Convention of 1787. They found little guidance in the history of English law as to who should be the Constitution's final interpreter. Although the Framers made it clear some sort of review of legislation needed to be established, the exact nature of the review was left undefined. In *Federalist Paper No. 78,* written by Alexander Hamilton (1757–1804) in 1788, the judiciary (courts) was described as the "least dangerous to the political rights of the Constitution." Hamilton saw the executive branch, the president, as carrying the "sword" and the legislative branch (Congress) carrying the "purse" which could be opened or closed at the political whim of the day. But, he noted the Supreme Court held neither and likely would be the fairest defender of liberty.

Madison was charged with not delivering judicial commisions left over from the previous secretary. Courtesy of the Library of Congress.

The answer came in 1803 in *Marbury,* a declaration that the Supreme Court would have the final say in guaranteeing that the intent of the Constitution was being carried out by the governmental branches. This decision was intertwined with the political scene of the day.

The Politics of 1800

In 1800, two political parties dominated America, the Federalists and the anti-Federalists, who were called the Democratic-Republicans at the time. The Federalists, in power at the time with John Adams (1797–1801) as president, believed in a strong national government to expand the country's economic and geographic interests and protect U.S. citizens. The anti-Federalists, a leading member being Thomas Jefferson, believed a strong central government would weaken the power of the states, and, therefore, the people. The anti-Federalists sought to halt further growth of the national government. Thomas Jefferson became the anti-Federalist's or Democratic-Republican party's candidate against John Adams in the presidential election of 1800.

The "Midnight Judges"

After a bitter battle, Thomas Jefferson emerged in February of 1801 as the presidential victor. Adams and his party feared Jefferson would undo everything the Federalists had accomplished the past twelve years. He decided to pack the federal courts with as many new Federalist judges as possible before the Jefferson administration took power in March. Adams appointed his Secretary of State John Marshall to be Chief Justice of the U.S. Supreme Court. However, Marshall would remain Secretary of State through the last day of Adams' term. Adams proceeded to nominate more that two hundred loyal Federalists to new judgeships including forty-two justices of the peace in the District of Columbia. The Senate confirmed the nominations of the justices of the peace on March 3, Adams' last day in office. Working late into the night, Adams signed the commissions and Secretary of State Marshall placed the official seal of the U.S. government on them then supervised their delivery. The new judges became appropriately known as the "midnight judges." During these moments of confusion, several of the commissions were not delivered, including one to William Marbury.

Writ of Mandamus

Jefferson became President the next day, March 4, and ordered the new Secretary of State, James Madison, not to deliver the remaining commissions. Marbury and several others who similarly did not receive their commission petitioned the Supreme Court, whose Chief Justice was now John Marshall, for a *writ of mandamus,* ordering Madison to deliver their commissions. An amusing twist to Marbury's petition to the Court was that it was Chief Justice Marshall who had failed to deliver the commission the night of March 3. The *writ of mandamus* is a court order requiring a government official to take action and carry out his duties. In the Judiciary Act of 1789, Congress had authorized the Supreme Court to issue to federal officials *writs of mandamus.*

A Skillfully Written Opinion

Chief Justice Marshall wrote the opinion for a unanimous Court. Marshall, who history remembers as the greatest chief justice to serve, managed to craft a skillful opinion amid a highly charged political atmosphere. Marshall hoped to avoid a direct conflict with Jefferson, Madison, and the anti-Federalist whom he feared would simply say no if he ordered them to deliver the commissions. At the time, the Supreme Court had little recognized power to actually force other branches of the government to comply with its decisions. In an attempt to aid the growth of the young governmental system by deciding who would be the ultimate interpreter of the Constitution, Marshall established the principle of judicial review. The new principle allowed the Supreme Court to have final word on the meaning and application of the Constitution.

Marshall's historic opinion was divided into five parts. The first three parts were simple. First, Marbury had a legal right to be a justice of the peace. Second, Secretary of State Madison violated this right by withholding the commission. Third, the *writ of mandamus* was a proper way to direct a government official to carry out his duty. But, the question of who could issue the writ led to the fourth part of the ruling.

A Cornerstone of the American System

The fourth and fifth parts of the *Marbury* decision, brilliantly reasoned, established a cornerstone of the United States' system of government. In the fourth part, Marshall considered whether or not the Supreme Court had the power, or in other words the jurisdiction, to issue a *writ of mandamus.* Article III of the U.S. Constitution gave the Supreme Court two types of jurisdiction, original and appellate. Original jurisdiction meant the Supreme Court could be the first court to receive a petition and hear the resulting case. Article III gave the Supreme Court original jurisdiction over politically sensitive issues such as those involving "ambassadors" or when one of the states was named as a party. In all other cases, the Supreme Court has appellate jurisdiction, meaning petitions or cases must work their way through the lower courts before arriving at the Supreme Court.

Yet, section 13 of the Judiciary Act of 1789 allowed the petitioning of the Supreme Court and all federal courts directly asking them to issue writs. Although Marbury was neither an ambassador nor a state government, the Judiciary Act gave him the right to petition the Supreme Court first. Marshall ruled that this legislation violated the intent of the Constitution by giving the Supreme Court original jurisdiction in matters not mentioned in Article III. He concluded the Judiciary Act was unconstitutional, therefore invalid and not enforceable by a court of law. As a result, the Supreme Court, in response to Marbury's petition, could not issue the writ. This decision avoided a direct conflict with the Jefferson administration. At the same time, it also negated an act passed by Congress. Marshall wrote that it would be absurd to insist that the courts must uphold unconstitutional acts of the legislature. No act of Congress could do something forbidden by the Constitution. Marshall's reasoning

THE GREAT CHIEF JUSTICE

From 1801 to 1835 John Marshall served as chief justice of the U.S. Supreme Court, writing 519 of the 1,100 opinions issued during that period. His personality dominated the Court and the justices who served with him. His opinions, brilliantly reasoned and masterfully written, transformed the Court into a powerful branch of the American government system.

Born and raised in Virginia, Marshall was mainly educated by his father. An avid reader, he educated himself in law, taking only one formal law course at the College of William and Mary in 1780. Marshall served in the Continental Army during the American Revolution for almost six years and endured the harsh winter with George Washington at Valley Forge. From 1781 until his appointment to the Supreme Court in 1801, he held various government service jobs, first in Virginia and later as U.S. minister to France from 1797 to 1798, U.S. representative from Virginia from 1799 to 1800, and U.S. Secretary of State from 1800 to 1801.

Marshall's greatest decisions form the heart of commentary on the U.S. Constitution. He established judicial review of the courts over laws enacted by Congress and over acts of state government when either was challenged as not obeying the Constitution. His judgements defended the reliability of contracts and protected private property rights. He also convincingly argued that the Constitution was the permanent supreme law of the United States, to be interpreted by the Supreme Court. Marshall died in Philadelphia, Pennsylvania while still serving on the Court on July 6, 1835.

established the Court's power to declare an act of Congress unconstitutional — a monumental first which became a cornerstone of the American democratic system.

Lastly, Marshall considered whether the judiciary was indeed the proper branch of government, as opposed to the executive (president) or legislative (Congress) to have the final authority to overturn unconstitutional legislation. Although by the year 2000 this had long been accepted, the Constitution did not actually identify which branch should have this power. Marshall, describing for the first time the doctrine of judicial review, stated that the federal courts, above all the Supreme Court, have the power to declare laws unenforceable if they violate the Constitution. Marshall wrote, "This is the very essence of judicial duty."

A Check on Legislative Power

In 1801, when John Marshall became Chief Justice, the Supreme Court was considered weak and unimportant. The *Marbury* decision began its transformation into the most powerful judiciary in the world. *Marbury* provided reasoning for constitutional examination of laws by the courts. Although scholars have extensively debated the legal reasoning behind *Marbury,* the significance has never been challenged. Judicial review provided a clear check on the exercise of legislative power over the people.

Suggestions for further reading

Clinton, Robert L. *Marbury v. Madison and Judicial Review.* Lawrence: University Press of Kansas, 1989.

Hobson, Charles F. *The Great Chief Justice: John Marshall and the Rule of Law.* Lawrence: University Press of Kansas, 2000.

Schwartz, Bernard. *A History of the Supreme Court.* New York: Oxford University Press, 1995.

McCulloch v. Maryland
1819

Appellant: James William McCulloch

Appellee: State of Maryland

Appellant's Claim: That a Maryland state tax imposed on the Bank of the United States was unconstitutional interference with federal government activities by the state.

Chief Lawyer for Appellant: Daniel Webster

Chief Lawyer for Appellee: Joseph Hopkinson

Justices for the Court: Gabriel Duvall, William Johnson, Henry B. Livingston, Chief Justice John Marshall, Joseph Story, Bushrod Washington

Justices Dissenting: None (Thomas Todd did not participate)

Date of Decision: March 7, 1819

Decision: Ruled in favor of McCulloch by finding that Congress had a constitutional power to establish a national bank and states could not legally interfere with federal law.

Significance: The ruling established the principle of implied powers through a broad interpretation of the U.S. Constitution, giving Congress an expanded role in governing the nation. The decision also reinforced the supremacy of federal law over state law when the two conflict. The landmark ruling became the basis for key Court decisions throughout the nineteenth and twentieth centuries supporting congressional activities.

Article I of the U.S. Constitution gives Congress power to make laws. Section 1 provides "all Legislative Powers herein granted shall be vested in a Congress of the United States, which shall consist of a Senate and a House of Representatives." Furthermore, Section 8 of Article I enumerates (specifically names or lists) the specific areas where Congress may exercise its law making powers. These include the power to declare war, raise and support armies, provide a navy, regulate commerce, borrow and make money, collect taxes, pay debts, regulate immigration and naturalization, pass bankruptcy laws, and provide for the common defense and general welfare of the United States. Clause 18 of Section 8 also declares that "Congress shall have Power . . . to make all Laws which shall be *necessary* and *proper*" for executing (carrying out) its powers.

Almost immediately after the birth of the new nation, a question inevitably arose concerning the list of enumerated powers. Was Congress' power limited by the "necessary and proper" clause to only a few laws needed to carry out the indispensable activities clearly listed in the Constitution? Or, did the clause actually grant Congress broader powers to do almost anything "necessary and proper" to provide for the welfare of its citizens?

The answer came in 1819 in *McCulloch v. Maryland. McCulloch* provided the U.S. Supreme Court its opportunity to define how broad Congress' power should be and, additionally, to what extent states could regulate activities which fell within the powers of the national government. In *McCulloch* the Court specifically was asked to consider if Congress had the constitutional power to charter a national bank, and, if so, could a state constitutionally impose a tax on that bank.

An Unpopular National Bank

Following the American Revolution War (1776–1783) the new country urgently needed a sound financial system. In response, Congress established in 1791 the First Bank of the United States, located in Philadelphia. Many argued that the Constitution did not give Congress the power to establish such a bank. However, the bank closed in 1811 and the issue largely died. The need for a second national bank soon became apparent again in 1816, after the expenses of the War of 1812 (1812–1814) pushed the country into a financial crisis. The second bank was established by an act of Congress and began providing loans to state banks and private individuals.

Foreshadowing a long period of up and down swings in the nation's economy, the boon created by the national bank loans soon turned to a bust. Mismanagement of the national bank plus its extension of too much credit forced the bank to call in many of its loans causing many state bank failures. The national bank became very unpopular among the states. Individual states attempted to restrict the bank's operation within their boundaries. Maryland chose to try to tax the national bank's branches out of existence by passing legislation which, in effect, applied to those branches only. The Maryland law provided that all banks not chartered in the state but operating within the state must issue their bank notes (paper money) on paper bearing the tax stamp of the state. The tax stamp was a 2 percent tax on the value of every note issued, or 2 cents on every dollar. James McCulloch, the cashier at the Baltimore branch of the national bank, continued to issue notes without paying the tax. The state of Maryland convicted and fined McCulloch for issuing bank notes without paying the appropriate state tax. He appealed to the U.S. Supreme Court which agreed to hear the case.

Daniel Webster's Argument

McCulloch's chief lawyer, Daniel Webster, argued Congress had the constitutional right to charter a bank and its branches even though the Constitution did not actually enumerate the power to charter a national bank. He further pointed out that a state could not tax a federal activity. If that were allowed, separate states could control federal government actions, greatly weakening the federal government. Maryland simply responded that Congress had no power to charter the bank, and the state indeed had power to tax the bank.

The Court had two questions before it. First, did the "necessary and proper" clause imply (hints at) that Congress had the power to charter a national bank? Secondly, could the states tax a national bank or should national activities be supreme?

To Endure for Ages

Chief Justice John Marshall, writing a brilliantly crafted opinion for the Court, established two key constitutional principles which still persisted in the year 2000. In the first, the implied powers principle, Marshall reasoned that congressional powers actually listed in the Constitution such as the powers to issue money, borrow money, collect taxes, and maintain armies *implied* that Congress could do whatever was "necessary and proper" to carry out these activities including chartering a national bank. As a result, the Necessary and Proper Clause is also known as the Implied Powers Clause. Marshall's reasoning enables Congress to undertake activities not specifically enumerated by the Constitution but nevertheless implied. Marshall wrote that as long as congressional actions had a "legitimate" basis consistent "with the letter and spirit of the Constitution" they were constitutional. This interpretation greatly expanded congressional authority.

Marshall emphasized in *McCulloch* the Constitution must be flexible and adapt to human needs. He wrote, the Constitution was "intended to endure for ages to come, and, consequently, to be adapted to the various crisis of human affairs."

The second principle, that of national supremacy, prohibits states from interfering with constitutional activities of the federal government. Marshall stated that allowing states to tax part of the national government disrupted the supremacy of the Constitution and of national laws over conflicting state laws. Hence, states could not tax the national bank.

A Long Document

In *McCulloch,* Marshall made it clear that the Constitution of the United States was to be applied by courts with flexibility and awareness of the nature of each problem. The Constitution was to be a living document, adapted to new conflicts and situations that arise through the years. It was not to be applied in a narrow fashion limiting legislative power to the exact words written in the Constitution. Many laws passed later by Congress throughout the nineteenth and twentieth centuries were enacted based on Marshall's broad interpretation of the Necessary and Proper Clause.

The *McCulloch* decision also strengthened the idea of nation supremacy. Although the Supreme Court became more supportive of states' rights after the American Civil War (1861–1865), by the late 1930s the Court shifted back toward Marshall's earlier position. It began to invoke the Supremacy Clause found in Article VI, Section 2 of the Constitution, and again firmly established that constitutional acts of Congress were supreme and state law must yield to them.

Marshall's words furnished an insightful beginning for the new nation in interpreting the Constitution regarding the evolving active nature of the document and the concept of supremacy of constitutional

DANIEL WEBSTER

"Liberty and Union, now and forever, one and inseparable!" These words were spoken by then-Senator Daniel Webster (1782–1852) in a 1830 debate with Senator Robert Y. Hayne of South Carolina in opposition to a South Carolina proposal to reverse a federal law.

Webster is one of the most eloquent and powerful speakers in American history. He also was a lawyer, representative, senator, and secretary of state. Born in Salisbury, New Hampshire on January 18, 1782, Webster graduated from Dartmouth College in 1801. Beginning a law practice in 1807 in Portsmouth, New Hampshire, he quickly became a spokesman for the business community. In 1817 he moved on to become an influential lawyer in Boston, Massachusetts.

As an attorney, Webster argued more cases before the U.S. Supreme Court than any other. Many of the cases, including *McCulloch v. Maryland,* have been the most important cases in U.S. legal history, defining the powers of government under the U.S. Constitution. Being a strong advocate for broad national government powers in opposition to states' rights proponents, Webster became known as the "Expounder of the Constitution." First appearing before the Court in 1814, he won in *Dartmouth College v. Woodward* (1819) which prohibited states from interfering with contracts, won in *McCulloch* the same year recognizing broad congressional powers, and won in ***Gibbons v Ogden*** (1824) which first defined federal powers over interstate commerce.

Webster's eloquent speaking skills were further demonstrated in Congress. He served in the U.S. House of Representatives from 1812 to 1817 and 1822 to 1827 and in the U.S. Senate from 1827 to 1841 and 1845 to 1850. Though unsuccessfully running for President in 1836, Webster did serve as U.S. Secretary of State from 1841 to 1845 and from 1850 to 1852 when he died at his farm in Marshfield, Massachusetts. Daniel Webster was truly one of the most influential politicians and lawyers in U.S. history.

national laws. Marshall's reasoning endures at the start of the twenty-first century.

Suggestions for further reading

Gunther, Gerald. *John Marshall's Defense of* McCulloch v. Maryland. Stanford, CA: Stanford University Press, 1969.

Hammond, Brag. "The Bank Cases." In *Quarrels That Have Shaped the Constitution,* edited by John A. Garraty, New York: Harper & Row, 1987.

Remini, Robert V. *Daniel Webster: The Man and His Time.* New York: W.W. Norton & Co., 1997.

Robarge, David. *A Chief Justice's Progress: John Marshall from Revolutionary Virginia to the Supreme Court.* Westport, CN: Greenwood Press, 2000.

McGrain v. Daugherty
1927

Appellant: John J. McGrain

Appellee: Mally S. Daugherty

Appellant's Claim: That the U.S. Senate had not exceeded its authority in requiring a private citizen to testify before its investigation committee concerning the Teapot Dome scandal.

Chief Lawyer for Appellant: George W. Wickersham

Chief Lawyer for Appellee: Arthur I. Vorys, John P. Phillips

Justices for the Court: Louis D. Brandeis, Pierce Butler, Oliver Wendell Holmes, James C. McReynolds, Edward T. Sanford, George Sutherland, Chief Justice William H. Taft, Willis Van Devanter

Justices Dissenting: None (Harlan Fiske Stone did not participate)

Date of Decision: January 17, 1927

Decision: Ruled in favor of McGrain by finding the Senate had an implied constitutional authority to carry out a congressional investigation of Daugherty.

Significance: The ruling clearly established Congress' power to conduct investigations even without stating a specific legislative purpose. The decision dramatically expanded Congress' ability to investigate the lives and activities of citizens. This power has been regularly exercised by Congress ever since. The decision was also considered the first to uphold the power of Congress or the courts to override on certain occasions claims of executive privilege if a president, his cabinet members, or presidential aides were called to testify.

In 1927 the U.S. Supreme Court issued a landmark ruling, *McGrain v. Daugherty.* The ruling firmly established Congress' power to conduct investigations, even without any specifically stated legislative (law making) purpose and to gather information by requiring private citizens to give testimony. The ruling arose out of a situation referred to as Teapot Dome. Teapot Dome was one of the most infamous (bad reputation) government scandals in U.S. history and became a symbol of corruption in the U.S. government.

The Teapot Dome Scandal

In 1909, President William Howard Taft (1909–1913) set aside three tracts of oil-bearing land, Elk Hills and Buena Vista in California and Teapot Dome in Wyoming, for use by the U.S. Navy in case of an emergency oil shortage. In 1921, President Warren G. Harding (1921–1923) took office and within a year transferred control of the three naval oil reserves to his good friend and newly-appointed Secretary of the Interior, Albert B. Fall. With neither congressional approval nor competitive bidding, in 1922 Fall leased the reserves at Elk Hills and Teapot Dome to private oil companies of Edward L. Doheny and Harry F. Sinclair. Fall received $100,000 from Doheny for helping to organize the Elk Hills transfer. For the Teapot Dome transfer Fall had received more than $300,000 in cash, bonds, and valuable livestock from Sinclair.

Fall resigned his post at the Interior Department in 1923 when an investigation uncovered his dealings and joined Sinclair's company. Not until 1929 was Fall convicted of bribery, fined $100,000 and sentenced to a one-year prison term. For the first time in U.S. history an officer in a president's cabinet had been convicted of a felony and served a prison sentence.

A Senate Investigation

For some time after his 1922 dealings with Doheny and Sinclair, Fall had enjoyed protection provided by other government officials including U.S. Attorney General Harry M. Daugherty. Press coverage of the scandal flamed public distrust of the Department of Justice and Daugherty. Many questioned Daugherty's failure to prosecute those involved in the scandal. Daugherty resigned his attorney general post in 1923.

In response to widespread charges that Daugherty had mismanaged the Department of Justice the Senate passed a resolution enabling a committee to investigate his activities. The Senate twice issued a subpoena (formal order to a person to give testimony) to Mally S. Daugherty, bank president and brother of the former attorney general and, to appear before the committee and bring his bank records. He refused to respond to the subpoenas. Congress declared Daugherty in contempt (deliberate disregard of public authority) and John M. McGrain, Sergeant-at-Arms of the Senate, placed him under arrest. Daugherty gained his release when a lower court declared that the Senate had exceeded its powers under the Constitution by requiring him to testify on a non-legislative issue. The court said the Senate was acting as if it was a court but it had no power to do that.

McGrain appealed directly to the U.S. Supreme Court which accepted the case. The Court addressed the issue of whether Congress had the power to make these demands on citizens when no specific provision existed in the Constitution for congressional investigations.

Essential to the Legislative Function

Upholding the Senate investigation and contempt conviction against Daugherty, the Court issued a unanimous 8-0 decision. Justice Willis Van Devanter, writing for the Court, broadly interpreted the implied power (not actually written in the Constitution but suggested) of Congress to conduct investigations and issue subpoenas even without stating a specific legislative law making purpose. The ruling extended, as never before, Congress' power to investigate the lives and actions of private citizens by requiring them to appear before investigating committees to answer questions involving the matters at hand.

The Court addressed two key questions in coming to this decision. First, could Congress demand a private person to appear before it to give testimony even though this power is not specifically written in the U.S. Constitution? Justice Van Devanter wrote that "the power of inquiry — with process to enforce it — is . . . essential and appropriate . . . to the legislative function." Van Devanter continued that a legislative body can not wisely legislate (make laws) without being informed about conditions which it seeks to change. Frequently, it must turn to others for this information and "some means of compulsion (demand) are essential to obtain what is needed." Yes, Congress could require a private person to testify.

Second, was the testimony requested for aid in a legislative function? Rejecting the lower court's ruling that the Senate had attempted to

CONTEMPT OF CONGRESS

In 1857 Congress passed a law making it a criminal offense to refuse to give information requested by either the U.S. House of Representatives or Senate. The law is still in effect in an amended form at the end of the twentieth century. The offending person is considered "in contempt" of Congress. The first Supreme Court case asserting the Court's right to review contempt cases and set standards for congressional investigations was *Kilbourn v. Thompson* (1881). The Court ruled that investigations had to be in subject areas over which Congress had authority, their purpose had to be related to the passage of legislation, and they could not simply probe into the private affairs of citizens. Sixteen years later in *In re Chapman* (1897) the Court eased the standard. The Court ruled that Congress did not have to specifically state the legislative purposes of its investigations and that witnesses could be questioned in more areas of their lives than allowed in *Kilbourn.* In *McGrain v. Daugherty* (1927) the Court firmly established Congress' power to obtain information by conducting legislative investigations and forcing private citizens to testify, even without a legislative purpose being stated.

The modern-day language of the law, known as Section 192, states that a person may be "summoned [called forth] as a witness by the authority of either House of Congress to give testimony or to produce papers upon any matter under inquiry before either House, or any joint committee established by . . . the two Houses of Congress, or any committee of either House of Congress . . . " If the summoned person fails to appear or refuses to answer any question relating to the inquiry subject, that individual will be guilty of a misdemeanor and punished "by a fine of not more than $1,000 nor less than $100 and imprisonment in a common jail for not less than one month or more than twelve months."

carry out a court function, Van Devanter concluded that the information gained from Daugherty's testimony could be used in creating future laws. "The only legitimate object the Senate could have in ordering the investigation was to aid it in legislating," he wrote. Van Devanter added that while it would have been desirable to state beforehand what the legislative purpose was, it was not absolutely necessary. So, a legislative goal did not have to be stated before an investigation is conducted.

However, while the Court gave Congress broad investigative power, it did establish limits. Van Devanter wrote, "A witness may rightfully refuse to answer where the bounds of the power are exceeded or the questions are not pertinent [do not apply] to the matter under inquiry."

An Often-Used Power

Although the phrase executive privilege had not yet come into use, *McGrain* is considered the first Supreme Court ruling to uphold the power of Congress to override this privilege on certain occasions when the president, his cabinet members, or his aides are requested to testify. The phrase, first used by Justice Stanley F. Reed in 1958, refers to the doctrine that a president may withhold certain information, documents, or testimony of aides from congressional investigation.

The investigative powers of Congress set out in *McGrain* were repeatedly put into action throughout the rest of the twentieth century. In the 1950s those suspected of being communists were called to testify before House and Senate committees during the McCarthy hearings. The next decades saw investigations of the Watergate break-in scandal, Iran-Contra arms deals, and finally the impeachment hearings of President Bill Clinton (1993–). Countless numbers of less publicized investigations took place as new laws were crafted by Congress.

Suggestions for further reading

Davis, Margaret L. *Dark Side of Fortune: Triumph and Scandal in the Life of Oil Tycoon Edward L. Doheny.* Berkeley: University of California Press, 1998.

Owen, Gordon R. *The Two Alberts: Fountain and Fall.* Las Cruces, NM: Yucca Tree Press, 1996.

Stratton, David H. *Tempest Over Teapot Dome: The Story of Albert B. Fall.* Norman: University of Oklahoma Press, 1998.

Barron v. Baltimore 1833

Appellant: John Barron

Appellee: The Mayor and city council of Baltimore, Maryland

Appellant's Claim: That Baltimore's city improvements severely damaged his harbor business constituting a taking of property without just compensation in violation of the Fifth Amendment.

Chief Lawyer for Appellant: Charles Mayer

Chief Lawyer for Appellee: Roger Brooke Taney

Justices for the Court: Gabriel Duvall, William Johnson, Chief Justice John Marshall, John McLean, Joseph Story, Smith Thompson

Justices Dissenting: None (Henry Baldwin did not participate)

Date of Decision: February 16, 1833

Decision: Ruled in favor of Baltimore by finding that the Supreme Court has no jurisdiction in the case because the Fifth Amendment only applies to federal government actions and not state disputes.

Significance: The ruling legally established the principle that the first ten amendments, the Bill of Rights, apply to and restrain the federal government's powers but do not apply to state governments. This legal doctrine was not reversed until the twentieth century when the Supreme Court gradually included the Bill of Rights into the Fourteenth Amendment guarantees.

FEDERAL POWERS AND SEPARATION OF POWERS

"Beware! Beware!—you are forging chains for yourselves and your children—your liberties are at stake." Words spoken by Elbridge Gerry, Massachuset's delegate to the Constitutional Convention in 1787.

Gerry was one of a handful of delegates refusing to sign the newly crafted Constitution. As did many citizens of the newly forming nation, he feared a domineering central government. Memories of British rule were fresh. The British army had forced owners of private homes to house soldiers, they assessed unfair taxes, and customs officials invaded homes to search for smuggled goods. The Constitution as written did not contain a bill of rights, a summary of the basic rights and liberties of the people. The lack of a bill of rights, which many believed would guard against a strong-arm central government, was the most serious obstacle to ratification by the states. Only after the federalists, who favored a strong central, or federal, government and believed a bill of rights was unnecessary, compromised and agreed to draft a list of basic rights to be added later to the Constitution was the tide turned toward ratification. Thus, one of the first acts of the new Congress in 1789 was to pass the first ten amendments (changes or additions) to the Constitution that came to be known as the Bill of Rights. Moreover, it was common knowledge of the day that the Bill of Rights was added because people feared the federal government and not because they dreaded abuses of power by their state governments.

Approximately forty years later in *Barron v. Baltimore* (1833) the U.S. Supreme Court was asked to decide if an amendment in the Bill of Rights applied to state governments as well as the federal government. Their decision started an argument that lasted well into the twentieth century.

Barron's Business, Baltimore's Needs

John Barron and John Craig were owners of a large and highly profitable wharf on the east side of the harbor in Baltimore, Maryland. Located in the deepest water of the harbor, the wharf was a popular docking place for ships to unload cargoes into nearby warehouses. Renting their wharf to ship owners, Barron and Craig collected large sums of money.

As Baltimore grew two city issues arose. First, the city needed new streets. Secondly, with the larger population the older sections of Baltimore's harbor became filled with stagnant water, garbage, and debris. Responding to the need for new streets and in an attempt to end the health hazard in the harbor, the city carried out an extensive public works program between 1815 and 1821. The program involved regrading and paving streets, building embankments, and diverting the natural course of streams. The stream diversions happened to lead right toward Barron's and Craig's wharf.

During storms those diverted streams carried large amounts of sand and soil which ended up at the front of Barron and Craig's wharf. Through time the water steadily grew shallower until large ships could no longer use the wharf. His profitable business ruined, Barron sued the city in the Baltimore County Court for money to compensate (pay him back) for his financial loses. His partner, John Craig, had died, so Barron represented Craig as well.

The Bill of Rights and State Governments

In the Baltimore County Court, Barron argued the city had violated his property rights but the city denied his claim. The city attorneys justified their projects by stating that the Maryland legislature had granted the city power to pave streets and regulate the flow of water. The silting up of the harbor was an unfortunate "nuisance" affecting all of Baltimore's residents but not directed specifically at Barron. The County Court found in favor of Barron and awarded him $4,500 in damages. The city appealed to the Maryland Court of Appeals which reversed the lower court decision and ruled against Barron. Barron took his case to the U.S. Supreme Court. Before the Court, one of the arguments presented on Barron's behalf dealt with the Fifth Amendment to the Constitution. Remember, the first ten amendments make up the Bill of Rights. After hearing arguments, the Court decided the case should focus only on the Fifth Amendment argument.

The Fifth Amendment states that "private property" shall not "be taken for public use without just compensation." Barron claimed the city of Baltimore had violated his constitutional rights under the Fifth Amendment by destroying his profitable business without compensating him. Barron contended that the Fifth Amendment "declares principles which regulate the legislation of the states, for the protection of the people in each and all the states . . . " The question before the Court was: Did the Fifth Amendment, or any part of the Bill of Rights, apply to and "regulate" the powers of state government as well as applying to the federal government or did the Bill of Rights only restrict actions of the federal government?

"Of Great Importance" But Not Difficult

Chief Justice John Marshall wrote the opinion of the unanimous Court. This was Marshall's last major constitutional decision and, unlike many of his previous opinions, it restricted rather than expanded federal authority over the states. Marshall began, "The question thus presented is of great importance, but not of much difficulty." Marshall concluded that the Bill of Rights was designed to regulate the activities of and avoid possible abuses of power by the federal government and was "not . . . applicable to the states." Conveying his reasoning for the decision, Marshall wrote that the people of each state had enacted their own constitutions to control their state and local governments. He also pointed out that, unlike certain parts of the Constitution, no language appeared in the Bill of Rights saying the amendments applied to the states. He believed if the authors had intended the Bill of Rights to apply to the states they would have specifically said so. Finally, Marshall reviewed "the history of the day," finding the Framers of the first ten amendments intended them to guard against abuse of power by "the general [federal] government—not against those of the local governments." Thus, the Fifth Amendment could not be used by Barron to require "just compensation" from Baltimore for making his wharf useless. The Fifth Amendment could only apply to cases involving the federal government.

Finding the Supreme Court could not apply the Fifth Amendment to Baltimore or Maryland, Marshall dismissed the case.

Enormous Significance

As Marshall had written, *Barron* was of enormous significance. Courts in future cases expanded the decision to include all amendments in the Bill of Rights. As a result, the courts prevented the federal government from interfering when a state violated an individual's basic liberties and rights. Not until 1868 with passage of the Fourteenth Amendment did Congress try to limit the powers of state governments and protect the rights of individuals. Yet, the Supreme Court did not begin using the Fourteenth Amendment's guarantee to all persons of equal protection of the laws and due process or fairness in application of those laws until well into the twentieth century. However, by the year 2000 the Court had ruled that almost every right and liberty contained in the Bill of Rights must be protected by state governments, like the federal government, under the Equal Protection and Due Process Clauses of the Fourteenth Amendment.

AMENDMENTS ALLOW FOR CHANGES

Realizing the nation would need to make changes to the Constitution, the Framers provided a way to amend it or make formal changes. A constitutional amendment can be proposed by a two-thirds vote of the House of Representatives and the Senate. Also, two-thirds of the state legislatures can call together a national convention to propose an amendment, but this method has never been used. Once Congress proposes an amendment, three-fourths of the state legislatures must ratify or approve it. A second path to ratification is by approval of three-fourths of the states meeting in special conventions, but this method has only been used once.

The first ten amendments were ratified in 1791 shortly after adoption of the U.S. Constitution. They are known as the Bill of Rights.

Approximately 9,000 resolutions for amending the Constitution have been proposed in Congress. However, only thirty-three have gone to the states for ratification. Only twenty-six amendments have been passed and made part of the Constitution. Amendments generally fill a need the Framers of the Constitution did not address. Examples are the Civil Rights Amendments (the Thirteen to Fifteen amendments), need for an income tax (the Sixteenth Amendment), the right to vote for women (the Nineteenth Amendment), and limits on presidential terms (the Twenty-second Amendment). The latest amendment, the Twenty-sixth, was ratified in 1971 and gave citizens eighteen to twenty years of age the right to vote.

Suggestions for further reading

Levy, Leonard W. *Origins of the Bill of Rights.* New Haven, CT: Yale University Press, 1999.

Nardo, Don, editor. *The Bill of Rights* (Opposing Viewpoints Digests). Greenhaven Press, 1998.

Quiri, Patricia R. *The Bill of Rights.* New York: Children's Press, 1999.

Veit, Helen E., Kenneth R. Bowling, Charlene B. Bickford, and Charles B. Bickford, editors. *Creating the Bill of Rights: The Documentary Record from the First Federal Congress.* Baltimore: John Hopkins University Press, 1991.

Dred Scott v. Sandford
1857

Plaintiff: Dred Scott

Defendant: John F.A. Sandford

Plaintiff's Claim: That Scott, a slave, became a free man when taken by his owner to a non-slave state as recognized by the Missouri Compromise.

Chief Lawyers for Plaintiff: Samuel M. Bay, Montgomery Blair, George T. Curtis, Alexander P. Field, Roswell M. Field, David N. Hall

Chief Lawyers for Defense: Hugh A Garland, H.S. Geyer, George W. Goode, Reverdy Johnson, Lyman D. Norris

Justices for the Court: John A. Campbell, John Catron, Peter V. Daniel, Robert C. Grier, Samuel Nelson, Chief Justice Robert B. Taney, James M. Wayne

Justices Dissenting: Benjamin Curtis, John McLean

Date of Decision: March 6, 1857

Decision: Ruled that Scott was still a slave and that slaves and their descendants were property and could never be U.S. citizens and can never become a citizen. The Court also found the Missouri Compromise unconstitutional.

Significance: Instead of settling the slavery issue, the decision fueled the controversy further. The ruling most likely hastened the start of the Civil War.

A slave is a person who works for another person against his or her will as a result of force. Dred Scott was a Missouri slave who attempted to gain his freedom through the courts. His case reached the U.S. Supreme Court and on March 6, 1857 the Court handed down a decision. The ruling in *Dred Scott v. Standford* has been described as the Court's greatest mistake, a tragic error, a political calamity. Not only did the opinion cast a dark shadow over the Court's trustworthiness and prestige, but it most likely hastened the beginning of the Civil War (1861–1865).

Born in Virginia in the late 1790s, Scott was owned by Peter Blow. A plantation owner, Blow took Scott to Alabama in 1819 then, after growing tired of farming, moved his family and slaves including Scott to the booming frontier town of St. Louis, Missouri in 1830. Scott was sold in 1833 to an army surgeon, Dr. John Emerson of St. Louis.

Missouri Compromise

Scott's travels west mirrored U.S. westward expansion during the same time period. Americans had pushed west from the original thirteen states to beyond the Mississippi River. Slavery, which was permitted by the U.S. Constitution, became a serious political problem as westward expansion continued. Northern states who had chosen to be free states, not allowing slavery, wanted to keep the new western territories free. Southern states, slave states, wanted to bring slavery and the plantation lifestyle to the territories. Both sides feared that as new states were admitted to the Union, the other side would gain a controlling vote in the Senate.

In 1818 the Territory of Missouri applied for admission to the United States. Slavery was legal in the territory and most people expected Missouri to enter as a slave state. At this time there were eleven free states and eleven slave states. Therefore, twenty-two senators were from free states and twenty-two senators from slave states. Admitting Missouri would tip the balance. In 1820 an agreement called the Missouri Compromise was reached in Congress between its Northern and Southern members. Missouri was admitted as a slave state and Maine was admitted as a free state. The Compromise also banned slavery from north of Missouri's southern boundary, except in the state of Missouri.

The Compromise proved far from a final solution as slavery remained an explosive issue for the next four decades. Many questioned if Congress had the authority to prohibit slavery in any territory. The con-

Dred Scott was a slave who, like most slaves, wanted his freedom.
Courtesy of the Library of Congress.

troversy would play a key role in the *Dred Scott* decision.

Scott's Travels North

Scott accompanied his new owner, Dr. Emerson, on his assignments. In 1834 Dr. Emerson took Scott out of Missouri to a military post in Illinois, a free state, where Scott served his owner until 1836. Emerson then took Scott with him to a new assignment at Fort Snelling in the Wisconsin Territory (in modern-day Southeast Minnesota). At that time, the territory of Wisconsin was free according to the Missouri Compromise. Dr. Emerson kept Scott as a slave at Fort Snelling until 1838 when they returned home to Missouri.

Within a few years of their return, Emerson died, leaving Scott to his widow. Mrs. Emerson moved to New York in the mid-1840s and left Scott in the care of Henry Blow, a member of the family that had originally owned him. Blow, opposed to the extension of slavery to the western territories, financially supported Scott to test in court whether living in the free state of Illinois and in the Wisconsin Territory had made him a free man. Scott brought suit in a Missouri court for his freedom, arguing that since he had been a resident of a free state and in a free territory, his status had changed. The Missouri court held in January of 1850 that Scott was a free man based on certain Missouri state court precedents (previous rulings) which said that, even though Missouri was a slave state, residence in a free state or territory resulted in a slave's emancipation (freedom). However, the Missouri Supreme Court in 1852 reversed that decision by stating that blacks were destined to be slaves.

In 1854 Mrs. Emerson arranged a sale of Scott to her brother John F.A. Sanford (the Supreme Court records misspelled Sanford's name as Sandford) who lived in the state of New York. The sale to Sanford enabled Scott to again file suit, this time in a federal circuit court. Suits may be brought in federal court if the two opposing parties are citizens of different states. Sanford was a citizen of New York and Scott needed to show he was a citizen of Missouri. The circuit court ruled that Scott, as a black slave, was not a citizen of Missouri, therefore he could not bring suit in federal court. Scott immediately appealed to the U.S. Supreme Court.

With the issue of slavery persisting and Congress unable to find a political solution, the Court felt mounting pressure to seek a final solution to the slavery question. Therefore, the Court agreed to hear the case. First argued before the Court in February of 1856, the justices decided to post-

Commentary on fugitive slaves often appeared in newspapers and pamphlets.
Courtesy of the Library of Congress.

pone their decision until after the November presidential election because of the political sensitivity. After a second round of oral arguments in December of 1856, a majority of seven decidedly pro-slavery justices favored a narrow ruling saying it was up to Missouri to determine if Scott was slave or free and the Court could not interfere with that decision. However, the two dissenting justices, John McLean and Benjamin R. Curtis, both fiercely antislavery, made it clear their dissents would be much more far reaching. They were preparing to consider whether or not a slave could ever become a citizen, whether living on free soil made a slave a free man, and whether Congress had the authority to ban slavery in the territories. In response, each of the seven majority justices decided to write their own opinions. Chief Justice Roger B. Taney's opinion was widely viewed as the official position of the majority.

Never a Citizen

First, Taney declared that never could Scott or any slave or his descendent be a citizen under the Constitution. Taney wrote that,

> **. . . they are not included and were not intended to be included under the word "citizens" in the Constitution, and can therefore claim none of the rights and privileges which that instrument provides for and secures to the citizens of the United States.**

Taney arrived at this conclusion by examining the historical view of slaves and the original intent of the Framers of the Constitution. With stinging words he wrote that slaves "had for more than a century before [the Constitution was ratified] been regarded as being of an inferior order . . . with no rights which the white man was bound to respect . . . " Further, Taney said that blacks were not included in the words of the Declaration of Independence, "all men are created equal." Not only were slaves not citizens but, Taney continued, that slaves were actually regarded in the Constitution as property.

Taney, having presented ample reasons why Scott could not be considered a citizen, could have stopped at this point and dismissed the case. For if Scott was not a citizen, he could not bring suit in federal court, just as the lower federal circuit court had ruled. However, in order to let the nation know where the Court stood, the Chief Justice felt it necessary to address the issues of the free man on "free soil" argument and of slavery in the territories. Taney dismissed the idea that a slave became free just because he entered a free state. Whatever claim to freedom Scott might have had in Illinois was lost when he left that state and Missouri was not obligated to enforce an Illinois law.

Taney next decided that the ban on slavery in territories by the Missouri Compromise was unconstitutional, therefore Scott's living in the Wisconsin Territory did not make him a free man. Taney had reasoned that Scott was property and the Fifth Amendment said that no one could deprive a person of his property without "due process of law [fair legal proceedings]" and "just compensation [payment]." For Congress to deprive slave owners their property just because they came into a free territory would be denying slave owners due process of law in violation of the Fifth Amendment. Hence, the Court declared the Missouri Compromise unconstitutional and said that Congress was bound to protect slavery in the territories. This was only the second time the Supreme Court had used the power of judicial review which allows the Court to declare an act of Congress unconstitutional. The first was ***Marbury v. Madison*** (1803).

Stage Set for Civil War

Intended to settle the legal question of slavery, the decision actually fueled the controversy over slavery and seriously damaged respect for the Court. Animosity heightened between the Northern and Southern states. The Democratic Party split into northern and southern wings over the slavery issue, allowing Republican Abraham Lincoln (1861–1865), strongly antislavery, to be elected President in 1860. Historians widely believe the Scott decision hastened the onset of the Civil War just four years later.

The outcome of the Civil War and the amendments Congress passed immediately following its conclusion overturned the Scott decision. Congress passed the Thirteenth Amendment, ratified in 1865, abolishing slavery. The Fourteenth Amendment, passed in 1866 and ratified in 1868, declared all persons born or naturalized in the United States were citizens of the United States and the state in which they lived. It also prohibited the states from depriving any person of life, liberty, or property without due process of law or denying any person equal protection of the laws. These guarantees, indirectly the legacy of the slave Dred Scott provided the basis for the emphasis on civil rights later in the twentieth century.

MAN OF CONTRADICTIONS

Roger Brooke Taney (1777–1864), the fifth chief justice of the United States serving from 1836 until his death in 1864, was born in Maryland in 1777. Taney's ancestors had settled in Maryland in the 1660s and his father was a prosperous tobacco plantation owner. Taney built a thriving legal practice in Maryland, and married Anne Phoebe Carlton Key, sister of the author of the "Star Spangled Banner," Francis Scott Key.

Taney was appointed to the Court by President Andrew Jackson (1929–1937), whom he staunchly supported, to fill the seat left by Chief Justice John Marshall's death. Taney often appeared to be a man of contradictions. Taney, the aristocrat, insisted on wearing ordinary trousers instead of formal knee britches under his judicial robes. Although a persuasive leader, Taney assigned important opinions to associate justices to write rather than issuing all opinions himself, a break from past tradition.

Taney adhered to the Jacksonian principle that power should be divided between the states and federal government and believed the Court must determine that split. Many feared he would dismantle Marshall's federalist vision of a strong central government. While he did transfer some power to the states, particularly in the area of commerce (trade), he did not completely break from the nationalism of the Marshall Court.

Although Taney served on the Court with great distinction, he is best remembered for his infamous decision in *Dred Scott v. Sandford* (1857) where he ruled that slaves were so inferior as to possess no rights, could never be citizens, were property, and that Congress was bound to protect slavery in the territories. Ironically, years earlier Taney had freed his own slaves at considerable financial sacrifice and stated that slavery was an "evil" and "a blot on our national character." Taney remained Chief Justice until his death a year before the end of the Civil War.

Suggestions for further reading

Fehrenbacher, Don E. *Slavery, Law and Politics: The Dred Scott Case in Historical Perspective.* New York: Oxford University Press, 1981.

Finkelman, Paul. *Dred Scott v. Sandford: A Brief History with Documents.* Bedford Books, 1997.

Freedman, Suzanne. *Roger Taney: The Dred Scott Legacy.* Enslow Publishers, Inc., 1995.

January, Brendan. *The Dred Scott Decision* (Cornerstones of Freedom). Children's Press, 1998.

Mississippi v. Johnson 1867

Plaintiff: State of Mississippi

Defendants: U.S. President Andrew Johnson, General Edward O. C. Ord P **laintiff's Claim:** That the president should be stopped from enforcing the Reconstruction Act of 1867 because it violated the U.S. Constitution.

Chief Lawyers for Plaintiff: W.L. Sharkey, R. J. Walker

Chief Lawyer for the Defense: U.S. Attorney General Henry Stanberry

Justices for the Court: Chief Justice Salmon P. Chase, Nathan Clifford, David Davis, Stephen J. Field, Robert C. Grier, Samuel F. Miller, Samuel Nelson, Noah H. Swayne, James M. Wayne

Justices Dissentig:

Date of Decision: April 15, 1867

Decision: Ruled in favor of President Johnson by finding that the Constitution's separation of powers prevents the Court from stopping the President in carrying out his executive duties.

Significance: The Court refused to limit a president's power to carry out the laws passed by Congress, keeping the separation of powers intact. The ruling was important in defining the executive's immunity from lawsuits designed to block his political duties. The decision also held that the Court could not stop a president from enforcing an act of Congress, but could rule on the constitutionality of an act once executed.

Executive immunity refers to a concept highly important to the nation's chief executive, the president. While exercising his executive powers, executive immunity shields the president from judicial (the courts) interference. A court cannot demand or require a president to take action or, on the other hand, stop action on any specific political duty such as enforcing laws made by Congress. The concept is part of the Constitution's system of separation of power. The three branches of federal government, the executive (president), the legislature (Congress), and the judicial (courts), are each protected from undue influence by the others. However, the president's immunity has limits from all challenge. Under Article II, Section 4 of the Constitution. Congress may impeach and remove a president from office if it finds him guilty of "Treason, Bribery, or other high Crimes and Misdemeanors."

A key U.S. Supreme Court ruling on executive immunity, *Mississippi v. Johnson* (1867), came during a difficult time in American history.

Reconstructing the South

Following the devastating Civil War (1861–1865), the country was trying to heal and address problems that came with the end of slavery. The governmental programs designed to restore order and rebuild the South were called Reconstruction.

Although the post-Civil War battles were fought with words and laws, not cannons and guns, Reconstruction policies pitted North against South, almost as fiercely as the war itself. The North, as the Civil War victor, clearly held an advantage. Following in the footsteps of President Abraham Lincoln (1861–1865), President Andrew Johnson (1865–1869) tried to make Reconstruction a healing process. But, by 1867 a group of politicians in Congress known as the Radical Republicans had taken control. Most of the Republicans had been strong abolitionists (anti-slavery) before the war. Controlling the beaten Confederacy (Southern states) and establishing rights of newly freed slaves was their primary concern and mission.

Reconstruction Act of 1867

One of the Radical Republicans' first major pieces of legislation was the Reconstruction Act of 1867. The act divided the Southern states into five military districts and required the President to assign an army officer as military governor to each district. Military courts would hear civil (non-military) disputes. Further, the President was to provide a sufficient military force to assist the officer in enforcing his authority within his district. As a condition for reentering the Union, the act required states to draft new constitutions giving former slaves the right to vote.

South Outraged

The Reconstruction Act outraged the South. Within a month of its passage, the state of Mississippi charged the act was overwhelmingly unconstitutional and challenged the president's authority to carry out its programs. The state asked the Supreme Court to issue a permanent injunction (court order to stop an action) to stop President Johnson and their area's military governor, Edward O. C. Ord, from carrying out the congressional programs outlined in the Reconstruction Act. Never before had an acting president been named as a defendant in a case heard before the Supreme Court.

The federal government had been in constitutional trouble only a year earlier by using military authority in civil issues. Calling it a "gross" misuse of power, the Court ruled in *Ex Parte Milligan* (1866) that the government could not declare martial law (military rule) in an area outside a war zone that already had existing civil governments and courts. Mississippi was no longer at war with the federal government and had its own civil government in place. Therefore, the *Milligan* ruling gave the South hope that the Court would also strike down the Reconstruction Act programs.

Before the Court, Mississippi referred to the precedent (previous ruling) of ***Marbury v. Madison.*** In that famous 1803 decision, Chief Justice John Marshall held that the Court could command executive officials to carry out "ministerial" duties in order to fulfill their legal obligations. A ministerial duty was thought of as a rather simple duty not open to an individual's personal judgement. Mississippi claimed carrying out the Reconstruction Act programs was merely ministerial and, therefore, the Court could order the president to stop them.

Mississippi Denied

The Supreme Court unanimously denied Mississippi's request for an injunction. Chief Justice Salmon P. Chase, writing for the Court, held that the judiciary (courts) could not stop the president from enforcing the Reconstruction Act, even if the act was unconstitutional. The Court chose not to focus on the constitutionality of the Reconstruction Act, but rather on its enforcement by the president. To prevent a president from enforcing acts of Congress would stop a president from carrying out his constitutional responsibilities to the legislative branch.

In his reasoning Chief Justice Chase first distinguished between "ministerial" duties and "political" duties. Chase defined ministerial duty as, " . . . one in respect to which nothing is open to discretion [judgement or question]. It is a simple, definite duty, arising under conditions admitted or proved to exist, and imposed by law." Chase continued by defining political duties,

> **Very different is the duty of the President in the exercise of power to see that the laws are faithfully executed, and among these laws the [Reconstruction Act} . . . {H}e is required to assign generals to command in the several military districts, and to detail sufficient military force to enable such officers to discharge their duties under the law . . . The duty thus imposed on the President is in no sense just ministerial. It is purely executive and political.**

Therefore, Chase disagreed with Mississippi that the actions required to set the Reconstruction Acts in motion were simply ministerial duties which, according to the *Marbury* decision, the Court could order the president to carry out or, in this case, to stop acting on. Rather, these duties were political requiring the exercise of political judgement. Any attempt by the Court to direct how a president must carry out his political duties was, in the language of John Marshall, "an absurd and excessive" interference with another branch of government. Preventing the president from acting on congressional legislation would cause a "collision . . . between executive and legislative departments of the government." The House would then have grounds for impeachment against the president. With this reasoning the Court kept the separation of powers intact.

Concerning the constitutionality of the Reconstruction Acts, the Court pointed out that the Constitution requires Congress to pass laws, the president to execute (carry out) them, and the Court to review them once they have been put into action. The Court had no power to review the Reconstruction Acts before they had even been put into action.

SALMON PORTLAND CHASE

Salmon Portland Chase (1808–1873) was born in New Hampshire, the eighth of eleven children. He served as the sixth chief justice of the Supreme Court from 1864 to 1873. Chase presided over the Court through America's bitter years of Reconstruction. His rulings generally empowered Congress to direct Reconstruction and rebuild the nation.

Chase graduated Phi Beta Kappa (with high honors) from Dartmouth College at eighteen years of age and built a successful law practice in Cincinnati, Ohio. By the 1830s slavery, which Chase fiercely opposed, was the burning issue. A deeply religious man, Chase was morally incensed by the treatment of slaves and defended those who protected runaway slaves. Elected to the Senate in 1849, he quickly became a leader of the antislavery movement helping to create the Republican Party. President Lincoln appointed Chase secretary of the treasury in 1860 and chief justice of the Supreme Court in 1864 to fill the vacancy left by the death of Roger B. Taney. His firm leadership and commitment to hard work helped regain some of the Court's prestige lost with Taney's *Dred Scott v. Sandford* decision. Chase pushed for voting rights for blacks, but took a moderate approach to Reconstruction winning the support of Democrats. It fell to Chase to preside over the impeachment trial of President Johnson. His fair legal procedure probably saved the Johnson presidency.

Chase was passed over three times for a presidential nomination in 1856, 1860, and 1868. Although his fellow justices often complained of what they considered his excessive political ambition, they regarded him as a strong, efficient leader with superior judicial abilities.

A Presidential Shield

Following the *Mississippi* decision, President Johnson did carry out the Reconstruction Act and in 1868 the state of Georgia filed a similar suit. At that point the Court could properly examine the act's constitutionality.

The Court let the act stand continuing to allow Congress to rebuild the nation in whatever ways it believed appropriate.

In a legal sense, *Mississippi* helped shape the notion of executive immunity. The president was now immune (shielded) from suits that tried to prevent him from carrying out a law. Ironically, President Johnson was personally very opposed to the Reconstruction Act but had felt Mississippi's action was a direct threat to presidential power. Therefore, he had ordered the U.S. attorney general to oppose the state's request.

In ***Nixon v. Fitzgerald*** (1982) the Court expanded presidential immunity by ruling that the president was immune to personal liability (responsibility) lawsuits for actions he took while carrying out his duties in office.

Suggestions for further reading

Hart, Albert B. *Salmon Portland Chase.* New York: Chelsea House, 1970.

Hoffman, Daniel N. *Governmental Secrecy and the Founding Fathers.* Westport, CN: Greenwood Publishing Group, 1981.

Niven, John. *Salmon P. Chase: A Biography.* New York: Oxford University Press, 1995.

Stampp, Kenneth M. *Era of Reconstruction, 1865-1877.* New York: Knopf, 1965.

Selective Draft Law Cases 1918

Appellants: Joseph F. Arver and others

Appellee: United States of America

Appellants' Claim: That the Selective Draft Act of 1917 violated various provisions of the U.S. Constitution including Section 8 of Article I and the First and Thirteenth amendments.

Chief Lawyers for Appellants: T.E. Latimer, Edwin T. Taliferro, Harry Weinberger

Chief Lawyer for Appellee: John W. Davis, Solicitor General

Justices for the Court: Louis D. Brandeis, John H. Clarke, William R. Day, Oliver Wendell Holmes, Joseph McKenna, James C. McReynolds, Mahlon Pitney, Willis Van Devanter, Chief Justice Edward D. White

Justices Dissenting: None

Date of Decision: January 7, 1918

Decision: Ruled in favor of the United States by finding that the act did not violate any section of the U.S. Constitution.

Significance: The case was the first to reach the Supreme Court challenging the federal government's legal power to draft men into the military. With the power confirmed, the military draft was used at various times throughout the twentieth century including the Vietnam War (1964–1975).

In 1917 as America entered World War I (1914–1918), patriotic songs sounded in the hearts and minds of young men enthusiastically answering the call to register for the newly-established draft. Encouraged by government posters as well as the songs, millions stood in long lines to sign up. Yet others chose to not heed the call and refused to register. America has a long history of using conscription (drafting citizens into military service) to raise short-term military forces in time of conflict. However, opposition to conscription by pacifists (those who believe disputes must be settled by peaceful means), members of certain religious groups, and opponents of particular wars has an equally long history.

Raising an Army

Historically, during times of tension, America has often relied on volunteers to fight its wars. But, even in colonial times men were sometimes conscripted to serve in local militias (army of citizens called together in emergencies). Though colonies sent local militia troops to fight in the Revolutionary War (1775–1783), they denied George Washington's (1732–1799) request to gather a national army by conscription. The U.S. Constitution, adopted in 1789, gave Congress the "power to raise and support armies" but it neither called for nor prohibited conscription.

Not until the American Civil War (1861–1865), did the need to maintain massive armies bring a taste of national conscription to America. In April of 1862, the Confederate Congress (Southern states) passed a conscription law requiring every white man aged eighteen to thirty-five to serve for three years. However, the law exempted men in certain occupations such as teachers, ministers, and overseers of large plantations. Congress followed with the Union Draft Law of 1863 making every male citizen between twenty and forty-five years of age subject to the draft. Avoiding the unpopular occupational exemptions allowed in the Confederate states, the Union (Northern) law allowed draftees to hire a substitute or pay $300 to escape service. Three hundred dollars was roughly equal to a worker's yearly wages.

In both the North and the South the principle behind the draft laws was the same. In a democracy when the security of a nation is in danger, every citizen has the duty to serve his country. On both sides a majority of citizens accepted the draft as necessary, but much opposition persisted. Many objected to exempting some men from the draft. Others claimed the draft was unfair to the poor because a man with money could hire someone else to fight for him or simply pay off his obligation. Draft riots broke out across the country with the worst occurring in New York City in July of 1863. Although very controversial, the draft laws were never tested in the Supreme Court. The legality of a national draft remained unchallenged until World War I.

"I Want You"

America entered World War I in February of 1917 and immediately faced the problem of how to mobilize (build) an army. A large army would have to be recruited and trained at short notice. In response, on May 17,1917 Congress passed the Selective Service Act. The act required young men aged twenty-one to thirty to register with the government so that some of them could be selected for compulsory (required) military service. Substitutes and pays-offs were not allowed. The 1917 draft law did allow for exemptions in essential industries and for conscientious objector (CO) status. CO status permitted men who opposed war for religious reasons to avoid combat. Although twenty-four million men registered for the draft, two to three million failed to register. Approximately 64,700 sought CO status. Almost 340,000 failed to report when called or deserted after arrival at training camp. The U.S. government arrested many of the men who tried to avoid military service and some of those arrested challenged the draft law.

Draft Resisters

Among the many Americans arrested for not registering for the draft was Joseph Arver. After his arrest, Arver and several other draft resisters from his home state of Minnesota brought suit against the federal government. The Supreme Court combined the cases of the draft resisters into one case commonly referred to as *Selective Draft Law Cases.* Arver and the others argued that the Constitution did not give Congress power to require men, by use of a compulsory (required) draft, to serve in the military. They also charged the conscientious objector status violated the First Amendment's prohibition against establishment of religion. Lastly, they claimed the draft was a form of involuntary servitude (lacking liberty to determine one's way of life) forbidden by the Thirteenth Amendment.

"Supreme and Noble Duty"

The unanimous (all members are in agreement) Court rejected all of the resisters' arguments and upheld the Selective Service Act. Chief Justice Edward D. White wrote the opinion which all of the justices signed. To answer the first argument, White examined Article I, Section 8 of the Constitution which gives Congress power "to raise and support armies" and "make all laws which shall be necessary and proper" to carry out that power. The words of the Constitution seemed perfectly clear to White. He commented,

> **As the mind cannot conceive an army without the men to compose it, on the face of the Constitution the objection that it does not give power to provide for such men would seem to be too frivolous for further notice.**

White continued by noting that while a "just government" has a duty to its citizens, the citizens have a "reciprocal obligation (a returned duty or commitment) . . . to render military service in the case of need." White concluded the Constitution indeed gives Congress the power to draft men into the military if the need arises.

Next came the justice's quick dismissal of Arver's second and third arguments. White could not imagine how the Act's religious exemption for conscientious objectors could be viewed as establishing a religion and, therefore, in conflict with the First Amendment. He observed this line of thinking was too unsound "to require us to do more."

Lastly, White saw no similarity between what the Thirteenth Amendment called involuntary servitude and military service. The Thirteenth Amendment was intended to prohibit certain kinds of forced labor such as slave labor. The Court ruled citizenship carried with it an obligation to perform the "supreme and noble duty of contributing to the defense of the rights and honor of the nation as the result of a war declared by the great representative body of the people." This obligation does not violate prohibitions of the Thirteenth Amendment.

The Draft's Long History

The *Selective Draft Law Cases* established the clear right of Congress to conscript citizens. Later challenges to the draft often focused on the conscientious objector status. Conscription into the military ended in

CONSCIENTIOUS OBJECTORS

At the end of the twentieth century federal law recognized two types of conscientious objectors, the traditional conscientious objector (CO) and the noncombatant CO. Both were required to register but, if drafted, could object on the basis of religious, ethical, or moral beliefs. Traditional COs objects to participation in war in any form and would normally perform alternative civilian service instead. The noncombatant CO objects to killing in war in any form but would accept noncombatant military duties such as being a medic.

As early as the 1660's members of pacifist religious groups such as the Quakers were exempted from serving in local militias. The Selective Service Act of 1917 provided for CO status and exemptions from military service for members of historically designated "peace churches" including Quakers, Mennonites, and Jehovah's Witnesses. Of the 64,000 men who applied, 57,000 were granted CO status. Of those COs drafted only 4,000 used their certificates of exemption and were placed in various alternative services. Four hundred and fifty of the 4,000 COs were sent to prison for refusal to accept alternative service.

At the onset of World War II (1939–1945), the 1940 draft law required that "religious training and belief" be present for CO status but not necessarily membership in a pacifist religious group. The percentage of inductees exempted as COs was approximately the same as in World War I. However, between 1965 and 1975 with mounting opposition to the Vietnam War resulting in over 100,000 draft evaders, the Supreme Court expanded the definition of CO to include not only religious objections but moral or ethical ones as well.

1973 as the Vietnam War came to an end. Registration for the draft temporarily ended in 1975, only to resume in 1980 under President Jimmy Carter (1977–1981) and continue toward the end of the twentieth century. The goal has been to maintain a list of available young men in case a need arises.

The Court heard two cases concerning draft registration in the 1980's. In *Rostker v. Goldberg* (1981), the Court denied a claim that draft registration was unconstitutional because it excluded women. In 1984 another draft case ruling gave Congress power to withhold federal student aid from men refusing to register.

Suggestions for further reading

Flynn, George Q. *The Draft 1940-1973.* Lawrence, Kansas: University Press of Kansas, 1993.

Freidel, Frank. *Over There.* New York: Bramhall House, 1964.

Gioglio, Gerald R. *Days of Decision.* Metuchen, New Jersey: Broken Rifle Press, 1989.

Tompkins, Vincent, ed: *American Decades 1910-1919.* Detroit: Gale Research, 1995.

United States v. Curtiss-Wright Export Corp.
1936

Appellant: United States

Appellee: Curtis-Wright Export Corporation

Appellant's Claim: That the president has constitutional authority to prohibit arms sales to foreign nations at war.

Chief Lawyers for Appellant: Homer S. Cummings, U.S. Attorney General; Martin Conboy

Chief Lawyer for Appellee: William Wallace

Justices for the Court: Louis D. Brandeis, Pierce Butler, Benjamin N. Cardozo, Chief Justice Charles E. Hughes, Owen J. Roberts, George Sutherland, Willis Van Devanter

Justices Dissenting: James Clark McReynolds (Harlan Fiske Stone did not participate)

Date of Decision: December 21, 1936

Decision: Ruled in favor of the United States by finding that the president holds unwritten powers to conduct foreign policy.

Significance: By broadly describing executive power in foreign affairs, the Court provided a justification for the president to act in foreign affairs without requiring congressional approval. The ruling laid the groundwork for the exercise of future presidential authority in decisions concerning U.S. activity in foreign countries.

FEDERAL POWERS AND SEPARATION OF POWERS

In keeping with the principle of separating power between the branches of the government, in 1787 the Framers of the U.S. Constitution assigned some foreign affairs powers to Congress and some to the president. However, much was left undefined, particularly responsibilities during peacetime. Congress can regulate international commerce (trade), declare war, and approve treaties signed by the president. The president is commander-in-chief of the military, appoints ambassadors to foreign nations, and negotiates foreign treaties. The role of the states and the courts in foreign affairs is fairly limited.

Through the nineteenth century, the United States was not a world power and foreign affairs not a primary concern. However, at the beginning of the twentieth century the United States began to emerge as a world power with the president often playing the main role in shaping and carrying out U.S. foreign policy. Congress began regularly assuming a lesser role in developing policy, instead primarily reacting to actions taken by the president such as, providing funds for presidential initiatives (programs) or approving treaties.

Bolivia and Paraguay at War

In the mid-1930s Bolivia and Paraguary, two South American countries, went to war over a dispute as to who controlled an area known as the Chaco region following the discovery of oil in the area. U.S. arms (weapons) manufacturers were selling weapons to both countries. Concerned about remaining officially neutral in the war, Congress passed a resolution in May of 1934 giving President Franklin D. Roosevelt (1933–1945) authority to impose an embargo (prohibit trade) on arms shipments to the two countries, particularly if he believed it might contribute to the ending of the war. Four days after passage of the resolution, Roosevelt, believing it would help restore peace, used the authority to proclaim an embargo.

Curtiss-Wright Export Corporation continued selling armed aircraft to Bolivia. The U.S. attorney general filed suit in federal district court to force Curtiss-Wright to comply with the embargo. The company argued the embargo was an illegal use of presidential power because Congress, as the regulator of interstate commerce, had unconstitutionally delegated its powers to the executive branch, in violation of the separation of powers doctrine. The district court ruled in favor of Curtiss-Wright and the United States appealed the decision to the Supreme Court.

Broad Executive Powers

Before the Court was the primary question: did Congress' resolution unconstitutionally delegate (give your authority to another) congressional powers to the executive branch? If so, how much power could Congress constitutionally delegate. Justice George Sutherland, writing for the 7-1 majority, noted that this case fell into an area of governing not specifically addressed by the Constitution. However, he found that simply by the Unites States being a sovereign (politically independent) nation before the Constitution was written, that it had certain inherent (natural) powers to conduct international relations regardless if written in the Constitution or not. The United States had to meet international responsibilities. Sutherland wrote,

> **[T]he investment of the federal government with the powers of [conducting foreign affairs] did not depend upon . . . the Constitution. The powers to declare and wage war, to conclude peace, to make treaties, to maintain diplomatic relations with other sovereignties, if they had never been mentioned in the Constitution, would have vested [fixed] in the federal government as necessary concomitants [parts] of nationality [being an independent nation] . . .**

Further, Sutherland wrote it was primarily the president's responsibility to carry out foreign policy and he did not need an act of Congress before taking action. Sutherland commented that the president has "plenary [absolute] and exclusive [not shared] power . . . as the sole organ of the federal government in the field of international relations — a power which does not require as a basis for its exercise an act of Congress." No specific grant of foreign affairs powers to the president needs to be provided in the Constitution. Unlike domestic issues where Congress must supply clear guidelines to the executive branch when delegating congressional powers, delegation of foreign affairs powers can be broad giving the president considerable discretion (choice) on how to proceed.

Since the nation needed strong and decisive leadership for conducting world affairs, Sutherland concluded that such national sovereign powers as dealing with foreign nations must be controlled by the executive branch of the federal government. Therefore, the Court ruled that Roosevelt was acting within his authority in establishing the embargo and the companies must comply.

JUSTICE GEORGE SUTHERLAND

The *United States v. Curtiss-Wright Export Corp.* (1937) decision was remarkable not only for recognizing very broad presidential powers in foreign affairs. It was also a rare instance for Supreme Court Justice George Sutherland (1862–1942) to write a Court opinion in support of an action taken by President Franklin D. Roosevelt (1933–1945). The justice had long been an obstacle to Roosevelt's governmental programs.

Sutherland was born in Buckinghamshire, England in 1862 and received a law degree from the University of Michigan Law School in 1883. He became a U.S. House representative from Utah from 1901 to 1903 and a Senator from 1905 to 1917. President Warren G. Harding appointed Sutherland to the U.S. Supreme Court in 1922.

A strong advocate for private rights and limited government, Sutherland was a key member of a conservative Court that repeatedly overturned laws regulating business activity, claiming they were an invasion of property and contract rights. Typically, in *Adkins v. Children's Hospital* (1923) Sutherland wrote the decision striking down a law setting minimum wage standards for female workers. Sutherland claimed it violated a woman's right to negotiate contracts. In the 1930s Sutherland and the Court consistently struck down federal acts passed to revive the nation's ailing economy as part of the New Deal program. With strong pressure from President Roosevelt and the public for the Court to adopt a more flexible perspective on economic regulation, Sutherland retired in 1938. He died in July of 1942 in Stockbridge, Massachusetts at the age of eighty years.

Controversial Interpretation

Justice Sutherland's finding was controversial for its assumptions that foreign policy power was so strongly located with the president. However, the landmark decision established the doctrine of inherent powers. With this sweeping view of presidential powers provided by the

Court, the decision provided justification for future presidents, on numerous occasions, to make foreign affairs decisions that were later sent to Congress only after the commitment had already been made. The Court has almost always supported presidential actions in foreign affairs and war actions. Twice the Court even upheld executive agreements that did not receive Senate ratification (formal approval).

Primary examples of executive foreign affairs power were presidential actions taken in the course of the Vietnam War (1957–1975). Rebellion and disarray escalated in the country of South Vietnam in the late 1950s and early 1960s. In 1964 Congress passed the Tonkin Gulf Resolution giving the president power to take "all necessary measures" and "to prevent further aggression" in South Vietnam. Through the remainder of the 1960s presidents Lyndon B. Johnson (1963–1969) and Richard M. Nixon (1969–1974) committed a half million American soldiers to Vietnam and ordered countless military actions in an attempt to halt a communist takeover of South Vietnam. Largely failing to achieve the set goals, the presidential actions came under increasing scrutiny by Congress and the American public. In 1973 Congress passed the War Powers Act in an effort to restrict presidential authority in committing American troops overseas without first reaching an agreement with Congress.

Overall, this landmark decision further added to the growth of presidential powers through U.S. history. The powers of the president over two hundred years had grown well beyond what the original Framers of the Constitution likely had envisioned. It also reaffirmed under the principle of the separation of powers the Court's commitment to stay out of foreign policy disputes. Foreign relations issues are to be resolved by the two political branches of government, the president and Congress.

Suggestions for further reading

Barber, Sotritos A. *The Constitution and the Delegation of Congressional Power.* Chicago: University of Chicago Press, 1975.

Briggs, Philip J. *Making American Foreign Policy: President-Congress Relations from the Second World War to Vietnam.* Lanham, MD: University Press of America, 1991.

Fitzgerald, John L. *Congress and the Separation of Powers.* New York: Praeger, 1986.

Oregon v. Mitchell
1970

Plaintiff: State of Oregon

Defendant: John N. Mitchell, U.S. Attorney General

Plaintiff's Claim: That certain provisions of the Voting Rights Act Amendments of 1970 were unconstitutional because the U.S. Constitution reserves the right to regulate elections to the states.

Chief Lawyer for Plaintiff: Lee Johnson

Chief Lawyer for the Defense: Erwin N. Griswold

Justices for the Court: Hugo L. Black, Harry A. Blackmun, William J. Brennan, Jr., Chief Justice Warren E. Burger, William O. Douglas, John Marshall Harlan II, Thurgood Marshall, Potter Stewart, Byron R. White

Justices Dissenting:

Date of Decision: December 21, 1970

Decision: Ruled largely in favor of the United States by finding that the eighteen-year-old minimum age requirement is valid for national elections but not for state and local elections. The act's ban on literacy tests and state residency requirements for voting in national elections was also upheld.

Significance: The decision allowed young adults eighteen years of age to vote in presidential and congressional elections, but left it to states to lower the age in their state and local elections. This split in authority created considerable confusion in state election systems.

Speaking to a U.S. Senate committee hearing in 1970, then Attorney General Ramsey Clark urged Congress to grant eighteen to twenty year old citizens the right vote. Forcefully, Clark noted,

> **Young people are skeptical . . . about our [government] institutions. But youth cares. Care as it may, it seems powerless . . . What can the 18-year-old do about war which seems unbearably cruel, starvation . . . racial discrimination . . . threats to the environment . . . Youth is excluded from the initial step in the decision process devised by our system of government — the vote . . . We must start our young people voting during their last year of high school . . . involve them in our system . . . in meaningful participation . . . If we do, the system will work . . . The 18-year-old vote is an essential element . . . of American democracy.**

(Quoted from *The Right to Vote.* (1972) by Bill Severn, pg. 1)

Young adults, eighteen to twenty years of age, would be the last block of American to receive the right to vote in all elections, federal, state, and local with the ratification of the Twenty-sixth Amendment in July of 1971.

The People's Struggle

At the birth of the United States, only white males with property or wealth could vote. The Founding Fathers who wrote the U.S. Constitution in the 1780s left it to the states to decide who could vote. Consequently, gaining the right to vote for most Americans, such as black Americans and women, became a step by step battle spanning almost two hundred years. Young adults would also struggle for decades to gain the right to vote.

Twenty-one Equals Adulthood Equals Right to Vote

The concept that twenty-one was the age at which a boy became a man was long rooted in English common law. In the eleventh century a young man was not considered strong enough to bear the weight of armor and, therefore, unable to take on adult responsibilities until twenty-one. English settlers brought to America the idea that twenty-one was the accepted age of adulthood and applied it to the age at which a young person could first vote. The Constitution did not set a voting age. The states, free to set their own voting qualifications including age limits, consistently adopted twenty-one as the standard age to first vote.

Arguments to lower the voting age were often heard during times of war and hardship. The American Civil War (1861–1865), World War I (1914–1918), the Great Depression (1929–1940), and World War II (1939–1945) all forced many young people to take on adult responsibilities and brought the cry for change in voting age.

"Fight at 18, Vote at 18"—Georgia's Slogan

Georgia became the first state to grant all those eighteen years of age the right to vote in 1943. By the mid-1950s opinion polls repeatedly showed a majority of Americans favored giving young men who had to fight the vote. Yet, it would be twelve years before the next state, Kentucky, joined Georgia in lowering the voting age to eighteen.

Beginning with President Dwight D. Eisenhower (1953–1961) in 1954, American presidents through the 1960s continuously called for a national constitutional amendment to lower the voting age for all young Americans, eighteen and older. Young people of the 1960s, faced with the Vietnam War (1964–1975), pushed hard for an amendment. Yet, all attempts to move a constitutional amendment through Congress failed.

Voting Rights Act of 1970

To avoid the slow and difficult process of a constitutional amendment, Senator Edward Kennedy of Massachusetts and Senator Mike Mansfield of Montana amazingly managed to add the eighteen-year-old vote onto the Voting Rights Act Amendments of 1970. The act extended the expiring Voting Rights Act of 1965, put a nationwide ban on literacy tests (ability to read and write), established uniform thirty-day state residency requirements for voting in a presidential election, and reduced the voting age to eighteen in all federal state and local elections after January 1, 1971. Congress based its action in reducing the voting age on the guarantees found in the Due Process and Equal Protection Clauses of the

Fourteenth Amendment to the Constitution. The Due Process Clause assures no rights may be taken away without fair legal hearings and equal protection guarantees persons in similar situations must be treated equally under the laws. Congress found that requiring a citizen to be twenty-one as a condition for voting "denies . . . the . . . constitutional rights of citizens eighteen years of age but not yet twenty-one years of age . . . [and] has the effect of denying . . . the due process and equal protection of the laws . . . "

Then Speaker of the House John McCormick called the day of the act's passage the "happiest day" in his long congressional career. He feared without the act eighteen-year-olds might be kept from voting for years. President Richard M. Nixon (1969–1974), although strongly favoring the eighteen-year-old vote, felt Congress had no constitutional power to enact it. He believed the decision should remain with each state until a constitutional amendment was passed. Nevertheless, Nixon signed the act and instructed U.S. Attorney General John Mitchell to force states to comply. A U.S. Supreme Court test followed within months in *Oregon v. Mitchell.*

A Flurry of Lawsuits

Oregon and Texas each sued Mitchell in an effort to prevent him from enforcing the act in their states. At the same time the U.S. government sued Arizona and Idaho on grounds that those two states refused to comply with the act. All four cases were combined in the Supreme Court opinion in *Oregon v. Mitchell.*

A Door Opened Part-Way

The states challenged three provisions (parts) of the 1970 amendments to the Voting Rights Act. The challenged provisions were the extension of voting rights to those eighteen years of age, the ban on state literacy tests, and the ban on state residence requirements for voting in presidential elections.

The states argued before the Court the provisions unlawfully took away constitutional power reserved for the states to set their own voting requirements.

On December 21, 1970, the Supreme Court issued its decision opening the door part way to voting by eighteen year olds. Four justices considered the voting age provision entirely constitutional for both federal and state and local elections. Four other justices believed it was entirely unconstitutional in any elections. Justice Hugo L. Black, writing for the Court, sided partly with one group and partly with the other. First, Black concluded,

> **Congress has the authority to permit 18 year old citizens to vote in national elections, under Article I, section 4, Article II, section 1 . . . of the Constitution since those provisions fully empower Congress to make or alter [change] regulations in national elections, to supervise such elections, and to set the qualifications for voters therein.**

But, Black further concluded, "under Article I, section 2, the States have the power to set qualifications to vote in state and local elections, and the whole Constitution reserves that power to the States" except where specific constitutional amendments have taken away the state's power. He found that the due process and the equal protection clauses in the Fourteenth Amendment on which Congress had relied in passing the act applied only to racial issues, not age issues.

Thus, Black's opinion resulted in a majority of five agreeing those young adults eighteen years of age could vote in federal elections and a majority of a different five agreeing those eighteen could not vote in state or local elections unless the states so decided. The justices, in agreement, upheld the provisions banning literacy testing nationwide and residency requirements in federal elections.

An Administrative Nightmare

The Court decision that those eighteen could vote in national elections but not state or local elections threw state election systems into confusion. All the states who had not allowed young citizens to vote would now have to establish two separate systems of registration and voting, one for national elections and another for state and local elections. Hundreds of additional state and municipal employees would have to be hired and millions of dollars spent on voting machines or separate paper ballots to carry out the dual system. Completing the task by 1972 elections seemed impossible. In addition, many people believed it was obviously unfair to say a young person was old enough to vote for those who run the nation but too young to know about issues closest to home. Pressure quickly mounted from the public for a constitu-

YOUTH VOTING AND VOLUNTEERISM

Ratification in 1971 of the Twenty-sixth Amendment, lowering the voting age to eighteen, opened the door to approximately eleven million new voters. Many political observers at the time predicted high numbers of young voters would have a profound effect on U.S. politics. However, those eighteen to twenty years of age have participated in elections at a significantly lower rate than the general population.

Youth voter turn-out in the 1998 elections was the lowest ever. According to exit polls, only 12.2 percent of those eighteen to twenty-four years of age voted in mid-term elections compared to 19 percent in 1994. While voter turnout had hit an all-time low, youth were volunteering in record numbers. The University of California at Los Angeles 1997 annual survey of college freshman found 73 percent had volunteered in 1996. Youth were making a difference in their communities where they could see immediate results from their efforts.

Compared to volunteering, studies indicate youth do not get the same empowering feeling when they go into a voting booth. The two-party system appears old and outdated. A majority of youth who register to vote, register as independent and of the most politically active groups up to 80 percent decline to name a party affiliation.

Suggestions to close the gap between the number of youth voting and volunteering include: (1) expanding the two-party system and (2) allowing registration on the same as elections.

tional amendment to set a uniform voting age of eighteen in all states for all elections.

The Twenty-sixth Amendment was proposed in Congress on March 23, 1971. The Senate and House overwhelmingly approved the amendment. By July 1, 1971 the amendment had been ratified by three-fourths of the states. The ratification period of 107 days was the shortest in American history.

Suggestions for further reading

Arrington, Karen McGill, and William L. Taylor, editors. *Voting Rights in America: Continuing the Quest for Full Protection.* Washington, DC: Joint Center for Political and Economic Studies, Inc., 1992.

Cultice, Wendell W. *Youth's Battle for the Ballot.* New York: Greenwood Press, 1992.

Kids Voting, USA. [Online] http://www.kidsvotingusa.org (Accessed August 18, 2000).

Severn, Bill. *The Right to Vote.* New York: Ives Washburn, Inc., 1972.

United States v. Nixon
1974

Appellant: United States

Appellee: Richard M. Nixon, President of the United States

Appellant's Claim: That the president must obey a subpoena requesting him to turn over tape recordings of conversations with his aides and advisors to a special prosecutor.

Chief Lawyers for Appellant: Leon Jaworski, Philip A. Lacovara

Chief Lawyer for Appellee: James D. St. Clair

Justices for the Court: Harry A. Blackmun, William J. Brennan, Jr., Chief Justice Warren E. Burger, William O. Douglas, Thurgood Marshall, Lewis F. Powell, Jr., Potter Stewart, Byron R. White

Justices Dissenting: None (William H. Rehnquist did not participate)

Date of Decision: July 24, 1974

Decision: Ruled against Nixon and ordered him to turn over the subpoenaed tapes to prosecutors.

Significance: The ruling established a constitutional basis for executive privilege. It also held that the president is not immune from judicial process, and must turn over evidence subpoenaed by the courts. The doctrine of executive privilege entitles the president to a high degree of confidentiality from the courts if the evidence involves matters of national security or other sensitive information, but the president cannot withhold evidence involving non-sensitive information when needed for a criminal investigation.

As daylight broke over Washington, D. C. on Wednesday, July 24, 1974, the threat of rain hung heavy in the hot, humid air. At 11:00 AM inside the packed U.S. Supreme Court chamber those who came to observe the day's proceedings sat in anxious anticipation. Suddenly, through the silent stately hall with its pillars and burgundy drapes, the voice of the Court marshal crackled,

> **Oyey! [give ear] Oyey! Oyey! All persons having business before the Honorable the Supreme Court of the United States are admonished to draw near and give their attention for the Court is now sitting. God save the United States and this Honorable Court!**

The opening word "Oyey" came from medieval France, was passed on to England, and now to the United States' highest court. Along with the words came a system of justice based on evidence. The matter of the day, involving seven close associates of President Richard M. Nixon (1969–1974), concerned whether those men could be judged fairly in a court of law when all evidence surrounding their case was not made available. Nixon held that evidence, in the form of tape recordings, and refused to release the tapes by claiming executive privilege.

Chief Justice Warren Burger, strong and steady but without expression, read the Court's decision. Upon completion, at precisely 11:20 AM, the gavel came down and the eight justices (William Rehnquist was not participating) slipped back behind the velvet curtains. The Supreme Court had decided by an 8-0 vote that the executive privilege claimed by the President was not absolute (having no restrictions). The tapes must be handed over to the special prosecutor. For a moment the chamber sat motionless in a hushed stupor, the clack of the gavel ringing in their ears.

Theodore H. White, in his 1975 book *Breach of Faith,* wrote:

> **. . . the Roman lawmakers had said, "Let Justice be done, though the heavens fall." Justice at every level of American power, was now under way: in two weeks a President would fall.**

A Privilege

Executive privilege is the right of the president to withhold certain information, documents, and testimony of members of the government's executive branch, from public and congressional investigation. Although the Constitution never mentions executive immunity, historically presidents have claimed it to keep information concerning national security confidential or to protect communications between high government officials. Presidents base their claim on the vaguely worded separation of powers principle in Article II which states, "The executive power shall be vested [guaranteed legal right] in a President of the United States of America" to "take care that the laws be faithfully executed [carried out]."

Claims of executive privilege have actually been used sparingly. Presidents have generally honored requests from Congress for information. Yet, claims do go as far back as George Washington (1789–1797), who refused to let the House see papers relating to the Jay Treaty. Likewise, Thomas Jefferson (1801–1809) withheld from the House private letters written to him concerning the Aaron Burr treason charges. Presidents Andrew Jackson (1829–1837), James K. Polk (1845–1849), Franklin Pierce (1853–1857), and Theodore Roosevelt (1901–1909) all withheld information requested by Congress. In 1927 the Supreme Court in ***McGrain v. Daugherty*** ruled that executive privilege, although the

Less than a month after this case was decided, President Nixon resigned from office. Reproduced by permission of AP/Wide World Photos.

actual term was not used, did not protect the executive branch from honest legislative investigation.

During the 1950s in an effort to shield the executive branch from the bullying questions of Senator Joseph R. McCarthy in hearings on communism in the United States, President Dwight Eisenhower (1953–1961) wrote a directive on the presidential privilege. The letter stated that communications between executive branch employees must remain confidential. Not until *Kaiser Aluminum & Chemical Corp. v. United States* (1958) was the phrase *executive privilege* was actually coined.

Presidents John F. Kennedy (1961–1963) and Lyndon B. Johnson (1963–1969) assured Congress that only the president could claim executive privilege. President Nixon also agreed to this principle.

Watergate Scandal

The Watergate scandal began during the 1972 presidential campaign between Democratic Senator George McGovern of South Dakota and the Republican President Nixon. On June 17, months before the election which Nixon won by a wide margin, a group of burglars broke into Democratic headquarters located in the Watergate building complex in Washington, D.C. *The Washington Post* after investigating the story suggested the break in could be traced to officials in the Nixon administration. Of course, the administration denied all charges but it steadily became more apparent that members of the administration and perhaps Nixon himself had been involved in an attempt to cover up the burglary.

Public and congressional pressure forced Nixon to appoint a special prosecutor, Archibald Cox, to look into the matter. Cox filed a subpoena to secure tapes Nixon had secretly taped in the Oval Office of the White House which he believed would shed light on the Watergate burglary. A subpoena is an order issued by a court requiring a person to do something. Furious, Nixon refused the request and immediately had Cox fired. However, public outrage forced Nixon to appoint a new special prosecutor, Leon Jaworski. Jaworski was charged with the responsibility of conducting the Watergate investigation for the government.

On March 1, 1974 a grand jury indicted (charged) U.S. Attorney General John N. Mitchell and six other persons, all senior Nixon administration officials or members of the Committee to Re-elect the President. They were charged with conspiracy to obstruct (get in the way of) justice by covering up White House involvement in the break-in at Democratic headquarters in the Watergate complex. A conspiracy is a combination of two or more persons to commit a crime or unlawful act. Nixon was named as an unindicted co-conspirator.

In April 1974, Jaworski obtained a subpoena ordering Nixon to release certain tapes and papers related to specific meetings between the President and those indicted by the grand jury. Those tapes and the conversations they revealed were believed to contain damaging evidence involving the indicted men and perhaps the President himself.

Hoping Jaworski and the public would be satisfied, Nixon turned over edited transcripts of forty-three conversations, including portions of twenty conversations demanded by the subpoena. James D. St. Clair, Nixon's attorney, then requested Judge John Sirica of the U.S. District Court for the District of Columbia to "squash" (stop) the subpoena. Sirica denied St. Clair's motion and ordered the president to turn the tapes over by May 31.

Both St. Clair and Jaworski appealed directly to the Supreme Court which heard arguments on July 8. St. Clair argued the matter should not be subject to "judicial [court] resolution" since the matter was a dispute within the executive branch. The branch should resolve the dispute itself. Also, he claimed Special Prosecutor Jaworski had not proven the requested materials were absolutely necessary for the trial of the seven men. Besides, he claimed Nixon had an absolute executive privilege to protect communications "between high Government officials and those who advise and assist them" in carrying out their duties.

Less than three weeks later the Court issued its decision. The justices struggled to write an opinion that all eight could agree to. The stakes were so high, in that the tapes most likely contained evidence of criminal wrongdoing by the President and his men, that they wanted no dissent. All contributed to the opinion and Chief Justice Burger delivered the unanimous decision. After ruling that the Court could indeed resolve the matter and that Jaworski had proven a "sufficient likelihood that each of the tapes contains conversations relevant [important] to the offenses charged in the indictment," the Court went to the main issue of executive privilege. The Court rejected Nixon's claim to an absolute, unqualified executive privilege from the judicial process under all circumstances.

The Court Says What the Law Is

In their discussion of executive privilege, the justices first restated the principle in ***Marbury v. Madison*** (1803), "We therefore reaffirm that it is the province and duty of this Court 'to say what the law is' with respect to the claim of privilege presented in this case."

Next, the Court confirmed that the concept of executive privilege, although not specifically named, is rooted in the Constitution. Burger stated,

> **the protection of the confidentiality of Presidential communications has . . . constitutional underpinnings . . . A President and those who assist him must be free to explore alternatives in the process of shaping policies and making decisions and to do so in a way many would be unwilling to express except privately. These are the considerations justifying a presumptive [supposed to be true] privilege for Presidential communications. The privilege is fundamental to the operation of Government and inextricably [forming a tangle] rooted in the separation of powers under the Constitution . . . to the extent . . . [the privilege] relates to the effective discharge [carrying out] of a President's powers, it is constitutionally based.**

However, Burger found that the claim of absolute privilege in the absence of "a claim of need to protect military, diplomatic, or sensitive national security secrets" failed when weighed against the need for evidence in criminal proceedings. Burger wrote, "the President's generalized assertion of privilege must yield to the demonstrated, specific need for evidence in a pending criminal trial." Burger ordered Nixon to turn over the tapes to Judge Sirica for inspection.

Presidency Doomed

Nixon, in San Clemente, California at the time, issued a statement that he would obey the Court's order. He turned over sixty-four tapes to Sirica. Portions of indeed revealed the president himself had clearly been involved in attempts to cover-up White House involvement in the Watergate burglary. One tape, recorded on June 23, 1972, produced the voice of Nixon directing the Central Intelligence Agency (CIA) to stop a Federal Bureau of Investigation (FBI) investigation of the burglary. This was a clear obstruction of justice. Realizing Congress was ready to impeach him and, his presidency doomed, Nixon resigned on August 9, 1974.

NIXON AND THE SUPREME COURT

In the presidential campaign of 1968, Richard Milhouse Nixon promised to reshape the Supreme Court. The Court under Chief Justice Earl Warren had taken what many, including Nixon, felt was a liberal turn, being too sympathetic to defendants in the criminal justice system. Determined to move the Court toward his more conservative views, Nixon appointed four justices including, upon Warren's retirement, Chief Justice Warren E. Burger in 1969. Burger had been a hard line, tough-on-criminals judge in the U.S. Circuit Court of Appeals for the District of Columbia. Nixon also appointed Harry A. Blackmun in 1970, and Lewis F. Powell, Jr., and William H. Rehnquist, both in 1971. In the year 2000, only Rehnquist remained on the Court serving since 1986 as its chief justice.

Nixon's presidency saw more legal confrontations with the Court over presidential powers than any other administration. Although four justices were his appointees, Nixon was dealt a series of setbacks from the Court in the 1970s. In *United States v. U.S. District Court* (1972) the Court rejected 6–2 Nixon's claim of presidential power to carry out electronic surveillance (wire-tapping) without a court warrant in order to investigate suspected subversive activities. In a catastrophic decision for Nixon in ***United States v. Nixon*** (1974), the Court voted 8–0 to reject Nixon's claim of executive privilege in withholding tape recordings in the Watergate scandal. Nixon resigned his presidency only weeks after the ruling.

During his presidency, Nixon had claimed broad authority to impound (hold and not spend) funds provided by Congress. In 1975, the Court in *Train v. City of New York* ruled unanimously that Nixon had overstepped his authority when he had refused to distribute $18 billion in state aid under the Water Pollution Control Act of 1972.

No Man Above the Law

United States v. Nixon established the constitutional basis for executive privilege but recognized it was not an absolute privilege covering all presidential communication. The doctrine could not prevent disclosure of evidence needed in criminal prosecution.

Interviewing Jaworski over lunch within an hour of the decision, White related in his book that Jaworski said he had pursued this process to the end not for fame but for America's young people. He observed that young people must believe in America's system of justice for it to survive. White quoted Jaworski, "What happened this morning proved what we teach in schools, it proved what we teach in colleges, it proved everything we've been trying to get across — that no man is above the law."

Suggestions for further reading

Friedman, Leon, editor. United States v. Nixon: *The President Before the Supreme Court.* New York: Chelsea House Publishers, 1974.

Kutlen, Stanley I., editor. *Abuse of Power: The New Nixon Tapes.* New York: Simon & Schuster, 1998.

White, Theodore H. *Breach of Faith: The Fall of Richard Nixon.* New York: Atheneum Publishers, 1975.

Woodward, Bob, and Carl Bernstein. *The Final Days.* New York: Simon & Schuster, 1976.

Nixon v. Fitzgerald 1982

Petitioner: President Richard M. Nixon

Respondent: Ernest Fitzgerald

Petitioner's Claim: That a president should not be held legally liable for his actions while performing the duties of his office.

Chief Lawyer for Petitioner: Herbert J. Miller, Jr.

Chief Lawyer for Respondent: John E. Nolan, Jr.

Justices for the Court: Chief Justice Warren E. Burger, Sandra Day O'Connor, Lewis F. Powell, Jr., William H. Rehnquist, John Paul Stevens

Justices Dissenting: Harry A. Blackmun, William J. Brennan, Jr., Thurgood Marshall, Byron R. White

Date of Decision: June 24, 1982

Decision: Ruled in favor of Nixon by holding that the president possesses absolute immunity from civil lawsuits while performing his official duties

Significance: The ruling expanded the principle of executive immunity first recognized by the Court in 1867. The president holds "absolute immunity" from civil liability for actions taken during the course of carrying out his constitutional duties. The Court held that the presidency is a special office worthy of special protections against civil lawsuits.

The first key U.S. Supreme Court ruling on executive immunity, ***Mississippi v. Johnson*** (1867) came amid the bitter years of Reconstruction. Congress and President Andrew Johnson (1865–1869) were attempting to carry out policies to rebuild the nation following the Civil War. Executive immunity shields the president from judicial (the courts) interference as he exercises his executive powers. In *Mississippi,* Chief Justice Salmon P. Chase acknowledged that, according the ruling in ***Marbury v. Madison*** (1803), the Court could order a president to perform a ministerial duty. A ministerial duty is a simple, specific duty to carry out a government function. This type of duty requires no political interpretation or judgement. But, Chase explained presidential actions which did involve political judgements were beyond the reach of judicial interference. In *Mississippi* the Court had been asked to stop President Johnson from carrying out an act passed by Congress, an activity which would require the president to make judgement calls. This, Chase said, the Court could not do. It could neither require the president to take specific action nor, on the other hand, prevent him from acting in such situations. This ruling had its roots in the Constitution's system of separation of power—allowing the three branches, executive (president), the legislature (Congress), and the judicial (courts) to function without undue influence from each other.

Over one hundred years later, the Court in *Nixon v. Fitzgerald* (1982) strengthened executive immunity further. The Court granted the president legal protection from civil liability lawsuits when his official presidential actions caused loses to another party. Civil liability are legal terms describing the situation of being subject to a legal obligation or responsibility such as having to pay damages (money) to an injured party when a dispute is settled. Civil means these disputes are between individuals in such areas as contracts, property, and family law. They do not involve criminal law. In *Nixon,* the Court decided on a very broad protection for the president from civil liability which they called "absolute immunity." The case arose from the predicament of Ernest Fitzgerald.

Ernest Loses His Job

Employed by the U.S. Air Force, Ernest Fitzgerald worked as a cost analyst, one who analyzes the spending of an agency or company. In the last months of President Lyndon B. Johnson's (1963–1969) administration, Fitzgerald testified before Congress that he had discovered serious cost overruns, excessive unbudgeted spending, on the C-5A transport plane development project. Angry over Fitzgerald's testimony, embarrassed officials at the Defense Department planned a way to eliminate his job. Supposedly, as part of a money saving reorganization effort, Fitzgerald's job was done away with in 1969 when President Richard M. Nixon (1969–1974) came into office. Nixon in a news conference said he was responsible for Fitzgerald's removal but later retracted (changed) that statement and denied responsibility. Fitzgerald believed he had lost his job directly because of his testimony on Capitol Hill. Fitzgerald complained to the Civil Service Commission which, although not finding a political plot, reinstated him saying he was removed for personal reasons. In 1982, Fitzgerald sued former President Nixon for damages.

The lower federal courts declared the president immune and dismissed Fitzgerald's suit. However, the court of appeals reversed the decision saying Nixon did not have immunity. Nixon appealed to the U.S. Supreme Court.

Many Important Questions

Many important questions were in front of the Court. Should the president be immune from actions taken in performance of official duties? If

Ernest Fitzgerald felt that his job was unfairly eliminated. Reproduced by permission of AP/Wide World Photos.

so, should the immunity be absolute (with no exceptions) or should there merely be limits set on when a president can be sued? Taking a different approach, should focus be on the actions themselves with some actions immune and others not? Or, finally, should a president simply be shielded from all suits because of the distraction and disruptions they would create? These were the important questions the Court considered.

An Easy Target

In a 5-4 decision, the Court ruled in favor of Nixon saying a president is immune from all civil lawsuits resulting from his actions as president. Justice Lewis F. Powell, Jr., wrote the majority opinion observing that the president's office was unique and different from all other executive offices. The president dealt with incredibly important issues often highly sensitive and highly charged, arousing citizens' passions. Powell commented,

> **In view of the visibility of his office and the effect of his actions on countless people, the President would be an easily identifiable target for suits for civil damages . . . this personal vulnerability [open to attack or criticism] frequently could distract a President from his public duties, to the detriment [harm] not only of the President and his office but also the Nation that the Presidency was designed to serve.**

Due to these "special" circumstances the Court found "absolute immunity" from all civil lawsuits appropriate. The Court rejected the line of thinking that immunity should be based on the action with some actions immune and others not. If this rule was adopted, every action a president takes would be subject to cries of unfairness. Therefore, the Court said the office as a whole, not individual actions, would be shielded with immunity.

Above the Law?

The dissenting justices believed the Court's opinion placed "the President above the law." To them the president could cause injury to "any number of citizens even though he knows his conduct violates a statute [law] or tramples on the constitutional rights of those who are injured."

Justice Powell responded by listing the many other ways besides a civil lawsuit that a president may be held accountable for his actions. The

EXECUTIVE IMMUNITY AND EXECUTIVE PRIVILEGE

While no mention of either is made in the U.S. Constitution, both executive immunity and executive privilege are important to the president as he exercises his power. Both immunities shield the president to a large degree from interference by the other two branches of government. Executive immunity and privilege are grounded in the Constitution's system of separation of powers.

Executive immunity protects the president from court interference with his policy-making duties. For example, a court cannot require a president to take action or, on the other hand, stop action on any specific political duty such as making policies to carry out laws passed by Congress. The president is also immune from any civil lawsuits brought against him for actions taken in performance of his duties.

Executive privilege allows the president to withhold, in certain instances, information, testimony of aides, and documents from public or congressional probes. This privilege was first used by George Washington, but not until ***United States v. Nixon*** (1974) did the Supreme Court recognize it formally as a limited privilege.

list included impeachment, scrutiny by the media, the desire to avoid misconduct or win reelection, and consideration of one's reputation in history.

Companion Case

Decided the same day as *Nixon* was the companion case *Harlow v. Fitzgerald.* In this case the Court held that the president's aides were not entitled to absolute immunity from civil lawsuits. Their immunity was qualified meaning they were protected unless their actions violated a clearly established law which a "reasonable person" should have been aware of.

Suggestions for further reading

Aitken, Jonathan. *Nixon: A Life.* Washington, DC: Regnery Publishers, 1996.

Berger, Raoul. *Executive Privilege: A Constitutional Myth.* Cambridge, MA: Harvard University Press, 1974.

Maroon, Fred J., and Tom Wicker. *The Nixon Years, 1969-1974: White House to Watergate.* New York: Abbeville Press, 1999.

Morrison v. Olson
1988

Appellant: Alexia Morrison

Appellee: Theodore B. Olson, Edward Schmults, Carol E. Dinkins

Appellant's Claim: That the Ethics in Government Act of 1978 which allowed for appointment of an independent counsel to investigate wrongdoing by federal officials did not violate the Appointment Clause of the Constitution or the principle of separation of powers.

Chief Lawyer for Appellant: Alexia Morrison

Chief Lawyer for Appellee: Thomas S. Martin

Justices for the Court: Harry A. Blackmun, William J. Brennan, Jr., Thurgood Marshall, Sandra Day O'Connor, Chief Justice William H. Rehnquist, John Paul Stevens, Byron R. White

Justices Dissenting: Antonin Scalia (Anthony M. Kennedy did not participate)

Date of Decision: June 27, 1988

Decision: Ruled in favor of Morrison by finding that the act was constitutionally valid.

Significance: The ruling reaffirmed the role of independent counsel in investigating federal officials, including the president. The Court determined that a judicial office within the executive branch of government did not violate the separation of powers concepts basic to the federal government.

"Whether ours shall continue to be a government of laws and not of men is now for Congress and ultimately the American people [to decide]." Words spoken by Archibald Cox immediately after being fired as special prosecutor investigating the Watergate scandal.

It all began in the summer of 1972 when someone broke into offices belonging to the Democratic Party in Washington's Watergate Complex. By 1973 newspaper stories suggested involvement by officials in the administration of President Richard M. Nixon (1969–1974). As a result, Attorney General Elliot L. Richardson, in May of 1973, selected Archibald Cox as special prosecutor to investigate the affair.

As the investigation widened, it appeared that White House officials had played a part and Cox requested from Nixon audio tapes of White House conversations. On Saturday night October 20, 1973 an outraged Nixon ordered Richardson to fire Cox. Refusing to carry out Nixon's order, Richardson and then his deputy attorney general, William D. Ruckleshaus, the top two officials of the Justice Department, resigned in protest. Later that night Robert Bock, the solicitor general, fired Cox. The night's events became known as the "Saturday Night Massacre" and left the American public reeling in dismay over Nixon's actions.

By the time the Watergate affair came to an end with Nixon's resignation in 1974, the foundation of the federal government had been shaken. Cover-ups, investigations, and controversies had pitted the three branches of government — executive, legislative, and judicial against each other. Controversy over the special prosecutor's power to investigate officials of the executive branch including the president had been particularly combative and disruptive. Congress decided an independent (free from others) prosecutor was indeed useful to investigate and check government misconduct but guidelines were needed to better define the appointment process and prosecutor's duties. Hence, as a last echo of Watergate, and largely triggered by the Saturday Night Massacre, Congress passed the Ethics in Government Act in 1978.

Ethics in Government Act

Title VI of the Ethics Act provided for the appointment of special prosecutor to investigate and, if necessary, prosecute high ranking government officials for violations of federal criminal law. The term special prosecutor was later changed to the less threatening term, "independent counsel."

Need for an independent counsel (lawyer) on occasion arose because of the severe conflict of interest that had become so clear during the Watergate matter. In the U.S. criminal justice system, prosecutors and law enforcement agencies work under supervision of government leaders in the executive branch. Should those government leaders be accused of misconduct, the federal attorneys and agencies are placed in the difficult position of upholding the law while remaining loyal to their supervisors. As the Saturday Night Massacre illustrated, they would labor under the real threat of being fired. Use of an independent counsel was suppose to avoid this conflict.

The act requires the Justice Department's attorney general (in the executive branch), upon receiving information concerning wrongdoing by a high government official, to conduct an investigation and report to a court of three judges in the judicial branch called the Special Division. The Special Division was placed by the act within the U.S. Court of Appeals for the District of Columbia. In his report, the attorney general may request appointment of an independent counsel to investigate the issue. If so, the Special Division, not the attorney general, chooses and appoints an independent counsel.

The counsel has "full power and independent authority to exercise all investigative and prosecutorial (legal trial proceedings) functions that are allowed any other officer of the Department of Justice." The counsel may be dismissed only by the attorney general and only for "good cause" with follow up reports to the Special Division. The office of independent counsel terminates (ends) when investigations or prosecutions are completed.

The independent counsel must also report on his or her activities from time to time to Congress (the legislative branch) so that Congress can watch over the official conduct of the counsel. The act allows congressional committees to request the attorney general to start the process of selecting an independent counsel to look into particular issues.

Independent Counsel Alexia Morrison

Following passage of the Ethics Act a controversy developed between the House of Representatives and the Environmental Protection Agency (EPA). The EPA only partly-supplied documents subpoenaed (formally ordered) by the House for an ongoing investigation. Upon looking further into the matter, the House Judiciary Committee found that an official in the attorney general's office, Theodore Olson, had most likely given false testimony during the course of the investigation. A copy of the Judiciary Committee's report was sent to the attorney general requesting appointment of an independent counsel to investigate Olson's actions. The attorney general found evidence of possible wrongdoing, and requested the Special Division to appoint an independent counsel. Alexia Morrison was appointed on May 29, 1986.

Morrison soon began investigating if others in the attorney general's office had joined with Olson to interfer with the House's EPA investigation. When, under Morrison's direction, a grand jury subpoenaed Olson, deputy attorney general Edward Schmults, and Carol E. Dinkins, the three refused to comply. They claimed the office of independent counsel was unconstitutional.

"How the Act Works in Practice"

Morrison went to court to have the subpoenas enforced. Having worked its way through the district court and court of appeals, the case found its way to the U.S. Supreme Court in April of 1988. Chief Justice William H. Rehnquist, writing for the majority in the 7-1 decision, commented that, "the proceedings in this case provide an example of how the Act [Ethics in Government Act] works in practice."

Three Constitutional Concerns

Chief Justice Rehnquist addressed three principle constitutional concerns with the act. The first issue related to the Appointments Clause found in Article II of the Constitution. The clause states, "Congress may by law vest [place authority in] the appointment of such inferior [lower ranking] officers, as they think proper, in the President alone, in the courts of law, or in the heads of departments." Although an earlier part of the clause allows only the president to make major appointments such as ambassadors, judges, the Supreme Court, and cabinet officials, this part permits Congress to give the President or a court of law power to select certain "inferior" officials. The Ethics Act indeed created a special court, the Special Division, to appoint an inferior official, the independent counsel. Rehnquist wrote the act did not violate the Appointment Clause as the Constitution clearly gave Congress power to allow a court of law to appoint an official in the executive department. However, the court of appeals had decided that the independent counsel was more than an "inferior" official because of the large amount of the counsel's legal power. Rehnquist disagreed. The independent counsel is an "inferior" officer since Morrison could be removed by the attorney general at any time and her office would terminate upon completion of her duties.

Secondly, Rehnquist ruled that the powers given to the Special Division to appoint an independent counsel did not violate Article III of the Constitution. Article III prevents the judiciary (courts) from taking over executive duties of a non-judicial nature in order "to maintain the separation between the Judiciary and the other branches of the Federal Government." Rehnquist wrote that the Special Divisions powers to "receive" reports from the counsel with no authority to act on or approve the reports, and to terminate the office only at the request of the attorney general in no way be considered as the courts taking over executive duties.

Lastly, Rehnquist addressed the issue of separation of powers. The attorney general's office claimed the act's limiting "the Attorney General's power to remove the independent counsel to only those instances in which he can show good cause" unconstitutionally interfered with "the President's exercise of his appointed functions." Rehnquist reasoned, "The congressional determination [through the act] to limit the Attorney General's removal power [and hence the President's power to suddenly fire the counsel] was essential . . . to establish the necessary independence of the office of independent counsel . . . [T]he Act, taken as a whole, does not violate the principle of separation of powers by unduly interfering with the Executive Branch's role."

Politically Charged

Considered a victory for Congress in general, the ruling strongly affirmed the role and power of independent counsels and gave support to other ongoing investigations into administration activities. The very nature of independent counsel removed politically charged since the counsel investigates executive branch officials and their operations. Through the 1980s and 1990s Congress was commonly controlled by one political party while the executive branch by the other, making the role of counsel even more controversial by appearing highly political. Yet, most politicians viewed the independent counsel as necessary to check misconduct and maintain a balance of power in government.

The list of federal government officials investigated by an independent

KENNETH W. STARR

The many pros and cons concerning the role of an independent counsel were dramatized through the 1990s. Prolonged investigations of President Bill Clinton's activities were primarily led by independent counsel Kenneth W. Starr. Starr became the focus of controversy over the usefulness of independent counsels. Born in Vernon, Texas in 1946, Starr attended Duke University Law School and became legal clerk for Supreme Court Chief Justice Warren E. Burger. In 1981 at the beginning of the Ronald Reagan (1981–1989) term, he joined the Justice Department and later appointed by Reagan as judge on the prestigious U.S. Court of Appeals for the District of Columbia. At thirty-seven years of age, Starr was the youngest person ever appointed to the court of appeals. In 1989 he became solicitor general for President George Bush's (1989–1993) administration, returning to private practice with election of Clinton.

In August of 1994 Starr was selected independent counsel to investigate the Whitewater bank scandal of Clinton and his associates. For the next six years Starr also investigated the death of White House counsel Vincent Foster, the firing of White House travel employees, and the Monica Lewinsky scandal. In 1996 during the travel investigation, Starr became the first to ever request the First Lady of the United States to testify before a grand jury. In 1998 Starr subpoenaed Clinton to testify before the grand jury regarding the Lewinsky scandal. Starr's investigation led to the impeachment trial of Clinton which ended in acquittal in February of 1999.

Starr's activities again raised all of the controversies over the appropriateness of independent counsels. He was criticized for being partisan in his inquiries and for running up major expenses, totaling $40 million by late 1998. For all of the expense and effort, few convictions actually resulted. Ironically, in 1999 Starr testified before Congress in opposition to extending the independent counsel portions of the Ethics Act.

counsel have steadily grown. Two White House aides to President Reagan were convicted of wrongdoing in 1987 and 1988. The *Morrison* decision acted to uphold their convictions though one of the convictions was later overturned. Reagan's attorney general Edwin Meese III resigned in 1988 following an investigation which reported possible wrongdoing by Meese. From 1986 to 1993 an independent counsel investigated what was known as the Iran-Contra Affair involving secretly selling arms to Iran and using the funds to finance a war in Nicaragua. Several Reagan administration officials were convicted of wrongdoing related to the operation. Perhaps best known were the ongoing investigations of President Bill Clinton (1993–) and his staff on numerous charges of wrongdoing, ranging from financial to sexual misconduct. Kenneth W. Starr served as independent counsel from 1994 to 2000.

Suggestions for further reading

Carville, James. *And the Horse He Rode In On: The People v. Kenneth Starr.* New York: Simon & Schuster, 1998.

Gormley, Ken, and Elliot Richardson. *Archibald Cox: Conscience of a Nation.* Reading, MA: Addison-Wesley, 1997.

Harriges, Katy J. *The Special Prosecutor in American Politics.* Second edition. Lawrence: University Press of Kansas, 2000.

Schmidt, Susan, and Michael Weisskopf. *Truth at Any Cost: Ken Starr and the Unmaking of Bill Clinton.* New York: HarperCollins, 2000.

Clinton v. Jones 1997

Petitioner: William J. Clinton, President of the United States

Respondent: Paula Corbin Jones

Petitioner's Claim: That the president of the United States during the term of his presidency is immune from a civil lawsuit challenging his actions prior to his taking office.

Chief Lawyer for Petitioner: Robert S. Bennett

Chief Lawyer for Respondent: Gilbert K. Davis

Justices for the Court: Stephen Breyer, Ruth Bader Ginsburg, Anthony M. Kennedy, Sandra Day O'Connor, Chief Justice William H. Rehnquist, Antonin Scalia, David H. Souter, John Paul Stevens, Clarence Thomas

Justices Dissenting: None

Date of Decision: May 27, 1997

Decision: Ruled in favor of Jones by finding that the president does not have immunity from civil lawsuits relating to personal conduct not part of his official duties.

Significance: The ruling asserted that although a president can not be sued for actions related to his official duties, the president is subject to the same laws regulating purely private behavior as the general population.

On May 8, 1991, twenty-four year old Paula Corbin Jones, a state clerical employee, was working at the registration desk for a conference given by Arkansas Industrial Development Commission at the Excelsior Hotel in Little Rock. About 2:30 PM Bill Clinton, then Governor of Arkansas passed by the desk while attending the conference to make a speech. Shortly afterward, State Trooper Danny Ferguson approached Jones and persuaded her to go upstairs to visit the governor. Jones followed Trooper Ferguson into the hotel elevator which took them to a business suite where Clinton was waiting. Once inside the suite, Jones would later claim Clinton made crude sexual advances, which she rejected and promptly left the room. Jones would also charge that her rejection of those advances led to punishment by her supervisor in the state job she held by changing her job duties. She also claimed the state police officer had later defamed (damaged) her reputation by stating that she had accepted Clinton's advances.

A Civil Lawsuit

Bill Clinton (1993–) was elected president of the United States in 1992. In May of 1994 Jones filed a civil lawsuit in the U.S. District Court for the Eastern District of Arkansas against Clinton alleging (charging) all of the above activities took place. A civil lawsuit is brought to enforce, make amends for violations, or protect rights of private individuals. It is not a criminal proceeding. Among her charges, Jones claimed her civil rights had been violated and asked for damages of $175,000.

Jones had waited until two days before the three year period of limitations would have expired ending the time period in which a lawsuit could be filed. Jones gave such reasons for not filing earlier as she was afraid of losing her job, the governor was in charge of the state so who could she trust, and now Clinton was the most powerful man in the country.

Clinton's attorneys immediately filed a motion to dismiss the charges based on presidential immunity. Presidential immunity shields the president from court interference as he carries out his executive duties and from any civil lawsuits brought against him *for actions taken in performance of duties.*

No Temporary Immunity

U.S. District Court Judge Susan Webber Wright denied the dismissal on immunity grounds but ordered the trial be postponed until after Clinton's presidency. Both parties appealed the decision to the U.S. Court of

CAN THE PRESIDENT BE SUED WHILE IN OFFICE?

The administration of President Bill Clinton, with its many attendant scandals, raised a number of issues concerning the presidency, ethics, and the law. Among these issues was the question, "Should civil suits against the president be stalled until he is out of office?" Given Clinton's enormous popularity, it is likely that the majority of Americans would have said "yes."

To look specifically at Clinton, Jones, or the suit, however, is to miss the point. In answering the question regarding presidents and civil suits, Americans should evaluate it without regard to personalities. Then they would be left with two issues: on the one hand, there was the fact that the president should not be above the law; on the other hand, responding to personal lawsuits brought against him would distract him from the important business of being president.

Appeals for the Eighth Circuit. The court of appeals affirmed (agreed with) Wright's decision that Clinton did not have immunity from the lawsuit but disagreed with the postponement. Post-poning any trial until the end of Clinton's presidency, Judge Bowman of the Eighth Circuit said, was a "temporary immunity." Finding no reason to grant this to Clinton, Bowman stated, "The President, like all other government officials, is subject to the same laws that apply, to all other members of our society." Judge Bowman could find no "case in which any public official ever has been granted any immunity from suit for his unofficial [not related to his governmental duties] acts." Judge Bowman pointed out that the issue at hand involved "only personal, private conduct by a President." Clinton then appealed to the U.S. Supreme Court which agreed to hear the case.

Court Rejects Clinton's Claims

On May 27, 1997, only months after Clinton's reelection as president, a unanimous Court affirmed the decision of the appeals court agreeing with Judge Bowman's reasoning. The Court rejected both of President Clinton's principle arguments, one involving presidential immunity and the other based on the doctrine of separation of powers.

No Immunity

In Clinton's first argument, he claimed "that [in] all but the most exceptional cases, the Constitution affords [allows] the President temporary immunity from civil . . . litigation [lawsuits] arising . . . even out of actions that happened before he took office." Clinton based this argument on a Supreme Court's earlier decision in ***Nixon v. Fitzgerald*** (1982). In *Nixon* the Court held that a president is entitled to absolute (without any restrictions) immunity from any civil lawsuit that challenges his official actions. In other words, the president cannot be sued for conduct which relates to his duties as president. This reasoning allows presidents to carry out their designated functions effectively without fear a particular action or decision will lead to a personal lawsuit. John Paul Stevens, writing for the Court, completely denied Clinton's claim of immunity saying *Nixon* could not be applied in this case. "This reasoning [in *Nixon*] provides no support for an immunity for *unofficial* conduct." Clinton's actions certainly were unofficial, not remotely involved with his presidential duties. Furthermore, the Court found no basis of precedent (previous decisions) to allow any immunity toward actions occurring before a president had taken office.

No Separation of Powers Conflict

President Clinton based his second argument on the separation of powers principle. The principle guides the division of power among the three branches of government, executive (the president), legislative (Congress), and judicial (courts). One branch may not unduly interfere with another branch. Stevens wrote, Clinton "contends that he occupies a unique office with powers and responsibilities so vast and important that the public interest demands that he devote his undivided time and attention to his public duties." Clinton continued that the separation of powers places limits on the judiciary not allowing it to burden the presidency with any action such as this lawsuit that would divert the president's energy and attention away from his executive duties. Clinton did not make any claim of being "above the law," he merely argued for a postponement of the court proceeding until completion of his presidency.

Although the Court accepted that the presidency is uniquely important, it found that the "separation-of-power doctrine does not require federal courts to stay [postpone] all private actions against the President until he leaves office." Stevens wrote that this case and any further legal action it might cause would not "place unacceptable burdens on the President that will hamper the performance of his official duties." The Court sent Jones' case back to district court for trial.

Paula Jones sought to take her case to court while President Clinton was still in office.
Reproduced by permission of AP/Wide World Photos.

An Important Reminder

The Supreme Court refused to allow a sitting president to avoid a civil lawsuit just because he is president. Instead, the president may claim immunity only where the questioned actions relate to official acts and duties of the presidency. The Court's decision was an important reminder that no person in a democratic nation, including the president, is above the law.

With the case back in district court, Jones' attorneys began the process of gathering information for their case. Wright agreed that any information bearing on Clinton's sexual relationships with other state or federal employees while governor and president was relevant. In January of 1998 Clinton gave testimony, the first president to ever do so as part of a trial while in office. On April 1, 1998, in a surprise move to both parties Judge Wright dismissed the Jones lawsuit by finding

PRESIDENT HELD IN CONTEMPT

"I did not have sexual relations with that woman, Miss Lewinsky," Clinton publicly proclaimed while giving formal testimony to federal district court in the Paula Jones sexual assault lawsuit. Giving testimony under oath in the Paula C. Jones sexual assault case in January of 1998, Clinton declared he had no past sexual relations with White House intern Monica S. Lewinsky.

Later, Clinton changed his story while giving testimony during a grand jury appearance in August of 1998. He admitted to "inappropriate intimate contact" with Lewinsky and misleading the public with his earlier statements. Clinton later faced an impeachment trial over the Lewinsky scandal before the U.S. Senate with Chief Justice William H. Rehnquist presiding. The trial ended with acquittal in February of 1999. With thoughts that his legal troubles might be over, U.S. District Court Judge Susan Webber Wright found Clinton in contempt of court on April 12, 1999 for intentionally giving false testimony about his relationship with Lewinsky during his January of 1998 testimony. Wright stated that the "record demonstrates by clear and convincing evidence that the president [gave] false, misleading and evasive answers that were designed to obstruct the judicial process." Wright concluded that Clinton had "undermined the integrity of the judicial system." Though no president had ever been found in contempt of court before, Wright found no constitutional restriction from doing so. She wrote, "the power to determine the legality of the President's unofficial conduct includes with it the power to issue civil contempt citations . . . for his unofficial conduct which abuses the federal [court] process." As the last chapter of the Jones case, in April of 1999 President Bill Clinton became the first sitting president to be found in contempt of court.

that Jones did not provide sufficient proof of emotional injury or discrimination at work. Jones prepared to appeal the decision, but negotiations began for a settlement. Finally, in November of 1998 Clinton agreed to pay Jones $850,000. Though Jones had originally demanded that Clinton issue an apology or admit guilt. Clinton did neither. The president sent a check for the amount in January of 1999.

Suggestions for further reading

Bugliosi, Vincent T. *No Island of Sanity: Paula Jones vs. Bill Clinton, the Supreme Court on Trial.* New York: Ballantine Books, Inc., 1998.

Conason, Joe, and Gene Lyons. *The Hunting of the President: The Ten Year Campaign to Destroy Bill and Hillary Clinton.* New York: Thomas Dunne Books, 2000.

Maraniss, David. *First In His Class: The Biography of Bill Clinton.* New York: Simon & Schuster, 1996.

Stephanopoulos, George. *All Too Human: A Political Education.* Boston: Little, Brown & Company, 1999.

FEDERALISM AND STATE POWERS

Throughout U.S. history, the division of power between the federal government and state governments has been the subject of continuous political and legal battles. After suffering from the British government's political and economic tyrannical policies applied to the American colonies that eventually led to the American Revolution (1775–1783), many Americans greatly distrusted centralized governmental powers. As a result, when the Continental Congress drew up the Articles of Confederation in 1781, the new central government was assigned few powers. The central government had little authority over commerce, no court system, and no power to tax. The states were essentially a loose union of sovereign (politically independent) governments, each free to regulate commerce as it saw fit, make money, and have their state courts hold judgement over national laws.

It soon became apparent to many Americans that such a fragmented governmental structure based almost solely on state powers would greatly hold back political and economic growth of the young nation. So, in 1787 a Constitutional Convention was called to restructure the government and create a national economy. Debates raged between federalists, those supporting a strong central government as proposed in a Virginia plan, and anti-federalists supporting continued strong state governments as proposed in a New Jersey plan which greatly resembled the Articles of Confederation. Finally, a compromise, known as the Great Compromise, was struck deciding on federalism as the basis for the governmental structure. Federalism is a dual (split in two) system of sovereignty, splitting power between a central government and various state governments. Both the federal and state governments can directly govern citizens through their own officials and laws. The resulting Constitution in recognizing the sovereignty of both federal and state governments gave to each some separate unique powers and some shared powers. Importantly, both the federal and state governments must agree to any changes to the Constitution.

Selling the Constitution

The new federal system proposed in the Constitution was so controversial in the states, that national leaders, both federalists and advocates for state powers (antifederalists) temporarily joined forces to convince the states to ratify the Constitution. Alexander Hamilton and James Madison along with John Jay wrote a series of eighty-five articles to support ratification of the Constitution. Initially they were published separately in New York newspapers. Collectively, the essays became known as *The Federalist* are considered one of the more important political documents in U.S. history. Purpose of *The Federalist* was to explain various provisions (parts) of the Constitution. As described by the authors, the basic principles of the new government included republicanism (representatives elected by the public), federalism (power split between a central and state governments), separation of powers (power split between two or more branches of government), and free government.

Many of the Constitutional Convention's delegates as well as public citizens feared that too strong of a central government was being established. For example, the Supremacy Clause in Article VI of the Constitution states that the Constitution, federal laws, and treaties are superior to state laws and constitutions. States can not ignore or take actions against federal law or the Constitution. In an effort to ease American's fears and to gain acceptance of the Constitution, therefore moving ratification (adoption by the states) along, the federalists and antifederalists agreed to a compromise. A list of basic rights was written with intentions of adding it to the Constitution. The Constitution then gained the required ratification of the states by 1788. One of the first acts of the new Congress was to add the list of basic rights to the

Constitution. The list contained ten amendments (changes or additions) to the Constitution and became known as the Bill of Rights. The Tenth Amendment in particular protected state powers and became the basis throughout American history for proponents of strong state powers to fight for their cause.

Powers Set Out in the Constitution

Articles I through VI of the Constitution largely define Federal powers and puts some restrictions on state powers. For example, only the federal government has power to coin money, declare war, raise armies and a navy, and govern Indian tribes. Concerning the federal court system, only the U.S. Supreme Court was specifically named in the Constitution, but Congress was given authority to establish other federal courts. The Tenth Amendment assigns all powers to the states not specifically given to the federal government. The amendment states that "powers not delegated to the United States by the Constitution, nor prohibited by it to the States, are reserved to the States respectively, or to the people." States also retain a common law "police power" to pass laws protecting the health and safety, and economic welfare of its citizens. Both the federal and state governments hold similar powers in some areas such as the power to tax and to borrow money.

Particularly important clauses of the Constitution that have played a key role in determining the boundary between federal and state powers have been the Commerce Clause, the Necessary and Proper Clause, the Supremacy Clause, and the Contract Clause. These clauses recognize the dominance of the central government. The Commerce Clause in Article I gives the federal government exclusive authority to regulate interstate commerce (business between states) and trade with foreign countries. The Necessary and Proper Clause of Article I states that Congress has the authority to "make all laws which shall be necessary and proper for carrying into execution the foregoing powers, and all other powers vested [granted] by this constitution in the government of the United States, or in any department, or officer thereof." The Supremacy Clause in Article VI states that "This Constitution, and the Laws of the United States . . . shall be supreme Law of the Land; and the Judges in every State shall be bound thereby." When the federal and state governments have passed laws on the same subject, the federal law takes priority if they come into conflict. The Contract Clause in Article I reads that "No State shall . . . make any . . . Law impairing the Obligation of Contracts."

Other limitations on state powers are included in Article IV. Each state must respect the laws, records, and court decisions of other states and that "citizens of each state shall be entitled to all privileges and immunities of citizens in the several states." States can not discriminate against the citizens of other states.

A Long, Intense Debate

Largely due to the intensity of debate between federalists and states' rights advocates (antifederalists), the Constitution did not precisely establish the line between federal sovereignty and state sovereignty. As a result, over two centuries of controversy and a bloody Civil War (1861–1865) have centered on attempting to resolve the differences between those advocating a strong central government and those advocating states rights. In fact, the first two political parties in the nation were based largely on this issue, the Federalist Party and the Democrat-Republican Party (antifederalists). The balance of power between the federal government and the states has steadily changed through time.

Survival of Federalism

With British domination over the colonies still fresh in peoples' minds, a strong public support for state powers persisted through early American history. When a U.S. Supreme Court ruling in *Chisholm v. Georgia* (1793) weakened states' powers by upholding the right of a citizen of one state to sue another state, Congress and the states responded with the Eleventh Amendment to the Constitution which was passed and ratified within only a few years. Overriding the Court's decision, the amendment limited the rights of citizens to sue state governments. However, at the beginning of the nineteenth century the tide would turn towards federalism.

The appointment in 1801 of John Marshall, a Federalist, as Chief Justice of the U.S. Supreme Court marked the beginning of Court decisions favoring a strong federal government over state government power. Chief Justice Marshall's opinions were brilliantly reasoned and masterfully written. In ***Marbury v. Madison*** (1803) Marshall fully recognized judicial review in which the Court is the government body to decide whether laws are constitutional—that is, in agreement with the principles and power established by the Constitution. In 1815, the state of Virginia challenged the Supreme Court's constitutional authority of judicial review, but lost in ***Martin v. Hunter's Lessee*** (1816). The heavily Federalist Court continued to interpret the Constitution as granting broad (extensive) powers to the national government. In ***McCulloch v. Maryland*** (1819) Marshall ruled that the Necessary and Proper Clause gave Congress power to make any laws considered necessary to carry out its duties in providing for the nation's welfare. This principle is referred to as implied powers, powers not actually written down in the Constitution but needed for the government to function. The decision also reinforced the supremacy of federal law over state law when the two conflict. Likewise, in ***Gibbons v. Ogden*** (1824), another decision limiting state powers, the Court recognized Congress' exclusive power to regulate a broad range of business activity that could affect interstate commerce (trade between states).

One of the earliest and most dramatic disputes involving states powers resulted in the ***Cherokee Nation v. Georgia*** (1831) decision. The state of Georgia even refused to attend the Supreme Court hearing and went ahead with execution of a tribal member in defiance of federal powers. Only a year later in ***Worcester v. Georgia*** (1832) the Court ruled that state sovereignty did not include power to regulate Indian lands. Only the federal government held such power over Indian nations.

During this early period of nationalism and recognition of broad federal powers, the basic provisions of the Constitution most often used by Marshall and the Court was the Necessary and Proper Clause, the Supremacy Clause, the Commerce Clause, and the Contract Clause.

A Turn to State Powers

Marshall, through his rulings favoring the federal governments strong role, has been largely credited for saving federalism during the early period of American history. However, his decisions still maintained a respect for state sovereignty as demonstrated in the ***Barron v. Baltimore*** (1833) decision. Marshall ruled that the restraints to governmental powers in the Bill of Rights did not apply to state governments but only protected Americans from abuses of power by the federal government. With John Marshall's death in 1835 while still serving as Chief Justice, the Court took a decided turn away from recognizing strong federal powers and began favoring protection of state police powers. This was at a time that Jacksonian politics favoring strong state powers and a weaker federal government dominated public thought. The emphasis on state powers, promoted by President Andrew Jackson (1829–1837), prevailed for several decades. Similarly, the Court adopted the doctrine of "dual federalism" meaning the federal and state governments have equal power with each having its separate authorities to operate under.

By the mid-nineteenth century, state powers became closely tied to the slavery issue. Dismayed with the Marshall decisions, particularly *McCulloch* affirming federal supremacy, the Southern states closely guarded their power to regulate slavery. Victory by Union forces in the American Civil War decided once and for all that the federal government was supreme over states and that under federalism no state has the power to secede (leave) the federal Union. Three new constitutional amendments, known as the Civil War Amendments, were designed to restrict state powers over U.S. citizens, in particular former slaves, and shift the balance of power from states to the federal government. The Thirteenth Amendment banned slavery. The Fourteenth Amendment, adopted in 1868, made the Bill of Rights apply to state governments as it had to the federal government since first adopted in 1791. The amendment states that "No State shall . . . deprive any person of life, liberty, or property without due process of law; nor deny to any person within its jurisdiction the equal protection of the laws." The Fourteenth Amendment also declared that former slaves were indeed citizens entitled to all the privileges of citizens. However, in respect to states' powers the Court did little in the late nineteenth century to enforce the amendment against state regulation and abuses of citizens' rights.

The power of businesses within states gained an upper hand during the late nineteenth and early twentieth century. A period of rapid industrial growth, the courts adopted a *laissez-faire* approach (business free of government regulation) to economic matters by restricting governmental regulation and intervention. The Court would use the Tenth Amendment to negate federal attempts at business regulation by protecting state interests, and would use the Due Process Clause of the Fourteenth Amendment to protect private property rights and freedom to contract from state regulation. For example, the Court in ***Lochner v. New York*** (1905) overturned a state law establishing working conditions including maximum hours for New York bakers by claiming it violated the "liberty of contract" protected under the Fourteenth Amendment's Due Process Clause.

Broad state police powers were recognized in *Euclid v. Ambler Realty Co.* (1926) to protect public health and safety, and to develop natural resources. The concept of dual federalism in the early twentieth century was perhaps most dramatically highlighted by the Court's decision in ***Hammer v. Dagenhart*** (1918). The ruling overturned a federal child labor law by claiming it was reserved as a state power under the Tenth Amendment. The Court continued to use the dual federalism doctrine to overturn economic recovery measures passed by Congress into the early 1930s.

The Twentieth Century Rise of Federal Government Powers

By the late 1930s the Court, under public and political pressure resulting from reform efforts to recover from the Great Depression resulted in a dramatic change. The idea of federalism and Marshall's earlier positions returned. In *West Coast Hotel Co. v. Parrish* (1937) the Court extended federal power to regulate some economic activities within states. Under a broadened Commerce Clause interpretation, federal powers expanded at the expense of state powers and emphasis on the Tenth Amendment declined. The Court in *NLRB v. United States* (1936) reaffirmed the Wagner Act which brought labor relations under federal oversight. In addition, the Social Security Act creating a national retirement fund, passed in 1935. Another fundamental shift in power had occurred.

Although by the end of World War II (1939–1945), the federal government's powers were clearly dominant over state powers, some important state powers remained. For example, the Court ruled in ***Erie Railroad Co. v. Tompkins*** (1938) that federal courts must recognize previous state court decisions as law. The decision in ***International Shoe Co. v. Washington*** (1945) expanded state powers over out-of-state businesses that operate within their boundaries.

Increased federal powers were further recognized in the 1950s and 1960s, primarily over the issue of racial discrimination. Through the 1940s the states had retained the primary responsibility for governing the rights of its citizens. Therefore, to protect individual rights from state abuses, the Supreme Court began issuing decisions limiting state powers related to freedoms of speech and religion, due process rights to fair trials, and equal protection of the law. The Supreme Court in ***Brown v. Board of Education of Topeka, Kansas*** (1954) barred racial segregation policies in public schools and brought local school districts under federal oversight. How the state and local governments create voting districts came under federal oversight in the *Baker v. Carr* (1962) decision. A 1965 ruling in *South Carolina v. Katzenbach* upheld the Voting Rights Act of 1965 that prohibited state-established voting requirements. Also in

1965, the protection of privacy from state powers was recognized in ***Griswold v. Connecticut*** setting the basis for later recognizing abortion rights. The ruling in ***Miranda v. Arizona*** (1966) and other Court decisions substantially changed state criminal justice systems. All of these cases and more focused on limiting state power over individual behavior. Interpretation of the Fourteenth Amendment's guarantee of equal protection of the laws and due process played a key role in these decisions, allowing the amendment to finally play a role in federalism.

By the late 1970s the pendulum began to swing back to the states. State power advocates joined in opposition to these federal court decisions restricting state rights. Efforts at racial desegregation attracted the most attention. Interest in increasing state powers through greater emphasis on the Tenth Amendment to limit federal powers arose. Opposition to federal welfare programs and limitations on the criminal justice system led to the rise of a states' rights movement in the 1980s under President Ronald Reagan (1981–1989). States began receiving more authority to experiment with social programs. This direction received an additional boost in 1994 with the first Republican-controlled, pro states' rights, House of Representatives since the 1940s. As a result the mid- and late-1990s saw further growth in state powers.

Federalism and State Powers Persist Side by Side

Despite the limiting of state powers under federalism through establishment of Supreme Court judicial review, broad commerce powers of Congress, and application of the Bill of Rights and the Fourteenth Amendment to states, the states maintained constitutional and political sovereignty at the end of the twentieth century. Although the supremacy of the federal government was well established, states were still free to govern much of their own political, economic, and social affairs in areas where Congress had not acted to establish consistency on a national level. Supreme Court decisions continue to either limit or support state powers depending on the particular issue at hand and the interpretation of federalism continues to change through time.

Suggestions for further reading

Elazar, Daniel J. *American Federalism: A View from the States*. New York: Harper & Row, 1984.

Katz, Ellis. *Federalism and Rights.* Lanham, MD: Rowman & Littlefield, 1996.

Levy, Leonard W. *Origins of the Bill of Rights.* New Haven, CT: Yale University Press, 1999.

Livingston, John C. *The Consent of the Governed.* New York: Macmillan Publishing Company, 1971.

McWilliams, Wilson C. *The Federalist, the Antifederalist, and the American Political Tradition.* New York: Greenwood Press, 1992.

Wood, Gordon S. *The Creation of the American Republic, 1776-1787.* New York: W. W. Norton & Company, 1969.

Martin v. Hunter's Lessee 1816

Plaintiff: Thomas Bryan Martin

Defendant: David Hunter

Plaintiff's Claim: That the state of Virginia could not disobey a Supreme Court order to overturn a state law illegally taking land from citizens loyal to the British during the Revolutionary War.

Chief Lawyer for Plaintiff: Jones (first name not recorded)

Chief Lawyer for Defense: Tucker (first name not recorded)

Justices for the Court: Gabriel Duvall, William Johnson, Henry B. Livingston, Joseph Story, Thomas Todd, Bushrod Washington

Justices Dissenting: None (John Marshall did not participate)

Date of Decision: March 20, 1816

Decision: Ruled in favor of Martin by finding that United States treaties with Great Britain constitutionally take priority over conflicting state law.

Significance: The ruling was a historic statement by the Court concerning the supreme judicial review powers of the U.S. Supreme Court over state courts and state law when federal issues are involved. It provided a precedence for numerous other Court decisions involving federal government powers through the following years.

After bitter political struggles with Great Britain over its dominating governmental policies resulting in the war for independence, many Americans opposed creating a strong new federal government. Consequently, the Articles of Confederation, written in 1781, gave the new national government few powers. The document stressed the states' sovereignty (political independence) calling the union between states "a firm league of friendship" and no more. The national government had no powers to tax or regulate commerce (business and trade) and no provisions were made for a federal court system. State courts would hear federal law cases. Each state interpreted federal law their own way leading to inconsistency and confusion with resulting financial and political chaos.

In response to the failures of the Articles of Confederation, a Constitutional Convention was called in 1787 to correct the weaknesses of the Articles. Much debate centered over how to split political power between the national government and the states. Those supporting a more even split in the power between a stronger central, or federal, government and the states were known as Federalists. Those opposed to a stronger national government and supporting continued strong state governments were simply known as anti-federalists. Ultimately, the delegates to the Convention chose a stronger central government.

Though the Constitution as written granted supremacy (higher in power) to the federal government in certain matters and established a Supreme Court, it did not precisely define the balance of power between the states and the federal government. Article VI of the Constitution proclaimed that this "constitution, and the laws of the United States . . . and all treaties made . . . under the authority of the United States, shall be the supreme law of the land." Article III of the Constitution established the Supreme Court. Section 2 of Article III states, "The judicial Power shall extend to all Cases . . . arising under this Constitution, the Laws of the United States, and Treaties made." After much debate in the states over the Constitution creating a stronger central government, it was ratified in 1788. The next year the Judiciary Act of 1789 defined what powers were given to the Supreme Court by the Constitution. The act declared the Court had the power to review state court rulings.

Following ratification of the Constitution, the federalist and anti-federalist debate became so intense that the two groups formed the core of the nation's two primary political parties. The Federalist Party was led by John Adams (1735–1826) and Alexander Hamilton (1755–1804) and the Democratic-Republicans (anti-federalists) by Thomas Jefferson (1743–1826) and James Madison (1751–1836).

Not surprisingly given the raging political debate over federalism, many aspects of the new government were constantly being tested during the first few decades of the nation's history. The early Supreme Court was dominated by judges who were Federalists. When Thomas Jefferson (1801–1809) became president he swore to replace the justices with those who were Democratic-Republicans so as to give greater support to states' rights issues. Although Jefferson failed in his efforts to transform the Court, his successor to the presidency, James Madison (1809–1817) was able to appoint Joseph Story, the Court's first Democratic-Republican justice. Many key early Court decisions addressed the supremacy of the federal powers. Two involved Denny Martin, *Fairfax's Devisee v. Hunter's Lessee* followed by *Martin v. Hunter's Lessee.*

Thomas Lord Fairfax's Land

Prior to the Revolutionary War (1775–1783), Thomas Lord Fairfax owned over five million acres of valuable land in the northern part of Virginia. Lord Fairfax, a citizen and resident of Virginia, had originally acquired the land through a charter from the English king. Upon his death in 1781 while the war was still raging, his property was left to his nephew, Denny Martin, a British citizen. Also during the war, the state of Virginia passed a law giving the state authority to confiscate (taking away for the public good) property of Loyalists (those colonists supporting Great Britain), such as Lord Fairfax. Denny Martin died sometime prior to 1803 and the property passed on to his heir, Thomas Bryan Martin. In the meantime, the state confiscated the land and sold it David Hunter. Thomas Martin filed a lawsuit with the state courts of Virginia challenging Hunter's right to the land.

The Virginia court found in favor of Hunter and Martin appealed the decision to the U.S. Supreme Court. The Court in 1813 in *Fairfax's Devisee v. Hunter's Lessee* decided in favor of Martin. Chief Justice John Marshall did not take part in the case because of a family connection to the Fairfax family. Joseph Story wrote the Court's opinion. Much to the dismay of his fellow Democratic-Republicans, Story held that the Virginia law was unconstitutional. Story found that Martin's ownership of the land was protected by the Treaty of Paris (1783) and Jay's Treaty (1794). Both treaties, signed by the United States and Great Britain following America's victory in the Revolutionary War, provided that property owned by Loyalists would be protected by the U.S. government. In his decision, Story noted that Article VI of the U.S. Constitution stated that treaties are, like laws of Congress, considered the "supreme Law of the Land." Article VI further states that "Judges in every State shall be bound" to the Constitution, federal laws, and treaties regardless of the "Laws of any State." In addition, Section 25 of the 1789 Judiciary Act provided the Supreme Court review power of state court decisions involving issues related to the Constitution, federal laws, and treaties.

Therefore, Story ruled that the treaties negotiated by the federal government took precedence (priority) over conflicting state laws. Martin was the true owner of the property. Story ordered the Virginia court to do the legal work necessary to pass ownership back to Martin. But, the Virginia judges refused. The judges claimed Section 25 violated the powers and rights of state governments.

As a result, Martin filed suit again. The case came back to the Supreme Court to address the constitutionality of the Judiciary Act including the Supreme Court's authority to review state laws and state court decisions. Virginia claimed a state had the right to defy federal treaties or court decisions that the state did not approve of. The Supreme Court, they contended, could only review decisions made by lower federal courts, not state laws or courts.

Story Rules Again

Once again Joseph Story wrote the Court's opinion. Story strongly held that the Supreme Court's appellate jurisdiction (the right to hear appeals of lower court decisions) indeed extended to all cases involving federal issues, both those decided previously in state courts and federal courts. Story wrote that Section 25 of the Judiciary Act was not only constitutional but necessary to guarantee federal laws and treaties were the supreme law of the land.

In rejecting Virginia's claim that states had equal sovereignty to the United States, Story asserted that the American people, not the states, had created the nation. Without the supremacy power of the United States over the states, there could be no nation since no uniform national policies would apply equally throughout the United States. Story wrote,

> **The constitution of the United States was ordained and established, not by the states in their sovereign capacities, but emphatically, as the preamble**

SUPREME COURT JUSTICE JOSEPH STORY

Joseph Story (1779–1845) was born in Marblehead, Massachusetts in September of 1779. After earning a degree at Harvard College and studying law in Boston, he served in the Massachusetts House of Representatives from 1805 to 1808 and in the U.S. House of Representatives from 1808 to 1809. Story became a member of the Democratic-Republican political party which strongly supported states rights in opposition to the Federalists. Because of his political views, he was appointed by President James Madison to the U.S. Supreme Court in 1811 in hopes of influencing the Court's decision in favor of states' rights.

Story served on the Court for thirty-four years during which time he made a lasting mark in U.S. legal history. Though his greatest opinion was in *Martin v. Hunter's Lessee* (1816), he became Chief Justice John Marshall's closest collaborator on many of Marshall's historic opinions. Much to the dismay of states' rights advocates he strongly supported Marshall's broad interpretations of the Constitution and supremacy of the federal government over state governments.

Story was considered the greatest legal scholar and educator of his time. He was instrumental in restructuring the Harvard Law School where he was a distinguished professor of law. He authored several books which influenced constitutional law throughout the nineteenth century. After Marshall's death in 1835, Story found himself often in the minority on Court decisions with an increased Court emphasis on states' rights. He served on the Court until his death in Cambridge, Massachusetts on September 10, 1845.

[introduction] of the constitution declares, by 'the people of the United States' . . . The constitution was not, therefore, necessarily carved out of pow-

ers already existing in state sovereignties, nor a surrender of powers already existing in state institutions . . . [T]he judicial power of the United States [is] . . . national, and . . . supreme . . . to act not merely upon individuals, but upon states; and to deprive them altogether of the exercise of some power of sovereignty, and to restrain and regulate them in the exercise of others.

A Landmark Decision

The opinion by Justice Story is considered the greatest argument ever made for the Supreme Court's judicial review powers over state courts and laws. The decision, which infuriated states' rights proponents, strongly supported the Federalist's position for a strong national government. The decision formed the basis for numerous later court decisions further defining the strong powers of the federal government.

Suggestions for further reading

Dudley, William, ed. *The Creation of the Constitution.* San Diego, CA: Greenhaven Press, Inc., 1995.

Dunne, Gerald T. *Justice Joseph Story and the Rise of the Supreme Court.* New York: Simon & Schuster, 1970.

Weissberg, Robert. *Understanding American Government.* New York: Rinehart and Winston, 1980.

Gibbons v. Ogden 1824

Appellant: Thomas Gibbons

Appellee: Aaron Ogden

Appellant's Claim: That a New York state law granting exclusive rights to individuals to operate steamships in New York waters while conducting interstate commerce violates the Constitution's Commerce Clause.

Chief Lawyers for Appellant: Thomas A. Emmet, Thomas J. Oakley

Chief Lawyers for Appellee: William Wirt, Daniel Webster, David B. Ogden

Justices for the Court: Gabriel Duvall, William Johnson, Chief Justice John Marshall, Joseph Story, Thomas Todd, Bushrod Washington

Justices Dissenting: None (Smith Thompson did not participate)

Date of Decision: March 2, 1824

Decision: Ruled in favor of Gibbons by finding that steamship navigation is part of commerce and that states could not pass laws regulating steamship traffic operating between two or more states.

Significance: The landmark ruling was the first to interpret federal powers under the Constitution's Commerce Clause. It provided a broad interpretation of what is commerce under the clause, holding that commerce was more than simply the buying and selling of goods and forming the basis for numerous rulings involving the Commerce Clause throughout the history of the United States.

"Dinner will be served at exactly 2 o'clock . . . Tea with meats . . . Supper at 8 in the evening . . . A shelf has been added to each berth, on which gentlemen will please put their boots, shoes, and clothes, that the cabin will not be encumbered." So read a handbill distributed to passengers on Robert Fulton's (1765–1815) steamship operating on the Hudson River in New York state.

Authority Over Interstate Commerce

Government regulation of business was a deep concern of colonists who had been subjected to the burdensome tax policies of Great Britain, a major issue leading to the Revolutionary War (1775–1783). Fear of national government control of local businesses led the colonists to be very restrictive in granting trade regulation power to a national government when drafting the Articles of Confederation in 1781. The only trade control given to Congress was that concerning trade with Indians. Regulation of interstate and foreign trade was reserved to the individual states. However, business competition between the states grew intense. Each state was more eager to build their own prosperity than seek agreement on trade policy. They each had their own tariff (import tax) policies on goods coming from other states or foreign countries. To further complicate matters, each state held authority to make their own money. Having thirteen currencies greatly inhibited trade. Another problem for businessmen was trying to collect on their bills when interstate trade was conducted. Local courts often proved protective of local businesses from their distant creditors.

The resulting chaotic trade situation was soon widely recognized as a major problem for the economic growth of the new nation. As a result the Framers of the U.S. Constitution during the Constitutional Convention of 1787 with little debate gave broader commerce powers to Congress. Commerce is commonly the conducting of economic trade or business between cities, states, or foreign nations. Clause 3 of Article I states that "Congress shall have the power . . . to regulate Commerce with foreign Nations, and among the several States, and with the Indian Tribes." The Supreme Court was not called upon to rule on the scope of the Commerce Clause until over thirty years later in 1824.

Rise of Steamship Commerce

A major new technology at the beginning of the nineteenth century began to make a major impact on interstate and foreign travel and trade, the

"OUR OVERWORKED SUPREME COURT"

Cartoonist Joseph Keppler depicted "Our Overworked Supreme Court" in a cartoon with that caption published in the humor magazine *Puck* on December 9, 1885. The scene showed the Supreme Court justices awash amidst a pile of paper. It symbolized the extraordinary caseload in which the court was regularly mired at the time.

In the Supreme Court of John Jay, the first chief justice (1789-95), the caseload was light, and Justices often spent time on administrative matters. By the time of the Civil War, the size of the docket had grown to some three hundred cases. By 1885, the Court was swamped with more than thirteen hundred cases.

In 1891, Congress passed the Circuit Court of Appeals Act, which established the appellate court system as a buffer between the lower courts and the High Court.

steam engine. In 1798 the state of New York passed a law giving Robert R. Livingston exclusive right to navigate steamboats in state waters. Exclusive use means no other business can hold the same right to operate steamships in those waters. It becomes a business monopoly. By 1802 Livingston took on inventor Robert Fulton as a partner. Fulton adapted a steam engine for large ships to carry passengers, greatly expanding the potential of earlier steam powered boats. Fulton and Livingston could also issue licenses to others to operate steamships in New York waters. Experiencing great success, they received the same type of grant in 1811 from the state of Louisiana. As a result, Fulton and Livingston controlled steamship access to two of the major seaports and waterways in the United States, New York City at the mouth of the Hudson River and New Orleans at the mouth of the mighty Mississippi River.

As more businessmen entered the steamship transport business, they too struck similar exclusive use deals with other states. As the new nation was rapidly expanding inland, the transportation of goods from one state to another involved different steamship companies in each state and became increasingly difficult. Public irritation over such inconvenience arose.

Aaron Ogden and Thomas Gibbons

In 1815 Aaron Ogden, a former New Jersey governor from 1812 to 1813, was in a struggling business partnership with Thomas Gibbons. Ogden purchased a license from Livingston to operate a steam-driven ferry line between New York City and Elizabethtown, New Jersey. Soon Gibbons began running his own steamships between New York and New Jersey, in direct competition with Ogden. Gibbons had obtained a license to operate his boats from the federal government under the Coastal Licencing Act of 1793 to operate in a "coasting" trade.

In 1819, Ogden sought a court injunction to block Gibbons' steamships from navigating in New York waters. Ogden claimed New York state law protected his monopoly and took precedence (priority) over the federal law. Gibbons countered that federal laws constitutionally overrode individual state laws.

A New York state court ruled in favor of Ogden by finding the state law took precedence in this case. The court asserted that federal commerce powers did not apply because ship navigation was not commerce. Only a federal law specifically regulating navigation could override the state steamship law, and no such law existed. The court issued the injunction ordering Gibbons to stop operating his steamships in New York waters. An injunction is a court order to stop an action from happening.

Supreme Court

Gibbons appealed to the U.S. Supreme Court. The case drew public attention for it pitted the Federalists who believed in establishing a strong national government against states' rights proponents, including former president Thomas Jefferson (1801–1809). Daniel Webster, famed lawyer and orator, presented Gibbons' case. Webster eloquently argued "that the power of Congress to regulate commerce was complete and entire, and, to a certain extent . . . exclusive." Also, he contended the term commerce included navigation necessary to conduct business transactions. Therefore, Gibbons' federal license took priority over New York law.

Chief Justice John Marshall, writing for the Court, saw things differently from the lower court and agreed with Webster. He saw the key question before the Court was just what kinds of activity did the Commerce Clause include. Also, could states regulate interstate commerce within their own waters? Marshall asserted three major points. First, the term "Commerce" in the Constitution was not just simply restricted to the actu-

JOHN FULTON AND THE STEAMSHIP

The *Gibbons v. Ogden* decision acknowledged the importance of steamship traffic to interstate commerce in the young nation. The ruling opened commerce to a wide range of steamship companies, thus promoting nationwide steamship travel and trade. The earliest steamboats began navigating on the Delaware River out of Philadelphia in 1787, but they were not commercially practical.

Robert Fulton (1765–1815), an American inventor, engineer, and artist, designed and built the first commercially successful steamboat in 1807, the *Clermont.* First he was interested in designing canal boats and a submarine in the 1790s. Having seen experimental steamships in France, Robert R. Livingston, the U.S. minister to France, interested Fulton in 1803 in the prospects of using steam engines on ships. Fulton ordered a steam engine from Britain and brought it to the United States in 1806. On August 17, 1807, the *Clermont* made its first successful voyage up the Hudson River from New York City to Albany. Soon the ship began providing passenger service on the river. Fulton later designed the first steam-operated warship, *Fulton the First,* to protect New York harbor in the War of 1812 (1812–1814) but died before its construction was completed. Fulton had greatly affected the growth of commercial trade in the nation and his statue now stands in Statutory Hall in the nation's Capitol Building.

al buying and selling of goods. It included navigation too when used to promote such buying and selling. Secondly, steamships significantly helped trade between states, hence were a part of interstate commerce when operating between two or more states. Thirdly, states could not pass laws restricting commerce between states, since this power was exclusively given to Congress by the Commerce Clause. Marshall declared that a primary objective in forming the federal government was authority to regulate interstate and foreign commerce. Marshall wrote, "The power over commerce, including navigation, was one of the primary objects for which the people . . . adopted their government." States retained the power to regulate "completely internal commerce [that] . . . does not extend to or affect other states." When a state law regulating commerce comes in conflict with a federal law, the federal always takes priority.

The lower court's ruling was overturned. Marshall dismissed the injunction against Gibbons and ruled the New York state law invalid since it was in conflict with the federal coastal licensing law.

From Steamships to the Internet

Despite the general acceptance of the Commerce Clause by the Framers of the Constitution, the Clause became the subject of more court cases than any other Congressional power. The publicly popular *Gibbons* decision has been called "the emancipation proclamation of American commerce." Interstate commerce was freed from the jumble of various restrictions imposed by numerous state governments. The decision established the importance of regulating interstate commerce by a central governmental authority, the national government rather than individual state or local governments.

States' rights proponents, including Jefferson, feared the decision would mark a trend toward the federal government taking over all rights believed reserved to the states. The broadening of commerce to include navigation provided a basis for later decisions involving communications, transportation, and manufacturing. Also, the ruling paved the way to consider new technologies that would come along as interstate commerce. Technologies never imagined by the Framers of the Constitution would include railroads, telegraphs, telephones, pipelines, airplanes, and by the 1990s, the Internet. Each new technology has relied upon the *Gibbons* ruling to protect their right to operate efficiently between states. By 2000 little economic activity remained beyond the regulatory authority of Congress under the Commerce Clause.

Suggestions for further reading

Baxter, Maurice G. *The Steamboat Monopoly,* Gibbons v. Ogden, *1824.* Philadelphia: Philadelphia Book Co., 1972.

Flexner, James T. *Steamboats Come True: American Inventors in Action.* Little Brown, 1978.

Philip, Cynthia O. *Robert Fulton: A Biography.* Watts, 1985.

Nebbia v. New York
1934

Appellant: Leo Nebbia

Appellee: State of New York

Appellant's Claim: That New York's Milk Control Act of 1934 violated the Fourteenth Amendment's Due Process Clause by unconstitutionally restricting business decisions.

Chief Lawyer for Appellant: Arthur E. Sutherland

Chief Lawyer for Appellee: Henry S. Manley

Justices for the Court: Louis D. Brandeis, Benjamin N. Cardozo, Charles Evans Hughes, Owen Josephus Roberts, Harlan Fiske Stone

Justices Dissenting: Pierce Butler, James Clark McReynolds, George Sutherland, Willis Van Devanter

Date of Decision: March 5, 1934

Decision: Ruled in favor of New York by finding that the state of New York had acted under its police powers in the best interest of its citizens.

Significance: The ruling established that any business activity could be subject to state regulation. The decision ended the long-standing distinction between businesses considered operating for the public good which could be regulated, and those not of direct public interest which could not be regulated. The decision marked the beginning of greater state government regulation of private economic activities.

"The powers not delegated to the United States by the Constitution, nor prohibited by it to the States, are reserved to the States respectively, or to the people." So reads the Tenth Amendment to the U.S. Constitution in its entirety. The amendment was written and adopted as part of the Bill of Rights in 1791 to soothe states' rights proponents during formation of the U.S. government.

Originally, the Articles of Confederation written in 1781 gave almost all governmental powers to the states with few to the federal government. The nation was a loose union of sovereign (politically independent) states. But in only a few years, it became evident that growth of the young nation, particularly business growth and economic development, needed consistency in rules and protection that only a strong central government could provide.

Delegates to the Constitutional Convention met in 1787 to correct this problem. After intense debate between supporters of a strong central government and proponents of states rights, a governmental structure with a strong central government was selected. With a great distaste for strong central governments lingering in the country following political battles and war with the British government, the first ten constitutional amendments were written to protect citizens and the states from potentially oppressive national government powers. The Tenth Amendment reserved all powers to the states that were not clearly given to the federal government.

Can States Regulate Business?

The Constitution established a governmental system based on the idea of federalism, in which power is split between a central federal government and the various states. However, the exact line between the powers of the federal and state governments was not precisely defined. Each would control certain areas. Early on, the Court recognized a broad police power (general authority) of states to protect its citizens and regulate business activities. Falling back on the Tenth Amendment the Court ruled in *Mayor of New York v. Miln* (1837) that a state had "undeniable and unlimited jurisdiction over all persons and things within its territorial limits . . . where the jurisdiction is not surrendered or restrained by the Constitution of the United States." But by the mid-nineteenth century as the industrialization (growth of big business) expanded, the Court became increasingly protective of property rights and took a narrower view of the state's power to regulate business. Use of the term "property" includes a person's business.

In a key 1877 decision supporting a state's police power over economic matters, the Court held in *Munn v. Illinois* that those business "in which the public has an interest," such as community agricultural grain storage structures, are subject to police power through state regulation. Other businesses are not. However, the "public interest" doctrine proved perplexing when applied in later cases as courts found difficulty in consistently identifying exactly what businesses held sufficient public interest.

Opponents to any state regulation of business argued such restrictions deprived people of their property rights by violating the Fourteenth Amendment's Due Process Clause. The clause states, "No state shall . . . deprive any person of life, liberty, or property without due process of law." Acceptance of this viewpoint grew and became known as "substantive due process" Substantive due process means that the Constitution protects certain rights, including property rights, from governmental interference. States became largely restricted from using police power over economic activity. Through the late nineteenth century and early twentieth century, this legal idea dominated many court decisions. The Court consistently ruled in favor of business interests when economic issues were involved.

Hard Times

With the collapse of the U.S. stock market in October of 1929, the nation entered a desperate economic period. Millions of people were out of work and many turned to the government for relief. The pro-business orientation of the Supreme Court became very unpopular, particularly with President Franklin D. Roosevelt (1933–1945) who was trying to lead the efforts for social and economic change. In the early 1930s, both the federal and state governments began taking action to control prices to ease the economic hardships. The state of New York created a Milk Board to set prices for milk. The resulting emergency legislation was the Milk Control Act of 1934 which set nine cents as the price to be charged for a quart of milk.

Grocer Leo Nebbia

Leo Nebbia owned and operated a small grocery store in Rochester, New York. One day Nebbia sold a quart of milk for more than nine cents. As a result he was charged with violating the Milk Control Act. Nebbia, claiming New York had no legal authority to control milk prices, lost his case in the county court and again before the New York Court of Appeals. He next appealed to the U.S. Supreme Court which agreed to hear his case.

Writing for the Court's majority on a close 5-4 vote, Justice Josephus O. Roberts revised the earlier *Munn* decision. He ruled that states could regulate all businesses, not just those businesses having public interest. Roberts wrote,

> **[I]n the absence of other constitutional restriction, a state is free to adopt whatever economic policy may reasonably be deemed to promote public welfare, and to enforce that policy by legislation adapted to its purpose. The courts are without authority . . . when it is declared by the legislature, to override it.**

Roberts held that states could regulate for the public good any business activity as long as the regulation was reasonable and effective. He wrote that a state "may regulate a business in any of its aspects, including the prices to be charged for the products . . . it sells." Therefore, the New York act did not violate the constitution and Nebbia was appropriately convicted of violating it.

So ended the domination of substantive due process ideas over court decisions concerning economic issues. In dissent, Justice James C. McReynolds still held on to the claim that the Due Process Clause gave the Supreme Court all the authority it needed to override any legislation restricting economic activity that it found unreasonable.

The Rise of Police Power Over Business

McReynolds, along with the other three dissenting justices in the case, Van Devanter, Sutherland, and Bulter, were highly unpopular for their very politically conservative views toward protecting businesses from government interference and regulation. Soon they lost their clout under pressure from Roosevelt and the public. The Court, supporting Roosevelt's programs for recovery, allowed more government regulation of business. Importantly, in 1937 in *West Coast Hotel Co. v. Parrish* the Court upheld the power of the federal government to regulate economic activities in states.

STATE POLICE POWER

Though not specifically mentioned in the U.S. Constitution, "police power" is a recognized general legal authority that states hold to govern their citizens, lands, or natural resources. Courts widely use the concept when considering the limits of state authority over its citizen's activities, or when establishing the line between federal and state regulation. Traditionally, the two main constitutional restrictions on the state use of police power has been the Commerce Clause and the Contract Clause. Only the federal government, not the states, can regulate interstate commerce, and state laws cannot interfere with private contractual relationships. Likewise, the right to freedom of expression and right to privacy are seen as primary limitations to state police powers.

Through the twentieth century, states have been given broader police power authority in protecting public health and safety, morals, and business activity. An early example of the Court recognizing state police power for public safety was by upholding a Massachusetts law requiring everyone to be vaccinated against certain disease. Police power was also recognized in the landmark ruling of *Euclid v. Ambler Realty Co.* (1926). The decision upheld a local government's power to establish zoning laws which allow certain kinds of activities in certain parts of the community. Despite its broad acceptance, police power continues to be a legal concept that cannot be precisely defined.

By the end of World War II (1939–1945), the federal government had become the dominant power in the U.S. governmental system. The Court's emphasis switched from property rights and business issues to issues of protecting individual civil rights from police power.

Suggestions for further reading

Davis, Kenneth S. *FDR, the New Deal Years, 1933-1937: A History.* New York: Random House, 1986.

Parrish, Michael E. *Anxious Decades: America in Prosperity and Depression, 1920-1941.* New York: W. W. Norton, 1992.

Watkins, Tom H. *The Great Depression: America in the 1930s.* Boston: Little, Brown, & Co. 1993.

Erie Railroad Co. v. Tompkins 1938

Petitioner: Erie Railroad Company

Respondent: Harry J. Tompkins

Petitioner's Claim: That state law rather than federal common law should determine the responsibility of a railroad to pay damages to an injured private citizen.

Chief Lawyer for Petitioner: Theodore Kiendl

Chief Lawyer for Respondent: Fred H. Rees

Justices for the Court: Hugo L. Black, Louis D. Brandeis, Charles E. Hughes, Owen J. Roberts, Harlan F. Stone, Stanley F. Reed

Justices Dissenting: Pierce Butler, James Clark McReynolds (Benjamin N. Cardozo did not participate)

Date of Decision: April 25, 1938

Decision: Ruled in favor of Erie Railroad reversing a lower court decision that had awarded damages to Tompkins

Significance: The ruling reversed a previous court decision made almost a century earlier recognizing a federal common law. The *Erie* decision held that no such law exists. Federal court decisions involving citizens from different states follow state law when neither constitutional issues nor acts of Congress are not involved. The decision also gave state high court rulings the same degree of importance as laws passed by state legislatures.

Common law is a collection of rules and principles that come from long-standing customs or traditions. In the United States, they often come from early English customs, general law, and judicial (court) decisions recognizing a custom. English common law, finally established in written form in England in the eighteenth century, forms the basis for U.S. law and still applies to many cases in modern America.

When the Framers of the Constitution were busy creating a new national governmental system, a major issue receiving considerable debate raged between the Federalists wanting a strong central government and states' rights supporters wanting most power to be held by state governments, not the central federal government. In creating the U.S. legal system, the Framers of the document established a U.S. Supreme Court in Article III and identified federal jurisdiction on specific kinds of cases. Though no other federal courts were established by the Constitution, it did give Congress power to establish federal courts as it saw the need. Quickly, Congress used their authority to establish a federal court system under the Judiciary Act of 1789. Federal district courts were established in each state. According to the act, federal courts must apply state laws, not create its own general law. The "laws of the several states" are to be "regarded as rules of decision" in civil actions in federal courts "in cases where they apply." In regard to civil (private noncriminal disputes) cases, federal courts could only accept cases involving citizens from different states, known as diversity jurisdiction.

An early idea that federal general law did exist for diversity jurisdiction cases was expressed by Supreme Court in *Swift v. Tyson* (1842). The Court believed that all decisions by state court judges actually did not create law. Therefore, federal judges could ignore state court rulings when making their own rulings. They create federal general law that would take priority over previous state court decisions. The *Swift* ruling gave federal judges considerable power over state law. The opinion, however, created much confusion within each state rather than uniformity in law that was intended, especially as the list of legal topics created under a new federal general law grew through time.

Tompkins Hit by Train

The Erie Railroad Company, a corporation chartered (an ownership license) in New York state, operated a railroad in northeastern United States. Under law, Erie would be considered a New York "citizen." One day while Harry J. Tompkins, a Pennsylvania citizen, was walking on a footpath alongside Erie railroad tracks in Pennsylvania when he was struck and injured by an open boxcar door on a passing train. Tompkins filed a lawsuit in a Pennsylvania federal district court seeking compensation (money payment) for his personal injuries. He claimed Erie was negligent (careless) in operating the railroad. Because the case involved diversity of citizenship, a Pennsylvania resident and a New York corporation, he filed the suit in federal court.

Because neither federal law nor any acts passed by the Pennsylvania state legislature existed covering such situations, the court had to determine what law should be applied in the case. A Pennsylvania court decision had previously established standard rules to guide courts in such cases. The rules stated that people using paths along railroads not at crossings would be considered trespassers. Railroads would not be liable (responsible) for injuries unless the trespassers were intentionally injured by reckless and deliberate acts of the railroads. Using the *Swift* decision, the district court judge refused to apply the Pennsylvania rule. Instead, he asked a jury to determine if the railroad was negligent. The jury found Erie negligent and awarded Tompkins $30,000 in damages, a substantial amount at that time. Erie appealed the district court decision to the federal Circuit Court of Appeals and lost again. Erie then appealed to the U.S. Supreme Court which accepted the case.

Erie posed two questions before the Court. First, should the federal judges have used a Pennsylvania state rule created by state judges to determine Erie's liability? Secondly, was not Tompkins to blame since he failed to pay attention to the warnings of a moving train including a horn and its headlight? Tompkins responded by focusing on the long-standing *Swift* rule that federal judges should not use state court rulings to guide their decisions. Federal law takes priority over state rules.

No Federal General Law

Justice Louis D. Brandeis, writing for the Court's 6-2 majority, declared that the doctrine established in the *Swift* ruling ninety-six years earlier was "an unconstitutional assumption of powers by the Courts of the United States." The earlier Court had mistakenly interpreted the act, according to Brandeis. Brandeis bluntly wrote, "There is no federal general common law." Referring to numerous legal studies critical of the *Swift* decision, Brandeis held that the Judiciary Act actually intended for federal courts to follow all laws of the state "unwritten as well as written," including those rules made by state courts. Brandeis contended that the *Swift* decision basically violated equal protection of the law since citizens could win some civil cases in a federal court that they could not have won in state courts. They could do this simply by moving to another state and filing the suit in a federal court as a diversity case. Corporations could even reestablish in a new state without actually moving. People or corporations could "shop around" for a federal court that would likely give the best ruling. As a result, plaintiffs (those filing a lawsuit) held a legal advantage over defendants (those the target of lawsuits). Brandeis noted that under the *Swift* rule, Tompkins' chances of winning an award depended on whether the railroad was a New York company or a Pennsylvania company, and that was not just. If Tompkins had filed suit in a Pennsylvania state court, he could not have received an award as he did from a federal court since the state court must follow the state rule. Brandeis also ruled that the *Swift* interpretation of the Judiciary Act was an unconstitutional invasion of state sovereignty. He wrote, the doctrine of federal general law "is an invasion of the authority of the state, and, to that extent, a denial of its independence."

In conclusion, Brandeis held that for diversity cases the proper law to apply is the law of the state. Whether that law was made by a state legislature or by a state court decision "is not a matter of federal concern." He could find nowhere in the Constitution that the federal government, Congress or the federal courts, can create rules of common law in states. Quoting from Justice Oliver Wendell Holmes' dissent in an earlier case, Brandeis wrote that the "authority and only authority is the State, and . . . the voice adopted by the State as its own . . . should utter the last word."

With the *Swift* precedent removed, Brandeis sent the case back to the lower court for review again. The lower court's ruling was not automatically overturned because the issue of negligence under state rule was to be resolved.

No Federal General Rules of Law

The *Erie* ruling significantly cut back the legal authority of federal judges in diversity jurisdiction cases. No longer could they create and apply a general common law at the federal level. Instead, federal judges must apply the state laws in which the federal court is located except when dealing with constitutional issues or matters specifically governed by acts of Congress. Federal courts in a sense became yet another level of state court in diversity cases not involving federal law.

DIVERSITY JURISDICTION

The Framers of the U.S. Constitution believed that for civil cases involving citizens from different states, some neutral means must be available to resolve disputes. As a result, Article III reads that "The [federal] Judicial Power shall extend . . . between Citizens of different States . . . " Section 34 of the act, which later became known as the Rules of Decision Act, established what cases the courts could hear and how law should generally be applied. The Judiciary Act of 1789 gave the newly established federal courts authority to hear such cases. The Judiciary Act considers corporations as citizens of the states in which they are chartered.

Though some believe the need for such protection no longer existed toward the end of the twentieth century, diversity jurisdiction for federal courts persisted. To keep the number of potential cases under control for federal courts, Congress sets minimum dollar figures for civil disputes to qualify for federal courts. In 1789 the amount was $500. By 1988 it was raised to $50,000.

In diversity cases, the federal courts must first look to apply the appropriate federal law. If no federal law for the particular situation exists, then the court must apply the law or principle of the state that is involved, whether established by the state legislature or the state's highest court of law. As a result, national uniformity only exists for situations where federal law applies. Otherwise, state's are free to develop their own rules federal courts must use in diversity cases. If no clear state law or rule exists, then the federal court must consider the way the state's highest court might decide the case.

The decision also put state court rulings on an equal footing as laws passed by state legislatures. The power of state courts was, therefore, substantially raised. The decision discouraged citizens from shopping around for a federal court in various states to file suit in that would likely give a more favorable ruling.

Suggestions for further reading

Elazar, Daniel J. *American Federalism: A View from the States.* New York: Harper & Row, 1984.

Hogue, Arthur R. *Origins of the Common Law.* Indianapolis: Liberty Press, 1986.

Levy, Leonard W., ed. *The Framing and Ratification of the Constitution.* New York: Macmillan Publishing Company, 1971.

International Shoe Co. v. State of Washington 1945

Appellant: International Shoe Company

Appellee: State of Washington

Appellant's Claim: That a state can not require a company based outside the state to contribute monies into the state's unemployment compensation fund simply for selling products in the state.

Chief Lawyer for Appellant: Henry C. Lowenhaupt

Chief Lawyer for Appellee: George W. Wilkins, Washington Assistant Attorney General

Justices for the Court: Hugo Lafayette Black, William O. Douglas, Felix Frankfurter, Frank Murphy, Stanley Forman Reed, Owen Josephus Roberts, Wiley Blount Rutledge, Harlan Fiske Stone

Justices Dissenting: None (Robert H. Jackson did not participate)

Date of Decision: December 3, 1945

Decision: Ruled in favor Washington by finding that International Shoe had sufficient contacts in the state to pay state unemployment tax.

Significance: The decision established an important rule to determine when an out-of-state company has enough presence in a state to come under that state's jurisdiction. The rule of "minimum contacts" established that very little contact by an out-of-state corporation was necessary to make it subject to state regulation.

If a person living in Oregon took a road trip across country and happened to cause a minor traffic accident in Ohio, the Ohio resident involved in the mishap could sue the Oregonian under the state laws of Ohio. The out-of-state driver could not claim that, as a resident of Oregon, he was bound only by decisions made in an Oregon court. In legal terms, this kind of problem is known as personal jurisdiction. Jurisdiction refers to a geographic area over which a government or court has authority. When the term personal is added to jurisdiction, the phrase refers to the power of a court to hear cases where the court is located based on the situation or amount of contact a person, the defendant, has within the court's jurisdiction.

A Shoe Company's Predicament

Now suppose that a large shoe company has several sales agents working in the state of Washington. The shoes are all made in St. Louis, Missouri. The company's headquarters are located in Delaware. The only thing the company does in Washington state is to have its salesmen sell shoes there. The question arises as to whether the shoe company must pay unemployment tax—a percentage of the salespeople's salaries—to the state of Washington.

In the 1930s, a time of high unemployment, Washington had passed a law setting up a state compensation (to make up for lost income) fund to pay unemployment wages to individuals who had lost their jobs through no fault of their own. To help with expenses of the program, companies who employed workers in the state were required to make annual contributions, known as the employment tax, to the program.

Should the Delaware shoe company be required to pay this tax to the state of Washington? The Supreme Court was faced with this problem in the case of *International Shoe Co. v. State of Washington.* The Court considered the case as a question of personal jurisdiction. The decision still carries enormous influence in settling problems of personal jurisdiction.

Personal Jurisdiction and Corporations

Legally a corporation is considered a person under U.S. law. Therefore, corporations are covered by personal jurisdiction laws. Chief Justice Harlan F. Stone commented in *International Shoe,* " . . . the corporate personality is a fiction although a fiction intended to be acted upon as though it were a fact."

Personal Jurisdiction and Minimum Contacts

Business in the late 1930s for International Shoe Company in the state of Washington was good. Between ten and thirteen salesmen employed by the company lived and worked in the state earning a total of $31,000 from 1937 to 1940, a large sum for the times. Washington wanted the tax due on those earnings. A state official personally delivered a notice to one of the company's salesmen living in the state and mailed a copy to the company's office in Delaware demanding that the company pay unemployment tax. The notice asserted the company owed back taxes from 1937 to 1940 when it had not paid unemployment tax.

The company refused to pay claiming that even though they had salesmen working in the state, they did not really have a corporate presence. No company offices were located in the state, no stocks of shoes were kept there, and no contracts of sale were actually signed there. All orders were normally sent by the salesmen to St. Louis where the orders were accepted and the shoes were then shipped from one of several places, all located outside the state of Washington. Since the company itself was not physically present in the state, the company claimed it should not come under Washington state jurisdiction. Therefore, it should not be required to pay unemployment tax.

In such a situation, the idea of a corporation as a person hence falling under personal jurisdiction laws becomes important. Returning to the example of an Oregonian causing a traffic accident which in Ohio, the Oregonian, upon receiving a summons at home in Oregon from Ohio, could argue that he is not present in Ohio, therefore Ohio has no personal jurisdiction over him. However, although the Oregonian was back home, it could be said that the traffic accident in Ohio established "minimum contacts" with Ohio. This minimum contact under personal jurisdiction laws in fact brings him under the jurisdiction of a Ohio state court. Similarly, did International Shoe Company's salesmen working in Washington establish enough contact for the company to fall under Washington state's jurisdiction?

The case first went to a Washington state Superior Court which ruled in favor of the state, ordering International Shoe to make the pay-

PERSONAL JURISDICTION

Personal jurisdiction refers to the legal power a court holds to hear and decide a civil law (private noncriminal) case based on the degree of contact that defendant (individual who is the target of a lawsuit) has in the area in which the court is located. Every state has personal jurisdiction over all its residents and all visitors within its boundaries. This includes residents who leave the state for a brief period of time or people from out-of-state who enter the state only briefly. This jurisdiction comes from the sovereign (politically independent) governmental powers held by each state. However, if the person named in a suit is located outside the state boundaries, then they must have made some form of contact within the state for the state's courts to take the case.

Questions of personal jurisdiction when dealing with individuals as defendants have been fairly straightforward. However, when corporations, who are considered "citizens" by law, are involved, complications can readily occur. For national corporations located in one state, but doing business in others, state courts sometimes have difficulty determining if they have jurisdiction. The corporation is always subject to personal jurisdiction in the state it is chartered. To conduct business in some states, out-of-state corporations have to sign agreements stating that they agree they are subject to personal jurisdiction. Other states require corporations to at least have an agent within the state to receive legal papers if a lawsuit should be filed against them. The general rule is that if a corporation wants the privilege of conducting business in a state, then it must accept responsibilities as well. Sometimes only a single contact made by a corporation within a state, such as a telephone call or letter can be sufficient contact to come under a state's personal jurisdiction. State laws establishing personal jurisdiction over out-of-state corporations are referred to as "long-arm statutes" for extending jurisdiction out long distances beyond state boundaries.

ments. International Shoe appealed the decision to the state supreme court which affirmed the lower court's decision. The company then appealed to the U.S. Supreme Court which accepted the case.

How Much Contact Is Enough Contact?

The Court was left to decide how much "contact" in a state is enough for a citizen, hence a corporation, to fall under that state's jurisdiction. Justice Harlan F. Stone wrote the Court's opinion in the unanimous 8-0 opinion. In finding in favor of Washington, Stone reasoned that by maintaining a sales staff and selling shows International Shoe had established enough contact with the state to require it to be subject to Washington laws for the activities it conducted in the state. These "minimum contacts" were sufficient whenever a corporation had "sufficient contacts or ties with the state . . . to make it reasonable and just, according to our traditional conception of fair play and substantial justice." Stone held that if a corporation enjoys the privilege of conducting business in a state, then it must also meet the obligations of doing business within the state. Also, if a company employs labor in a state, it should be expected to contribute taxes to the unemployment program.

A Major Precedent

The ruling set a major precedent (principles set by earlier court decisions) for determining personal jurisdiction matters. International Shoe made it significantly easier for states to seek jurisdiction over out-of-state corporations. Following the decision, states passed numerous laws defining state jurisdiction over out-of-state businesses. These laws have normally received favorable review in the courts, which strengthens state powers in this area. However, the issue of just what constitutes "minimum contact" was left for courts to explore further in future cases.

The growth of the Internet in the 1990s raised more complex questions concerning what qualifies as corporate contact in a state. The application of state sales taxes to electronic commerce in cyberspace became a major issue among state governments. This question and other new ones in an era of rapid developments in telecommunications pose new problems concerning state regulation of out-of-state businesses.

Suggestions for further reading

Dawson, Paul A. *American Government: Institutions, Policies, and Politics.* Glenview, IL: Scott, Foresman, 1987.

Ferguson, John H., and Dean E. McHenry. *The American Federal Government.* New York: McGraw-Hill Book Company, 1977.

Weissberg, Robert. *Understanding American Government.* New York: Rinehart and Winston, 1980.

Puerto Rico v. Branstad
1987

Petitioner: Commonwealth of Puerto Rico

Respondent: Terry Branstad, Governor of Iowa, et al.

Petitioner's Claim: That Iowa violated the Extradition Clause of the U.S. Constitution by refusing to extradite Ronald Calder, who was wanted for murder in Puerto Rico.

Chief Lawyer for Petitioner: Lino J. Saldana

Chief Lawyer for Respondent: Brent R. Appel

Justices for the Court: Harry A. Blackmun, William J. Brennan, Jr., Thurgood Marshall (writing for the Court), Sandra Day O'Connor, Lewis F. Powell, Jr., William H. Rehnquist, Antonin Scalia, John Paul Stevens, Byron R. White

Justices Dissenting: None

Date of Decision: June 23, 1987

Decision: The Supreme Court said federal courts could require Iowa to extradite Ronald Calder to Puerto Rico.

Significance: With *Branstad,* the Supreme Court said federal courts have the power to order state governments to obey the U.S. Constitution and federal laws.

The Extradition Clause of the U.S. Constitution requires states to extradite fugitives who are hiding in their states. A fugitive is someone who escapes from law enforcement and fails to appear to be tried for a crime. When a state extradites a fugitive, it arrests him and delivers him to the state where he is wanted for a crime. In 1793, Congress passed the Extradition Act, which requires states and territories of the United States to obey the Extradition Clause.

In *Kentucky v. Dennison* (1861), the U.S. Supreme Court issued a strange ruling about the Extradition Clause. It said states must obey the clause, but the federal government may not enforce the clause or punish states for disobedience. The Supreme Court said state and federal governments are equal sovereign powers, so one cannot order the other to do anything. In *Puerto Rico v. Branstad* (1987), the Supreme Court had to decide whether *Dennison* was still good law.

The Fugitive

Ronald Calder was an air traffic controller from Iowa who worked for the Federal Aviation Administration in San Juan, Puerto Rico. On 25 January 1981, Calder got into an argument with Antonio de Jesus Gonzalez in the parking lot of a grocery store. An angry Calder got into his car and drove it into Gonzalez and Gonzalez's pregnant wife, Army Villalba. After striking the couple, Calder backed his car up over Villalba's body two or three times. Gonzalez survived, but Villalba and her unborn child died.

Puerto Rican authorities arrested Calder, charged him with first-degree murder and attempted murder, and released him on $5,000 bail. Calder did not think a white American could get a fair trial in Puerto Rico, so he fled to his family's home in Iowa. Puerto Rico notified Iowa that Calder was wanted in Puerto Rico to stand trial for murder.

On April 24, 1981, Calder surrendered to authorities in Iowa. On May 15, the governor of Puerto Rico asked Governor Robert Ray of Iowa to extradite Calder to Puerto Rico. Governor Ray held an extradition hearing, at which Calder argued that he could not get a fair trial in Puerto Rico. Governor Ray then tried to get Puerto Rico to reduce the charges against Calder. When Puerto Rico refused, Governor Ray denied the extradition request. Terry Branstad, who became governor in Iowa after Ray, also denied Puerto Rico's extradition request.

In 1984, Puerto Rico sued Iowa in federal court. Puerto Rico wanted to force Governor Branstad to extradite Calder to Puerto Rico. Relying on *Kentucky v. Dennison,* both the trial court and the court of appeals said they were powerless to order Iowa to obey the Extradition Clause. Puerto Rico took the case to the U.S. Supreme Court.

FEDERALISM AND STATE POWERS

The Justice

With a unanimous decision, the Supreme Court ruled in favor of Puerto Rico. Writing for the Court, Justice Thurgood Marshall said it was time to overrule *Dennison.* When the Supreme Court overrules a prior case, it announces a new rule of law that replaces the rule from the old case.

Justice Marshall said the Supreme Court decided *Dennison* shortly before the American Civil War began, when the federal government was its least powerful point in American history. With the United States falling apart, there was no way the Supreme Court could have ruled that the federal government could order states to obey the Constitution.

In cases decided after the Civil War, the Supreme Court found the courage to make such rulings. As an example, Justice Marshall referred to the famous case of ***Brown v. Board of Education*** (1955). In *Brown,* the Supreme Court ordered the states to end segregation—the practice of separating white and black students in different public schools. The Court said segregation violated the Equal Protection Clause under the Fourteenth Amendment. According to *Brown* and many other cases,

Governor Terry Branstad refused to extradite a man who was wanted for murder.
Reproduced by permission of AP/Wide World Photos.

KENTUCKY V. DENNISON

In 1861, the United States was on the verge of the American Civil War. Southern states wanted to maintain power by keeping slavery, which made southern agriculture highly profitable. Northern states wanted to abolish slavery. By 1861, many southern states had ceded from, or left, the union of the United States to form a separate Confederacy. In the midst of this turmoil, the U.S. Supreme Court had to decide a case concerning a slave who escaped from captivity.

Charlotte was a slave girl who lived in Louisville, Kentucky. One day she was allowed to go with her owner, C.W. Nichols, to visit her mother in Wheeling, Virginia, where Nichols had business. On their way to Wheeling, Charlotte and Nichols passed through Ohio, which had abolished slavery. While in Cincinnati, Charlotte met some people who helped her escape from Nichols and she became a free woman in Ohio.

Kentucky believed that Willis Lago, a free African American in Ohio, helped Charlotte escape from Nichols. Kentucky Governor Beriah Magoffin asked Ohio Governor William Dennison to arrest Lago and send him to Kentucky to face charges of assisting the escape of a slave. When Dennison refused, Kentucky sued him in federal court.

With tension over the slavery issue high, the question of whether federal courts could order states to comply with the Constitution was difficult. When the case made it to the Supreme Court, the Court said Ohio was required to send Willis Lago to Kentucky to face criminal charges. The Court also said, however, that the federal government had no power to force Ohio to send Lago to Kentucky. Lago escaped charges, the United States fought a civil war, and it took another 125 years for the Supreme Court to overturn *Dennison in* Puerto Rico v. Branstad.

when a state violates the U.S. Constitution, the federal government can force it to obey. Marshall said the idea that state and federal governments are equal sovereign powers is no longer true.

Iowa, then, had a duty to obey the Extradition Clause and the Extradition Act of 1793 by sending Calder to Puerto Rico. If Iowa denied Puerto Rico's request, the federal courts could issue an order giving Iowa no other choice. By reversing *Dennison,* the Supreme Court made sure no state could become a safe haven for fugitives from the law.

Suggestions for further reading

Johnson, Joan. *Justice.* New York: Franklin Watts, 1985.

Karson, Jill, ed. *Criminal Justice: Opposing Viewpoints.* San Diego: Greenhaven Press, 1998.

Mikula, Mark, and L. Mpho Mabunda. *Great American Court Cases.* Detroit: The Gale Group, 1999.

Owens, Lois Smith, and Vivian Vedell Gordon. *Think about Prisons and the Criminal Justice System.* Walker & Co., 1992.

LABOR AND LABOR PRACTICES

The role of labor organizations in modern U.S. industrialized society has its roots in the European merchant and craft guilds of the Middle Ages. The guilds were associations of people with common interests, usually setting prices and quality standards for their goods and wage rates for their employees. The guilds grew to have considerable political power before eventually dying out by the seventeenth century.

Early efforts in the United States for employees to organize into organizations seeking better pay, fewer working hours, and improved working conditions met with fierce opposition. Labor organizers were often considered criminals. This early conflict between employers and unions shaped labor law and labor relations throughout U.S. history.

Early organized labor actions in the United States included efforts by Philadelphia shoemakers in 1792 to improve their work conditions. Their actions met with little success as their organization was ruled illegal by a Pennsylvania court. Unions were considered illegal conspiracies. President Andrew Jackson (1829–1837) even sent U.S. troops in 1834 to break up a strike by canal construction workers in Ohio. A strike by employees is an organized refusal to work. Jackson claimed the strike interfered with interstate commerce (trade across state lines) by threatening not to complete the canal construction. Finally, in 1842 a Massachusetts court recognized a worker's right to strike and that unions were legally valid organizations, the first such ruling in the nation.

Labor organizations began to appear in the mid-nineteenth century. Skilled laborers were the first to organize with the railroad workers leading the way. Railroad workers held a particular edge in that they could potentially cause large scale economic disruptions.

Industrialization and Labor Unrest

Following the American Civil War (1861–1865) industrialization (growth of large manufacturers) expanded rapidly. Rapid changes in technology spurred the growth of capitalism (an economic system in which businesses are privately owned and operated for profit) in which the newly emerging large corporations were much more concerned with profits than employee comfort and safety. As a resul, interest in labor unions grew. In 1869, the Noble Order of the Knights of Labor became one of the first national labor organizations. The eight-hour work day and restrictions on child labor were two of its objectives.

Many still considered unions as obstacles to capitalism and, therefore, un-American. Translating new Darwinian theories of biological evolution to society in general, many believed in a social version of survival of fittest. Those persons who did not prosper on their own initiative were obviously deficient in character and should not be aided by organized groups. A *laissez-faire* economic system which was based on freedom from of governmental or labor union interference was considered most desirable for economic success. The unhampered marketplace was to dictate business success and workers were to perform based on the market needs. In the factories and sweatshops twelve hour workdays and six-day workweeks were common with wages barely at subsistence levels. Working conditions were dangerous and unsanitary. Death and injury were common in industrial accidents.

By the 1880s European immigration escalated providing an increased labor force for the industrialists. Unskilled workers and their families living in crowded slums became common. Support for social reform grew more and the public began to push for protective legislation. Confrontations between laborers and their employers and police began to turn violent in the late 1870s continuing in a series of strikes through the

1880s. Federal troops were called to stop one strike. Finally, police killed dozens of strikers in a 1894 incident. Public acceptance of unions decreased with each incident. In addition, discrimination against the immigrants was prevalent. Typical of the labor movement in general, the Knights of Labor declined, disappearing by 1900.

Two notable developments during this period were the formation of the American Federation of Labor (AFL) in 1886 and passage of the Sherman Antitrust Act in 1890. The AFL was a loose organization of twenty-five national trade unions representing skill workers. Stressing cooperation with employers, the AFL represented over 300,000 workers.

Congress passed the Sherman Antitrust in 1890 with intentions of breaking up the business monopolies. Ironically, courts tended to apply the prohibitions against workers' strikes rather than against business activity ruling that strikes were illegal restraints of trade. With strikes proving ineffective and attracting much public scorn, the use of boycotts soon became a popular alternative. Boycott is an organized effort to convince people not to purchase or handle products made by a particular business. Regional or national boycotts proved more effective than localized strikes, but they also met with much legal opposition. In *Loewe v. Lawlor* (1908) the Court ruled that coordinated boycotts by combinations of workers, like strikes, violated the Sherman Antitrust Act of 1890. Even the publicizing of a proposed boycott was considered in violation of the act despite claims of First Amendment free speech rights by the organizers. The First Amendment protection of the freedom of assembly prevented the banning of unions altogether.

Labor and the Courts

The main court activity in the late nineteenth and early twentieth centuries involved the issuing of injunctions (court order to stop an action) against union activities and rulings often striking down reform legislation. Rulings, such as ***Lochner v. New York*** (1908) striking down a state law setting maximum hours of work for bakers, were normally unfavorable to labor because of the court's desire to define and protect the "liberty of contract," as interpreted in the due process clauses of the Fifth and Fourteenth Amendments. The clauses state "No person shall be . . . deprived of life, liberty, or property, without due process of law." The right of an employer to contract for labor with employees was considered a "liberty" protected by the clause.

Employers commonly used court injunctions to stop strikes and hinder organizing efforts. The first came in 1877 against railroad workers. In a national boycott of railway cars built and owned by the Pullman company, a series of injunctions were issued by federal courts. The injunctions were upheld by a unanimous (all justices agree) Supreme Court in *In re Debs* (1895). Likewise, in *Gompers v. Buck's Stove & Range Co.* (1911) the Court reaffirmed the legality of labor injunctions. Between 1880 and 1930 approximately 4,300 court orders were issued against labor activities.

Persistent court losses led labor leaders to begin lobbying Congress for protective laws including prohibition of injunctions against labor activities. To seek improved working conditions, Congress created the U.S. Department of Labor in 1913. The following year Congress passed the Clayton Act of 1914 barring courts from issuing injunctions against peaceful strikes or boycotts. Formation of unions was no longer to be considered a violation of antitrust law. However, the act proved of little help as it was too vaguely worded for lower courts to apply effectively. Use of injunctions continued. In addition, a common means of controlling union activity was yellow-dog contracts. Employers required employees and those applying for jobs to sign an agreement that they were not and would not become union members. The Court upheld yellow dog contracts in *Coppage v. Kansas* (1915). Union membership correspondingly declined from over five million in 1920 to 3.5 million in 1929.

A desire to protect the "vulnerable" (person who could easily be harmed) did exist through this period. In ***Muller v. Oregon*** (1908) a state maximum hour law for women was upheld. But federal child labor laws did not fair as well. In ***Hammer v. Dagenhart*** (1918), the Court ruled that such laws fell outside congressional authority and should be left to the states. Yet, states were unwilling to pass laws prohibiting child labor since children were popular sources of cheap labor for businesses operating in their boundaries. Despite some limited gains with state reform laws, any effort to recognize broad reforms for all workers was found unacceptable. One result was that laws allowing protection of women only led to a gender-based division in America's working class.

Maintaining Peaceful Labor Relations

Finally, greater recognition of unions and protection of workers rights came in the 1930s. The Great Depression brought a decline in business influence and increased strife among workers. Congress passed the Norris-LaGuardia Act in 1932 more clearly restricting use of injunctions. With improved protection of unions, unskilled workers began to have a voice with the rise of the Congress of Industrial Organizations (CIO).

A truly new era in labor relations and labor law arrived in 1935 with the Wagner Act, also known as the National Labor Relations Act. The act is the most important labor legislation in U.S. history guaranteeing workers "the right to self-organization, to form, join, or assist labor organizations, to bargain collectively, through representatives of their own choosing, and to engage in other concerted activities for . . . mutual aid or protection." Collective bargaining is when the employer and employees' representatives negotiate a labor agreement concerning work conditions including wages, hours, and safety. Employers are required to bargain with their employees' elected representatives. Importantly, the act also prohibited employers from committing "unfair labor practices" that would violate these employee rights. Yellow-dog contracts were outlawed. The act created the National Labor Relations Board (NLRB), a federal agency to enforce the act's provisions. The NLRB has power to investigate employees' complaints and issue orders for employers to stop certain labor practices. The Board can go to a federal appeals court for enforcement of its orders if need be. The NLRB can also conduct elections to determine which union is to represent employees of a particular company.

With the Supreme Court's rejection of a National Industrial Recovery Act only two months before passage of the Wagner Act, the new act received few favorable rulings in the lower courts for two years until a case finally made it to the Supreme Court. Due largely to considerable political pressures from President Franklin D. Roosevelt (1933–1945) and the public, the Court made one of its most dramatic constitutional shifts in U.S. history. Suddenly, the *laissez-faire* economic concepts and protection of business from labor actions was largely abandoned, replaced by recognition of workers' rights and role of government in regulation of economic activities. The Court first abandoned the liberty of contract doctrine in *West Coast Hotel Co. v. Parrish* (1937) by upholding a state law setting minimum wages for women. Then, in ***National Labor Relations Board v. Jones & Laughlin Steel Corp.*** (1937) the Court upheld the NLRA, greatly expanding federal authority to regulate economic matters. The Court for the first time recognized that individual workers were at a disadvantage in negotiating with employers over work conditions. Unions and government intervention were now considered appropriate to make labor relations more balanced.

In *Hague v. Congress of Industrial Organizations* (1939) the Court went further in using First Amendment protections to protect union organizing activities. Freedom to discuss labor issues was recognized as crucial to a modern industrial society. As follow-up to *Hague,* the Court soon ruled in support of peaceful picketing in *Thornhill v. Alabama* (1940). Picketing is physically interfering with a particular business to influence the public against purchasing its products. As a result of the NRLA and sudden favorable Court rulings, union membership substantially grew for the next several decades.

Unfortunately for labor, the favorable rulings came largely from the Court's concern about the public being informed of key labor issues through picketing, strikes, and boycotts and maintaining labor peace than actually protecting workers' rights. This perspective supported substantial government regulation of labor unions and workers' rights. Two key revisions (amendments) to the Wagner Act occurred in 1947 and 1959 which served to restrict union activities. The Taft-Hartley Act of 1947, also known as the Labor Management Relations Act, applied unfair labor practice prohibitions against labor unions, just as the Wagner Act had against employers. For example, unions and union members could not threaten or intimidate other employees into supporting union activities. It also restricted workers' rights to select their own representatives partly in fear of Communist infiltration of labor unions with onset of the Cold War (1946–1991). These restrictions were upheld in *American Communications Association v. Douds* (1950) in the name of protecting commerce from the threat of disruption. Picketing was also limited by the act.

By the late 1950s workers' rights had declined with the government still emphasizing labor peace. Use of injunctions against union activities reappeared. The AFL and CIO merged in 1955 to form the AFL-CIO to increase its power in the face of increased restrictions. The 1959 Landrum-Griffin Act, also known as the Labor Management Reporting and Disclosure Act, curbed abuses of power by union leaders and regulated how labor unions conduct their internal affairs. Still, a strong U.S. economy in the 1960s, based largely on manufacturing industries which dominated the world economy, led to growth of union membership. The workforce also began to change. Passage of the Civil Rights Act of 1964 opened up employment as well as union memberships to both racial minorities and women. But, unfavorable legal rulings toward labor continued as the Court in *American Ship Building Co. v. NLRB* (1965) upheld an employer's right to "lockout" employees as part of collective bargaining pressure on workers. Lockout means refusal to allow employees to enter their workplace.

Propelled by the Wagner Act and its amendments, the field of labor law grew, focusing on the rights of employees, employers, and labor unions. The process of organizing unions, conducting elections for union representatives, spending union monies, negotiating labor contracts, and resolving disputes became well established. Though both unions and employers are required to bargain when one or the other requests it, there is no requirement that workers and employers must reach agreement on a labor contract. Federal or state government mediators (officials stepping in between the two sides) may even be called upon to help with negotiations. Strikes or boycotts could result from failed negotiations. If disputes threaten public health or safety, the U.S. president has authority to obtain an eighty day injunction from federal courts against strikes or lockouts. This power was often used in the 1950s and 1960s, but much less so after 1970. Almost every labor contract that is established includes a grievance (complaint) procedure designed to settle disputes between workers and employers. Failure of immediate solution may lead to arbitration, meaning another person not connected to the two sides decides the issues. The resulting solution is considered final and both sides must comply with it.

A Changing Economy

Labor relations continued to change in the late twentieth century. A decline of union membership and activity occurred through the 1970s and 1980s. A combination of economic slowdowns, increased automation in factories, and shift of manufacturing jobs to less developed countries with cheaper labor costs contributed to the change. The U.S. economy shifted from manufacturing to service jobs, including health care, food service, information technology, and insurance which generally pay less for lesser skilled employees and are more temporary in nature. In addition, women who were generally less inclined to participate in union activities entered the workforce in substantially larger numbers. Almost 35 percent of the U.S. workforce claimed union membership in 1954 compared to less than 15 percent in 1995.

Changes in the U.S. economy in the 1990s led to more cooperative working relations between employers and labor unions, including agreements in some instances to reduce wages in tradeoff for greater job security. Some employers began giving unions a greater voice in company policies. The NLRA, built on the notion that labor and employers always have opposing viewpoints and goals, became viewed as outdated by both labor and business as some new workplace cooperative practices were ruled in violation of the act. Some called for repeal of the NLRA and restructuring of labor law to better conform to the changing work environment in the twenty-first century.

Suggestions for further reading

Boyett, Joseph H. *Beyond Workplace 2000.* New York: Dutton Books, 1995.

Foner, Philip S. *History of the Labor Movement in the United States.* New York: International Publishers, 1974.

Foner, Philip S. *Women and the American Labor Movement From World War I to the Present.* New York: The Free Press, 1980.

Milkman, Ruth, ed. *Women, Work and Protest: A Century of U.S. Women's Labor History.* Boston: Routledge & Kegan Paul, 1985.

Tilley, Chris. *Work Under Capitalism.* Boulder, CO: Westview Press, 1998.

Trattner, Walter L. *Crusade for the Children: A History of the National Child Labor Committee and Child Labor Reform in America.* Chicago: Quardrangle Books, 1970.

Yellen, Samuel. *American Labor Struggles.* New York: Arno Press, Inc., 1967.

Lochner v. New York
1905

Appellant: Joseph Lochner

Appellee: State of New York

Appellant's Claim: That New York's Bakeshop Act was an unreasonable exercise of state police power to regulate the working conditions at bakeries.

Chief Lawyers for Appellant: Frank Harvey Field, Henry Weismann

Chief Lawyer for Appellee: Julius M. Mayer, Attorney General of New York

Justices for the Court: David J. Brewer, Henry B. Brown, Melville W. Fuller, Oliver Wendell Holmes, Joseph McKenna, Rufus W. Peckham

Justices Dissenting: William Rufus Day, John Marshall Harlan I, Edward Douglass White

Date of Decision: April 17, 1905

Decision: Ruled in favor of Lochner by finding that the Bakeshop law unconstitutionally restricted an employer's liberty to contract for labor.

Significance: The decision recognized a sweeping new freedom of contract loosely drawn from the due process clauses of the Fifth and Fourteenth amendments. The decision had a major effect on twentieth century society to the detriment of the workingman. In the late 1930s, the Court shifted its focus to protection of individual rights over economic interests.

The way in which the courts interpret the U.S. Constitution changes greatly through time as society changes. From the birth of the nation in the 1780s until the 1870s, courts interpreted the Due Process Clause of the Fifth Amendment as applying primarily to how fairly federal laws were applied, not so much what the intent of the law was. The amendment states that no person shall "be deprived of life, liberty, or property, without due process of law." Citizens should receive sufficient notice and fair legal hearings before government could take action. Individual rights, such as freedom from discrimination, were not a concern as in modern America.

Liberty of Contract

In 1868 the Fourteenth Amendment was added to the Constitution which also contained a Due Process Clause. Aimed at protecting individuals from state actions, the amendment came at a time the American Industrial Revolution was well underway with industry rapidly growing. Major changes in society were also occurring including an ever widening gap between the rich and poor. While employers were accumulating wealth, employees were working longer and longer hours, often in unhealthy conditions. Few laws existed for health and safety standards in places of employment.

Typical of this industrialization trend, many bakers in New York worked twelve hours a day for seven days a week. Conditions in city bakeries, often located in the basements of tenement houses, were cramped and filthy. With little time for rest, many workers essentially lived in their kitchens, sleeping at their workbenches. With poor ventilation, disease and early deaths were common. Believing that unsanitary and unsafe conditions affected the bakers and their products, the New York legislature passed the Bakeshop Act in 1895. Besides setting minimum sanitation standards, the act stated that no employee "shall be required or permitted to work in a biscuit, bread, or cake bakery . . . more than sixty hours in any one week, or more than ten hours in any one day."

Joseph Lochner

Joseph Lochner owned a small bakery in Utica, New York that produced biscuits, breads, and cakes for early-morning customers. Lochner's employees were frequently required to work late into the night, sometimes sleeping in the bakery before rising early to prepare the products for the customers. In April of 1901, one of his bakers, Aman Schmitter worked over sixty hours in one week. A complaint was filed with the police who arrested Lochner and charged him in violation of the Bakeshop Act.

Ten months after his arrest, Lochner's case went to trial in Oneida County Court. Intending to appeal to a higher court to challenge the law, Lochner refused to plead guilty or not guilty, and offered no defense to the charge. Judge W. T. Dunmore found Lochner guilty and sentenced him to pay a fifty dollar fine or spend fifty days in jail. Lochner immediately appealed the decision to the Appellate Division of the New York Supreme Court.

Before the five appeals court judges, Lochner argued that because of the Bakeshop Act he could not freely make a contract with his employees concerning pay and hours of work. This interfered with his right to earn a living and pursue a lawful trade as protected by the Fourteenth Amendment's Due Process Clause. Three of the five judges were unconvinced with his arguments and upheld his conviction. They ruled the law was a proper exercise of the state's police powers to protect

Lochner's Home Bakery in New York. Courtesy of the Library of Congress.

the health and safety of its citizens. Lochner appealed the decision to the New York Court of Appeals, but lost again.

Lochner next appealed to the U.S. Supreme Court which agreed to hear his case. Lochner also decided to change lawyers, hiring Henry Weismann. Weismann was an interesting choice for in the 1890s he had been a lobbyist for the Journeyman Bakers Union and editor of the union's newsletter, the Bakers' Journal. Weismann was an advocate for laws limiting bakers' hours to eight hours a day. Leaving the union in 1897, Weismann opened two bakeries of his own leading a complete change in personal interests. He joined the Retail Bakers' Association to fight enforcement of the Bakers Act.

Before the Court, Weismann argued the law violated Lochner's "liberty of contract." He claimed that employers and employees had a basic right to negotiate a contract over conditions of their labor free from state restrictions as long as they did not interfere with another person's liberty of contract. Weismann asserted that baking was not a dangerous occupation. Therefore, the law was an inappropriate use of police powers depriving bakery owners of their due process rights.

New York countered that state restrictions to protect the health and well-being of workers and general public were nothing new. For example, physicians were required to obtain a license before practicing medicine. Using statistics, the state also argued baking was less healthy than many occupations. It involved heavy lifting and carrying while breathing air containing flour dust and germs. Lung diseases including tuberculosis were common. Because employees had less bargaining power than their employers when negotiating labor contracts, laws were needed for the public good to protect workers from being unfairly exploited.

The Court was left to decide between the right to contract versus the employees protection from poor working conditions. Justice Rufus Peckham delivered the findings of the Court in a close 5–4 decision. Peckham declared the act interfered with the right "to make contracts regarding labor upon such terms as they may think best, or upon which they may agree." Under the Fourteenth Amendment, people were free to purchase and sell labor without state restrictions, contended Peckham. Regarding the state's assertion that baking was an unhealthy occupation, Peckham stated, "The trade of a baker is not unhealthy . . . to such a degree which would authorize the legislature . . . to cripple the ability of the laborer to support himself and his family" by restricting his work.

Concluding that a direct relationship between the act and the health and welfare of New York bakers was not sufficient, Peckham wrote,

> **There is no reasonable ground for interfering with the liberty of a person or right of free contract, by determining the hours of labor, in the occupation of a baker . . . A law like the one before us involves neither the safety, the morals, nor the welfare of the public . . .**

A Strong Dissent

In dissent, Justice John Marshall Harlan believed that baking was a hard occupation. Though agreeing that the due process clause does protect the liberty to contract, the state's have power to regulate that liberty for the health and safety of its citizens. He pointed to many state mining laws limiting miners to eight hour days.

Justice Oliver Wendell Holmes pointed out that the peoples' rights are routinely limited by state laws. Holmes wrote,

> **The liberty of the citizens to do as he likes so long as he does not interfere with the liberty of others to do the same . . . is interfered with by school laws, by the Post Office, by every state or municipal institution which takes his money for purposes thought desirable, whether he likes it or not.**

Holmes asserted that the state's have broad rights to restrict activities and the courts should be very cautious in overturning them.

Lochner's Legacy

For the next thirty-two years federal courts used *Lochner* to overturn numerous laws attempting to regulate various aspects of business, employment, and property interests. The decision launched a new era of constitutional interpretation lasting until 1937. During this time, public sentiment strongly supported the idea that government should minimally interfere with the newly evolving industrial capitalistic market, an idea known as *laissez-faire* economics.

Following the stock market crash of 1929, President Franklin D. Roosevelt began to attempt to establish a social and economic reform

JUDICIAL RESTRAINT

Article III of the U.S. Constitution describes how U.S. courts of law should operate. It directs the U.S. Supreme Court to keep a sharp distinction between its duties and that of Congress. The Court must restrain (to hold back) itself from doing Congress' job of making policy. To legal scholars the *Lochner v. New York* decision represents the best example of the lack of "judicial restraint" shown by the Court. The Court should give Congress and state legislatures the benefit of the doubt when interpreting laws. It should never overturn a law unless clearly violating some part of the Constitution. Rulings should not promote new ideas or preferences of the justices. The Court should rely only on precedents (previous decisions) or long established common law rather than attempting to promote some general public good considered important at the time. That is the legislature's role.

In *Lochner,* the Court's majority was reflecting the general public mood at the time of a growing young industrialist society based on a capitalistic economy. People believed the least amount of government regulation would allow the economy to grow "naturally." To support this idea in *Lochner,* the Court created an unwritten right from a loose reading of the Constitution, the right to contract. Decades later, the Court adopted a greater role of self-restraint by changing its interpretation of the Due Process Clause and overturning *Lochner.*

program based on a series of new federal laws. The Court, using the *Lochner* decision, and consistently overturned the laws much to the dismay of the president and much of the public.

Finally, in 1937 the Court embraced Holmes' dissent in *Lochner* in the case of *West Coast Hotel Co. v. Parrish.* In letting stand a Washington state law setting a minimum wage for women, the Court ruled the freedom to contract was not unlimited. For the rest of the twentieth century, governments were given freedom to regulate the workplace and other economic affairs.

Suggestions for further reading

Ken, Paul. Lochner v. New York*: Economic Regulation on Trial.* Lawrence: University Press of Kansas, 1998.

Leslie, Douglas L. *Labor Law in a Nutshell.* St. Paul, MN: West Publishing Group, 1992.

Terrell, Leo J. *The Things Your Boss Won't Tell You: Your Rights at the Work Place.* Beverly Hills, CA: L. Terrell Enterprises, 1998.

Muller v. Oregon
1908

Appellant: Curt Muller

Appellee: State of Oregon

Appellant's Claim: That an Oregon law prohibiting women from working more than ten hours a day is unconstitutional.

Chief Lawyers for Appellant: William D. Fenton, Henry H. Gilfry

Chief Lawyers for Appellee: H. B. Adams, Louis Brandeis

Justices for the Court: David J. Brewer, William R. Day, Melville W. Fuller, John Marshall Harlan, Oliver Wendell Holmes, Joseph McKenna, William H. Moody, Rufus W. Peckham, Edward D. White

Justices Dissenting: None

Date of Decision: February 24, 1908

Decision: Ruled in favor of Oregon by agreeing with a lower court that women are a "special class" of citizens in need of protection at the workplace.

Significance: The classification of women as a special class brought mixed results. The decision paved the way for men and children to later receive similar protections under state laws regulating workplace conditions. But, the ruling also reinforced sexual discrimination in the workplace experienced by many women through the rest of the twentieth century.

For years women have fought cultural stereotypes depicting females as the "weaker sex." Such perceptions have long been a part of English tradition dating back at least to the medieval period of history. Women were considered primarily as wives and mothers, to be protected from the rough world outside the home. In marriage a wife's identity would be fully merged into the husband's. This idea carried forward until the mid-nineteenth century when states began recognizing wives more as separate persons. Still unable to vote in elections, the growing feminist political movement of the mid-nineteenth century focused on gaining voting rights.

Other issues also began to attract attention as well. During the industrial expansion following the American Civil War (1861–1865), workers' conditions were often deplorable. By the late nineteenth century, mass immigration from Europe to the U.S. industrial cities led to many women seeking work in the factories. "Sweat shops" became common. Almost twenty states passed laws placing women in a special legal class for protection from such harsh work conditions. Among these was Oregon which passed a law in February of 1903 setting the maximum number of hours a woman could work in a day. The act stated that "no female [shall] be employed in any mechanical establishment, or factory, or laundry in this state more than ten hours during any one day."

At the beginning of the twentieth century, the growing public demand for regulation of businesses collided with the prevailing legal ideas that the "liberty of contract" as provided in Section 10 of Article I of the Constitution prohibited just about all forms of government interference in business. The liberty of contract is a basic freedom to make agreements with others. Many claimed the freedom to contract for labor was protected from state regulation by the Due Process Clause of the Fourteenth Amendment which reads that the state shall not "deprive any person of life, liberty or property, without due process of law." The Supreme Court in ***Lochner v. New York*** (1905) negated a New York law setting maximum hours a week that bakers could work based on this concept.

Mrs. Elmer Gotcher

Not long after the *Lochner* decision, Joe Haselbock, foreman at Portland's Grand Laundry required Mrs. Elmer Gotcher, a launderer, to work more than ten hours on September 4, 1905. Gotcher filed a complaint against the shop's owner, Curt Muller, claiming that the laundry

LABOR AND LABOR PRACTICES

violated the Oregon maximum hours law. On September 18, the Multnomah County Court ruled in favor of Gotcher and fined Muller ten dollars. Muller appealed his conviction to the Oregon state supreme court which affirmed the sentence in 1906. Muller then decided to challenge the constitutionality of the state law and appealed to the U.S. Supreme Court.

Oregon Case Attracts National Attention

With similar hours laws under attack in other states, the case attracted considerable attention of national feminist groups who promoted women's issues. The National Consumers' League, with Florence Kelley as executive secretary and Josephine Goldmark an active member, supported the Oregon law. Kelley and Goldmark believed long hours of work was harmful to female workers, particularly pregnant workers and mothers. However, other feminist groups opposed the Oregon law. Alice Paul and the National Woman Party believed that to treat women differently would make it difficult for women to compete with men for jobs. Special protection could hinder their efforts for gaining equality in the work-

Mrs. Gotcher was demanded to work long hours at a local laundry.
Courtesy of the Library of Congress.

place. Other groups opposing the Oregon law were those not so much involved in women's issues, but more concerned about government interference in business and defending the "liberty of contract."

Kelley and Goldmark contended that states held a "special interest" in helping workers in dangerous occupations. Fearful that the recent *Lochner* decision could be a precedent (setting a principle for later court decisions) and restrain states' abilities to enact laws dealing with women's working conditions, they turned to Goldmark's brother-in-law and successful Boston lawyer, Louis D. Brandeis, to argue their case before the Court. Brandeis had gained a strong reputation for effectively arguing in favor of legal protection of people's social needs and had represented several states in defending their wage and hour laws.

Brandeis accepted the case but required the National Consumers' League provide him a massive amount of information within two weeks on the connection between women's health and long hours of factory work. Goldmark and Kelley labored around the clock to produce a 113-page brief (document for the Court) drawing information of many sources including the medical field.

Women Deserve Special Protection

Before the Court, Muller argued that the Oregon law denying women the right to work more than ten hours a day interfered with their liberty to make contracts and ability to support themselves. In addition, the Oregon law directly conflicted with another Oregon law giving men and women equal personal rights. Referring to the Fourteenth Amendment, Muller argued the Oregon law was unconstitutional since "the statute [law} does not apply equally to all persons . . . "

Brandeis, using the lengthy brief, countered that women as a group needed special protection. Brandeis attempted to show that unlike the situation in the *Lochner* case which dealt with mostly male bakers, the Oregon law was justified in protecting the health, safety, and welfare of women. Basing his argument on the notion that women are the "weaker sex," Brandeis stated it was "common knowledge" that permitting women to work more than ten hours a day in such workplaces as factories and laundries was "dangerous to public health, safety, morals [and] welfare." Extended periods of manual labor produced damaging physical and mental effects in women. Consequently, the state indeed had a valid interest in women's health.

Justice David J. Brewer, writing for the unanimous Court, stated that the mere fact that so many states had adopted such laws reflected "a widespread belief that woman's physical structure, and the functions she performs in consequence thereof, justify special legislation restricting or qualifying the conditions under which she should be permitted to toil."

In a statement that seemed progressive (forward thinking) at the time, but paternalistic (overly protective) ninety years later, Brewer wrote,

> **That woman's physical structure . . . place her at a disadvantage in the struggle for subsistence is obvious. This is especially true when the burdens of motherhood are upon her. Even when they are not . . . continuance for a long time on her feet at work, repeating this from day to day, tends to injurious effects upon the body, and, as healthy mothers are essential to vigorous offspring, the physical well-being of woman becomes an object of public interest and care in order to preserve the strength and vigor of the race.**

Brewer concluded that a woman "is properly placed in a class by herself, and legislation designed for her protection may be sustained." The Court unanimously affirmed the lower court decision. Muller was ordered to pay the fine plus court costs.

Mixed Results

The *Muller* decision opened the door for states to pass more laws regulating work conditions. Brandeis' argument also set a new standard for presenting information in support of reform laws addressing social conditions. The Court's role influence on reform laws was far from over. Still very protective of business interests, the Court ruled in *Adkins v. Children's Hospital* (1923) that state laws regulating workplace conditions were unconstitutional. But the Court changed direction again fourteen years later in *West Coast Hotel v. Parrish* (1937) by upholding a Washington state minimum wage law for women and children, essentially overturning the *Adkins* decision and returning to *Muller*. The sweeping protection of "liberty of contract" had finally declined in favor of protecting the health and safety of citizens. Congress passed the Fair Labor Standards Act in 1938 extending to men the same wage and hour restrictions earlier applied to women. The Court in ***United States v. Darby*** (1941) affirmed the constitutionality of minimum wage laws.

LOUIS D. BRANDEIS

Louis Dembitz Brandeis (1856–1941), a brilliant lawyer and eventual Supreme Court justice, had a lifelong commitment to social reform. Born in 1856 in Louisville, Kentucky to well-to-do European immigrant parents, Brandeis was an excellent student. He graduated from Harvard Law School in 1877 at the top of his class. Brandeis established a highly successful private law practice in Boston. Highly involved in the Progressive Movement at the beginning of the twentieth century and dedicated to social reform, he provided legal services for many causes.

In the *Muller v. Oregon* case, Brandeis introduced a whole new form of legal brief, one that was lengthy including much data from many subjects. The style became known as the Brandeis Brief. In 1916 Brandeis was appointed by President Woodrow Wilson (1913–1921) to the Supreme Court on which he served for twenty-three years. The first Jewish American Court nominee and a staunch supporter of social reform in a time of strong pro-business interests among the American leaders. The writer of many eloquent dissents while on the Court, Brandeis fought for individual rights laying the groundwork for recognition decades later of the right to privacy. Brandeis retired from the Court in 1939 and died in 1941. Widely considered one of the great justices in Supreme Court history, in 1948 a new private university, Brandeis University in Massachusetts, was named in his honor.

Though the *Muller* decision was welcomed by many earnestly trying to protect women from deplorable work conditions, it did add support to the "weaker sex" notion and hindered women from competing with men in many jobs. Women were commonly relegated to low-paying, temporary, unskilled jobs. Women could not deliver the mail, work in foundries and mines, run elevators, sell liquor, and work as streetcar conductors or printers in print shops. In reaction to the *Muller* decision, the *New York Times* wrote in its February 28, 1908 edition, "We leave to the advocates of women suffrage to say whether this decision makes for, or against, the success of their cause." The Nineteenth Amendment granting women voting rights was added twelve years later in 1920, but other feminist issues continued unresolved. The practice of treating women differently in the workplace continued through the remainder of the twentieth century.

Suggestions for further reading

Goldstein, Leslie F. *The Constitutional Rights of Women.* Madison: The University of Wisconsin Press, 1989.

Hoff, Joan. *Law, Gender, and Injustice.* New York: New York University Press, 1991.

Mezey, Susan G. *In Pursuit of Equality: Women, Public Policy, and the Federal Courts.* New York: St. Martin's Press, 1992.

Hammer v. Dagenhart
1918

Appellant: W.C. Hammer, U.S. Attorney for the Western District of North Carolina

Appellee: Roland Dagenhart

Appellant's Claim: That Congress had constitutional authority under the Commerce Clause to pass and enforce the Keating-Owen child labor law.

Chief Lawyers for Appellant: John W. Davis, U.S. Solicitor General; Roscoe Pound, Dean of Harvard Law School

Chief Lawyer for Appellee: Junius Parker

Justices for the Court: William Rufus Day, Joseph McKenna, Mahlon Pitney, Willis Van Devanter, Edward Douglas White

Justices Dissenting: Louis D. Brandeis, John Hessin Clarke, Oliver Wendell Holmes, James Clark McReynolds

Date of Decision: June 3, 1918

Decision: Ruled in favor of Dagenhart by finding that Congress had no authority under the Commerce Clause to restrict manufacturing activities involving children.

Significance: The decision was a strong statement in favor of state powers. The Court continued taking unpopular positions on attempts by the federal government to regulate business and protect workers' rights. Though another child labor law was overturned again four years later, by the late 1930s protection of children in the workplace finally became accepted by the courts.

LABOR AND LABOR PRACTICES

With expansion of industrialization in the late nineteenth century, conditions for workers on the job were often harsh. The Supreme Court justices during this time largely believed in the idea of *laisse-faire* economy, meaning business and industry were free to grow largely unaffected by government regulation. This position led to many unpopular Court decisions blocking government regulation and efforts to promote workers' rights.

In the absence of child labor laws, many children worked long hours at difficult and dangerous jobs in mines and factories and on farms. In 1900, one out of every six children between the ages of ten and fifteen worked for money. Often jobs required children to work ten or more hours a day and paid only a few cents an hour. Chief among these was the South's growing textile industry which heavily relied on the cheap labor of children.

Social reform movements began to grow in reaction to the harsh working conditions, with particular concern focused on the effects on women and children as well as the long range implications for U.S. society. Though a proposed child labor law was unsuccessful in Congress in 1907, it drew increased national attention to the issue. However, reformists faced two major obstacles. One was that labor contracts were considered personal matters outside the authority of government to regulate. For the government to say that children should not work more than ten hours a day, or that children under fourteen years of age should not work at all would be considered interference with a parent's and employer's right to enter into a contract. Second, such matters were considered the responsibility of states to regulate. The Tenth Amendment to the Constitution states that all powers not specifically given to the federal government are reserved for the states. But states were not likely to restrict labor. Since child labor was cheaper than adult wages, influential business interests opposed state laws restricting child labor. They feared that if the state prohibited child labor their businesses would be non-competitive with businesses in other states not restricted by such laws. Businesses in states without child labor laws could likely sell their products at a lower cost.

Keating and Owen

Representative Edward Keating and Senator Robert L. Owen proposed a different legal route to protect children from working long hours for low wages in hazardous conditions. They decided to use federal authority under the Commerce Clause to avoid the issue of regulating work conditions or contracts. The Commerce Clause, included in Article I of the Constitution, gives the federal government authority to regulate interstate commerce (business conducted across state lines). They proposed and soon passed the Keating-Owen Act, commonly known as the Child Labor Act of 1916. The act prohibited the interstate shipment of products made in factories or mines that employed children under fourteen years of age or that allowed children between fourteen and sixteen years of age to work more than eight hours a day. Employers were also prohibited from requiring children to work six days a week, after 7:00 P.M. or before 6:00 A.M. Companies could not ship products until these labor conditions had ceased for at least thirty days.

Immediately opponents to the act rallied to challenge it. Among these was David Clark. Clark was publisher of a trade journal in Charlotte, North Carolina, a major center of the textile industry, and a member of the Executive Committee of Southern Cotton Manufacturers. Looking for a test case to challenge the new law, Clark found Roland Dagenhart who worked with his two teenaged sons at the Fidelity Manufacturing Company, a small cotton mill in Charlotte. Dagenhart's older son, Reuben, was fifteen years of age, and his younger son was thirteen years of age.

Child laborers were not uncommon in the early years of the 1900s. Courtesy of the Library of Congress.

Under the new federal law, Reuben would have to greatly reduce the number of hours worked in a week. The younger son could not work at all.

When Fidelity Manufacturing indicated it would follow the new law, Dagenhart with encouragement from Clark filed a lawsuit in U.S. District Court for the Western District of North Carolina against the company and against W. C. Hammer, the U.S. Attorney who would likely be the person enforcing the law in that area. Dagenhart sought an injunction (a court order to stop an action) to prevent the company from obeying the act and to keep Hammer from enforcing it. The district ruled the act was unconstitutional and issued an injunction to stop enforcement of it. Hammer appealed the decision to the Supreme Court which accepted the case.

Before the Supreme Court, Hammer argued how destructive child labor was to both the children and their families. He also argued that states were unable to pass such protective laws individually because of the fear of losing business to other states. Only the federal government could pass such a law that would be equally applied to everyone. The Keating-Owen Act was, therefore, necessary to protect the public good.

Justice William R. Day wrote the opinion of the Court's bitterly divided 5-4 majority in favor of Dagenhart. Typical for the Court during this time period, Day held a very narrow (restricted) view of federal government authority under the Commerce Clause. Day wrote that the power to regulate commerce is the power "to control the means by which commerce is carried on," not the "right to forbid commerce" as the Keating-Owen Act did. Hammer argued that interstate prohibitions had already been successfully applied to other forms of commerce related to lottery tickets, contaminated food, and kidnaped persons. None of these could be transported between states. However, Day responded that for these situations "the use of interstate transportation was necessary" for harmful activities to occur. However, in the Dagenhart case, Day asserted "the goods shipped are of themselves harmless" therefore the actual transportation of goods is not the problem at hand.

Day concluded that though states who passed child labor laws would likely be more disadvantaged economically than those who did not pass such laws, "this fact does not give Congress the power to deny transportation in interstate commerce." The Tenth Amendment allowed states to freely make their own choices. The first child labor law passed in the United States was overturned.

Justice Oliver Wendell Holmes, known as the Great Dissenter for his frequent disagreements with the Court's majority, wrote one of the

When it was legal, companies often hired children for simple jobs that many adults couldn't or wouldn't do. Courtesy of the Library of Congress.

CHILD LABOR LAWS

Children have worked to help their families since ancient times, commonly on farms. Social problems with child labor began to rise with the coming of industrialization in the eighteenth century in Britain and the nineteenth century in the United States. Kept out of school, children often worked in filthy, dimly-lighted mines, mills, and factories. The British Parliament passed the first British child labor law in 1802 aimed at protecting pauper children (children dependent on charity). In the United States, by 1832 about 40 percent of New England factory workers were between the ages of seven and sixteen. Massachusetts was the first state to pass a child labor law, in 1836, but few other states adopted laws in the nineteenth century and those few were generally not enforced.

After the Keating-Owen Act, the first federal child labor law, was overturned in the Supreme Court; a national child labor law did not pass successfully until the 1930s. By the year 2000, all fifty states had child labor laws to protect children from risk of injury. The laws vary widely, but generally set a minimum general employment age, a higher age for hazardous work, and limits on hours. Violation of child labor regulations can lead to criminal prosecution. An accused employer can not claim innocence of the child's age as a defense. They have a responsibility to know the age of their workers. Child labor among farmworkers remains a key issue.

best known dissents in Supreme Court history. Holmes passionately wrote, "It does not matter whether the supposed evil precedes or follows the transportation . . . It is enough that in the opinion of Congress that transportation encourages the evil."

An Unpopular Decision

The Court decision in *Hammer* was met with public outrage. The *New York Evening Mail* called the decision a "victory of sordidness [unwholesomeness] over our little ones." Congress responded by looking at its other authorities such as the power to tax. In February of 1919, Congress passed a revenue act applying a stiff 10 percent excise tax on products made with child labor. However, that law was also struck down in *Bailey v. Drexel Furniture Co.* (1922) with the Court ruling that Congress had no taxing authority for business activities occurring fully within a state.

With a major change in Court direction in the late 1930s supporting federal regulation of many activities, the Court reversed the *Hammer* decision in ***United States v. Darby*** (1941).

Interestingly, five years later at age twenty Reuben Dagenhart made the following comment during an interview about the case,

> **I don't see that I got any benefit. I guess I'd have been a lot better off if they hadn't won it. Look at me! A hundred and five pounds, a grown man and no education. I may be mistaken, but I think the years I've put in the cotton mills have stunted my growth. They kept me from getting any schooling. I had to stop school after the third grade and now I need the education I didn't get . . . It would have been a good thing in this state if that law they passed had been kept.**

Suggestions for further reading

Bartoletti, Susan C. *Growing Up in Coal Country.* Boston: Houghton Mifflin Co., 1996.

Freedman, Russell. *Kids at Work: Lewis Hine and the Crusade Against Child Labor.* New York: Clarion Books, 1994.

Greene, Laura O. *Child Labor: Then and Now.* New York: F. Watts, 1992.

National Labor Relations Board v. Jones & Laughlin Steel Corp. 1937

Appellant: National Labor Relations Board

Appellee: Jones & Laughlin Steel Corporation

Appellant's Claim: That Congress has the constitutional authority under the Commerce Clause to pass legislation protecting the rights of organized labor.

Chief Lawyers for Appellant: U.S. Attorney General Homer S. Cummings, U.S. Solicitor General Stanley F. Reed, and J. Warren Madden

Chief Lawyer for Appellee: Earl F. Reed

Justices for the Court: Louis D. Brandeis, Benjamin N. Cardozo, Chief Justice Charles Evans Hughes, Owen Josephus Roberts, Harlan Fiske Stone

Justices Dissenting: Pierce Butler, James Clark McReynolds, George Sutherland, Willis Van Devanter

Date of Decision: April 12, 1937

Decision: Ruled in favor of the National Labor Relations Board by finding that Congress has authority under the Commerce Clause to regulate labor relations.

Significance: The landmark ruling signaled a radical change in the Supreme Court's acceptance of Congressional power to regulate economic matters.

The right of workers to ban together seeking better working conditions was not traditionally recognized in U.S. history. For decades Supreme Court decisions supported a *laissez-faire* form of economy in which businesses operate with minimal government interference, letting the marketplace guide economic growth. The Commerce Clause in Article I, Section 8, of the Constitution did give Congress power to "regulate Commerce . . . among the several states." But the clause was typically interpreted very narrowly by the Court, restricting the power of the federal government in economic matters.

Likewise, the courts did not interfere with the freedom of an employer to contract for labor with his employee. According to the courts, employers and employees had the right to bargain free of government interference under the Due Process Clause of the Fifth Amendment. The clause states that "No person shall be . . . deprived of life, liberty, or property, without due process of law." In addition the Contract Clause in Article I reads, "No State shall . . . make any . . . Law impairing the Obligation [responsibility] of Contracts." Therefore, the Court used the Fifth's Due Process Clause to limit federal regulation of business activities and the Contract Clause to limit state regulation.

Employers were free to take a variety of actions to discourage employees from joining organizations, such as labor unions. Labor unions are groups of workers who have joined together to seek better work conditions. One of the more common means to discourage an employer from forming a labor union was known as yellow-dog contracts. Employers forced employees to sign these contracts agreeing to not join unions, or to quit unions if already a member. Employees could be fired if they did not comply with the contract. The Supreme Court ruled in *Adair v. United States* (1908) that yellow-dog contracts were legal under the "liberty of contract" concept.

Labor and the New Deal

With major economic problems plaguing the nation during the Great Depression of the 1930s, Congress passed various laws designed to guide social and economic reform. The laws, collectively known as the New Deal, gave Congress unprecedented control of the nation's economy. Authority for New Deal legislation largely drew from the Commerce Clause.

LABOR AND LABOR PRACTICES

In 1935 Congress passed the National Labor Relations Act, more commonly known as the Wagner Act. The act, for the first time, recognized the right of workers to organize and bargain collectively with their employers. Collective bargaining is when an employer and a representative of his employees negotiate an agreement concerning work conditions, including wages, hours, and safety. Considered one of the more dramatic pieces of New Deal legislation, the bill was introduced by Senator Robert F. Wagner, a Democrat from New York. President Franklin D. Roosevelt (1933–1945) first feared that strong labor organizations might interfere with the nation's economic recovery. But, he became a supporter of the proposed act when passage became evident. In fact, fear that labor unrest might slow the flow of interstate commerce and economic recovery led, in part, to its passage. The act applied to all businesses conducting interstate commerce (business conducted across state lines) or who were affected by interstate commerce.

The Wagner Act created the National Labor Relations Board (NLRB) to enforce its provisions (parts), The new federal agency was charged with resolving disputes between employees and employers. The

Organized labor unions work democratically to ensure that workers get a say in their work conditions. Reproduced by permission of the Corbis Corporation.

NLRB hears cases involving charges of unfair labor practices and makes decisions which may be appealed to the federal court of appeals.

The Wagner Act outlawed various employer practices aimed at discouraging union participation by its employees including yellow dog contracts. It was now illegal for a company to fire employees because they belonged to unions. It also required employers to bargain with unions chosen by their employees. The act recognized as lawful strikes and other peaceful actions taken by employees to pressure employers into agreement. The act also set up procedures for workers to organize and elect representatives by secret ballot to conduct negotiations.

The idea of a law protecting labor unions seemed in direct conflict with the prevailing mood of the Court. Prior to 1937 the Court had overturned almost every important piece of New Deal legislation. Angry, Roosevelt unsuccessfully led a charge to change the Court. However, Roosevelt's threats and public pressure finally led two justices to retire and two others to alter their attitudes. New justices aapointed by Roosevelt held views supportive of government regulation.

Jones & McLaughlin

Jones & Laughlin Steel Corporation produced steel and shipped it across state lines. In a climate of social unrest throughout the nation in the mid-1930s, relations between Jones & Laughlin and employees at its Aliquippa, Pennsylvania plant deteriorated. Employees decided to form a bargaining unit affiliated with the national American Federation of Labor (AFL) labor union to represent their interests. The company wanted to keep more employees from joining. In July of 1935, four days after President Roosevelt signed the Wagner Act into law, Jones & McLaughlin fired ten workers who were union leaders at the plant. Local 200 of the Amalgamated Association of Iron, Steel, and Tin Workers of America filed a complaint with the NLRB accusing the company of engaging in unfair labor practices by firing union members. The NLRB upheld the complaint by finding that Jones & Laughlin's actions violated the Wagner Act. The Board ordered the company to reinstate the men and provide back pay for their time off. When the company refused to comply, the NLRB filed a petition with the Fifth Circuit Court of Appeals to enforce the order. The appeals court, finding the act unconstitutional, ruled in favor of Jones & Laughlin and refused to enforce the order. The NLRB appealed the decision to the U.S. Supreme Court.

Protecting Interstate Commerce

Before the Court, Jones & Laughlin again argued that Congress did not have authority under the Commerce Clause to regulate labor relations between workers and their employers. They also contended the act violated the Due Process Clause of the Fifth Amendment protecting the "liberty of contract." They claimed federal government had no power to interfere with the rights of the private property owners and their employees.

Chief Justice Charles E. Hughes wrote the opinion for the majority in a close 5-4 decision in favor of the NLRB. Hughes found that the act neither went beyond Congress' powers under the Commerce Clause nor violated due process. He wrote,

> **The congressional authority to protect interstate commerce from burdens and obstructions is not limited to transactions which can be deemed to be an essential part of a "flow" of interstate or foreign commerce. Burdens and obstructions may be due to injurious action springing from other sources . . . That power may be exerted to protect interstate commerce no matter what the source of the dangers which threaten it.**

Hughes believed that labor unrest could lead to strikes which in turn could lead to disruption of interstate commerce. Such interference would be particularly harmful to the nation during such a time of economic crisis.

Most importantly, Hughes found that workers held a "fundamental right" to organize. The Wagner Act paid a particularly beneficial role by requiring employers to negotiate agreements with their workers. This requirement actually increased the employees' protection under the law by having power to negotiate with employers through democratically elected representatives.

Union Power

The landmark ruling gave labor unions the power to organize and negotiate with employers. The Jones ruling also proved to be the major turning point in the battle between Roosevelt and the Supreme Court over federal powers. The Court finally supported Roosevelt's belief that the federal government had authority to regulate the nation's economic affairs by

LABOR UNIONS IN U.S. HISTORY

Labor unions are organizations of workers who join together to improve their working conditions and their lives. Unions began to appear in the United States at the end of the eighteenth century when Philadelphia shoemakers united to obtain higher wages, shorter work hours, and better work conditions. They were largely unsuccessful as a Pennsylvania state court ruled that labor unions violated conspiracy laws. In 1834 workers went on strike refusing to complete construction of a canal in Ohio, but President Andrew Jackson (1829-1837) sent U.S. troops to break up the strike believing it interfered with interstate commerce.

The first state court ruling recognizing the legitimacy of unions and their right to strike came in Massachusetts in 1842. As industrialization (growth of large industry) grew rapidly following the Civil War (1861–1865), work conditions in many factories greatly declined. In reaction, union activity increased as well. Violent strikes resulted on several occasions beginning in 1877. In 1894 dozens of strikers were killed by police. Each time labor came away with decreased public support. Union membership declined significantly after 1894. One of the few large unions prospering during this time was the American Federation of Labor (AFL) which stressed cooperation with business while seeking improved work conditions.

Union membership declined further following World War I (1914–1918) faced with organized opposition from industry and fears of political radicals within some unions. The grim economic condition of the country in the 1930s again renewed interest in union activity. A peak in union membership reached 21 million in 1971. However, with the decline in manufacturing jobs through the 1980s and 1990s and with public sentiment opposed to union activity, membership again dropped by the end of the twentieth century.

broadening its interpretation of the Commerce Clause. With passage of the Wagner Act and the favorable ruling in Jones, union membership grew from 4.7 million in 1936 to 8.2 million in 1939 and continued to increase into the early 1970s. At the end of the twentieth century the Wagner Act remained the most important piece of labor legislation passed in the U.S. history.

Suggestions for further reading

Cortner, Richard C. *The Jones & Laughlin Case.* New York: Knopf, 1970.

Foner, Philip S. *History of the Labor Movement in the United States.* New York: International Publishers, 1974.

Freeman, Richard B., and James L. Medoff. *What Do Unions Do?* New York: Basic Books, 1984.

Geohagen, Thomas. *Which Side Are You On?* New York: St. Martin's Press, 1993.

Darby v. United States 1941

Appellant: United States

Appellee: Fred W. Darby

Appellant's Claim: That under the Commerce Clause of the Constitution, Congress may regulate workers' wages and hours.

Chief Lawyer for Appellant: Robert H. Jackson, U.S. Attorney General

Chief Lawyer for Appellee: Archibald B. Lovett

Justices for the Court: Hugo Lafayette Black, William O. Douglas, Felix Frankfurter, Charles Evans Hughes, Frank Murphy, Stanley Forman Reed, Owen Josephus Roberts, Harlan Fiske Stone (writing for the Court)

Justices Dissenting: None (James Clark McReynolds did not participate)

Date of Decision: 3 February 1941

Decision: The Supreme Court upheld the Fair Labor Standards Act.

Significance: *Darby* allowed Congress to use its power under the Commerce Clause, which involves business, to enact laws for public welfare.

In 1938, Congress passed the Fair Labor Standards Act. It was the last important piece of the New Deal. The New Deal was President Franklin D. Roosevelt's plan to improve social and economic conditions in the United States during the Great Depression.

The Fair Labor Standards Act set maximum working hours and minimum wages for workers making products that would travel in interstate commerce. Interstate commerce means commerce or business that crosses state lines. The Commerce Clause of the U.S. Constitution gives Congress the power to regulate interstate commerce.

Associate Justice Harlan Fiske Stone.
Courtesy of the Library of Congress.

Industrial Evolution

Fred W. Darby was an industrialist in Georgia. Darby's company made lumber from timber. Much of the lumber was shipped in interstate commerce for sale in other states.

Soon after Congress passed the Fair Labor Standards Act, the federal government charged Darby with violating the Act. The government said Darby's workers received less than the minimum twenty-five cents per hour. It also said Darby's workers worked more than the maximum forty-four hours per week without getting increased pay for overtime.

Darby fought the lawsuit by asking the federal district court to dismiss the case. Darby said that under the Commerce Clause, Congress only had power to regulate businesses that actually crossed state lines. Darby's company manufactured lumber entirely within the state of Georgia.

Darby said it was up to Georgia to decide whether to regulate his business. After all, the Tenth Amendment of the Constitution says the

THE NEW DEAL

Upon taking office in 1933, Roosevelt kept his promise. He helped Congress enact federal programs for relief, recovery, and reform. Relief programs such as the Works Progress Administration (WPA) created jobs by funding federal construction projects. Recovery programs such as the Agricultural Adjustment Administration (AAA) sought to improve agriculture, business, and employment. Reform programs such as the Fair Labor Standards Act and the National Labor Relations Act sought to improve working conditions for Americans.

In the end, the New Deal did not cure the Great Depression. Expanded production for World War II did that. Roosevelt's New Deal, however, left Americans with new public welfare programs such as Social Security that now are part of everyday life.

states have all power not given to Congress. Because Georgia had not enacted minimum wages or maximum hour laws, Darby did not think he had to obey any. The federal district court agreed and dismissed the entire case, so the United States appealed to the U.S. Supreme Court.

Affecting Commerce

With an 8–0 decision, the Supreme Court reversed and upheld the Fair Labor Standards Act. Justice Harlan Fiske Stone delivered the Court's opinion. Justice Stone said the Commerce Clause does not limit Congress to regulating items as they are shipped in interstate commerce. It allows Congress to regulate anything that affects interstate commerce. Manufacturing lumber from timber affects interstate commerce because some of the lumber eventually will be shipped across state lines. Congress, then, had power to regulate Darby's business.

Justice Stone admitted that the purpose of the Fair Labor Standards Act was to improve minimum standards of living necessary for health and general well being. Health and well being are not part of interstate commerce. Justice Stone said, however, that Congress's goal does not affect whether a law is within its power. The result was important for the future of federal public welfare legislation.

Suggestions for further reading

Joel, Lewin G. *Every Employee's Guide to the Law.* New York: Pantheon Books, 1993.

Lawson, Don. *FDR's New Deal.* New York: Crowell, 1979.

Leuchtenburg, William Edward. *Franklin D. Roosevelt and the New Deal, 1932-1940.* New York: Harper & Row, 1963.

Repa, Barbara Kate. *Your Rights in the Workplace.* Berkeley: Nolo Press, 1996.

Schraff, Anne E. *The Great Depression and the New Deal.* New York: Franklin Watts, 1990.

Stewart, Gail B. *The New Deal. New York: New Discovery Books, 1993.*

Corning Glass Works v. Brennan 1974

Petitioner: Corning Glass Works

Respondent: Peter J. Brennan, U.S. Secretary of Labor

Petitioner's Claim: That the Court of Appeals erred by ruling that Corning violated the Equal Pay Act.

Chief Lawyer for Petitioner: Scott F. Zimmerman

Chief Lawyer for Respondent: Allan Abbot Tuttle

Justices for the Court: William J. Brennan, Jr., William O. Douglas, Thurgood Marshall (writing for the Court), Lewis F. Powell, Jr., Byron R. White

Justices Dissenting: Harry A. Blackmun, Warren E. Burger, William H. Rehnquist (Potter Stewart did not participate)

Date of Decision: June 3, 1974

Decision: The Supreme Court said Corning violated the Equal Pay Act by paying male nightshift inspection workers higher wages than female dayshift inspection workers.

Significance: With *Corning,* the Supreme Court reinforced the policy of "equal pay for equal work."

Corning Glass Works was a company with production plants in Corning, New York, and Wellsboro, Pennsylvania. Prior to 1925, Corning operated its Wellsboro plant only during the day. The employees who inspected finished products were all female.

LABOR AND LABOR PRACTICES

Between 1925 and 1930, Corning began to use automatic production equipment, which made finished products faster than people made them. It became necessary for Corning to hire nightshift inspectors to keep up with the increased production. Corning, however, had two problems. Under New York and Pennsylvania law, women were not allowed to work at night. In addition, men thought inspection work was inferior work for women. Men would not do inspection work unless they got more money than female inspectors received. Corning gave the male nightshift inspectors more money.

Fair Labor Standards

In 1963, Congress passed the Equal Pay Act. The law required companies to pay men and women equally for similar work. By then, New York and Pennsylvania had gotten rid of the laws that prevented women from working at night.

In June 1966, Corning began to allow women to get the higher paying nightshift inspection jobs. Then in January 1969, Corning signed an

Practicing fair labor standards has always been a problem with businesses. Reproduced by permission of the Corbis Corporation.

agreement to pay dayshift and nightshift inspectors the same money. The agreement, however, contained an exception for nightshift workers hired before January 1969. Those workers, most of whom were men, still received higher pay than dayshift inspectors.

The U.S. Secretary of Labor filed two lawsuits against Corning, one in federal court in New York and one in Pennsylvania. The Secretary charged Corning with violating the Equal Pay Act by paying male nightshift inspectors higher wages than female dayshift inspectors. The Secretary said Corning could not fix the problem just by opening up nightshift jobs for women. He wanted Corning to give raises to the dayshift inspectors to make their wages equal to those of the nightshift inspectors.

Corning fought the lawsuit. The Equal Pay Act said companies could pay different wages for people working under different "working conditions." Corning said it paid nightshift workers more because working at night was less desirable. After trials and appeals, the federal court of appeals in New York ruled in favor of the United States while the one in Pennsylvania ruled in favor of Corning. The U.S. Supreme Court decided to review both cases.

The Equal Rights Amendment would ensure that all people would be treated the same, whether they were male or female. Reproduced by permission of Archive Photos, Inc.

THURGOOD MARSHALL

Thurgood Marshall was born on July 2, 1908 in Baltimore, Maryland. The son of a schoolteacher and club steward, Marshall left Baltimore in 1926 to attend the all-black Lincoln University. When Marshall tried to get into law school at the University of Maryland, the school turned him down because he was African American. Marshall attended law school at Howard University in Washington, D.C., where he graduated first in his class.

Marshall practiced law in Baltimore from 1933 to 1938. There he fought for civil rights by working as counsel for the Baltimore branch of the National Association for the Advancement of Colored People ("NAACP"). In 1939, Marshall became director of the NAACP's Legal Defense and Education Fund. In that role, Marshall argued and won many important civil rights cases before the U.S. Supreme Court. His most important case, ***Brown v. Board of Education*** (1954), ended segregation, the practice of separating black and white students in different public schools.

In 1961, President John F. Kennedy nominated Marshall to the U.S. Court of Appeals for the Second Circuit. Southern opposition to Marshall's appointment delayed it for one year. In 1965, President Lyndon B. Johnson appointed Marshall to be U.S. Solicitor General, the attorney who represents the United States in federal court. Two years later President Johnson chose Marshall to be the first African American justice on the U.S. Supreme Court. Many southern senators again opposed Marshall's nomination and again were defeated. During his twenty-five years on the Supreme Court, Marshall regularly voted in favor of individual civil and constitutional rights.

Equal Pay for Equal Work

With a 5–3 decision, the Supreme Court ruled in favor of the Secretary of Labor. Justice Thurgood Marshall delivered the Court's opinion. Marshall said Congress passed the Equal Pay Act to end the notion that men, because of their role in society, should get paid more than women for the same work. "Equal work should be rewarded by equal wages."

The problem, of course, was deciding whether nightshift and dayshift inspection was equal work. The Supreme Court said it was. Inspectors at night had the same surroundings and same hazards as inspectors during the day.

Marshall emphasized that Corning was free to pay nightshift workers more if working at night had added psychological or physical demands. Corning, however, had not proved that those demands existed. Its pay differential was a relic of the days when men were paid more because they were men. That was illegal sex discrimination under the Equal Pay Act. Corning would have to raise the pay rates for dayshift inspection workers.

Suggestions for further reading

Bourgoin, Suzanne Michele, and Paula Kay Byers. *Encyclopedia of World Biography.* Detroit: Gale Research, 1998.

Cary, Eve. *Women and the Law.* Skokie: National Textbook Company, 1984.

Hanmer, Trudy J. *Taking a Stand against Sexism and Sex Discrimination.* New York: Franklin Watts, 1990.

Shaw, Victoria. *Coping with Sexual Harassment and Gender Bias.* New York: Rosen Publishing Group, 1998.

Weiss, Ann E. *The Glass Ceiling: A Look at Women in the Workforce.* Twenty First Century Books, 1999.

Williams, Mary E. *Working Women: Opposing Viewpoints.* San Diego: Greenhaven Press, 1998.

Witt, Elder. *Congressional Quarterly's Guide to the U.S. Supreme Court.* District of Columbia: Congressional Quarterly Inc., 1990.

The American military includes the Army, Navy, Air Force, and Marines. Military law applies to people who work in the military. It differs in many ways from civilian law, which governs regular citizens. Civilian law tries to maintain peace by resolving disputes and punishing criminal activity. Military law strives to promote order, morale, and discipline.

Origins of Military Justice in the United States

Like civilian law, military law has its origins in Roman law dating back to the first century B.C. Civil and military law in the Roman empire were part of one system. In the eleventh century, William the Conqueror introduced Roman law into England. As the military grew over the next few centuries, so did the desire to create separate systems for civil and military law. In 1649, England created a separate national system for military justice.

The American colonies that would form the United States created a military justice system even before declaring independence. Just weeks after American and British troops clashed at Lexington and Concord in

April 1775, the Second Continental Congress formed an American army. Later that year, George Washington helped write the Articles of War. The colonies based the Articles of War on the military justice systems of the British and ancient Roman empires, which enjoyed great success as powerful empires.

The U.S. Constitution, which the United States adopted in 1787, made the military subject to civilian control through the president and congress. The president is commander-in-chief of the armed forces. That gives him ultimate authority for operating the military in both peacetime and war. Congress is responsible for raising, supporting, and making rules for the armed forces. Congress also has the power to declare war.

Military Law

The main goal of the Articles of War was to maintain discipline in the military forces. For that purpose it covered military crimes such as mutiny, or rebelling against military authority. Originally the Articles did not cover regular crimes such as murder, rape, and theft. In 1863, Congress revised the Articles to cover regular crimes, but only in times of war or rebellion.

In 1950, Congress replaced the Articles of War with the Uniform Code of Military Justice. The Uniform Code combined different laws for the various military branches into one code of 140 articles. The Code governs criminal and other unlawful military conduct in both peacetime and war. It covers regular crimes such as murder, rape, and theft, as well as conduct that is unlawful only in the military.

Offenses that are unique to the military include being absent without leave, or AWOL, the most common military offense. The Code also covers violation of orders, disrespect for officers, insubordination, mutiny, desertion, and conduct unbecoming an officer. Desertion is avoiding hazardous duty or an important assignment. The Code does not define conduct unbecoming an officer, but the offense generally covers conduct that harms the military's reputation. In *Parker v. Levy* (1974), the U.S. Supreme Court said the offense of conduct unbecoming an officer is not too vague to be enforced.

Court-Martials

In the military, a person charged with misconduct often faces a proceeding called a court-martial. A court-martial resembles a criminal trial under civilian law. Instead of a jury, however, military personnel hear and decide cases. These personnel are called members instead of jurors.

Under the Articles of War, commanding officers had great power to handle court-martials. They could convene a court, select its members, and review the court's decision with authority to disapprove the sentence and send the case back for reconsideration. Following World War II in 1945, servicemen complained that the military justice system was too harsh and unfair, often giving excessive punishments. When Congress passed the Uniform Code in 1950, it changed the court-martial system in response to these complaints.

The Uniform Code created three types of court-martials: summary, special, and general. The summary court-martial is for enlisted personnel who are accused of minor offenses. One officer hears and decides cases with an abbreviated form of trial. The maximum sentence the court may impose is confinement for one month and a small fine. Enlisted personnel can refuse trial in a summary court-martial and ask for a special or general court-martial.

The special court-martial is for enlisted personnel and officers in all cases except capital cases, those in which the death penalty is available. Special court-martials use three or more members, counsel for both sides, and sometimes a military judge to referee the case. The maximum sentence the court may impose is bad-conduct discharge, confinement for up to six months, and loss of two-thirds pay for the same time. Enlisted personnel can insist that one-third of the members who decide their cases also be enlisted personnel. Members, however, must be ranked higher than the accused.

General court-martials can hear cases for any violation of the Uniform Code, including capital offenses. A general court-martial has five or more members, counsel for both sides, and a military judge. Available sentences include death, dishonorable discharge, bad-conduct discharge, dismissal of an officer, imprisonment, and loss of rank, pay, and allowances.

During a court-martial, the accused has many of the constitutional rights that criminal defendants have. He has the Sixth Amendment right to a speedy, public trial. In special and general court-martials he has the right to counsel. The accused enjoys the Fifth Amendment right against self-incrimination, which means he cannot be forced to confess or to testify against himself. The Fourth Amendment prevents the government from conducting unreasonable searches and seizures. The military cannot use evidence obtained in violation of the Fourth Amendment during a court-martial.

The Uniform Code allows the military to handle many violations outside the court-martial process. Nonpunitive measures allow commanding officers to discipline personnel for minor offenses such as shoplifting, intoxication, and fighting. Nonpunitive measures include withholding privileges, counseling, reductions in rank, and reassignment of duties. Nonjudicial punishment is more severe and is reserved for cases in which nonpunitive measures are inadequate.

The Military Draft

The military draft is the government's way of building its military forces. The federal government conducted its first draft during the American Civil War from 1861 to 1865.

During World War I in 1917, Congress passed the Selective Service Act to build an army. Many Americans challenged the law by saying the draft violated the Thirteenth Amendment, which prohibits slavery and involuntary servitude. The Supreme Court rejected this argument in the *Selective Draft Law Cases* (1918). It said the Thirteenth Amendment does not protect Americans from fulfilling civic duties such as military service and jury duty.

Following World War II, Congress enacted a peacetime draft with the Universal Military Training and Service Act of 1948. The law exempted people who were opposed to war for religious reasons. It gave no exemption, however, for people who opposed war for moral reasons unrelated to religious beliefs. In *Welsh v. United States* (1970), the Supreme Court said Congress violated the Constitution by distinguishing between religious and non-religious objections to war. As a result of *Welsh,* conscientious objectors can avoid the draft if they oppose war in any form because of deeply held religious, philosophical, or moral beliefs.

After the United States withdrew from the Vietnam War in 1973, Congress ended the military draft. America's military forces since then, including those that fought in the Persian Gulf War in 1991, have been voluntary. Young men age eighteen to twenty-five, however, still must register with the Selective Service System in case the government needs to reactivate the draft and recruit Americans for war.

Gays and Women in the Military

In 1916, the Articles of War made homosexual conduct a military crime. The military believed homosexuality ruined morale among heterosexual personnel. Since then homosexuals have been discharged from military service in great numbers. In the 1980s alone, over 15,000 homosexuals were discharged from the military.

In 1993, President William J. Clinton used his power as commander-in-chief to try to end discrimination against homosexuals in the military. Congress reacted by including a "don't ask, don't tell" policy in military legislation. The policy prevents military authorities from asking military personnel about their sexual orientation. In turn, homosexual military personnel are not supposed to reveal their orientation or engage in homosexual conduct. Keeping everyone silent is supposed to limit the number of homosexuals who get discharged for their sexuality. People on both sides of the issue have criticized the policy.

In 1948, Congress excluded women from combat roles with the Women's Armed Services Integration Act. Because the military academies were designed to produce combat officers, women were excluded there as well. When the draft ended in the mid-1970s, the military found it necessary to include more women in non-combat roles.

Congress and the judiciary finally ended the exclusion at military academies in 1991. President Clinton opened combat roles to women in the Air Force in 1993 and in the Navy in 1994. Only Army and Marine units engaged in direct ground combat remained closed to women. Women and men alike applauded these changes and urged further reform. Critics, however, claimed that a feminist social agenda was hurting the military and national security.

Suggestions for further reading

Encyclopedia Americana, 1993 ed., s.v. "Court-martial."

Sherrill, Robert. *Military Justice is to Justice as Military Music is to Music.* New York: Harper & Row, 1970.

Suro, Robert. "Military's Differing Lesson Plans Reflect Unease on Gay Policy." *Washington Post,* March 4, 2000.

World Book Encyclopedia, 2000 ed., s.v. "Court-martial."

Toth v. Quarles
1955

Petitioner: Audrey M. Toth

Respondent: Donald A. Quarles, Secretary of the U.S. Air Force

Petitioner's Claim: That Congress violated the Constitution by allowing the military to hold court-martials for civilians who used to be military personnel.

Chief Lawyer for Petitioner: William A. Kehoe, Jr.

Chief Lawyer for Respondent: Simon E. Sobeloff, U.S. Solicitor General

Justices for the Court: Hugo Lafayette Black (writing for the Court), Tom C. Clark, William O. Douglas, Felix Frankfurter, John Marshall Harlan II, Earl Warren

Justices Dissenting: Harold Burton, Sherman Minton, Stanley Forman Reed

Date of Decision: November 7, 1955

Decision: The Supreme Court ordered the Air Force to release Robert Toth from custody.

Significance: With *Toth,* the Court said the military does not have power to try civilians for military crimes.

Robert Toth was an enlisted airman in the U.S. Air Force during the Korean War. On 27 September 1952, Toth was on guard duty with Airman Thomas Kinder at an airbase in South Korea. That day the airmen found a Korean civilian, Bang Soon Kil, who appeared to be drunk.

The airmen took Bang Soon into custody and drove him to base headquarters in a jeep.

On the way to headquarters, Bang Soon grabbed at Toth's arm. Toth allegedly stopped the jeep and pistol-whipped Bang Soon. When the airmen arrived at headquarters, their commanding officer, Lieutenant George Schreiber, ordered them to take Bang Soon away and shoot him.

By the time military authorities discovered the murder, Toth had been honorably discharged from service. Schreiber and Kinder, however, were still in the Air Force. Both men faced a court-martial, which is a military trial for violation of the Uniform Code of Military Justice. The court-martial found Schreiber guilty and sentenced him to life in prison, but the Air Force reduced the sentence to five years in prison, forfeiture of pay, and a dishonorable discharge. The court-martial also gave Kinder a life sentence, but the Air Force reduced it to two years in prison and a dishonorable discharge.

Civil Court-Martial?

After being honorably discharged from the Air Force, Toth returned to his home in Pittsburgh, Pennsylvania, and got a job in a steel plant. He had been there five months when Air Force police arrived at the plant to arrest him for Bang Soon's murder. The Air Force put Toth on an airplane for South Korea to stand trial in a military court-martial.

Civilian courts had no power to try servicemen for crimes committed in the military. Article 3(a) of the Uniform Code allowed the military to court-martial a former serviceman for military crimes that were punishable by at least five years in prison. If Toth was guilty, a court-martial was the only way to bring him to justice.

After the Air Force took Toth to South Korea, his sister, Audrey M. Toth, filed for a writ of *habeas corpus* in federal court in the District of Columbia. A writ of *habeas corpus* is an order to release a prisoner who is in custody in violation of the Constitution. Toth's sister said the Uniform Code violated the Constitution by allowing civilians to be court-martialed by the military. It allowed Toth to be tried without the benefits of a grand jury accusation, a neutral judge, and a jury of his peers.

The federal court granted the writ and ordered the Air Force to release Toth. It said the Air Force had no power to take Toth to South Korea for trial without first holding a hearing. The court of appeals, however, reversed. It said the power to hold the court-martial gave the

Air Force the power to transport Toth to South Korea for trial. Faced with a court-martial in South Korea, Toth took the case to the U.S. Supreme Court.

Court-Martial Lacks Power

With a 6–3 decision, the Supreme Court ruled in favor of Toth. Justice Hugo Lafayette Black wrote the Court's opinion. Black said the Constitution gave Congress the power to make rules and regulations for the land and naval forces. Those rules, however, can apply only to people who are in the military forces. Once a serviceman leaves the military and becomes a regular citizen, the military has no power to court-martial him.

Black said allowing the military to court-martial civilians would deprive them of constitutional rights. Article III of the Constitution creates a judicial system run by independent, neutral judges. The Fifth Amendment gives citizens the right to be charged by a grand jury before standing trial for a crime. The Sixth Amendment says criminal trials must be jury trials so that citizens will be judged by their peers in the community. Military court-martials do not use independent judges, grand juries, or jury trials. Letting the military court-martial civilians would deprive them of those rights.

The government argued that the Court's decision would allow military criminals to escape justice. The Court rejected this argument. It said Congress could enact legislation to allow civilian courts to try civilians for crimes committed in the military. The military, however, was not allowed to make up for the lack of such legislation by hauling regular citizens into military court.

Necessary and Proper

Three justices dissented, which means they disagreed with the Court's decision. Justice Stanley Forman Reed wrote a dissenting opinion. Reed did not agree that the military lacked power to try civilians for crimes committed in the military. He thought it was unfair for Toth to escape a trial just because he got out of the Air Force before it discovered the murder.

The Necessary and Proper Clause of the Constitution gives Congress the power to do anything reasonable to carry out its specific powers. One of those specific powers is the authority to make rules and regulations for the military forces. Justice Reed thought it was reasonable

MURDER OF BARRY WINCHELL

Pfc. Barry Winchell was a soldier in the U.S. Army at Fort Campbell on the Kentucky-Tennessee border. Winchell also was homosexual. In the early morning hours of 5 July 1999, fellow soldier Calvin N. Glover beat Winchell to death with a baseball bat as Winchell lay asleep in his barracks. One night earlier, Winchell had beaten Glover in a fist fight that Glover started. When friends teased that he had been beaten by a "fag," Glover vowed to get Winchell back. The murder followed months of anti-gay harassment, which Winchell reported to his superiors to no avail. Gay rights activists called the murder a hate crime. Winchell's parents considered suing the Army for failing to protect their son.

for Congress to promote discipline by allowing the armed forces to court-martial former servicemen for military crimes.

Aftermath

Nobody was punished seriously for Bang Soon Kil's murder. Air Force Secretary Harold E. Talbott dismissed Schreiber from the service after Schreiber had served only twenty months of his five year sentence. Talbott suspended Kinder's dishonorable discharge, allowing Kinder to return to the service. Toth, who insisted that he was not present when Bang Soon was killed, escaped trial as a result of the Supreme Court's decision.

Suggestions for further reading

Eilperin, Juliet. "Parents of Slain GI Consider Suing Army." *Washington Post,* January 10, 2000.

Encyclopedia Americana, 1993 ed., s.v. "Court-martial."

Pressley, Sue Anne. "Hate May Have Triggered Fatal Barracks Beating." *Washington Post,* August 11, 1999.

Sherrill, Robert. *Military Justice is to Justice as Military Music is to Music.* New York: Harper & Row, 1970.

"Soldier's Sentence Allows Parole." *Washington Post,* December 10, 1999.

World Book Encyclopedia, 2000 ed., s.v. "Court-martial."

Goldman v. Weinberger 1986

Petitioner: S. Simcha Goldman

Respondent: Caspar W. Weinberger, U.S. Secretary of Defense, et al.

Petitioner's Claim: That Air Force regulations preventing him from wearing a yarmulke while on duty violated his First Amendment religious freedom.

Chief Lawyer for Petitioner: Nathan Lewis

Chief Lawyer for Respondent: Kathryn A. Oberly

Justices for the Court: Warren E. Burger, Lewis F. Powell, Jr., William H. Rehnquist (writing for the Court), John Paul Stevens, Byron R. White

Justices Dissenting: Harry A. Blackmun, William J. Brennan, Jr., Thurgood Marshall, Sandra Day O'Connor

Date of Decision: March 25, 1986

Decision: The Supreme Court said the Air Force regulations did not violate the Constitution.

Significance: *Goldman* allows the military to sacrifice religious freedom for uniformity to maintain discipline and morale.

S. Simcha Goldman was an Orthodox Jew and an ordained rabbi. In 1973, Goldman joined the Armed Forces Health Professions Scholarship Program. The program gave him financial support to study psychology for three years at Loyola University in Chicago, Illinois.

After getting a Ph.D. in 1976, Goldman became a commissioned officer in the U.S. Air Force. He served as a clinical psychologist at the mental health hospital at March Air Force Base in Riverside, California. From 1976 to 1981, Goldman's performance was praiseworthy.

Religious devotion

As an Orthodox Jew, Goldman wore the yarmulke required by his religion. A yarmulke is a skullcap that covers the top of the wearer's head in God's presence. It serves as a reminder to serve God at all times.

Air Force regulation 35-10 made it unlawful for officers to wear headgear indoors. Goldman, however, wore his yarmulke in the hospital without any problems from 1976 to 1981. In April 1981, Goldman testified at a court-martial hearing while wearing his yarmulke. Afterwards a court lawyer complained to Colonel Joseph Gregory, Goldman's commanding officer, that Goldman's yarmulke violated Air Force regulations in the courtroom and in the hospital.

Colonel Gregory told Goldman about the violation and ordered him to refrain from wearing the yarmulke everywhere except in the hospital. When Goldman's lawyer protested to the Air Force General Counsel, Colonel Gregory revised the order to prohibit Goldman from wearing the yarmulke even in the hospital.

Goldman requested permission to wear civilian clothes, including his yarmulke, until the dispute was resolved. The Air Force denied his request. The next day Goldman received a letter of reprimand and a warning that further violations of regulation 35-10 could result in a court-martial. Colonel Gregory also withdrew a recommendation to extend Goldman's active service and submitted a negative recommendation instead.

Goldman sues

Goldman filed a lawsuit against Caspar Weinberger, the U.S. Secretary of Defense, and other government and military officials. Goldman said regulation 35-10 violated his religious freedom under the First Amendment. The First Amendment says "Congress shall make no law . . . prohibiting the free exercise" of religion. It prevents the government from interfering with religious belief and activity unless it has a compelling (very strong) reason for doing so.

Caspar Weinberger upheld the Air Force rule that prevented Airman Goldman from wearing a yarmulke while on duty.
Reproduced by permission of the Corbis Corporation.

After a full hearing, the federal court in the District of Columbia ruled in favor of Goldman. The court of appeals, however, reversed. It said the regulation was permissible to serve the military's interest in uniformity. By requiring everyone to wear similar uniforms, the military discourages individualism and builds a uniform, disciplined military. Faced with having to violate his religion while serving his country, Goldman took his case to the U.S. Supreme Court.

Military uniformity

With a 5–4 decision, the Supreme Court ruled in favor of Weinberger and the Air Force. Justice William H. Rehnquist delivered the Court's opinion. Rehnquist said military personnel do not give up all constitutional rights. The military, however, must foster discipline, obedience, and unity. That is the only way to make sure personnel will follow orders without hesitation in times of war.

To foster unity, Air Force regulations require personnel to wear standard uniforms. Those regulations make it unlawful to wear religious headgear. Exceptions for yarmulkes would foster individualism, not unity. Justice Rehnquist said Goldman's religious freedom was not more important than the military's need to develop unity.

In the armed forces there are strict codes of dress and conduct that aim to keep everyone and everything the same. Courtesy of the Library of Congress.

Rehnquist noted that Air Force regulations did not prohibit all religious clothing. Goldman could wear his yarmulke during indoor religious ceremonies. Commanding officers were allowed to permit officers to wear religious headgear in their living quarters. Commanding officers also could allow officers to wear nonvisible religious clothing of any kind. Air Force regulation 35-10, however, served the military goal of uniformity by forcing officers on duty to wear the standard Air Force uniform. That did not violate religious freedom under the First Amendment.

CHAPLAIN FIRST AMENDMENT CASE

In the summer of 1996, the Roman Catholic Church launched the "Project Life Postcard Campaign." The Church's goal was to defeat President William J. Clinton's veto of a bill that would have banned certain abortions. The Church asked its priests to urge parishioners to send postcards to Congressmen asking them to override the veto.

Father Vincent J. Rigdon was a Roman Catholic priest and lieutenant colonel in the Air Force Reserve who preached at Andrews Air Force base in Washington, D.C. In response to the Church's campaign, the military ordered Rigdon and all other chaplains not to participate in the postcard campaign. The military said the campaign violated rules that prevent military personnel from lobbying for or against legislation in Congress.

Rigdon sued the armed forces to challenge the order. He said it violated his First Amendment rights to free speech and religion. A Catholic officer, an Air Force rabbi, and the Muslim American Military Association joined Rigdon in his lawsuit. They feared the order would prevent chaplains from discussing important issues during sermons, counseling, and confessions.

The military said the order did not prevent chaplains from discussing moral issues during sermons and religious teaching. On 7 April 1997, however, the federal district court ruled against the military and in favor of Rigdon and his fellow chaplains. The court said chaplains are allowed to urge congregants to write letters to Congress on important moral issues. The court said, "There is no need for [the government's] heavy handed censorship."

Irrational military rationale

Four justices dissented, which means they disagreed with the Court's decision. Justice William J. Brennan, Jr., wrote a dissenting opinion. Brennan said the government needs a compelling reason to interfere with religious freedom. Here Brennan said the government could not even offer a good reason. There was no evidence that Goldman would hurt military discipline by wearing a yarmulke.

There also was no evidence that the military needed to maintain absolute uniformity in dress. In fact, Air Force regulations said, "Neither the Air Force nor the public expects absolute uniformity of appearance. Each member has the right, within limits, to express individuality through his or her appearance. However, the image of a disciplined service member who can be relied on to do his or her job excludes the extreme, the unusual, and the fad." Brennan said there was nothing extreme, unusual, or faddish about wearing a yarmulke. By prohibiting yarmulkes, the military and the Supreme Court forced American Orthodox Jews to choose between obeying their religion and serving their country.

Suggestions for further reading

Adde, Nick. "Chaplains Launch Free Speech Suit." *Navy Times,* November 4, 1996.

"Chaplains Can't Be Muzzled." *Navy Times,* May 5, 1997.

Evans, J. Edward. *Freedom of Religion.* Minneapolis: Lerner Publications Company, 1990.

Farish, Leah. *The First Amendment: Freedom of Speech, Religion, and the Press.* Enslow Publishers, Inc., 1998.

Gay, Kathlyn. *Church and State: Government and Religion in the United States.* Brookfield: Millbrook Press, 1992.

Hirst, Mike. *Freedom of Belief.* New York: Franklin Watts, 1997.

Jolkovsky, Binyamin L. "Military Bans Pulpit Politicking." *Christian Science Monitor,* October 16, 1996.

Klinker, Philip A. *The First Amendment.* Englewood Cliffs: Silver Burdett Press, 1991.

"Military Chaplains Plumb Church-State Tar Pit." *National Catholic Reporter,* October 18, 1996.

"Military Chaplains Win Speech Case." *Christianity Today,* June 16, 1997.

Sherrow, Victoria. *Freedom of Worship.* Brookfield: Millbrook Press, 1997.

Clinton v. Goldsmith 1999

Petitioner: William J. Clinton, President of the United States, et al.

Respondent: James Goldsmith

Petitioner's Claim: That the Court of Appeals for the Armed Forces lacked authority to review President Clinton's decision to drop an officer from the Air Force.

Chief Lawyer for Petitioner: Michael R. Dreeden

Chief Lawyer for Respondent: John M. Economidy

Justices for the Court: Stephen Breyer, Ruth Bader Ginsburg, Anthony M. Kennedy, Sandra Day O'Connor, William H. Rehnquist, Antonin Scalia, David H. Souter (writing for the Court), John Paul Stevens, Clarence Thomas

Justices Dissenting: None

Date of Decision: May 17, 1999

Decision: The Supreme Court reversed the Court of Appeals' order, which had stopped President Clinton from dropping Goldsmith from the Air Force.

Significance: With *Clinton,* the Court said military officers must follow the proper legal channels to challenge a decision by the president of the United States.

MILITARY LAW AND ISSUES

James Goldsmith was a major in the U.S. Air Force. Goldsmith also was HIV-positive, which means he had the virus that causes AIDS. Because people can transmit HIV during sexual intercourse, Goldsmith's superior told him to inform his sexual partners about his condition. Goldsmith's superior also told him to take precautions during sexual intercourse to avoid giving the virus to his partners.

Goldsmith violated this order by having unprotected sexual intercourse with a fellow officer and a civilian. The Air Force court-martialed Goldsmith for his disobedience. The court-martial convicted Goldsmith of disobeying an order from a superior officer, aggravated assault with means likely to produce death or serious harm, and battery. Goldsmith received a sentence of six years in prison and forfeiture of $2,500 of his salary each month for six years.

Roll call

Officers who spend a lot of time in military jail are costly to the federal government because they still receive pay. In 1996, Congress passed a law giving the President power to drop officers from the rolls after they spend six months in jail as a result of a court-martial sentence. Officers dropped from the rolls forfeit all military pay. In 1996, the Air Force notified Goldsmith that he was going to be dropped from the Air Force's rolls.

At the time, Goldsmith said he was having trouble getting his HIV medication in jail. Goldsmith filed a case with the Air Force Court of Criminal Appeals (AFCCA) under the All Writs Act to get his medication. The All Writs Act allows federal courts to issue orders needed to carry out their powers.

The function of the AFCCA, however, is to review cases decided by court-martials. The AFCCA is not a place for individual requests, like Goldsmith's request for medication. Because of this, the AFCCA ruled that it lacked jurisdiction, or power, to grant Goldsmith's request.

Goldsmith appealed to the Court of Appeals for the Armed Forces (CAAF), which reviews decisions by courts in the military branches. Because the Air Force released Goldsmith from confinement before the CAAF decided the case, the CAAF did not have to consider Goldsmith's request for HIV medication.

Goldsmith, however, argued that President William J. Clinton and the Air Force would violate the Constitution if they dropped him from

The Court decided that President Bill Clinton had final say on whether or not an officer was removed from the Air Force.
Reproduced by permission of AP/Wide World Photos.

the Air Force's rolls. Goldsmith said dropping him would violate the Double Jeopardy Clause, which prevents the government from punishing people twice for the same crime. Goldsmith said it also would violate the Ex Post Facto Clause, which prevents the government from using a law to convict a defendant for something that was not a crime when the defendant did it. When Goldsmith violated his superior's order, there was no law that the President could drop Goldsmith from the rolls. Congress enacted that law later.

The CAAF ruled in Goldsmith's favor. Using the All Writs Act, it ordered President Clinton and various other executive officials not to drop Goldsmith from the Air Force's rolls. President Clinton and the executive officials took the case to the U.S. Supreme Court. The issue was whether the CAAF had the power to prevent President Clinton from acting under Congress's law.

Clinton prevails

With a unanimous decision, the Supreme Court ruled in favor of President Clinton. Justice David Souter delivered the Court's decision. Justice Souter said Congress created the CAAF to review sentences imposed by court-martials. Dropping Goldsmith from the rolls was not part of his court-martial sentence. It was independent action by President Clinton under a law of Congress. The CAAF had no power to

DON'T ASK, DON'T TELL DOESN'T WORK

Homosexual conduct is unlawful in the military and is grounds for being court-martialed and discharged. When William J. Clinton became president in 1993, he wanted to end discrimination against homosexuals in the military. Political pressure, however, forced him to accept a new policy called "Don't ask, don't tell." Congress made the policy a law in 1994.

Under the policy, military authorities are not supposed to ask officers or enlisted members about their sexual orientation. In return, homosexuals are not supposed to reveal their sexuality or engage in homosexual conduct. Keeping everyone silent was supposed to permit homosexuals to serve in the military. It also was supposed to reduce anti-gay harassment, which historically is a problem in the military.

Six years later, people on both sides of the issue agreed that the policy had failed. In December 1999, President Clinton said the policy was "out of whack" and not working as it was supposed to work. In March 2000, the Pentagon revealed a survey of 71,500 service personnel worldwide. Eighty percent of those surveyed said they heard anti-gay comments in the military during the previous year. Thirty-seven percent said they saw anti-gay harassment. Eighty-five percent said they believed the military tolerated verbal abuse of homosexuals.

Failure of the "Don't ask, don't tell" policy led Vice President Al Gore to call for its repeal. Gore vowed to end discrimination against homosexuals in the military if he was elected president in November 2000.

review that action.

Justice Souter noted that Goldsmith had not yet been dropped from the rolls. If that happened, Goldsmith would be allowed to challenge the decision before the Air Force Board of Correction for Military Records. If the Board ruled against him, Goldsmith could appeal the case to a federal court. What Goldsmith could not do was get relief from the CAAF, which had no power to tell President Clinton what to do.

Suggestions for further reading

Connolly, Ceci, and Bradley Graham. "Gore Vows New Policy on Gays in Military." *Washington Post,* December 14, 1999.

Encyclopedia Americana, 1993 ed., s.v. "Court-martial."

Sherrill, Robert. *Military Justice is to Justice as Military Music is to Music.* New York: Harper & Row, 1970.

Suro, Roberto. "Harassment of Gay GIs Tolerated, Study Finds." *Washington Post,* March 25, 2000.

World Book Encyclopedia, 2000 ed., s.v. "Court-martial."

The term Native American is commonly used to refer to American Indians living within the United States, though it also includes Hawaiians and some Alaskan natives not considered American Indians. When referred to in general, American Indians often prefer to be called by their tribal names, such as Nez Perce, Navajo, Sioux, or Oneida.

The place of Native Americans in the U.S. legal system is highly unique. Tribes are formally recognized sovereign (politically independent) nations located within the boundaries of the United States. By the 1990s over 2 percent of lands within the United States were actually governed by Native American tribal governments. Such lands under tribal jurisdiction are referred to as Indian Country.

Tracing the history of U.S.-Indian relations from the nation's early years reveals that present-day Native American legal standing in the United States is not the result of a well-organized body of legal principles, but rather an accumulation of policies coming from many sources over time. Although many similarities do exist, each tribe has its own unique cultural and legal history. For over two hundred years, U.S. Indian policy shifted between periods of supporting tribal self-government and economic self-sufficiency apart from U.S. society to periods of forced Indian social and economic assimilation (inclusion) into the dominant society.

The Growth of Indian Law

The basis for what is known as Indian law, which is actually U.S. law about Indians and not by Indians, was established well before the birth of the United States. During the seventeenth century British and Spanish colonies began negotiating treaties with the New World's native peoples, treating them as politically independent groups. The treaties recognized Indian ownership of lands they were living on and using. The United States, after independence from Great Britain, inherited this age-old European international policy. As a result, tribal sovereignty, recognized well before the birth of the United States, became the basis for future U.S.-Indian relations.

Fresh from victory over Britain in the American Revolution (1775–1783), the fledgling new government made establishment of peaceful and orderly relations with American Indians one of its first items of business. The 1787 Northwest Ordinance, enacted by the Continental Congress, recognized existing Indian possession of the newly gained lands from Britain that were not part of the original colonies. Attempting to end the practice of private individuals or local governments negotiating treaties with or buying lands directly from the sovereign Indian nations, the Ordinance stated that only the federal government could legally carry out such activities.

Recognition of tribal sovereignty was directly addressed in the U.S. Constitution, adopted in 1788. Authority for the federal government's legal relationship with tribes was placed in the Commerce Clause of Article 1 which reads simply that Congress has power "to regulate Commerce with foreign Nations and . . . the Indian Tribes." The Constitution also recognizes the legal status of Indian treaties in Article VI by stating, "This Constitution, and the Laws of the United States . . . and all Treaties made . . . shall be the supreme Law of the Land." This means congressionally ratified (approved) treaties have the same legal force as regular federal laws. Further reflecting the importance of Indian relations to the new nation, one of the first acts passed by the first U.S. Congress was the Indian Trade and Intercourse Act of 1790. Exercising its new constitutional authority, Congress proclaimed treaty-making policy and brought all interactions between Indians and non-Indians under federal control.

U.S. Indian policy became further defined by three landmark Supreme Court decisions between 1823 and 1832. Known as the Marshall Trilogy after then-Chief Justice John Marshall, the cases of ***Johnson v. McIntosh*** (1823), ***Cherokee Nation v. Georgia*** (1831), and ***Worcester v. Georgia*** (1832) affirmed the tribal right to occupy and govern their lands, tribal sovereignty from state jurisdiction within Indian reservations, and defined a moral trust responsibility of the United States toward the tribes. Marshall described tribes as "domestic dependent nations" essentially free of state controls. The trust relationship toward Indian nations meant the United States is responsible for Indian health and welfare.

Later Court decisions further defined Indian policy. A reserved rights doctrine was established in *United States v. Winans* (1905) meaning that Indians retain certain inherent (native) rights until explicitly taken away by Congress. But, the Court in *Lone Wolf v. Hitchcock* (1903) also gave Congress "plenary" (absolute) power over Indian peoples. Plenary power meant Congress could on its own change U.S. Indian policy, even change treaties and end specific rights without consent of the tribes. However, the trust responsibility requires careful exercise of this absolute power, using it only when considered beneficial to Indian peoples. To resolve legal disputes over treaty interpretations, the "canons of construction" recognized in *Winters v. United States* (1908) state that unclear treaty language should always be interpreted by the courts from the tribal perspective.

U.S. governmental policy concerning Indians proceeded from the Marshall Trilogy to the year 2000 along a zig-zag pathway of alternating goals. Policy swerved from isolation and protection on reservations, to forced integration (assimilation) into American farming society, to recognition of reorganized tribal governments and relations with the federal government, to termination of trust status, and finally to support for tribal self-determination and integrity.

Treaties, Removal, and Reservations

Despite the seemingly protective U.S. Indian policies developed through the first few decades of the nation's history, in reality Indian peoples suffered catastrophic loss of economies, lands, and life during the persistent westward push of white settlements. One of the more tragic examples of U.S. government actions was the 1830's removal policy directed by President Andrew Jackson (1829–1837). Under this policy, the United

States forcefully removed the Five Civilized Tribes from the Southeastern United States to a newly created Indian Territory in what later became Oklahoma. Thousands of deaths directly resulted.

U.S. removal policies continued through the 1850s and 1860s as more treaties were made with tribes in the West. The western treaties created a vast reservation system in which the inherent rights of Native Americans would presumably persist within certain defined territories, called reservations. Some treaties also reserved Indian hunting, fishing, and gathering rights outside reservation boundaries to help maintain traditional economies. Although not written in the treaties, water rights were also implicitly included as later interpreted by the Court in *Winters*. Honoring these treaties conflicted with the promotion of non-Indian settlement and economic development in newly gained U.S. territories.

As opposed to rights of tribal governments, the legal rights of Indian individuals was a major concern of neither the federal government nor the courts throughout much of the nineteenth century. With tribal relations largely guided by the treaties rather than standard U.S. law, legal dealings with Indian individuals were generally avoided. As a result, a system for policing and punishment of Indians developed largely beyond the reach of U.S. courts. Indian agents having ready access to the military, exercised broad authority, often detaining and executing numerous individuals for a wide range of alleged actions.

The End of Treaty-Making

In 1871, Congress ended treaty-making, closing a major chapter in U.S.-Indian relations. By this time, the Indian population had largely been isolated by the U.S. government into remote areas, out of the way of U.S. expansion and settlements. Distant from U.S. markets, as well, prospects for economic recovery were slim at best. Consequently, the fortunes of Indian peoples was only to decline further through the next sixty years. Greed for more lands led to further damaging federal policies. Continued U.S. expansion brought increased natural resource needs and gold discoveries making the remote reservation lands suddenly attractive to Westerners.

In addition, by the 1870s Indian issues rose more in the national public eye as social reformers shifted attention from slavery. Demands for humanitarian action gathered momentum. An 1879 federal court ruling in *United States ex rel. Standing Bear v. Crook* asserted that Indians off-reservation were "persons" having the same constitutional due process and equal protection rights under the Fourteenth Amendment as U.S. citizens. The U.S. army no longer held broad authority to detain Indians without full civilian constitutional protections. However, much about the legal standing of Indian individuals still remained poorly defined. In 1884 the Supreme Court ruled the Fourteenth Amendment of the Constitution had not automatically granted citizenship to Indians.

Assimilation

A major period of forced cultural assimilation began with the General Allotment Act of 1887 and lasted into the 1930s. Assimilation means the U.S. government tried to blend Native Americans into the mainstream U.S. society. Many believed the Indian tradition of communally-owning property was a key barrier to Indians adopting Western ways. As a result, Congress passed the Allotment Act, also known as the Dawes Act, authorizing the Bureau of Indian Affairs (BIA) to divide all reservation lands into smaller parcels. The agency then allotted (assigned) 160-acre parcels to families and eighty-acre parcels to single adults over eighteen years of age. Indians receiving allotments also received U.S. citizenship. U.S. policymakers reasoned that when people owned their own property they would most likely become farmers and adopt the U.S. farming lifestyle.

Given the still relatively extensive land holdings of the Indians in 1887, much land was left over after every tribal member had received their allotment. Those unallotted lands were declared "surplus" and sold by the United States to non-Indians. In addition to the loss of vast amounts of "surplus" lands, much allotted land went into forfeiture (banks claim ownership) when many Indians could not pay taxes on their often remote unproductive desert properties. Even if the land was productive, markets were usually still too distant. The allotment policy became an economic disaster to Indian peoples, reducing Indian Country in the United States from 138 million acres in 1887 to forty-eight million acres by 1934. In many cases, the more agriculturally productive lands on reservations had passed out of tribal control.

In a further effort to assimilate Indians, all Indians born in the United States became U.S. citizens through the Indian Citizenship Act of 1924. The act also made Indians citizens of the states in which they resided. Although able to vote and hold state office, they are not subject to state law while on Indian lands. The Constitution's Bill of Rights, however, did not apply to protecting Indians from their tribal governments as it did from federal and state actions because of tribal sovereignty. As a result, tribal members could be subjected at times to harsher legal penalties from their own tribal governments than non-Indians in U.S. society for the same crimes.

Reorganizing Tribal Governments

By the 1930s the calamity of the allotment policy had become apparent. In an effort to end assimilation efforts, U.S. policy returned to stressing tribal sovereignty. The Indian Reorganization Act of 1934 ended the allotment process, stabilized remaining tribal land holdings, and promoted tribal self-government. The act encouraged tribes to adopt U.S.-style constitutions and form federally-chartered corporations. Although many tribes elected to organize under the rules of the act, many others rejected developing constitutions. Some organized new governments under their own tribal rules. However, even this seemingly friendly policy of encouraging formation of modern tribal governments had harmful social effects in Indian Country. The newly established more modern governments often came in conflict with the traditional tribal political leaders.

Urban Indians and Termination

Following World War II (1939–1945), other traditions began changing also. With thousands of Indians returning from military service abroad or working in defense plants, their exposure to mainstream U.S. society made life on poverty-ridden reservations less acceptable. Also, the GI Bill provided educational opportunities. More Indians began moving off-reservation into the newly expanding urban areas, seeking greater economic opportunity. The welfare of these urban Indians became an increasing concern of the federal government under its trust responsibilities.

In a few cases, tribes still held a sufficient land base with marketable natural resources such as timber began to develop an economic base and prosper. However, greed for Indian-owned assets of value rose again. By 1953 U.S. governmental policy significantly shifted back to assimilation, this time through "termination" policies. Termination of a tribe meant ending the special trust relationship and loss of reservation lands. The lands, some very productive, were sold to non-Indians and access to federal health and education services was taken away. The economic base for those Indian communities was devastated. In addition to termination, Congress also passed Public Law 280 in 1953. The act expanded state jurisdiction onto tribal lands in selected states, decreasing tribal sovereignty yet more in those areas.

Tribal Self-Determination

Congressional support for termination did not last long as U.S. Indian policy again took a dramatic shift back in the 1960s toward a tribal government self-determination (govern own internal affairs) era. Influenced by the black American civil rights movement, a series of Congressional hearing in the 1960s focused on the lack of consistent civil rights protections offered by tribal governments to their members.

As a result, Congress passed the Indian Civil Rights Act (ICRA) of 1968 extending most of the Bill of Rights to Indian peoples including free speech protections, free exercise of religion, and due process and equal protection of tribal government laws. Not extended to Indians was the right to a jury trial in civil cases, free legal counsel for the poor, search and seizure protections, and prohibition on government support of a religion. Issues such as gender discrimination in tribal laws still could not be challenged under federal law. The act also cut back some of the states' authorities granted in Public Law 280. In respect for tribal sovereignty, interpretation of ICRA is left to the tribes and tribal courts, not federal courts. Federal courts can only review tribal court decisions in certain types of criminal cases.

Other legal distinctions for Indians were also identified. Title VII of the 1964 Civil Rights Act explicitly exempted Indian hiring preferences from its due process protections in some instances. The 1974 Court ruling in *Morton v. Mancari* affirmed that American Indians can be treated differently from other U.S. citizens by the federal government despite anti-discrimination laws. Tribes are political not racial groups on occasions when the U.S. government bases it actions on its trust responsibilities to protect Indian interests and promote tribal sovereignty. If the Indian preference laws were only designed to help Indians as individuals, they then could be determined illegal.

With civil rights protections different from other U.S. citizens, determining who is Indian has important legal consequences. Constituting a political rather than racial group, tribal members may gain membership to a tribe through birth or marriage and may have substantial non-Indian ancestry. Conversely, a person of total Indian ancestry who has never established a relationship with a tribe may not enjoy Indian legal status. Each of the over 550 recognized tribes in the United States is responsible to determine membership as an exercise of their tribal sovereignty. In general, an Indian is anyone with some degree of Indian ancestry, considered a member of an Indian community, and promoting themselves as Indian.

The biggest boost in support of tribal sovereignty and self-sufficiency came in 1975 when Congress passed the Indian Self-Determination and Education Assistance Act. The act gave tribes much greater opportunity to administer federal programs benefitting Indian peoples that were previously administered by the BIA. Many of these programs provided health and education services.

Through the rest of the twentieth century Congress continued passing acts protecting tribal rights and interests, including the American Indian Religious Freedom Act (1978), Indian Mineral Development Act (1982), Indian Gaming Regulatory Act (1988), the Native American Graves Protection and Repatriation Act (1990), and the Indian Self-Governance Act (1994). By the 1990s, tribes could form and reorganize their own governments, determine tribal membership, regulate individual property, manage natural resources, provide health services, develop gaming businesses, regulate commerce on tribal lands, collect taxes, maintain law enforcement and establish tribal court systems. By the end of the twentieth century, tribal court systems had greatly expanded as many tribes gained greater economic and political power. However, due to the broad diversity of tribal legal systems, the meaning of justices and the way it was applied differed from tribe to tribe. Besides those patterned after United States models, some tribes retained traditional systems and others no system at all.

By 2000, the resulting branch of U.S. law, commonly called Indian Law, was a very peculiar part of the U.S. legal system with tribal governments and their peoples possessing a unique legal status. Members of federally recognized tribes were both U.S. and tribal citizens, simultaneously receiving benefits and protections from federal, state, and tribal governments.

Suggestions for further reading

Hirschfelder, Arlene, and Martha K. de Montano. *The Native American Almanac: A Portrait of Native America Today.* New York: Prentice Hall, 1993.

Prucha, Francis P. *The Great Father: The United States Government and the American Indians.* Lincoln: University of Nebraska Press, 1986.

Red Hawk, Richard. *A Trip to a Pow Wow.* Sacramento, CA: Sierra Oaks Publishing Co., 1988.

Riley, Patricia, editor. *Growing Up Native American.* New York: Morrow, 1993.

Washburn, Wilcomb E., editor. *Handbook of North American Indians: History of Indian-White Relations, Vol. 4.* Washington, DC: Smithsonian Institution Press, 1988.

Weatherford, Jack. *Indian Givers: How the Indians of the Americas Transformed the World.* New York: Fawcett Columbine, 1988.

Wilkinson, Charles F. *American Indians, Time, and the Law: Native Societies in a Modern Constitutional Democracy.* New Haven: Yale University Press, 1987.

Johnson v. McIntosh 1823

Appellants: Johnson and Graham

Appellee: William McIntosh

Appellant's Claim: That title to land purchased by private individuals directly from Indian tribes before the United States gained independence should be recognized by the United States.

Chief Lawyers for Appellants: Harper and Webster

Chief Lawyers for the Appellee: Winder and Murray

Justices for the Court: Gabriel Duvall, William Johnson, Chief Justice John Marshall, Joseph Story, Smith Thompson, Thomas Todd, Bushrod Washington

Justices Dissenting: None

Date of Decision: February of 1823

Decision: Ruled in favor of McIntosh by denying recognition of land purchases from Indian tribes by individuals.

Significance: This landmark ruling established the legal basis by which the United States could establish its land base. Chief Justice John Marshall had to piece together the concept of discovery as used by early European explorers and Indian sovereignty (governmental independence). Being sovereign governments, the rights to lands that Indians physically possessed could only be acquired by the U.S. government, not by private individuals or states.

When European explorers began arriving on the eastern shores of North America in the sixteenth century, they found numerous long-established Indian societies, each with their own governments, laws, and customs. Although the explorers asserted the "doctrine of discovery" to claim control of lands they "discovered" for their rulers, European colonists who later followed the explorers still had to deal with the question of Indian land possessions. By 1532 Spain officially declared that Indians held a certain right to land that foreign nations could not take simply through "discovery." Actual possession of land occupied and used by American Indians could only be gained by signing a treaty or by waging a "just war."

Mr. Johnson and Mr. Graham

Prior to the Revolutionary War (1776–1783) while the thirteen American colonies were still under British rule, the Illinois and Piankeshaw Indian tribes lived in the Ohio Valley region to the west. During the period of European exploration, France had claimed the region through discovery. A 1763 treaty ending the French and Indian War (1754–1763) between France and Great Britain over North American lands transferred claim to the region to Great Britain. A number of years later, in 1773 and 1775, Mr. Johnson and Mr. Graham, two individuals acting on their own, purchased lands northwest of the Ohio River directly from the two tribes.

At the outbreak of the Revolutionary War in 1776, numerous conflicts erupted between tribes, the colonies, and their citizens. Many of the tribes were sympathetic to the British. Attempting to establish claim and some control over the Ohio Valley to its west, the state of Virginia passed a law proclaiming exclusive right to large tracts of land. Included were the two parcels owned by Johnson and Graham. Consistent with existing legal principles, the law recognized that the Indians held a right of possession to continue living in the region until the lands could be purchased by Virginia. The act also provided that all previous land transactions by Indians to private individuals for their own use were not valid. Additionally, upon defeat, Great Britain gave up its claim to the Ohio River area.

The newly established United States immediately began to address land ownership issues on its frontier. It also needed a national policy for Indian relations as ruthless conflicts continued among tribes and frontier populations. The 1787 Northwest Ordinance established U.S. claim to the newly gained lands and recognized Indian rights of possession to their existing holdings on those lands. The Ordinance established how newly acquired lands from the British, not previously part of the original colonies, would be governed. Individual state claims, such as Virginia's, were no longer valid. The Ordinance stated that Indian "lands and property shall never be taken from them without their consent." The U.S. Constitution, adopted in 1789, further recognized Indian nations as one of three types of sovereign governments in the United States, the other two being the states and the federal government. Article 1 of the Constitution gave Congress authority to "regulate commerce with . . . the Indian Tribes" and Article VI recognized Indian treaties along with acts of Congress as the "supreme law of the land."

Questions persisted, however, as to just what kind of title to land did tribes hold and how could that title be transferred to others. In an attempt to further address this issue, one of the first laws passed by the first U.S. Congress in 1790 was the Indian Trade and Intercourse Act. The act recognized the federal government's role in negotiating Indian treaties and prohibited tribes from selling lands to anyone else except the U.S. government. The U.S. government immediately began negotiating treaties with the tribes as equal sovereigns, seeking to establish peace and acquire a land base.

William McIntosh

With the general framework in place for securing peace and acquiring Indian lands on the U.S. frontier, the United States acquired the Ohio Valley area. Selling the land to raise money and encourage frontier settlement, the United States soon sold to William McIntosh some of the land including the original parcels earlier acquired by Johnson and Graham. With McIntosh laying claim to his new lands, Johnson and Graham filed a lawsuit in the District Court for Illinois challenging McIntosh's ownership. Johnson and Graham argued they had legally purchased the parcels directly from the tribes before the United States had gained control of the region. The court rejected their argument and ruled in favor of McIntosh. Johnson and Graham appealed to the U.S. Supreme Court.

The Discovery Doctrine

In a landmark decision establishing the basic principles of property ownership in the new nation, legendary Chief Justice John Marshall wrote the Court's opinion. Supporting the lower court's decision in favor of

THE "TRAIL OF TEARS"

Of the many injustices visited by the United States on Indian tribes, the removal of the Cherokee nation from their Georgia homeland to Oklahoma in the winter of 1838–39 was one of the most inexcusable. Over the course of their journey, on a route called the "Trail of Tears,"one-quarter of the Cherokee people died.

The Cherokee had been almost unique among Indians in their establishment of a European-style government. Hoping in vain to preserve their lands in northwest Georgia against the spread of white settlement, in the early 1800sthey adopted many of the features that they hoped would qualify them as "civilized" in the eyes of the federal government. Not only did they become the only Native American group with a written language, thanks to the efforts of the linguist Sequoyah, they also established a parliamentary and constitutional form of government with a capital at New Echota. In addition, they took up cattle-raising and farming, a departure from the traditional Native American hunter-gatherer economy.

But these efforts proved futile. In 1828, Georgia declared void all Cherokee laws, and claimed their lands for the state.

McIntosh, Marshall carefully detailed the basic rules for land acquisition along the expanding frontier. First, Marshall returned to the early European concepts of discovery that led to settlement of the colonies. Marshall wrote, "that discovery gave title to the government by whose subjects it was made, against all other European governments [which] necessarily gave to the nation making the discovery the sole right of acquiring the soil from the natives." In other words, the key importance of the doctrine of discovery was establishing which European nation held the right to acquire particular lands from Indian groups who actually lived on it.

Then Marshall described the implication of discovery to the tribes. According to Marshall, the tribes

> **were admitted to be the rightful occupants of the soil, with a legal as well as just claim to retain possession of it, and to use it according to their own discretion [choice]; but their rights to complete sovereignty, as independent nations, were necessarily diminished, and their power to dispose of the soil at their own will, to whomever they pleased, was denied by the original fundamental principle, that discovery gave exclusive title to those who made [the discovery].**

Although the tribes held right of possession, the individual European countries held a title by discovery. That title of discovery was clearly held by nations and not by individuals. Marshall contended these principles underlying discovery were recognized by all European nations during colonization in the seventeenth and eighteenth centuries.

Regarding Johnson's and Graham's properties, Marshall asserted that title of discovery to the two parcels was held by Great Britain after 1763, but "was forfeited by the laws of war" to the United States. Marshall claimed, "It is not for the courts of this country to question the validity of this [the United States'] title." Consequently, Marshall assumed the United States held clear title of discovery, and the 1790 Indian Intercourse Act established that only the United States could acquire right of possession from the tribes and sell the lands to private individuals. The United States held such a discovery right of acquisition to the Ohio Valley following the Revolution.

Since a national control of lands can only pass from one government to another government, individuals such as Johnson and Graham could not have gained a valid U.S. legal title from the tribes. Their right of ownership could only be recognized under tribal law, not U.S. law. Their title, therefore, "cannot be recognized in the courts of the United States." Marshall declared McIntosh the rightful owner since he had purchased the land from the United States after the United States acquired it from the Indian nations through treaty.

U.S. Expansion

The *Johnson* decision served to more fully interpret the Indian Trade and Intercourse Act. A process was defined for recognizing tribal land rights and the orderly transfer to the United States. The ruling held that

MODERN INDIAN CLAIMS IN THE ORIGINAL STATES

The *Johnson v. McIntosh* (1823) decision laid the legal groundwork for U.S. expansion through the next several decades. Because many of the original thirteen states and their European predecessors had acquired millions of acres directly from Indian tribes without ever gaining approval of Congress, Marshall had hoped to minimize the effects of the ruling on previous land acquisitions. However, the controversy of land ownership in the original thirteen states returned over a century later. In the 1970s tribes began challenging those early land acquisitions of the original colonies. Tribes filed twenty-one lawsuits in seven eastern states as well as Louisiana. They claimed their right of possession as recognized in *Johnson* by Chief Justice John Marshall was never legally acquired by the United States.

As an example, in 1972 several lawsuits sought 7.5 million acres and $150 million in damages for the alleged illegal land transfers in Maine and Massachusetts alone. The Supreme Court in *Passamaquoddy Tribe v. Morton* (1975) confirmed that tribes had legal authority to pursue such claims. Out of court negotiations led to the Maine Indian Claims Settlement Act of 1986 in which the Maine tribes received over $81 million for lost lands.

For claims in the state of New York, the Court ruled in *County of Oneida v. Oneida Indian Nation* (1985) that the 1795 acquisition of 100,000 acres by New York from the Oneida was invalid because it never received congressional approval. These cases highlighted the complex historical relationship between the tribes and eastern states.

Indians did not hold absolute title to their lands, but a lesser right of occupancy. Indians were also restricted in how they could dispose of their lands. They could only sell to the U.S. government or to other parties with approval of the United States. Therefore, the United States held exclusive right to acquire Indian lands, either "by purchase or conquest." In practicality, this ruling recognized that Indian nations retained national sovereignty, but in some limited way. Marshall would soon more specifically define the nature of that sovereignty in ***Cherokee Nation v. Georgia*** (1831) in which he would describe tribes as "domestic dependent nations."

In a third ruling establishing the basis of U.S. Indian law, Marshall ruled in ***Worcester v. Geogia*** (1832) that tribal sovereignty meant that states could not enforce their laws on tribal lands. Tribes could govern their own internal affairs, restricted only by Congress which held ultimate legal power. The rulings of *Johnson, Cherokee Nation,* and *Worcester* have been described as Marshall's Trilogy of Indian court cases legally defining U.S.-Indian relationships for most of the next two centuries.

The ruling in someways was a compromise. Discovery did not end tribal ownership but the Indians did not retain full title either. Marshall placed Indian land claims into a European land ownership system.

Suggestions for further reading

National Congress of American Indians. [Online] http://www.ncai.org (Accessed July 31, 2000).

Wilson, James. *The Earth Shall Weep: A History of Native America.* New York: Atlantic Monthly Press, 1999.

Wunder, John R. editor. *Native American Law and Colonialism, Before 1776 to 1903.* New York: Garland Publishing, Inc., 1996.

Cherokee Nation v. Georgia
1831

Plaintiff: Cherokee Indian Nation

Defendant: State of Georgia

Plaintiff's Claim: That the U.S. Supreme Court, using its constitutional powers to resolve disputes between states and foreign nations, stop Georgia from illegally and forcefully removing the Cherokee Nation from its lands.

Chief Lawyer for the Plaintiff: William Wirt

Chief Lawyer for the Defendant: None

Justices for the Court: Henry Baldwin, William Johnson, Chief Justice John Marshall, John McLean

Justices Dissenting: Smith Thompson, Joseph Story (Gabriel Duvall did not participate)

Date of Decision: March 5, 1831

Decision: Ruled in favor of Georgia by finding that the Supreme Court had no legal authority to hear the dispute because Indian tribes are "domestic dependent nations," not foreign nations.

Significance: By refusing to hear the case, the Court left the Cherokees at the mercy of the state of Georgia and its land-hungry citizens. In late 1838 the Cherokee were forcefully marched under winter conditions from their homes in northwest Georgia to lands set aside in Oklahoma. Four thousand died in military detention camps and along the infamous "Trail of Tears." The forced removal of Indian tribes from the Southeastern United States was completed by 1858.

"The whole scene since I have been in this country has been nothing but a heart-rendering one . . . I would remove every Indian tomorrow beyond the reach of the white men, who, like vultures, are watching, ready to pounce on their prey and strip them of everything they have . . . " U.S. General John Ellis Wood in charge of the Cherokee removal quoted in "The Time Machine." *American Heritage,* September/October 1988.

Before settlement by European colonists in the seventeenth and eighteenth centuries, the Cherokee Indians lived along much of North America's southeastern coast. By the 1780s, war, disease, and starvation had killed most American Indians living along much of North America's eastern coastline. The Cherokee population shifted further inland and negotiated treaties with the U.S. government to protect their remaining homelands. Based on a treaty signed with the United States in 1791, the Cherokee were settled on traditional lands in the hills of northwest Georgia and western North Carolina.

As U.S. settlement pressed further inland in the early nineteenth century, many surviving Indian groups forcefully resisted further land loss. Some even sided with Britain against the United States in the War of 1812 (1812–1814). However, the United States won the war in 1814 and General Andrew Jackson (1767–1845) promptly led the U.S. military to victory over the Creeks and other Indian groups who had actively opposed the United States.

In contrast to the Creeks, the Cherokee had early accepted U.S. presence as inevitable and adopted a more peaceful policy of coexistence. In dealing with European intrusion into their lands, the Cherokee sought to hold their ground by adopting many of the white ways. During the early 1800s the Cherokee went through a remarkable period of cultural change. They adopted a farming economy including cattle-raising in place of traditional hunting and gathering. Some Cherokee even became plantation owners with slaves. Others became involved in commerce, managing stores, mills and other businesses. Cherokee children were sent to American schools and mixed marriages with non-Indians were allowed. Seeing the benefits of reading and writing, a Cherokee silversmith, Sequoya, created a Cherokee alphabet that was quickly adopted. They became the only Indian nation in North America with a written language. By the 1820's, the Cherokee had established written laws, a constitution, and a capitol at New Echota.

As the Cherokee became a flourishing independent nation within Georgia's state boundaries, resentment grew among white settlers.

Cherokee Nation v. Georgia

PROTECTION

CHEROKEE PHŒNIX.

VOL. I. NEW ECHOTA, THURSDAY APRIL 10, 1828. NO. 8.

The case involving the Cherokee Nation was followed in the local Cherokee newspaper. Courtesy of the Library of Congress.

Already eager to grab the rich agricultural lands of the Cherokee, the discovery of gold in Cherokee country in 1828 further escalated the greed for land and wealth. In addition, President Andrew Jackson signed the Indian Removal Act of 1830 that provided funds for removal of eastern Indians to the west beyond the Mississippi River.

The state of Georgia began enacting laws declaring all Cherokee laws void and seeking to remove the Cherokee from their lands. In reaction to Georgia's actions, the Cherokees hired white lawyers led by

NATIVE AMERICANS

William Wirt to defend their interests. With the state's antagonism toward the tribe, Wirt clearly did not want to have to defend the Cherokee case in Georgia state courts. Noting that Article III, Section 2 of the U.S. Constitution gives the U.S. Supreme Court original jurisdiction (the geographic area over which a government or court has authority) in cases for which a state is a party, Wirt took the Cherokee case straight to the Court. He requested an injunction (a court order stopping an action) forbidding Georgia from removing the Cherokees. A complicating factor was that all Indians including the Cherokee were not recognized as U.S. citizens. Section 2 restricts Supreme Court jurisdiction only to cases involving American citizens by stating that it may only hear disputes "between a State, or the Citizens thereof, and foreign States . . . " Since the Cherokee Nation was not a state and the Cherokees were not U.S. citizens, Wirt decided to take the position that the Cherokee Nation was a foreign nation, thus placing the case under the Court's jurisdiction.

On the other side, the state of Georgia believed the federal courts had no business judging their state laws. They believed so strongly in states' rights that they refused to send anyone to legally represent them before the Supreme Court.

A political cartoon showing injustice and cruelty against the Cherokee Nation. Reproduced by permission of the Corbis Corporation.

In arguing for foreign nation status on March 5, 1831, Wirt stressed that the Cherokee's "boundaries were fixed by treaty, and what was within them was acknowledged to be the land of the Cherokees. This was the scope of all treaties." On a more human level, Wirt pleaded that,

> **The legislation of Georgia proposes to annihilate [the Cherokee}. As its very end and aim . . . If those laws be fully executed, there will be no Cherokee boundary, no Cherokee nation, no Cherokee lands, no Cherokee treaties . . . They will all be swept out of existence together, leaving nothing but the monuments in our history of the enormous injustice that has been practised towards a friendly nation.**

Responding that very same day, Chief Justice John Marshall delivered the Court's 4–2 decision. Attempting to finally resolve the legal status of Indian tribes within the United States, Marshall stated that tribes such as the Cherokee are "domestic dependent nations," not foreign nations. Marshall wrote that through the doctrine of discovery applied by European nations when exploring North American lands in the seventeenth and eighteenth centuries, the tribes had partially lost their sovereignty as nations when the European nations had laid claim to their lands. Consequently, tribes were no longer fully independent foreign nations. The Indians had essentially become wards (dependent subjects) of the federal government for whom the United States held a special legal responsibility to protect, a trust responsibility. Marshall concluded that since the Cherokee were not a fully independent nation, the Supreme Court holds no jurisdiction to hear the Cherokee claims.

Tragic Consequences

Unable to gain legal support from the American court system, the Cherokee were at the mercy of the state of Georgia and Jackson's removal policy. After years of harassment and antagonism, a small group of Cherokee in 1835 led by Major Ridge and his son ceded by treaty all Cherokee lands. The Cherokee peoples were given two years to leave their traditional lands and move to a special Indian territory created by Congress in 1834 in what latter became Oklahoma. By 1838 the Cherokees were stripped of all their lands in the Southeast.

Under watch of 7,000 U.S. troops, the Cherokee peoples were forced from their homes and marched a thousand miles during the win-

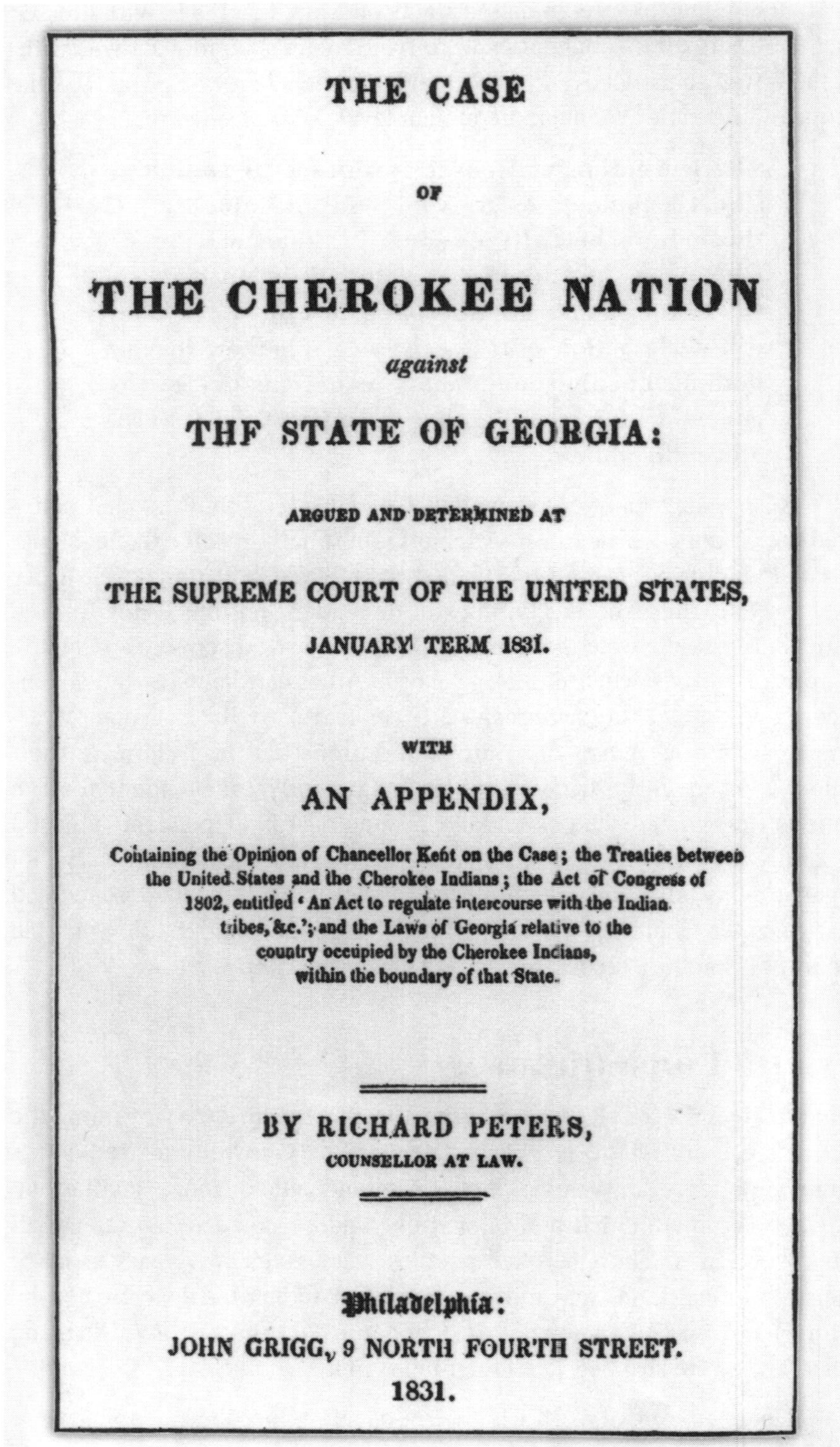

THE CASE

OF

THE CHEROKEE NATION

against

THF STATE OF GEORGIA:

ARGUED AND DETERMINED AT

THE SUPREME COURT OF THE UNITED STATES,

JANUARY TERM 1831.

WITH

AN APPENDIX,

Containing the Opinion of Chancellor Kent on the Case; the Treaties between the United States and the Cherokee Indians; the Act of Congress of 1802, entitled 'An Act to regulate intercourse with the Indian tribes, &c.'; and the Laws of Georgia relative to the country occupied by the Cherokee Indians, within the boundary of that State.

BY RICHARD PETERS,

COUNSELLOR AT LAW.

Philadelphia:

JOHN GRIGG, 9 NORTH FOURTH STREET.

1831.

The title page of the case involving the Cherokee Nation. Reproduced by permission of Northwind Photos.

TRAIL OF TEARS

Many Cherokee resisted the government's efforts to remove them from their lands. As the deadline for removal approached in 1837 President Martin Van Buren (1837–1841) ordered federal authorities to force the Cherokee from their homes and place them in temporary detention camps. They remained in the camps through 1838 during a typically hot sweltering Southern summer. Diseases began to spread. Suffering from dysentery, measles, and whooping cough, some two thousand died in the camps.

That October, over fifteen thousand men, women and children began a six month thousand mile journey to the very unfamiliar country of Oklahoma. Most marched overland from northwest Georgia, across central Tennessee, western Kentucky, southern Illinois, southern Missouri and northern Arkansas to eastern Oklahoma. A smaller number were taken by flatboat down the Tennessee River to the Mississippi River and then up the Arkansas River. Lacking adequate food, shelter, and clothing while en route, another two thousand died from exposure, disease, and exhaustion. The Cherokee buried their dead along the route that became known as the Trail of Tears. The forced march became one of the most tragic events in U.S.-Indian relations. The Trail of Tears was later designated a National Historic Trail by Congress.

ter of 1838 and 1839 to the Oklahoma territory. Thousands died as it became known in history as the "Trail of Tears." During their removal, a thousand or more Cherokee fled into remote areas of the East, including the Great Smoky Mountains. They later gained federal recognition as the Cherokee of the North Carolina Qualla Reservation. The massive relocation still stands as one of the saddest moments in U.S.-Indian relations.

Following their tragic journey, the Cherokee reestablished their farming society in the hills of northeastern Oklahoma. They quickly setup a new government and signed a constitution in 1839. Tahlequah, Oklahoma became the capital for the displaced peoples.

Removal of the Cherokee Nation left behind only scattered Indian groups in the Southeast. By 1842, most of the Five Civilized Tribes' peoples of the Southeast, the Cherokee, Chickasaw, Choctaw, Creek, and Seminole, had been taken from their prosperous farms and plantations and resettled to government-assigned lands in Oklahoma. The last of the Seminoles of Florida were removed in 1858.

The Cherokee's forced removal dramatized the fate of Indian peoples in the face of U.S. expansion. The tide of U.S. expansion eventually overwhelmed even those tribes with peaceful policies and firmly established economies.

Suggestions for further reading

Gilbert, Joan. *The Trail of Tears Across Missouri.* Columbia: University of Missouri Press, 1996.

McLoughlin, William G. *After the Trail of Tears: The Cherokees' Struggle for Sovereignty, 1839-1880.* Chapel Hill: University of North Carolina Press, 1993.

Rice, Horace R. *The Buffalo Ridge Cherokee: A Remnant of a Great Nation Divided.* Bowie, MD: Heritage Books, 1995.

Wilkins, Thurman. *Cherokee Tragedy: The Ridge Family and the Decimation of a People,* Second Edition. Norman: University of Oklahoma Press, 1986.

Worcester v. Georgia 1832

Appellant: Samuel A. Worcester

Appellee: State of Georgia

Appellant's Claim: That the state of Georgia had no legal authority to pass laws regulating activities within the boundaries of the Cherokee Nation, a nation recognized through treaties with the United States.

Justices for the Court: Garbriel Duvall, William Johnson, Chief Justice John Marshall, John McLean, Joseph Story, Smith Thompson

Justices Dissenting: Henry Baldwin

Date of Decision: March 3, 1832

Decision: Ruled in favor of Worcester overturning his lower court conviction for living on Cherokee Nation lands without a state of Georgia permit.

Significance: This ruling was the third key decision by Chief Justice John Marshall since 1823 establishing the political standing of Indian tribes within the United States. The ruling recognized the sovereign (politically independent) status of tribes. States did not have jurisdiction to pass laws regulating activities on Indian lands located within their state boundaries. This reaffirmation of tribal sovereignty became the basis for many Court decisions over the next 160 years and eventually helped lead to dramatic Indian economic recovery by the late twentieth century. Despite winning in Court, the Cherokee were still forced from their homeland by the federal government and resettled in Oklahoma.

After the United States gained independence from Great Britain in the late eighteenth century, landownership issues became an even greater concern. Indian nations, still many and strong, held military supremacy over the new fledgling and economically broke United States. The young nation did inherit from Great Britain several international principles guiding Indian relations. First, tribes have sovereignty, meaning they are politically independent of other nations and free to govern their own internal affairs by their own laws and customs. Secondly, tribes held a pre-existing right to the land they occupied which they could give to others. Third, land could only be exchanged between national governments. Neither private citizens nor state governments could acquire land from tribes.

Congress, Georgia, and the Cherokee

Following the basic international principles of Indian relations, the U.S. Constitution granted exclusive authority to deal with tribes to Congress, not the states. The authority was primarily included in Article 1 of the Constitution which gave Congress sole power to "regulate commerce with . . . the Indian Tribes." Article VI of the Constitution also recognized Indian treaties along with acts of Congress as the "supreme law of the land." Like federal laws, Indian treaties would carry greater weight than state laws. To exercise its authority to regulate activities on Indian lands and to affirm internationally recognized tribal sovereignty, the first U.S. Congress passed the Indian Trade and Intercourse Act in 1790. The act and its basic principles were further affirmed by the Supreme Court ruling in ***Johnson v. McIntosh*** (1823). Consequently, the Indians were considered free and independent nations within their own traditional territories. Although free of U.S. common law, they were subject to congressional oversight.

The state of Georgia during the nation's early years took a hard position on states' rights. Georgia vigorously opposed federal government oversight of state activities. The state equally disliked the Indian presence within its boundaries. Following gold discoveries on Cherokee Nation lands in 1828, a series of laws were passed to antagonize the Cherokee and gain control over them and their lands. One law was titled, "An Act to prevent the exercise of assumed and arbitrary power by all persons, under pretext [claim] of authority from the Cherokee Indians." The act stated that all white persons wishing to live on Cherokee Nation lands must first obtain a license or permit from the state of Georgia and take a state oath. Minimum sentence for violators was four years of hard labor.

Samuel A. Worcester

Samuel Worcester, a Vermont citizen and missionary of the American Board of Commissioners for Foreign Missions, traveled to the Cherokee Nation in the early nineteenth century to pursue his missionary calling. However, soon he and six other white persons were arrested by Georgia officials and physically removed from tribal lands. Worcester was charged "for residing on the 15th of July, 1831, in that part of the Cherokee Nation attached by the laws of the State of Georgia, without license or permit, and without having taken the oath to support and defend the constitution and laws of the state of Georgia." Worcester, in his defense, argued he was preaching the gospel under authority of the President of the United States and with permission of the Cherokee Nation. He also contended that Georgia had no jurisdiction since the United States recognized the Cherokee as a sovereign nation through several treaties. Consequently, he stressed that the Georgia laws regulating activities on Cherokee lands violated the Indian Trade and Intercourse Act and were invalid.

The superior court, disagreeing with Worcester's arguments, found him and the others guilty and sentenced them to four years of hard labor in a prison camp. Worcester appealed his conviction to the U.S. Supreme Court.

A Independent Nation

Chief Justice John Marshall delivered the Court's 6-1 decision. Marshall believed the case raised two important questions. First, legislatures normally have very limited legal powers that extend beyond their established geographic area of jurisdiction. Usually, that power is limited to the actions of their own citizens. Therefore, Georgia's actions amounted to application of jurisdiction over the Cherokee Nation which they did not have. Cherokee lands were not within state jurisdiction and Worcester was not a Georgia citizen.

Secondly, Marshall stressed that the relationship between the federal government and the American Indian nations was inherited from Great Britain following independence by the United States. The several treaties between the United States and the Cherokees affirmed the Cherokee Nation's sovereignty and right to self-government. As a result, the United States and the Cherokee considered the Indian nation to be under the protection of the United States only. The Cherokee was a "distinct community occupying its own territory." Because the treaties were recognized in the U.S. Constitution as the supreme law of the land, like acts of Congress, they had greater authority than state laws when they came in conflict. Marshall concluded that Georgia had no legal right to exert control over Cherokee internal affairs and the state law under which Worcester had been prosecuted was void.

Marshall concluded that "Indian nations are distinct political communities, having territorial boundaries, within which their authority is exclusive [total], and having a right to all the lands within those boundaries, which is not only acknowledged, but guaranteed by the United States."

Marshall added that the forcible seizure of Worcester, without the Cherokee's permission or approval of the President of the United States, while he was residing in Cherokee territory violated the U.S. Constitution as well.

Indian Sovereignty

The *Worcester* decision represented the third decision presented by Chief Justice Marshall between 1823 and 1832 establishing the foundation for U.S. Indian law. Known as the Marshall Trilogy, the rulings would influence U.S.-Indian relations for over a century. The cases of *Johnson v. McIntosh,* ***Cherokee Nation v. Georgia,*** and *Worcester* resolved the Indian right of possession to lands they occupied within the European concept of discovery, established the political nature of tribal nations as "domestic dependent nations," and reaffirmed tribal sovereignty to rule its own internal affairs free of state jurisdiction. Tribal regulation of its own activities was limited only by treaties and acts of Congress. The Court recognized Congress' plenary (total) power over tribal rights and activities.

Despite winning their case in court, the Cherokee lost in real life. The federal government pressed to remove the Cherokee which they finally did six years later in one of the more tragic stories in U.S. history.

Through the following 160 years relations between the United States and Indian tribes was to progress through many dramatically different phases. Indian social and economic recovery from disastrous federal policies would not gain momentum until the 1970s with the increased emphasis on tribal self-determination. The self-determination policies gave tribes increasing authority and responsibility to manage

JOHN ROSS

John Ross (1790–1866), though seven-eighths non-Indian by birth and that mostly Scottish, became a long-standing political leader of the Cherokee Nation. Ross was born in present-day Alabama in 1790 and grew up outside native traditions. As a young man, he became a merchant in the present-day Chattanooga, Tennessee area and northwestern Georgia where the Cherokee Nation was centered. In the 1810s Ross became involved in Cherokee political affairs as they established a European form of parliamentary government. By 1828 he was elected principal chief of the Cherokee. The year 1828 is also when gold was discovered in Cherokee country and the state of Georgia stepped up its efforts to remove the Cherokee. The Cherokees became split on how to respond to the mounting pressures for removal. Ross favored resistance. But a Cherokee leader of a smaller group, Major Ridge, signed the 1835 Treaty of New Echota with President Andrew Jackson (1829–1837). The highly unpopular treaty sold all Cherokee lands for $5 million to the United States and agreed to move to lands west of the Mississippi River. Ross tried to cancel the treaty, but without success. In 1838 the Cherokee began their forced, one thousand mile journey under harsh winter conditions. Later known as the Trail of Tears, almost one fourth of the tribe's members died.

Ross continued his prominent role as a Cherokee leader after resettling in Oklahoma. The tribe experienced difficult times adjusting to the new home and loss of many tribal members. Finally, peace within the tribe came in the 1850s only to end with the outbreak of the American Civil War (1861–1865). For still unknown reasons, Ross supported the Confederacy. Following the war, Ross took part in negotiations with the United States leading to an 1866 treaty preserving the Cherokee Nation.

their own internal affairs free from federal oversight. This late twentieth century policy was largely based on *Worcester* and other Marshall decisions almost a century and a half earlier. Numerous Court decisions throughout the twentieth century would further define the highly unique political status that American Indians hold. The Marshall Trilogy provided the foundation for many of those decisions.

Suggestions for further reading

Bruchoc, Joseph. *The Trail of Tears.* New York: Random House, 1999.

Ehle, John. *Trail of Tears: The Rise and Fall of the Cherokee Nation.* New York: Doubleday, 1988.

King, Duane H. ed. *The Cherokee Indian Nation: A Troubled History.* Knoxville: University of Tennessee Press, 1979.

Moulton, Gary E. *John Ross, Cherokee Chief.* Athens: University of Georgia Press, 1978.

Governments need money so they can provide important services to their citizens. Such services can include national defense from foreign threats, police and fire departments, public schools and libraries, health and sanitation systems, roads, and many others. Governments at all levels, including city, state, and federal, charge citizens and businesses for these services through taxes. The raising of funds through taxes is called taxation. Taxes have been raised as long as governments have existed.

In primitive societies, community members supported common services largely through voluntary labor, to build roads and other facilities. In early European history, payment of tribute (forced payments) to leaders, such as feudal lords, for protection was common. With increasing private ownership of property and businesses, taxation was introduced. Taxes assessed by early European monarchies were often harshly, and unequally, imposed. Taxation was a key point of dispute between the United States and Great Britain leading to the American Revolutionary War (1776–1783). Colonists claimed they were being taxed without having any say regarding the taxes forced on them by the mother country. "Taxation Without Representation" began a popular slogan at the time.

Following independence from Great Britain, the nation's Founding Fathers addressed taxation in Article 1 of the U.S. Constitution. Adopted in 1786, the Constitution included the Tax and Spending Clause giving Congress power to "lay and collect Taxes, Duties, Imposts [duties on imported foreign goods], and Excises [taxes on domestic goods], to pay the Debts and provide for the common Defence and general Welfare of the United States." The rise of democratic societies, such as in the United States, required that taxation be more fairly applied in order for taxpayers to cooperate. The growth of trade and commerce led to a more complex taxation system. The change of the U.S. economy in the nineteenth century from agrarian (based on agriculture and farms) to industrial (factories) brought yet new kinds of taxes, and even more complexity including greater difficulty in record keeping and tax collection. Recognizing the importance of taxation to the well-being of the nation, the Court has traditionally interpreted Congress' taxing powers very broadly. Not only does the Tax and Spending Clause give Congress taxation powers, but other parts of the Constitution does also including the Commerce Clause as recognized in the ***Head Money Cases*** (1884) ruling. The Commerce Clause gives Congress power to regulate trade between states and with foreign nations and Indian tribes.

Taxation can take many forms. The federal government relies on import (tariffs), excise taxes, personal income and corporate (business) taxes, and Social Security taxes in addition to other revenues. State governments rely primarily on personal and corporate income taxes, sales taxes, and certain fees, such as hunting and fishing licenses. The property tax is primarily used by local governments. Other taxes include estate, inheritance, and gift taxes.

Federal Government Tariffs

Prior to the American Civil War (1861–1865) funding support for the U.S. government came primarily from tariffs. Tariffs are taxes placed on goods that one nation imports from another. Tariffs date back at least to the 1200s when the European Christian Crusades brought increased trade between Europe and the Middle East. Early tariff agreements were struck between Italian merchants and commercial partners in Asia and Africa. With the discovery in 1492 of New World populations and resources by European powers, foreign trade greatly increased. High tariffs were put in place by European countries.

High tariffs charged by Great Britain on goods exported from the colonies was a major factor leading American colonists to rebel against British domination. Shortly after gaining independence in the American Revolutionary War (1776–1783), Congress passed the Tariff Act of 1783. Tariffs were established to protect the newly emerging American industries and to raise revenue for the government, impoverished from the war effort.

The industrialization period of the nineteenth century led to increased production of goods, particularly in the North. The nation became split over tariff policies. Northern states wanted to raise prices of foreign goods through higher tariff rates to promote sales of their own goods. Southern states sought low tariffs since they still imported much of their goods from Britain. The tariff dispute was one factor besides slavery that led to the American Civil War (1861–1865).

Besides raising revenue for the federal government, tariffs also serve to protect U.S. industries from foreign competition. The tariff taxes increases the price of foreign goods, making U.S. made goods more attractive to buyers. By selling more goods, the tariffs encourage increased production by U.S. firms. The U.S. Constitution prohibits tariffs on exports from the United States to other nations.

Tariffs also can serve political purposes, such as protesting the policies of another nation by increasing the prices of their goods into the country. For example, in the 1990s the United States placed high tariffs on Japanese produced goods because of Japan placing strict limits on the amount of U.S. goods going into their country.

International agreements are often signed between nations setting low tariffs, or maybe even no tariffs at all, on each others goods. The United States maintains special tariff agreements with countries it extends most-favored-nation (MFN) status to. Low, preferential, tariffs may also be applied to underdeveloped nations to assist in their economic development.

In addition to tariffs charged on foreign goods sold in the United States, U.S. citizens also may have to pay duties to the U.S. Customs Service for certain goods purchased.

Excise Taxes

Whereas tariffs deal with foreign made goods, taxes placed on the purchase of domestic goods, goods made within the United States, are called excise taxes. Such taxed items include alcohol, firearms, tobacco, gasoline, and diesel fuel. In 2000, the federal tax on gasoline was 18.4 cents per gallon, on truck diesel fuel 24 cents a gallon. States also add taxes that vary from state to state. Revenues from taxes on gasoline and diesel fuel sales are specially directed to road construction projects. For a long time the United States also had a luxury tax applied to such items such as automobiles. However, the tax has been steadily phased out and will end altogether in 2002.

Income Tax

The most commonly known form of tax in modern America is the tax on incomes, both on individuals and corporations. Taxable income can include wages and salaries, rent, interest earned, and corporate earnings.

The personal income tax was first used in the United States during the American Civil War to pay for war expenses. Passed by Congress in 1862, the tax was repealed (canceled) a few years later. In 1894 Congress brought back the income tax on individuals and companies, assessing 2 percent of income. However, the following year the U.S. Supreme Court declared the tax unconstitutional. The Court ruled in ***Pollock v. Farmer's Loan and Trust Company*** (1895) that such a tax would be violating Article I since the revenue gained was not be distributed to services in the states in direct proportion to each state's population as directed by the Article.

Consequently, no national income tax existed until adoption of the Sixteenth Amendment in 1913. The amendment gave Congress authority to levy (collect) taxes on any form of income without the requirement of distributing the funds among the states in proportion to their populations. With its new power, Congress passed the Tariff Act of 1913 creating a tax system for individual and corporate incomes.

Individual, or personal, income taxes are a form of "progressive taxes." The higher a person's income, the higher the percentage of his income is collected for taxes. Therefore, people with higher incomes and a greater ability to pay provide most of the income tax revenue. By the late twentieth century, those with lower incomes paid 15 percent of their income in taxes, the highest incomes paid 40 percent. Corporate income taxes were based on profits and not as progressive as the personal income tax structure.

Social Security and Medicare

In 1935 Congress passed the landmark Social Security Act. The act provides old-age benefits and health insurance, known as Medicare, for people over sixty-five years of age. To fund these government programs, a payroll tax was created. Employers are responsible for paying these taxes instead of the workers. Money is deducted (withheld, subtracted) from an employee's wages before she receives her paycheck. The employers then must equally match that amount of funding from their own funds. The employers pay these taxes directly to the U.S. Treasury. People self-employed (working for themselves) have to pay income, Social Security, and Medicare taxes from their earnings. The tax and spending powers of Congress to withhold money from people's paychecks for retirement benefits was immediately challenged in 1937 after the Social Security Act was passed. The powers were affirmed by the U.S. Supreme Court in ***Helving v. Davis*** (1937).

State and Local Taxes

State and local governments are given authority through the Tenth Amendment to raise revenue in a variety of ways. Under the Tenth Amendment, states can claim powers not specifically reserved for the federal government nor denied to the states. Like the federal government, most states also have income taxes. These taxes are charged at a lower rate than the federal government.

Many state and local governments largely rely on sales taxes. Most goods and services purchased are assessed a certain tax level. Because of the sales tax effect on the poorer citizens, some goods considered essentials, such as food, clothing, and medicine, are exempt from the sales tax or are taxed at a lower rate. Property taxes are also a key means of raising revenue. Land and buildings, such as homes, are taxed a certain percentage based on their assessed (estimated) value. Many local governments rely heavily on property taxes to fund public schools.

Corporations and manufacturers are also assessed business taxes by states and local governments. In addition, various stages of production and distribution of goods can be taxed. These taxes add to the value of the final product and increases the costs paid by the purchasers. Also, companies can be assessed franchise taxes, the cost on the privilege of doing business in the state. Companies must also pay taxes to operate state unemployment compensation programs, government insurance established by the Social Security Act of 1935 for those who lose their jobs through no fault of their own. The unemployed receive a certain amount of money weekly for a limited period of time.

State and local governments will also charge set fees to professionals for obtaining a license to practice their profession.

Estate, Inheritance, and Gift Taxes

The federal and state governments also assess different kinds of taxes on money and property passing from deceased persons to their heirs. An estate tax is charged for the privilege of transferring property from people who have died to their heirs. It is assessed on the entire estate before it is distributed. The inheritance tax is paid by each heir for the privilege of receiving property from a deceased. A person pays a gift tax if they decide to give a valuable gift to another person.

Collecting Taxes

The Internal Revenue Codes include federal laws directing how the various types of taxes are paid, whether income, business, or estate. The Internal Revenue Service (IRS), first created in 1862, is part of the U.S. Department of Treasury and responsible for collecting federal taxes. It is called Internal Revenue because it collects tax money from sources within the United States. Perceived abuses of the IRS in collecting taxes led to passage of the Taxpayer Bill of Rights in 1988 which was expanded in 1996. Many states passed similar state laws regarding collection of state taxes. The Taxpayer Bill of Rights gives taxpayers greater ability to question IRS findings and to be represented by lawyers or accountants.

Tax Disputes

Considerable debate surrounds the tax systems found in the United States. Fundamental concerns about taxation focus on equality and fairness. The burden of taxation must be imposed as equally as possible on all classes of people. This requirement led to progressive rate income tax systems. Higher rates are charged to people with higher incomes. However, the idea of equality of taxation does not mean that all the people must equally to enjoy the benefits of governments services. For example, couples who do not have schoolchildren still must pay taxes to support local schools.

The U.S. federal tax laws had become incredibly complex by the late twentieth century. The amount of time spent by individuals and corporations to compute and pay taxes was estimated to cost billions of dollars each year. Those supporting tax reform charge that the complexity leads to higher rates of tax avoidance with wealthy individuals and companies taking advantage of numerous legal opportunities to lessen their taxes paid. This is considered unfair to those in the middle and lower income levels with less opportunity to decrease their tax burden. Some want to shift a greater tax burden onto corporations, but others argue that these taxes would generally be passed on to individuals through higher prices for goods and services.

Also, many argue that the income tax which includes a tax on interest gained from savings accounts substantially discourages saving. The United States has the lowest saving rate among the western industrial countries. This situation forces corporations to seek loans outside the country. Many also claim that property taxes discourages home ownership. Reliance on property taxes also means wealthier communities have better schools and better government services.

A major push for tax reform forced consideration of alternative means of taxing. One alternative was the flat-rate tax system which would greatly simply the process. All citizens would pay taxes at a set rate and corporations would pay at a lower rate. However, opponents to the flat-tax claimed this alternative would potentially shift a larger tax burden onto the lower income population. Another alternative would be replacing the federal income tax with a national sales tax. This system could encourage saving but again place a greater burden on lower income citizens.

Tax Court System

Article I of the Constitution also gave Congress authority to establish a tax court system. The U.S. Tax Court was originally established by the Revenue Act of 1924. State and federal tax courts deal solely with tax disputes. Such disputes typically involve arguments over the assessment of property values or tax status of certain organizations. Decisions of the tax courts may be appealed to the U.S. courts of appeals and the U.S. Supreme Court.

Tax evasion is a criminal offense under federal and state laws. Prison sentences and fines may be imposed on those convicted. In order to gain criminal conviction, a deliberate attempt to illegally avoid paying taxes must be proven as ruled by the Supreme Court in *Spies v. United States* (1943). The decision in *Sansone v. United States* (1969) set further standards for proving criminal conduct.

Suggestions for further reading

Brown, Roger H. *Redeeming the Republic: Federalists, Taxation, and the Origins of the Constitution.* Baltimore: The Johns Hopkins University Press, 1993.

Brownlee, W. Elliott. *Federal Taxation in America: A Short History.* New York: Cambridge University Press, 1996.

Internal Revenue Service. [Online] http://www.irs.ustreas.gov (Accessed July 31, 2000).

Webber, Carolyn, and Aaron Wildavsky. *A History of Taxation and Expenditure in the Western World.* New York: Simon & Schuster, 1986.

Head Money Cases 1884

Appellants: Edye & Another, Cunard Steamship Company

Appellee: W. H. Robertson

Appellants' Claim: That the Immigration Act of 1882 establishing a tax on immigrants entering the nation was unconstitutional.

Chief Lawyer for Appellants: Edwards Pierrepoint, Phillip J. Joachimsen, George DeForest Lord Chief Lawyer for

Appellee: Samuel Field Phillips, U.S. Solicitor General

Justices for the Court: Samuel Blatchford, Jospeh P. Bradley, Stephen J. Field, Horace Gray, John Marshall Harlan I, Stanley Matthews, Samuel F. Miller, Chief Justice Morrison R. Waite, William B. Woods

Justices Dissenting: None

Date of Decision: December 8, 1884

Decision: Ruled in favor of the Robertson and the United States by finding that Congress had authority to tax immigrant entry through its power to regulate commerce.

Significance: The decision supported Congress' power to regulate immigration into the country. It also recognized that Congress not only had power to tax through the Tax and Spending Clause of Article I of the U.S. Constitution, but also through the Commerce Clause as well. Congress passed numerous other laws regulating immigration through the following century.

TAXATION

Immigration is the act of people coming to live in a foreign country. Often the term is confused with emigration which refers to people leaving their own country to live in another. Immigration to the United States has increased and declined in various time periods since the early colonists to the New World in the seventeenth century.

Through the nineteenth century until the 1930s the world experienced extensive immigration of peoples from one country to another. Over half of those immigrants came to the United States. Though many reasons spurred people to immigrate to a new country, searching for better jobs and economic opportunity was most common.

Through much of the nineteenth century, the U.S. government made little effort to regulate immigration as the California gold rush of 1849 attracted many Chinese laborers. Neither passports nor visas were required. Though immigration had long been central to American settlement, concern over it grew through the 1850s. Immigrants served as a source of inexpensive labor and it was believed took jobs away from U.S. citizens. Also, many immigrants did not readily blend into U.S. society causing considerable suspicion and fear among the general public. Although an economic depression in the United States in the 1870s greatly slowed immigration, Congress passed it first immigration law in 1875 barring entry to convicts and prostitutes.

With improving economic conditions by 1880, America once again became attractive. Immigration increased dramatically as did public concerns over the effects of immigration. Due to a shortage of farmland and increasing poverty in northwestern Europe, the new wave of immigration included many citizens of Denmark, Norway, and Sweden.

Responding to public pressure, Congress began passing more measures in 1882 to regulate immigration. One bill, the Chinese Exclusion Act, prohibited Chinese laborers from entering the country. On August 3, 1882, Congress passed another bill, the Immigration Act. The act read,

> **That there shall be levied, collected and paid a duty of fifty cents for each and every passenger, not a citizen of the United States, who shall come by steam or sail vessel from a foreign port to any port within the United States.**

The purpose of the tax, known as "head money," was to establish "a fund to be called the Immigrant Fund . . . to defray the expenses of regulating immigration under this Act and for the care of immigrants . . . for the relief of such as are in distress."

IMMIGRATION REGULATION TODAY

As of 1998, immigration regulation is governed by the Immigration Act of 1990, also known as IMMACT. IMMACT established a limit of six hundred seventy-five thousand immigrant that will be allowed to move into the United States each year. This limit does not include people who are seeking refuge, asylum, or people who want to come into the United States for other humanitarian-based reasons. There also are no limits for immigrants who are spouses, minor children, or parents of people who are already U.S. citizens.

Under IMMACT, one hundred forty thousand of the total annual admissions may be for employment-based reasons. The act favors the admission of immigrants who are professionals and investors, and places an annual limit of ten thousand on admission of lesser-skilled persons.

IMMACT also has a diversity component that reserves fifty-five thousand annual admissions for immigrants from countries that traditionally do not have strong family or job ties to the United States. Each diversity-based immigrant must have a high school degree or its equivalent, or two years of experience in an occupation requiring two years of training.

Immigrants who enter the United States by commercial aircraft or vessel pay a six dollar fee when their ticket for travel is issued. The U.S. Immigration and Naturalization Service enforces the immigration laws and manages the various admissions.

The Dutch Steamer Leerdam

Two months later, on October 2, 1882, the Dutch steamship *Leerdam* arrived in New York Harbor from Rotterdam, Holland. The ship contained 382 immigrants who planned to settle in the United States. The company of Funch, Edye & Co. which was responsible for the ship in the United States was charged $191 head money on October 12th by William H. Robertson, the customs collector for the port of New York. The com-

TAXATION

pany paid the tax so they could enter the harbor, but within a few days appealed the fee to the Secretary of Treasury. The Secretary denied their appeal. Funch next filed a lawsuit U.S. Circuit Court against Robertson claiming the charge was unconstitutional. The court ruled in favor of the customs collection.

When appealed to the U.S. Supreme Court, the lawsuit was combined with two other similar cases and titled *Head Money Cases.* The shipping companies raised three arguments in their case. First, Congress exceeded its constitutional powers by regulating immigration with an immigrants' entry tax. Article I of the Constitution stated that *Congress shall have the power to lay and collect taxes, duties, . . . and excises, to pay the debts and provide for the common defense and the general welfare of the United States; but all duties . . . and excises shall be uniform throughout the United States.* The companies argued the head tax was not for general welfare and common defense, therefore Article I did not support a head tax. Besides, immigration, the companies argued, is not a business. The United States did not argue the Article I challenge, for it was the Commerce Clause giving Congress power to regulate trade that was used to pass the act. The Commerce Clause, also located in Article I

As new immigrants entered into the United States they had to be given a thorough health screening including shots to ensure they weren't bringing illness and disease into the country. Courtesy of the Library of Congress.

of the U.S. Constitution, gives Congress the power "to regulate Commerce with foreign Nations and among the . . . states." Commerce refers to producing, selling, and transporting goods.

Secondly, the companies argued the tax was applied only at ports where immigrants entered the country. As Article I stated, all taxes levied by Congress must be uniformly applied. Therefore, the tax was unconstitutional because it did not apply to all ports.

Thirdly, the Immigration Act was illegal because it conflicted with existing international treaties between the United States and other nations which permitted immigration. They claimed the tax inhibited immigration.

The Business of Immigration

The Court ruled unanimously, 9–0, in favor of the United States. Justice Samuel F. Miller, writing for the Court, stated that Congress clearly had authority to regulate immigration. Since the Court had ruled in a previous case that states do not have that power, then the federal government must. Miller wrote that it would be unthinkable "that the ships of all nations . . . can, without restraint or regulation, deposit here . . . the entire European population of criminals, paupers, and diseased persons, without making any provision to preserve them from starvation . . . even for the first few days after they had left the vessel." Miller also found that indeed immigration was a business and a very profitable one at that. Consequently, it was not unreasonable to expect those profiting from immigration to bear some of the burden in helping those immigrants who were poor and protecting U.S. states and cities from an excessive financial burden.

Secondly, Miller asserted that the tax was uniformly applied since "it operates with the same force and effect in every place where [immigration] . . . is found." The main concern would be that all ships carrying immigrants was taxed the same way and Miller found that to be the situation.

Lastly, Miller could not see where any treaty had been violated since no foreign country had complained. Besides, Congress had the power to change treaties if it so desired anyway, much like changing its own laws. Miller concluded that the purpose of the act "is humane, is highly beneficial to the poor and helpless immigrants and is essential to the protection of the people in whose midst they are deposited by the steamships." The immigrant tax act was upheld.

IMMIGRATION REGULATION OF THE 1990S

Congress repeatedly exercised its constitutional powers as recognized in *Head Money Cases* to regulate immigration. The Immigration Act of 1990, known as IMMACT, regulated immigration into the United States through the 1990s. The act was administered by the U.S. Immigration and Naturalization Service. IMMACT set a limit of 675,000 immigrant entries per year. The IMMACT limit did not apply to refugees, those seeking political asylum, or other humanitarian admissions, or to spouses, minor children, and parents of U.S. citizens. IMMACT set a limit of 140,000 per year for employment reasons. Various categories of workers were included in the limits, favoring more professionals. Only 10,000 of the 140,000 could be lesser-skilled workers. IMMACT also distinguished among countries from which the immigrants are leaving. Striving for diversity in America, a total of 55,000 admissions were reserved for immigrants from countries that do not traditionally enter the country. Such immigrants had to have high school or equivalent education or two years of experience in an occupation requiring two years of training. "Head money" is still applied in the form of a six dollar fee added to tickets for immigrant travel by commercial airlines or boat.

Immigration Restrictions Continue

From 1881 to 1920, over twenty-three million immigrants came to America from throughout the world. The population of the United States in 1880 was slightly over fifty million. By 1900 the U.S. population had grown by 50 percent to almost 76 million with immigration being a major contributor to the dramatic increase. Given support by the Supreme Court in *Head Money Cases,* regulation of immigration remained a hot issue before Congress throughout the twentieth century.

Until the mid-1890s most immigrants had arrived in the United

States from northern and western Europe. With a major shift then to southern and eastern Europe as a key source, the new immigrants less readily blended into American society. Public concern over immigration escalated again. Quota laws (placing number limits) were passed in the early twentieth century favoring immigration from northern and western Europe. Another wave of immigration came again during the latter part of the twentieth century with many arriving from Asia.

Suggestions for further reading

Archdeacon, Thomas A. *Becoming American: An Ethnic History.* New York: Free Press, 1983.

Briggs, Vernon N., Jr. *Mass Immigration and the National Interest.* Armonk, NY: M.E. Sharpe, 1992.

Daniels, Roger. *Coming to America: A History of Immigration and Ethnicity in American Life.* New York: HarperCollins, 1990.

Killian, Pamela. *Ellis Island: Gateway to the American Dream.* New York: Crescent Books, 1991.

Portes, Alejandro, and Ruben G. Rumbaut. *Immigrant America: A Portrait.* Berkeley: University of California Press, 1996.

Sandler, Martin W. *Immigrants.* New York: HarperCollins, 1995.

Pollock v. Farmers' Loan & Trust Company 1895

Appellant: Charles Pollock

Appellee: Farmers' Loan & Trust Company

Appellant's Claim: That the Income Tax Act of 1894 violated the tax powers of Congress as provided in Article I of the U.S. Constitution.

Chief Lawyers for Appellant: William D. Guthrie, Clarence A. Seward, Joseph H. Choate

Chief Lawyers for Appellee: Herbert B. Turner, James C. Carter

Justices for the Court: David Josiah Brewer, Henry Billings Brown, Stephen Johnson Field, Chief Justice Melville Weston Fuller

Justices Dissenting: Horace Gray, John Marshall Harlan I, George Shiras, Jr., Edward Douglas White (Howell Edmunds Jackson did not participate)

Date of Decision: May 20 1895

Decision: Ruled in favor of Pollock by finding the general income tax provision of the act unconstitutional.

Significance: After striking down the income tax law, the income tax issue did not fade. Demand for a constitutional amendment grew to give Congress power to levy an income tax. Eighteen years later the Sixteenth Amendment was adopted authorizing Congress to impose income taxes without the taxing restrictions originally written in the Constitution.

During the latter decades of the nineteenth century, the U.S. economy was completing its transition to a more industrialized society. Big business, run by a few elite industrialist leaders, was gaining control of the nation's economy which had earlier been based largely on farming and agriculture earlier. An agrarian reform movement grew in the 1870s and 1880s for the purpose of defending the interests of farmers from the potential economic threats of big business. During the 1890s the agrarian (farming) movement gave way to a broader political reform movement called Populism. The movement included not only farmers, but workers, small business owners and anyone else subject to economic policies of big business.

A key goal of the Populists was passage of an income tax which would place a greater burden on the wealthy to finance government services. An income tax is a charge applied to the money made by individuals and corporations coming from business, investments, real estate earnings, and other sources. A national income tax had existed earlier, created in 1862 to raise revenue to pay expenses of the American Civil War (1861–1865). But, it was repealed in 1872.

With a national economic crisis in 1893 declining government revenues made adoption of an income tax system more attractive to a broader population. The following year, Congress passed the Income Tax (Wilson-Gorman Tariff) Act of 1894, establishing the first peacetime income tax. A two percent tax was placed on incomes over $4,000, which actually affected only about two percent of the wage earners in the nation. The tax was not well received by the wealthier citizens.

Charles Pollock

The Farmers' Loan & Trust Company was an investment bank that bought stocks and bonds and properties. Under the new law, it had to pay an income tax on its profits, including income gained from real estate and New York City bonds. In reaction to the newly passed income tax, Charles Pollock, a Massachusetts investor who owned shares in the company, devised a plan to legally challenge the tax act. With full cooperation of Farmers' Loan and on behalf of the other company stockholders, Pollock filed a lawsuit in a New York federal district court against the company to prevent it from paying the tax. Pollock charged the tax act violated the Tax and Spending Clause of Article I of the Constitution. Congress was exceeding its limited constitutional tax powers.

Though the district court ruled against him, it did allow Pollock to appeal the decision directly to the U.S. Supreme Court. In recognition of the importance of the issue concerning the constitutionality of a national income tax, the Supreme Court accepted the case but with two exceptions to normal Court procedures. First, the Court did not normally accept cases in which both parties were agreeable to the suit. Secondly, the Court allowed the U.S. attorney general to argue the case for Farmers' Loan even though the U.S. government was not named in the suit.

A Major Public Concern

With great public fanfare, case arguments began on March 7, 1895. Only eight justices were present with Justice Howell E. Jackson away ill with tuberculosis. The Court's gallery was overflowing with interested observers and major newspapers closely followed the proceedings. Pollock's lead attorney, Joseph Hodges Choate, had considerable flair and passion in presenting a convincing argument to the justices.

Choate presented three arguments to the Court. First, the income tax was applied to profits from state and municipal bonds. This, he claimed, intruded on constitutionally recognized state powers and their ability to raise revenues.

Secondly, Choate claimed tax on profits from real estate was a "direct tax." Direct taxes are taxes levied by government directly on property, including personal income. The amount of tax is determined by the financial worth of the property. In contrast, indirect taxes by government are applied to certain rights or privileges, such as sales taxes, customs duties, and license fees. They are usually set fees. According to the Tax and Spending Clause of Article I of Constitution, all revenue from direct taxes must be divided among the states in proportion to their populations. The more population a state has, the more federal tax revenue it receives to provide public services. The distribution of revenue from indirect taxes was less restricted. The tax system established by the act did not intend to distribute the revenue back to the states proportionally as directed in Article I.

Thirdly, Article I required that direct taxes must be uniformly applied to all individuals and businesses and this tax was not. Choate claimed the tax was unfair and a threat to traditional American values by taxing people differently. Because the tax in effect would redistribute the nation's wealth by taxing the rich, Choate exclaimed the tax was " . . . communistic in it purposes and tendencies, and is defended here upon principles as communistic, socialistic — what I should call them — populistic as ever have been addressed to any political assembly in the world."

The Court agreed with Pollock and Choate that the tax indeed infringed on states by taxing state bonds. Also, the Court agreed that the tax on real estate earnings was direct. It was essentially a tax on the land itself. Therefore, it was subject to the Article I limitations. The eight justices were split, 4-4, however over the question of uniformity and whether a tax on income from personal property was direct or not. The Court ignored its earlier ruling in *Springer v. United States* (1881) that the income tax collected during the Civil War was indirect, hence not subject to the limitations in Article I. Because of the importance of the decision and lack of a decisive ruling by the Court, Chief Justice Melville W. Fuller requested a rehearing of the case.

Back to Court

Arguments were presented again on May 6, 1895. A decision resulted two weeks later. Chief Justice Fuller again presented the Courts opinion from a 5-4 decision. Fuller clearly expressed his economically conservative views in denouncing the tax as unconstitutional. He reaffirmed the previous decision regarding the tax on land as direct, and added that the tax on personal property was also a direct tax. Since taxes on land and personal property were the main taxes in the bill, he struck down the entire act. Fuller asserted that such a tax "would leave the burden of the tax to be borne by professions, trades, employment, or vocations; in that way . . . a tax on occupations and labor."

In reversing the earlier district court ruling, the Court ruled the tax act void and sent the case back to district court for final resolution.

The four justices objecting to the decision wrote separate dissenting opinions. The harshest came from Justice John Marshall Harlan. The *New York Times* reported that Harlan gestured wildly at Fuller with "thinly disguised sneers." Harlan aggressiveness, including pounding on the desk, shocked many of the lawyers present in the courtroom. Harlan emphasized that the Court's ruling placed most Americans at a disadvantage with the wealthy. Harlan stated that,

> **undue and disproportioned burdens are placed upon the many, while the few, safely entrenched**

JOHN MARSHALL HARLAN I

John Marshall Harlan, born on June 1, 1833 to a wealthy and prominent family in Boyle County, Kentucky, was named for the great chief justice of the U.S. Supreme Court, John Marshall (1801–1835). Harlan's father was a lawyer and politician, serving as U.S. congressman and state attorney general. Harlan received a college degree from Centre College in 1850 and studied law from 1851 to 1853 at Transylvania University. With solid family connections, Harlan quickly assumed governmental positions including county judge in Franklin County, Kentucky in 1858, and attorney general of Kentucky from 1863 to 1867.

An active member of the Republican Party, Harlan worked for Rutherford B. Hayes (1877–1881) in his successful bid for U.S. president in 1876. As a reward for his political efforts, Harlan was appointed by Hayes to the U.S. Supreme Court in October of 1877. Harlan became known as the Great Dissenter opposing several important decisions during his thirty-four years on the Court. Besides his emotional opposition to the decision in *Pollock v. Farmers' Loan & Trust Company* (1895), Harlan's eloquent dissent the following year in ***Plessy v. Ferguson*** (1896) as the only justice opposing the Court's decision supporting state required racial segregation was supported almost sixty years later in the landmark decision of ***Brown v. Board of Education***. Harlan served until his death on October 14, 1911. His grandson, John Marshall Harlan II, also served on the Supreme Court, from 1955 to 1971.

behind the rule of [Article I] . . . are permitted to evade their share of the responsibility for the support of government ordained for the protection of the rights of all. I cannot assent to an interpretation of the Constitution that . . . cripples . . . the national government in the essential matter of taxation, and at the same time discriminates against the greater part of the people of our country.

An Unpopular Decision

The Court's ruling was not well received by the public. Some legal scholars disagreed with the decision. Taxation remained a controversial political issue, even becoming a topic for the next presidential race. Many recognized that the Constitution needed amending to permit a federal income tax without the requirement dividing revenue among the states proportionately to their individual populations. After eighteen more years of debate, the Sixteenth Amendment to the Constitution was adopted in 1913 giving Congress power to tax income without the distribution requirement to the states. The first revenue gained from income taxes came in 1916. The continued goal of the income tax continued to be a fair distribution of the tax burden among all citizens raising revenue for government.

Suggestions for further reading

Adams, Charles. *Those Dirty Rotten Taxes: The Tax Revolts That Built America.* New York: Free Press, 1998.

Bartlett, Donald L., and James B. Steele. *America: Who Really Pays the Taxes?* New York: Simon & Schuster, 1994.

Shlaes, Amity. *The Greedy Hand: How Taxes Drive Americans Crazy and What To Do About It.* New York: Random House, 1999.

Whitte, John F. *The Politics and Development of the Federal Income Tax.* Madison: University of Wisconsin Press, 1986.

Helvering v. Davis
1937

Petitioner: Guy T. Helvering,
U.S. Commissioner of Internal Revenue

Respondent: George P. Davis

Petitioner's Claim: That the Social Security Act of 1935 authorizing payroll taxes to fund a national old-age benefits program neither violates the Tax and Spending Clause of the Constitution nor takes away from powers reserved to the states in the Tenth Amendment.

Chief Lawyer for Petitioner: Homer S. Cummings,
U.S. Attorney General

Chief Lawyer for Respondent: Edward F. McClennan

Justices for the Court: Louis D. Brandeis, Benjamin N. Cardozo, Chief Justice Charles Evans Hughes, Owen Josephus Roberts, Harlan Fiske Stone, George Sutherland, Willis Van Devanter

Justices Dissenting: Pierce Butler, James Clark McReynolds

Date of Decision: May 24, 1937

Decision: Ruled in favor of Helvering and the United States by finding that Congress has constitutional powers to establish a Social Security program for the aged.

Significance: In upholding the constitutionality of the Social Security Act, the Supreme Court signaled a major shift by supporting President Franklin D. Roosevelt's New Deal programs. The act introduced a new era in American history by establishing a responsibility of society to care for the aged, unemployed, impoverished, and disabled.

"By 1932, the unemployed numbered upward of thirteen million. Many lived in the primitive conditions of a preindustrial society stricken by famine. In the coal fields of West Virginia and Kentucky, evicted families shivered in tents in midwinter; children went barefoot. In Los Angeles, people whose gas and electricity had been turned off were reduced to cooking over wood fires in back lots . . . At least a million, perhaps as many as two million were wandering the country in a fruitless quest for work or adventure or just a sense of movement." From *Franklin Roosevelt and the New Deal:1932-1940* (1963) by William E. Leuchtenburg, New York: HarperCollins.

A New Deal

The Great Depression, beginning with the U.S. stock market crash in October of 1929, was a worldwide business slump leading to the highest unemployment in modern times. With stores, banks, and factories shut down, millions of Americans became jobless and broke. The substantial economic hardships on American citizens through the following years extended to those too old to work.

In 1932 with the economy continuing to suffer, the nation elected Franklin D. Roosevelt (1933–1945) president. To address the nation's economic plight, Roosevelt soon introduced an ambitious program for social and economic reform that became known as the New Deal. Central to reform was the substantially increased federal government role in the country's internal affairs at home.

However, progress toward carrying out the programs was slow. The Supreme Court repeatedly declared unconstitutional (did not follow the intent of the Constitution) the legislation passed to create federal relief programs. The Court ruled the measures exceeded Congress' constitutional authority. Much to Roosevelt's frustration, most of the Supreme Court justices held conservative views on federal government power and were not favorable to the proposed reforms. Reorganizing his efforts in 1935, Roosevelt unveiled a renewed long-term New Deal plan that included social security. A key to the reform was passage of the Social Security Act of 1935. Designed to bring greater economic stability to the population, Title II of the act created an old age benefits program. Title VIII established a way to fund the program by requiring companies to withhold a certain amount of money from employees' paychecks. That money, matched with an equal amount from the employer, would be paid to the U.S. Treasury and placed in a national trust fund. The fund would then provide monthly benefits to retired workers over the age of sixty-five if they had worked and paid taxes into the program. The act was primarily aimed at industry with Title VIII exempting certain types of employees, such as agricultural workers, from the program.

Bolstered by winning reelection in 1936, President Roosevelt focused attention on reorganizing the Supreme Court to get more favorable rulings on his programs. Under political pressure some justices in disfavor with the President and public chose to retire while others altered their views on Roosevelt's reform programs.

George P. Davis

George P. Davis was a shareholder for the Edison Electric Illuminating Company of Boston, an electrical power company. When Edison began to deduct money from its employees' wages to comply with the newly passed Social Security Act, Davis filed a lawsuit in the U.S. District Court for the District of Massachusetts against the company. Davis claimed "old age benefits [was] not a purpose for which the Congress has power to tax." He sought "to restrain the corporation from making the payments, and deductions from wages." Davis stated, "The deductions from the wages of the employees will produce unrest among them and will be followed . . . by demands that wages be increased . . . The corporation and its shareholders will suffer irreparable loss, and many thousands of dollars will be subtracted from the value of the shares."

The district court permitted Guy T. Helvering, commissioner of the U.S. Internal Revenue Service (IRS), to intervene (come in to represent) in the suit representing Edison Electric. The district court dismissed Davis' lawsuit. He appealed to the U.S. First Circuit Court of Appeals which ruled in his favor by holding that Title II was an invasion of state reserved powers. Helvering appealed the appeals court decision to the U.S. Supreme Court which agreed to hear the case.

Social Security Secured

Davis argued before the Supreme Court that the Social Security Act inappropriately expanded Congress' power to tax under the Taxing and Spending Clause of Article I of the U.S. Constitution. The clause states, that Congress has power to "lay and collect Taxes, Duties, Imposts [duties on imported foreign goods], and Excises [taxes on domestic goods], to pay the Debts and provide for the common Defence and general Welfare of the United States." More specifically, Davis charged the act violated the Tenth Amendment which grants powers to the states not specifically reserved to the U.S. government. Providing for social security was such a state power, he contended.

Justice Benjamin N. Cordozo wrote the opinion for the Court in a 7-2 decision. Cordozo stressed that monies spent on the general welfare of the nation's population was indeed the responsibility of the federal government, not state governments. He stated that the severe economic depression of the 1930s was "plainly national" requiring a nationwide solution. Cordozo wrote, "the ill is . . . not greatly different whether men are thrown out of work because there is no longer work to do or because the disabilities of age make them incapable of doing it." Cordozo concluded that the "laws of the separate states cannot deal with it effectively . . . States and local governments are often lacking in the resources that are necessary to finance an adequate program of security for the aged."

The old age benefits program provided by the Social Security Act was indeed constitutionally valid. Cordozo wrote, "Congress may spend money in aid of the 'general welfare.'" In addition, the tax on employers "is an excise tax and thus within the power conferred upon [given to] Congress by . . . the Constitution."

The New Deal Lives

At the time the Court delivered the *Helvering* decision, it also announced a decision in *Steward Machine Co. v. Davis* which challenged another section of the Social Security Act involving unemployment benefits. The two decisions were vital to Roosevelt's programs designed to put America back to work and protect those most affected by the depression. However, it took the demands of World War II (1939–1945) for industrial production of war materials that to ultimately bring the Depression to a close. Though always controversial, the Social Security Act became a major lasting part of U.S. domestic policy.

Days before the *Helvering* decision was presented, Justice Willis Van Devanter, one of the politically conservative justices opposing Roosevelt's programs announced his retirement. Roosevelt was free to select a new justice more supportive of his programs.

THE NEED TO SECURE SOCIETY

Continued expansion of the Industrial Revolution during the nineteenth century brought many basic changes to home life. No longer did the typical family work together on a farm with relatives and other closely associated families. Instead of living in small farming communities, many families moved to newly established industry centers seeking a better life. Fathers would go off to the factories for long work days leaving the wife to raise the children and take care of the home. Fewer economic "safety nets" existed for workers who grew too old to be as productive or if a sudden traumatic event occurred such as death or disability of the breadwinner. The need for social security programs grew to aid such distressed families and provide a more stable society in the industrial workforce. Germany, the first industrial country to establish such a social security program in the 1880s, required sickness and old age insurance. Similar plans were introduced through the few decades in other European and some Latin American countries.

In the United States, "beneficial associations" grew composed of workers joining together to provide sickness, old age benefit, and funeral insurance. With the crash of the stock market in 1929 and prolonged decline of the economy, President Franklin D. Roosevelt included the Social Security Act as a key element of his social and economic reforms. In the 1950s Social Security was expanded to include farmers and those self-employed. Health insurance benefits, known as Medicare, were added in 1965 as well as federally-assisted state unemployment compensation programs.

By the 1990s fears mounted over the future of the Social Security with estimates it would eventually go broke. The president and Congress both worked toward solutions to the problem. The program had become a major part of modern life in America with 90 percent of all workers covered by Social Security in 1997 and 42 million receiving benefits.

Suggestions for further reading

Freidel, Frank. *Franklin D. Roosevelt: A Rendezvous with Destiny.* Boston: Little, Brown and Company, 1990.

Terkel, Studs. *Hard Times: An Oral History of the Great Depression.* New York: Pantheon Books, 1986.

Watkins, T. H. *The Great Depression: America in the 1930s.* Boston: Little, Brown and Company, 1993.

General Bibliography

Aaseng, Nathan. *Great Justices of the Supreme Court*. Minneapolis: Oliver Press, 1992.

Arthur, Joe. *Justice for All: The Story of Thurgood Marshall*. New York: Yearling Books, 1995.

Bains, Rae. *Thurgood Marshall: Fight for Justice*. Mahwah, NJ: Troll Assoc., 1993.

Bernstein, Richard, and Jerome Agel. *Into the Third Century: The Supreme Court*. New York: Walker & Co., 1989.

Cornelius, Kay. *The Supreme Court*. New York: Chelsea House Publishers, 2000.

Coy, Harold. *The Supreme Court*. New York: Franklin Watts, 1981.

Deegan, Paul J. *Anthony Kennedy*. Edina, MN: Abdo & Daughters, 1992.

——. *Antonin Scalia*. Edina, MN: Abdo & Daughters, 1992.

——. *Chief Justice William Rehnquist*. Edina, MN: Abdo & Daughters, 1992.

——. *David Souter*. Edina, MN: Abdo & Daughters, 1992.

——. *Supreme Court Book*. Edina, MN: Abdo & Daughters, 1992.

Deegan, Paul J., and Bob Italia. *John Paul Stevens*. Edina, MN: Abdo & Daughters, 1992.

——. *Sandra Day O'Connor*. Edina, MN: Abdo & Daughters, 1992.

Feinburg, Barbara Silberdick. *Constitutional Amendments*. Twenty First Century Books, 1996.

General Bibliography

Friedman, Leon. *The Supreme Court.* New York: Chelsea House, 1987.

Friedman, Leon, and Fred L. Israel. *The Justices of the United States Supreme Court: Their Lives and Major Opinions.* New York: Chelsea House Publishers, 1995.

Goldish, Meish. *Our Supreme Court.* Brookfield: Millbrook Press, 1994.

Harrison, Michael. *Landmark Decisions of the United States Supreme Court.* San Diego: Excellent Books, 1991.

Health, David. *The Supreme Court of the United States.* New York: Capstone, 1998.

Holland, Gini. *Sandra Day O'Connor.* Austin: Raintree/Steck Vaughn, 1997.

Irons, Peter H. *The Courage of Their Convictions: Sixteen Americans Who Fought Their Way to the Supreme Court.* New York: Penguin, 1990.

Italia, Bob, and Paul Deegan. *Ruth Bader Ginsburg.* Edina, MN: Abdo & Daughters, 1994.

Kallen, Stuart A. *Thurgood Marshall.* Edina, MN: Abdo & Daughters, 1993.

Kent, Deborah. *Thurgood Marshall and the Supreme Court.* Chicago: Children's Press, 1997.

Krull, Kathleen. *A Kids' Guide to America's Bill of Rights: Curfews, Censorship, and the 100-Pound Giant.* New York: Avon Books, 1999.

Macht, Norman L., Christopher E. Henry, and Nathan I. Huggins. *Clarence Thomas: Supreme Court Justice.* New York: Chelsea House Publishers, 1995.

Peterson, Helen Stone. *The Supreme Court in America's Story.* Scarsdale: Garrard Pub. Co., 1976.

Prentzas, G.S. *Thurgood Marshall.* New York: Chelsea House Publishers, 1994.

Prolman, Marilyn. *The Constitution.* Chicago: Children's Press, Inc., 1995.

Reef, Catherine. *The Supreme Court.* New York: Dillon Press, 1994.

Rierden, Anne B. *Reshaping the Supreme Court: New Justices, New Directions.* New York: Franklin Watts, 1988.

Sagarin, Mary. *Equal Justice under Law: Our Court System and How It Works.* New York: Lothrop, Lee & Shephard Co., Inc., 1966.

Stein, R. Conrad. *The Powers of the Supreme Court.* Chicago: Children's Press, Inc., 1995.

——. *The Bill of Rights.* Chicago: Children's Press, Inc., 1992.

White, G. Edward. *Oliver Wendell Holmes: Sage of the Supreme Court.* New York: Oxford University Press Children's Books, 2000.

Justices of the Supreme Court

The Justices are listed by year of appointment and in what way they served the court—as an Associate Justice or Chief Justice.

- **John Jay (Chief: 1789 - 1795)**
- **John Rutledge (Associate: 1790 - 1791, Chief: 1795 - 1795)**
- **William Cushing (Associate: 1790 - 1810)**
- **James Wilson (Associate: 1789 - 1798)**
- **John Blair (Associate: 1790 - 1795)**
- **James Iredell (Associate: 1790 - 1799)**
- **Thomas Johnson (Associate: 1792 - 1793)**
- **William Paterson (Associate: 1793 - 1806)**
- **Samuel Chase (Associate: 1796 - 1811)**
- **Oliver Ellsworth (Chief: 1796 - 1800)**
- **Bushrod Washington (Associate: 1799 - 1829)**
- **Alfred Moore (Associate: 1800 - 1804)**
- **John Marshall (Chief: 1801 - 1835)**
- **William Johnson (Associate: 1804 - 1834)**
- **Brockholst Livingston (Associate: 1807 - 1823)**
- **Thomas Todd (Associate: 1807 - 1826)**

Justices of the Supreme Court

Gabriel Duvall (Associate: 1811 - 1835)
Joseph Story (Associate: 1812 - 1845)
Smith Thompson (Associate: 1823 - 1843)
Robert Trimble (Associate: 1826 - 1828)
John McLean (Associate: 1830 - 1861)
Henry Baldwin (Associate: 1830 - 1844)
James M. Wayne (Associate: 1835 - 1867)
Roger B. Taney (Chief: 1836 - 1864)
Philip P. Barbour (Associate: 1836 - 1841)
John Catron (Associate: 1837 - 1865)
John McKinley (Associate: 1838 - 1852)
Peter V. Daniel (Associate: 1842 - 1860)
Samuel Nelson (Associate: 1845 - 1872)
Levi Woodbury (Associate: 1845 - 1851)
Robert C. Grier (Associate: 1846 - 1870)
Benjamin R. Curtis (Associate: 1851 - 1857)
John A. Campbell (Associate: 1853 - 1861)
Nathan Clifford (Associate: 1858 - 1881)
Noah Swayne (Associate: 1862 - 1881)
Samuel F. Miller (Associate: 1862 - 1890)
David Davis (Associate: 1862 - 1877)
Stephen J. Field (Associate: 1863 - 1897)
Salmon P. Chase (Chief: 1864 - 1873)
William Strong (Associate: 1870 - 1880)
Joseph P. Bradley (Associate: 1870 - 1892)
Ward Hunt (Associate: 1873 - 1882)
Morrison R. Waite (Chief: 1874 - 1888)
John M. Harlan (Associate: 1877 - 1911)
William B. Woods (Associate: 1881 - 1887)
Stanley Matthews (Associate: 1881 - 1889)
Horace Gray (Associate: 1882 - 1902)

Samuel Blatchford (Associate: 1882 - 1893)
Lucius Q.C. Lamar (Associate: 1888 - 1893)
Melville W. Fuller (Chief: 1888 - 1910)
David J. Brewer (Associate: 1890 - 1910)
Henry B. Brown (Associate: 1891 - 1906)
George Shiras, Jr. (Associate: 1892 - 1903)
Howell E. Jackson (Associate: 1893 - 1895)
Edward D. White (Associate: 1894 - 1910, Chief: 1910 - 1921)
Rufus Peckham (Associate: 1896 - 1909)
Joseph McKenna (Associate: 1898 - 1925)
Oliver W. Holmes, Jr. (Associate: 1902 - 1932)
William R. Day (Associate: 1903 - 1922)
William H. Moody (Associate: 1906 - 1910)
Horace H. Lurton (Associate: 1910 - 1914)
Charles E. Hughes (Associate: 1910 - 1916, Chief: 1930 - 1941)
Willis Van Devanter (Associate: 1911 - 1937)
Joseph R. Lamar (Associate: 1911 - 1916)
Mahlon Pitney (Associate: 1912 - 1922)
James C. McReynolds (Associate: 1914 - 1941)
Louis D. Brandeis (Associate: 1916 - 1939)
John H. Clarke (Associate: 1916 - 1922)
William Howard Taft (Chief: 1921 - 1930)
George Sutherland (Associate: 1922 - 1938)
Pierce Butler (Associate: 1923 - 1939)
Edward T. Sanford (Associate: 1923 - 1930)
Harlan Fiske Stone (Associate: 1925 - 1941, Chief: 1941 - 1946)
Owen J. Roberts (Associate: 1930 - 1945)
Benjamin N. Cardozo (Associate: 1932 - 1938)
Hugo L. Black (Associate: 1937 - 1971)
Stanley Reed (Associate: 1938 - 1957)
Felix Frankfurter (Associate: 1939 - 1962)

Justices of the Supreme Court

William O. Douglas (Associate: 1939 - 1975)
Frank Murphy (Associate: 1940 - 1949)
James F. Byrnes (Associate: 1941 - 1942)
Robert H. Jackson (Associate: 1941 - 1954)
Wiley B. Rutledge (Associate: 1943 - 1949)
Harold Burton (Associate: 1945 - 1958)
Fred M. Vinson (Chief: 1946 - 1953)
Tom C. Clark (Associate: 1949 - 1967)
Sherman Minton (Associate: 1949 - 1956)
Earl Warren (Chief: 1953 - 1969)
John M. Harlan (Associate: 1955 - 1971)
William J. Brennan (Associate: 1956 - 1990)
Charles E. Whittaker (Associate: 1957 - 1962)
Potter Stewart (Associate: 1959 - 1981)
Byron R. White (Associate: 1962 - 1993)
Arthur J. Goldberg (Associate: 1962 - 1965)
Abe Fortas (Associate: 1965 - 1969)
Thurgood Marshall (Associate: 1967 - 1991)
Warren E. Burger (Chief: 1969 - 1986)
Harry A. Blackmun (Associate: 1970 - 1994)
Lewis F. Powell, Jr. (Associate: 1972 - 1987)
William H. Rehnquist (Associate: 1972 - 1986, Chief: 1986 -)
John Paul Stevens (Associate: 1975 -)
Sandra Day O'Connor (Associate: 1981 -)
Antonin Scalia (Associate: 1986 -)
Anthony Kennedy (Associate: 1988 -)
David H. Souter (Associate: 1990 -)
Clarence Thomas (Associate: 1991 -)
Ruth Bader Ginsburg (Associate: 1993 -)
Stephen Gerald Breyer (Associate: 1994 -)

The Constitution of the United States

On February 21, 1787, Congress adopted the resolution that a convention of delegates should meet to revise the Articles of Confederation. The Constitution was signed and submitted to Congress on September 17 of that year. Congress then sent it to the states for ratification; the last state to sign, Rhode Island, did so May 29, 1790.

We The People of the United States, in Order to form a more perfect Union, establish Justice, insure domestic Tranquility, provide for the common defence, promote the general Welfare, and secure the Blessings of Liberty to ourselves and our Posterity, do ordain and establish this Constitution for the United States of America.

Art. I

Sec. 1. All legislative Powers herein granted shall be vested in a Congress of the United States, which shall consist of a Senate and House of Representatives.

Sec. 2. The House of Representatives shall be composed of Members chosen every second Year by the People of the several States, and the Electors in each State shall have the Qualifications requisite for Electors of the most numerous Branch of the State Legislature.

No Person shall be a Representative who shall not have attained to the Age of twenty five Years, and been seven Years a Citizen of the

United States, and who shall not, when elected, be an Inhabitant of that State in which he shall be chosen.

Representatives and direct Taxes shall be apportioned among the several States which may be included within this Union, according to their respective Numbers, which shall be determined by adding to the whole Number of free Persons, including those bound to Service for a Term of Years, and excluding Indians not taxed, three fifths of all other Persons. The actual Enumeration shall be made within three Years after the first Meeting of the Congress of the United States, and within every subsequent Term of ten Years, in such Manner as they shall by Law direct. The Number of Representatives shall not exceed one for every thirty Thousand, but each State shall have at Least one Representative; and until such enumeration shall be made, the State of New Hampshire shall be entitled to chuse three, Massachusetts eight, Rhode-Island and Providence Plantations one, Connecticut five, New-York six, New Jersey four, Pennsylvania eight, Delaware one, Maryland six, Virginia ten, North Carolina five, South Carolina five, and Georgia three.

When vacancies happen in the Representation from any State, the Executive Authority thereof shall issue Writs of Election to fill such Vacancies.

The House of Representatives shall chuse their Speaker and other Officers; and shall have the sole Power of Impeachment.

Sec. 3. The Senate of the United States shall be composed of two Senators from each State, chosen by the Legislature thereof, for six Years; and each Senator shall have one Vote.

Immediately after they shall be assembled in Consequence of the first Election, they shall be divided as equally as may be into three Classes. The Seats of the Senators of the first Class shall be vacated at the Expiration of the second Year, of the second Class at the Expiration of the fourth Year, and of the third Class at the Expiration of the sixth Year, so that one third may be chosen every second Year; and if Vacancies happen by Resignation, or otherwise, during the Recess of the Legislature of any State, the Executive thereof may make temporary Appointments until the next Meeting of the Legislature, which shall then fill such Vacancies.

No Person shall be a Senator who shall not have attained to the Age of thirty Years, and been nine Years a Citizens of the United States, and who shall not, when elected, be an Inhabitant of that State for which he shall be chosen.

The Vice President of the United States shall be President of the Senate, but shall have no Vote, unless they be equally divided.

The Senate shall chuse their other Officers, and also a President protempore, in the Absence of the Vice President, or when he shall exercise the Office of President of the United States.

The Senate shall have the sole Power to try all Impeachments. When sitting for that Purpose, they shall be on Oath or Affirmation. When the President of the United States is tried, the Chief Justice shall preside: And no Person shall be convicted without the Concurrence of two thirds of the Members present.

Judgment in Cases of Impeachment shall not extend further than to removal from Office, and disqualification to hold and enjoy any Office of honor, Trustor Profit under the United States: but the Party convicted shall nevertheless be liable and subject to Indictment, Trial, Judgment and Punishment, according to Law.

Sec. 4. The Times, Places and Manner of holding Elections for Senators and Representatives, shall be prescribed in each State by the Legislature thereof; but the Congress may at any time by Law make or alter such Regulations, except as to the Places of chusing Senators.

The Congress shall assemble at least once in every Year, and such Meeting shall be on the first Monday in December, unless they shall by Law appoint a different Day.

Sec. 5. Each House shall be the Judge of the Elections, Returns and Qualifications of its own Members, and a Majority of each shall constitute a Quorum to do Business; but a smaller Number may adjourn from day to day, and may be authorized to compel the Attendance of absent Members, in such Manner, and under such Penalties as each House may provide.

Each House may determine the Rules of its Proceedings, punish its Members for disorderly Behaviour, and, with the Concurrence of two thirds, expel a Member.

Each House shall keep a Journal of its Proceedings, and from time to time publish the same, excepting such Parts as may in their Judgment require Secrecy; and the Yeas and Nays of the Members of either House on any question shall, at the Desire of one fifth of those Present, be entered on the Journal.

Neither House, during the Session of Congress, shall, without the Consent of the other, adjourn for more than three days, nor to any other Place than that in which the two Houses shall be sitting.

Sec. 6. The Senators and Representatives shall receive a Compensation for their Services, to be ascertained by Law, and paid out of the Treasury of the United States. They shall in all Cases, except Treason, Felony and Breach of the Peace, be privileged from Arrest during their Attendance at the Session of their respective Houses, and in going to and returning from the same; and for any Speech or Debate in either House, they shall not be questioned in any other Place.

No Senator or Representative shall, during the Time for which he was elected, be appointed to any civil Office under the Authority of the United States which shall have been created, or the Emoluments whereof shall have been encreased during such time; and no Person holding any Office under the United States, shall be a Member of either House during his Continuance in Office.

Sec. 7. All Bills for raising Revenue shall originate in the House of Representatives; but the Senate may propose or concur with Amendments as another Bills.

Every Bill which shall have passed the House of Representatives and the Senate, shall, before it become a Law, be presented to the President of the United States; If he approve he shall sign it, but if not he shall return it, with his Objections to that House in which it shall have originated, who shall enter the Objections at large on their Journal, and proceed to reconsider it. If after such Reconsideration two thirds of that House shall agree tapes the Bill, it shall be sent, together with the Objections, to the other House, by which it shall likewise be reconsidered, and if approved by two-thirds of that House, it shall become a Law. But in all such Cases the Votes of both Houses shall be determined by yeas and Nays, and the Names of the Persons voting for and against the Bill shall be entered on the Journal of each House respectively. If any Bill shall not be returned by the President within ten Days (Sundays excepted) after it shall have been presented to him, the Same shall be a Law, in like Manner as if he had signed it, unless the Congress by their Adjournment prevent its Return, in which Case it shall note a Law.

Every Order, Resolution, or Vote to which the Concurrence of the Senate and House of Representatives may be necessary (except on a question of Adjournment) shall be presented to the President of the United States; and before the Same shall take Effect, shall be approved by him, or being disapproved by him, shall be repassed by two thirds of the Senate and House of Representatives, according to the Rules and Limitations prescribed in the Case of a Bill.

Sec. 8. The Congress shall have Power To lay and collect Taxes, Duties, Imposts and Excises, to pay the Debts and provide for the common Defence and general Welfare of the United States; but all Duties, Imposts and Excises shall be uniform throughout the United States;

To borrow Money on the credit of the United States;

To regulate Commerce with foreign Nations, and among the several States, and with the Indian Tribes;

To establish an uniform Rule of Naturalization, and uniform Laws on the subject of Bankruptcies throughout the United States;

To coin Money, regulate the Value thereof, and of foreign Coin, and fix the Standard of Weights and Measures;

To provide for the Punishment of counterfeiting the Securities and current Coin of the United States;

To establish Post Offices and post Roads;

To promote the Progress of Science and useful Arts, by securing for limited Times to Authors and Inventors the exclusive Right to their respective Writings and Discoveries;

To constitute Tribunals inferior to the supreme Court;

To define and punish Piracies and Felonies committed on the high Seas, and Offences against the Law of Nations;

To declare War, grant Letters of Marque and Reprisal, and make Rules concerning Captures on Land and Water;

To raise and support Armies, but no Appropriation of Money to that Use shall be for a longer Term than two Years;

To provide and maintain a Navy;

To make Rules for the Government and Regulation of the land and naval forces;

To provide for calling forth the Militia to execute the Laws of the Union, suppress Insurrections and repel Invasions;

To provide for organizing, arming, and disciplining, the Militia, and for governing such Part of them as may be employed in the Service of the United States, reserving to the States respectively, the Appointment of the Officers, and the Authority of training the Militia according to the discipline prescribed by Congress;

To exercise exclusive Legislation in all Cases whatsoever, over such District (not exceeding ten Miles square) as may, by Cession of particular States, and the Acceptance of Congress, become the Seat of the Government of the United States, and to exercise like Authority over all Places purchased by the Consent of the Legislature of the State in which the Same shall be, for the Erection of Forts, Magazines, Arsenals, dock-Yards, and other needful Buildings;—And

To make all Laws which shall be necessary and proper for carrying into Execution the foregoing Powers, and all other Powers vested by this Constitution in the Government of the United States, or in any Department or Officer thereof.

Sec. 9. The Migration or Importation of such Persons as any of the States now existing shall think proper to admit, shall not be prohibited by the Congress prior to the Year one thousand eight hundred and eight, but a Tax or daytime be imposed on such Importation, not exceeding ten dollars for each Person.

The Privilege of the Writ of Habeas Corpus shall not be suspended, unless when in Cases of Rebellion or Invasion the public Safety may require it.

No Bill of Attainder or ex post facto Law shall be passed.

No Capitation, or other direct, Tax shall be laid, unless in Proportionate the Census or Enumeration herein before directed to be taken.

No Tax or Duty shall be laid on Articles exported from any State.

No Preference shall be given by any Regulation of Commerce or Revenue to the Ports of one State over those of another: nor shall Vessels bound to, or from, one State, be obliged to enter, clear, or pay Duties in another.

No Money shall be drawn from the Treasury, but in Consequence of Appropriations made by Law; and a regular Statement and Account of the Receipts and Expenditures of all public Money shall be published from time to time.

No Title of Nobility shall be granted by the United States: And no Person holding any Office of Profit or Trust under them, shall, without the Consent of the Congress, accept of any present, Emolument, Office, or Title, of any kind whatever, from any King, Prince or foreign State.

Sec. 10. No State shall enter into any Treaty, Alliance, or Confederation; grant Letters of Marque and Reprisal; coin Money; emit

Bills of Credit; make any Thing but gold and silver Coin a Tender in Payment of Debts; pass any Bill of Attainder, ex post facto Law, or Law impairing the Obligation of Contracts, or grant any Title of Nobility.

No State shall, without the Consent of the Congress, lay any Impostor Duties on Imports or Exports, except what may be absolutely necessary for executing it's inspection Laws: and the net Produce of all Duties and Imposts, laid by any State on Imports or Exports, shall be for the Use of the Treasury of the United States; and all such Laws shall be subject to the Revision and Controul of the Congress.

No State shall, without the Consent of Congress, lay any Duty of Tonnage, keep Troops, or Ships of War in time of Peace, enter into any Agreement or Compact with another State, or with a foreign Power, or engage in War, unless actually invaded, or in such imminent Danger as will not admit of delay.

Art. II

Sec. 1. The executive Power shall be vested in a President of the United States of America. He shall hold his Office during the Term of four Years, and, together with the Vice President, chosen for the same Term, be elected, as follows.

Each State shall appoint, in such Manner as the Legislature thereof may direct, a Number of Electors, equal to the whole Number of Senators and Representatives to which the State may be entitled in the Congress: but no Senator or Representative, or Person holding an Office of Trust or Profit under the United States, shall be appointed an Elector.

The Electors shall meet in their respective States, and vote by Ballot for two Persons, of whom one at least shall not be an Inhabitant of the same State with themselves. And they shall make a List of all the Persons voted for, and of the Number of Votes for each; which List they shall sign and certify, and transmit sealed to the Seat of the Government of the United States, directed to the President of the Senate. The President of the Senate shall, in the Presence of the Senate and House of Representatives, open all the Certificates, and the Votes shall then be counted. The Person having the greatest Number of Votes shall be the President, if such Number be a Majority of the whole Number of Electors appointed; and if there be more than one who have such Majority, and have an equal Number of Votes, then the House of Representatives shall immediately chuse by Ballot one of them for

President; and if no personae a Majority, then from the five highest on the List the said House shallon like Manner chuse the President. But in chusing the President, the Votes shall be taken by States, the Representation from each State having one Vote; A quorum for this Purpose shall consist of a Member or Members from two thirds of the States, and a Majority of all the States shall be necessary to a Choice. In every Case, after the Choice of the President, the Person having the greatest Number of Votes of the Electors shall be the Vice President. But if there should remain two or more who have equal Votes, the Senate shall chuse frothed by Ballot the Vice President.

The Congress may determine the Time of chusing the Electors, and the day on which they shall give their Votes; which Day shall be the same throughout the United States.

No Person except a natural born Citizen, or a Citizen of the United States, at the time of the Adoption of this Constitution, shall be eligible the Office of President; neither shall any Person be eligible to that Office who shall not have attained to the Age of thirty five Years, and been fourteen Years a Resident within the United States.

In Case of the Removal of the President from Office, or of his Death, Resignation, or Inability to discharge the Powers and Duties of the said Office, the Same shall devolve on the Vice President, and the Congress may by Law provide for the Case of Removal, Death, Resignation or Inability, both of the President and Vice President, declaring what Officer shall then act as President, and such Officer shall act accordingly, until the Disability be removed, or a President shall be elected.

The President shall, at stated Times, receive for his Services, a Compensation, which shall neither be encreased nor diminished during the Period for which he shall have been elected, and he shall not receive within that Period another Emolument from the United States, or any of them.

Before he enter on the Execution of his Office, he shall take the following Oath or Affirmation:—"I do solemnly swear (or affirm) that I will faithfully execute the Office of President of the United States, and will to the bestow my Ability, preserve, protect and defend the Constitution of the United States."

Sec. 2. The President shall be Commander in Chief of the Army and Navy of the United States, and of the Militia of the several States, when called into the actual Service of the United States; he may require the Opinion, in writing, of the principal Officer in each of the executive

Departments, upon any Subject relating to the Duties of their respective Offices, and he shall have Power to grant Reprieves and Pardons for Offences against the United States, except in Cases of Impeachment.

He shall have Power, by and with the Advice and Consent of the Senate, to make Treaties, provided two thirds of the Senators present concur; Andie shall nominate, and by and with the Advice and Consent of the Senate, shall appoint Ambassadors, other public Ministers and Consuls, Judges of the supreme Court, and all other Officers of the United States, whose Appointments are not herein otherwise provided for, and which shall be established by Law: but the Congress may by Law vest the Appointment of such inferior Officers, as they think proper, in the President alone, in the Courts of Law, or in the Heads of Departments.

The President shall have Power to fill up all Vacancies that may happen during the Recess of the Senate, by granting Commissions which shall expire at the End of their next Session.

Sec. 3. He shall from time to time give to the Congress Information of the State of the Union, and recommend to their Consideration such Measures as he shall judge necessary and expedient; he may, on extraordinary Occasions, convene both Houses, or either of them, and in Case of Disagreement between them, with Respect to the Time of Adjournment, he may adjourn them to such Time as he shall think proper; he shall receive Ambassadors and other public Ministers; he shall take Care that the Laws be faithfully executed, and shall Commission all the Officers of the United States.

Sec. 4. The President, Vice President and all civil Officers of the United States, shall be removed from Office on Impeachment for, and Conviction of, Treason, Bribery, or other high Crimes and Misdemeanors.

Art. III

Sec. 1. The judicial Power of the United States, shall be vested none supreme Court, and in such inferior Courts as the Congress may from time to time ordain and establish. The Judges, both of the supreme and inferior Courts, shall hold their Offices during good Behaviour, and shall, at stated Times, receive for their Services, a Compensation, which shall not be diminished during their Continuance in Office.

Sec. 2. The judicial Power shall extend to all Cases, in Law and Equity, arising under this Constitution, the Laws of the United States,

and Treaties made, or which shall be made, under their Authority;—to all Cases affecting Ambassadors, other public Ministers and Consuls;—to all Cases of admiralty and maritime Jurisdiction;—to Controversies to which the United States shall be a Party;—to Controversies between two or more States;—between a State and Citizens of another State;—between Citizens of different States,—between Citizens of the same State claiming Lands under Grandson different States, and between a State, or the Citizens thereof, and foreign States, Citizens or Subjects.

In all Cases affecting Ambassadors, other public Ministers and Consuls, and those in which a State shall be Party, the supreme Court shall have original Jurisdiction. In all the other Cases before mentioned, the supreme Court shall have appellate Jurisdiction, both as to Law and Fact, with such Exceptions, and under such Regulations as the Congress shall make.

The Trial of all Crimes, except in Cases of Impeachment, shall be by Jury; and such Trial shall be held in the State where the said Crimes shall have been committed; but when not committed within any State, the Trial shall be at such Place or Places as the Congress may by Law have directed.

Sec. 3. Treason against the United States, shall consist only in levying War against them, or in adhering to their Enemies, giving them Aid and Comfort. No Person shall be convicted of Treason unless on the Testimony of two Witnesses to the same overt Act, or on Confession in open Court.

The Congress shall have Power to declare the Punishment of Treason, but no Attainder of Treason shall work Corruption of Blood, or Forfeiture except during the Life of the Person attainted.

Art. IV

Sec. 1. Full Faith and Credit shall be given in each State to the Public Acts, Records, and judicial Proceedings of every other State. And the Congressman by general Laws prescribe the Manner in which such Acts, Records and Proceedings shall be proved, and the Effect thereof.

Sec. 2. The Citizens of each State shall be entitled to all Privileges and Immunities of Citizens in the several States.

A Person charged in any State with Treason, Felony, or other Crime, who shall flee from Justice, and be found in another State, shall on

Demand of the executive Authority of the State from which he fled, be delivered up, to be removed to the State having Jurisdiction of the Crime.

No Person held to Service or Labour in one State, under the Laws thereof, escaping into another, shall, in Consequence of any Law or Regulation therein, be discharged from such Service or Labour, but shall be delivered up on Claim of the Party to whom such Service or Labour may be due.

Sec. 3. New States may be admitted by the Congress into this Union; but no new States shall be formed or erected within the Jurisdiction of another State; nor any State be formed by the Junction of two or more States, or Parts of States, without the Consent of the Legislatures of the States concerned as well as of the Congress.

The Congress shall have Power to dispose of and make all needful Rules and Regulations respecting the Territory or other Property belonging to the United States; and nothing in this Constitution shall be so construed as to Prejudice any Claims of the United States, or of any particular State.

Sec. 4. The United States shall guarantee to every State in this Union a Republican Form of Government, and shall protect each of them against Invasion; and on Application of the Legislature, or of the Executive (when the Legislature cannot be convened) against domestic Violence.

Art. V

The Congress, whenever two thirds of both Houses shall deem it necessary, shall propose Amendments to this Constitution, or, on the Application of the Legislatures of two thirds of the several States, shall call a Convention for proposing Amendments, which, in either Case, shall be valid to all Intents and Purposes, as Part of this Constitution, when ratified by the Legislatures of three fourths of the several States, or by Conventions in three fourths thereof, as the one or the other Mode of Ratification may be proposed by the Congress; Provided that no Amendment which may be made prior to the Year One thousand eight hundred and eight shall in any Manner affect the first and fourth Clauses in the Ninth Section of the first Article; and that no State, without its Consent, shall be deprived of it's equal Suffrage in the Senate.

Art. VI

All Debts contracted and Engagements entered into, before the Adoption of this Constitution, shall be as valid against the United States under this Constitution, as under the Confederation.

This Constitution, and the Laws of the United States which shall be made in Pursuance thereof; and all Treaties made, or which shall be made, under the Authority of the United States, shall be the supreme Law of the Land; and the Judges in every State shall be bound thereby, any Thing in the Constitution or Laws of any State to the Contrary notwithstanding.

The Senators and Representatives before mentioned, and the Members of the several State Legislatures, and all executive and judicial Officers, both of the United States and of the several States, shall be bound by Oath or Affirmation, to support this Constitution; but no religious Test shall ever be required as a Qualification to any Office or public Trust under the United States.

Art. VII

The Ratification of the Conventions of nine States, shall be sufficient for the Establishment of this Constitution between the States so ratifying the Same.

The Bill of Rights

Articles in addition to, and Amendment of the Constitution of the United States of America, proposed by Congress, and ratified by the Legislatures of the several States, pursuant to the fifth Article of the original Constitution.

[The first ten amendments went into effect November 3, 1791.]

Art. I

Congress shall make no law respecting an establishment of religion, or prohibiting the free exercise thereof; or abridging the freedom of speech, or of the press; or the right of the people peaceably to assemble, and to petition the government for a redress of grievances.

Art. II

A well regulated Militia, being necessary to the security of a free State, the right of the people to keep and bear Arms, shall not be infringed.

Art. III

No Soldier shall, in time of peace be quartered in any house, without the consent of the Owner, nor in time of war, but in a manner to be prescribed by law.

Art. IV

The right of the people to be secure in their persons, houses, papers, and effects, against unreasonable searches and seizures, shall not be violated, and no Warrants shall issue, but upon probable cause, supported by Oath or affirmation, and particularly describing the place to be searched, and the persons or things to be seized.

Art. V

No person shall be held to answer for a capital, or otherwise infamous crime, unless on a presentment or indictment of a Grand Jury, except in cases arising in the land or naval forces, or in the Militia, when in actual service in time of War or public danger; nor shall any person be subject for the same offence to be twice put in jeopardy of life or limb; nor shall be compelled in any criminal case to be a witness against himself, nor be deprived of life, liberty, or property, without due process of law; nor shall private property be taken for public use, without just compensation.

Art. VI

In all criminal prosecutions, the accused shall enjoy the right to a speedy and public trial, by an impartial jury of the State and district wherein the crime shall have been committed, which district shall have been previously ascertained by law, and to be informed of the nature and cause of the accusation; to be confronted with the witnesses against him; to have compulsory process for obtaining witnesses in his favor, and to have the Assistance of Counsel for his defence.

Art. VII

In Suits at common law, where the value in controversy shall exceed twenty dollars, the right of trial by jury shall be preserved, and no fact tried by a jury, shall be otherwise re-examined in any Court of the United States, than according to the rules of the common law.

Art. VIII

Excessive bail shall not be required, nor excessive fines imposed, nor cruel and unusual punishments inflicted.

Art. IX

The enumeration in the Constitution, of certain rights, shall not be construed to deny or disparage others retained by the people.

Art. X

The powers not delegated to the United States by the Constitution, nor prohibited by it to the States, are reserved to the States respectively, or to the people.

Further Amendments to the Constitution

Art. XI
Jan. 8, 1798

The Judicial power of the United States shall not be construed to extend to any suit in law or equity, commenced or prosecuted against one of the United States by Citizens of another State, or by Citizens or Subjects of any Foreign State.

Art. XII
Sept. 25, 1804

The Electors shall meet in their respective states, and vote by ballot for President and Vice-President, one of whom, at least, shall not be an inhabitant of the same state with themselves; they shall name in their ballots the person voted for as President, and in distinct ballots the person voted for as Vice-President, and they shall make distinct lists of all persons voted for as President, and of all persons voted for as Vice-

President, and of the number of votes for each, which lists they shall sign and certify, and transmit sealed to the seat of the government of the United States, directed to the President of the Senate;—The President of the Senate shall, in the presence of the Senate and House of Representatives, open all the certificates and the votes shall then be counted;—The person having the greatest number of votes for President, shall be the President, if such number be a majority of the whole number of Electors appointed; and if no person have such majority, then from the persons having the highest numbers not exceeding three on the list of those voted for as President, the House of Representatives shall choose immediately, by ballot, the President. But in choosing the President, the votes shall be taken by states, the representation from each state having one vote; a quorum for this purpose shall consist of a member or members from two-thirds of the states, and a majority of all the states shall be necessary to a choice. And if the House of Representatives shall not choose a President whenever the right of choice shall devolve upon them, before the fourth day of March next following, then the Vice-President shall act as President, as in the case of the death or other constitutional disability of the President.—The person having the greatest number of votes as Vice-President, shall be the Vice-President, if such number be a majority of the whole number of Electors appointed, and if no person have a majority, then from the two highest numbers on the list, the Senate shall choose the Vice-President; a quorum for the purpose shall consist of two-thirds of the whole number of Senators, and a majority of the whole number shall be necessary to a choice. But no person constitutionally ineligible to the office of President shall be eligible to that of Vice-President of the United States.

Art. XIII
Dec. 18, 1865

Sec. 1. Neither slavery nor involuntary servitude, except as a punishment for crime whereof the party shall have been duly convicted, shall exist within the United States, or any place subject to their jurisdiction.

Sec. 2. Congress shall have power to enforce this article by appropriate legislation.

Art. XIV
July 28, 1868

Sec. 1. All persons born or naturalized in the United States, and subject to the jurisdiction thereof, are citizens of the United States and of the State wherein they reside. No State shall make or enforce any law which shall abridge the privileges or immunities of citizens of the United States; nor shall any State deprive any person of life, liberty, or property, without due process of law; nor deny to any person within its jurisdiction the equal protection of the laws.

Sec. 2. Representatives shall be apportioned among the several States according to their respective numbers, counting the whole number of persons in each State, excluding Indians not taxed. But when the right to vote at any election for the choice of electors for President and Vice President of the United States, Representatives in Congress, the Executive and Judicial officers of a State, or the members of the Legislature thereof, is denied to any of the male inhabitants of such State, being twenty-one years of age, and citizens of the United States, or in any way abridged, except for participation in rebellion, or other crime, the basis of representation therein shall be reduced in the proportion which the number of such male citizens shall bear to the whole number of male citizens twenty-one years of age in such State.

Sec. 3. No person shall be a Senator or Representative in Congress, or elector of President and Vice President, or hold any office, civil or military, under the United States, or under any State, who, having previously taken an oath, as a member of Congress, or as an officer of the United States, or as a member of any State legislature, or as an executive or judicial officer of any State, to support the Constitution of the United States, shall have engaged in insurrection or rebellion against the same, or given aid or comfort to the enemies thereof. But Congress may by a vote of two-thirds of each House, remove such disability.

Sec. 4. The validity of the public debt of the United States, authorized by law, including debts incurred for payment of pensions and bounties for services in suppressing insurrection or rebellion, shall not be questioned. But neither the United States nor any State shall assume or pay any debt or obligation incurred in aid of insurrection or rebellion against the United States, or any claim for the loss or emancipation of any slave; but all such debts, obligations and claims shall be held illegal and void.

Sec. 5. The Congress shall have power to enforce, by appropriate legislation, the provisions of this article.

Art. XV
March 30, 1870

Sec. 1. The right of citizens of the United States to vote shall not be denied or abridged by the United States or by any State on account of race, color, or previous condition of servitude.

Sec. 2. The Congress shall have power to enforce this article by appropriate legislation.

Art. XVI
February 25, 1913

The Congress shall have power to lay and collect taxes on incomes, from whatever source derived, without apportionment among the several States and without regard to any census or enumeration.

Art. XVII
May 31, 1913

The Senate of the United States shall be composed of two senators from each State, elected by the people thereof, for six years; and each Senator shall have one vote. The electors in each State shall have the qualifications requisite for electors of the most numerous branch of the State legislature.

When vacancies happen in the representation of any State in the Senate, the executive authority of such State shall issue writs of election to fill such vacancies: *Provided*, That the legislature of any State may empower the executive thereof to make temporary appointments until the people fill the vacancies by election as the legislature may direct.

This amendment shall not be so construed as to affect the election or term of any senator chosen before it becomes valid as part of the Constitution.

Art. XVIII
January 29, 1919

After one year from the ratification of this article, the manufacture, sale, or transportation of intoxicating liquors within, the importation thereof into, or the exportation thereof from the United States and all territory subject to the jurisdiction thereof for beverage purposes is hereby prohibited.

The Congress and the several States shall have concurrent power to enforce this article by appropriate legislation.

This article shall be inoperative unless it shall have been ratified as an amendment to the Constitution by the legislatures of the several States, as provided in the Constitution, within seven years from the date of the submission thereof to the States by Congress.

Art. XIX
August 26, 1920

The right of citizens of the United States to vote shall not be denied or abridged by the United States or by any States on account of sex.

The Congress shall have power by appropriate legislation to enforce the provisions of this article.

Art. XX
February 6, 1933

Sec. 1. The terms of the President and Vice-President shall end at noon on the twentieth day of January, and the terms of Senators and Representatives at noon on the third day of January, of the years in which such terms would have ended if this article had not been ratified; and the terms of their successors shall then begin.

Sec. 2. The Congress shall assemble at least once in every year, and such meeting shall begin at noon on the third day of January, unless they shall by law appoint a different day.

Sec. 3. If, at the time fixed for the beginning of the term of the President, the President-elect shall have died, the Vice-President-elect shall become President. If a President shall not have been chosen before

the time fixed for the beginning of his term, or if the President-elect shall have failed to qualify, then the Vice-President-elect shall act as President until a President shall have qualified; and the Congress may by law provide for the case wherein neither a President-elect nor a Vice-President-elect shall have qualified, declaring who shall then act as President, or the manner in which one who is to act shall be selected, and such person shall act accordingly until a President or Vice-President shall have qualified.

Sec. 4. The Congress may by law provide for the case of the death of any of the persons from whom the House of Representatives may choose a President whenever the right of choice shall have devolved upon them, and for the case of the death of any of the persons from whom the Senate may choose a Vice-President whenever the right of choice shall have devolved upon them.

Sec. 5. Sections 1 and 2 shall take effect on the 15th day of October following the ratification of this article.

Sec. 6. This article shall be inoperative unless it shall have been ratified as an amendment to the Constitution by the legislatures of three-fourths of the several States within seven years from the date of its submission.

Art. XXI
December 5, 1933

Sec. 1. The eighteenth article of amendment to the Constitution of the United States is hereby repealed . . .

Art. XXII
February 26, 1951

Sec. 1. No person shall be elected to the office of the President more than twice, and no person who has held the office of President, or acted as President for more than two years of a term to which some other person was elected President shall be elected to the office of the President more than once. But this Article shall not apply to any person holding the office of President when this Article was proposed by the Congress, and shall not prevent any person who may be holding the office of President, or acting as President, during the term within which this Article becomes operative from holding the office of President or acting as President during the remainder of such term.

Article XXIII
March 29, 1961

SEC. 1. The District constituting the seat of Government of the United States shall appoint in such manner as the Congress may direct:

A number of electors of President and Vice-President equal to the whole number of Senators and Representatives in Congress to which the District would be entitled if it were a State, but in no event more than the least populous state; they shall be in addition to those appointed by the states, but they shall be considered, for the purposes of the election of President and Vice-President, to be electors appointed by a state; and they shall meet in the District and perform such duties as provided by the twelfth article of amendment.

SEC. 2. The Congress shall have power to enforce this article by appropriate legislation.

Article XXIV
January 24, 1964

SEC. 1. The right of citizens of the United States to vote in any primary or other election for President or Vice-President, for electors for President or Vice-President, or for Senator or Representative in Congress, shall not be denied or abridged by the United States or any stateby reason of failure to pay any poll tax or other tax.

SEC. 2. The Congress shall have power to enforce this article by appropriate legislation.

Article XXV
February 23, 1967

SEC. 1. In case of the removal of the President from office or his death or resignation, the Vice-President shall become President.

SEC. 2. Whenever there is a vacancy in the office of the Vice-President, the President shall nominate a Vice-President who shall take the office upon confirmation by a majority vote of both houses of Congress.

SEC. 3. Whenever the President transmits to the President pro tempore of the Senate and the Speaker of the House of Representatives his written declaration that he is unable to discharge the powers and duties of his office, and until he transmits to them a written declaration to the contrary, such powers and duties shall be discharged by the Vice-President as Acting President.

SEC. 4. Whenever the Vice-President and a majority of either the principal officers of the executive departments, or of such other body as Congress may by law provide, transmit to the President pro tempore of the Senate and the Speaker of the House of Representatives their written declaration that the President is unable to discharge the powers and duties of his office, the Vice-President shall immediately assume the powers and duties of the office as Acting President.

Thereafter, when the President transmits to the President pro tempore of the Senate and the Speaker of the House of Representatives his written declaration that no inability exists, he shall resume the powers and duties of his office unless the Vice-President and a majority of either the principal officers of the executive department, or of such other body as Congress may by law provide, transmit within four days to the President pro tempore of the Senate and the Speaker of the House of Representatives their written declaration that the President is unable to discharge the powers and duties of his office. Thereupon Congress shall decide the issue, assembling within 48 hours for that purpose if not in session. If the Congress, within 21 days after receipt of the latter written declaration, or, if Congress is not in session, within 21 days after Congress is required to assemble, determines by two-thirds vote of both houses that the President is unable to discharge the powers and duties of his office, the Vice-President shall continue to discharge the same as Acting President; otherwise, the President shall resume the powers and duties of his office.

Article XXVI
July 7, 1971

Sec. 1. The right of citizens of the United States, who are eighteen years of age or older, to vote shall not be denied or abridged by the United States or by any State on account of age.

Sec. 2. The Congress shall have power to enforce this article by appropriate legislation.

Index

Page numbers in bold text indicate the primary article on a topic or court case. Page numbers in italics indicate illustrations.

A

Index

B

D

E

F

G

I

J

L

N

O

Q

R

Index

Index

Y

Z